MW01242021

GLOBAL CONSTITUTIONALISM FROM EUROPEAN AND EAST ASIAN PERSPECTIVES

Global constitutionalism argues that parts of international law can be understood as being grounded in the rule of law and human rights, and insists that international law can and should be interpreted and progressively developed in the direction of greater respect for and realization of those principles. Global constitutionalism has been discussed primarily by European scholars. Yet without the engagement of scholars from other parts of the world, the universalist claims underlying Global constitutionalism ring hollow. This is particularly true with regard to East Asia, where nearly half of the world's population and a growing share of global economic and military capacities are located. Are East Asian perspectives on Global constitutionalism similar to European perspectives? Against the background of current power shifts in international law, this book constitutes the first cross-cultural work on various facets of Global constitutionalism and elaborates a more nuanced concept that fits our times.

TAKAO SUAMI is a professor at Waseda University Law School, Tokyo, Japan. He studied law at the University of Tokyo (LLB), Cornell Law School (LLM) and the University of Leuven (KU Leuven) (LLM). He was a visiting professor at Duke University Law School and the University of Pennsylvania Law School. He served as President of the European Union Studies Association – Japan, and is currently a member of the board of trustees of the Japanese Society of International Law. His teaching and research interests lie in EU law, international economic law and judicial policymaking in Japan.

ANNE PETERS is Director at the Max Planck Institute for Comparative Public Law and International Law, Heidelberg, a professor at the universities of Heidelberg, FU Berlin and Basel, and a William C. Cook Global Law Professor at the University of Michigan. She has been a member of the European Commission for Democracy through Law (Venice Commission) in respect of Germany (2011–2015) and served as President of the European Society of International Law (2010–2012). Her current research interests relate to public international law including its history, global animal law, global governance and global constitutionalism.

DIMITRI VANOVERBEKE is a professor at Leuven University (Belgium) and Director of the Department of East Asian and Arabic Studies. He lectures in Japanese studies (law, politics and society) and also lectures in the Europe–Asia: Interactions and Comparisons module of the Master of Arts in European Studies at KU Leuven (East Asian politics). His current research interests relate to law and society and to the political dynamics in Japan and in South-East Asia. Aside from publishing on the past and present of the legal system in Japan, he also publishes on the relationship between Japan and the European Union.

MATTIAS KUMM is the Inge Rennert Professor of Law at New York University Law School as well as Professor for Rule of Law in the Age of Globalisation at Humboldt University and Managing Director of the Center of Global Constitutionalism at the WZB Social Science Research Center in Berlin. His research focuses on basic issues and contemporary challenges in global, European and comparative public law and legal philosophy. He was a professor at Harvard, Yale and the European University Institute (EUI) and is a co-founder and co-editor in chief of *Global Constitutionalism.*

GLOBAL CONSTITUTIONALISM FROM EUROPEAN AND EAST ASIAN PERSPECTIVES

Edited by

TAKAO SUAMI
Waseda University, Japan

ANNE PETERS
Max Planck Institute for Comparative Public Law and International Law, Germany

DIMITRI VANOVERBEKE
Katholieke Universiteit Leuven, Belgium

MATTIAS KUMM
Humboldt University and NYU School of Law, Berlin

CAMBRIDGE
UNIVERSITY PRESS

CAMBRIDGE
UNIVERSITY PRESS

University Printing House, Cambridge CB2 8BS, United Kingdom

One Liberty Plaza, 20th Floor, New York, NY 10006, USA

477 Williamstown Road, Port Melbourne, VIC 3207, Australia

314–321, 3rd Floor, Plot 3, Splendor Forum, Jasola District Centre,
New Delhi – 110025, India

79 Anson Road, #06–04/06, Singapore 079906

Cambridge University Press is part of the University of Cambridge.

It furthers the University's mission by disseminating knowledge in the pursuit of
education, learning, and research at the highest international levels of excellence.

www.cambridge.org
Information on this title: www.cambridge.org/9781108417112
DOI: 10.1017/9781108264877

© Cambridge University Press 2018

First published 2018

Printed and bound in Great Britain by Clays Ltd, Elcograf S.p.A.

A catalogue record for this publication is available from the British Library.

Library of Congress Cataloging-in-Publication Data
Names: Suami, Takao, 1954– editor. | Peters, Anne, 1964– editor. | Kumm, Mattias, editor. |
Vanoverbeke, Dimitri, editor.
Title: Global constitutionalism from European and East Asian perspectives / edited by Takao
Suami, Waseda University, Japan; Anne Peters, Max-Planck-Institut fur auslandisches
offentliches Recht und Volkerrecht, Germany; Mattias Kumm, Humboldt-Universitat zu
Berlin; Dimitri Vanoverbeke, Katholieke Universiteit Leuven, Belgium.
Description: Cambridge, United Kingdom ; New York, NY, USA : Cambridge University
Press, 2018.
Identifiers: LCCN 2018018158 | ISBN 9781108417112
Subjects: LCSH: Constitutional law – Europe. | Constitutional law – East Asia. | Comparative
law. | Law and globalization.
Classification: LCC K3165 .G583 2018 | DDC 342.4–dc23
LC record available at https://lccn.loc.gov/2018018158

ISBN 978-1-108-41711-2 Hardback

CONTENTS

CONTRIBUTORS

GUIMEI BAI, LLM (1982) and PhD (1997), a professor of international law and Executive Director of the Research Centre for Human Rights and Humanitarian Law, Peking University Law School, has been teaching a general course of public international law since 1983, the course on theories of international law for the master's programme since 1986 and the course on mechanisms of human rights protection since 2000. She is the author of *International Law* (all editions of 2006, 2010 and 2015, in Chinese), *Self-Determination in International Law* (1999, in Chinese) and several articles on theories of international law and human rights in major Chinese law journals.

DR MATTHIEU BURNAY is a lecturer in global law at Queen Mary University of London. He has an interdisciplinary background in law, political science and history. He holds a PhD in law from the University of Leuven and a double MSc degree in international affairs from Peking University and the London School of Economics. His main research interests are in global law and governance; the study of the political and legal aspects of EU–China relations in global governance; as well as the comparative study of the rule of law in Europe and Asia.

KAZUYORI ITO is an associate professor at the Public Policy School, Hokkaido University, Japan. His academic and public activities include serving as a council member of the Japan Association of International Economic Law; a member of the Study Group on the WTO Dispute Settlement Reports, organized by the Ministry of Economy, Trade and Industry, Japan; and a member of the Study Group on International Economic Disputes, organized by the Ministry of Foreign Affairs, Japan. He is the coauthor of *Anti-Dumping Laws and Practices of the New Users* (2007) and *Managing Development: Globalization, Economic Restructuring and Social Policy* (2006).

LOUIS J. KOTZÉ is a research professor of law at the Faculty of Law, North-West University, South Africa, and a visiting professor of environmental law at Lincoln University, United Kingdom. His research focuses on the Anthropocene, environmental constitutionalism, human rights and global environmental law and governance. He is a co-editor of the *Journal of Human Rights and the Environment* and has been awarded a European Curie Horizon 2020 Marie Curie Individual Fellowship in 2018 to conduct research at the University of Lincoln. This project endeavours to construct a framework for global ecological law in the Anthropocene.

MATTIAS KUMM (editor) is the Inge Rennert Professor of Law at New York University Law School as well as Professor for Rule of Law in the Age of Globalisation at Humboldt University and Managing Director of the Center of Global Constitutionalism at the WZB Social Science Research Center in Berlin. His research and teaching focus on basic issues and contemporary challenges in global, European and comparative public law. He has been a visiting professor at Harvard, Yale and the European University Institute (EUI) and is a co-founder and co-editor in chief of *Global Constitutionalism*.

BIN LI is a professor of law at Beijing Normal University. His ongoing research projects focus on such topics as the transformation of Chinese law on private property; the interaction between Chinese law and international law; globalization and the development of international law, human rights, business and the reform of the transnational investment legal regime; and comparative study on legal cultures. He teaches in the field of international law, in particular public international law, human rights, international economic law and legal aspects of transnational business transactions.

AXEL MARX is Deputy Director of the Leuven Centre for Global Governance Studies at KU Leuven (University of Leuven). His publications focus on global governance, sustainability standards, non-state market regulation, labour rights, trade governance and comparative case methods. He recently co-edited the books *Global Governance of Labor Rights* (2015, with Jan Wouters, Glenn Rayp and Laura Beke) and *Global Governance through Trade* (2015, with Jan Wouters, Bregt Natens and Dylan Geraets). As an expert for policymakers, he has contributed to reports for inter alia the United Nations Industrial

Development Organization (UNIDO), the International Labour
Organization (ILO), the European Commission, the European
Parliament, the Committee of the Regions and several national
governments.

TOSHIKI MOGAMI, PHD, University of Tokyo, was a professor and
Director of the Peace Research Institute, International Christian
University, Tokyo, and is a professor at Waseda University, Tokyo, in
international law and organization. He previously served as President of
the Japan Peace Research Association and currently is President of the
Japan Chapter of the Asian Society of International Law. He is the author
of *International Organisation* (first edition published in 1996 and
currently in its fourth edition), *Humanitarian Intervention* (2001) and
The UN and USA (2005), all in Japanese, as well as many others including
articles written in English. He was a visiting researcher at the Max Planck
Institute for International Comparative Law, 2016–2017, and a visiting
professor at the Institute for European International Studies, University
of Basel, 2017–2018.

KAORU OBATA is a professor at Nagoya University, Japan, and
a member of the UN Human Rights Council Advisory Committee. He
studied law at the University of Kyoto (LLB and LLM) and received an
LLD (Kyoto) in 2016. His publications in English include 'The European
Human Rights System beyond Europe: Interaction with Asia' (2015) 23
Journal für Rechtspolitik 36–43 and 'Historical Functions of Monism with
Primacy of International Law: A View Based on Japanese Experience
during the Early Period of the Allied Occupation' (2006) 49 *Japanese
Annual of International Law* 1–35.

ANNE PETERS (editor) is Director at the Max Planck Institute for
Comparative Public Law and International Law, Heidelberg,
a professor at the universities of Heidelberg, FU Berlin and Basel, and
a William C. Cook Global Law Professor at the University of Michigan.
She has been a member of the European Commission for Democracy
through Law (Venice Commission) in respect of Germany (2011–2015)
and served as President of the European Society of International Law (
2010–2012). Her current research interests relate to public international
law including its history, global animal law, global governance, global
constitutionalism and the status of humans in international law.

DR CHRISTINE SCHWÖBEL-PATEL is Senior Lecturer at the School of Law, University of Liverpool, and Director of the Critical Approaches to International Criminal Law research cluster. She has published widely on global constitutionalism, including the monograph *Global Constitutionalism in International Legal Perspective* (2011). Christine is also the editor of *Critical Approaches to International Criminal Law* (2014).

YOON JIN SHIN is an assistant professor at Seoul National University School of Law. She served as a judge in South Korea before she studied at Yale Law School for her JSD (2015) and LLM (2011) degrees. Shin worked at New York University School of Law as Hauser Post-Doctoral Global Fellow (2015–2016) and at the Berlin Social Science Center (WZB) as a senior researcher (2016–2017). Her research and teaching focus on human rights, transnational law and global constitutionalism. Her recent publications include the monograph *A Transnational Human Rights Approach to Human Trafficking: Empowering the Powerless* (2017).

TAKAO SUAMI (editor) is a professor at Waseda University Law School, Tokyo, Japan. He studied law at the University of Tokyo (LLB), Cornell Law School (LLM) and the University of Leuven (KU Leuven) (LLM). He was a visiting professor at Duke University Law School and the University of Pennsylvania Law School. He served as President of the European Union Studies Association – Japan, and is currently a member of the board of trustees of the Japanese Society of International Law. His teaching and research interests lie in EU law, international economic law and judicial policymaking in Japan.

GEIR ULFSTEIN is a professor of international law at the Department of Public and International Law and Co-Director of PluriCourts – Centre for the Study of the Legitimate Roles of the Judiciary in the Global Order, University of Oslo. Ulfstein has published in different areas of international law, including the law of the sea, international environmental law, international human rights and international institutional law. He is Co-Chair of the International Law Association's Study Group on the Content and Evolution of the Rules of Interpretation and has been a member of the Executive Board of the European Society of International Law (2010–2016).

DIMITRI VANOVERBEKE (editor) is a professor at Leuven University (Belgium) and Director of the Department of East Asian and Arabic Studies. He lectures in Japanese studies (law, politics and society) and also lectures in the Europe–Asia: Interactions and Comparisons module of the Master of Arts in European Studies at KU Leuven (East Asian politics). His current research interests relate to law and society and to the political dynamics in Japan and in South-East Asia. Aside from publishing on the past and present of the legal system in Japan, he also publishes on the relationship between Japan and the European Union.

XIGEN WANG, doctor of law, is President of the Human Rights Institute at Wuhan University (the National Human Rights Base). He is the Changjiang Distinguished Professor (a title for the national leading scholar in philosophy and social sciences granted by the State Council of China). Invited by the United Nations, Wang serves as a high-level consultant on the right to development and has participated in the drafting of the standards of the right to development and related activities of the UN several times since 2007.

JAN WOUTERS is a full professor of international law and international organizations, Jean Monnet Chair, Director of the Institute for International Law and Leuven Centre for Global Governance Studies at KU Leuven, and President of the university's Board for International Policy. He is an adjunct professor at Columbia University and a visiting professor at SciencesPo, LUISS and the College of Europe. A member of the Belgian Royal Academy and of counsel at Linklaters, he has published widely on international and EU law, international organizations and global governance. He conducts many international research projects, advises and trains international organizations and governments and is often asked to comment on international events in the media.

HYUCK-SOO YOO, professor, teaches international law and international economic law at Yokohama National University in Japan. He holds a doctorate in law from the University of Tokyo (1991). He was a visiting researcher of Harvard Law School and visiting scholar of the School of Advanced International Studies (SAIS), Johns Hopkins University. He has published many books and articles about international law and international economic law. He is a member of the Japanese Society of International Law, a standing director of the Japanese Association of International Economic Law and the Korean International Trade Law Association. His current research interests relate to global governance and international legal order and to the status of aliens and nationality in international law.

ACKNOWLEDGMENTS

The idea for this project emerged in the fall of 2012. Takao Suami suggested opening a discussion on constitutionalism beyond states between established (and mostly European) scholars in this field and East Asian scholars. Soon, Miguel Poiares Maduro expressed support for this initiative and collaborated with Suami to push the project forward. In April 2013, Maduro was appointed a minister for the Portuguese government and was forced to leave the project. Instead of Maduro, Mattias Kumm, Anne Peters and Dimitri Vanoverbeke joined the organizing team and launched the project at an international workshop at the University of Leuven (KU Leuven) in Belgium in February 2014 and deepened the discussion in a second workshop at the same location in February 2015. The dynamics and exchanges that were set in motion resulted in too many lectures and workshops to enumerate here. Gradually this volume took shape.

Not only the authors but also many others have made important contributions to the project. The editors would like to express their profound gratitude to Carl Baudenbacher, President of the European Free Trade Association (EFTA) Court and a professor at the University of St. Gallen in Switzerland, for his relevant suggestions and help in recruiting European scholars as contributors. Furthermore, Chang-fa Lo, professor at National Taiwan University and Justice at the Constitutional Court in Taiwan; Akio Shimizu and Tamio Nakamura, both professors at Waseda University; Keun-Gwan Lee, professor at Seoul National University; and Yueyao Zhang, PhD candidate at the Max Planck Institute for Comparative Public Law and International Law in Heidelberg, actively participated in discussions at the aforementioned international workshops. Their contributions offered important insights on the subjects that are tackled in this book. Without their input, this work would not have taken the shape it has now. Furthermore, we express our gratitude to the Leuven Centre for Global Governance Studies. The centre provided us with various types of practical assistance for the workshops. Yota Negishi, a visiting fellow at the Max Planck Institute for Comparative Public Law and International Law and an assistant professor at Seinan Gakuin University, significantly contributed to the editing and realization of this volume. Without his efficient assistance in controlling the editing procedures, this volume would not have been possible. We also thank Dr Malcolm Maclaren, University of Zurich, for correcting and polishing the English writing of non-native speakers. We thank Anette Kreutzfeld for invaluable assistance in the proof-reading stage. The Max Planck Institute for Comparative Public Law and International Law, Heidelberg, financed the language-editing process. We also thank our editor at Cambridge University Press, Joe Ng, for guiding us patiently through the review, editing and production processes. Last but not least, we are grateful to the Japan Society for the Promotion of Science which provided a Grant-in-Aid for the Scientific Research Project (Grant No. 23243003) that supplied the main financial basis of the international workshops.

This book had a very long gestation phase, during which the landscape of international law changed, and with it also the attitudes and expectations of contributing scholars. We as editors are convinced that the conversation we tried to begin with this volume is more needed than ever before.

~

Global Constitutionalism from European and East Asian Perspectives

An Introduction

ANNE PETERS, TAKAO SUAMI, DIMITRI VANOVERBEKE
AND MATTIAS KUMM

1 Current challenges

In the past decade, international crises have triggered fundamental questions about the current sociopolitical and economic order in all regions of the world. The worldwide financial crisis of 2007–2008 stimulated questions about monetary policies and more fundamentally about the existing economic model. The Euro-crisis caused in 2010 by the Greek public deficit and the mass influx of refugees into Europe since 2015 have been challenging the political leaders in the EU, which is the prime model for regional cooperation. How can we find a solution to the problems that Greece has been facing and – more important maybe – how can we prevent the crisis from spreading to other parts of Europe? The list of crises continues: Europe is the stage for numerous terrorist attacks, and Russia poses a mounting threat at Europe's eastern borders. These lead some to doubt the viability of the European strategy for peace building and peace preservation. Facing the new challenges, some EU member states such as Hungary and Poland seem to drift away from the rule of law, human rights and democracy and are thus shaking the very foundation of the EU.

East Asia has not been spared similar afflictions. The monetary and financial crisis of 1997–1998 and then the global financial crisis of 2007–2008 raised the question of how the region could establish or reform institutional structures in order to prevent similar problems from occurring in the future. More recently, several disputes about maritime boundaries, sovereignty, exploitation of resources and navigation in the seas of this region have destabilised the peaceful relationship among nations in East Asia. Above all and most recently, the nuclear threat by North Korea presents a major challenge in the region.

In a row of states in Europe and in East Asia, the rule of law is undermined by populist governments. In their foreign relations, some nation states seem to try to develop a more 'realist' discourse in which they notably question the role of international organisations. Alternatives to international organisations such as the UN and the EU have been ventilated by assertive nations or by subnational regions seeking to restore their past grandeur. These alternatives emphasise self-rule and are sceptical about transnational modes of decision making.

The year 2016 was crucial, a turning point. In Europe, after a referendum, the United Kingdom decided to leave the EU – an unprecedented move. In the United States, the least expected outcome of the presidential elections became a reality. Donald Trump, a businessman-turned politician, had only one short message: 'America first'. That message runs against cooperation between nations and joining forces to face global challenges. It appears as if we have moved from an inclusive world to an exclusive world, from internationalism to nationalism. The Doha Round negotiations on international trade law, which began in 2001, have not produced any fruitful result yet and are today almost forgotten. Moreover, the US administration decided in 2017 to pull out of the negotiations for a Transatlantic Trade and Investment Partnership (TTIP) agreement and to shelve the recently negotiated text of a Transpacific Partnership (TPP) agreement.

All these events reflect the apparent rise of the BRICSAM (Brazil, Russia, India, China, South Africa and Mexico) states and a concomitant decline of the United States and Europe. It has been pointed out that the political and economic shift has also brought about 'power shifts *in* international law'.[1] This cannot leave untouched the process of constitutionalisation which has arguably been transforming the structure and essence of international law.[2] So was this transformative momentum

---

[1] William W. Burke-White, 'Power shifts in international law: structural realignment and substantive pluralism' (2015) 56 *Harvard International Law Journal* 1–80 (emphasis added).

[2] Jerzy Zajadło and Tomasz Widłak, 'Constitutionalisation: a new philosophy of international law?', in Andrzej Jakubowski and Karolina Wierczyńska (eds.), *Fragmentation vs the Constitutionalisation of International Law: A Practical Inquiry* (London: Routledge, 2016), pp. 15–31, p. 30.

only 'a hallmark of the period of U.S. leadership'[3] whose phasing out is accompanied by a reassertion of state sovereignty – against constitutionalist aspirations? This seems to be the thrust of the Chinese scholar and judge at the International Court of Justice Hanquin Xue, who insists on the centrality of the state for the functioning of international law: 'States are the crucial actors at both national and international level. . . . Any weakening of the status and role of the State, as demonstrated in many a case, could only mean more misery and sufferings for individuals'.[4] In a different context and with regard to Chinese courts, another author pointed out that the courts' 'involvement in foreign affairs is likely to remain limited by China's desire to maintain its authoritarian regime'.[5] Although 'China is increasingly applying international law granting rights to individuals in relation to public authorities, the Chinese judicial policy toward these rights appears rather conservative. . . . China's rise has produced a judicial policy that is open to the application of international law, but only when it poses little threat to executive authority.'[6]

The (re)emphasis on the importance of states may have been aided in part by the violation of basic Westphalian principles such as territorial integrity and the prohibition on the use of force by leading powers (e.g. the intervention in Iraq by the United States in 2003 and the annexation of Crimea by Russia in 2014). Similarly, the humanitarian intervention in Kosovo in 1999 is widely seen to have overstretched international law, and the application of the doctrine of the responsibility to protect in Libya in 2011 has not improved the situation of the population but has contributed to a profound destabilisation of the region.

It may well be that for a host of international legal rules and regimes seeking to advance constitutional objectives, such as the protection of human rights, 'the return of the state will likely have pronounced negative consequences. Over time these regimes may be ratcheted back as international law returns closer to its Westphalian origins as a system of

---

[3] Burke-White (n. 1), p. 77.

[4] Hanquin Xue, 'Comments on Hurrell', in James Crawford and Sarah Nouwen (eds.), *Select Proceedings of the European Society of International Law 3* (Oxford: Hart, 2012), pp. 27–29, p. 28. Likewise, in post-Soviet Russian international legal scholarship, a 'statist' school now seems to be dominant in the intellectual centres, and this fits with the political climate under President Putin (Lauri Mälksoo, *Russian Approaches to International Law* (Oxford: Oxford University Press, 2015), p. 99).

[5] Congyan Cai, 'International law in Chinese courts during the rise of China' (2016) 110 *American Journal of International Law* 269–288, at 288.

[6] Ibid.

sovereignty, among sovereigns.'[7] Ingrid Wuerth has even argued that
the international legal system needs to be recalibrated to fit our 'post-
human rights era'. Her observation is that the doctrinal and theoretical
expansion of international human rights norms, coupled with a weak to
non-functioning implementation machinery and with selective, politi-
cised enforcement, has fuelled resentment against Western double
standards and – importantly – undermines the normative power of
international law as a whole, in analogy to the broken windows theory
in criminology.[8]

At first sight, all these developments are unfavourable to global constitutionalism. However, international law remains indispensable for
resolving coordination problems among interdependent nation states
and societies and for facilitating cooperation. Networks of both states
and other actors continue to contribute to economic and social wealth.
Multinational enterprises, civil society and individuals (both natural and
legal persons) crossing borders influence the functioning of international
society and domestic societies. Despite a 'souring' of the political and
media discourse on globalisation,[9] the economic, social and political
interconnectedness of states and societies is a persistent fact.[10]

In the face of strong bottom-up currents that are not restricted to one
nation, states cannot simply reverse the trends by mere state-induced
policies. Even the major powers of the world such as the United States
and China seem incapable of turning the tide. For example, US President
Trump declared that the United States intends to exercise its right to
withdraw from the Paris Agreement on Climate Change as soon as the

---

[7] Burke-White (n. 1), at 77.
[8] Ingrid Wuerth, 'International law in the post-human rights era' (2017) 96 *Texas Law
Review* 279–349.
[9] See for an excellent account of the current globalisation-sceptical political and media
discourse: Nikil Saval, 'Globalisation: the rise and fall of an idea that swept the world',
The Guardian, 14 July 2017.
[10] See the KOF Swiss Economic Institute's measurements of globalisation in its economic,
social and political dimensions. According to that institute's indicators, globalisation is
ongoing. See for the methodology (indices and variables) of the KOF Index of
Globalization: http://globalization.kof.ethz.ch/media/filer_public/2017/04/19/vari
ables_2017.pdf based on Axel Dreher, Noel Gaston and Pim Martens, *Measuring
Globalization: Gauging Its Consequences* (New York: Springer, 2008). See for nuanced
assessment of the depth and breadth of *economic* globalisation (measured in terms of the
mobility of goods and persons and financial flows): Pankaj Ghemawat, *Globalization in
the Age of Trump* (Boston, MA: Harvard Business Review, 2017). Ghemawat identifies
'semiglobalization': international (economic) interactions are significantly fewer than
domestic interactions.

state is eligible to do so[11] 'unless the United States identifies suitable terms for reengagement'.[12] This phrase might indicate that the United States seeks to avoid abandoning the international climate regime completely. The Japan–EU economic partnership on which agreement in principle was reached in July 2017 and the decision in November 2017 of eleven nations to move ahead with the TPP, without the United States, demonstrate that new alliances can be forged. Both moves aim at keeping the option open for the United States to rejoin the negotiation table on the TPP initiative. Path dependent choices of the past cannot easily be undone. International cooperation in the fields of security, development, trade and investment, environment, fair competition and technology seems necessary and cannot be simply abandoned, because all nations face these issues. A coherent and common approach appears to be the only way to tackle the problems. In other words, global problems can be effectively solved only by global responses. Before discussing the specific contribution of global constitutionalism to problem solving, the challenges of coordination and the need for a European–East Asian dialogue in this context, we need to clarify some key concepts, which will also inform the discussions in the following chapters.

2 Key concepts[13]

Global constitutionalism, as an '-ism', is a set of ideas (or an ideology) which encourages various types and directions of legal analysis. It first reads and reconstructs some features and functions of international law (in the interplay with domestic law) as forming constitutional bits and pieces and as fulfilling a constitutionalist programme (positive analysis). Second, global constitutionalism seeks to provide arguments for the further development of institutions and procedures in a specific direction (normative analysis). The positive analysis lies in

---

[11] Under Art. 28 of the Paris Agreement, this is possible three years after the entry into force of the agreement for the United States, and that will be on 4 November 2019.

[12] United Nations, Depositary Notification, Communication of the United States, 4 August 2017, UN Doc. C.N.464.2017.TREATIES-XXVII.7.d, https://treaties.un.org/doc/Publication/CN/2017/CN.464.2017-Eng.pdf.

[13] See for an overview of the literature on global constitutionalism, global (or international) constitutional law and constitutionalisation: Thomas Kleinlein and Anne Peters, 'International constitutional law', in Anthony Carty (ed.), *Oxford Bibliographies in International Law*, 2nd ed. (Oxford: Oxford University Press, 2017). See most recently Anthony F. Lang and Antje Wiener (eds.), *Handbook on Global Constitutionalism* (London: Elgar, 2017).

(re-)describing parts of international law – in their interplay with domestic law – as reflecting complementary constitutionalist principles, notably the rule of law, human rights and democracy (the constitutionalist 'trinity'[14]). The normative contribution lies in the employment of these constitutionalist principles as a benchmark for the critique of international law as it stands and in the vision that the international legal order (its institutions and procedures) can and should be interpreted and progressively developed in the direction of greater respect for and realisation of those principles. Thus, global constitutionalism serves as a heuristic tool, as a vocabulary of critique and as a carrier of a normative agenda.[15]

Global constitutionalism has roots in the historic political movement of 'constitutionalism', which, in eighteenth- and nineteenth-century Europe and America, called for written constitutions for nation states. The basic purpose of the constitution then was to subdue political power to the law, hence to create a government of laws, not of men. In order to reach that objective, the constitution was to embody certain material principles, most importantly the separation of powers or checks and balances. Article 16 of the French Declaration of the Rights of Man and Citizens of 26 August 1789 views the protection of human rights and separation of powers as the necessary contents of a constitution ('Toute société dans laquelle la garantie des droits n'est pas assurée, ni la séparation des pouvoirs déterminée, n'a point de constitution').

Constitutionalism of the twenty-first century seeks to realise a political space governed by constitutional law, which would functionally correspond to the 'thick' conception of a constitution.[16] So constitutionalism is wedded to the foundational idea of free and equals governing

---

[14] Mattias Kumm, Anthony Lang, James Tully and Antje Wiener, 'How large is the world of global constitutionalism?' (2014) 3 *Global Constitutionalism* 1–8, at 3.

[15] See for a quest for a more normatively conscious employment of 'constitutionalisation theory' with a moral compass: Garrett Wallace Brown, 'The constitutionalization of what?' (2012) 1 *Global Constitutionalism* 201–227.

[16] Some authors prefer a still 'thicker' (or 'narrower') conception of a constitution which would call a given legal text a constitution only if it has been made by a *pouvoir constituant* in a kind of constitutional big bang (as a manifestation of popular sovereignty); see, e.g., Dieter Grimm, 'The achievement of constitutionalism and its prospects in a changed world', in Petra Dobner and Martin Loughlin (eds.), *The Twilight of Constitutionalism?* (Oxford: Oxford University Press, 2010), pp. 3–22. Such a constitution is not present on the international realm, and it is doubtful whether this conception fits to the global sphere.

themselves through law, both within the state and beyond it.[17] This idea is translated into a commitment to human rights, democracy and the rule of law, as mentioned. Different conceptions of constitutionalism then reflect different accounts of how these principles are spelt out in more concrete terms (e.g. with regard to the idea of a demos or demoi and a constituent power as points of reference and origin, the role of the international community, the formality of the law in its relationship to background principles and so on). The endorsement of constitutionalism beyond the state may require novel and modified institutions and procedures to implement the mentioned foundational idea of free and equals governing themselves through law. For example, the mechanisms of democratic governance as exercised in some nation states might be unworkable in the international realm or in some regions of the world. Proxies might be other forms of inclusive, deliberative and participatory governance, if based on transparent institutions and procedures. Finally, a (domestic, regional or global) society of free and equal individual human beings seems to require a minimum of social security and solidarity mechanisms to allow for 'social citizenship' in the various nested and overlapping polities we live in.

The idea of global constitutionalism does not necessarily comprise the claim that there is an international 'Constitution' with a capital C. Obviously, international constitutional law lacks the typical (albeit not indispensable) formal features of constitutional law, namely the quality of 'higher law' (trumping ordinary law and being more difficult to amend than ordinary laws) and its codification in one single document called Constitution. However, we find institutions, processes and principles within the international legal order (e.g. in the UN Charter[18] but arguably also in non-state-made or hybrid regimes[19]) which fulfil typical

---

[17] See on the continuities and similarities of 'nation-state constitutionalism' and 'global constitutionalism', seeking to avoid a mere 'expansion' to the global realm: Michel Rosenfeld, 'Is global constitutionalism meaningful or desirable?' (2014) 25 *European Journal of International Law* 177–199, at 192 and 199.

[18] See for a reading of the UN Charter as 'the constitution of the international community' Bardo Fassbender, 'International constitutional law: written or unwritten?' (2016) 15 *Chinese Journal of International Law* 489–515, at 513, with further references also to his prior seminal work. Julian Arato, 'Constitutionality and constitutionalism beyond the state: two perspectives on the material constitution of the United Nations' (2012) 10 *International Journal of Constitutional Law* 627–659 usefully distinguishes between a juridical and a political notion of the UN Charter as a constitution.

[19] The idea of 'societal constitutionalism' stemming from reflexive or autopoietic processes of norm creation by societal transnational actors has been most elaborated by Gunther Teubner. See Gunther Teubner, *Constitutional Fragments: Societal Constitutionalism and*

constitutional functions. These functions are to found, to organise, to integrate and to stabilise a political community, to contain political power, to provide normative guidance and to regulate the governance activities of law-making, law application and law enforcement.

In this context, the concept of 'constitutionalisation' denotes both legal processes in the real world of law and the accompanying discourses (mostly among academics, less among judges and even less among political law-making actors).[20] The evolution from an international order based on some organising principles such as state sovereignty, territorial integrity and consensualism to an international legal order which acknowledges and has creatively appropriated and – importantly – modified principles, institutions and procedures of constitutionalism may be qualified as a kind of constitutionalisation 'within' international law (and even within particular international organisations[21]) and discourse. This evolution necessarily presupposes some intertwinement of international law with domestic law, but it is by no means irreversible.

Globalization (Oxford: Oxford University Press, 2012). See along this line of thought, e.g., Kolja Möller, 'Formwandel des Konstitutionalismus: Zum Verhältnis von Postdemokratie und Verfassungsbildung jenseits des Staates' (2015) 101 *Archiv für Rechts- und Sozialphilosophie* 270–289.

[20] The idea of constitutionalisation implies that a constitution (or constitutional law) can come into being in a process extended through time. It also implies that a legal text (or various legal texts) can acquire (or eventually lose) constitutional (and constitutionalist) properties in a positive feedback process. A text can therefore be more (or less) constitution-like and more or less satisfy principles of constitutionalism. Garrett Wallace Brown usefully distinguishes between 'constitutionalisation' understood as a mapping exercise and 'global constitutionalism' as a more critical and normative shaping activity (Brown (n. 15), at 227).

[21] See on two waves of 'organisational' constitutionalism underscoring first the constitutive and enabling function of constitutional law and later its constraining and checking function: Anne Peters, 'International organizations and international law', in Jacob Katz Cogan, Ian Hurd and Ian Johnstone (eds.), *The Oxford Handbook of International Organizations* (Oxford: Oxford University Press, 2016), pp. 33–59. See also Viljam Engström, *Constructing the Powers of International Institutions* (Leiden: Martinus Nijhoff, 2012), pp. 145–183 (chapter 6 on 'Constitutionalism as a framework for debating powers'). See on the WTO recently Joanna Langille, 'Neither constitution nor contract: understanding the WTO by examining the legal limits on contracting out through regional trade agreements' (2011) 86 *New York University Law Review* 1482–1518. Armin von Bogdandy, Matthias Goldmann and Ingo Venzke, 'From public international to international public law: translating world public opinion into international public authority' (2017) 28 *European Journal of International Law* 115–145 ask for a legal framework for pursuing the quest for the effectiveness and legitimacy of international institutional law and are sceptical of global constitutionalism because they find it too focussed on human rights (ibid. at 128–130).

3 A European–East Asian dialogue

Our book confronts global constitutionalism, which is considered to be Eurocentric, with East Asian critiques. The perception of Eurocentrism flows from the fact that until now, global constitutionalism in its various forms has been defined, defended and discussed primarily by European (and to a lesser extent by US) scholars. Scholars in many other parts of the world have not been fully implicated in this discussion. It is therefore unsurprising that notably Asian scholars have mentioned 'Western bias and hegemony' as one of the major challenges to global constitutionalism.[22] The Nepalese scholar Surendra Bhandari stresses that 'the emergence of constitutionalism in international law ... is neither Eurocentric in its concept and nature nor typically American, Latin American, African, or Asian. It is rather fashioned by the common and universal aspirations of humankind. Nevertheless, the practical realm of designing concepts and transmuting them into the construct of international rules has overwhelmingly been westernized, which is one of the reasons for the global disenchantment and backlash to global constitutionalism.'[23]

Without the engagement of scholars from other parts of the world, the universalist claims underlying global constitutionalism ring hollow. One region not sufficiently represented in the discussion on global constitutionalism is East Asia where nearly half the world's population and a growing share of global economic and military capacities are located. This region is important not only because of the increasing coherence through many integrative economic, political and sociocultural processes but also because of the intensity of the discussion on the role of law in the development of this region and because of important dissident voices.

We are aware that caution is warranted when using the concept of East Asia and juxtaposing it to Europe. In Christopher Dent's words: 'East Asia is probably the most diverse region in the world in terms of economic development asymmetry, mixed political regimes and socio-religious traditions and characteristics.'[24] The impact of history on the region is important as well and must not be neglected in the discussion on global constitutionalism in East Asia. Dent stresses that East Asia 'is

---

[22] Surendra Bhandari, *Global Constitutionalism and the Path of International Law: Transformation of Law and State in the Globalized World* (Leiden: Brill, 2016), pp. 41–44.

[23] Ibid., pp. 266–267.

[24] Christopher M. Dent, *East Asian Regionalism* (London: Routledge, 2016) (originally published in 2008), p. 3.

a region marked by historic animosity between rival nations, where conflicts still persist between old and new states alike, and where nationalism remains a potent force in many countries of the region'.[25]

The title of this book does not intend to imply that 'East Asia' is one coherent and delimited entity. We are critical of such a point of view. On the other hand, we need to realise, with Peter Katzenstein, that 'the absence of full agreement on the boundaries of "Europe" and "Asia" has not stopped political actors from invoking and politically exploiting regional terminology'.[26] How then to conceptualise East Asia? Katzenstein explains that 'in the case of Asia, for example, the definition of the region that includes Southeast and Northeast Asia – essentially the Association of Southeast Asian Nations (ASEAN) plus China, North and South Korea, and Japan – and that excludes North America, Australia and New Zealand, and South Asia – that is, the lands of British colonial settlement and imperial control – has both been contested and proved durable in most political initiatives for bringing about Asian or East Asian regionalism'.[27] Our employment of the concept 'East Asia' will mostly refer to developments of East Asia as a region including the aforementioned South-East and North-East Asian nations. The book contains the viewpoints of mostly North-East Asian scholars who do not reflect a common view of East Asia.

False essentialism needs to be avoided not only with regard to Asia or East Asia as regions but also with regard to purported regional approaches to international law. The Indian scholar Bhupinder S. Chimni rightly points out that 'both an essentialist cultural/civilizational explanation and a crude materialist understanding of an Asian approach to international law need to be rejected. There are no pure western or non-western ideas, cultures and civilizations. The "Asian Civilization" or rather "Asian Civilizations", like all other civilizations, is a complex configuration of diverse and multiple cultures and innumerable interpretations of it.'[28]

---

[25] Ibid.
[26] Peter J. Katzenstein, *A World of Regions: Asia and Europe in the American Imperium* (Ithaca, NY: Cornell University Press, 2015), p. 11.
[27] Ibid.
[28] Bhupinder S. Chimni, 'Is there an Asian approach to international law? Questions, thesis, and reflections' (2008) 14 *Asian Yearbook of International Law* 249–264, at 250. He also points out that 'an Asian approach to international law must distinguish between the civilizational values embedded in the life, world and struggles of Asian peoples and the practices of Asian States' (ibid., p. 251).

Yet, dynamics towards more cooperation and interdependency can be recorded in the region. Since the 1980s, international production networks have been forged and have transformed the East Asian region into a network economy.[29] Moreover, free trade agreements have been proliferating to such an extent that it has been labelled a 'noodle bowl'.[30] Multilateral regional institutions for cooperation (e.g. ASEAN, APT, APEC, ARF, EAS) are manifold in East Asia. This shows a drive towards cooperation despite diversity, divisions and the legacy of history.[31]

Also noteworthy are new concepts that are launched to overcome a cooperation deficit in various fields. A case in point is 'human security'. According to a UN Development Programme (UNDP) report of 1994, this concept includes 'safety from such chronic threats as hunger, disease and repression' and 'protection from sudden and hurtful disruptions in the patterns of daily life – whether in homes, in jobs or in communities'.[32] It thus aims at enhancing the livelihood of all citizens beyond the confines of a nation state. The norms and values embedded in this concept are in line with the earlier mentioned constitutional functions. However, the concept is quite vague.[33] Global constitutionalism could play a role in giving it more solidity and significance. Understanding human security in the light of constitutionalist principles would arguably lead to its qualification as a principle of international constitutional law which places the individual human being in the centre without overblowing human rights. Importantly for the context of our book, the concept of 'human security can claim a significant Asian pedigree'.[34] It has become prominent in East Asia since the end of the 1990s. This shows that the region was in dire need of some global and non-state-centred concept that could be the stepping stone for initiatives to improve and guarantee welfare of the citizens in East Asia.[35] At the same time, the rise and

[29] Dent, (n. 24).
[30] Cf. Richard E. Baldwin, 'Managing the noodle bowl: the fragility of East Asian regionalism' (2008) 53 *The Singapore Economic Review* 449–478.
[31] Cf. Simon Chesterman, 'Asia's ambivalence about international law and institutions: past, present and futures' (2016) 27 *European Journal of International Law* 945–978.
[32] United Nations Development Programme, Human Development Report, 1994 (New York: Oxford University Press, 1994), p. 23.
[33] Martin Wählisch, 'Human security: concept and evolution in the United Nations' (2014) 18 *Max Planck Yearbook of United Nations Law* 3–31.
[34] Amitav Acharya, 'Human security: East versus West' (2001) 56 *International Journal* 442–460, at 459.
[35] See Japanese Ministry of Foreign Affairs, Diplomatic Bluebook, 1999, chapter 2, section 3. Quoted in Roland Paris, 'Human security: paradigm shift or hot air?' (2001) 26 *International Security* 87–102.

persistence of human security is an example for an East Asian contribution to global constitutionalism.

But besides this example, East Asian voices, perspectives and symbolism are basically absent in the discourse on global constitutionalism. This has left numerous questions so far unanswered. First of all, it is not clear whether, how and why the understanding and assessment of global constitutionalism by scholars from East Asian nations differ from the views of their European counterparts.[36] If the views diverge, how do claims of global constitutionalism resonate once they are espoused or criticised by East Asian voices shaped by their own specific historical experiences and aspirations? How do these new outlooks and prospects enrich established understandings of what global constitutionalism is or might be? What critiques of global constitutionalism in East Asia are most salient? What kind of understanding is fostered by bringing East Asia into the discussion? Does a normatively thick constitutionalist understanding of international law withstand a confrontation with the realities and readings of international law in East Asia?

By pursuing these questions, we seek to implement Bhupinder Chimni's programme of a 'simultaneous *critique* of "western" ideas and concepts, and their *enrichment* through non-western practices' in order to 'help produce transcultural universal categories of international law. The dialogue between civilizations must take place on the basis of equality, mutual understanding and open-endedness.'[37] Indeed, the dialogue between European and East Asian scholars, as attempted in this volume, aims at de-Europeanising global constitutionalism by including suggestions and insights by scholars from China, Korea and Japan, focussing on developments of the role of law in East Asia.

4   The power and potential of global constitutionalism

Global constitutionalism has been subject to serious criticism from various viewpoints.[38] In times of ruthless globalisation, one of the most

---

[36] See – along a similar vein – for the contention (based inter alia on lab experiments) that different 'Eastern' and 'Western' systems of perceptions and thought exist: Richard Nisbett, *The Geography of Thought: How Asians and Westerners Think Differently . . . and Why* (New York: Free Press, 2003). Nisbett expresses the hope that both intellectual traditions are meeting and will transform each other and themselves in this encounter so that the best elements of both cultures will be retained (ibid., p. 229).

[37] Chimni (n. 28), at 251 (emphasis added).

[38] Jean d'Aspremont even diagnoses an 'anti-constitutionalist fury' among international lawyers (Jean d'Aspremont, 'International legal constitutionalism, legal forms, and the

salient policy objections seems to be that the constitution-like agreements in the field of trade and investment 'lock in' neo-liberal frameworks of accumulation. This critique highlights the mismatch between the market-enabling global rules that secure and protect global markets on which global capital moves and the national market-constraining regimes. The mismatch is that the lower-level (national) policies designed to redistribute wealth and correct market failures will be constrained by the outmigration of firms and therefore run aloof.[39]

Against the background of these and other attacks on constitutionalism, both in the domestic and the global realm, we insist on the power and potential of this framework.[40] Global constitutionalism, i.e. the extension of constitutionalism to the sphere beyond the state, bears some potential for understanding and explaining a number of changes newly emerging in the development of international legal order and for developing solutions to numerous problems in international society, and if only because attractive and viable alternative approaches are not in sight.[41]

Olivier de Frouville has aptly described the catch-22 in which the globalised world finds itself: economic globalisation has led to the loss of autonomy of states and their peoples, to the domination of the political order by the economy and to the loss of meaning of political life within the states' borders.[42] The only way to regain the primacy of the political order over the economy would be a full constitutionalisation of the international sphere, by building a federal scheme which would sufficiently constrain its components

need for villains', in Anthony F. Lang and Antje Wiener (eds.), *Handbook on Global Constitutionalism* (London: Elgar, 2017), pp. 155–169, p. 155). D'Aspremont's critique is most sophisticated, reading the debate among constitutionalists and anti-constitutionalists as the expression and continuation of a debate about the role of legal forms in international law (ibid., p. 166).

[39] Stephen Gill and A. Claire Cutler (eds.), *New Constitutionalism and World Order* (Cambridge: Cambridge University Press, 2014).

[40] See for the need to strengthen and revitalise the UN Charter as the constitutional foundation of international law especially in a time of accelerated political and economic change and a reconfiguration of power with a high potential for destabilisation: Fassbender (n. 18), at 514–515.

[41] Mattias Kumm, Jonathan Havercroft, Jeffrey Dunoff and Antje Wiener, 'The end of the West and the future of global constitutionalism' (2017) 6 *Global Constitutionalism* 1–11.

[42] Olivier de Frouville, 'On the theory of international constitution', in Denis Alland, Vincent Chetail, Olivier de Frouville and Jorge E. Viñuales (eds.), *Unité et diversité du droit international: Ecrits en l'honneur de professeur Pierre-Marie Dupuy* (Leiden: Brill, 2014), pp. 77–103, p. 103.

and which would be at least weakly democratic (through deliberations, transparency and inclusion). However, it seems (currently or
intrinsically) impossible to realise both effective political global governance and global democracy.[43] And, tragically, the available
options of building effective (but hardly democratic) global institutions and maintaining the (globally unjust) status quo *both* give rise
to dissatisfaction and motivate nationalism and religious or pseudo-
religious extremism.[44]

Exactly this contemporary constellation compels a continuous discussion on developing shared governing principles. In such discussions, the
formal principle of state equality (Article 2(1) UN Charter) can to some
extent mitigate the unequal bargaining power of states and can thus
contribute to facilitating the acceptance of negotiated solutions.
It therefore seems that common problems can be addressed better when
the rules of the game guarantee that the state parties around the negotiating
table are on an equal footing. Moreover, the principle of state equality
prohibits double standards, i.e. the application of different standards to
otherwise similar situations, e.g. with regard to trade barriers or human
rights. Based on historical experience of unequal treatment, East Asian
states today insist on state equality.[45]

Importantly, both proponents and opponents have pointed out that
global constitutionalism, intentionally or unintentionally, relies on
Western constitutionalism. This is true as a matter of historical evolution.
However, a regional origin and genesis of ideas does not – as a matter of
principle – foreclose their spread to and their adaptation and appropriation by other cultures. Concerns could be voiced that global constitutionalism is similar to a 'legal transplant' inside the field of international
law. Alan Watson had coined the term in 1974, describing 'the common
phenomenon of one country adopting, in whole or in part, another
country's established law, legal procedure, legal institution, or legal

---

[43] Dani Rodrik, *The Globalization Paradox: Democracy and the Future of the World Economy* (New York: Norton, 2011).
[44] De Frouville (n. 42), p. 103.
[45] See point 6 of the Declaration of the Russian Federation and the People's Republic of China on the Promotion of International Law of 25 June 2016 (UN Doc. S/2016/600) condemning double standards. Hanquin Xue explains Chinese insistence on non-intervention as a reaction to double standards applied by the West (Hanquin Xue, 'Chinese contemporary perspectives on international law: history, culture and interna-tional law' (2011) 355 *Recueil des Cours/Collected Courses of The Hague Academy of International Law* 41–233, at 153). See also Philipp W. Chan, *China, State Sovereignty and International Legal Order* (Leiden: Brill Nijhoff, 2014).

system'.[46] Legal 'transplantation' has come under the critique of being an artificial insertion of foreign tissue which will likely be repelled by the receiving body politic. A newer and more subtle technique is the 'legal translation'.[47] This technique seems more in line with global constitutionalism, because it accommodates the varying sensitivities and differing connotations associated with law in general and with constitutional law and constitutionalism in particular. This suggests that constitutional principles and procedures, and a constitutionalist mindset, should be not transplanted but rather translated to fit into East Asia. In fact, constitutionalism as an ideational system and mode of governance is today no longer exclusively possessed by Western states. Rather, constitutionalism is pervasive throughout the world. However, non-Western constitutionalism is not necessarily identical to Western constitutionalism.[48] A closer study and integration of non-Western constitutionalism may open up a new path for the development of global constitutionalism.

In sum, keenly aware of the need for inclusion and equality, we seek to offer a more diverse academic platform for analysing, in a more inclusive way, various facets of global constitutionalism. Importantly, the critical reflection on global constitutionalism with a focus on East Asia and the critical analysis of global constitutionalism by East Asian scholars will bring to light the weaknesses, strengths and the potential of global constitutionalism. The book thereby aspires to contribute to the elaboration of a more nuanced concept that fits our times.

5   Overview of the book

The book consists of three parts. Each part brings together related research topics that develop cumulatively the book's approach to global constitutionalism.

---

[46] Alan Watson, *Legal Transplants: An Approach to Comparative Law* (Athens, GA: University of Georgia Press, 1974). Also quoted in Valerie P. Hans, 'Trial by jury: story of a legal transplant' (2017) 51 *Law & Society Review* 471–704, at 471.

[47] Maximo Langer, 'From legal transplants to legal translations: the globalization of plea bargaining and the Americanization thesis in criminal procedure' (2004) 45 *Harvard International Law Journal* 1–64.

[48] An important difference might relate to the constitutional status of religion in various non-European countries. See, e.g., Benjamin Schonthal, 'Formations of Buddhist constitutionalism in South and Southeast Asia' (2017) 15 *Journal of International Constitutional Law* 705–733; Rainer Grote and Tilmann J. Röder (eds.), *Constitutionalism in Islamic Countries: Between Upheaval and Continuity* (Oxford: Oxford University Press, 2012).

The first part examines the theoretical foundations of global constitutionalism. In this part, groundwork is done for a further explication of global constitutionalism by examining the context in which global constitutionalism has so far been discussed and by reconstructing existing arguments for global constitutionalism. How might confronting arguments and narratives formulated by East Asian scholars modify the positions defended by European scholars? What experiences and concerns inform East Asian scepticism about global constitutionalism? To what extent does talking of an international society that shares certain common (possibly constitutionalist) values make sense?

Toshiki Mogami, in Chapter 1, reviews the contributions and the so far unnoticed limits of global constitutionalism. Being apparently so new, this theory has been highly esteemed as truly innovative. Was it, however, wholly innovative, in terms of either its power to explain facts or its capability to prescribe a design for the future? Mogami casts doubt on this estimation and shows that there was a predecessor to global constitutionalism which deserves to be remembered and referred to. At the same time, the chapter calls attention to the theoretical validity of the conventional concepts of multilateralism, and after enriching multilateralism normatively, it connects this 'normative multilateralism' with the concept of critical constitutionalism and presents 'normative multilateralism' as a viable alternative for the survival of global constitutionalism.

In Chapter 2, Bin Li analyses China's socialist rule of law and connects this to the discussion on global constitutionalism. Li states that constitutionalism as such has evolved unevenly since being introduced into China's legal rhetoric. China's past and current attitudes towards constitutionalism during the state- and institution-building process have had an important impact on China's strategic choices regarding fundamental principles such as the rule of law, human rights, democracy and global governance. It is questionable whether *global* constitutionalism would be able to accommodate the politics and forms of constitutional practice in China. China's conservative domestic position on constitutionalism is echoed globally by its scepticism regarding the function of international law as a way to contain power and politics. The country is therefore unlikely to be persuaded by the merits of global constitutionalism, except to the extent that global constitutionalism is actually able to compensate for the limits of international law in subordinating politics to law and power to justice. Entering the twenty-first century, China – as a rising major power – is no longer satisfied with preserving its national autonomy passively; it aims to acquire more 'power of language' and even leadership in global affairs. It remains to be seen, however, whether China is prepared, theoretically and practically, for such a profound change.

Christine Schwöbel-Patel (Chapter 3) contributes to this volume's groundwork by problematising the mutually reinforcing relationship between global constitutionalism and neo-liberalism in the East Asian context. The nexus is explained as based on the insistence on separating the public and the private in both constitutionalism and neo-liberalism. The central question is whether global constitutionalism's predisposition towards neo-liberalism (in the sense of privileging the separation of the state from the market and, with that, a separation of the political from the economic) would be strengthened and deepened by global constitutionalism's extension to East Asia. Alternatively, could this new dialogue provide an opportunity for 'decolonising' global constitutionalism and its political economic bias? In the fourth chapter, Takao Suami takes a more 'positive' approach by examining the European legal experience with regional integration in the past and questioning whether this can contribute to constitutionalism beyond Europe. Suami notes that most claims of global constitutionalism are inspired by this experience, especially by the constitutionalisation of EU law. He argues, however, that legal achievements in Europe should not be automatically considered universalisable and that we must be careful about channelling European experiences into the formulation of global theories. Suami argues that nonetheless we must recognise that they do teach other regions many lessons and may be useful for a globalised world, because the unique features of EU law are not decisive in distinguishing EU law from international law. It is the *substance* of constitutional principles that is specific to Europe, though most countries elsewhere are formally committed to constitutional principles. The distinction between constitutional principles and specific standards embodying the principles is useful in developing constructive dialogue between Europe and East Asia for the acceptance of global constitutionalism.

Concluding the first part (Chapter 5), Mattias Kumm retraces the history of global constitutionalism, explaining that narratives are very much part and parcel of the history of Western legal and political thought and have been connected to periods of Western hegemony. With such a historical background, can global constitutionalism be sufficiently civilisationally and culturally inclusive? Can it be relevant when

Western hegemony seems to be receding and the balance of power shifting in favour of other regions, most notably Asia? After clarifying concepts, the chapter provides some basic ideas towards an affirmative genealogy of global constitutionalism. Drawing on examples from Asian and European history, it shows first that universal categories and their meaning have often been shaped by contestations and conflicts between different actors, not simply dictated by 'the West'. It shows also that anti-constitutionalist claims, often made in the name of national tradition, culture or sovereignty, have – both in postcolonial contexts and in the West – served as a cover for the continuation of practices of domination by national elites and as a shield for these from challenges by the oppressed. Finally, the chapter shows that to the extent that international legal structures perpetuate forms of domination, constitutionalism has demonstrated the internal resources to criticise these and to guide efforts of progressive development and reform.

In the second part of this book, core constitutionalist values (or principles), such as human rights and the rule of law, and their implications for global constitutionalism in the three main North-East Asian nations are discussed. Fundamental to the 'thick' form of global constitutionalism is the transposition of values developed in national constitutionalism. 'Thick' global constitutionalism is essentially value oriented. For global constitutionalism to 'hold true' (i.e. to be an epistemically plausible and normatively persuasive concept), certain values and principles commonly shared by the global world must be identified. This qualification is particularly important for East Asia, since the societal and legal reality in it (including laws, democracy, culture, economic development and religion) is very diverse.

In Chapter 6, Dimitri Vanoverbeke looks more closely at East Asia's first experience with constitutionalism by explicating the process of constitutionalism in Japan. In this chapter, he argues that constitutionalism has two dynamics: top down and bottom up or state centred and society centred. Constitutionalism includes a complex, long-term process of the transformation of goals and ideas, and this process determines how future developments and reforms regarding constitutionalism are approached in a given society. Japan's experience is important in understanding how historical paths have a lasting impact on constitutionalism and on the understanding of the global constitutionalism debate.

Vanoverbeke also goes beyond the case of Japan to analyse the recent dynamics of institution building in South-East Asia, where principles and constitutional norms are debated and conferred in new formal systems related to the Association of Southeast Asian Nations (ASEAN). The dynamics that he uncovers in the recent ASEAN institutional reforms conform with the long-term developments regarding constitutionalism in Japan and should be considered in revisiting strong criticism from East Asian scholars of global constitutionalism.

Matthieu Burnay (Chapter 7) focuses on China and analyses Chinese perspectives on the rule of law. In a context where China has re-emerged as a central actor in global governance, understanding the development of the socialist rule of law with Chinese characteristics is necessary to understand the prospects for China's contribution to global constitutionalism and the constitutionalisation of international law. The chapter argues that China's legal system can be characterised as a 'multiple-speeds legal system', in which respect for the rule of law varies depending on the rules' impact on the country's legal, political, economic and social stability. The chapter holds that zooming out of the triangle of the rule of law, democracy and human rights will help us to understand the Chinese perspective on the rule of law – which is critical of the rule of law developed internationally. The Chinese emphasis has been on the rule of law as a self-standing principle rather than as a complement to human rights and democracy. The accomplishment of a fully fledged rule of law will require China to reflect on its political system and its perspective on human rights.

Chapter 8 (by Yoon Jin Shin) analyses South Korea and more specifically 'cosmopolitanising' rights practices in the country and explores their implications for global constitutionalism. The chapter first shows how international human rights law interacts with constitutional law in rights contestation and adjudication processes before the Korean Constitutional Court. It then examines the court's changing attitude towards comparative constitutional law and foreign rights practices and notes the court's evolving, transnational self-identity vis-à-vis the wider world. The subsequent section reflects on the encounter of (Asian) tradition and culture with constitutional rights and principles, and it discusses the merits of constitutional rights review in accommodating both the locality of contexts and the universality of rights norms. Finally, the role of individual rights-holders is emphasised in Korea's cosmopolitanising rights practices. The mutually empowering relationship between global-minded individuals and the Constitutional Court is highlighted. This chapter concludes that the overall development in South Korea exemplifies a practice of bottom-up and locally grown global constitutionalism emerging outside Europe. It provides a counterweight to the oft-levelled charges that global constitutionalism is an elitist and Eurocentric enterprise. Korea may provide a promising perspective from which to understand and advance global constitutionalism as a truly global project.

The book's third part considers specific legal constellations in terms of global constitutionalism. It focuses on the interrelated issues of trade, environment and development. Global constitutionalism considers crucial 'horizontal' relationships among international organisations and legal regimes, because global constitutionalism purports to offer a comprehensive and cross-cutting framework. For example, the legal design of the relationships between the World Trade Organization (WTO) and other international forums impacts how trade or investment and non-trade concerns, such as protection of the environment and labour, are accommodated within international trade law. Some legal aspects arising in bilateral trade and interstate investment relations might also be included in this category of constitutional issues.

In this part's first chapter (Chapter 9), Anne Peters argues that the traditional trinity of global constitutionalism can and should be extended to cover a fourth aspect, a social limb. Just as national constitutionalism has embraced the social question, global constitutionalism must do so too in times of globalisation fatigue. Here, global constitutionalism can build on and promote important trends in the post-2015 international legal order, notably the emerging cross-border social responsibility for individuals. The study of inter- and transnational social law standards and entitlements through the lens of global constitutionalism facilitates cross-fertilisation between social and liberal constitutional principles and works against playing out those dimensions against each other in a false competition. By absorbing the social question, global constitutionalism can mitigate its neo-liberal tilt and is rescued from being reduced to a project to deepen the power of capital and to extend a market civilisation in which the transnational investor is the principal political subject. With such a renovation from within, global constitutionalism can form part of a fresh 'post-neo-liberal imagination' of international law.

Hyuck-Soo Yoo (Chapter 10) addresses the issue of international development in the discourse of global constitutionalism. First, the history of international development in international society after World War II is sketched. It is noted that the concept, contents and dimension of development have been changed and that development is no longer a problem of developing countries alone but of the whole world, including developed countries. Next, the large gap between the level of goals and objectives of development and the level of individual and concrete rules to achieve it is shown. The chapter examines in turn how and to what extent global constitutionalism can redescribe and reconstruct international law in the field of development as containing constitutional bits and pieces. Yoo points out that its redescription and reconstruction have their own limitations and that we need a thick version of the 'constitutional order'. In conclusion, he argues that we should change our paradigm of international development and try to pursue feasible alternative designs of the global economic order by which today's imbalance among countries could be largely avoided.

In Chapter 11, Wang Xigen argues that 'the right to development approach' should be applied in constructing the global legal mechanism to implement the right to development. A new way of thinking – people-centred development with justice – should be introduced. In terms of the rule of law, both the existing radicalism and conservatism should be abandoned, and a new way of thinking should be adopted, namely the 'double-track approach', which integrates soft law with hard law. Hard law must be applied in two steps. The first step is to make use of the existing mechanism of human rights. Before the promulgation of the specific hard law on the right to development, the Declaration on the Right to Development in 1986 could be linked to the system of individual communications and to the reporting, evaluation, monitoring and collaboration mechanism in the two human rights covenants of 1966. The second step is to establish the specific hard law mechanism in two forms, namely the international convention on the right to development at the public law level and the bilateral contract on the right to development at the private law level.

In view of the remarkable rise in legal discipline under the WTO Agreement and investment treaties, theorists speak of the 'constitutionalisation' of international economic law. A pluralist insight reveals, however, that the advancement of certain constitutional values, such as economic freedom, would inevitably involve the sacrifice of other societal values. Accordingly, constitutionalism associated solely with the evolution of a specific treaty regime would have a mixed impact on the global society as a whole. In Chapter 12, Kazuyori Ito focuses on the mixed character of constitutionalism in the international economic legal order and argues that the concept of constitutionalisation itself must be reformulated. The constitutional character of a global economic institution should be assessed according to the extent to which the institution allows equal and serious consideration of inputs from around the world. If global constitutionalism seeks to enhance human liberty and autonomy in the global legal arena, it should be careful not to narrow its ambition to the promotion of specific values attainable through the development of specialised international norms; it should concern itself with the issue of autonomy and self-determination of people in the broader society, particularly through safeguarding the political process of deliberation.

The core thesis of Louis J. Kotzé's Chapter 13 is that the Anthropocene's deepening global socioecological crisis underlines the urgency of revisiting the potential of constitutionalism to achieve some of the global regulatory interventionist outcomes needed to maintain an ordered coexistence and to improve global socioecological security. To this end, a case can be made in support of globalising environmental constitutionalism, which would require exploring how far this idea manifests itself in the global regulatory space. Kotzé seeks specifically to make clear how global environmental constitutionalism currently manifests itself in a regional environmental law and governance setting, both in the European Union and in the Association of Southeast Asian Nations. The chapter thereby offers a perspective on the potentially different manifestations of global environmental constitutionalism in a comparable, but distinct, regional setting. At the same time, the chapter provides common ground for global constitutionalism and environmental law discourses and thus seeks to bridge the separation of the two issue areas.

The book's fourth part discusses the implementation and enforcement of international law within a constitutionalised system. Enforcement is integral to a possible process of constitutionalisation since a lack of enforcement prejudices the effectiveness of any legal system. This part focuses on how constitutional principles guide or constrain the international and domestic enforcement of international law. Its chapters focus on the important role played by international courts and tribunals as well as on the functioning of private governance schemes.

Kaoru Obata (Chapter 14) argues that present-day global constitutionalism and its non-hierarchical character often presuppose the validity of the principle of 'functional complementarity'. This principle means coordinating national and international jurisdictions according to their procedural effectiveness in providing redress. It seems to have been established in Europe, mainly in EU law and the European Convention on Human Rights. It entails, however, an unsolved problem in its antithetical functioning for 'core' and 'peripheral' members. Obata also casts doubt on its universal applicability through analysing the jurisdictional immunity of international organisations as well as the theory and practice of admissibility before the International Criminal Court. The principle is felt not to be sufficiently valid in relation to unreliable jurisdictions mainly in Africa and Asia. The arguments for exclusive jurisdiction over the UN's own peace operations or original jurisdiction of the international community over 'core crimes' sometimes rule out any applicability of the principle. Obata analyses whether or not, given these actual limitations of the principle of functional complementarity, the global constitution, even in its pluralistic version, will work coherently and harmoniously.

Guimei Bai's Chapter 15 probes the role of Chinese human rights nongovernmental organisations (CHRNGOs) in the context of global constitutionalism. Although it seems that China is reluctant to accept the ideas of global constitutionalism and human rights, the situation is actually much more complex. There has been a heated, ongoing debate on constitutionalism and democracy in the Chinese academy and government, but China has gradually become accustomed to participating in matters of international human rights. Against this backdrop, human rights NGOs, especially CHRNGOs, have also been following a long and winding path of development in China for decades. On one hand, CHRNGOs are at present increasingly active in promoting human rights education and in engaging in China-related international human rights procedures. On the other, they are destined to face simultaneously a variety of institutional challenges such as registration, funding and political sensitivity. Proposing several solutions, the chapter points to a considerable opportunity to consolidate the survival and contribution of CHRNGOs in a changing China.

In Chapter 16, Axel Marx and Jan Wouters take as a point of departure that while there is no lack of constitutional norms in international law, it is far more challenging to ensure their effective implementation. The authors' main thesis is that private governance schemes can act to enforce fundamental rules of public international law efficiently. In a globalised world, the monopoly of rule making and enforcement no longer lies with sovereign states alone. An increasing number of private actors play a role here, as a significant body of literature describes. These private initiatives establish transnational mechanisms that enforce international law and global constitutional norms. A focus on non-state actors enriches our understanding of how constitutionalisation processes might work 'beyond the state', since these actors enforce international norms, even when the norms are contested or rejected by sovereign states. Marx and Wouters substantiate this argument by focusing on a specific type of private action 'voluntary sustainability standards'.

Geir Ulfstein (Chapter 17) discusses whether the rule of law as known from the national constitutional context is also useful internationally. He examines whether an international rule of law should be seen as part of global constitutionalism. The significance of international courts and tribunals for the rule of law in the Asian context is then dealt with. The strong regional courts in Europe are compared with the weak development of regional courts in Asia. The question is raised whether the use by Asian states of global dispute settlement mechanisms may compensate for the lack of regional courts. The chapter reflects on why the regional Asian judiciary is so weak and considers if more regional judicialisation may be expected in the future. It also asks whether viable alternative Asian procedures for dispute resolution exist. This discussion is used to assess the status of the rule of law in Asia but also the possibility that the Asian states' sceptical approach to international judicialisation may weaken the global rule of law.

In the book's concluding Chapter 18, Takao Suami tackles the question whether global constitutionalism might be useful in promoting certain principles specifically in East Asia. He asserts that, given its universal character, global constitutionalism has not yet been discussed from the perspective of any particular region. The level of constitutionalisation differs in each region. Accordingly, the impact of global constitutionalism, which covers domestic and international law, differs from region to region. Against this background, his chapter details how and to what extent global constitutionalism is significant for East Asia. After a summary of the situation of East Asia overall, the second section focuses on the discussion in wartime Japan of 'overcoming modernity'. This discussion demonstrates a serious analytic and normative flaw of the postulate of 'Asian values'. Based on insights from the second section, the last section studies the situation of the constitution of Japan. It concludes that global constitutionalism may have a positive impact on the constitutional protection for individuals. As a whole, Suami's chapter asserts that the traditional West–East dichotomy is theoretically meaningless in analysing ongoing problems in international society.

6 Conclusion

The scarceness of regional approaches to global constitutionalism leaves a gap in legal scholarship. This book attempts to begin closing this gap by giving a voice to scholars researching constitutionalism in East Asia and engaging in a debate with long-time advocates of global constitutionalism.

The ultimate question is how and to what extent global constitutionalism is significant for East Asia. The answer is mixed, to say the least. True, some legal developments in East Asia in the past decades can be characterised as manifestations of constitutionalisation, e.g. the mentioned concept of human security, the free trade agreements and the regional multilateral institutions for enhanced cooperation. Besides these rather exceptional phenomena, however, most developments remain at the stage of mere legalisation, understood as the 'densening' of legal elements in the international relations among East Asian states.[49] We might mention both state-centred initiatives such as the 2007 ASEAN Charter and private initiatives pushing for further legalisation in the region.[50] Legalisation is an important starting point for constitutionalisation, but constitutionalisation proper would need to go beyond this stage. Many East Asian nations and East Asia as a region have so far been unable to move beyond this first stage because they are so far not relying on constitutional values when interpreting and applying international law. Additionally, a Westphalian-type sovereignty is still widely acclaimed in East Asia; many East Asian states insist on non-interference with domestic affairs.

In the current – maybe transitory – phase, two mutually incompatible trajectories of the international scene are conceivable: either we will see deeper integration triggered by further globalisation, accompanied by

---

[49] Cf. Judith Goldstein, Miles Kahler, Robert O. Keohane and Anne-Marie Slaughter, 'Introduction: legalization and world politics' (2000) 54 *International Organization* 385–399.

[50] Cf. Tamio Nakamura (ed.), *East Asian Regionalism from a Legal Perspective: Current Features and a Vision for the Future* (London: Routledge, 2009).

global constitutionalism, or we will move towards an Asia-dominated world in which the values of sovereignty and non-interference prevail. But there is also a third possibility, as Tom Ginsburg points out: 'Both claims, that of global constitutionalization and that of Asian dominance, may be compatible. This possibility would require an acceleration of integration in Asia itself and the adoption of a set of norms and preferences among peoples of the region that is compatible with the constitutionalist vision. It is a vision of convergence, in which Asian values become European values and vice versa.'[51] Global constitutionalism – if embraced in East Asia – would, we claim, help to solve regional issues. Yet, the likelihood for global constitutionalism to catch root at the national level seems small in view of specific sensitivities of the region. Not in the least, there is historical animosity, which creates political tension, and distrust, which has led to the dismissal of even faint proposals for transnational decision making that is not based on absolute consensus. How can global constitutionalism contribute to peace and prosperity for all individuals in East Asia as it arguably has in other parts of the world? How can the historical and sociopolitical tensions that bar cooperation and fuel misunderstandings be overcome so as to give a fair chance to global constitutionalism to be considered a relevant legal tool for East Asia, too? This volume is a first attempt to offer clues for first answers and trigger a discussion in East Asia about international law in general and global constitutionalism in particular.

With these contributions, our book seeks, first, to refine (maybe reshape or even downsize) the positive findings and, second, to promote or adjust the normative agenda of global constitutionalism. The ultimate purpose of adjustments in both dimensions is to turn global constitutionalism into a truly global framework, which is capable of working towards the resolution of problems of human society that can be national, regional or international. The overall objectives of law and governance, namely to contribute to the preservation of peace and to foster the livelihood of individuals, can be supported by global constitutionalism on the condition that it overcomes its real or perceived Eurocentrism. We are pleased if readers will find that this book succeeded in challenging dominant Western narratives and in paving the way to a richer, more inclusive understanding of international law and of what global constitutionalism is or might be.

---

[51] Tom Ginsburg, 'Eastphalia as the perfection of Westphalia' (2010) 17 *Indiana Journal of Global Legal Studies* 27–45, at 45.

PART I

Groundwork

Interplay Between European Ideas and East Asian Perspectives

Perpetuum Mobile

Before and After Global Constitutionalism

TOSHIKI MOGAMI

1 By way of stocktaking

The notion of global or international constitutionalism (hereafter 'global constitutionalism') has never been unidefinitional. Its definition and description have always caused trouble for both global constitutionalists and their critics. Yet, for the sake of convenience, a dichotomy of global constitutionalism can be established between the descriptive/cognitive category and the normative/prescriptive one: the former suggests that there exists a constitution (or a body of laws equivalent to a constitution), and the latter asserts that certain defective aspects of international law must be rectified, not in terms of political convenience but in terms of norms as universal as possible in accordance with basic values that enjoy societal legitimacy.[1]

The descriptive/cognitive category has been represented outstandingly by Bardo Fassbender who holds that the United Nations Charter is the constitution of the international community,[2] though this recognition has not been shared by many, even among the global constitutionalists. Despite his establishment of a simple and discernible milestone from which to start arguments, it seems to overlook a few important points. A criticism, among others, is that this theory fails to pay due attention to the fact that the UN Charter system is devoid of any legal mechanism with which the exercise of power by the Security Council (SC), including the use of force in the form of enforcement actions or the authorisations

---

[1] For a more detailed account of this dichotomous categorisation, see Toshiki Mogami, 'Towards *jus contra oligarchiam*: a note on critical constitutionalism' (2012) 55 *Japanese Yearbook of International Law* 371–402, esp. at 373–376.
[2] Bardo Fassbender, *The United Nations Charter as the Constitution of the International Community* (Leiden: Martinus Nijhoff Publishers, 2009).

thereof for a portion of member states, can be controlled. Since the statutory control of power is the essence of a constitution, the Charter, absent this essence, is by definition not a constitution.[3] Moreover, the system also does not guarantee equality among the member states.

On the other hand, the normative/prescriptive category is not monolithic, and authors talk about a variety of issues relying on their own notions of constitutionalism: some emphasise the primacy of human rights; others are more interested in the construction of more or less centralised systems of global governance, such as the dispute settlement mechanism of the World Trade Organization (WTO); and still others tend to shed light on the degree of robustness of the activities of international organisations, such as the activation of the UN Security Council's Sanctions Committees or the enlivenment of the International Criminal Court. In short, it cannot be said that in this category, either, there exists a definite and unanimous definition and description of what global constitutionalism connotes.[4]

At the same time, this theorisation, discrete in notions as it may be, has brought about a rich variety of international agendas that should be attached importance: for example, the participation of non-state actors in global governance, the primacy of the rights of human beings or the equipment of judicial procedures in all sorts of fora. However discrete its notion may be, global constitutionalism has succeeded in indicating the vital foci of international life, particularly in the alleged post–nation state era.

The problem is, even in defiance of the ambiguity about definitions and descriptions, the achievements of global constitutionalism itself remain ambiguous, too. What are the outcomes that global constitutionalism was able to produce better than other approaches? What has been the real conceptual innovation which otherwise would have been impossible? True, an intellectual world that includes global constitutionalism is much better than one in which violent unilateralism is rampant, one in which humanity is simply trampled with impunity, one in which nobody cares about peaceful resolutions of conflict or one in which uncritical worship of absolute state sovereignty persists. Yet, there is little evidence

---

[3] Mogami (n. 1), at 374–375.

[4] Perhaps with the exception of Anne Peters, who has tried to construct the definition of the term as precisely and extensively as possible in her works listed in this chapter, although it is not certain how widely her definition(s) and characterisations are shared by those scholars engaged in global constitutionalism. See, e.g., Anne Peters, 'The merits of global constitutionalism' (2009) 16 *Indiana Journal of Global Legal Studies* 397–411.

that all the credit could be ascribed to global constitutionalism, either. It is also why there have been consistent criticisms against this theory.

However, the validity of these criticisms does not appear solid. One criticism was levelled against the 'value orientation' of global constitutionalism,[5] another directed at its 'lack of realism'[6] and still another against its 'utopianism'.[7] Each has its own truism, depending on the kind of global constitutionalism each one chooses as the target, yet none of them has proved sufficient to annihilate altogether the validity and necessity of (a certain kind of) global constitutionalism.

Thus, this chapter aims to take stock of the trajectory so far of global constitutionalism: Whether and how was it necessary? What were its achievements? Was it really innovative? What is desired of it if it is to sustain its validity?

First, was global constitutionalism necessary, and if so, how? The theorisation came about in Europe, when the euphoria for the post–Cold War era was largely betrayed, with the outbreak of ethnic conflicts, human rights violations by tyrannical regimes, the outburst of refugees as a result thereof, environmental destruction, economic crises and so on. The world apparently needed solutions for these conundrums. Global constitutionalism was part of the answer. Although a legal theorisation cannot by itself be a panacea, reacting to the situation with notions such as 'global' and 'constitutional' was not without reason, for it was the basic, overall structure of the world, as well as effective and ineffective principles governing it, that were at stake.

Thus, it could be said that the birth of the theory *was* necessary in view of the scale of the global problematique. On the other hand, if necessity is defined as the ability of the theory to solve the problems, the necessity of global constitutionalism was not guaranteed from the outset, as with any theory. If it *was* necessary, it meant only that the international legal world needed that sort of theory as it had been confronted with several sorts of fragmentation (in the sense of unequal and disintegrated developments/ underdevelopments) as well as a lack of effectiveness in controlling the legally dubious acts. The problematique was systemic; hence a systemic reaction such as 'global' (in scope) and 'constitutional' (in nature) was hoped for.

---

[5] See, e.g., Matej Avbelj, 'Can European integration be constitutional and pluralist: both at the same time?', in Matej Avbelj and Jan Komárek (eds.), *Constitutional Pluralism in the European Union and Beyond* (Oxford: Hart Publishing, 2012), pp. 381–409.

[6] See, e.g., Jan Klabbers, 'Constitutionalism lite' (2004) 1 *International Organization Law Review* 31–58.

[7] See, e.g., Nico Krisch, *Beyond Constitutionalism* (Oxford: Oxford University Press, 2010).

Second, what were the expected outcomes of this kind of seemingly holistic theory? Characterising itself as global and constitutional, this theory was destined to aim at prescribing for international (principally legal) *order*, international *justice* (in the ethical sense) and international *organising* (as opposed to fragmenting) of states. They are *goals* that the theory should take upon itself, rather than *values* that it is predicated upon. Among them, the goal of order necessitates the theory to tackle the problem of peace, particularly negative peace, or the avoidance or minimisation of war/use of force and other forms of international violence; the goal of international justice should essentially relate to the eradication of inequality between human beings as well as states, not only for the present generation but also for the future and even past generations, which would inevitably involve the difficult process of elucidating the meaning of time in international law beyond the age-old formula of applying only legal norms which were valid in the period when the acts in question were done.[8]

It should be clear that these goals are theoretically deducible ones, not the goals that the existing theories of global constitutionalism proclaim to achieve. Here again the existing theories are too diverse to be presumed to contain a (largely) identical set of goals. On the contrary, I would submit that the existing theories have dealt with those goals only insufficiently, and far from comprehensively, though a few of them have succeeded in clearly presenting the values on which the theory is based.[9]

As regards *order*, the question of international security has not been the focal point of global constitutionalism with the exception of a few theories.[10] As regards *justice*, research has been accumulated concerning

---

[8] This is the problem known as intertemporal law, and only half of it. As is well elucidated by, for example, Rosalyn Higgins, 'Time and the law: international perspectives on an old problem' (1997) 46 *International & Comparative Law Quarterly* 501–520, the limitation to apply the contemporaneous law as regards territorial title is only half of the principle formulated by Max Huber in his Palmas case award of 1928 (*USA v. the Netherlands*), where he equally said that distinction should be made 'between the creation of rights and the existence of rights' and that the 'continued manifestation' of rights 'should follow the conditions required by the evolution of the law'. For the development of this question, see n. 11.

[9] See, e.g., Anne Peters, 'Compensatory constitutionalism: the function and potential of fundamental international norms and structures' (2006) 19 *Leiden Journal of International Law* 579–610; Erika de Wet, 'The emergence of international and regional values systems as a manifestation of the emerging international constitutional order' (2006) 19 *Leiden Journal of International Law* 611–632.

[10] See, e.g., Erika de Wet, *Chapter VII Powers of the United Nations Security Council* (Oxford: Hart Publishing, 2004).

the contemporary protection of human rights, which may be extrapo-
lated into the future, but little has been discussed about rectifying historical injustices such as slavery and the slave trade, sexual slavery in time of
war and other sorts of human degradation and inhuman deprivation; the
question is not simply that of policy proposals but also, for lawyers at
least, the question of whether we can juridico-theoretically redefine the
effect of *time* by which we may be able to apply the current legal norms to
past acts without unduly shaking legal stability.[11] And finally, as regards
organising the global society, somehow the linkage between global constitutionalism and international organisations has not been manifestly
focused upon: for example, whether existing organisations such as the
UN are involved with global constitutionalisation and in what way, or
whether a high degree of integration such as that enjoyed by the EU is
synonymous with global constitutionalisation or is opposed to it.
The answers are yet to be found.

2 Predecessors and alternatives

2.1 Revisiting WOMP

Before discussing the points insufficiently dealt with by the major global
constitutionalism theories, we should first consider whether there were
theoretical predecessors of global constitutionalism which appeared after
the turn of the century. The answer is positive, although people had the
false impression (at least this was the constitutionalist authors' preten-
sion) that it was original and innovative. The predecessor is the World

---

[11] Higgins herself, in her article (n. 8), is rightly cautious about interpreting this 'second
limb' of the principle as oversetting the 'first limb' (of applying solely the law in effect at
the time of the original act), but the relativisation by Huber was latently capable to incur
a new development in international law. Even if the first limb of the principle remains
valid it is founded on the presumption that the act *was* legal at that time, but it could also
be the case that the legality was only imposed on the weaker by the stronger, as in the case
of slavery and other examples. If so, the lapse of time may be interpreted differently, as
allowing or obligating international law to wind back time and judge past acts by criteria
of the law developed later. This has much to do with what putative global constitutionalism can be expected to explore in relation to the realisation of global social justice.
In this regard, Jan Klabbers refers to Art. 31 of the Vienna Convention on the Law of
Treaties and correctly indicates that this article has 'an emancipatory potential'.
Jan Klabbers, 'Reluctant Grundnormen: Article 31 (3)(c) and 42 of the Vienna
Convention on the Law of Treaties and the fragmentation of international law', in
Matthew Craven, Malgosia Fitzmaurice and Maria Vogiatzi (eds.), *Time, History and
International Law* (Leiden: Martinus Nijhoff Publishers, 2011), pp. 141–161, p. 161.

Order Models Project (WOMP), which was most active between the 1960s and the end of the Cold War approximately.

Christine Schwöbel once pointed out that 'the majority of scholars concerned with constitutionalism are Germans or other continental Europeans'.[12] This could only be true if we forget about WOMP, which originated in the United States, gathered a number of scholars from many parts of the world and was ardently engaged in the discussion and ideation of global constitutionalism in the 1970s and 1980s. This intellectual movement could be regarded as a precursor of the global constitutionalism that became prevalent in the twenty-first century, either in Germany or in some parts of Europe as well as in a few non-European areas.

The idea of global constitutionalism was not accepted enthusiastically by the WOMPers at the outset when the term was taken to mean the advocacy of world government or world federalism, which had been espoused by Saul Mendlovitz, one of the key persons of the group. However, towards the quasi-end of its existence (it has not yet been formally disbanded), there was seen a growing interest in global constitutionalism defined in WOMP's own way, clearly separated from world government. The book *The Constitutional Foundations of World Peace*,[13] published in 1993, with authors also from outside WOMP, consciously developed the global constitutionalist framework and was well representative of the change in tide.

At WOMP, global constitutionalism was newly defined 'broadly and synergistically as a set of transnational norms, rules, procedures and institutions designed to guide a transformative politics dedicated to the realisation of world order values both within and between three systems of international politics in an interdependent world', where the 'three' meant (1) the state system, (2) international governmental institutions and (3) non-state groups and individuals. We (I was part of it) also meant by the term 'something broader and wider than the nineteenth-century tendency to advocate a war/peace system as a blueprint, and something less legalistic than a positivist or Austinian (only rules backed by effective sanctions qualify as "law") extension of effective law enforcement to a global scale'.[14] The definition also included in it 'a process dedicated

---

[12] Christine Schwöbel, *Global Constitutionalism in International Legal Perspective* (Leiden: Martinus Mijhoff Publishers, 2011), p. 107.

[13] Richard A. Falk, Robert Johansen and Samuel S. Kim (eds.), *The Constitutional Foundations of World Peace* (Albany, NY: State University of New York Press, 1993).

[14] Ibid., p. 9.

to deepening and widening democracy both within and across state boundaries, as well as insinuating democratic practices into all levels of political activity, including that associated with international institutions'.[15]

Although this definition, or the WOMPers' commitment, may not have been identical with that of the present-day constitutionalism (most typical and representative ones), we can perceive much proximity with the latter. First, it was predicated on 'values': what the WOMPers called 'world order values' were (1) the minimisation of large-scale collective violence; (2) the maximisation of social and economic well-being; (3) the realisation of fundamental human rights and conditions of political justice; and (4) the rehabilitation and maintenance of environmental quality.[16] Second, it was consciously concerned about justice and order, as exemplified by Richard Falk's pronouncement that 'our concern with global constitutionalism implies a conception of justice and order'.[17] Third, the theoretical axis for its orientation towards a 'just world order' was clearly legal: both the four-volume series *The Strategy of World Order* compiled and published in the 1960s and the five-volume series *Studies on a Just World Order* from the 1980s contained a volume titled 'International Law', evidently because the group was led principally by international lawyers such as Mendlovitz and Falk, to be supplemented by a few more later. Fourth, the attention to 'transnational actors' was manifest from the beginning, something quite innovative in those days. Put differently, there was something 'cosmopolitan' in it,[18] and thus the undertaking as a whole was full of 'beyond the nation state' ethos, sustaining its adherence to overcoming the 'logic of Westphalia'.[19] Fifth, overall, being 'normative' and upholding 'normativity', in the sense of aspiring to 'change for the better', were always the banner of the project.[20] Or else, it kept being 'critical and diagnostic'[21] to the status quo of the day.

---

[15] Ibid.
[16] See, e.g., Richard Falk, *A Study of Future Worlds* (New York: Free Press, 1975), pp. 11–31. Later, the value of 'participatory politics' came to be counted.
[17] Richard A. Falk, 'The pathways of global constitutionalism', in Falk et al. (eds.) (n. 13), p. 15.
[18] Richard A. Falk, Robert C. Johansen and Samuel S. Kim, 'Global constitutionalism and world order', in Falk et al. (eds.) (n. 13), p. 4.
[19] E.g. Falk (n. 16), pp. 59–69.
[20] See, e.g., Toshiki Mogami, 'Normativity: domestic and international dimensions' (1987) 12 *Peace and Change* 39–49; Falk, Johansen and Kim (n. 18), p. 5.
[21] Falk et al., ibid., p. 6.

2.2 A comparison

I would not dare to compare the one-time global constitutionalism to the contemporary one for the simple reasons that the two are in agreement in opposing world government and they share many essential orientations such as the enshrinement of human rights, democracy and the rule of law. Yet, their similarity is undeniable, which renders it hardly possible to say that the contemporary version has been truly innovative.

There are differences as well that could distinguish the two, both positive and negative. First, the scope of WOMP's global constitutionalism was much wider than the present one: WOMP was made up of not only lawyers but also political scientists, sociologists and philosophers. It was interdisciplinary in the true sense of the term. Accordingly, its global constitutionalism was not restricted to the legal sphere, but instead tended to include many political ideals and societal aspirations, regardless of whether they could legitimately be part of legal discourse. Being widespread, its notion of global constitutionalism turned out to be no less ambiguous than the current one, though there was much to be inherited, such as the 'critical' and 'normative' posture which I myself did inherit. At the same time the notion of global constitutionalism alone was no panacea to solve all the global problems, and the WOMPers had to cope with each and every global problem in a concrete way with absolutely the same perspective or cosmology, which was global constitutionalism. But does it not hold true, too, with the contemporary version? We could only say that WOMP failed to narrow down the concept of global constitutionalism to an operational level, which is not really different from the current situation.

WOMP's interest in international legal aspects was conspicuous, as was noted before. The notable characteristic of its 'international legal studies' was that it was much less Black Letter law studies, 'foreign office international law' or formalistic jurisprudence than was legal positivism. Contemporary global constitutionalism may resemble this, yet WOMP's global constitutionalism was much farther from positivism than that, possibly allowing legal positivists to contend that WOMP's version was no longer international legal studies. But those who are more progressive and oriented towards legal alternatives for the betterment of the world may find it quite stimulating and judge that a plethora of hints are scattered around for the enrichment of global constitutionalism even today.

Second, mingled with a variety of political ideals, there certainly was some tendency in WOMP to be sympathetic with the Third World as the 'underdog'[22] of the world. This naturally invited criticisms against its alleged 'Third World orientation',[23] which did not appear fair, for the interest had to do with the 'human interest' as opposed to a specific national interest.[24] Whether fair or not, this was a difference from the contemporary global constitutionalism, which at present is more legalistic than the predecessor. It was in the last analysis an intellectual and practical endeavour to search for *alternatives* to the here and now, even going beyond a framework of analysis and the conceptualisation of the contemporary version, though the two share the same ethos.

Tragically enough, quite often WOMP also was accused of 'imposing an unavoidable Western and Northern slant' because of its 'U.S. funding and administration of the project'.[25] Although there is a hint of truthfulness in it, the criticism yet appears to contradict the charge against the group's 'Third World orientation' as well as its attraction of authors from the non-North-Western world who enriched the cultural/intellectual diversity with works such as *Footsteps into the Future* (Rajini Kothari, 1974) and *Revolution of Being* (Gustavo Lagos and Horacio Gody, 1977), together with a few participants from Japan. It is the academic orientation and products, as well as the designed trajectory for the future, that determine the North-Western slant of this academic endeavour, not the nationalities of its leading members.

Third, although this ancestral version of global constitutionalism shares much in common with the present-day version (which is cognisably more jurisprudential as noted before), there is a significant difference between the two: the importance they each attach to the issue of traditional international security. In WOMP, peace was always at the core, beginning with the title of volume 1 of its first series, *Toward a Theory of War Prevention*.[26] Whatever topic it was engaged in, it never failed to include global security issues, both legal and institutional. War prevention, regulation of the use of force, conflict resolution and

---

[22] Johan Galtung, *The True Worlds: A Transnational Perspective* (New York: Free Press, 1980), chapter 5.

[23] Falk, Johansen and Kim (n. 18), p. 8.

[24] See, e.g., Robert Johansen, *The National Interest and the Human Interest: An Analysis of U.S. Foreign Policy* (Princeton, NJ: Princeton University Press, 1980).

[25] Falk, Johansen and Kim (n. 18), p. 7.

[26] Richard A. Falk and Saul H. Mendlovitz (eds.), *Toward a Theory of War Prevention* (New Brunswick, NJ: World Law Fund, 1966).

disarmament including denuclearisation were the primary concern for WOMP, equally in the context of its global constitutionalism. In contrast, this peace/security does not seem to be a central issue in the theoretical framework of the contemporary version. One discernible exception is Erika de Wet's book cited before,[27] along with a few more related articles, which come into line with my own 'critical constitutionalism' argument and the 'against oligarchy'[28] paradigm, too. However, there has not been much more systematic handling of the issue in the present-day context.

I do not imply that the ancestral global constitutionalism centred exclusively around the issue of traditional international security, but WOMP as a whole was doing so with considerations of a number of related and equally essential issues, which laid the conceptual foundation of WOMP's global constitutionalism. Needless to say, there are always priority decisions to be made in any academic undertaking, and thus any theoretical work does not have to deal with all the issues. But global constitutionalism is first and foremost about global *order*, in my understanding at least – preferably, and theoretically necessarily, a *just* world order. If so, there is no good reason for constitutionalism to avoid a systematic handling of the security issue.

Here again, it is fair to recognise that by incorporating the security issue at the centre of global constitutionalism WOMP was not necessarily successful in finding viable solutions for the anomaly in that field. The discourse of global constitutionalism itself is not, I repeat, a panacea. Yet it is imperative to relate any global constitutionalist framework with the issue of security, first with traditional security and then with non-traditional security including human security.

As regards traditional (usually military) security, an anomaly is being perceived currently on two fronts, both factual and legal. On the factual side, the so-called collective security is dysfunctional: many domestic wars and acts of violence are being perpetrated, and violence by non-state actors is being exerted, against which 'wars on terror' are being waged either unilaterally or collectively, to little avail. Nuclear proliferation continues. Thus, any theory of order and security is required to decide at least whether we should revitalise (UN) collective security, or else, search for an alternative to the current collective security. The trouble

---

[27] De Wet (n. 10), chapter VII, 'Powers'.
[28] Mogami (n. 1). The term 'oligarchy' is also used by Anne Peters in 'Dual democracy', in Jan Klabbers, Anne Peters and Geir Ulfstein (eds.), *The Constitutionalization of International Law* (Oxford: Oxford University Press, 2009), pp. 263–341, esp. pp. 286–289.

with the first option, which is related to the anomaly on the legal side, is that it is not clear *what kind* of collective security should be revitalised. In other words, the notion of collective security has never been uniquely defined, rendering it almost impossible to talk about the revitalisation nonchalantly: *Which* collective security are we to revitalise?

The conventional meaning of collective security is supposedly military and/or non-military enforcement actions taken by international organisations with public authority, such as the League of Nations or the United Nations.[29] However, there is no mention, and therefore definition, of the term in the League Covenant and the UN Charter. It is known by now that there was not even the term when the League was established.[30] Thus, peaceful (pacific) settlement of disputes (chapter VI of the Charter, for instance) was excluded from the notion of collective security as if naturally, without legal basis. The exclusion came about only accidentally when at Yalta the wartime United Nations' Big 3 had to agree on the scope of applicability of veto,[31] with the result that peaceful settlement of disputes is regarded as conceptually different from collective security, which itself has been undefined. Also, activities such as UN peacekeeping have been regarded as something outside the collective security framework, without legal basis. (That there is no mention of it in the Charter is one thing, but whether it can be part of collective security or not is another.)

In contrast to these condensations of the concept, there is also an opposite trend to expand the notion so as to include even collective self-

---

[29] See, for a classical example, Hans Kelsen, *Collective Security under International Law* (Washington, DC: Naval War College, 1954), reprinted by the Lawbook Exchange (Union, NJ: 2001), esp. pp. 1–2. It is worth pointing out that when he first published his pioneering work *The Law of the United Nations* (New York: Frederick A. Praeger, 1950), reprinted by the Lawbook Exchange (Union, NJ: 2000), he only discussed 'enforcement action' without using the term 'collective security', reflecting the relative anonymity of the concept that basically resulted from its non-existence in the Charter. It was only when he published in 1951 a supplement to this book (contained in the same reprint) that he consciously started employing that concept, distinguishing it from collective self-defence.

[30] George W. Egerton, 'Great Britain and the League of Nations: collective security as myth and reality', in *The League of Nations in Retrospect: Proceedings of the Symposium* (Berlin; New York: Walter de Gruyter, 1983), pp. 95–117, p. 95, although other authors use this concept rather unknowingly. As regards the origin of the consolidation of the concept, see Maurice Bourquin (ed.), *La sécurité collective* (Paris: Institut International de Coopération Intellectuelle, Société des Nations, 1936), esp. pp. 7–39.

[31] See, e.g., Bruno Simma, Daniel-Erasmus Khan, Georg Nolte, Andreas Paulus (eds.) and Nikolai Wessendorf (assistant ed.), *The Charter of the United Nations*, 3rd ed. (Oxford: Oxford University Press, 2012), Article 27 (Andreas Zimmermann), esp. p. 880.

defence as part of it. According to this trendy explication, collective security and collective self-defence are essentially selfsame in that they are reactions against aggression.[32] It may arguably be so, but collective security ought to be understood as multilateral and public exercise of power, whereas collective self-defence is essentially an (collectively executed) individual and private act, even if endorsed by law. The latter can, under current law, be launched without any public authorisation, and if it is equated with collective security it would mean that any states can initiate collective security at their own discretion without legal control at least at first. This is tantamount to the negation of the rule of law.[33]

What is required of any theory of global constitutional order is at least to streamline this conceptual anomaly, on the basis of which we would be able to ideate some improvements for global security institution. The WOMPers often went so far as to plan and show the concrete strategies and routes towards a 'preferred' condition in any given field including global security; this may not be a prerequisite for any theory, but the enlightening of the conceptual obscurity is.

Last but not least, WOMP was consciously interested in the *organising* or institutionalisation of international society, with a principal emphasis on the United Nations. This orientation is well symbolised by the fact that volume 3 of the 1966 world order series was titled *The United Nations*, and volume 3 of the 1991 series was titled *The United Nations and a Just World Order*. Though addressing the work of the UN frontally, the posture of WOMP was not necessarily one of uncritical endorsement of all the activities and policies or even founding principles of the existing UN. Rather, it was a sort of critical endorsement of the world organisation, with the more essential target being how to organise the possibly disintegrative and mutually conflictive world. The 1966 compilation contained many chapters that simply introduced the structure of the UN system, but the 1991 one was a mixture of articles supportive of the UN activities *and* those sceptical or even critical of them.[34] The slide from support to scepticism/criticism in twenty-five years was apparent, which

---

[32] See, e.g., Yoram Dinstein, *War, Aggression and Self-Defence*, 2nd ed. (Cambridge: Cambridge University Press, 1994), esp. p. 277; also, Nicholas Tsagourias and Nigel D. White, *Collective Security: Theory, Law and Practice* (Cambridge: Cambridge University Press, 2013), p. 83.

[33] Despite what is referenced in n. 32, Tsagourias and White at the same time correctly point to the possible inappropriateness of equating the two without recognising the essential and qualitative difference between the two. Ibid.

[34] See, e.g., Marc Nerfin's chapter in the volume, 'The Future of the United Nations: Some Questions on the Occasion of an Anniversary', pp. 519–534.

became even clearer in other books published in 1993 and 1994.[35] Yet the interest in and surveillance of this multilateral organisation persisted. Equally notable is that the interest in the UN was already interlinked with the felt need to bring about 'social justice', which the UN was called upon to realise, by going beyond being an instrument for big power dominance.[36]

Thus, with all of contemporary global constitutionalism's normative contributions to the world of international law, I wonder if it has been truly innovative as theory. Seen from the viewpoint that bestrides both WOMP and the present global constitutionalism, there appears to be something atavistic in the latter. The conspicuous difference is that the latter has chosen to be juridical above all as a discipline, while WOMP was much more bloated, covering even issues that were not the subjects of legal science. It cannot be said that a multidisciplinary framework is definitely superior to a uni-disciplinary one, as the former has its own drawbacks as social science. However, there were merits generated from WOMP's deliberate self-identification as a science for a just world order: that is, the wilful orientation towards global *order* and global *justice*, which unfortunately are somewhat missing in the contemporary constitutionalism.

In relation to the preceding discussion, I will now relate the constitutionalist undertaking to another conventional framework: multilateralism.

3 Normative multilateralism: global constitutionalism as a theory of international organisation

3.1 Historical role of international organisation

The interest in the ordering of the world does not necessarily require employing as bold an approach as federalism or constitutionalism but allows one to take a more conventional and modest view, that is, employing a multilateralist framework. As this notion covers a wide range of meanings, we have to begin with narrowing it down to an operational level. In my view, it should go far beyond the naïve meaning of friendly relations or cooperation among states. It is not the simple existence of international organisations or a network of international treaties, whose enforcement capability is not always guaranteed. My understanding is

[35] Falk et al. (eds.) (n. 13); Yoshikazu Sakamoto (ed.), *Global Transformation: Challenges to the State System* (Tokyo; New York: United Nations University Press, 1994).
[36] See, e.g., Toshiki Mogami, 'Grafting the past onto the future of the United Nations system', in Falk et al. (eds.) (n. 13), pp. 129–146.

that the concept of multilateralism is essentially normative, designating a few fundamental modes of action, that is, collective decision making and collective action, both based on common rules. It thus represents several different aspects of the rule of law.[37] This set of principles is derived from the understanding that multilateralism is the opposite of unilateralism, rather than bilateralism, unlike what is asserted in the textbook dichotomy of treaties. Thus, multilateralism becomes normative, and by being so it is converted into an ordering principle. Moreover, it is multilateral and not multi-state, so it can and should also encompass non-state actors, challenging the age-old state-centrism.

When we employ this concept of normative multilateralism, the first entity we should analyse today is the most global organisation, the UN. There are a few presuppositions for this: it is not the most integrated or efficient organisation; its Charter is not the constitution of the world; and it is not an equivalent to a world government, with limited powers as a whole (except for the permanent members of the Security Council). It is only multilateralist, by which measure we are expected to evaluate its performance. But being normatively multilateralist is already a tall order.

The attribution of the adjective 'normative' is not arbitrary but is empirically induced from the history of international organisations, particularly the global (or 'universal') ones. Thus, before going into the evaluation of multilateralism à la UN, we should take a look at the history of international organisation in a nutshell, as far as it is closely related to the analysis here.

The history of international organisation began with constitutional thought, 'constitutional' in the sense of forming a certain polity, either a transnational government or parliament. We can cite Pierre Dubois, Georg von Podiebrad, Emeric de Crucé, William Penn, Abbé de Saint-Pierre or Immanuel Kant as the representative advocates of the ideas along that line.[38] These people ideated some kind of organisation for peace (absence of war) in the form of a regional parliament or state association. If we set aside those actual entities that are regarded by some as the forerunners of international organisation, such as the ancient Greek Amphiktyonia or, closer to the present, the Hanseatic League, we

---

[37] Toshiki Mogami, 'Takokukanshugi to Hou no Shihai' (Multilateralism and the rule of law) (2004) 23 *Yearbook of World Law* 93–123, at 113-116.

[38] For this, see F. Parkinson, *The Philosophy of International Relations* (Beverly Hills, CA: Sage Publications, 1977), pp. 45–48; Pierre Gerbet, 'Rise and development of international organization: a synthesis', in Georges Abi-Saab (ed.), *The Concept of International Organization* (Paris: UNESCO, 1981), pp. 27–49, pp. 28–30.

will see that the origin of international organisation was ideological – not in the Marxist, class-oriented sense but in the sense of competitions vying for social legitimacy.[39]

The development of international organisation was, however, not linear; the comparatively 'modern' international organisations that appeared in history, the so-called public international unions (or international administrative unions) of the nineteenth century,[40] were more 'functional' than 'constitutional'. In other words, they were severed from the original ideas of those thinkers.

It was only after the emergence of the League of Nations and the United Nations that the actual phenomena of international organisation became able to be linked to the goal of peace and, to that extent, to constitutional thought. But even this reality was not enough to firmly establish an academic framework that grasps the phenomena from an ideological viewpoint, roughly for the reason that despite the existence of these organisations the sovereign nation-state system remained intact, leaving less need to think of the phenomena in ideological/constitutional terms. Moreover, after World War II the three European Communities were inaugurated which, with their 'supranational' set-up and powers, appeared to exhibit a revolutionarily political and 'constitutional' reconfiguration, engendering a kind of academic enthusiasm for the theme of supranationalism.[41]

Yet it remained and remains meaningful to grasp the existence of international organisations as a whole on a normative dimension. First, since the appearance of the public international unions, the notion of

---

[39] This may be similar to what Eagleton listed as 'ideas which help to legitimate a dominant political power' (Terry Eagleton, *Ideology* (London; New York: Verso, 1991), p. 1) but should connote also something more constructive of social structure that would serve best the social interest. More closely related to my own discussion is Herren's eminent article from 2016 where she talks about 'the ideological framework international organizations were based on', which she elaborates on pp. 97–101 (quotation at 93); Madeleine Herren, 'International organizations, 1865–1944', in Jacob K. Cogan, Ian Hurd and Ian Johnstone (eds.), *The Oxford Handbook of International Organizations* (Oxford: Oxford University Press, 2016), chapter 4.

[40] For a general account of public international unions, see Bob Reinalda, *Routledge History of International Organizations: From 1815 to the Present Day* (London; New York: Routledge, 2009), pp. 83–135.

[41] Toshiki Mogami, 'Oushuu Kyoudoutai no Soshiki Kouzou' (The organisational structure of the European Community) (1981) 81 *Journal of International Law and Diplomacy* 30–67, at 49. See also Inis Claude Jr, *Swords into Plowshares: The Problems and Progress of International Organization*, 4th ed. (New York: Random House, 1971), pp. 102–117, esp. pp. 109–110.

'common interest' has inseparably been attached to the enterprise of international organisation, whatever the notion may mean. The notion is political, because the notion of common interest does not assuredly entertain a unique definition; on the contrary there can always be disagreement as to its meaning as will be shown later. But precisely because of this possible disagreement, the search for common interest becomes ideological.

Second, starting from a grandiose design like that of a world federation and moving to a more modest one of the promotion of common interest, there is an undercurrent running through these endeavours: exonerating the international community from the Hobbesian state of nature, that is, 'during the time men live without a common Power to keep them all in awe, they are in that condition which is called Warre; and such a warre, as is of every man, against every man'.[42] If exercised in a freewheeling manner, this 'natural right' would result in innumerable wars; thus such a state has to be overcome eventually. The historic objectives were the same; the idea of world federation was an idealistic and structural answer to this challenge, and the idea of the promotion of common interest was a more realistic and gradualistic one.

On the other hand, the attempt to exonerate the international community was to 'modernise' the international community in the sense that the attempt was imbued with the intent to rationalise the anarchical dispersion of power and equip the community with a more articulate and unitary order, though it is clear that such a reform would not be attained in an instant. Interestingly enough, the sovereign nation state itself was the product of modernity, in the sense that it was an institution to liberate the European societies from the feudalistic or religious order of the Middle Ages, as was expressed by Hobbes. Thus there exist two 'modernities' that are mutually opposed: one is the sovereign nation state as an undertaking to overcome the Middle Ages; the other is the international organisation as an undertaking to overcome the sovereign nation-state system.[43] Since modernity was not simply a chronal periodisation but an ideological perception, the phenomenon of international organisation as a new modernity was also ideological, instead of being just a functional and mechanistic occurrence.

[42] Thomas Hobbes, *Leviathan* (1651), Revised Student Edition (Cambridge: Cambridge University Press, 1997), p. 88.

[43] For an extensive discussion on this point, see Toshiki Mogami, *Kokusai Kiko Ron* (International Organisation) (Tokyo: Iwanami Shoten, 2016) (first published in 1996), pp. 41–44.

Third, the extraction of 'common interest' itself has an ideological dimension. True, it could be said that the exoneration from the state of nature could itself be a common interest in the international community, but what constitutes common interests is not always clear, and making this decision becomes an important role for international organisations. For example, the WTO was established to promote sustainable development and free trade as common interests,[44] but what concrete policies can be accepted as common interests by the member states is not self-evident. Some may stick to perfectly free trade, and others may regard the additional incorporation of protectionist measures as more common. It is not only an opposition of national interests but is related to the more ideological question of how best to organise the divided world.

At this phase 'common interest' is no longer a neutral and mechanical notion that is established a priori. Rather it becomes a catalyst that urges competition among several concepts of world order around the definition of the notion. Of course, such competition does not contradict the cardinal object of the formation of order, for it is not extraordinary that an order is established through a dialectic process and as a result of the competition among different concepts. The point is that the competition or confrontation of several concepts of order attributes, precisely because it is competition or confrontation, an ideological dimension to the whole process. In other words, since the 'axiomaticity' of common interest in actual international organisations is no more than presumed and therefore ideological, its clarification also embroils another round of ideological conflict in the arena of international organisations.

3.2   Ideological role of international organisation

Against this historical and theoretical backdrop we can start discussing the particular ideological role that is assigned to international organisation and/or multilateralism, before and after the inauguration of the UN, particularly the latter.

---

[44] For example, the agreement establishing the World Trade Organization in its Preamble says: 'Recognising that their relations in the field of trade and economic endeavor should be conducted with a view to raising standards of living, ensuring full employment and a large and steadily growing volume of real income and effective demand, and expanding the production of and trade in goods and services, while allowing for the optimal use of the world's resources in accordance with the objective of sustainable development . . .'. This is already too complex and contains many mutually incompatible objectives.

First, the sovereign nation-state system has been liberalistic by nature – 'liberalistic' in a limited sense, for it only implies the freedom of action of the international legal subjects (conveniently designated, even self-appointed as such, by the power-wielding states in each period) but does not involve the constitutional element such as parliamentary democracy. It is, in short, economic liberalism named capitalism and political liberalism that authorises the freedom of political decision making and action, which includes military freedom. This last qualification used to include even the freedom to resort to war up until recently.

This state of affairs marks a sharp contrast between liberalism on the international plane and one on the domestic plane, particularly the modern European seedbed of the state-sovereignty system.[45] The birth of the 'sovereign state' in Europe in about the seventeenth century was triggered by the states' need to be liberated from the reign of universal authority, either religious (Church) or secular (Holy Roman Empire), but in the resultant state-sovereignty system the leitmotif of the liberation from centralised universal authority was lacking and kept losing its relevance as the system became increasingly universalised even outside Europe. The universal authority to be resisted no longer existed in the international community, so the central function of state sovereignty was to guarantee the individual state's external independence and legal supremacy.[46] This fixed a new relationship between international liberalism and the sovereign state: that is, numerous sovereign states are not born because the international community (of sovereign states) is predicated on the liberalistic principle to liberate sovereign actors from universal authority; instead, the international community cannot but be liberalistic, or laissez-faire to be precise, because numerous (quasi-absolute) sovereign states exist.

Thus, while the modern (European) nation state *as such* did not simply destroy the *ancien régime* but instead domestically posited constitutionalism or parliamentary democracy as the institutional security with which to destroy and reorganise the regime, the sovereign nation-state *system* began with schism from the outset which then was steadily multiplied almost globally.[47] And because this system lacked a prototype

[45] For this, see, e.g., Ignacio de la Rasilla del Moral, 'International legal theory: the shifting origins of international law' (2015) 28 *Leiden Journal of International Law* 419–440, at 424–432.

[46] Mogami (n. 43), esp. pp. 41–44.

[47] This is euphemistically paraphrased as either 'admission to the family of nations' or 'admission to the international legal community'. See, for this, Wilhelm G. Grewe, *The Epochs of International Law* (Berlin; New York: Walter de Gruyter, 2000) (original German version published in 1944), chapter 4 of parts 1 to 6 and chapter 5 of part 7.

system to be reconfigured, there was no likelihood from the beginning that something like representative democracy was to be among its founding principles, forcing any endeavour to organise the entire world to be inaugurated out of nothing. As a result, the attempt to modernise the international community and to exonerate it out of the state of nature had to aim, first and foremost, to *restrain* sovereign freedom. With the modern sovereign state, the expansion of the freedom of its components (the nation) was the meaning of 'modernity', while with the sovereign nation system, the restraint of states' sovereign freedom became the meaning of 'modernity'. The task of this restraining was largely assigned to international law and international organisation, at least ideally and/or ideologically.

3.3 Multilateralism as an ideology

Multilateralism as a concept or ideology appeared in the context described previously as an instrument with which to constrain power of an international nature: first, state sovereignty as authenticated legally by international law,[48] and second, international organisation as soon as it is endowed with power to govern, direct, or enforce its member states and/or their nationals. As long as international organisations are not endowed with this power, multilateralism means simple cooperation among states, but once they are empowered that way, the meaning of multilateralism changes accordingly and becomes rather an ideology and principle according to which state sovereignty ought to be controlled by the organisation so that the rule of law can be maintained, and, in addition, the power of the organisation has to be distributed in a democratic way and controlled in a constitutional way.[49]

This is how the notion of normative multilateralism assumes its particular role. The performance of this role may be measured with

[48] It is common to refer to the Peace Treaties of Westphalia as the origin of this principle in international law. However, the treaties were at best the beginning of the process of consolidation. The principle was never established or consolidated instantaneously. On the contrary, as Lesaffer justly indicates, neither the principle of state sovereignty nor that of equality of states was 'introduced, or even appear as principles of international relations' in those treaties; Randall Lesaffer, 'The classical law of nations (1500–1800)', in Alexander Orakhelashvili (ed.), *Research Handbook on the Theory and History of International Law* (Cheltenham: Edward Elgar, 2011), chapter 14, p. 414.

[49] Peters discusses this problem as one of the 'accountability' of international organisations with a role attribution of 'law as constrainer'; Anne Peters, 'International organizations and international law', in Cogan et al. (eds.) (n. 39), chapter 2, esp. pp. 41 et seq.

every international organisation in each historic period, but particular emphasis should be placed on the UN, given its (the Security Council's) enormous power to give orders to the member states. This was not necessarily a happy outcome for the entire world; it simply reflected an inevitable stage in the history of the nation-state system, where the constraint of quasi-absolute state sovereignty had to be entrusted to those who were *more sovereign* than the formal peers.[50]

The attribution of an enormous power to a few 'chosen' states in the UN was not only a result of their victory in the war just ended but also the reflection of a particular ideology of international organisation, that is, to create an international power for an otherwise anarchical international society. Since the peace theories of the thirteenth century onward, the idea to organise the world has been coupled with the idea to create a central power. Its extreme (perhaps most logical) expression in the form of the creation of a world government or federation has been constantly sidestepped because it was regarded to be the least realistic. In its stead, the endowment of an enforcement power was chosen as *modus vivendi*, based on the recognition of sovereign equality among members yet setting a tacit discrimination among those 'equals', on the basis of less-than-federal multilateralism, which was also un-egalitarian towards its members in reality. Judging by the standard of a just world order, this is an *unauthentic multilateralism*, for multilateralism is expected as a matter of principle to perform a more equalising and democratising role.

At this juncture, the emphasis of multilateralism shifts from *power creation* to *power control*.[51] The creation of certain international power may be necessary, yet at the same time it has to be subject to democratic standards: both are the expressions of multilateralism, and the former should not be realised without the latter.

This normative multilateralism has not been fully operative in the UN because of the near impossibility of the relinquishment of the permanent members' prerogatives through the revision of Article 27 of the Charter. On the other hand, this deficit of interstate democracy was counter-balanced by another phenomenon: the rise of the General Assembly (GA) since the end of the 1960s. The increase of the newly independent member states, most of which were non-aligned, implied that the General

---

[50] I have long called this a 'weighted sovereignty system', on the analogy of the weighted voting system. See, e.g., Mogami (n. 43), esp. p. 92.

[51] Mogami (n. 1), at 382–384.

Assembly was to gain salience in place of the Security Council.[52] Of course, this power did not entail any enforcement power like that of the Security Council but was just symbolic and representative of the majority. But the increase in the representativity of the majority was sufficient to shift, if temporarily, the power centre from the SC to the GA: now the will of the General Assembly can be regarded as the legitimate will of the organisation or of the international community as a whole. I have called this the 'second-generation legitimacy' of the UN, as opposed to the 'first-generation legitimacy' which had been founded on the real power of the winners of World War II, as embodied in the Charter.[53]

This new 'will' of the organisation (or of the international community) manifested itself in the form of several GA resolutions, particularly 'declarations', as well as some treaties, that were expressive of the aspirations, desires and interests of the GA's majority, largely developing Third World states. These include, among others, the Declaration on the Granting of Independence (GA Resolution 1514(XV)), Declaration on Principles of International Law Concerning Friendly Relations (GA Resolution 2625 (XXV)), Resolutions on Permanent Sovereignty over Natural Resources (GA Resolutions 1803 (XVII), 2158 (XXI), 3171 (XXVIII)), Declaration on the Establishment of a New International Economic Order (GA Resolution 3201 (S/VI)) and Charter of Economic Rights and Duties of States (GA Resolution 3281 (XXIX)). There was apparently a power shift within the General Assembly from big power dominance to the dominance by the have-nots, which I have called 'in-organisational hegemony' – hegemony somewhat in the Gramscian sense,[54] to the extent that it involved imposing the moral, political and cultural values of the 'class' which bore this hegemony on other 'classes', though it was less than Gramscian, for this takeover was not fully successful.

---

[52] For a general account of this phenomenon, see, e.g., Harold Jacobson, *Networks of Interdependence: International Organizations and the Global Political System*, 2nd ed. (New York: Alfred A. Knopf, 1984), pp. 108–115; and for the shift in the emphasis of activities in the UN, in conjunction with this numerical change, see, e.g., Reinalda (n. 40), part XI.

[53] I have long relied upon these conceptions of legitimacy inside the UN system. See, e.g., Mogami (n. 43), esp. pp. 108–111.

[54] James Joll, *Gramsci* (London: Fontana/Collins, 1977), chapter 9, esp. at p. 99, where he holds: 'The hegemony of a political class meant for Gramsci that the class had succeeded in persuading the other classes of society to accept its own moral, political and cultural values.'

This power shift took place only inside the General Assembly: hence 'in-organisational'; it was just virtual and unreal outside of it. And needless to say, this shift was not in itself a manifestation of normative multilateralism, as it incurred frustration on the part of those who once possessed the hegemonic status inside and outside the organisation, particularly the United States.[55] However, this shift exemplified that the age-old notion of order by power – military, political, economic, cultural – was not always legitimate and may have to be replaced or at least supplemented by an alternative concept of order based on a different yardstick. As the aspiration behind the in-organisational hegemony was of egalitarian nature, this trend as a whole finally became an inevitable aspect of normative multilateralism. The world remained unequal, so was the organisation: hence the legitimacy of the aspiration towards more equality.

However, this in-organisational hegemony was offset by the behaviours of its claimants and was overturned by the fluctuation of the locus of legitimacy inside the UN after the end of the Cold War. First, despite the legitimacy of the aspiration towards true equality, the domestic behaviours of some of the developing states were not always praiseworthy; some were charged with the violation of fundamental rights and freedoms, and others were found uncaring about (even exacerbating) the inequality among their own nations; still others were often engaged in armed conflicts with their neighbouring countries, all of which helped diminish the legitimacy of their otherwise legitimate aspirations. Second, with the Gulf War of 1991 par excellence, the legitimacy of the big powers was retrieved when it was demonstrated that peace was to be attained with military might as at the conclusion of World War II, which had instituted the legitimacy of the monopoly of enforcement powers by the big powers.

Thus, the legitimacy claimed by the developing countries from the 1960s onward came to be downplayed, although the aspiration towards it remained valid and legitimate *and* unfinished.[56] And then, the newly

---

[55] There are an innumerable number of books and articles about the disputes between the United States and the UN system, which were discussed under the entry of the 'crisis' or 'reform' of the UN, among which I deem highly worth reading Pierre de Senarclens, *La crise des Nations Unies* (Paris: Presses Universitaires de France, 1988). I myself wrote a book on that topic titled *UNESCO no Kiki to Sekai Chitsujo* (The UNESCO Crisis and World Order) (Tokyo: Token Syuppan, 1987).

[56] On this topic, see Toshiki Mogami, 'The United Nations system as an unfinished revolution' (1990) 15 *Alternatives* 177–197.

regained legitimacy by the big powers, though persuasive on the surface, turned out to be just temporary, for its banner-bearer, the United States, did not persist in utilising or activating the UN after the war. On the contrary, this utilisation incurred another problem of legitimacy as it demonstrated also the illegitimacy of the monopoly of power in the UN or a kind of international oligarchy.[57] So the renewed (first-generation) legitimacy did not take over the second-generation legitimacy entirely; only, this time the assertion of the second-generation legitimacy was not powerful enough to challenge the seemingly renewed old legitimacy. Theoretically, the problem of normative multilateralism remained on both sides: the aspiration to make the world more equal and the need to control the big powers.

4 From normative multilateralism to critical constitutionalism

For me global constitutionalism has signified, first and foremost, critical constitutionalism. And this critical constitutionalism was meant to connote *jus contra anarchiam* and *jus contra oligarchiam*,[58] meaning 'law for the constraint and minimisation of (originally) interstate violence' and 'law for the constraint of oligarchical internationally institutionalised power', respectively. In other words, global constitutionalism for me was not much more than this, not a blueprint for an overarching legal order, nor a comprehensive explanatory scheme of international law. And critical constitutionalism originated in normative multilateralism, which intellectually derived largely from the conceptual framework of WOMP; only the notion of normative multilateralism was much more confined in scope than the all-inclusive WOMP activities.

Admittedly, the restriction to *jus contra anarchiam* and *jus contra oligarchiam* is conspicuously narrow, yet it is essential enough for a theory of international law to tackle. If a theory of international law ought not to be satisfied with presenting the entire list of sample problems either to be just concerned about or to give idealistic solutions to, certain delimitations had better be drawn that can guide the theory to be involved in problems for which it can come up with viable solutions. In view of this, it is only natural that we should concern ourselves with overcoming international anarchy, which has been the constant task of international law, though it has also been accompanied by roles to

---

[57] See Mogami (n. 1). Peters has also spoken about oligarchy. See Peters (n. 28), pp. 286–288.
[58] See, for an overall discussion on this, Mogami (n. 1).

buttress international anarchy. Though the situation is ambivalent, the primary emphasis has been placed on its overcoming instead of strengthening, hence the legitimacy of characterising international law as *jus contra anarchiam*.

Equally, the search for *jus contra oligarchiam* has become a focal point especially after the end of the Cold War, when the second-generation legitimacy was frustrated and the first generation resurged. But its resurgence with the Gulf War was in a way ostensible: the UN policy of the 'winner' of the war, the United States, was shaky and inconsistent even after this 'victory'. It did not lead to the construction of a more objective, UN-centred and rule of law–based international order. In the meantime international terrorism became more widespread and rampant, which added to the plausible legitimacy of the first generation, even outside the UN. Being partly a leftover by-product of the Gulf War which disturbed the geopolitical stability of the Middle East, the spread of international terrorism invited and legitimised to some extent the violent reactions by the militarily big powers, now with the institutional stage of the Security Council, acquiescing in 'wars' against terror and imposing sanctions through Sanctions Committees.[59] Thus the apparent international anarchy has been revived instead of being suppressed, and the counter-anarchy has taken root in the form of essentially an international oligarchy, as was prescribed by the UN Charter in 1945, but all this deteriorated with the war against Iraq in 2003 waged without even an SC authorising resolution on the pretence that Iraq was hiding weapons of mass destruction.[60]

Critical constitutionalism was directed particularly against these two phenomena, overlapping normative multilateralism to a considerable degree. However narrow this perspective may be, these phenomena appeared much more urgent than any other international law problems. It would of course be wrong to pretend, based on this narrower perspective which may sound more realistic, that a global constitutionalism with

---

[59] For a discussion on the UN sanctions system after the end of the Cold War, including the work of the SC Sanctions Committees, see Tsagourias and White (n. 32), chapter 10. See also Antonios Tzanakopoulos, *Disobeying the Security Council: Countermeasures against Wrongful Sanctions* (Oxford: Oxford University Press, 2011) for a critical and superb overview of the UN sanctions system.

[60] For harsh yet legitimate criticisms against this use of force, see, among a plethora of others, Thomas Franck, 'What happens now? The United Nations after Iraq' (2003) 97 *American Journal of International Law* 607–620, and Richard Falk, 'What future for the UN Charter system of war prevention' (2003) 97 *American Journal of International Law* 590–598. These are typically global constitutionalist arguments.

a wider perspective was not meaningful enough. However, if global constitutionalism, aiming either to be equipped with an overall explanatory power for international law or to consolidate the value basis for it, was not in itself truly innovative and not further advanced than its predecessors such as WOMP, then we should say that global constitutionalism as an academic movement has had limits which it has not overcome.

Even if the contemporary global constitutionalism confines itself to the reaffirmation of fundamental values on which to build international legal order, such as the trinity of democracy, human rights and rule of law, it still cannot be groundbreaking. On the contrary, the assertion of these 'orthodox' values may only remind people of Article 2 of the Treaty of the European Union which declares itself founded on the values of human dignity, freedom and equality in addition to the aforementioned three, thus strengthening if inadvertently the impression that global constitutionalism is akin to Eurocentrism. In either event a reaffirmation of the fundamental values is just a beginning for a theory, not the culmination or final destination. If a theory cannot go beyond that, then it ceases to deserve being called a theory. And in this sense, too, the WOMP movement had its merits in attempting to be as concrete as possible, either in the minimisation of domestic and international violence (or 'peace' in short, which is somehow missing in the value list of global constitutionalism at large) or in the maximisation of social justice, even if there might have been something quixotic about it.

A strategy of constriction like this may not be the right tactic, but it seems inevitable that global constitutionalism will make clear what its essence is and what it aims at as a theory. If the aim is to be heuristic/explanatory, it will be required to prove how this overall framework can best explain the actual functioning or dysfunctioning of most, if not all, branches of international law. It is what, most typically, the theories of natural law and legal positivism have done. Since then there has not been any comparable 'theory' of this scale except, perhaps, the theory of hegemonic international law (HIL).[61] If, on the other hand, the aim is to present to the world of international law an alternative imagery of international law such as the WOMP type of constitutionalism, New Haven School, Third World approaches to international law (TWAIL) or

---

[61] For the theory of HIL, see, e.g., Detlev L. Vagts, 'Hegemonic international law' (2001) 95 *American Journal of International Law* 843–848.

feminist approaches to international law,[62] then it should be more clearly determined to follow the path, by articulating what is to be legally desired rather than what is currently the legal reality. In my interpretation, global constitutionalism has so far been halfway, containing the elements of both approaches.

Yet there has been something aspirational in searching for more or better legal order, inheriting the intellectual tradition of the WOMP type. It is why I characterise it as being in *perpetuum mobile* of this normative kind of theorisation. It may not be wholly innovative, yet it has some elements inherited from the past theories that are to be maintained. Maybe something a bit more modest may fit the real picture at this juncture, which either is confined to 'the critical' (critical constitutionalism) or returns to and consolidates the more conventional yet more mature concept of multilateralism (normative multilateralism). Little would change by doing so, as far as global constitutionalism remains at the halfway stage.

5   A modest but constructive way ahead

If we agree to move forward along this line, it would be good to take into consideration the kind of criticism against global constitutionalism levelled from the viewpoint of multilateralism, either consciously normative or less so. For example, there is one gentle criticism which seems to exemplify neatly what global constitutionalism should have been headed for, by pointing to the self-reflective and constructive path for global constitutionalism. It concerns Garrett W. Brown's 'The constitutionalization of what?'[63]

Like myself, he indicates that there is 'a general ambiguity about what the term means' and 'a general neglect regarding what exactly is being constituted by the processes of constitutionalisation'.[64] Moreover, 'this continued ambiguity has serious implications for the concept of constitutionalisation when used as a normative claim', for the concept can obscure, among other items, 'whether we *should* be enthusiastic about the concept of constitutionalisation as globally minded cosmopolitans'.[65]

---

[62] For the most recent comprehensive account of these theories, see Anne Orford and Florian Hoffmann (eds.), *The Oxford Handbook of the Theory of International Law* (Oxford: Oxford University Press, 2016).

[63] Garrett Wallace Brown, 'The constitutionalization of what?' (2012) 1 *Global Constitutionalism* 201–228.

[64] Ibid., at 202.

[65] Ibid. (italics original).

According to him, the prevailing logic in constitutionalism is that 'more international law and more international institutions represent a more robust form of constitutionalisation'.[66] This observation may sound a little bit simplistic, yet it merits serious consideration when broken down in the following manner.

First, there can be an alternative interpretation which holds that 'more law . . . and more international institutions can actually disperse legal authority horizontally in ways that can contradict a "vertical" constitutionalisation process'.[67] Or else, that kind of aggrandisement may invite powerful states to 'create new international institutions . . . in order to sidestep existing legal and institutional regimes that no longer serve their interests'.[68] Second, the incremental sort of constitutionalism 'seemingly ignores a pathway-dependent dark-side associated with constitutionalism', which means that 'the establishment of formal legal processes where legal rights and duties are codified and where the authoritative mechanisms for legal adjudication are clearly delineated . . . lock (the legal subjects) into this (legal) relationship'.[69] Third, Brown suggests that, because of its concern about the role of power, 'constitutionalisation could represent nothing more than a form of neo-imperialism' by 'entrenching Western political and economic power'. It also exhibits 'universalising and pro-Western orientation'. He echoes some other 'liberally minded scholars' and says that 'by conceptualising constitutionalisation as universally oriented, it [constitutionalism] runs the risk of also "dressing up strategic power-plays" as having a progressive form'.[70]

The first point could be relativised with a remark that all the theories of constitutionalism are not verticality minded. The second point shares the basic tenet of authors such as Christine Schwöbel[71] and may have some truism in it, although it is not clear to what extent the existing constitutionalism is contented with the existing reality. But the third point seems to deserve serious consideration, for this aspect has little been squarely confronted by global constitutionalism. It can even be said that in many cases the universalisability of

---

[66] Ibid., at 211.

[67] Ibid.

[68] Ibid.

[69] Ibid., at 212.

[70] Ibid., at 215–216.

[71] Schwöbel (n. 12) also expresses strong criticism against global constitutionalism's orientation towards 'stability' and replaces 'fluidity' with it (p. 164), by employing Jacques Derrida's idea of 'the future as a promise without content' (p. 124). Both Brown and Schwöbel appear to be deeply concerned about a kind of locked-in syndrome, where we will be locked into the present forever, that global constitutionalism is supposed to incur.

the constitutionalist framework and constitutionally made norms tends to be taken for granted, even when the arguments are put forward with good intentions, like a submission that 'the most advanced manifestation of the normative superiority of a regional value system is that of the ECHR',[72] which appears in an otherwise excellent theory that is correctly critical of the formation of international hierarchy. In view of the political and structural hierarchy and asymmetry between the Occident and non-Occident, such generalisability is not self-evident, politically if not academically and cognitively.

Brown points out two problems par excellence. First, there is no guarantee that the sovereign state system, even if it may be constitutionally overcome, will not regress to the *status quo ante*: he asks 'why is it that jurisgenerative politics automatically moves toward universal cosmopolitan principles and what keeps it from moving regressively toward an opposing nationalistic narrative?'[73] Second, criticising Benhabib, he brings attention to the dark side of contemporary history: 'Many of the injustices involved with the global system stem from the very same democracies that Benhabib relies upon to constitutionalise a cosmopolitan rule of law.'[74] Democracies can also behave badly, he discloses. Take a look, for example, at the extraordinary rendition performed by the United States.[75]

Thus, while acknowledging many favourable global conditions that constitutionalisation can produce, he holds onto his most fundamental criticisms. Highly important is the question as to 'whether constitutionalisation *should* refer to all laws and institutions or whether it *should* refer to only those instruments that can capture a certain normative component'.[76] Norms to be globally constitutionalised will have to be percolated and selected. Brown advocates rightfully that we need 'a *more normatively sensitive* global constitutionalism' that can respond to key questions about 'whether we are constitutionalising the right legal terms, if we are creating the right international institutions, and, most importantly, whether these regimes actually reflect any *sense of global justice*'.[77] This may just be a criticism, but it is also where global constitutionalism stands.

---

[72] De Wet (n. 9), at 617.
[73] Brown (n. 63), at 224.
[74] Ibid., at 224–225.
[75] Ibid., at 225. For this critical account that is highly apropos, see Edward Newman, *A Crisis of Global Institutions?: Multilateralism and International Security* (London: Routledge, 2007), esp. chapter 2.
[76] Brown (n. 63), at 227 (italics original).
[77] Ibid., at 227–228 (italics mine).

6   By way of conclusion

With these self-critical re-examinations, it seems that we have finally reached the starting point – the realisation of *global order and justice*, if confined to the legal dimension. The questions are how global order and justice are to be defined and what kind of (legal) problems are there to be faced, legal as well as historical. And if these are the problems to be tackled by global constitutionalism, has this paradigm been truly innovative, without academic precedents? I reiterate that there were precedents, dooming global constitutionalism to be not particularly innovative yet placing it in the long vein of reformative theories. The motivation has been right, and the next question is to determine how we can meaningfully confine our focus of research.

2

China's Socialist Rule of Law and Global Constitutionalism

BIN LI

1 Introduction

The idea of global constitutionalism embodies a constitutionalist approach to international law. Such an approach sets out a normative framework that claims the principles of the rule of law, a separation of powers, fundamental rights protection, democracy and solidarity, together with institutions and mechanisms securing and implementing those principles, for the purpose of constructing a legitimate international legal order.[1] Not being opposed to pluralism, global constitutionalism's function is to compensate or complete constitutionalism at the national level[2] or to put constraints on national constitutions and political practices through 'a cosmopolitan turn' or 'global legitimacy'.[3] In other words, global constitutionalism lays down the limits and frontiers on national constitutions and legal orders in a top-down fashion. In that respect, global constitutionalism aims to build a legitimate international legal order that reflects the ideology of subduing political power to the law and of creating a government of laws in lieu of mankind, thus reviving the political movement of the seventeenth and eighteenth centuries in the Western world.

The ideology of 'law prevailing over power' accords with the objective of China's legal reform process in the past thirty years since the 1980s, which is often described as introducing the model of 'rule by law' and rejecting that of 'rule by mankind'. Through the amendments adopted in

---

[1] Anne Peters, 'Global constitutionalism', in Michael T. Gibbons (ed.), *The Encyclopedia of Political Thought*, 1st ed. (London: Wiley-Blackwell, 2014), pp. 1484–1487.

[2] Anne Peters, 'Compensatory constitutionalism: the function and potential of fundamental international norms and structures' (2006) 19 *Leiden Journal of International Law* 579–610.

[3] Mattias Kumm, 'The cosmopolitan turn in constitutionalism: an integrated conception of public law' (2013) 20 *Indiana Journal of Global Legal Studies* 605–628, at 605.

1999, 'socialist rule of law' was inserted into Article 5 of the current constitution. Socialism is thereby stressed and put before the rule of law, which means that the rule of law in China should follow the socialist ideology. Socialist rule of law has the objective and function of 'taming power with law' or of opposing 'rule by mankind', which also fall within the ambit of global constitutionalism arguments. The approximate convergence between the normative claims of global constitutionalism and China's pursuit of the authority of law as ruling instrument cannot, however, hide many other discrepancies: China's perception of a just and legitimate international legal order and its consequential practices could amount to a sort of resistance to the normative framework of global constitutionalism that embodies substantially liberal values. This chapter intends to highlight discrepancies that cannot be overlooked or absorbed into the apparently convergent rhetoric of rule of law, human rights or democracy. In fact, even though those fundamental notions of classic constitutionalism are universally referred to in almost all arguments for political legitimacy, the very connotation and legal interpretation of those notions could vary significantly at the local level. China's theory and practice of socialist rule of law could be perceived as a sort of pluralist challenge to global constitutionalism,[4] which must be addressed by arguments that strive for globalising constitutionalism. The global constitutionalism that aims to set forth a standard of evaluation of national legal orders as regards what it conceives as the legitimate global legal order is likely inadequate, since it lacks efficient measures to prevent abusive interpretations or even manipulations of the fundamental notions of liberal constitutionalism.

Some scholars argue that global constitutionalism remains a good approach even if it may be refuted by political powers. In other words, global constitutionalism does not intend to give effect to its 'normative force' through stimulating the positive transformation towards the constitutionalisation of the global legal order. This modesty could also be understood in light of the difficulty currently involved in building a genuinely global legal order when divergent and even conflicting approaches to international law coexist for political, historical and cultural reasons.

---

[4] Authors supporting pluralism believe that it 'has significant strengths in providing adaptability, creating space for contestation, and offering a possibility of steering between conflicting supremacy claims of different polity levels'. See Nico Krisch, *Beyond Constitutionalism: The Pluralist Structure of Postnational Law* (Oxford: Oxford University Press, 2010), p. 70.

Even if global constitutionalism is reduced to a pure cognitive or
normative framework that is deprived of any transforming function
and whose effectiveness depends on the change of spirit or mindset of
the subjects of international law, the authority of the argument remains
problematic: it focuses on the redescription of international law or on the
ascription of constitutional norms to current international legal principles following national constitutional paradigms. The purpose of global
constitutionalism is essentially to transplant the national constitutional
paradigms to international law, while ignoring the limit and difficulty in
such transplantation. On one hand, the fundamental norms proposed by
global constitutionalism could find their embodiment in international
legal instruments through proactive interpretations, such as human
rights and rule of law. Global constitutionalism may be therefore
regarded as reproducing the fundamental principles of modern international law. On the other, global constitutionalism faces the same obstacles
that international law does in promoting the universality of those fundamental rules. Though as a normative framework, global constitutionalism does not oppose but embraces pluralism, acknowledging the
different types of constitutionalism at the nation-state level, it proposes
little to nothing on the methods of conciliation between universalism and
pluralism.[5] It fails in particular to address the limits or boundaries of the
pluralistic interpretation of the constitutional norms. With pluralism and
its impact on universalism inadequately addressed, the argument of
global constitutionalism runs the risk either of devolving into
a disguised legal hegemony in the name of universality through unduly
dissimilating the divergences or of reifying legal relativism through
opposing constitutionalism with non-/anti-constitutionalism.

Such risks can be particularly felt in considering that liberal constitutionalism – which the idea of global constitutionalism draws on – generally 'acquires its legitimacy in relation to a socio-political reality
oriented towards conflicting poles of identity and difference' and that 'a
working constitutional order must revolve around a predominant
identity'.[6] If the 'clash between constitutional identity and other relevant

---

[5] For example, in her recent research paper, Anne Peters asserts that 'pluralism' alone is not
sufficient as a guideline for ordering a society, because it says nothing about its own limits.
See Anne Peters, 'Constitutionalisation', in Jean d'Aspremont and Sahib Singh (eds.),
Concepts for International Law: Contributions to Disciplinary Thought (London: Edward
Elgar, forthcoming 2018).
[6] Michel Rosenfeld, 'Modern constitutionalism as interplay between identity and diversity:
an introduction' (1993) 14 *Cardozo Law Review* 497–531, at 498, 500.

identities, such as national, ethnic, religious, or cultural identity, is made inevitable by the confrontation between contemporary constitutionalism's inherent pluralism, and tradition',[7] such a clash is by no means less inevitable at the global level given the plurality of the constitutional subjects. In the same vein, the argument for the constitutionalisation of international law is often criticised as overambitious in the debate about the legitimacy of the value-laden hierarchy of norms in international law.[8] The idea of global constitutionalism, in its search for the common premise or *Grundnorm* of a global legal order, should thus shift its focus from its substantial contents to the problems relating to its global dimension; global constitutionalism as a movement towards the constitutionalisation of global or transnational legal order might be reconsidered as a movement towards the globalisation of constitutional norms from the perspective of reconciling identity and difference.

The application of constitutional norms at a global level is especially difficult: even though the legitimacy of liberal constitutional norms may be less contested at a local level, their de-territorialised legitimatisation at a global level could be more questionable. The practical and political resistances to the idea of global constitutionalism shed light on this difficulty, as shown in the case of China's approaches to constitutionalism and international law. The analysis in this chapter may be subject to the criticism that the domestic–international nexus method is not applied in a rigorous but rather liberal fashion.[9] This chapter does not, however, attempt to map out clearly the multiple links between domestic affairs and China's compliance with international legal rules. Instead, it attempts to map out the common conceptual pattern and highlight the main features that underlie China's position on constitutionalism, in both domestic and global contexts. The result may be criticised as overly simplistic, but it could offer an insight into the eventual correlation between China's strategies on both local and global constitutionalism.

In brief, the central question in the chapter is whether constitutionalism could be globalised when confronted with divergent or even conflicting understandings of international law and with the underpinning

---

[7] Michel Rosenfeld, 'The identity of the constitutional subject' (1995) 16 *Cardozo Law Review* 1049–1110, at 1051.
[8] Erika de Wet, 'The constitutionalisation of public international law', in Michel Rosenfeld and András Sajó (eds.), *The Oxford Handbook of Comparative Constitutional Law* (Oxford: Oxford University Press, 2012), p. 1228.
[9] Roda Mushkat, 'China's compliance with international law: what has been learned and the gaps remaining' (2011) 1 *Pacific Rim Law & Policy Journal* 41–69, at 65.

values at both local and global levels. The challenge arises not merely from the disagreement on the common premise of constitutionalism but more importantly from the fragmentation of the building process involving different subjects.

2   Can constitutionalism be globalised? The case of China's specificity

The outdated discourses on Asian values that emphasise Asian countries' cultural and political singularities no longer raise powerful resistance to the efforts of globalising constitutionalism. The idea of local specificity has, however, changed its focus. As the Chinese case shows, it is the usefulness of global constitutionalism as a normative framework in measuring a nation state's legal development as regards constitutionalism that is now in question. The enquiry about the capacity of the constitutionalisation of international law to protect national interests also has an impact on China's decision whether to embrace the idea of global constitutionalism. In other words, considered in terms of the relationship between domestic law and international law, China's position towards global constitutionalism is pragmatic rather than normatively inspired.

2.1   Globalising constitutionalism and 'Asian values'

Differing from constitutionalisation, which describes an ongoing phenomenon or process of normative evolution, constitutionalism is an attitude, a frame of mind, a philosophy of striving towards some form of political legitimacy, typified by respect for a constitution.[10] European scholars have debated over the problem and task of the 'translation of constitutionalism into the postnational context'[11] that will inevitably affect the universality of the values pursued by constitutionalist thought. Accordingly, the same issue arises now in the larger context insofar as East Asian states' approaches to constitutionalism are at stake. There are

[10] Jan Klabbers, 'Setting the scene', in Jan Klabbers, Anne Peters and Geir Ulfstein (eds.), *The Constitutionalization of International Law* (Oxford: Oxford University Press, 2011), p. 10.

[11] Joseph H. H. Weiler, *The Constitution of Europe* (Cambridge: Cambridge University Press, 1999), p. 270; Neil Walker, 'Postnational constitutionalism and the problem of translation', in Joseph H. H. Weiler and Marlene Wind (eds.), *European Constitutionalism beyond the State* (Cambridge: Cambridge University Press, 2003), p. 35.

intriguing questions such as 'is there Asian specificity making an essential difference to global constitutionalism?' and, if yes, 'what would be the special values to which Asian states adhere and which would be proposed by Asian states to global constitutionalism?' This manner of questioning is, however, problematic due to the overgeneralisation that opposes 'Western civilisation' to 'Asian values' and reduces the question to the grand dichotomy or 'clash of civilisations'. Moreover, 'Asian values' should be also considered through a diversified prism, as Sen has contended that there are no such 'Asian values' that justify authoritarianism.[12] The discourse on 'Asian values' should be refreshed through considering diversity and variation in Asian countries' constitutional options and no longer be used as a political pretext to reject constitutionalism outright. A necessarily new understanding of 'Asian values' will appear when the complexity of constitutionalism in China is taken into account.

When the notion 'Asian values' is used here, it is used to explain China's position towards rule of law and, more, to stress that China's history and culture should be preserved and be given due consideration in the modernisation process, which includes the building of the socialist rule of law. The specificity of 'local knowledge' is shown by the fact that China attaches much importance to the function of morality or moral norms in guiding individuals' conduct and in maintaining social order, while acknowledging the limit of law in both respects. Moral norms and rule of law are seen practically as two inseparable aspects of the guideline for governing the state, building the society and educating the citizens. Put otherwise, rule of law can never work alone in the Chinese context. It probably explains also the position of the socialist rule of law as the prevailing discourse; this purports to preserve an inextricable link between state, society and individual citizens in China.

The 'Asian values' discourse may also be contested by the fact that, during the twentieth century, the successive political regimes in China devoted themselves without exception to drafting their own constitutional charter. Such a scenario means that the constitution as the written basis for sovereignty was recognised by international law and that China was no longer a universal empire but a state intending to stand on equal footing with all the others. In other words, there is no doubt that modern China accepted to follow the formal rule of the game in international relations between states.

---

[12] Amartya Sen, 'Human rights and Asian values' (1997) 217 *The New Republic* 33–40, at 33.

2.2   Measuring China's complex attitudes towards constitutionalism

As far as China is concerned, answers to the preceding questions are by no means straightforward. The questions are not only premised on an uncontested legitimacy of global constitutionalism, but they also postulate that China's practices on constitutionalism and on international law are consistent and rigid, from which one can deduce a clear position or strategy. However, China's practices are evolving and are sometimes summarised, following a selective approach, as having experienced an incomplete shift,[13] in which remarkable progress and setbacks coexist. It has also been suggested that while China has the developmental potential towards constitutionalism, China's constitutional option is 'too complex, too chaotic and too spontaneous to be completely captured by human comprehension, either positively or negatively'.[14] The uncertainty is likewise felt in the account of the tensions between 'a moderated transition favouring cosmopolitanism' and 'a return to a pre-constitutional era', reflecting the complex and profound changes taking place in Chinese constitutionalism within the larger context of powerful international developments. 'China therefore reveals the powerful impulse towards and the formidable limits to cosmopolitan constitutionalism.'[15] When China's complexities, uncertainty and changing features in the understandings and practices of constitutionalism are set against the backdrop of global constitutionalism, global constitutionalism's usefulness as a parameter for measuring China's compatibility is questionable. (See Section 4.) The complexities of China's attitude towards constitutionalism can be better explained by the fact that constitutionalism is closely connected with the Western liberal political ideology supporting the separation of powers, liberal democracy, capitalism, etc.: in short, 'Western constitutionalism' has political implications that are in diametrical conflict with China's socialist ideology and political system. This is the very reason why China attaches fundamental importance to the socialist rule of law and at the same time strongly opposes Western constitutionalism perceived as a tool for promoting Western political values.

[13] Remarks by Jacques deLisle, 'China and international law' (2013) 107 *American Society of International Law Proceedings* 345–357, at 348–349; Mushkat (n. 9), at 68.
[14] Stéphanie Balme and Michael Dowdle, 'Introduction: exploring for constitutionalism in 21st century', in Stéphanie Balme and Michael Dowdle (eds.), *Building Constitutionalism in China* (New York: Palgrave Macmillan, 2009), p. 10.
[15] Haig Patapan, 'Towards a cosmopolitan constitutionalism: on universalism and particularism in Chinese constitutionalism' (2015) 3 *The Chinese Journal of Comparative Law* 78–96, at 96.

2.3 Constitutionalisation of international law and national interests

When confronted with the question whether China would embrace global constitutionalism from the perspective of China's approach to international law, a pragmatic literature on the role of international law would probably give different answers depending on whether international law's constitutional turn could effectively safeguard China's legitimate national interests. China's reaction to the question could be better understood from a historical perspective. It is often suggested that the formation and development of the Chinese attitude towards international law reflect China's historical transformation.[16] If history matters, however, in understanding China's approach to international law, it is not a narrowly legal history of generally unhappy encounters with the Western-created system over the last century and a half. It is rather the history of a long and rich tradition of Chinese approaches to international relations. This history has wisely illustrated that Chinese classical Confucian and Legalist thoughts and practices shared the conviction that domestic and international orders were closely linked. The Confucian idea advocates that different types of interstate order should, would or must govern relations within the Chinese world and between China and the outside world.[17] In fact, historic experiences marked by 'unequal treaties' have exerted great influence on China's perception of the relationship between China on one hand and the world as well as international law on the other. The political emotion arising from the history of humiliation is, however, fading away with time and being replaced by the up-to-date discourses such as 'new great power'.[18] China's rise has led to the new claims that China should speak louder in global affairs and international law. China has recently advocated its concept of the shared future or common fate of the human community at international forums.[19] This advocacy shows that China is becoming more active in the effort to construct the world order and in strengthening its soft power in global affairs. In short, China's recent diplomatic practices, from

[16] Li Zhaojie, 'The impact of international law on the transformation of China's perception of the world: a lesson of history' (2012) 27 *Maryland Journal of International Law* 128–153; see also Phil C. W. Chan, 'China's approaches to international law since the Opium War' (2014) 27 *Leiden Journal of International Law* 859–892.
[17] Jacques deLisle, 'China's approach to international law: a historical perspective' (2000) 94 *American Society of International Law Proceedings* 267–295, at 268–269.
[18] Congyan Cai, 'New great powers and international law in the 21st century' (2013) 24 *The European Journal of International Law* 755–795.
[19] UNSC Resolution 2344 (2017) formally referred to 'a community of shared future for mankind' and endorsed the Belt and Road Initiative as a development initiative contributing to the regional economic cooperation (para. 34).

the G20 summit to the Silk Road Economic Belt and the twenty-first-century Maritime Silk Road (the Belt and Road) Initiative, have a significant impact on China's position towards international law. Its international legal practice will certainly reflect this trend, which calls for the emergence of new or adjusted international legal rules, particularly concerning regional economic cooperation. The traditional understanding of linkage or connection between domestic and international orders will no longer suffice to guide the interaction between Chinese law and international law. Such interaction could probably be reinvigorated in the globalisation context, whereby a 'merger of two systems'[20] would be conceivable through the mutual adjustment of domestic and international orders.

Briefly recalling the evolution of China's state power and of its influence on the changing discourses about the relationship between China and international law reveals that many international lawyers since the late Qing Empire have been sensitive to the power politics behind international law. Such a mindset is in line with the understanding of the linkage between domestic law and international law from a state-governing perspective. As the government's legitimacy is determined by its performance and achievements within both domestic and international fora, the government's ability to effectively defend the national interest in resorting to international law is generally felt to be a key issue. Consequently, one cannot say that China does not care about the role of international law in pursuing global justice; China's foremost concern is rather the function as well as the limits of international law in safeguarding national interest. (See Section 5.) China's defensive approach may extend to the idea of global constitutionalism that purports to lay down the constitutional foundation of international law. Furthermore, China's defence of national interests highlights the limit of global constitutionalism, in that it overstresses the normative aspect without making constructive proposals on enhancing the effectiveness. In other words, when considered in terms of the interaction between domestic law and international law, the divergence between China's practices and the idea of global constitutionalism relates less to acknowledging the *legitimacy and authority* of the idea itself than to perceiving its *function and effect*. The confrontation between China's pragmatic and functionalist approaches to international law and the analytical and normative

---

[20] Kevin Herrick, 'The merger of two systems: Chinese adoption and Western adaptation in the formation of modern international law' (2005) 33 *Georgia Journal of International and Comparative Law* 685–703.

framework of global constitutionalism also calls into question the necessity as well as the possibility of converging or reconciling the two different
legal approaches.

3 Constitution without constitutionalism: China's constitutional option in state governing

Although the words 'constitution' and 'constitutionalism' as legal concepts have been only recently imported into the Chinese language, one
can still perceive the functional analogy between China's traditional ideas
related to state governing and the Western constitutionalist concepts of
political legitimacy and authority: the constitutional functions of the idea
that ruling power is subject to some higher norms roughly correspond to
each other. Nonetheless, China's current constitutional option diverges
from the requirements of modern constitutionalism in many respects.
China's contemporary history has determined the current political system and its functioning, notably the understanding of political legitimacy
and the leadership of the Communist Party of China (CPC).
The preceding considerations are not developed through, but beyond,
the constitutionalist discourse and thinking.

3.1 Constitution and constitutionalism as imported Western legal concepts

Chinese authors tend to perceive the constitution as a symbol and
element of modern democracy.[21] The word 'constitution' (宪) appeared
in a very early stage of Chinese history, but it never distinguished itself
from the ordinary statutes and never acquired the meaning of a set of
fundamental principles or rules that it stands for in the modern era. Both
constitution and constitutionalism are regarded as notions from Western
culture and outcomes of the bourgeois revolution; there are no convincing materials and evidence to support the idea that constitution and
constitutionalism had existed before Western constitutional thoughts
were imported into China from the end of the nineteenth century.[22]

---

[21] Xu Chongde, *The History of the Constitution of the People's Republic of China* (中华人民共和国宪法史), Vol. 1 (Fuzhou: Fujian Renmin Chubanshe, 2005), p. 2.
[22] Zhang Jinfan, *The Chinese History of Constitution* (中国宪法史) (Beijing: People Press, 2011), pp. 7–8. See also Xiaohong Xiao-Planes, 'Of constitutions and constitutionalism: trying to build a new political order in China, 1908-1949', in Balme and Dowdle (eds.) (n. 14), p. 38.

The constitution as an imported concept is also affirmed by historians. For example, Kuhn uses the expression 'constitutional agenda' to designate the changing consensus and actions in the process of building a modern state in the Chinese context. He distinguishes the formal or written constitution from the substantial and non-written constitution that originates from people's political attitudes and manners of living, considering the latter as the true fundamental law and the main cause of the evolution of China's constitutional structure.[23] It is also suggested that the Western idea of constitution closely parallels the Chinese concept of *fatong* (法统), which combines the ideas of 'law' (*fa*) and 'succession' (*tong*). The concept refers to the set of rules and institutions that constituted and legitimated the dynastic state. 'Traditionally, a *fatong* was created by the founder of a dynasty, and was then maintained by his descendants. A change in the dynasty marked its *fatong*'s formal termination, even while institutional borrowings from one dynasty to another were often numerous. Although intimately associated with imperial governance, the notion of *fatong* expressed a juridico-political orthodoxy that continued to influence the spirit and the rhetoric of China's political world well into the Republican era.'[24] Although the word and concept of constitution were imported relatively recently, the constitution's function in state building could be found by analogy in China's past.

In his historical studies of the late Ming dynasty, Pierre-Étienne Will acknowledged that 'there was no such thing in Imperial China as a coherent legal text that would impose itself on the holders of political power as well as on the ordinary citizens, and that would have to be referred to in order to verify the legality of the decisions and actions of the government and the regulations it promulgated'. Nonetheless, Will contended that in Chinese history, there had been 'beyond the strict definitions of modern law, not only notions and texts playing a role similar to that of a constitution, but also institutions and procedures whose aim would be comparable with that of constitutional control in our own systems', and he concluded that a 'virtual constitutionalism' had existed in China. Will confessed that 'any historian of China knows that speaking of a Constitution, or of constitutionalism, or of constitutional control in Imperial China (late or otherwise), as I do, can only be by analogy'.[25]

---

[23] Philip A. Kuhn, *Origins of the Modern Chinese State*, translated into Chinese by Chen Jian and Chen Zhihong (Beijing: Sanlian Shudian, 2013), preface of the Chinese version, p. 4.

[24] Xiao-Planes (n. 22), p. 38.

[25] Pierre-Étienne Will, 'Epilogue: virtual constitutionalism in the late Ming dynasty', in Balme and Dowdle (eds.) (n. 14), p. 261.

The 'by analogy' understanding of constitutionalism advocates the putative convergence between China's traditional concept of *fatong* and Western constitutionalism. It follows that the substantial functions of constitutionalism exist in China or that the Western idea of constitutionalism could be translated into China's local institutions and procedures that perform similar functions (and vice versa).

That said, the 'by analogy' method is limited in that it overstates the ability of institutions and procedures established at the founding stage of a dynasty to restrict emperors much later and in that it ignores the fact that constitutionalism is by essence a normative discourse. Such discourse embodies the values, often non-stated, that underlie the material and institutional provisions in a specific constitution; at an even deeper level, constitutionalism is a self-referential concept – not a reflection of something that contains or embodies something else (like values) but the reflection of the very thing itself.[26] In fact, the Chinese traditional concept of *fatong* can hardly be regarded as the embodiment of the values of Western constitutionalism, much less as the value itself. Just as in the late Ming dynasty, where the emperor's personal discretion or abuse of power was resisted and restricted in the name of institutions set forth by the dynasty's founding fathers, such a scenario could be better explained as the embodiment of traditional Chinese moral values, such as filial piety, rather than Western liberal values. Moreover, the lack of constitutional discourses in the Chinese context helps to explain why debates on constitutionalism in contemporary China are attentive to the political implications and are generally connected to institution building and state governing. The pragmatic and functionalist comprehension of constitutionalism should be further nuanced, since such comprehension could contain the dynamism against liberal values.

3.2 Constitutionalism through the prism of the constitution's enforcement

As to the question whether there is constitutionalism in China, answers can vary greatly. Those who stress the significant progress in China's lawmaking contend that China's constitutional framework has undergone important evolution since the adoption of the constitution of 1982 with its political, social and economic development. They also contend that

---

[26] Joseph H. H. Weiler and Marlene Wind, 'Introduction: European constitutionalism beyond the state', in Weiler and Wind (eds.) (n. 11), p. 3.

up-to-date, recognisable constitutional structures are being built in
China: administrative litigation; documentary constitutional endorsement of private enterprise, private property, the rule of law and even
human rights; and an emerging popular constitutional consciousness
that is able, at least at times, to use this budding constitutionalism to
constrain governmental hubris.[27] By contrast, Henkin has concluded that
the constitutions of the former Union of Soviet Socialist Republics and of
the People's Republic of China may be said to serve purposes that are not
closely related to the concerns of constitutionalism.[28] Although more
than thirty years have passed since China's launching of economic
reform and the open policy, accompanied by the legal reform, Henkin's
critique remains for many authors a baseline in understanding China's
attitudes towards constitutionalism. Some affirm that 'the presence of
a vital tradition of socialist constitutions' is what makes Asia a region
distinctive in constitutional terms, that China is the centre of such
analysis and that the overall sense 'is of an authoritarian legality'.[29]
Similarly, others criticise that 'having a constitution without constitutionalism is a condition in which China has long been stuck' and that the
lack of judicial review or of popular participation in the enforcement of
the constitution is the most obvious and direct cause for the lack of
constitutionalism.[30] The divergence of views relates to the constitution's
implementation or its effective binding force, with emphasis put on the
enforcement mechanism and issues. It is, however, the political implications of the constitutionalism that call into question the acceptability of
liberal values in the Chinese context.

The translation of 'constitutionalism' into Chinese Xianzheng (宪政)
emphasises these political implications. It does not mean merely the
supremacy of the constitution – which, among other things, implies
that the public power shall be limited by the constitution. It means
more profoundly a model of state governing, i.e. 'governing the state in
accordance with the constitution', which means setting constraints on
the exercise of state powers. Some argue that building constitutionalism
in China requires political reform, the success of which rests on the

[27] Michael W. Dowdle, 'Of comparative constitutional monocropping: a reply to Zhang
Qianfan' (2010) 8 International Journal of Constitutional Law 977–984, at 981.

[28] Louis Henkin, The Rights of Man Today (London: Stevens and Sons, 1978), pp. 55–73.

[29] Rosalind Dixon and Tom Ginsburg (eds.), Comparative Constitutional Law in Asia
(London: Edward Elgar, 2014), pp. 9–10.

[30] Zhang Qianfan, 'A constitution without constitutionalism? The paths of constitutional
development in China' (2010) 8 International Journal of Constitutional Law 950–976.

spontaneous endeavours of its citizens.[31] Although the Party has never officially endorsed the concept of constitutionalism, it has affirmed that rule of law requires 'governing the state in accordance with the constitution' in the recent political resolution on rule of law adopted on 23 October 2014, during the fourth plenary session of the 18th Congress. That affirmation is particularly significant given that the resolution is generally regarded as the most important political agenda on legal reform in China. Soon after the Party's resolution on rule of law, on 1 November 2014, the Standing Committee of the 12th National People's Congress designated 4 December as National Constitutional Day. The political significance is that stronger importance shall be attached to the constitution's supremacy and that the constitution's authority shall be safeguarded, as it is warranted by rule of law. More recently, the 19th National Congress of the CPC pronounced the objective to set up a central leading group for advancing law-based governance in all fields, which includes, inter alia, strengthening the implementation of the constitution. This move has been widely welcomed because it confirms the expectation that China's constitution should be effectively applied. Concrete reform measures, especially implementation mechanisms, are expected to be in place in order to improve the constitution's effectiveness or the constitution's authority.

3.3 Constitutionalism and China's political system

The strategy of improving the constitution's implementation without mentioning constitutionalism is explained by the fact that constitutionalism remains a politically contentious concept.[32] In 2013, *Red Flag Manuscript*, a Chinese academic journal of political theories directed and run by the Central Committee of the CPC, published an article entitled 'A Comparative Study on Constitutionalism and People's Democracy System', whose main idea was that constitutionalism is the fundamental framework of the occidental political systems and that constitutionalism's core values and ideology are capitalism and dictatorship of the bourgeoisie. In short, constitutionalism is stated to be

---

[31] Cai Dingjian, 'The development of constitutionalism in the transition of Chinese society' (2005) 19 *Columbia Journal of Asian Law* 1–29, at 25.

[32] For further analysis of the ongoing debate over the constitutionalism issue, see Samson Yuen, 'Debating constitutionalism in China: dreaming of liberal turn?' (2013) 4 *China Perspectives* 67–72.

contrary to the people's democracy system.[33] The author contends that constitutionalism is not just a legal but more essentially a political concept, notably in the Chinese context, especially since constitutionalism could be exploited to overthrow the Party's leadership. Moreover, the idea of constitutionalism defended by Western scholars hardly takes account of China's history of state building, which forges the basic understanding of political legitimacy. Maintaining the Party's leadership is the most fundamental principle of China's politics, and the Western understanding of constitutionalism seems to be too parochial in not fully recognising this. It may even become subversive to the Party's leadership through negating the Party's theory and doctrine in governing the state. Constitutionalism should be therefore subordinated to the Party's leadership, and the Party's legitimacy is premised on its mission and the CPC's representation of the general will of the people. Both the constitution and laws should be made under the Party's leadership for people's interest and in accordance with the lawful procedures.

In order to reconcile the Party's leadership with the constitution's authority, two proposals have been put forward. First, the Party should itself behave within the limits set down by the constitution and laws, a basic principle recognised by the Party's constitution.[34] Second, the Party should be considered as 'de facto sovereign', playing the key role in the constitution's functioning. The Party's constitution becomes the integral part of the effective constitution under China's state–party political system,[35] or the Party leadership and constitution's authority may at least converge.

According to the preceding arguments, the Chinese understanding of constitutionalism, if any, may greatly differ from the traditional views regarding the constitution as the guardian of fundamental rights through constraining government powers, including limited government, separation of powers, checks and balances, and independent judicial review.[36] The main raison for the Party's resistance to constitutionalism is to

[33] Yang Xiaoqing, 'A comparative study on constitutionalism and People's democracy system' (宪政与人民民主主义制度之比较研究) (2013) 10 Red Flag Manuscript (红旗文稿) 4–10.

[34] Constitution of the Communist Party of China, amended and adopted at the 18th National Congress on 14 November 2012, General Program, para. 28.

[35] Jiang Shigong, 'How to explore the Chinese path to constitutionalism? A response to Larry Catá Backer' (2014) 40 Modern China 196–213.

[36] Louis Henkin, 'A new birth of constitutionalism: genetic influence and genetic defects', in Michel Rosenfeld (ed.), Constitutionalism, Identity, Difference, and Legitimacy: Theoretical Perspective (Durham, NC: Duke University Press, 1994), p. 39.

prevent traditional Western constitutionalism from becoming the prevailing ideology and eroding the very foundation of China's current political system. However, the phrase 'governing the state in accordance with law', as proclaimed by Article 5 of the Chinese constitution and often translated as 'rule of law', reflects the expectation of legal constraints being imposed on state power. Similarly, China's constitution affirms by Article 33, paragraph 3, that the 'State respects and guarantees human rights'. These two examples show that China's constitution shares certain features of a liberal constitution. Some argue that 'China presents an interesting variant of constitutionalism – at least at the theoretical level. It suggests the possibility of authoritarian constitutionalism, that is, of constitutionalism with an extreme variant of Western-style democratic values.'[37] Nonetheless, upholding Party leadership – the Party's authority either within or beyond the constitution – remains the dividing line between the Chinese way of asserting the constitution's authority and Western liberal constitutionalism. The division is largely related to different considerations of political legitimacy in the state-building context.

3.4 Constitutionalism and political legitimacy in the Chinese context

China's experiences in making modern constitutions are closely connected to making the modern state. The state-building perspective may offer insight into the differences between China and the Western world as regards constitutionalism. The constitution's functional role, as it is emphasised and developed in the Chinese context, confirms the prevailing viewpoints that constitution and legislation are used as instruments for building the state, i.e. that they are treated as political tools rather than as the embodiment of fundamental values underpinning a political regime.[38] In a larger context, China's instrumental approach of not giving the constitution any autonomy from the political sphere resembles the approaches of other East Asian states whose constitution-making experiences can be described as efforts at promoting democracy, national

---

[37] Larry Catá Backer, 'Party, people, government and state: on constitutional values and the legitimacy of the Chinese state-party rule of law system' (2012) 30 *Boston University International Law Journal* 331–408, at 404.

[38] A recent comparative study shows that China's constitution is among the most ideologically 'statist' constitutions in the world. In contrast to libertarian constitutions, statist constitutions both presuppose and enshrine a far-reaching role for the state in a variety of domains by imbuing the state with a broad range of powers as well as responsibilities. See David S. Law and Mila Versteeg, 'The evolution and ideology of global constitutionalism' (2011) 99 *California Law Review* 1163–1257, at 1229.

independence or national inclusion.[39] For those East Asian states that are
said to have taken the route of liberal democracy, their practices of
developing constitutionalism in response to the transitional arrangements, rather than of accepting the core values of liberal democracy,
expand scopes and create new functions that have not yet been recognised in the development of modern constitutionalism. It is also argued
that 'unlike classical limiting functions of constitutions, transitional
constitutionalism may function as managing reform agendas, substitut-
ing violent revolutions and even facilitating social and political
integration'.[40] A common feature in East Asian states is precisely that
'the building of a constitutional state was often undertaken rather instru-
mentally as an inevitable part of modernization'.[41] Against that backdrop, Chinese constitutional history reveals a 'constant tension between
constraints imposed by centralized leadership and the search for institutional mechanisms to peacefully regulate political competition, differences of opinion, and the inevitable conflicts of interests'.[42]
The establishment of the CPC's leadership in 1949 did not end the
process of state building, which is also largely characterised as modernisation. The evolution of China's constitutions shows that political
ideology and culture have been the primary forces in writing successive
constitutions and amendments. The Party's political ideology may take
over or supplant a constitution, or equally, a constitution may emerge by
affirming or demanding compliance with such ideology. Modern
Chinese constitutionalism is shrouded and obscured by the theory and
political ideology of the CPC. Indeed, there is an inherent possibility
that the CPC will write its entire ideology into the constitution.[43]
The implications are two-fold: constitutional amendments concretise
the Party's leadership through legal form or discourses and at the same

[39] Wen-Chen Chang, 'East Asian foundations for constitutionalism: three models
reconstructed' (2008) 9 *National Taiwan University Law Review* 111–141, at 134.
[40] Wen-Chen Chang and Yeh Jiunn-Rong, 'The changing landscape of modern constitutionalism: transitional perspective' (2009) 3 *National Taiwan University Law Review*
145–183, at 148, 176.
[41] Jiunn-Rong Yeh and Wen-Chen Chang, 'The emergence of East Asian constitutionalism:
features in comparison' (2011) 59 *American Journal of Comparative Law* 805–840.
[42] Xiaohong Xiao-Planes, 'Constitutions and constitutionalism: trying to build a new political order (1908–1949)', in Mireille Delmas-Marty and Pierre-Étienne Will (eds.), *China,
Democracy, and Law: A Historical and Contemporary Approach*, translated by
Naomi Norberg (Leiden; Boston: Brill, 2012), p. 294.
[43] M. Ulric Killion, 'China's amended constitution: quest for liberty and independent
judicial review' (2005) 4 *Washington University Global Studies Law Review* 34–80, at 45.

time consolidate or crystallise the Party's political legitimacy in state governing in a contemporaneous manner.

Adherence to Party leadership in the constitutional construction and discourse of 'ruling the state by law' distinguishes China's constitutional practice from liberal constitutionalism. The debate on whether China has the transformative potential for constitutional development[44] calls into question the methodology in analysing China's specialty on constitutional issues. It has been suggested that 'China is unlikely to found constitutionalism on a rejection of its past' and that China's commitment to a constitutional future is likely to be framed in terms of an accompanying commitment to its socialist past. 'For better or worse, this is China's most visibly distinct history. As such, it cannot be abandoned or denied without abandoning constitutionalism itself.'[45] Nevertheless, the recourse to history to justify a Chinese constitutionalism calls for prudence. China's historical background should not be artificially limited to the communist past in the narrow sense. Only through a more general observation could one identify the place and role of the constitution and law in that polity, while the place and role of the constitution reflect the seemingly distinctive collection of values and concerns that distinguish one nation from another. Here, it seems useful to recall Unger's analysis on the role of law in pre-imperial China and sinologists' criticism of that analysis.[46] They offer an insight into the Chinese understanding of constitutionalism as fundamental value or superior law. In rebutting Unger's conclusion that the rhetoric of constitutionalism found in the West never existed in the Chinese discourse, it should be emphasised that the Mandate of Heaven had been deeply rooted in China's political, social and religious context since pre-imperial Chinese society; its function can be considered comparable to that of the natural law in the Western context. The idea of the Mandate was that Heaven had endowed an earthly representative with the authority and responsibility to govern all civilised peoples. That awesome authority, and the duty of loyalty and obedience among the people that went with it, imposed on the ruler – indeed, could only be justified by – an even more awesome responsibility

---

[44] Michael W. Dowdle, 'Of parliament, pragmatism, and the dynamics of constitutional development: the curious case of China' (2002) 35 *New York University Journal of International Law & Politics* 1–200.

[45] Michael W. Dowdle, 'Constitutional listening' (2013) 88 *Chicago-Kent Law Review* 115–156, at 153.

[46] William P. Alford, 'The inscrutable occidental? Implications of Roberto Unger's uses and abuses of China's past' (1986) 64 *Texas Law Review* 915–972.

to work for the welfare of the people. If the ruler failed to discharge that responsibility, as measured against universal and discernible standards that transcended the ruler, the people could express their displeasure. Heaven would then remove its Mandate from the ruler and provide it to one who would better heed the people and serve their welfare.[47] It follows that since the pre-imperial stage, China had developed a greater belief in a cosmopolitan standard by which to evaluate state law and to restrict whoever rules. Further historical research confirms that, though notions such as constitution, natural law or rule of law were alien to Chinese legal tradition,[48] there were different kinds of regimes in China's past to hold the ruler accountable to the law.[49] In those researchers' opinion, the effective restraints on power that governed society in China's past imply that the Chinese society shares to a certain degree the concept of fundamental law enjoying authority superior to the imperial power and that history could be seen as an indicator of 'constitutional tradition' in the Chinese context. From that perspective, redefining constitutionalism beyond the narrow Western sense paves the way for understanding China's constitutional tradition. Similarly, 'constitutionalism' can be defined as a basic structure of laws in accordance with values widely accepted in a society.[50] The fundamental law or 'basic structure of laws' stands for norms of superior authority than ordinary statutes or legislation. It comprises norms of moral or philosophical rather than legal nature, since Confucianism, the dominant intellectual tradition in China and some other East Asian countries, had grave reservations

[47] Ibid., 936.
[48] Chinese scholar Yu Keping has stated that Chinese traditional culture paid much attention to 'rule by law' but not to 'rule of law'. The two concepts, though seemingly similar, are substantially different. Rule by law means handling events strictly in accordance with the law, which was an important element of traditional culture. Apart from emphasising strict accordance with the law, the essence of rule of law is that no person or group can override the law. The principle of rule of law never appeared in traditional culture and was inconsistent with the logic of traditional culture. By nature, this was the culture of an absolute monarchy, which presupposed that the emperor was above the law. See Yu Keping, 'The developmental logic of Chinese culture under modernization and globalization' (2008) 35 *Boundary* 157–182, at 160.
[49] Qiang Fang and Roger Des Forges, 'Were Chinese rules above the law? Toward a theory of the rule of law in China since early times to 1949 CE' (2008) *Stanford Journal of International Law* 101–146. See also Pierre-Etienne Will, 'Checking abuses of power under the Ming Dynasty', in Delmas-Marty and Will (eds.) (n. 42), pp. 117–167; Chaihark Hahm, 'Ritual and constitutionalism: disputing the ruler's legitimacy in a Confucian polity' (2009) 57 *American Journal of Comparative Law* 135–203.
[50] Wm. Theodore De Bary, 'The "constitutional tradition" in China' (1995) 9 *Journal of Chinese Law* 7–34, at 7.

about law as a fundamental solution to the problems of human society.[51] Following the view that the Confucian idea of ritual propriety or *li* (礼) could nourish civic virtue and inform the normative standard for evaluating the ruler's legitimacy, it is even argued that ritual propriety played the functional role as the constitutional norm in Chinese imperial history. Such functional understanding of Confucianism should be, however, tempered by the recognition that Confucian heritage was and is continuously reinterpreted and re-presented to meet the challenges of the day.[52] In fact, the reinterpretation and re-presentation of Confucianism is often analogised to the modern constitution's function, with no importance being attached to either conflict or concordance between Confucian ideas and the liberal values of the modern constitution. Furthermore, it has been pointed out that 'there is a certain danger in applying categories derived from modern Western experience to pre-modern East Asia': 'a careful consideration suggests that there are some materials in the East Asian tradition that do approximate those features associated with the modern concepts of constitutions and constitutionalism. This is especially true if we focus less on the enlightenment norms

---

[51] For example, the case of Korea is considered particularly instructive for the study of the interaction between law, culture and Confucianism. The Korean culture is generally regarded as the most Confucian of all Asian cultures, and the current Korean cultural discourse is becoming a hybrid of traditional Confucian signs, symbols and narratives – allegedly according to which 'law' was the least preferred means for settling disputes or governing a state – and a newer set of idioms and references provided by the ideal of rule of law. See Chaihark Hahm, 'Law, culture, and the politics of Confucianism' (2003) 16 *Columbia Journal of Asian Law* 253–302, at 259. As far as imperial Vietnam is concerned, research reveals numerous constitutional norms as the embodiment of the Confucian *li* (rites) used to restrain the royal authority, namely the models of ancient kings, the political norms in the Confucian classics, the ancestral precedents and the institutions of the preceding dynasties. See Bui Ngoc Son, 'Confucian constitutionalism in Imperial Vietnam' (2013) 9 *National Taiwan University Law Review* 373–427. Japan's constitutionalisation process is marked by alteration and adaptation, i.e. of foreign legal models to Japan's local culture. See Christopher A. Ford, 'The indigenization of constitutionalism in the Japanese experiences' (1996) 28 *Case Western Reserve Journal of International Law* 3–62. It is noted that 'after nearly three centuries, Confucian ideals implemented throughout the Tokugawa feudal structure became engraved in Japanese culture. Among these ideals was the primacy of the group which grew out of the principles of filial piety and compromise. Its influence continues.' See Dean J. Gibbons, 'Law and the group ethos in Japan' (1990) 3 *Legal Perspectives* 98–126, at 124. It is also affirmed that 'for the Japanese, Constitutionalism is a foreign culture imported during the Meiji Era'. See Annen Junji and Lee H. Rousso, 'Constitutionalism as a political culture' (2002) 11 *Pacific Rim Law & Policy Journal* 561–576, at 570.

[52] Hahm Chaihark, 'Constitutionalism, Confucian civic virtue, and ritual property', in Daniel L. Bell and Hahm Chaibong (eds.), *Confucianism for the Modern World* (Cambridge: Cambridge University Press, 2003), pp. 45–47.

of liberal rights and more on the structural features of precommitment.'[53]
'Precommitment' means a type of self-restraint for the sake of future
welfare. Only from the perspective of precommitment could one perceive
the functional convergence between Chinese traditional notions such as
the Mandate of Heaven or ritual propriety and the Western concepts of
political legitimacy and authority. Such convergence, however, is only
partial, if the rich substantial connotations of modern constitutionalism
are accounted for. As for the current official discourse on Party leadership, the presumption that adherence to Party leadership in China's
contemporary constitutional construction reflects the traditional scepticism about the role of law and constitution is hard to rebut.[54]
The corollary of this presumption is that adherence to Party leadership
could be analogised to re-present the relationship between the ruler and
his Mandate of Heaven in China's past. Like rulers holding the supreme
power but at the same time subordinate to the Mandate of Heaven and
ritual propriety, the Party's leadership draws its legitimacy from the
source beyond its control, i.e. the people's support as last resort. That
also explains why the Party attaches so much importance to its mission in
representing the fundamental interest of the vastest people, as informed
by the theory of 'Three Representatives' (or 'Three Represents' according
to the constitution of the CPC), which was recognised by constitutional
amendment in 2004. Since the 18th National Congress, the Party's effort
to strictly enforce the disciplinary rules among its members shows
further the Party's concern with consolidating its political legitimacy.
The promotion of political instruction such as 'the Party shall exercise
strict self-governance in every respect' and 'maintain strict political
discipline in the Party', as well as the elaboration of disciplinary rules
including Regulations of the Communist Party of China on Internal
Oversight, Code of Conduct for Intraparty Political Life under New
Circumstances, etc. demonstrates that the Party prioritises the upholding
of its authority through disciplinary measures. The Party's implementation of the disciplinary sanctions a priori is very much like the enforcement of the state law in the Chinese context.

That said, there is in China a popular belief in values with authority
superior to any man-made rules – including the constitutional

---

[53] Tom Ginsburg, 'Constitutionalism: Eastern Asian antecedents' (2012) 88 *Chicago-Kent Law Review* 11–33, at 30.
[54] Moreover, the Chinese pronunciation of the word 'constitution' is '*xian fa*' (宪法). Phonetically, the word is misleading, since it gives the impression that the constitution is just one of the enacted laws (*fa*, 法), without authority as fundamental law.

provisions – which measure the legitimacy and determine the sub-sistence of the ruling power. One can infer from such belief that the functional meaning of constitutionalism does exist in Chinese legal tradition, and such a constitutionalist function probably calls for innovation in the discourse beyond the formal constitutionalism. In so much as a constitutionalist function exists, the core issue is to identify the values embracing the fundamental rules governing the operation and evolution of the positive law. In the Chinese context, those values have not only institutional functions as regards state building and governing but are more essentially moral norms guiding individuals' conduct and behaviour: they serve to preserve social order and achieve the aspired-to ideal society. In other words, the values underlying the legal and political system are themselves a set of social norms. Since the 18th Congress of the CPC, the core socialist values have been nationally promoted; they are best seen as the overarching principles for the state, society and individual citizens. These core socialist values are described in twenty-four words and phrases including prosperity, democracy, civility, harmony, freedom, equality, justice, rule of law, patriotism, dedication, integrity and friendship. The normative, but not simply aspirational, character of those socialist core values relies on the fact that they are substantiated in the application of the legal principles and rules and that they are really followed by the citizens as norms of conduct. How those socialist core values are understood and interpreted in practice is a question per-taining to China's position towards the normative values of global constitutionalism, and it is a question of effectiveness. The process of constitutionalisation in the field of international law raises further questions about the compatibility of the values underpinned by Chinese tradition with global constitutionalism; it also highlights China's specificity in dealing with global constitutionalism beyond the national level.

4 China's perspective on international law and global constitutionalism

In international law, constitutionalisation is analysed as a process inspired by constitutionalist thought.[55] The main considerations speak-ing for the constitutionalisation of international law include the

---

[55] Klabbers (n. 10), pp. 5, 10.

following. First, the principle of sovereignty is being ousted from its position as the foremost principle of international law. Second, the principle of state consent is being partly replaced by majoritarian decision making. Third, the formal acceptance of universal treaties enshrining constitutional values is not the end, but rather the beginning, of the constitutionalisation of international law, which requires consensus in the details. Fourth, the settlement of international disputes is increasingly legalised and juridified, though the juridification needs further clarification.[56] Other signs are the constitutionalisation of international legal subjects, the constitutionalisation of sources such as *jus cogens* and *erga omnes* norms, the constitutionalisation of legal processes of participation and transparency, as well as the emergence of constitutional goods and principles.[57] These proposed indicators of global constitutionalism are, however, challenged as avowedly aspirational rather than descriptive of existing international law.[58] In other words, global constitutionalism, inasmuch as it is a good idea, is not yet sufficiently endorsed by state practices. This section aims to reassess China's approach to international law in light of the intellectual movement of global constitutionalism, which interprets some features of the status quo of international relations as 'constitutional' and even 'constitutionalist' and which seeks arguments for their further development in a specific direction.[59]

The discrepancy between the Chinese perspective and the idea of global constitutionalism starts with the concept of sovereignty. Sovereignty is said to be still the main source of legitimacy of international legal norms, despite what Peters calls the 'erosion' of the requirement of consent by such developments as obligations *erga omnes*, 'objective regimes' and 'legislation' by the Security Council. It is far too early to conclude from relatively recent developments in international law that sovereignty has been displaced by a 'hybrid' international constitution in which it plays a subsidiary role.[60] China has persistently stood for the primacy of state sovereignty and, correlatively, the principle of non-intervention. This stance has deep roots in the miserable experience of modern Chinese

---

[56] Anne Peters, 'The merits of global constitutionalism' (2009) 16 *Indiana Journal of Global Legal Studies* 397–411, at 398–399.

[57] Anne Peters, 'Are we moving towards constitutionalization of the world community?', in Antonio Cassese (ed.), *Realizing Utopia: The Future of International Law* (Oxford: Oxford University Press, 2012), pp. 121–124.

[58] James Crawford, *Chance, Order, Change: The Course of International Law: General Course on Public International Law*, Collected Courses of The Hague Academy of International Law, Vol. 365 (Leiden; Boston: Brill; Nijhoff, 2013), p. 451.

[59] Peters (n. 57), p. 119.

[60] Crawford (n. 58), p. 451.

history,[61] i.e. China's being constrained by the 'unequal treaties' imposed by the Western superpowers after the First Opium War (1839–1842). Due to this history China is said to be a most enthusiastic champion of the principle of state sovereignty.[62] Xue Hanqin, Chinese judge on the International Court of Justice, once stressed that the debate over the principles of sovereignty and non-interference boils down to ideological and cultural differences and to the basic conception of world order.[63] Her critics point to the substantial inequality among different states, especially to developing states' lack of the political and economic power to influence the world order that Western superiors have. Departing from that point of view, Xue concludes that the principles of sovereignty and non-interference mean that 'each State has the *autonomy* to freely choose the development model it deems suitable for its own country and that choice should not be subject to external scrutiny and interference. The internal self-determination is intrinsically linked with the concept of sovereignty and external self-determination.'[64] In fact, China deems state autonomy as the core of sovereignty, and such autonomy is closely connected to state building. Moreover, Xue points out that the difficulty with the normative claim of the existence of an international community lies in the fact that in reality, 'common interests of the international community' have to be displayed in concrete instances. The question as to who is entitled to represent the interests of the international community and to act on its behalf is not novel, but it remains unsettled.[65] Xue's account of national sovereignty is typical among Chinese scholars. China's emphasis on state autonomy and scepticism about the international community explain why it insists on the absolute jurisdictional immunity of states in foreign courts, while acknowledging that the matter of state immunity now turns on the relationship between the immunity rule and substantive law as regards serious violations of international law and peremptory norms.[66] China remains critical about humanitarian intervention and the responsibility to protect.[67]

[61] Samuel S. Kim, 'Sovereignty in the Chinese image of world order', in Roland St. J. Macdonald (ed.), *Essays in Honor of Wang Tieya* (Leiden: Martinus Nijhoff Publishers, 1994), pp. 428–429.
[62] Wang Tieya, 'International law in China: historical and contemporary perspectives' (1990) 221 *Recueil des cours* 195–370, at 288.
[63] Xue Hanqin, *Chinese Contemporary and Perspectives on International Law: History, Culture and International Law*, Collected Courses of The Hague Academy of International Law, Vol. 355 (Leiden; Boston: Brill; Nijhoff, 2012), p. 93.
[64] Ibid., p. 95 (emphasis added).
[65] Ibid., p. 102.
[66] Ibid., pp. 89–90.
[67] Ibid., pp. 104, 106.

This chapter chooses the International Criminal Court, the World Trade Organization and international human rights regimes to illustrate China's adherence to state sovereignty and autonomy. Although China shows more openness and flexibility in other fields of international law (such as in accepting investor–state disputes settlement by international investment arbitration), these three examples are more useful in deducing China's position on global constitutionalism.

4.1 State autonomy and the International Criminal Court

China's striving for state autonomy is exemplified by its position on the creation and operation of the International Criminal Court (ICC). China had been actively involved in the negotiations, but the Chinese delegation cast a negative vote at the end of the Rome Conference. Among Chinese scholars, it is widely accepted that 'the challenge provided by the advent of the ICC is immense for the national legal order of China, and [that] ripples of the work of the body will transcend this and other legal systems, surging against the barriers, if any, of sovereignty of countries of today's world'.[68] The desire to maintain the barriers of sovereignty likely underlies China's cautious reaction about the ICC's jurisdiction,[69] the prosecutor's *proprio motu* power and discretion, and the ICC's competence over internal armed conflict,[70] issues that will compromise the state's autonomy in trying and punishing the most serious crimes. The optimistic view is that 'China's position is similar to that of an observer who is looking at the growth of an institution in whose founding

[68] Xu Hong, 'The regime of international judicial cooperation under the framework of the International Criminal Court' (国际刑事法院框架内的国际司法合作制度), in *Chinese Yearbook of International Law 1999* (中国国际法年刊 1999) (Beijing: Law Press China, 2002), p. 164.

[69] In explaining China's abstention in adopting UNSC Resolution 1593 (2005), Chinese Ambassador Wang Guangya had pointed out: 'China, which was not a party to the Rome Statute, had major reservations regarding some of its provisions and had found it difficult to endorse the Council authorization of that referral.' Available at http://www.un.org /press/en/2005/sc8351.doc.htm.

[70] The Taiwan issue is perceived as the most significant potential conflict between China and the ICC. The ICC's jurisdiction over war crimes in internal armed conflicts could result in interference in China's internal affairs. Tibet, Xinjiang, *Falun Gong* and deficiencies in its national judicial system are other, lesser concerns for China vis-à-vis the ICC. See Jing Guan, 'The ICC's jurisdiction over crimes in internal armed conflict: an insurmountable obstacle for China's accession' (2010) 28 *Penn State International Law Review* 703–754, at 705, 706. See also Bingbing Jia, 'China and the International Criminal Court: the current situation' (2006) 10 *Singapore Year Book of International Law* 87–97, at 94–96.

he has played a role. It will soon learn of the benefits or disadvantages of the institution to *its* interests.'[71] China's approach to the ICC may be best described as pragmatic. For China's pragmatism to be justified, what those interests are and whether China's interests could converge with the interest of justice in face of the most serious international crimes need to be clarified. China does acknowledge that the principle of sovereignty does not mean that sovereignty is absolute and that sovereignty should operate within the domain of law.[72] Indeed, China's reservations are based mainly on political considerations. As regards the ICC's universal jurisdiction, it is believed that 'the overriding objective of universal jurisdiction is not purely justice-oriented. Its application is always fraught with political motivation and may be misused through politics.'[73] Some argue from a different perspective that it is political constraints that hinder the application of universal jurisdiction in practice.[74] The different reactions to political influence in applying international legal rules reflect China's specificity in dealing with the relationship between law and politics: China accepts only those rules of international law whose application can be kept immune from political misuse; otherwise China refuses to be subjected to the law and opts for maintaining state autonomy in order to shelter itself from injustices of international law. In other words, the principle of sovereignty is still a barrier against, not a means for redressing, the injustice in international relations.

Since China's strategy of realpolitik in maintaining state sovereignty is also backed by its past submissive history, globalisation is making a profound difference in some aspects of the relationship between China and international law. With the development of international law, particularly the emergence of special international regimes, China's defensive strategy has undergone significant evolution, mainly in the field of international trade and investment as well as human rights protection. Although this evolution is not linear, reflecting to a certain degree the so-called fragmentation of international law, it presents new trends in China's perspective on international law.

---

[71] Ibid., at 97 (emphasis added).

[72] Xue (n. 63), p. 86.

[73] Zhou Lulu, 'Brief analysis of a few controversial issues in contemporary international criminal law', in Morten Bergsmo and Ling Yan (eds.), *State Immunity and International Criminal Law* (Brussels: Torkel Opsahl Academic Publisher, 2012), p. 45.

[74] Alexandre Skander Galand, 'Book review: Morten Bergsmo and Ling Yan (eds.), *State Immunity and International Criminal Law*' (2014) 25 *European Journal of International Law* 625–629, at 625.

4.2 Regulatory autonomy and the World Trade Organization

In the field of international trade law, China's accession to the World Trade Organization (WTO) in 2001 is often perceived as the most remarkable event in the relationship between China and international law. It is true that the benefit from free trade is the main motive for China's decision to become a WTO member and that China is prepared to restrict or even cede its autonomy for that benefit through accepting limits on its power to regulate trade issues, which include investment and intellectual property protection. The legally binding decisions adopted through the dispute settlement mechanism constitute the most incisive constraint on China's state power in trade affairs.[75] It should be noted, however, that China's accession to the WTO was also motivated by the consideration that the WTO, as a rule-based organisation with a full-fledged legal framework, could directly or indirectly play a positive role in China's internal legal reform, since the WTO both imposes on China and spurs it to take obligatory steps and measures in regulating trade and commerce through well-established and qualified legal rules rather than discretionary policies. Such evolution constitutes an important aspect of the reform of ruling the state by law, even though often misunderstood as the 'rule of law'.[76] Indeed, the then widely held expectation was that compliance with WTO obligations could induce China to achieve the goal of a 'thin' rule of law in terms of transparency, impartial application of laws and judicial review.[77] After more than a decade of membership, China's practices in dealing with WTO legal rules have, however, proved that the WTO's impact on China's international legal reform towards rule of law is more complex than was generally imagined. Some contend

---

[75] For example, the DSB's decision in *China-Distribution Services* (DS363) is considered to have immeasurable impact on China's services market, foreign investment and related laws. It illustrates 'the relationship between services and investment, how international norms, concepts and principles are domesticated, and to what extent the implementation of domestic laws is affected by the principles and understanding of the international community'. See Wang Guiguo, *Radiating Impact of WTO on Its Members' Legal System: The Chinese Perspective*, Collected Courses of The Hague Academy of International Law, Vol. 349 (Leiden; Boston: Brill; Nijhoff, 2011), p. 246.

[76] For example, soon after China's accession to the WTO, China's chief prosecutor Cao Jianming had predicted that 'China's entry into the WTO will not only profoundly impact the rule of law in China, but will also call for higher standards for China's judicial system'. See Cao Jianming, 'WTO and the rule of law in China' (2002) 16 *Temple International and Comparative Law Journal* 379–390.

[77] See Wang Jiangyu, 'The rule of law in China: a realistic view of the jurisprudence, the impact of the WTO, and the prospects for future development' (2004) 2 *Singapore Journal of Legal Studies* 347–389.

that 'China has not been willing to grasp the WTO opportunity for domestic legal reforms as much as observers, and some Chinese leaders, had hoped for. This incomplete normative revolution now creates tensions between WTO members, as evidenced by an increasing number of disputes shedding a direct light on the lack of transparency in the Chinese legal system.'[78]

The dispute settlement mechanism puts by far the most obvious and tangible constraints on China's state autonomy in regulating international trade. Two recent disputes, namely *China–Raw Materials*[79] and *China–Rare Earths*,[80] have shown the impact of the Dispute Settlement Body (DSB), especially of the Appellate Body, on China's domestic industrial and trade policies – though the Appellate Body's legal reasoning in those two high-profile decisions has been criticised, and its judicial authority was considered under threat.[81] China has adopted measures to comply with the DSB decisions,[82] thus accepting that its regulatory autonomy is restricted by the WTO rules.[83] Against that backdrop, it has been argued that 'China joined the WTO in 2001 under exceptionally unfavourable, non-reciprocal and asymmetric terms of membership.

[78] Leïla Choukroune, 'The compromised "rule of law by internationalisation"' (2012) 1 *China Perspectives* 9–14.

[79] WTO, *China–Measures Related to the Exportation of Various Raw Materials*, Appellate Body Reports of 30 January 2012, WT/DS394, 395, 398/AB/R.

[80] WTO, *China–Measures Related to the Exportation of Rare Earths, Tungsten and Molybdenum*, Appellate Body Reports of 7 August 2014, WT/DS431, 432, 433/AB/R.

[81] The criticism focuses on the WTO-plus obligations imposed on China by virtue of the Appellate Body's problematic interpretation of the relationship between the WTO rules and China's accession protocol, which deprived China of the right to invoke the justifiable exceptions to its trade restrictive measures, mainly the export quotas on some raw materials and rare earths for considerations of environmental protection. See Julia Ya Qin, 'Judicial authority in WTO law: a commentary on the Appellate Body's decision in China-Rare Earths' (2014) 13 *Chinese Journal of International Law* 639–651; Liu Ying, 'The applicability of environmental protection exceptions to WTO-Plus obligations: in view of the China-Raw Materials and China-Rare Earths cases' (2014) 27 *Leiden Journal of International Law* 113–139; Bin Gu, 'Applicability of GATT Article XX in China-Raw materials: a clash within the WTO Agreement' (2012) 15 *Journal of International Economic Law* 1007–1031.

[82] China abolished the export quotas on rare earths at the end of 2014. A news report is available at http://epaper.jinghua.cn/html/2015-01/06/content_159650.htm, last consulted on 22 January 2015.

[83] It is asserted that if the generalised application of Article XX outside of the GATT is permitted, it would do needless violence to the delicate balance between trade facilitation and regulatory autonomy that WTO members agreed to. See Danielle Spiegel Feld and Stephanie Switzer, 'Whither Article XX? Regulatory autonomy under non-GATT agreements after China-Raw Materials' (2012) 38 *The Yale Journal of International Law Online* 16–30.

China's less-than-equal status raises difficult legal questions with respect to
the rule of law in the WTO, as they call into question the normativity of the
fundamental principles that underlie the WTO system.'[84] Similarly, there
have been warnings that the 'WTO-plus' packages on safeguards and anti-
dumping rules may weaken WTO discipline and that an aggressive use of
the WTO-plus provisions would substantially reduce China's expected
gains and undermine China's incentive to maintain its WTO implementation efforts.[85] The preceding views, which may be a revival of the 'unequal
treaty' discourse, express unease with the fairness of the process of China's
WTO accession but, more profoundly, question the legitimacy of the
current international trade system in terms of China's political willingness
and ability to protect national interests. Essentially, China's scepticism
about the Appellate Body's judicial authority is closely connected to the
unresolved issues of the appropriate allocation of decision-making competence and China's institutional capacity to handle certain kinds of
decisions. These are the broad contexts in which China's role in the
WTO must be assessed or reassessed.[86] Those cases relating to an aspect
of sovereignty could prompt reflection on the best place for making
decisions. To a certain degree, it is an issue of a constitutional nature.
China has shown much flexibility over the WTO, particularly the dispute
settlement mechanism's influence on its regulatory autonomy. China's
current reactions do not, however, imply any Chinese initiative or agenda
of constitutional nature on the WTO's future reform.

China's concern about the WTO's constraints is intensified by disputes
in which DSB rulings and recommendations are felt to have spillover
effect on regulation that is traditionally considered to be related to
domestic social-political affairs. China's awareness of the WTO's influence on domestic affairs would lead to an attitude shift towards judicial
decision-making under the framework of the multilateral trading system.
In *China–Audiovisual Services*,[87] China's censorship was at stake,

[84] See Xiaohui Wu, 'No longer outside, not yet equal: rethinking China's membership in the
World Trade Organization' (2011) 10 *Chinese Journal of International Law* 227–270.
[85] See Graeme Thomson, 'China's accession to the WTO: improving market access and
Australia's role', in Deborah Z. Cass, Brett G. Williams and George Barker (eds.), *China
and the World Trading System: Entering the New Millennium* (Cambridge: Cambridge
University Press, 2003), pp. 68–82; Ian Dickson, 'China's interests in the World Trade
Organization's deregulation of international textile trade', ibid., pp. 175–201.
[86] J. H. Jackson, 'The impact of China's accession on the WTO', ibid., p. 28.
[87] WTO, *China–Measures Affecting Trading Rights and Distribution Services for Certain
Publications and Audiovisual Entertainment Products*, Report of the Appellate Body of
21 November 2009, WT/DS363AB/R.

because its restrictions on trading rights and market access to a service for distribution of cultural products violated provisions of China's accession protocol.[88] In implementing the DSB's rulings and recommendations, China stated that it 'was disappointed and has serious concerns with Reports of the Appellate Body and the Panel on this dispute', because 'this dispute involves a number of Chinese administrative measures on cultural products and is embodied with more complexity and sensitivity than other disputes'.[89] Following this case, some drew attention to the fact that

> China maintains a social-political governance regime that is quite different from that of many other WTO members and because China's trade policies are sometimes designed for political purposes, changes in trade policies may have unexpected social-political impacts. For this reason, China often appears more vulnerable to the spill-over impacts of WTO dispute settlement than many other countries. Given China's current social-political governance regime, it is highly likely that China will confront more WTO cases with spill-over impacts.[90]

With due respect, the spillover of the DSB rulings and recommendations is somewhat exaggerated. The disputed regulatory measures did cover China's censorship of cultural products, but those measures had been contested as regards their effect or impact; they were disputed only to the extent that they amounted to a restriction on trading rights and discrimination against foreign service providers in market access.[91] Furthermore, both the Panel and Appellate Body found that China could pursue its censorship regime and 'public morals' in a less trade restrictive manner. Finally, *China–Audiovisuals* leaves open the question of whether the protection of cultural goods can or should be actually justified under the General Agreement on Tariffs and Trade (GATT) and WTO rules. The Appellate Body confirmed a general 'right to regulate' pursuant to GATT Article XX. The exact scope of this 'right to regulate' and whether it must be explicitly referred to in WTO obligations remain unclear. Such an approach 'would certainly harness the regulatory

---

[88] China did invoke GATT Art. XX (a) ('public morals') to justify certain restrictions on trading rights found to violate China's accession protocol. See WTO, *China–Measures Affecting Trading Rights and Distribution Services for Certain Publications and Audiovisual Entertainment Products*, Report of Panel of 12 August 2009, WT/DS363/R, para. 4.112.

[89] WTO, *Status Report by China of 15 March 2011*, WT/DS363/17/Add.2.

[90] See Chi Manjiao, 'China's participation in WTO dispute settlement over the past decade: experience and impacts' (2012) 15 *Journal of International Economic Law* 29–49.

[91] WTO, *Request for Consultations by the United States* (16 April 2007), WT/DS363/1.

autonomy of WTO members'.[92] Further analysis indicates that international trade disputes relating to censorship – such as Google's departure from China, which triggered the argument that Internet censorship is an illegal trade barrier to foreign service providers[93] – are indifferent to the freedom of expression and ultimately promote economic interests with little, if any, restriction on speech.[94] Other opinions focus on the transparency and due process aspects, because the secrecy and opacity of China's censorship could raise WTO inconsistency issues.[95] Leaving aside the diverging analyses about the possible influence of the DSB ruling and recommendation on China's domestic regulatory power, China's experiences in dispute settlement under the WTO show that the boundary between local politics and global governance is no longer clearly drawn, with domestic regulation subject to greater external constraints than ever before. Inversely, China is increasingly required to take into consideration externalities to ensure the internal measures' compatibility with WTO rules.

The interaction between China and the WTO shows most clearly and concretely how pursuit of national policies can generate 'externalities' of international adjudication that national law cannot assess. That said, the multilateral trading system based on the WTO, though functionally effective compared to other international regimes, does not yet present a big obstacle to convincing China to give up its scepticism on global

---

[92]   Paola Conconi and Joost Pauwelyn, 'Trading cultures: Appellate Body report on China-Audiovisuals (WT/DS363/AB/R, adopted 19 January 2010)' (2011) 10 *World Trade Review* 95–118, at 105. Joost Pauwelyn contended that the DSB's ruling can 'facilitate importation and distribution of material that passes Chinese censorship, but leaves China's substantive content review intact and may even make it worse'. Joost Pauwelyn, 'Squaring free trade in culture with Chinese censorship: the WTO Appellate Body Report on China – Audiovisuals' (2010) 11 *Melbourne Journal of International Law* 119–140, at 135. Julia Ya Qin, 'Pushing the limits of global governance: trading rights, censorship and WTO jurisprudence: a commentary on the China – Publications Case' (2011) 10 *Chinese Journal of International Law* 271–322, at 287.

[93]   See Cynthia Liu, 'Internet censorship as a trade barrier: a look at the WTO consistency of the Great Firewall in the wake of the China-Google Dispute' (2011) 42 *Georgetown Journal of International Law* 1199–1238. See also Anonymous, 'A dual track approach to challenging Chinese censorship in the WTO: the (future) case of Google and Facebook' (2013) 34 *Michigan Journal of International Law* 857–891.

[94]   See Tomer Broude and Holger P. Hestermeyer, 'The first condition of progress? Freedom of speech and international trade law' (2004) 54 *Virginia Journal of International Law* 295–321.

[95]   Ya Qin (n. 92), at 285. *Contra*, Michael Ming Du, 'Has the WTO Appellate Body pushed the limits of global governance in the China-Publications Case? A reply to Julia Ya Qin' (2012) 11 *Chinese Journal of International Law* 227–234.

constitutionalism. It is arguably even more difficult to persuade China to fully embrace the idea that global constitutionalism 'has to take a cosmopolitan turn', since 'only a cosmopolitan state – a state that incorporates and reflects in its constitutional structure and foreign policy the global legitimacy conditions for claims to sovereignty – is a legitimate state'.[96] One explanation could be found in the criticism that the WTO has a democracy deficit and excludes non-trade interests;[97] a better one is that China tends to maintain its autonomy in judging the values underpinning cosmopolitanism and to shelter itself from the pervasive global constitutionalism or cosmopolitism discourses.

It is interesting to note that while China insists on its state autonomy, it has not prepared itself well to participate more actively and even to contribute to the global constitutionalisation process. China's unpreparedness is illustrated to some degree by the academic debates over the issue. When appraising a reconceptualisation of constitutionalism through a transformation of the WTO into a democratic trading system with development as its primary goal,[98] some Chinese scholars maintain a classic stance and advocate that the quest for democratic trading systems should be based on and guided by national interest.[99] China's preference for state autonomy and national interests can be considered outdated given the widely accepted finding that 'all the economics is international',[100] and its defensive approach to the constitutionalisation process at the global level reflects somewhat its conservative policies on constitutionalism and democracy issues at the domestic and local level. It remains uncertain as to what extent China's internal policies on constitutionalism could evolve due to China's interaction with the ongoing process of global constitutionalism by means of voluntary adaptation or adjustment. The uncertainty arises mainly from China's both pragmatic and selective approach in adapting itself to the external normative constraints. This approach is characterised by the imbalance

---

[96] Kumm (n. 3), at 605.

[97] Sarah Joseph, *Blame It on the WTO? A Human Rights Critique* (Oxford: Oxford University Press, 2013), pp. 88–89.

[98] Deborah Z. Cass, *The Constitutionalization of the World Trade Organization: Legitimacy, Democracy and Community in the International Trading System* (Oxford: Oxford University Press, 2005), pp. 243–244.

[99] Zuo Haicong and Fan Xiaoying, 'Constitutionalization of WTO: from "judicial constitutionalisation" to "democratic trading system"' (WTO 宪政化: '从司法宪法论' 到 '贸易民主论') (2013) *Contemporary Law Review* (当代法学) 148–157, at 149.

[100] Peter F. Drucker, 'Trade lessons from the world economy' (1994) 73 *Foreign Affairs* 99–108, at 99.

between an open, utilitarian and flexible political choice as regards the international legal rules embodying merchandise values on one hand and a prudent and defensive strategy over international legal rules of non-merchandise values on the other. China's treatment of human rights and sovereignty issues may highlight the aforementioned pragmatic and selective approach.

4.3   State sovereignty and human rights

The relationship between China and the international human rights regime is often described as a mixture of engagement and resistance. While China undertakes human rights obligations through joining many international human rights instruments and mechanisms, China also contends that it is held to a double standard and stigmatised as a human rights violator.[101] Setting aside here the controversy on the methods and criteria used in assessing a state's human rights performance, there are substantial reasons for China's resistance, which relate to the concept of human rights, the prioritisation of certain rights and particularly the approach to the relationship between state sovereignty and human rights.

When addressing the question whether the concept of human rights is compatible with Chinese cultural tradition, Chinese scholars often assert that the Confucian tradition has moral content overlapping with international human rights in their three generations. In addition, Confucian moral and political thought could make further contributions, which include strengthening a more communitarian-receptive understanding of civil-political liberties as empowerment aimed at community involvement and flourishing; supporting the thesis about the interdependence and indivisibility of the three generations of human rights; and promoting developmental-collective human rights particularly concerned with matters of peace, harmony and ecological responsibility.[102] Nowadays, the debate on the compatibility of Chinese cultural heritage with human

---

[101] See Randall Peerenboom, 'Assessing human rights in China: why the double standard?' (2005) 38 *Cornell International Law Journal* 71 164. Based on empirical studies, Peerenboom concludes that China is unjustifiably treated and held to a double standard of human rights performance by the West, and he offers some explanations for that situation.

[102] See Sumner B. Twiss, 'A constructive framework for discussing Confucianism and human rights', in Wm. Theodore de Bary and Tu Weiming (eds.), *Confucianism and Human Rights* (New York: Columbia University Press, 1998), pp. 45–46.

rights is less extensive than before, since China's constitutional amendments in 2004 provide that, among other things, the state respects and protects human rights. Following these, China adopted state action plans on human rights in 2009 and 2012. These events mark the official endorsement of the human rights idea. There has been an evolution of the literature on China's human rights protection. The prevailing discourse on human rights in China attaches much importance to the historical perspective of Chinese legal development.[103] Scholars nowadays argue that human rights, together with rule of law and democracy, are the components of constitutionalism, i.e. that human rights are the guaranteed goal of constitutionalism.[104] The evolution of the status of human rights is only a snapshot of the profound changes that Chinese law has undergone in the past sixty years. Much attention is, however, turning to the fact that China's human rights practices do not fully conform to the letter and spirit of the international or 'universal' human rights regime; consequently, more research should be done on the question of how to narrow the gaps.[105]

China's understanding of the relationship between state sovereignty and human rights, which reflects its lasting concern about protecting state autonomy from external control and from the influence of international human rights mechanisms, remains a major obstacle to the country's full engagement. China's abstention from international human rights complaints procedures is an expression of this concern. As between periodic review based on the submission of national reports and individual complaints procedures, China obviously prefers the former. The latter would eventually reduce China's autonomy in conducting the human rights review and would offer opportunities to those who want to shame China and cause it to lose face on the international stage. Abstention could also be explained by many other reasons, mainly related to domestic law and policies. For example, China signed but has yet to ratify the International Covenant on Civil and Political Rights (ICCPR), and there is no clear timeline for ratification. China has confirmed that it will ratify the Covenant after modifying certain domestic laws in order to comply with Covenant obligations. As some have observed, 'the weakest aspect of China's international law record is its

[103] Xue (n. 63), p. 123.
[104] Li Buyun, 'Constitutionalism and China', in Yu Keping (ed.), *Democracy and the Rule of Law in China* (Leiden: Brill, 2010), p. 199.
[105] Roda Mushkat, 'Non-democratic state learning of human rights: reconfiguring Chinese patterns' (2013) 27 *Temple International and Comparative Law Journal* 63–110, at 70.

conduct relating to domestic political and civil rights, which so intimately implicates the country's criminal justice system'.[106] It is precisely the tension or incompatibility between domestic law and international human rights norms that hinders China's acceptance of certain international human rights obligations. Conditioning the ICCPR's ratification on domestic legal reforms characterises China's pragmatic approach to international law. China's prudence and resistance to international human rights mechanisms also suggest that China has yet to substantially endorse the idea that human rights mechanisms can be evoked against the state. Accordingly, it would be even harder for China to fully embrace the opposability of human rights to the state on the international level. By contrast, the Universal Periodic Review mechanism under the Human Rights Council and state reporting practices under various human rights bodies (such as the Human Rights Committee, the Committee on Economic, Social and Cultural Rights, etc.) seem more acceptable to China, because they can strike a balance between the state's obligations to protect human rights under international monitoring and state autonomy in implementing those international obligations.[107]

At the domestic level, international human rights instruments are rarely invoked and directly applied by the courts in their decisions. As Chinese scholars observe, China's

> new judicial policy still provides little room for the application of rules granting substantive rights to individuals vis-à-vis the state in general, and human rights treaties in particular . . . little progress can be expected in the near future. China continues to support the position that a strong executive authority is necessary for its rise. Therefore, China's ratification of future treaties, including those governing the relationship between individuals and the state, will likely be accompanied by measures to neutralize the judicialisation of such treaties.[108]

China's reservation about judicial enforcement of international human rights instruments may be explained also by the concern for state autonomy in human rights issues. In the Chinese context, such autonomy can be better preserved if the government takes constructive measures in

---

[106] Jerome A. Cohen, 'Friedmann memorial award address' (2010) 49 *Columbia Journal of Transnational Law* 17–33, at 30.

[107] On China and Eastern states' perspectives on implementing core international conventions of human rights, see Guimei Bai, 'Human Rights NGOs and Global Constitutionalism from a Chinese Academic Perspective' (Chapter 15 in this volume).

[108] Cai Congyan, 'International law in Chinese courts during the rise of China' (2016) 110 *American Journal of International Law* 269–288, at 287.

promoting human rights. The underlying belief that judicial enforcement of human rights against state and government would undermine the latter's legitimacy and the 'stability imperative'[109] becomes counterproductive in practice. Put otherwise, human rights, especially economic and social, can be better promoted by a strong state and an efficient and responsive government. The key idea is captured in the phrase 'sovereignty prevails over human rights'. Here, though, the verb 'prevails' should be understood as accentuating the fundamental importance of state and government in achieving human rights goals and not the state's power and privilege in 'trumping' human rights. It is crucial in the Chinese context to avoid misconceiving the preceding phrase. In that respect, global constitutionalism contains the normative arguments in favour of human rights and can serve as the benchmark in understanding the relationship between state and human rights.

China's two state action plans on human rights reiterate that the government prefers the compromise between an international examination of the national implementation of human rights obligations on one hand and state autonomy about the same on the other. The plans reaffirm a theory of Deng Xiaoping as the overarching principle guiding the protection and promotion of human rights in China. Deng's thoughts and well-known speeches stressed that the state is the crucial guarantor of human rights and that human rights will become an illusion to the people if a state loses its sovereignty; accordingly, if protecting human rights is imperative, then state sovereignty should enjoy priority over human rights. Deng's words were then perceived as orienting China's human rights policy. Recalling Deng's critique on the relationship between state sovereignty and human rights not only helps to complete the historical perspective but also sheds light on China's current ambiguity in dealing with the international human rights protection mechanisms. Deng had underscored that the Chinese understanding of human rights is totally different from the Western; he warned that criticism from the West of China's human rights performance was nothing but the disguised interference that would undermine China's state sovereignty. In brief, the 'state's right is far more important than human rights', and 'state sovereignty and national security shall always be given the top priority'.[110] The defensive mindset on human rights had in fact taken shape already,

---

[109] Sarah Biddulph, *The Stability Imperative: Human Rights and Law in China* (Vancouver: UBC Press, 2015), p. 7.

[110] *Selected Works of Deng Xiaoping, Tome III* (邓小平文选第三卷) (Beijing: China People's Publishing House (人民出版社), 2001), pp. 345–348.

on some diplomatic occasions, before Deng's official pronouncement. At the beginning of the 1980s, scholars had been advocating that the socialist human rights concept was both more substantive and wider than the capitalist one and that China should rely on the essential meaning of human rights to fight against imperialism and hegemony in international political relations.[111] Nowadays, though the idea of the human rights struggle in international relations is no longer expressed publicly, it is too early to conclude that China has reconceptualised the relationship between state sovereignty and human rights.[112] China is increasingly involved in human rights affairs and activities on the international stage, but it remains, strictly speaking, sceptical about the constitutionalist notion that state sovereignty is legitimately premised on the respect of human rights. The risk for China's approach to human rights issues is that its credibility on human rights engagement would be called into question. Although Chinese authorities no longer refer explicitly to Deng's political dictum that state sovereignty prevails over human rights, the 'human rights struggle' mindset – i.e. the idea that human rights discourse could become the cause of political interference and counter-interference in international relations – has not substantially changed, and it continues to hinder China from taking a further step towards more serious human rights engagements.

5 Concluding remarks

The debate and divergent opinions on constitutionalism within China's domestic context show that the liberal constitutionalist thoughts are suspected and rejected by China. There is a historically and culturally deep-rooted Chinese belief that norms of authority exist and are superior to positive rules. However, the belief in norms of superior authority is neither expressed through the formal discourse of constitutionalism nor practised through constitutional mechanisms (such as judicial review or other functionally similar control and exam procedures). Politics in China does not perceive the legitimacy question from the perspective of constitutionalism; in Claude Lefort's words, the 'political form' of

[111] Xin Chunying, 'Human rights in modern international political struggles' (现代国际政治斗争中的人权问题) (1981) 1 *Study and Reflections* (学习与思考) 49–52, at 52.
[112] See Men Jing, 'Between human rights and sovereignty: an examination of EU-China political relations' (2011) 17 *European Law Journal* 534–550, at 537, 540. Men argues that while the European Union respects human rights as a universal value, China emphasises sovereignty and collective rights.

Chinese society does not originate from the social representations of constitution. Instead, the legitimacy of the ruling power and the political regime that it creates and operates is essentially evaluated by their performance in the functions of state governing and social control, even though China's current political regime is often depicted as authoritarian. The advent of constitutionalism postulates the transplantation of Western ideology into Chinese legal culture, which perceives the legitimacy of political power pragmatically rather than by reference to Western dogma. In other words, the question of China's specificity in terms of constitutional values should be channelled into a pluralist understanding of the nexus of political legitimacy and law in order to accommodate China's refusal of a formal interpretation of constitutionalism. It requires not simply a reformulation or invention of words but a reconceptualisation of the idea of constitutionalism. The merits of global constitutionalism should be revaluated according to its ability in 'ordering pluralism', going beyond the relative and the universal, and not according to the values it affirms and promotes. The shift of focus will stimulate further reflections over new methods of normativity, as well as the pluralist criterion of legitimacy. As Ricoeur has put it, 'the universalism and contextualism are not opposed to each other on the same plane but stem from two different levels of morality, that of a presumed universal obligation and that of a practical wisdom that takes into account the diversity of cultural heritages'.[113] The idea of constitutionalism should further take into account the diversity of cultural heritages in inventing a pluralist criterion of legitimacy in order to avoid reducing it to the clash of civilisations.

Moreover, China's perception of the legitimacy question from the constitutional perspective at the domestic level resonates with its approach to global constitutionalism, since China's practices of international law are imbued with pragmatic and functionalist ideas. Yet the prolongation of China's pragmatism and functionalism from the domestic to the global context is marked by the 'shift of concerns', i.e. from the concern about the ruling power's performance in state governing and social control to the concern about international law's effectiveness and efficacy, where the notion of ruling power becomes more elusive on the international stage. In fact, China's return to the international community – as marked by its active participation in globalisation – goes

[113] Paul Ricoeur, *Reflections on the Just*, translated by David Pellauer (Chicago: University of Chicago Press, 2007), p. 248.

together with a more flexible and utilitarian position on state sovereignty. China has incontestably accepted constraints of different degrees on its state sovereignty in many fields and aspects of international law. With China's rise as a big power, however, the effectiveness and efficacy of international law become more crucial than ever for it to sustain its influence internationally. China will become more reliant on international law due to its changing position in world politics and economics; in particular, China will further explore the instrumental function of international law in pursuing its national interests.[114] Although China's experience with international law is relatively brief and shallow rooted, its history – ranging from the period of the 'unequal treaties', through the re-entry to the UN after its membership had been disregarded due to the Taiwan issue, to the accession to the WTO – does shape and alter China's conception and policies of international law.[115] It is true that 'in post-Mao China, international law has become part of the effort to catch up with the rest of the world', but it is also true that 'there still remains the shadow of the past – China's perennial concern with its status, security and sovereignty'.[116] Some argue that China has already displayed a penchant for striking a balance between the principle of sovereignty and the ideal of rule of law in international relations.[117] China's stress on sovereignty or state autonomy is particularly salient as regards international adjudication. This is often deemed a key element of the international rule of law, and it has even been argued that 'international courts and tribunals have themselves become new social actors, ones that contribute to evolutions in the state of human consciousness and actions'.[118] Officially China considers itself as 'a staunch defender and builder of the

---

[114] Japan's transition from a defensive to a more offensive approach towards international law since the mid-nineteenth century also supports the author's view that China's empowering will lead to the more active exploitation of international law for serving the national interests. See R. P. Anand, 'Family of "civilized" states and Japan: a story of humiliation, assimilation, defiance and confrontation', in R. P. Anand, *Studies in International Law and History: An Asian Perspective* (Dordrecht: Springer-Science +Business Media, B.V., 2004), pp. 24–102.

[115] Cohen (n. 106), at 29–32.

[116] Samuel S. Kim, 'The development of international law in post-Mao China: change and continuity' (1987) 1 *Journal of Chinese Law* 117–160, at 157; Hungdah Chiu, 'Chinese attitudes toward international law in the post-Mao era, 1978–1987' (1987) 21 *The International Lawyer* 1127–1166, at 1165.

[117] Bingbing Jia, 'Remarks: China and international law' (2013) 107 *American Society of International Law Proceedings* 346–348, at 347.

[118] Philippe Sands, 'Reflections on international adjudication' (2016) 27 *European Journal of International Law* 885–900, at 889.

international rule of law'[119] and adheres to the principle of peaceful settlement of international disputes. Nonetheless, it remains reserved about the jurisdiction of international courts and tribunals for disputes relating to sovereignty and territorial integrity issues. Such reserve is exemplified in the recent Sino–Philippines arbitral proceedings on maritime jurisdiction.[120] China suspects that international adjudication may not be immune from politics and that politics will eventually undermine its impartiality. In that respect, the criticisms of international courts and tribunals[121] are relevant for understanding China's position on international adjudication, especially when the 'high-profile' cases with political implications are involved. A cultural perspective on international adjudication can also explain China's prudence about international courts and tribunals. These are considered imbued with Western notions of law and justice and to have administered jurisprudence 'in a monocultural mould'.[122] Furthermore, the public law theory of international adjudication provides a democratic perspective for considering the legitimacy problem of international adjudication,[123] which could usefully explain China's prudence in settling interstate disputes through adjudication. In fact, China's relatively weak involvement in the constitution, functioning and activities of international courts and tribunals is felt to have the consequence that China's legitimate interests may not be adequately represented and preserved through international adjudication. The debate on the legitimacy of international adjudication may help somewhat to shelter China, as well as some other countries, from the blame of 'exceptionalism' to international courts and tribunals.

[119] See Wang Yi, 'China: a staunch defender and builder of the international rule of law' (2014) 13 *Chinese Journal of International Law* 635–638.

[120] PCA, *South China Sea Arbitration*, Award of 12 July 2016, case N°2013-19. On 12 July 2016, the ad hoc tribunal adopted the award on merit. China's position paper on the arbitral proceedings is available at http://www.fmprc.gov.cn/mfa_chn/ziliao_611306/tytj_611312/t1217143.shtml.

[121] See Geoffrey Palme, 'The difficulties of third-party adjudication for political people' (2003) 97 *Proceedings of the Annual Meeting (American Society of International Law)* 289–293, at 289. Davis R. Robinson, 'The role of politics in the election and the work of judges of the International Court of Justice' (2003) 97 *Proceedings of the Annual Meeting (American Society of International Law)* 277–282, at 277.

[122] C. G. Weeramantry, 'Some practical problems of international adjudication' (1996) 17 *Australian Yearbook of International Law* 1–18, at 11, 12.

[123] See Armin von Bogdandy and Ingo Venzke, 'In whose name? An investigation of international courts' public authority and its domestic justification' (2012) 23 *European Journal of International Law* 7–41. Armin von Bogdandy and Ingo Venzke, *In Whose Name? A Public Law Theory of International Adjudication* (Oxford: Oxford University Press, 2014).

Nonetheless, how the exception or even resistance strategy could be replaced by more constructive measures remains unsettled. It is questionable whether concern over the legitimacy of international adjudication could always justify the exceptionalism.

Besides dispute settlement under the WTO, China accepts international arbitration on state–investor disputes, since these are no longer generally perceived as putting state sovereignty at risk due to China's fast rise in outward investments.[124] China's changing position can be explained by its scepticism on the fairness of international adjudication but also by its awareness of the limits of international law in the face of power politics. To a degree, its position also reflects Chinese traditional legal thought acknowledging the limits of law in governing state and society. Moreover, China's pragmatic and functionalist approach to international law tolerates the flexible interpretation of state sovereignty, permitting broad acceptance of international adjudication on issues of trade and investment but not territory or human rights. China's selective adaptation to the phenomenon of the constitutionalisation of international law implies that the gap between the practices of international law on one hand and the embrace of global constitutionalism as both a good idea and a cognitive framework on the other remains to be further narrowed. It is not yet certain that China's empowerment could lead to the evolution of its approach to international law. China, like many other international actors, probably needs enlightenment instead of empowerment to change its perception of the relationship between the nation state and the world community. As it first emerged, global constitutionalism was perceived by some US scholars as a source of trouble with 'the potential to profoundly alter domestic constitutional balances governing the making and enforcement of American law'.[125] Global constitutionalism is, in this sense, not simply normative but descriptive of reality. Dealing with the fact of global constitutionalism is not a matter of empowerment, since even a state as powerful as the United States must face the 'trouble' arising from the penetration of international law into

---

[124] See Stephen W. Schill, 'Tearing down the Great Wall: the new generation investment treaties of the People's Republic of China' (2007) 15 *Cardozo Journal of International and Comparative Law* 73–118.

[125] Ernest A. Young, 'The trouble with global constitutionalism' (2003) 38 *Texas International Law Journal* 527–545, at 528. See also Julian Ku and John Yoo, *Taming Globalization: International Law, the U.S. Constitution, and the New World Order* (Oxford: Oxford University Press, 2012), p. 10. Ku and Yoo argue that the 'best way to approach globalization is to tame it by subjecting its domestic effects to the same separation-of-powers and federalism rules that apply to any other law'.

domestic law. Thus, China can only engage with global constitutionalism by other means than power. Critics of the idea of global constitutionalism contend, however, that the invocation of a constitutional discourse may be a rhetorical strategy designed to invest international law with the power and authority that domestic constitutional structures and norms possess and that the constitutional turn may be self-defeating in that it 'is less a sign of international law's flourishing than of it being in a state of crisis'.[126] The constitutional discourse reveals the existing challenges to both international law's effectiveness and its foundation. China's current approach towards constitutionalism domestically and globally also show-cases China's scepticism on the effectiveness issue. China's realist view will render it difficult to embrace fully the idea that global constitution-alism remains a good legal concept even if it is politically resisted. Consequently, transforming global constitutionalism into the practices of international law would be a further and important step towards obtaining China's support for the idea.

---

[126] Jeffrey L. Dunoff, 'Constitutional conceits: the WTO's "constitution" and the discipline of international law' (2006) 17 *The European Journal of International Law* 647–675, at 669.

3

Global Constitutionalism and East Asian Perspectives in the Context of Political Economy

CHRISTINE SCHWÖBEL-PATEL[*]

1 Introduction

Global constitutionalism is, in a manner of speaking, unchartered territory for East Asia. In the following, I explore the potential consequences of expanding the debate on global constitutionalism to East Asia. While there is the potential of enriching the debate through this geographical expansion, there is also a danger that it could further naturalise an already dominant form of political-economic organisation, namely neo-liberalism.

Not only has political economy been a neglected site of enquiry in the debate on global constitutionalism, and therefore merits further exploration in itself, it is an issue which becomes particularly pertinent in conversation with East Asian perspectives on global constitutionalism.[1] The argument is built on the assumption that consensus between Western and Asian actors is often sought in commercial relations (doing business together). On this assumption, a consequence of a global constitutional debate could be the further depoliticisation of the dominant mutual language of business.

[*] Senior Lecturer, University of Liverpool, C.Schwobel@liverpool.ac.uk. Many thanks to Robert Knox for comments on an earlier draft. All websites were last visited on 23 March 2017.

[1] As with all geographical and cultural references of this scope, the term 'East Asia' is difficult to define or to fix. 'East Asia' is often taken to mean the ten ASEAN member countries (Brunei Darussalam, Cambodia, Indonesia, Lao PDR, Malaysia, Myanmar, the Philippines, Singapore, Thailand, Viet Nam) and China, Japan and Korea, the so-called ASEAN Plus Three. Depending on the issue, it may include some neighbouring countries. Tamio Nakamura (ed.), *East Asian Regionalism from Legal Perspective: Current Features and a Vision for the Future* (London: Routledge, 2009). According to the Project Framing Paper, this project is particularly interested in the ASEAN Plus Three (Framing Paper on file with the author).

It is no secret that global constitutionalism has, to date, been a debate largely confined to European origins and audiences, with particular enthusiasm expressed by German scholars.[2] It is also no secret that the debate on global constitutionalism has largely been a values-oriented debate, foregrounding the search for a common normative agenda.[3] Superficially, these two features of the dominant global constitutional orientation already have exclusionary effects for East Asian scholars and practitioners: Seemingly, it is a debate taking place outside of its geography, and given the foregrounding of both territorial sovereignty and an enduring 'Asian values' understanding of several East Asian states, a universal norms debate is politically (and ideologically) seemingly a dead end. Depending on one's point of view, one could label this type of exclusionary effect as 'hegemony', a colonial hangover from the Western perspective. Alternatively, one could label it as nationalist and isolationist from an East Asian perspective. Regardless, the global constitutional debate in an East Asian context does, to date, not carry much momentum. The unequal distribution of global constitutional scholars in Europe vis-à-vis other parts of the world appears to be perpetuating this exclusionary effect. This collection of essays is therefore very welcome in beginning a debate which extends beyond this geographical (and ideological) bias. And yet, apart from a positive diversifying of the debate, it also seems that much is at stake with this conversation.

This chapter voices the concern that the dialogue on global constitutionalism between international lawyers from the West and international lawyers from East Asia could further naturalise neo-liberal biases and forms of organisation. My concern about this potential is based on two observations: first, that the dominant ideas of global constitutionalism, although diverse and multiform, all share the liberal tenet of the separation between public and private authority, which is mapped onto a separation of political and economic activity and state and civil society. This separation privileges the deregulation and ultimately the depoliticisation of private economic activity – one of the main precepts of neo-

---

[2] Among others, see work by Bardo Fassbender, Andreas Fischer-Lescano, Mattias Kumm, Stefan Oeter, Anne Peters, Antje Wiener and myself.

[3] This includes ideas of particular human rights, *jus cogens* norms and other treaty norms as constitutional, notwithstanding an emphasis by some authors on procedure over substance (see Anne Peters, 'Constitutional fragments: on the interaction of constitutionalization and fragmentation of international law', *Centre for Global Constitutionalism University of St. Andrews Working Paper 2015*, available at http://papers.ssrn.com/sol3/papers.cfm?abstract_id=2591370).

liberalism. Given that the conversation with East Asian international lawyers on global constitutionalism is unlikely to take place on the footing of a common values debate (regardless of whether this is a good or bad thing), it means that a debate would most likely take place on an economic basis. Despite the differences between the states in question and their approach to political economy, they nevertheless appear to agree on the division of political and economic activity in law and international relations.

The second observation concerns the almost universal reach of neo-liberalism as the dominant business model as well as its pervasiveness beyond business, reaching to all aspects of life. 'Neo-liberalism' is a term commonly used to describe the political-economic form of organisation which prioritises private property and enterprise over public goods; it has a preoccupation with markets and profits and with the individual (and individual freedoms); and it furthers a declining appreciation and understanding of ideas of community and commonality; and consequently it furthers the domination of a small class of ruling elite who have gained and maintained their wealth at the expense of the rest. These priorities not only are evident in commercial relations (the so-called private sphere) but are also becoming more and more evident in previously public spaces such as health care, education and other public and social services. East Asia occupies an interesting space here – and certainly China's economic model of a so-called socialist market economy could not be described as neo-liberalism in the 'Washington Consensus' sense of the term.[4] What the East Asian economies, including China, have in common with neo-liberalism, however, is a general consensus on 'the need for less government intervention in the economy'.[5]

Could, therefore, a dialogue between East and West on global constitutionalism have the effect of strengthening the global appeal of neo-liberalism? Global constitutionalism in this sense would act as a vehicle for neo-liberalism, squeezing out any space for resistance or dissent. Or, alternatively, and more optimistically, does this dialogue provide an opportunity? Given the differing economic and political means of

[4] The Washington Consensus is a set of economic policy prescriptions agreed upon by the International Monetary Fund (IMF), the World Bank and the US Treasury Department (all based in Washington, DC) which promote a strongly market-based approach to international relations and development.
[5] He Li, 'The Chinese path of economic reform and its implications' (2005) 31 Asian Affairs 195–211.

organisation, could global constitutionalism, through an impetus from East Asia, be 'decolonised', freeing it of its liberal-democratic assumptions, bringing the economic into political debates and ultimately providing a space for considering alternative political-economic models?

2   Global constitutionalism and international law and political economy

Establishing a link between global constitutionalism and political economy arguably becomes clearer with a step-by-step analysis of enquiring into (1) the link between global constitutionalism and international law, then (2) the link between international law and political economy and finally (3) the relationship between global constitutionalism and political economy.

2.1   Global constitutionalism and international law

The debate on global constitutionalism is interdisciplinary, spanning political theory, international relations, social sciences and international law. However, much of the debate and many of the leading voices in the debate are rooted in international law.[6] This provides global constitutionalism with a distinctly normative, as opposed to a descriptive, flavour. The debate on global constitutionalism is, therefore, largely about questions of how constitutional features (the rule of law, democracy, human rights) can be applied in a global context for standard-setting and problem-solving purposes. The question at the heart of this is: Can global constitutionalism contribute to addressing some of the world's largest problems? In other words, can it contribute to a more equal, prosperous, sustainable and overall better life for humankind? And it is laudable to pose these questions. These are, after all, a set of questions which demonstrate a desire for harmony among people based on a common fabric, whatever that may be. On this basis, global constitutionalism has been described as one of the 'master narratives' of international law, which attempts to construct 'meaningful totalities out of scattered events'.[7]

---

[6] Influential scholars from outside international law include Anthony Lang, Antje Wiener and Michael Zürn.

[7] Matthew Windsor references Ricoeur's distinction between narrative's successional (progress) and configurational (totalities) dimensions in this context. Matthew Windsor, 'Narrative kill or capture: unreliable narration in international law' (2015) 28 *Leiden Journal of International Law* 743–769, at 748. See Paul Ricoeur, 'The narrative function',

I have previously argued that, although diverse and multiform, the predominant global constitutionalism projects from an international legal perspective share some important properties in the privileging of: (1) the limitation of power, (2) the institutionalisation of power, (3) social idealism (meaning an idea for the future based on societal values), (4) the standard-setting capacity of constitutions in the sense of a systematisation of law and (5) the recognition of individual rights.[8] In these constitutional traditions, the listed features all form part of public law, i.e. the area of law which is regulated by the state and concerns relations between the state and individuals. Together, these features can further be condensed to a general *liberal-democratic* idea of global constitutionalism as the pre-eminent interpretation of global constitutionalism among international lawyers today.[9] This should, in and of itself, not be surprising. It is after all the extrapolation of national constitutional principles, largely originating in the French Constitution of the first French Republic, the United States Constitution and the post–World War II German Constitution, which have been reproduced in many constitutions across the world.

However, these constitutional principles need to be placed into both a colonial as well as an ideological context. Although it may not be directly intended by the participants to the debate, global constitutionalism has the potential to act as a vehicle of hegemony through the engagement of a *civilising rhetoric*. Global constitutionalism is an idea which purports to be universal, yet it is a debate largely originating in Europe and entrenched in European Enlightenment thinking. It therefore sits comfortably in a progress narrative which subscribes to the progressive nature of European legal thought and suggests the application of this thought to the non-European world. The *legal* nature of this form of universalism is important since it implies a form of sanction/enforcement should a violation/non-compliance be determined.

As we have learned from recent scholarship in international law, the discipline and its central principles not only were constituted by asymmetries of power between colonial powers and colonial subjects but continue to create and naturalise these asymmetries. Antony Anghie, a critical international legal historian and leading figure of the orientation

---

in John B. Thompson (ed.), *Hermeneutics & The Human Sciences* (Cambridge: Cambridge University Press, 1981), p. 274. I would argue that constitutionalism has both successional as well as configurational dimensions.

[8] Christine Schwöbel, *Global Constitutionalism in International Legal Perspective* (Leiden: Martinus Nijhoff/Brill, 2011).
[9] Ibid.

which calls itself Third World approaches to international law (TWAIL), argues that the international legal order was founded on a structural bias of differentiation between European and non-European states beginning in the sixteenth century. Anghie places the colonial encounter as a crucial time in which such differentiation was established. The European standard of civilisation was, as Anghie found, the standard by which non-European countries (in particular Latin American colonies) were measured. 'Technical' terms or terms of expertise, most notably 'sovereignty', helped institutionalise and naturalise a division between what was considered civilised and what was considered uncivilised. This 'dynamic of difference', according to Anghie, continues to be the basis of exploitation of the global South.[10]

In the past years, perhaps as a response to the recognition of the Eurocentric nature of the global constitutional debate, there has emerged both a discontent about global constitutionalism[11] as well as growing purchase of *pluralism* as opposed to *hierarchy* in constitutionalism. In light of a changed international and national landscape, Nico Krisch proposes a conceptualisation of pluralism to make sense of the new legal ordering. Instead of hierarchy, pluralism, according to Krisch, enables ongoing contestation and open-endedness for principles.[12] The rise of critical voices and the continued search for other legal principles to make sense of a diverse and decentred world have led to global constitutionalism taking on a slightly different, less hierarchical tone.[13] Some are

---

[10] Anthony Anghie, *Imperialism, Sovereignty, and the Making of International Law* (Cambridge: Cambridge University Press, 2005). See also Sundhya Pahuja, *Decolonising International Law: Development, Economic Growth and the Politics of Universality* (Cambridge: Cambridge University Press, 2011); Balakrishnan Rajagopal, *International Law from Below: Development, Social Movements and Third World Resistance* (Cambridge: Cambridge University Press, 2003).

[11] There are varying forms of critique and reengagement. Examples of a critical stance include Richard Collins, 'Constitutionalism as liberal-juridical consciousness: echoes from international law's past' (2009) 22 *Leiden Journal of International Law* 251–288; Schwöbel (n. 8); Kolja Möller, 'Formwandel des Konstitutionalismus: Zum Verhältnis von Postdemokratie und Verfassungsbildung jenseits des Staates' (2015) *Archiv für Rechts- und Sozialphilosophie* 270–289.

[12] Nico Krisch, *Beyond Constitutionalism: The Pluralist Structure of Postnational Law* (Oxford: Oxford University Press, 2010); Alec Stone Sweet claims that the distinction between constitutionalism and pluralism is in fact a 'false dichotomy'; see Alec Stone Sweet, 'Constitutionalism, legal pluralism, and international regimes' (2009) 16 *Indiana Journal of Global Legal Studies* 621–645.

[13] See also the recent special edition in the journal *Global Constitutionalism* on Julia Morse and Robert Keohane's conception of 'contested multilateralism' and global

already declaring the debate on global constitutionalism outdated.[14] It seems, however, that there will continue to be rises and falls, trends and countertrends in this debate. Whether we are riding a wave of rising or of falling appeal to global constitutionalism will in part depend on what the most pressing issues of international law and politics are. In the current trend of increased nationalism accompanied by a suspicion of multilateralism, we may soon be experiencing a renewed interest in the supposedly unifying language of global constitutionalism. In any event, global constitutionalism remains a largely theoretical debate which is shaped by current affairs, even if this is unconsciously so.

2.2 International law and political economy

David Kennedy has observed that the central questions today are not political questions (regarding questions to be addressed by governments alone) and they are not economic questions (regarding questions to be addressed by the operations of markets alone), but rather they concern questions which can best be addressed by 'thinking of politics and economics as intertwined projects and close collaborators in the distribution of political authority and economic reward'.[15] The political economy of international law is a topic which has only recently attracted attention among international lawyers, largely as a delayed response to globalisation and the attendant growth of relevant organisations and practices. In international law, this is mostly captured in the sub-disciplines of international economic law, as the law regulating cross-border and business transactions, and international investment law, as the law regulating behaviour of foreign investors and sovereign states. Jeffrey Dunoff and Joel Trachtman have argued that the relationship between globalisation (the process of an increase in the flow of people, capital, goods, services and ideas across borders) and

constitutionalism (2016) 5 *Global Constitutionalism* 295–350. See also Julia Morse and Robert Keohane, 'Contested multilateralism' (2014) 9 *Review of International Organizations* 385–412. Contested multilateralism concerns the claim that new institutions are developing to challenge the institutional status quo.

[14] Global constitutionalism has been described as no longer 'fashionable'; Thomas Kleinlein, 'Between myths and norms: constructivist constitutionalism and the potential of constitutional principles in international law' (2012) 81 *Nordic Journal of International Law* 79–132.

[15] David Kennedy, 'Law and political economy of the world' (2013) 26 *Leiden Journal of International Law* 7–48, at 7–8.

international law is 'mutually reinforcing'. The activities associated with globalisation increase the demand for international law, particularly international economic law, and in turn international economic law facilitates the international flow of goods, capital, people and ideas.[16] This mutual reinforcement implies a win-win situation for market liberalisation: government restrictions become increasingly relaxed through a ceding of sovereignty to international organisations and rules, the environment for privatisation is improved through deregulation, competitive forces decide on the success or failure of enterprise and wages are suppressed. The state has a crucial role in this, at once expected to construct walls around the market as well as expected to not interfere with these walls once they are erected.

> [The state] must set up those military, defence, police and legal structures and functions required to secure private property rights and to guarantee, by force if need be, the proper functioning of markets. . . . State interventions in markets (once created) must be kept to a bare minimum.[17]

These economic preferences and the role of the state in particular are embedded at the International Monetary Fund (IMF), the World Bank and the World Trade Organization (WTO). This economic programme, associated with several post–World War II phenomena and the Chicago economists Friedrich Hayek and Milton Friedman, is today mostly referred to as neo-liberalism. Neo-liberalism from this vantage point of structural programmes which become naturalised in the economic and then the non-economic sphere in order to protect the interests of a capitalist class is to be understood as a political project.[18]

It is worth noting that a strict adherence to this economic programme is largely recommended for and required of developing countries.[19] At the same time, Western industrialised countries often adopt protectionist measures (government subsidies, trade

---

[16] Jeffrey L. Dunoff and Joel P. Trachtman (eds.), *Ruling the World? Constitutionalism, International Law, and Global Governance* (Cambridge: Cambridge University Press, 2009), p. 5.

[17] David Harvey, *A Brief History of Neoliberalism* (Oxford: Oxford University Press, 2005), p. 2.

[18] Ibid., p. 2.

[19] In the narrow meaning of the 'Washington Consensus' as set out by John Williamson in 1990 'to refer to the lowest common denominator of policy advice being addressed by the Washington-based institutions to Latin American countries as of 1989' (www.cid.harvard .edu/cidtrade/issues/washington.html).

tariffs, restricted patents) which allow them to privilege some of their national products and services without subjecting them to the tough global competitive market.[20] US agricultural subsidies are one example of this double standard. This is often described as socialism for the rich, capitalism for the poor.

As Claire Cutler expertly argues in *Private Power and Global Authority*, international law and neo-liberalism are not only mutually reinforcing, but the former is effectively rendering private economic activity 'apolitical' and neutral.[21] Particularly since the end of the Cold War, globalisation has accelerated and taken on the cloak of neo-liberalism. What was previously regarded as the economic theory, or even ideology, of neo-liberalism has been transformed into common sense. Constitutionalism comes into this equation as a governance project at the local, regional and global level. It is the 'juridical foundation for the global expansion of capitalism'.[22] Cutler and Gill identify the ways in which constitutionalism institutionalises neo-liberalism at all these levels by employing the concept of 'new constitutionalism'.[23] For them, 'new constitutionalism' is a project which institutionalises the huge contradictions and crises which form part of the neo-liberal political project. The social forces and practices which constitute neo-liberalism include, for example, increases in inequality, despite the accumulation of capital, and the socialisation of large investors and firms, despite the free movement of capital. But, Cutler and Gill also identify resistance to such 'new constitutionalism' in the form of contestation, innovation and transformation.

It is widely acknowledged by international organisations,[24] civil society organisations[25] and economists alike[26] that neo-liberalism is

---

[20] Ha-Joon Chang, *Bad Samaritans: The Guilty Secrets of Rich Nations and the Threat to Global Prosperity* (London: Random House Business, 2008).

[21] A. Claire Cutler, *Private Power and Global Authority: Transnational Merchant Law in the Global Political Economy* (Cambridge: Cambridge University Press, 2003).

[22] A. Claire Cutler, 'New constitutionalism and the commodity form of global capitalism', in Stephen Gill and A. Claire Cutler (eds.), *New Constitutionalism and World Order* (Cambridge: Cambridge University Press, 2014), p. 45.

[23] Gill and Claire Cutler (eds.) (n. 22), p. 3.

[24] 'In it together: why less inequality benefits all', 21 May 2015, OECD report, http://www.oecd.org/social/in-it-together-why-less-inequality-benefits-all-9789264235120-en.htm.

[25] 'An economy for the 1%: how privilege and power in the economy drive extreme inequality and how this can be stopped', 18 January 2016, Oxfam report on structural inequalities, http://policy-practice.oxfam.org.uk/publications/an-economy-for-the-1-how-privilege-and-power-in-the-economy-drive-extreme-inequ-592643.

[26] Thomas Piketty's book *Capital in the Twenty-First Century* (Cambridge, MA: Harvard University Press, 2014) was particularly influential.

experiencing a crisis of sorts. Most notably, the IMF has itself published reports which question its utility, particularly in terms of its propensity to increase income inequality.[27] Not only did the global financial crisis expose the weaknesses of a global neo-liberal capitalist model, more importantly, neo-liberalism is causing deep income inequalities. The rich are becoming richer, and the poor are becoming poorer. And arguably, what begins as financial crisis can spill over into conflict and social upheaval.[28] With law standing at the heart of the neo-liberal model, it seems that much is at stake to unsettle the taken-for-granted and common-sense attitude of lawyers to neo-liberalism. This also means questioning the instrumental place that such revered notions as 'constitutionalism' can have in creating a deeply socially unjust structure.

2.3   Global constitutionalism and political economy

Applying, then, the emerging debates on the connections between international law and political economy to global constitutionalism may reveal the inner workings and biases of the global constitutional debate. The Framing Paper for this project names the following keywords: sovereignty, nation state, global legal order, global or international constitutionalism, constitutional pluralism, regional integration, public international law, international economic law, World Trade Organization, free trade agreement, human rights protection, legal culture and international cooperation.[29] An enquiry into political economy is a means to bring together all these keywords.

It may seem puzzling that the introduction asserted a neglect of an analysis into the political economy of global constitutionalism when much of the discourse on international constitutionalism began with a scholarly debate on the constitutionalisation of the WTO. In the early 2000s, several scholars engaged in the question of whether the legalisation of the WTO (particularly given its highly legalised

---

[27] Jonathan D. Ostry, Prakash Loungani and Davide Furceri, 'Neoliberalisms: oversold?' (2016) 53 *Finance and Development* 38–41. Available at http://www.imf.org/external/pubs/ft/fandd/2016/06/pdf/ostry.pdf.

[28] For an interesting short video overview, see Paul Mason, 'Capitalism is failing: it's time to panic', 12 August 2015, http://www.theguardian.com/commentisfree/video/2015/aug/12/paul-mason-capitalism-failing-time-to-panic-video.

[29] Takao Suami, Project Framing Paper, January 2013 (on file with the author).

dispute settlement system) meant/should mean/should not mean the constitutionalisation of the WTO and the economic order more generally.[30] This literature was, however, largely concerned with the constitutionalisation of the trade regime, not of the international legal order as a whole. Given that neo-liberal precepts have so permeated thinking on a national, inter- and transnational level, one cannot separate the economic order as pertaining simply to a commercial or trade sphere. The neo-liberal order is at present the only true contender for global reach and due to this monopoly on the institutions, regulations and imagination have become naturalised as the only way of ordering globally interconnected affairs. It follows therefore that those writing on global constitutionalism would not be aware of the particular political-economic model they are assuming – they would most likely not have given it any thought. With this chapter, I hope to make a small contribution to changing this taking-for-granted of the neo-liberal dimension of global constitutionalism.

The point of departure which I propose lies in the public/private dichotomy. Global constitutionalism and neo-liberalism arguably meet and intertwine in the separation of the public and the private spheres. Ideas of constitutionalism have historically entailed a public/private division whereby the public sphere is considered as the political sphere and the private sphere is the sphere of the economic.[31] Neo-liberalism encapsulates this division by promoting

---

[30] Ernst-Ulrich Petersmann, 'Constitutionalism and international organizations' (1997) 17 *Northwestern Journal of International Relations* 398–469; Robert Howse and Kalypso Nicolaidis, 'Legitimacy and global governance: why constitutionalizing the WTO is a step too far', in Roger B. Porter, Pierre Sauvé, Arvind Subramanian and Americo Beviglia Zampetti (eds.), *Efficiency, Equity, and Legitimacy: The Multilateral Trading System at the Millennium* (Washington, DC: Brookings Institution Press, 2001), pp. 227–252; Neil Walker, 'The EU and the WTO: constitutionalism in a new key', in Grainne de Burca and Joanne Scott (eds.), *The EU and the WTO: Legal and Constitutional Issues* (Oxford: Hart Publishing, 2001), pp. 31–57; Ernst-Ulrich Petersmann, 'Human rights, constitutionalism and the World Trade Organization: challenges for World Trade Organization jurisprudence and civil society' (2006) 19 *Leiden Journal of International Law* 633–667.

[31] A prominent and familiar debate in which the collapse of the public into the private is emphasised could undermine the salience of the public/private distinction in constitutionalism. See, e.g., Martha Minow, *Partners Not Rivals: Privatization and the Public Good* (Boston, MA: Beacon Press, 2002). This often concerns the privatisation of public services such as education and health care. However, the abstract and symbolic distinction of the two spheres is still very much present in notions of global constitutionalism and, significantly, serves a particular ideological function.

policies aimed at keeping the market separate and protected from state intervention. This private sphere of the economy is taken out of state control and therefore out of a form of democratic control. The private sphere, the sphere of the economic, is accordingly depoliticised. This rationale of the private sphere and deregulation is connected to the guiding principle of 'the invisible hand' – creating the fiction that law is not present in this sphere.[32]

The public/private distinction, as one of the 'grand dichotomies' of Western thought,[33] is not a single paired opposition but rather a complex network of oppositions.[34] To narrow the possible interpretations of this opposition down, I am interested in its evolution in legal history, in particular constitutional history as it relates to international law. There are several historical moments which have been explored in this regard. One might start with Roman law; one might start with Grotius and his discussions of the mercantile rights in the law of nations. I will follow Morton J. Horwitz's starting point of the 'double movement in modern political and legal thought'.[35] The significance in law appears to have evolved *conceptually* in new ideas of territorial sovereignty in the sixteenth and seventeenth centuries and *practically* with the Industrial Revolution and the notion of the market. As a response to the emergence of the nation state and notions of sovereignty (prompting ideas of a distinct public realm) in the sixteenth and seventeenth centuries, there also emerged a desire for a sphere which should be free from the power of the state (prompting ideas of a distinct private realm). John Locke had a profound impact on the distinction, advocating for a right to private property, which he derived from labour. However, as Horwitz states, it was not until the emergence of the market as a central legitimating institution in the nineteenth century that the public/private distinction was brought into the core of legal discourse.[36]

---

[32] Möller (n. 11), at 275.
[33] Norberto Bobbio, *Democracy and Dictatorship: The Nature and Limits of State Power*, translated by Peter Kennealy (Oxford: Polity Press, 1997).
[34] Jeff Weintraub, 'The theory and politics of the public/private distinction', in Jeff Weintraub and Krishan Kumar (eds.), *Public and Private in Thought and Practice: Perspectives on a Grand Dichotomy* (Chicago, IL: The University of Chicago Press, 1997), pp. 1–2.
[35] Morton J. Horwitz, 'The history of the public/private distinction' (1982) 130.6 *University of Pennsylvania Law Review* 1423–1428.
[36] Ibid., at 1424.

Horowitz writes of the American legal academy furthering the separation between the different branches, designating public law fields (constitutional, criminal, regulatory law) and private law fields (torts, contracts, property, commercial law). This is attributed to a powerful contingent of orthodox judges and jurists who aimed to create a legal science that would sharply separate law from politics.[37] This project of creating a neutral and apolitical science of law was certainly not restricted to the United States but was also (previously) pursued in Europe.[38] Law was to be separated 'from what was thought to be the dangerous and unstable redistributive tendencies of democratic politics'.[39] Politics, then, is present in public law but repressed as that which is irrational and biased, and is entirely missing in private law. Law schools have continued to teach this strict public/private divide and have caused the reproduction of the depoliticisation of law. Duncan Kennedy has highlighted that the core law school subjects – contract law, criminal law, property law, tort law – are not built on the foundation of neutral reasoning but are 'the ground-rules of late nineteenth-century laissez-faire capitalism'.[40] The primacy of property and restrictions on interference with the market are foregrounded as central values.[41] The rights to be protected are those reflecting the interests of private property owners, businesses, multinational corporations and financial capital. Private law, in this understanding, is a neutral system which facilitates voluntary market transactions and vindicates injuries to private rights.

The ideological meaning given to the public/private divide is two-fold. First, the public must not intervene in the market. Second, law is apolitical. Law is regarded as a rational mechanism which can speak reason to power. Law is thought to have *progressed* to become rational.[42] Although

---

[37] Ibid., at 1425.

[38] See Martti Koskenniemi, *The Gentle Civiliser of Nations: The Rise and Fall of International Law 1870–1960* (Cambridge: Cambridge University Press, 2001) for an account of this trend in international law, particularly chapter 1, 'The legal conscience of the civilized world', pp. 11–97.

[39] Horowitz (n. 35), at 1425.

[40] Duncan Kennedy, 'Legal education and the reproduction of hierarchy' (1982) 32 *Journal of Legal Education* 597.

[41] See also Christine Schwöbel-Patel, 'Teaching international law critically: critical pedagogy and *Bildung* as orientations for learning and teaching', in Bart van Klink and Ubaldus de Vries (eds.), *Academic Learning in Law: Theoretical Positions, Teaching Experiments and Learning Experiences* (Cheltenham: Edward Elgar, 2016), pp. 99–120.

[42] See Francis Fukuyama, *The End of History and the Last Man* (London: Penguin, 2012).

the emphases and interpretations of global constitutionalism vary, the division between the political and the economic is largely assumed to be post-political, requiring no further justification. In global constitutionalism, it is taken for granted. Global constitutionalism, then, is employed, perhaps largely unwittingly, as a vehicle for neo-liberalism.

3   Global constitutionalism and East Asian perspectives

This collection sets out to rethink 'how both EU and East Asia can contribute to the construction of global legal order'.[43] Moreover, it advances from the assumption that East Asian scholars have not *yet* joined the discussion on global constitutionalism.[44] The question which emerges from a political economy lens is: Would the debate with East Asian scholars imply a further naturalisation of the public/private divide and therewith a bias for neo-liberalism? Or, alternatively, could this new dialogue provide an opportunity for decolonising global constitutionalism and its political-economic bias?

3.1   Political Economy of East Asia

These sections can provide only a rough overview, with much detail omitted[45] East Asia is not a monolithic whole, and certainly the political-economic emphases vary greatly. In regard to the ASEAN Plus Three, one could generally state that Japan and South Korea are more closely aligned with Western political and economic models (and it merits emphasising here that just as East Asia is not a monolithic whole, nor is the West with varying degrees of social democratic ideals incorporated) than China which is described as a socialist market economy.

It is relevant in this context that despite its peaks and troughs, overall East Asia has experienced economic success in the past few decades.[46] China's economic reforms (often referred to as 'reform

---

[43] Suami (n. 29).

[44] Ibid.

[45] See other chapters in this collection for a more complete view.

[46] Some of the troughs include Japan's economic crisis in the 1990s as well as widespread scepticism as to whether China has really grown at the rate that the national statistical office professes. Moreover, at the time of writing, there is debate over the end of China's four-decade 'growth miracle'.

and opening up') beginning in the late 1970s, and implemented in two stages, introduced market principles in the form of decollectivisation of agriculture, allowing private entrepreneurialism, allowing the privatisation of state-owned industry and opening up the country to foreign investment. Politically, the Communist Party of China has been the sole ruling party since 1949. Japan is a constitutional monarchy, which draws much of its current political patterns from the time of the Allied occupation at the end of World War II. Overall, Japan is more integrated into the international legal system. South Korea is East Asia's most developed country according to the Human Development Index.[47] Overall, East Asia has emerged as one of the strongest regions in terms of economic clout and political influence.

The political economy of East Asia is of course a vast topic, which for lack of space and expertise cannot be developed further here. Two issues of political economy are particularly relevant to this study: first, Deng Xiaoping, the Paramount Leader of China who led China through its major economic reforms, pursued the dictum that disputes regarding sovereignty and territorial integrity should be put to one side in order to further economic opening and modernisation. This effectively created a distinction and isolation between the political and the economic where doing business together was enabled through a setting aside of territorial disputes.[48] Given that the separation of the political and the economic is in line with neoliberal and global constitutional tenets, this continued policy of China allows an insight into the potential dialogue on global constitutionalism with East Asia. Second, it is also relevant here that the East Asian states in question were central in displacing the relative hegemony of the North Atlantic political and economic centre. Given that the hegemonic potential (and possibly nature) of global constitutionalism has been exposed, it would seem relevant that a discourse between the former economic hegemon and the current economic hegemon would take place largely on terms most familiar to the former hegemon.

---

[47] United Nations Development Programme, Human Development Reports, http://hdr .undp.org/en/composite/HDI.
[48] Jacques deLisle, 'Remarks by Jacques deLisle' (2013) 17 *Proceedings of the Annual Meeting (American Society of International Law)* 348–352.

3.2   East Asia and international law

Asia's relationship to international law has been described as both 'ambivalent' as well as 'selective'.[49] Simon Chesterman argues that Asia 'benefits most from the security and economic dividends provided by international law and institutions and yet is the wariest about embracing those rules and structures'.[50] Regardless of whether one subscribes to this cost–benefit view, Asian countries are certainly cautious about certain aspects of international law and at the same time receptive to others. Although at risk of overgeneralisation (particularly as regards Japan), it can be claimed that East Asian states commonly assert traditional sovereign prerogatives. This approach to international law along the traditional Westphalian parameters of sovereignty, sovereign equality and non-intervention is sometimes described as 'Eastphalia'.[51]

This ambivalence towards international law is often presented in its historical context. As noted previously, international law played a central role in the imperial project, echoes of which are still evident in international law today. The exclusion of non-European states from full participation in international law was constructed on the basis of a civilisation bias which affected East Asian states profoundly.[52] Japan was more successful than China in being admitted into the circle of civilised states. It was of course itself an imperial power (and the only non-Western world power in the late nineteenth and early twentieth century), ruling over Korea until defeated by the Allies in World War II. However, Japan came to experience its otherness in its post–World War II occupation and transformation.[53] In the meantime, China suffered what it refers to as 'the century of humiliation' from the mid-nineteenth to the mid-twentieth century.[54] This began with the Opium Wars between China and, first and foremost, Britain. The Opium Wars were military

---

[49] Simon Chesterman, 'Asia's ambivalence about international law and institutions: past, present, futures' (2017) 27 *European Journal of International Law* 945–978; Jacques deLisle, 'China's approach to international law: a historical perspective' (2000) 94 *American Society of International Law Proceedings* 267–275.

[50] Ibid.

[51] Ibid. Chesterman rightly observes that the sovereign prerogative, which is often coined an 'Asian approach' to international law or 'Eastphalia', is in fact a traditional idea of Westphalian international law.

[52] Chesterman (n. 49).

[53] Ibid. In regard to the racial issues associated with the Tokyo trials, at 954.

[54] Eric Yong-Joong Lee, 'Early development of modern international law in East Asia: with special reference to China, Japan, and Korea' (2002) 4 *Journal of the History of International Law* 42–76.

interventions waged for the purpose of securing China as a trading 'partner' for the import of opium from Britain's colony India. The quest was to legalise opium and to exempt it from any trade duties. In addition, Britain wanted access to Chinese tea, silk and porcelain.[55] The unequal treaties and the ceding of Hong Kong to Britain which resulted from China's defeat in the Opium Wars were bitter defeats. Chesterman observes that in order to understand Asian attitudes to international law it is important to note not only the humiliation which comes with colonisation but also the fact that the vast majority of Asian states 'literally did not participate in the negotiation of most of the agreements that define the modern international order'.[56]

There are significant differences within East Asia as regards their attitudes to international law, but China's position in particular deserves some attention given China is the largest in terms of territory and population and has experienced such remarkable economic growth.[57] Notably, the Chinese view on international law is described as instrumentalist in that it considers international law as an instrument of the state rather than a check on it.[58] Despite a prominent Asian values debate in the 1990s, and a subsequent embrace of relativism and/or pluralism, China today appears more flexible in regard to what has been termed 'conceptual' aspects of sovereignty as opposed to 'spatial'.[59] The latter refers to current territorial disputes in the South and East China Sea as well as ongoing claims over Taiwan, Xinjiang and Tibet. In terms of 'conceptual' aspects, China has signed most major UN-centred international human rights conventions as well as issuing a Human Rights White Paper, Action Plans and other informal documents which engage with human rights obligations[60] It is, however, also conceded that despite this official stance, China may in part be paying lip service to conceptual aspects of sovereignty, given that sovereign discretion is still largely

---

[55] P. W. Fay, *The Opium War 1840–42* (Chapel Hill, NC: University of North Carolina Press, 1975); Brian Inglis, *The Opium War* (London: Hodder and Stoughton, 1976); Alain Peyrefitte, *The Immobile Empire – The First Great Collision of East and West – The Astonishing History of Britain's Grand, Ill-Fated Expedition to Open China to Western Trade, 1792–94* (New York: Alfred A. Knopf, 1992).

[56] Chesterman (n. 49), at 949. Examples he notes are the Hague Peace Conferences of 1899 and 1907, the signing of the League of Nations in 1919, the Bretton Woods Conference in 1944 and the establishment of the United Nations itself.

[57] Indeed, there are fears that China's current economic slowdown could have a major impact on the world economy.

[58] Chesterman (n. 49), at 952.

[59] DeLisle (n. 48), at 351.

[60] Ibid., at 351.

maintained.[61] One area of international law in which China is particularly active is in bilateral investment treaties (BITs). China is party to the second largest number of BITs overall, displaying a clear preference for (1) economic agreements and (2) bilateral as opposed to multilateral regimes. Although there has been a problematising and pushback against the reigning supreme of neo-liberal tenets in investment treaties and its fundamental investor-friendly approach,[62] there is still no apparent alternative regime which contests the hegemony of the Washington Consensus.

Against this background of an 'Eastphalian' system of sovereignty, it is relevant that East Asia has generally not been at the forefront of efforts to 'decolonise' international law.[63] Only a few TWAIL scholars come from East Asia. This seems to point to an understanding of the instrumentalist vision of international law rather than an interest in it as a possible instrument for resisting hegemonic power of Western military and economic states. Naturally, this must be seen in relation to China's position as, at the very least, a regional hegemon. Given these preconditions, it would seem that there would be only minor interest in discussions on global constitutionalism from a scholarly perspective and even less so from a political perspective.

3.3   East Asia and Global Constitutionalism

This section sets the lack of political will to one side and questions what East Asian approaches to global constitutionalism may likely look like from a theoretical and practical perspective.

Domestic perspectives on constitutionalism are relevant here, just as they are for the Western scholars writing on global constitutionalism. It can generally be said that in parallel to international law's European origins, constitutionalism is also a legal phenomenon brought to East Asia by the West, although not necessarily through colonialism. Japan's

---

[61] Ibid., at 352.

[62] See, e.g., Muthucumaraswamy Sornarajah, *The International Law on Foreign Investment*, 3rd ed. (Cambridge: Cambridge University Press, 2010).

[63] Although it is notable that China played an important role at the Bandung Conference of 1955. On Bandung and international law, see Luis Eslava, Vasuki Nesiah and Michael Fakhri (eds.), *Bandung, Global History and International Law: Critical Pasts and Pending Futures* (forthcoming: Cambridge University Press). The relationships forged at the Bandung Conference are sometimes invoked to explain China's economic engagement in Africa ever since. See Denis M. Tull, 'China's engagement in Africa: scope, significance and consequences' (2006) 44 *Journal of Modern African Studies* 459–479.

constitutional history is interesting in this regard and tells a complex story. The Constitution of the Empire of Japan, or the Meiji Constitution, came into force in 1890 after a Japanese study mission was sent to various states (including the United States, France, Spain, the United Kingdom and Germany) to enquire into the most appropriate form of constitutionalism for Japan. This study mission found the Prussian model to be particularly suitable to the Japanese context in its mix of constitutional and absolute monarchy. This is not a story of direct imperialism. In contrast, the Meiji Constitution's successor, Japan's constitution of 1947, is widely regarded as 'imposed' on it as part of US General MacArthur's post–World War II plans for economic, political and social change. Although studies have softened the 'imposition' supposition,[64] it can still be presumed that the occupying power exercised a great deal of influence on the initiation, drafting and content of the constitution – not least given the fact that it was first written in English and only then translated into Japanese. Despite this, the Japanese post-war constitution is largely regarded a success, finding legitimacy with the Japanese people and considered an effective means of ensuring the rule of law.

Turning again to China: China's current constitution, the Constitution of the People's Republic of China, was adopted in 1982 under Deng Xiaoping's leadership. It is modelled largely on the 1936 Constitution of the Soviet Union, and China is declared a 'socialist state under the people's democratic dictatorship led by the working class and based on the alliance of workers and peasants'.[65] Despite having a constitution, China is criticised as not having constitutional*ism* given the absence of judicial review and the lack of popular participation in the enforcement of the constitution.[66] A central issue continues to be the question whether the constitution has the capacity to put a check on the actions of the Party and its leadership. As a general matter, China is suspicious of liberal constitutionalism.

A functioning or emergent regional constitutional regime is often viewed as a precursor to global constitutionalist thinking, hence the

---

[64] Justin Williams, 'Making the Japanese Constitution: a further look' (1965) 59 *American Political Science Review* 665–679.

[65] Art. 1, Constitution of the People's Republic of China. The English text of the Constitution is available here: http://www.npc.gov.cn/englishnpc/Constitution/2007-11/15/content_1372963.htm.

[66] Zhang Qianfan, 'A constitution without constitutionalism? The paths of constitutional development in China' (2010) 8 *International Journal of Constitutional Law* 950–976.

frequent reference to EU constitutionalism from advocates of its global interpretation. Asia has, as a general matter, not embraced regional unity through common regional institutions. According to its Charter, the Association of Southeast Asian Nations (ASEAN) serves legal and political purposes to promote greater political, security, economic and socio-cultural cooperation.[67] Despite the various intentions set out in the Charter, 'a noticeable lack of discourse over the role of law and institutions in promoting regionalism in this macro-region' has been observed.[68] This lack of enthusiasm for the role of law and institutions in East Asian regionalism may be indicative of a larger lack of enthusiasm for cooperation on constitutionalism on an international plane.[69]

Hence, Domestic and regional constitutionalism do not offer fertile ground for a flourishing debate on global constitutionalism in East Asia. The inflections of constitutionalism and international law which go beyond an instrumentalist approach are seen with suspicion, particularly by China. This has not, of course, inhibited economic relations. Indeed, one could say that economic relations are flourishing, with East Asia being a major export and import region; in addition, investments in the region as well as by its constituent states in other parts of the world are thriving.[70] Overall, one could state that given the accepted differences in regard to the public-political landscape, a consensus is commonly sought within the economic sphere. As was mentioned previously, this is reflected in the comparatively high number of bilateral trade agreements vis-à-vis multilateral treaties around common rights.[71] The economic is the area in which East–West relations are at their least contested. But this also tells us something about the division of the political and economic in that trade and investment agreements are largely regarded as *apolitical*. This seeming neutrality of the market is, as was argued previously, a distinct feature of neo-liberalism. Despite their having different ideological foundations, the inherent neo-liberal flavour of a separation of the public from the private and the attendant separation of the political from the economic reign supreme. In other words, although its economic influence is not based on a straight-out neo-liberal programme which

---

[67] Art. 1(2) of the ASEAN Charter.
[68] Nakamura (ed.) (n. 1), p. xv.
[69] Ibid. for an effort to address this.
[70] The establishment of the Asian Infrastructure Investment Bank (AIIB) of 2015 is of note here.
[71] Tommy Koh, 'International law and the peaceful resolution of disputes: Asian perspectives, contributions, and challenges' (2011) 1 *Asian Journal of International Law* 57–60.

tries to minimise state intervention in the market, China is also not posing a threat to the unrivalled Washington Consensus paradigms.[72]

Constitutionalism is revealed, then, to be a distinctly political project, on the domestic, regional and global levels. As a political (and social) project, constitutionalism serves the interests of some over others. In the global context, which we are interested in, constitutionalism in East Asia is far more likely to serve private interests, corporate interests and their institutions rather than follow a universal higher moral code. This is because (1) the constitutional form is already biased towards a separation of the public and private, thus depoliticising the sphere of the private, and (2) the constitutional form has the ability to 'lock in' or 'fix' programmes and principles which serve certain purposes and interests.[73] The implication of an East–West dialogue on global constitutionalism would then, perhaps inadvertently, be a further deepening of the separation of the market and therefore the continued inaccessibility of mechanisms of redistribution in the political sphere. Such a trend in thinking, or in the institutionalisation of this thinking through global constitutionalism, could ultimately mean the deepening of economic and social inequality.

3.4 Opportunities?

The conversation with East Asian scholars and practitioners regarding global constitutionalism may, on the other hand, provide opportunities: it may unearth the hitherto neglected debate on political economy, requiring that which has been naturalised to be spelled out. Neo-liberalism's limits have, particularly in the past years, become prominent. Sovereign debt, the global financial crisis, the Greek and other European crises, rising economic inequality and the rise of national populism are all symptoms of the problems with neo-liberalism. This realisation could not only provide the opportunity to rethink global constitutionalism, it could also provide the opportunity to rethink the basis of the predominant economic order. Could this be the introduction of the political into the economic/private sphere?

---

[72] Sarah Babb, 'The Washington Consensus as transnational policy paradigm: its origins, trajectory and likely successor' (2013) 20 Review of International Political Economy 268–297.

[73] Stephen Gill, 'New constitutionalism, democratisation and global political economy' (1998) 10 Pacifica Review: Peace, Security & Global Change 23–28.

Despite the appeal of this proposition, there are some hurdles which are almost impossible to overcome. First, a common lowest denominator, however loose, would need to capture not only the diverse international laws and practices but also, crucially, the transnational laws and practices on a non-normative basis. Even in a loose form of constitutionalism, that of an 'attitude, a frame of mind',[74] some form of fixing within moving processes is required. And if one takes values out of the debate and takes the legal form out of the debate, what does this leave us with? Only again an agreement that 'doing business' without enquiring into values has worked in the past. The political in terms of a democratic and inclusive process would most likely, in practical terms, be factored out. An example of this may be detected in China's approach to the disputes arising from the territorial claims made on the South and East China Seas. Chinese policy is to 'set aside' sovereignty questions to seek cooperation on practical matters such as resource development.[75]

Second, the close link between global constitutionalism and international law would, it seems, be an inhibitor. A common framework, even in a minimalist sense, would need to somehow capture laws and practices which derive from increasingly diverse and multiple local, regional and global locations involving both state and non-state authorities and state and non-state law.[76] Not even international law is able to capture these multiform processes and events,[77] so why would a global constitutionalism? So long as international law is unable to account for the role of law in the *constitution* (as in construction) of local and global political economies, its decolonisation through a debate on commonalities with non-Western actors is unlikely. Notwithstanding the fantastic efforts of scholars from the Global South to engage in this largely Eurocentric debate,[78] I believe that the likelihood for opening global constitutionalism to a truly global idea is slim.

---

[74] Jan Klabbers, 'Setting the scene', in Jan Klabbers, Anne Peters and Geir Ulfstein (eds.), *The Constitutionalization of International Law* (Oxford: Oxford University Press, 2009), p. 10.
[75] DeLisle (n. 48), at 352.
[76] Claire Cutler (n. 21), p. 2 describes this as the 'new transnational legal order'.
[77] Ibid. And this brings us, in a somewhat circular fashion, to the debate on global governance. Dunoff has observed in this context that the constitutional debate is self-defeating in that it 'is less a sign of international law's flourishing than of it being in a state of crisis'; Jeffrey L. Dunoff, 'Constitutional conceits: the WTO's "Constitution" and the discipline of international law' (2006) 17 *European Journal of International Law* 645–675, at 669.
[78] See, e.g., Daniel Bonilla-Maldonadlod, *Constitutionalism of the Global South: The Activist Tribunals of India, South Africa and Colombia* (Cambridge: Cambridge University Press, 2013).

Third, and in a related vein, the necessity for constitutionalism's form to capture dynamic processes, even if for a short time only, arguably has a depoliticising effect. Constitutionalism is in this sense 'a mechanism for withdrawing controversial and potentially destabilising issues from the parry and thrust of ordinary politics to a less inclusive constitutional domain'.[79]

Finally, aside from these structural biases of the global constitutionalist idea, the existence of a concomitant political will relating to such efforts is questionable. Global constitutionalism remains a scholarly debate, and there is not a whiff of governmental, civil society or policy interest in it to date.

4 Conclusion

At the beginning of this chapter, it was asserted that the debate on global constitutionalism has at its core the question of whether it can contribute to addressing some of the world's largest problems. In other words, can it contribute to a more equal, prosperous, sustainable and overall better life of humankind? This chapter has highlighted how the neglected enquiry into the political economy of global constitutionalism is a crucial element in order to get a little closer to answering these ambitious questions. It was found that global constitutionalism, with its central parameters of political liberalism emphasising the division of the public and the private, plays into the hands of a neo-liberal political project by depoliticising the economic sphere. Global constitutionalism, if enforced or institutionalised beyond its European birthplace, would be unlikely to democratise or decolonise international affairs. Rather, it would more likely be a further vehicle for the naturalisation of neo-liberalism and at the very least maintain the status quo.

---

[79] Jeffrey L. Dunoff, 'The politics of international constitutions: the curious case of the World Trade Organization', in Dunoff and Trachtman (eds.) (n. 16), p. 179.

4

Global Constitutionalism and European Legal Experiences

Can European Constitutionalism Be Applied to the Rest of the World?

TAKAO SUAMI [*]

1 Introduction

This chapter examines the significance of the legal experiences in European regional integration for international society as a whole and seeks to explain whether and how these can form a building block for constitutionalism beyond Europe.

Global constitutionalism is grounded in the observation of various ongoing changes named globalisation in international society. It is unquestionable that globalisation has generally reduced the importance of national borders in many respects. Yet the speed, scope and content of these changes are not similar in all regions. In the face of the recent changes in East Asia, East Asians are being expected to listen to a discussion on global constitutionalism that is launched almost exclusively by non-Asian scholars. Most claims of global constitutionalism are indeed inspired by the legal experiences of European integration in the past decades after the end of World War II, especially by the constitutionalisation of European Union law (EU law) on the basis of legal doctrines developed by the European Court of Justice (ECJ), currently the Court of Justice of the European Union (CJEU).[1] Beyond a doubt, Europe has accumulated very

---

[*] Professor of European Law, Waseda Law School (suamilaw@waseda.jp). I express my sincere thanks to my colleagues Anne Peters, Mattias Kumm and Dimitri Vanoverbeke for their comments on an early draft of this chapter.

[1] Weiler explains that due to the development of 'supremacy, direct effect, implied powers, and human rights scrutiny by the ECJ', the basic treaties of the EU have been transformed into the constitutional charter of the polity (Joseph H. H. Weiler, *The Constitution of Europe: 'Do the New Clothes Have an Emperor?' and Other Essays on European Integration* (Cambridge: Cambridge University Press, 1999), pp. 8–9, 12, 19–29, 295; Joris Larik,

advanced and unique legal experiences through the process of its regional integration, which are affluent in hints and clues to develop new legal theories in many fields of law. If, indeed, the European experiences were always universalizable, no intellectual difficulties would arise. But this assumption is doubtful, because the transferability of European achievements to other regions has not been fully studied yet.[2] If European experiences rest on facts that are specific to Europe, then the possibility of truly global constitutionalism would inevitably have to be reconsidered. Therefore, we must be more careful in feeding European experiences into the formulation of theories with a global aspiration. With the awareness of these concerns, the main focus of this chapter is to differentiate European achievements that have a universal reach from those that are non-universal or local ones. This chapter shows that some of the European experiences are assets that can be shared, while others are not. The former ones alone are entitled to constitute a foundation for global theories including global constitutionalism.

This chapter consists of two main sections and proceeds as follows. In order to fully understand the theory of global constitutionalism, it is necessary to follow the genealogy of this theory. Considering that, the first section provides a brief overview of how the development of constitutional pluralism in the EU has been absorbed into global constitutionalism. In doing so, it argues that a series of targeted-sanction cases before the EU courts have played a crucial role in encouraging the merger of two legal theories. The second section looks more closely at both the universality and the specificity of European experiences and reconstructs global constitutionalism in terms of its value aspect. On the one hand, the progress of EU law demonstrates that constitutionalism can be applied in transnational spaces beyond the borders of states, but on the other hand, the value aspect of European experiences cannot be automatically transferred to those spaces. In general, the former is mainly addressed to non-Europeans including East Asians, and the latter is more suggestive to Europeans. In sum, this chapter as a whole will try to shed new light on global constitutionalism through studying European legal experiences themselves from an East Asian point of view and to contribute to its further development in order to make it a more universally accepted legal theory.

'Shaping the international order as an EU objective', in Dimitry Kochenov and Fabian Amtenbrink (eds.), *The European Union's Shaping of the International Legal Order* (Cambridge: Cambridge University Press, 2014), pp. 62, 79–80).
[2] Ester Herlin-Karnell, 'EU values and the shaping of the international legal context', in Kochenov and Amtenbrink (eds.), ibid., pp. 89, 101.

2   The origins of global constitutionalism and its developmental path

2.1   The background of global constitutionalism

Fully comprehending the evolutionary process of debates on global constitutionalism will provide a solid foundation for a more nuanced debate on this theory. Many aspects of international law and society have undergone fundamental changes in the last few decades after the fall of the Berlin Wall and the subsequent end of the Cold War. Those changes embraced 'globalisation', 'the fragmentation of international law' and 'the development of international organizations including the EU'.[3] They actually constituted the backdrop for the development of the 'constitutionalization of international law', and the emergence of global constitutionalism has been a response to them.

The origin of constitutionalism beyond states goes back to the period between World Wars I and II. For example, Alfred Verdross discussed the constitution of the international legal order from the 1920s. He discussed international constitution in a different context from the current debate. Nevertheless, his argument has given many suggestions to international law scholars and has influenced contemporary debates on global constitutionalism.[4] As a matter of fact, global constitutionalism is not the same as his theory. By way of having preliminary debates about the constitutionalisation of international law, current scholars began putting forward global constitutionalism with a view to properly handling the aforementioned fundamental changes.

2.2   Global constitutionalism as a descriptive and normative theory

Global constitutionalism is still a controversial conception, and it is difficult to define it uniformly at present. To begin, global constitutionalism presents a new paradigm for the recognition of international legal

---

[3] Jeffrey L. Dunoff and Joel P. Trachtman, 'A functional approach to international constitutionalization', in Jeffrey L. Dunoff and Joel P. Trachtman (eds.), *Ruling the World? Constitutionalism, International Law, and Global Governance* (Cambridge; New York: Cambridge University Press, 2009), pp. 3, 5–9.

[4] Henry Janzen, 'The legal monism of Alfred Verdross' (1935) 29 *American Political Science Review* 387–402, at 397–401; Aoife O'Donoghue, 'Alfred Verdross and the contemporary constitutionalization debate' (2012) 32 *Oxford Journal of Legal Studies* 799–822, at 814–821; Thomas Kleinlein, 'Alfred Verdross as a founding father of international constitutionalism?' (2012) 4 *Goettingen Journal of International Law* 385–416, at 389–407.

order, but this aspect is nothing but a part of global constitutionalism. According to Anne Peters who is one of the leading advocates, global constitutionalism not only recognises some features of international relations as being constitutional but also, in a mindset of constitutionalism, insists on 'the application of constitutional principles, such as the rule of law, checks and balances, human rights protection, and democracy in the international legal sphere'.[5] For international organisations, global constitutionalism requests that they have a particular kind of constitution that satisfies constitutionalist standards by enshrining these principles.[6]

Probably most global constitutionalists presume that there are commonly or universally shared values which are held by the international community[7]. A related claim is 'the ultimate, international legal subjects are individuals'.[8] As the term 'values' indicates, constitutionalism has normative and subjective dimensions.[9] Thereby, global constitutionalism can be distinguished from international legalisation or judicialisation.[10] By reason of its normative nature, global constitutionalism encourages interpretation of international law in compliance with constitutional standards and gives international lawyers who encounter many policy or legal problems all sorts of clues as to how to improve on the present international laws and organisations. In this way, this theory not only rightly appreciates what is happening in the world but also guides the future of international society in a particular direction.

---

[5] Anne Peters, 'Compensatory constitutionalism: the function and potential of fundamental international norms and structures' (2006) 19 *Leiden Journal of International Law* 579–610, at 582–584.

[6] Anne Peters, 'The constitutionalisation of international organisations', in Neil Walker, Jo Shaw and Stephen Tierney (eds.), *Europe's Constitutional Mosaic* (Oxford: Hart Publishing, 2011), pp. 253–254.

[7] Jan Klabbers, 'Setting the scene', in Jan Klabbers, Anne Peters and Geir Ulfstein (eds.), *The Constitutionalization of International Law* (Oxford; New York: Oxford University Press, 2009), p. 26; Jan Klabbers, 'The European Union in the global constitutional mosaic', in Walker, Shaw and Tierney (eds.) (n. 6), p. 300.

[8] Anne Peters, 'Are we moving towards constitutionalization of the world community?', in Antonio Cassese (ed.), *Realizing Utopia: The Future of International Law* (Oxford: Oxford University Press, 2012), pp. 118–119 and 129; Anne Peters, 'Humanity as the A and Ω of sovereignty' (2009) 20 *European Journal of International Law* 513–544, at 514, 518, 533–540.

[9] Peters, 'Are we moving towards constitutionalization' (n. 8), p. 119.

[10] Klabbers, 'Setting the scene' (n. 7), pp. 7–9; Geir Ulfstein, 'The international judiciary', in Klabbers, Peters and Ulfstein (eds.) (n. 7), pp. 126, 141.

2.3   Contemporary global constitutionalism: hierarchy or non-hierarchy within the international legal order

Global constitutionalism may have a friendly relationship with the idea of there being a constitution which has a higher status in the international legal order.[11] One formal element which is shared by most constitutions is their quality of being a supreme legal norm over ordinary law, although the most famous exception is the English 'unwritten' constitution which can be amended by ordinary parliamentary laws. Accordingly, global constitutionalism seemingly encourages the building up of a hierarchical structure within international law.[12] This is indicated by the fact that some scholars describe *jus cogens* norms as being constitutional in the international legal order and that furthermore they tend to seek something higher (e.g. the UN Charter, WTO law and ILO law) inside the international legal order.[13]

In contrast to such a predominant image yielded by the wording of a 'world constitution' or 'global constitution', only a few advocates of global constitutionalism do adhere to the hierarchical structure of the international legal order. Taking into account decentralised features inherent in international law, global constitutionalists are generally more flexible than those claiming a strict hierarchy such as domestic legal orders. For instance, Peters takes a view that global constitutionalism is a multi-level constitutionalism, which is nested rather than hierarchical or monolithic.[14] Her argument is not limited to the inner part of international law. Not following the traditional view with a strict distinction between international law and domestic law, she extends her multi-level constitutionalism to the relationship between national law and international law.[15] Jan Klabbers also takes a pluralistic view of global

---

[11] Klabbers, 'Setting the scene' (n. 7), pp. 11–19.

[12] Jessica C. Lawrence, 'Contesting constitutionalism: constitutional discourse at the WTO' (2013) 2 *Global Constitutionalism* 63–90, at 67.

[13] Christine E. J. Schwöbel, *Global Constitutionalism in International Legal Perspective* (Leiden; Boston: Martinus Nijhoff Publishers, 2011), pp. 29–34 and 39; Bardo Fassbender, 'Rediscovering a forgotten constitution: notes on the place of the UN Charter in the international legal order', in Dunoff and Trachtman (eds.), *Ruling the World?* (n. 3), pp. 133, 137–147.

[14] Peters (n. 6), p. 285.

[15] She presents the non-hierarchical, network type and pluralistic relationship between 'the multiple constitutions on the national and global level' and points out that 'the absence of hierarchy is accompanied by the absence of a single authority to decide on eventual conflicts of norms' (Anne Peters, 'Dual democracy', in Klabbers, Peters and Ulfstein (eds.) (n. 7), pp. 263, 336–338). She states in another article that instead of hierarchy, one can see 'a loosely knit global constitutional network' (Peters (n. 5), at 601–602).

constitutionalism.[16] The cited views show that it is nowadays widely accepted that global constitutionalism should be pluralist.[17] Although pluralism is a term with multiple meanings, 'pluralism' in this chapter means an idea which rejects the existence of one ultimate authority, which provides for the legitimacy of all legal orders. Pluralism understands that authorities are exercised on various levels as well as in different places.[18]

2.4 Constitutional pluralism in EU law and global constitutionalism

2.4.1 Merging constitutional pluralism in EU law with global constitutionalism

Global constitutionalism was first discussed as an international law subject within a circle of international law scholars. While, from the beginning, they paid certain attention to the constitutionalisation of EU law in the context of reconceptualising the founding treaties of international organisations as their constitutional norms, the importance of EU law for global constitutionalism was rather limited and remained in a similar position as other international organisations such as the World Trade Organization (WTO) and the United Nations (UN).[19]

In contrast, nowadays, the constitutionalisation of EU law is more frequently referred to by global constitutionalists as being the most visible example of global constitutionalism.[20] This fact proves that global constitutionalism currently has close relevance to the theory of EU law, in particular to its 'constitutional pluralism'.[21] In fact, global constitutionalism in international law has been gradually growing in parallel with constitutional pluralism in EU law. As a result, it is rather difficult to

---

[16] According to him, 'a constitutional global order needs to be a pluralistic global order' in the sense that 'it will have come to terms with its own heterarchy' (Klabbers, 'Setting the scene' (n. 7), pp. 43–44).

[17] Michel Rosenfeld, 'Is global constitutionalism meaningful or desirable?' (2014) 25 European Journal of International Law 177–199, at 190–191.

[18] Klabbers, 'Setting the scene' (n. 7), p. 44.

[19] Peters (n. 5), at 595–597.

[20] Peters (n. 6), pp. 266–272; Mattias Kumm, 'The cosmopolitan turn in constitutionalism: on the relationship between constitutionalism in and beyond the state', in Dunoff and Trachtman (eds.), Ruling the World? (n. 3), pp. 258, 279–288; Schwöbel (n. 13), pp. 47–48.

[21] Jean L. Cohen, 'Sovereignty in the context of globalization: a constitutional pluralist perspective', in Samantha Besson and John Tasioulas (eds.), The Philosophy of International Law (Oxford: Oxford University Press, 2010), pp. 261, 262 and 276; Jean L. Cohen, Globalization and Sovereignty: Rethinking Legality, Legitimacy, and Constitutionalism (Cambridge: Cambridge University Press, 2012), pp. 66–76.

understand the essence of global constitutionalism without properly understanding constitutional pluralism in EU law. Metaphorically speaking, European global constitutionalists are now a mixture of two types of legal scholars, namely international lawyers and EU lawyers. Two different streams of ideas have actually merged into one larger stream of global constitutionalism. In order to prove this assumption, we must study constitutional pluralism in EU law first. In this chapter, 'constitutional pluralism' always means a legal theory of EU law.

2.4.2   Constitutional tension in EU law

It is quite well known that there has been unresolved constitutional tension between EU law and national constitutions of the member states from the outset of the European Communities (EC). Since the early 1960s, the ECJ has firmly established the primacy of EU law over all domestic laws including national constitutions without any explicit textual basis.[22] Inasmuch as the member states established the ECJ as a final adjudicator of EU law by concluding the EU's founding treaty, non-compliance with the ECJ's rulings cannot be justified under international law as well as under EU law.[23]

Yet, national courts, particularly constitutional courts in the member states, have not accepted the absolute primacy of EU law as such and still retain their powers to intervene in conflicts between EU law and national law in the light of their constitutions.[24] The German Constitutional Court (GCC) has virtually led other constitutional courts in the EU. As every European scholar knows well, a series of GCC judgments indicate how the relationship between EU law and domestic constitutions has evolved over four decades, and they have also expressed the GCC's firm intention to protect the core of the German Constitution. Initially, the main point in dispute concerned the protection of human rights enshrined in the Constitution.[25] Due to the change in the GCC's attitude as well as the improvement of human rights protection at the EC

---

[22] Case C6/64, *Costa v. ENEL* [1964] ECR585, 593; Case 11/70, *Internationale Handelsgesellschaft* [1970] ECR1125, para. 3; Case 106/77, *Amministrazione delle Finanze dello Stato v. Simmenthal* [1978] ECR629, paras. 17–22.

[23] Weiler (n. 1), pp. 291, 298–317.

[24] Paul Craig and Gráinne De Búrca, *EU LAW: Text, Cases and Materials*, 5th ed. (Oxford: Oxford University Press, 2011), pp. 268–300; Koen Lenaerts and Piet Van Nuffel, *European Union Law*, 3rd ed. (London: Sweet and Maxwell, 2011), pp. 772–809 (edited by Robert Bray and Nathan Cambien).

[25] In the *Solange I* judgment of 1974, the GCC claimed jurisdiction to control the constitutionality of EC acts from that perspective ([1974] 2 CMLR 540, 549–550).

level, the disparity between the GCC and the ECJ had actually narrowed in the late 1980s.[26]

Unfortunately, the relatively peaceful relationship between the two courts did not last for a long time. The turning point was the GCC's *Maastricht* judgment of 1993. Besides human rights review, in this judgment, the GCC raised a new jurisdiction for reviewing EC acts to 'see whether they remain within the limits of the sovereign rights conferred on them or transgress them' (*ultra vires* review).[27] It is also worth noting that many constitutional or supreme courts in the EU have followed the GCC's approach by and large.[28] In 2009, the GCC made more progress with the *Lisbon* judgment, which announced that the GCC would carry out a third type of constitutional review of EU law in the light of the inviolable core of the Constitution (identity review).[29] After all, it follows that national courts do not resist day-to-day application of EU law[30] but

[26] After the *Solange I* judgment, all EC institutions had made efforts to improve their protection of human rights. Namely, the ECJ recognised as part of EC law human rights deriving from both common constitutional traditions in the member states and international human rights treaties concluded by them, in particular the European Convention on Human Rights (Case 29/69, *Stauder* [1969] ECR419, para. 7; Case 11/70, *Internationale Handelsgesellschaft*, para. 4). Other EC institutions also made their commitment to the protection of human rights (Joint Declaration of the European Parliament, the Council and the Commission, OJ 1977, C 103/1). Then, in the *Solange II* judgment of 1986, the GCC renounced temporarily ('as long as') on exercising its jurisdiction over EC acts on the condition that the ECJ would generally ensure 'an effective protection of fundamental rights' which was similar to domestic protection (*Solange II* [1987] 3 CMLR 225, 265).

[27] *Brunner v. European Union Treaty* [1994] 1 CMLR 57, paras. 13 and 49.

[28] For example, Danish Supreme Court, Case No. 1361/1997, 6 April 1998, para. 9.6; Corte costituzionale, Judgment of No. 103 of 2008, 12 February 2008, para. 7; French Constitutional Council, Décision no 2007–560 DC, 27 December 2007, para. 9; Czech Constitutional Court, Pl. ÚS 5/12: Slovak Pensions, 31 January 2012.

[29] Namely, the issue is 'whether or not the inviolable-core content of the constitutional identity' of the German Constitution (Arts. 1, 20 and 79(3)) was duly respected (*Lisbon*, 2 BvE 2/08, 2 BvE 5/08, 2 BvR 1010/08, 2 BvR 1022/08, 2 BvR 1259/08 and 2 BvR 182/09, 30 June 2009, para. 240); Daniel Thym, 'In the name of sovereign statehood: a critical introduction to the Lisbon judgment of the German Constitutional Court' (2009) 46 *Common Market Law Review* 1795–1822; Mehrdad Payandeh, 'Constitutional review of EU law after *Honeywell*: contextualizing the relationship between the German Constitutional Court and the EU Court of Justice' (2011) 48 *Common Market Law Review* 9–38, at 16–19. In addition, the GCC's recent judgment of December 2015 on the execution of the European Arrest Warrant brings a new element into the identity review (2 BvR 2735/14, 15 December 2015, Bundesverfassungsgericht, Press Release No. 4/2016 of 26 January 2016).

[30] The Czech Constitutional Court's judgment in the Slovak Pensions case is the sole example of explicit opposition to the primacy of EU law (n. 28). In 2012, the Czech Constitutional Court overturned the ECJ's preliminary ruling by reason of its

constantly express that 'they could set aside EU law for constitutional grounds under certain circumstances'.[31] After the early 1990s, all things considered, the gap between the ECJ and the national courts has not become narrower at all. The divergence concerning their positions has consolidated and is not likely to disappear in the foreseeable future.

2.4.3   The birth and development of constitutional pluralism

Against such a backdrop, constitutional pluralism in EU law was born in the early 1990s, and it has become much more popular in this century. Constitutional pluralism is a legal theory which explains and justifies the constitutional tension in the EU, and it has the following major features.[32]

In the first place, according to Miguel Poiares Maduro, the starting point of constitutional pluralism is that no ultimate authority for uniformly resolving the constitutional tension can be found in the territory of the EU.[33] The essential point here is that constitutional pluralism

constitution (Robert Zbíral, 'Czech Constitutional Court, judgment of 31 January 2012, Pl. ÚS 5/12, a legal revolution or negligible episode? Court of Justice decision proclaimed *ultra vires*' (2012) 49 *Common Market Law Review* 1475–1491). But this incident is still an exception. In contrast, in 2014, following the ECJ's ruling on the EU Charter of Fundamental Rights, the Spanish Constitutional Court modified its established interpretation of the right to a fair trial in the Spanish Constitution (Spanish Constitutional Court, Judgment 26/2014, 13 February 2014; Case C-399/11 *Melloni v. Ministerio Fiscal*, 26 February 2013); Aida Torres Pérez, '*Melloni* in three acts: from dialogue to monologue' (2014) 10 *European Constitutional Law Review* 308–331.

[31] Mattias Kumm, 'The jurisprudence of constitutional conflict: constitutional supremacy in Europe before and after the Constitutional Treaty' (2005) 11 *European Law Journal* 262–307, at 263.

[32] Neil MacCormick, *Questioning Sovereignty: Law, State, and Practical Reason* (Oxford: Oxford University Press, 1999), pp. 113–121 and 131–133; Miguel Poiares Maduro, 'Europe and the Constitution: what if this is as good as it gets?', in Joseph H. H. Weiler and Marlene Wind (eds.), *European Constitutionalism beyond the State* (Cambridge: Cambridge University Press, 2003), pp. 74–102; Miguel Poiares Maduro, 'Contrapunctual law: Europe's constitutional pluralism in action', in Neil Walker (ed.), *Sovereignty in Transition* (Oxford: Hart Publishing, 2003), pp. 501–537; Franz C. Mayer, 'Multilevel constitutional jurisdiction', in Armin von Bogdandy and Jürgen Bast (eds.), *Principles of European Constitutional Law* (Oxford: Hart Publishing, 2006), pp. 281–333; Joakim Nergelius, *The Constitutional Dilemma of the European Union* (Groningen: Europa Law Publishing, 2009), pp. 36–37; Paul Kirchhof, 'The European Union of states', in Armin von Bogdandy and Jürgen Bast (eds.), *Principles of European Constitutional Law*, 2nd rev. ed. (Oxford: Hart Publishing, 2010), pp. 735–761.

[33] Miguel Poiares Maduro, 'Three claims of constitutional pluralism', in Matej Avbelj and Jan Komárek (eds.), *Constitutional Pluralism in the European Union and Beyond* (Oxford: Hart Publishing, 2012), pp. 67, 75–77; Neil MacCormick, 'The Maastricht Urteil: sovereignty now' (1995) 1 *European Law Journal* 259–266, at 264–265.

accepts the idea that the EU has the legal authority which is comparable to those held by its member states. Accordingly, the ECJ is responsible for interpreting EU law, and the highest national courts likewise assume the final responsibility for interpreting their national laws. Both EU law and national constitutions are equally legitimate in their primacy claims. Thus, within the EU, there is no higher authority to resolve conflicts between the ECJ and the highest national courts. In the second place, EU law and national laws are distinct legal orders but interact with each other within a single legal framework.[34] There is no federal style of hierarchy between them, though they coexist in the same geographical space. Instead, they constitute a non-hierarchical relationship irrespective of the primacy of EU law. Consequently the principle of the EU law's primacy against national laws has become comparable to the conflict of laws which controls the interface among different national laws.[35] This understanding of the primacy justifies a possibility that, even under the primacy of EU law, national laws will not be necessarily subordinate to EU law, in the case where EU law is defective in its legitimacy.[36] In the third place, inasmuch as conflicts between EU law and national law cannot be totally resolved by the primacy of EU law, they must be solved by either political agreement or international law.[37] This solution clearly suggests that it is essential to avoid any occurrences of real conflicts through mutual accommodation. For that reason, having institutionalised judicial dialogues between the ECJ and national courts through the preliminary ruling procedure (Art. 267 of TFEU) is crucial. The ECJ has encouraged national courts to ask for preliminary rulings on EU law prior to holding any constitutional review,[38] and notably not a few constitutional courts have taken a more positive attitude towards the

---

[34] Elke Cloots, 'Germs of pluralist judicial adjudication: Advocaten voor de Wereld and other references from the Belgian Constitutional Court' (2010) 47 *Common Market Law Review* 645–672, at 647–648.

[35] Herwig C. H. Hofmann, 'Conflicts and integration: revisiting *Costa v ENEL* and *Simmenthal II*', in Miguel Poiares Maduro and Loïc Azoulai (eds.), *The Past and Future of EU Law: The Classics of EU Law Revisited on the 50th Anniversary of the Rome Treaty* (Oxford: Hart Publishing, 2010), pp. 60–68; Matej Avbelj, 'Supremacy or primacy of EU law: (why) does it matter?' (2011) 17 *European Law Journal* 744–763, at 750–752.

[36] Mattias Kumm, 'Rethinking constitutional authority: on the structure and limits of constitutional pluralism', in Avbelj and Komárek (n. 33), pp. 39, 42–43 and 55.

[37] MacCormick (n. 32), pp. 120–121.

[38] Joined Cases C-188/10 and C-189/10, *Melki and Abdeli*, 22 June 2010, paras. 52–56; Rostane Mehdi, 'French Supreme Courts and European Union law: between historical compromise and accepted loyalty' (2011) 48 *Common Market Law Review* 439–473, at 470–471.

reliance on this procedure.[39] Constitutional pluralism never gives up the pursuit of coherence and consistency within the European legal order, however. Constitutional pluralists anticipate that constitutional principles (e.g. human rights, democracy and the rule of law) underlying EU law as well as national laws will guide both the ECJ and national courts to find mutually acceptable solutions for constitutional conflicts.[40] In this context, the fact that the normative principles are mutually shared within the EU (Art. 2 of the Treaty on European Union (TEU)) is essentially important. Both the EU and its member states have been jointly engaged in developing common constitutional traditions.[41] In addition, it must be noted that the member states agreed to establish the EU at the outset, and later they did not insert into the founding treaties a provision which overturned the primacy of EU law on the occasions of treaty revisions. In view of the obvious fact that they have mostly respected the primacy of EU law, national courts will be more likely to follow the primacy of EU law in principle from now on.

2.4.4   Constitutional pluralism and global constitutionalism

While European experiences of regional integration generally constitute the background of global constitutionalism, it can be further thought that constitutional pluralism in EU law is closely associated with global constitutionalism.

More than anything else, the arguments of constitutional pluralism are very similar to those of global constitutionalism. If one compares constitutional pluralism with global constitutionalism in terms of the contents, it is easy to discover that both of them have features in common, namely: (1) the lack of ultimate constitutional authority in the transnational space, (2) the non-hierarchical and pluralistic relationships between or among different constitutions, (3) the sharing of constitutional principles (such as the rule of law, democracy and human rights) derived mainly from national constitutions and international treaties and (4) the pursuit of consistency between or among different constitutional orders. These are the four common core features between the two legal theories and show that there are strong resemblances between the two theories. One of the distinctions between them is that as compared with constitutional pluralism, global constitutionalism places less stress on

---

[39] Corte costituzionale, Judgment of No. 103 of 2008 (n. 28), paras. 34–36; *Honeywell*, BVerfG, 2 BvR 2661/06, 6 July 2010, paras. 58–61; Payandeh (n. 29), at 21–27; Tribunal Constitucional de España, Order 86/2011, 9 June 2011; Torres Pérez (n. 30), at 310–311.
[40] Kumm (n. 31), at 286; Maduro (n. 33), p. 82.
[41] Kumm (n. 31), at 288–292.

judicial dialogues among various courts including both national and international courts. This derives mainly from the lack of an institutio- nalised mechanism for judicial dialogues at the international level. But this does not mean that judicial dialogues have no relevance to global constitutionalism. This question will be mentioned later in this chapter.

The close relationship between the two theories is reinforced by the confluence of constitutional pluralists into global constitutionalists. Several EU law scholars who argue constitutional pluralism for the EU also argue global constitutionalism for international society. They began studying constitutional pluralism in the context of the EU, but since their ideas on EU law were transferrable to much broader settings beyond the EU, they have broadened their interests to cover the entire international society at a later stage. Namely, an original constitutional pluralist, Miguel Poiares Maduro, joined the group of editors for a new legal journal named *Global Constitutionalism* in 2012.[42] Furthermore, some others have insisted on both ideas in parallel. Neil Walker, for example, argues European and global constitutionalism in the same framework of 'postnational constitutionalism'.[43] According to him, constitutionalism in the EU is part of the broader picture of constitutionalism. These personal overlaps also evidence an intimate interconnection between the two theories.

Why has constitutionalism at the European level been able to affect constitutionalism at the global level? This is because manifestly, Europe is an advanced area of international law. Since the end of World War II, European countries have consistently promoted regional integration mainly through the European Communities (the EC, later the EU) and the European Convention on Human Rights (ECHR). The lasting process of the European integration, in particular the foundation of the Internal

---

[42] Miguel Poiares Maduro first discussed constitutionalism in the EU (Maduro, 'Europe and the constitution' (n. 32), pp. 74–102). But many aspects of his idea can be transferred to the global arena (Antje Wiener, Anthony F. Lang Jr., James Tully, Miguel Poiares Maduro and Mattias Kumm, 'Why a new journal on global constitutionalism?' (2012) 1 *Global Constitutionalism* 1–15). Mattias Kumm also started from constitutional pluralism in the EU and then reached cosmopolitan constitutionalism (Kumm (n. 36), pp. 39–65).

[43] Neil Walker has a broader picture on constitutionalism from the outset of this century (Neil Walker, 'The EU and the WTO: constitutionalism in a new key', in Gráinne de Búrca and Joanne Scott (eds.), *The EU and the WTO: Legal and Constitutional Issues* (Oxford: Hart Publishing, 2001), pp. 31–57). He translated the concept of constitution- alism from the state to the European Union's setting and further expanded it to other international settings (Neil Walker, 'Postnational constitutionalism and the problem of translation', in Weiler and Wind (eds.) (n. 32) pp. 27–54; Neil Walker and Stephen Tierney, 'Introduction: a constitutional mosaic? Exploring the new frontiers of Europe's constitutionalism', in Walker, Shaw and Tierney (eds.) (n. 6), pp. 1–18).

Market, is a regional precedent for globalisation. During the process for the Internal Market, Europe before others confronted a great deal of problems which were similar to those that international society is currently facing in the progress of globalisation,[44] and consequently it accumulated plenty of experience and know-how on transnational constitutionalism. Hence it can be reasonably inferred from Europe's preceding experiences that the similarities between the two theories were derived from the expansion of European ideas to the global sphere. All things considered, constitutional pluralism and global constitutionalism share similar essential attributes and are based upon the same idea. On the one hand, the differences between them are nothing but a matter of degree reflecting the difference in legal nature between the EU and international society. On the other hand, mutual interaction between them has especially made the theory of global constitutionalism more fertile.

2.4.5   Targeted-sanction cases as a turning point

Constitutional pluralism discusses 'constitutionalism beyond the states' in the realm of the EU, and it is not originally addressed to international society as a whole. Therefore, one question of why constitutional pluralism has started affecting global constitutionalism arises. In fact, although the EC/EU was referred to as an example of constitutionalisation of an international organisation,[45] the connection between the two theories in the initial stage of debates was not as strong as it is today.

The turning point seemed to be a series of well-known *Kadi* cases which were held before the European Court of First Instance (CFI) and the ECJ.[46] The issue in these cases was the legality of targeted-sanction

---

[44] For example, in the context of free movement of goods, the EC has confronted an issue on how to accommodate free movement and public interests such as environmental protection and consumer protection from the 1970s (Case C-120/78, *Cassis de Dijon* [1979] ECR649, para. 8). Since the foundation of the WTO in 1995, the WTO members have been forced to deal with similar issues including those on trade and environment as well as trade and labour.

[45] Peters (n. 5), at 595.

[46] Case T-315/01, *Kadi v. Council and Commission*; Case T-306/01, *Yusuf and Al Barakaat International Foundation v. Council and Commission*, 21 September 2005; Joined Cases C-402/05 P and C-415/05 P, *Kadi and Al Barakaat International Foundation v. Council*, 3 September 2008 (*Kadi I*); Case T-85/09, *Kadi v. Commission*, 30 September 2010; Joined Cases C-584/10 P, C-593/10 P and C-595/10 P, *Commission and Council v. Kadi*, 18 July 2013 (*Kadi II*); Daniel Halberstam, 'Local, global and plural constitutionalism: Europe meets the world', in Gráinne De Búrca and Joseph H. H. Weiler (eds.), *The Worlds of European Constitutionalism* (Cambridge: Cambridge University Press, 2012), pp. 150, 175–193.

measures based upon the UN Security Council Resolutions against individual suspects.[47] With a view to implementing these Resolutions, the EU legislature adopted the EC Regulations which ordered a freeze on the funds of listed individuals including Mr. Kadi. It was manifest that the UN Sanctions Committee's procedures did not satisfy the requirements of human rights under EU law.[48] Nonetheless, in 2005, the CFI concluded that the Security Council's Resolutions fell outside the ambit of its human rights review, on condition that they observed *jus cogens*, because it attached great importance to the primacy of obligations under the UN Charter (Article 103).[49] However, in 2008, in response to Mr. Kadi's appeal, the ECJ overruled the CFI's judgment and annulled the contested Regulation by reason of human rights violations (*Kadi I* judgment).[50] The ECJ's judgment has two remarkable features. First, unlike the CFI, the ECJ expressed a pluralistic and non-hierarchical view on the relationship between UN law and EU law by denying the primacy of the UN Charter over the autonomous EU legal order.[51] Second, in a similar way as the constitutional review of EU law by national constitutional courts, the ECJ concluded that it could make a full judicial review of the EU secondary legislation implementing the UN Resolutions on the basis of EU human rights.[52] Thereafter, the *Kadi I* judgment was confirmed by the General Court and the Court of

---

[47] Christina Eckes, 'Individuals in a pluralist world: the implications of counterterrorist sanctions' (2013) 2 *Global Constitutionalism* 218–236.

[48] After the ECJ's judgment in 2008, procedures at the Sanctions Committee were considerably improved in favour of the protection of human rights. But the EU courts have maintained a view that the new procedures do not meet such requirements (Case T-85/09, *Kadi v. Commission* (n. 46), para. 128; Joined Cases C-584/10 P, C-593/10 P and C-595/10 P, *Kadi II* (n. 46), paras. 83–84 and 133–134).

[49] The CFI judgment was almost equivalent to the refusal of pluralism and applied a monistic view as in *Costa v. ENEL* to the relationship between EU law and UN law (Case T-315/01, *Kadi v. Council and Commission* (n. 46), paras. 225 and 230–231; Kumm (n. 36), pp. 43–47).

[50] Joined Cases C-402/05 P and C-415/05 P, *Kadi I* (n. 46).

[51] The ECJ held in its *Kadi I* judgment that an international agreement cannot affect the autonomy of the Community legal system (Joined Cases C-402/05 P and C-415/05 P, *Kadi I* (n. 46), para. 282). Since respect for human rights is a condition of the lawfulness of Community acts (ibid., para. 284), the obligations imposed by an international agreement cannot have the effect of prejudicing the constitutional principle including respect for fundamental rights (ibid., para. 285); N. Türküler Isiksel, 'Fundamental rights in the EU after Kadi and Al Barakaat' (2010) 16 *European Law Journal* 551–577, at 560–562.

[52] Joined Cases C-402/05 P and C-415/05 P, *Kadi I* (n. 46), paras. 299–300 and 326.

Justice (*Kadi II* judgment) again,[53] and the position of the *Kadi I* judgment became firmly established case law in the EU.

2.4.6   The acceleration of interactions between constitutional pluralism and global constitutionalism

What aspect of the ECJ's *Kadi I* judgment is meaningful for the interaction between constitutional pluralism and global constitutionalism? In its reasoning, the ECJ underscored the autonomy of EU law that makes EU law unaffected by an international agreement.[54] In its conclusion, the ECJ accepted the equivalent role as that of national constitutional courts as being a guardian of human rights in the setting of the EU's external relationship with the UN. Advocate General Maduro's opinion clearly observes 'the duty of the Court of Justice is to act as the constitutional court of the municipal legal order that is the Community'.[55] Taken all together, as far as the inapplicability of higher law is concerned, this judgment shifted the view taken by constitutional courts of the member states about the relationships between EU law and national constitutions to the global arena, namely the relationships between UN law and EU law.

In sum, until the *Kadi I* judgment, constitutional pluralism had been mostly discussed in the realm of EU law. However, the idea of constitutional pluralism is essentially applicable not only to the EU but also in other transnational situations. Therefore, the *Kadi I* judgment could apply the logic of the constitutional courts' judgments to the UN–EU relationship.[56] As a consequence of this judgment, both the EU courts

[53] Case T-85/09, *Kadi v. European Commission* (n. 46), paras. 121–126; Joined Cases C-584/10 P, C-593/10 P and C-595/10 P, *Kadi II* (n. 46), 18 July 2013, para. 97; Armin Cuyvers, '"Give me one good reason": the unified standard of review for sanctions after *Kadi II*' (2014) 51 *Common Market Law Review* 1759–1788, at 1765–1767.

[54] AG Opinion Maduro, Case C-402/05 P, *Kadi v. Council and Commission* (n. 46), paras. 21 and 37; Joined Cases C-402/05 P and C-415/05 P, *Kadi I* (n. 46), paras. 282 and 314–315.

[55] AG Opinion Maduro, Case C-402/05 P, *Kadi v. Council and Commission* (n. 46), para. 37. This reference indicates the role of the ECJ against the UN legal order. Furthermore, on an analogy with the practice of constitutional courts in the member states, AG Opinions pointed out a possibility that the ECJ might defer to the institutions of another system (ibid., para. 44) and actually applied the reasoning in the *Solange I* judgment to the case concerned (ibid., para. 54) (Daniel Halberstam (n. 46), pp. 192–193; Charles F. Sabel and Oliver Gerstenberg, 'Constitutionalising an overlapping consensus: The ECJ and the emergence of a coordinate constitutional order' (2010) 16 *European Law Journal* 511–550, at 512–513). In contrast, the ECJ's *Kadi I* judgment is less clear about this analogy than the AG Opinion of Maduro.

[56] Armin Cuyvers, 'The *Kadi II* Judgment of the General Court: the ECJ's predicament and the consequences for member states' (2011) 7 *European Constitutional Law Review* 481–510, at 497–498.

and national constitutional courts have become able to respond to inter-ferences of external laws in a similar way.[57] Due to this analogical applica-tion, to say the least, the *Kadi I* judgment has caused the application of constitutional pluralism to the international legal order in general and has strengthened the interactions between constitutional pluralism and global constitutionalism. This causal relationship is indicated by the fact that the *Kadi I* judgment attracted enormous attention from many of the current global constitutionalists.[58] In other words, one can understand that the *Kadi I* judgment has enlarged the size of the window through which the accumulation of constitutional discussions at the European level could flow into discussions at the global level. Nowadays, it seems that constitu-tional pluralism is supplying global constitutionalism with a lot of clues, hints and ideas. For instance, the EU has a much more centralised legal structure than the present international society has, because the EU is supported by sophisticated decision-making procedures as well as by various well-developed executive, legislative and judicial institutions. Moreover, EU law is much more effective than international law because of its applicability in the member states. Constitutional pluralism, none-theless, reveals that one cannot assume a monolithic and hierarchical relationship between EU law and national law. If that is so, it is almost impractical to assume a hierarchical relationship among various constitu-tions in a highly diversified world. Hence, it is quite natural that global constitutionalists do not consider global constitutionalism as being based upon the idea of hierarchical-constitutional order.

3   European legal experiences: universality and particularity: what can we learn from the regional integration taking place in Europe?

3.1   Dependence on European legal experiences: good or bad?

Thanks to the *Kadi I* judgment, constitutional pluralism for the EU has become more linked to global constitutionalism for the entire international society. As the intimate connection between global constitutionalism and

---

[57] Such phenomena could be found before the *Kadi I* judgment (Florence Giorgi and Nicolas Triart, 'National judges, community judges: invitation to a journey through the looking-glass: on the need for jurisdictions to rethink the inter-systemic relations beyond the hierarchical principle' (2008) 14 *European Law Journal* 693–717, at 709) but did not fall under the constitutionalism debate.

[58] The *Kadi I* judgment clearly constitutes a major reason why the new journal of global constitutionalism was launched (Antje Wiener et al. (n. 42), at 1–2; Halberstam (n. 46), pp. 185–187; Klabbers, 'Setting the scene' (n. 7), pp. 1–3).

constitutional pluralism indicates, the current idea of global constitutionalism considerably relies upon the development of the EU legal order. If we take into account the hollowing out of national constitutions in the EU as well as the constitutionalisation of EU law, it makes sense that global constitutionalists keep their eyes on legal experiences concerning the European integration. That is because constitutional discourse is very suitable and persuasive when it explains what is taking place in the EU.

In contrast, there is widespread scepticism about the universality of European constitutional experiences among East Asian scholars.[59] To be frank, interest in global constitutionalism is not so strong in East Asian countries. The general indifference to global constitutionalism seems to be derived partly from a strong tradition of positivism in East Asia. Doubts about the applicability of the EU style of regional integration to East Asia also constitute another basis of that scepticism.[60] It is certain that Europe is unique in various respects, so it, accordingly, differs much from other regions, in particular from East Asia. First of all, Europe is covered and controlled by much denser legal networks than those in East Asia. In Europe, multiple regional legal systems with their own courts horizontally coexist, overlap and interact with each other. What's more is that each of them vertically interacts with national legal systems through their respective institutionalised procedures. As a result of such coexistence with overlap and interaction, the risk of judicial conflicts has become very high. Therefore, in order to avoid the occurrence of contradictory judicial decisions, these courts have to take part in a 'judicial dialogue', whether one likes it or not[61]. Second, as compared with East

---

[59] For example, Hanquin Xue, a Chinese judge of the International Court of Justice, expressed her deep suspicion about the Western origin of international law (Hanquin Xue, 'Meaningful dialogue through a common discourse: law and values in a multi-polar world' (2011) 1 *Asian Journal of International Law* 13–19, at 15, 17).

[60] Most East Asian scholars take a view that the EU cannot be a model of East Asian regional integration (Tamio Nakamura, 'Proposal of the draft charter of the East Asian community: an overview and the basic principles', in Tamio Nakamura (ed.), *East Asian Regionalism from a Legal Perspective: Current Features and a Vision for the Future* (London: Routledge, 2009), pp. 193–214).

[61] Anthony Arnull, 'Judicial dialogue in the European Union', in Julie Dickson and Pavlos Eleftheriadis (eds.), *Philosophical Foundations of European Union Law* (Oxford: Oxford University Press, 2012), pp. 109–133; Vassilios Skouris, 'The role of the Court of Justice of the European Union in the EEA single market', in The EFTA Court (ed.), *The EEA and the EFTA Court: Decentered Integration* (Oxford; Portland, OR: Hart Publishing, 2014), pp. 3–12; Juliane Kokott and Daniel Dittert, 'European Courts in dialogue', in The EFTA Court (ed.) (ibid.), pp. 43–52; Giuseppe Martinico, 'What lies behind Article 4(2) TEU?', in Alejandro Saiz Arnaiz and Carina Alcoberro Llivina (eds.), *National Constitutional Identity and European Integration* (Cambridge: Intersentia,

Asian countries, European countries have already succeeded in sharing common constitutional values and principles, although not to a full extent,[62] through their long-standing participation in various regional systems. With respect to human rights, thanks to the ECHR, they have almost reached similar, if not identical, judicial interpretations and standards on any individual rights.[63] A high level of their affinity in understanding constitutional principles constitutes an essential prerequisite for having effective dialogues between various courts in Europe, because it is difficult for such dialogues to work well without having a common foundation.[64] It is evident that in these respects, East Asia is quite dissimilar from Europe. Above all, the situation in North-East Asia is the opposite. Although it is a fact that even in East Asia, legalisation has increased during the twenty-first century, there is no regional legal framework covering the whole of East Asia (China, Korea and Japan).[65]

Against such a backdrop, how should we evaluate the meaning of European legal experiences for the entire international society from the viewpoint of global constitutionalism? First of all, the fact that a theory predominantly originates from any particular region or state does not in itself undermine its universalizability. East Asian scholars tend to stress East Asian particularity against European universality, but the claim of particularity cannot be a fundamental criticism against that of universality. As long as any particularity has to be assessed on the basis of universality, the former cannot help complementing the latter. In other words, there is no hostile relationship between 'particularism' and

2013), pp. 93–108; Christian Tomuschat, 'The defence of national identity by the German Constitutional Court', in The EFTA Court (ed.) (ibid.), pp. 205–219; François-Xavier Millet, 'How much lenience for how much cooperation? On the first preliminary reference of the French Constitutional Council to the Court of Justice' (2014) 51 *Common Market Law Review* 195–218.

[62] It cannot be denied that many differences between the EU member states still exist in terms of constitutional values (Sionaidh Douglas-Scott, 'The problem of justice in the European Union: values, pluralism, and critical legal justice', in Dickson and Eleftheriadis (eds.) (n. 61), p. 412). 'Sharing values' is always a matter of degree.

[63] Guy Harpaz, 'The European Court of Justice and its relations with the European Court of Human Rights: the quest for enhanced reliance, coherence and legitimacy' (2009) 46 *Common Market Law Review* 105–141, at 108–115, 125–130; Armin von Bogdandy, Mattias Kottmann, Carlino Antpöhler, Johanna Dickschen, Simon Hentrei and Maja Smrkolj, 'Reverse Solange: protecting the essence of fundamental rights against EU member states' (2012) 49 *Common Market Law Review* 489–520, at 509–514.

[64] Harpaz (n. 63), at 125–126.

[65] Takao Suami, 'Regional integration in East Asia and its legalization: can law contribute to the progress of integration in East Asia?', in Nakamura (ed.), *East Asian Regionalism from a Legal Perspective* (n. 60), pp. 169–170, 173–176.

'universalism', and these two ideas reinforce and supplement each other.[66] In contrast, in case East Asians attempt to reject European universality itself, the issue whether European experiences are universal has to be examined. As the history shows, any legal theory has to be born and develop not in a vacuum but in a particular cultural, social and historical environment.[67] To put it differently, any local or regional theory embraces a potential to develop into a worldwide theory. A good example is international law.[68] Therefore, even if we assume that global constitutionalism is predominantly based upon the theory of EU law, this does not in and of itself seem to injure its universality. It is the same with other cases of social science theories which were developed in Europe. In brief, the fact that a theory was born in Europe cannot necessarily undermine its universalist claim.

On the other hand, however, we have to be careful of the risk that too much dependence upon European experiences produces a possibility that global constitutionalism will deviate from being a genuinely universal theory. At the time of its inception, any theory tends to be inevitably influenced by miscellaneous variables which are locally or regionally induced, even if that theory is intended to be universally applied[69]. Through the subsequent process of development, the theory usually extinguishes its non-universal elements and finally acquires its true universality. Global constitutionalism is not an exception to this truism. In various regions throughout the world, Europe is considered to be the most advanced region from the viewpoint of international law, and it is likely to be the first region to face novel legal problems. It is probable that other regions will follow the same path of progress as Europe at some later time, but there is no assurance that this will always happen. Hence, it is necessary to distinguish universal elements of European experiences from those which are specific only to Europe. The important question to

---

[66] Naoki Sakai, 'Modernity and its critique: the problem of universalism and particularism' (1988) 87 *The South Atlantic Quarterly* 475–504, at 480, 487.

[67] Malcolm N. Shaw, *International Law*, 6th ed. (Cambridge: Cambridge University Press, 2008), p. 24.

[68] Modern international law was born in the seventeenth century of Europe, but the scope of its application has been expanded since the nineteenth century, and finally it has become a universal instrument (Stephen C. Neff, *Justice among Nations: A History of International Law* (Cambridge, MA: Harvard University Press, 2014), pp. 310–319).

[69] Emmanuelle Jouannet, 'French and American perspectives on international law: legal cultures and International Law' (2006) 58 *Maine Law Review* 292–335, at 301–323; Anne Peters, 'International legal scholarship under challenge' (2016) *MPIL Research Paper Series No. 2016-11* 1–28, at 2–4.

be answered is how to make a distinction between the two types of experiences.

3.2 The universality of European experiences

3.2.1 Preliminary issue: the legal nature of EU law

3.2.1.1 The sui generis nature of EU law The core of European legal experiences is the development of EU law. What aspects of EU law can be considered to be fruitful for the entire international society? In order to answer this question, one has to begin by examining the legal nature of EU law. Assuming that EU law is completely different from international law, the impact of EU law theory on global constitutionalism cannot avoid being limited, and on the contrary, if the EU law is akin to international law, EU law theory can fairly affect the theory of international law. Actually, it seems that global constitutionalists are not strongly concerned about this, but whether or not EU law is substantively distinct from public international law has been still an unsolved question.[70] For that reason, the legal nature of EU law has to constitute a starting point for examining the transferability of EU law experiences to international law in general.

The EU was founded as an international organisation on the basis of an international treaty among the member states. Because of this origin, close connections are presumed between EU law and international law. Nevertheless, the ECJ established the identity of EU law as a sui generis legal order in the 1960s, and thereafter it repeatedly emphasised the stark differences between EU law and public international law in terms of legal nature.[71] Besides the ECJ's case law, most scholars of EU law consider EU law something different from international law, irrespective of their use of the terminology 'sui generis' or 'supranational'.[72] As Joseph Weiler

---

[70] Weiler (n. 1), pp. 296–297.

[71] Case 26/62, *Van Gend en Loos v. Nederlandse Administratie der Belastingen* [1963] ECR1, 12; Case 6/64, *Costa v. ENEL* (n. 22); Case 14/68, *Wilhelm v. Bundeskartellamt* [1969] ECR1, para. 6; Opinion 1/91, *Draft Treaty on the Establishment of a European Economic Area* [1991] ECR I-6102, paras. 14–22; Joined Cases C-402/05 P and C-415/05 P, *Kadi I* (n. 46), paras. 281–282; Commission of the European Communities, *Thirty Years of Community Law* (Luxembourg: Office for Official Publications of the European Communities, 1983), pp. 33–41.

[72] Lenaerts and Van Nuffel (n. 24), pp. 16–19; Robert Schütze, *European Constitutional Law* (Cambridge: Cambridge University Press, 2012), pp.77–79; Sionaidh Douglas-Scott, *Constitutional Law of the European Union* (Harlow: Longman, 2002), pp. 277–281; Allan Rosas and Lorna Armati, *EU Constitutional Law: An Introduction*, 2nd rev. ed.

rightly mentioned, after the constitutionalisation of EU law, American and European scholars of international law took less interest in EU law, because it was no longer considered international law.[73] It is to be noted that this tendency is more obvious in East Asia. To be sure, the attributes of EU law are different from those of ordinary international law in several important respects, including: (1) the centralised system of legislation, (2) the compulsory jurisdiction of the EU courts, (3) the evolution of human rights protection and (4) the primacy and the direct effect of EU law.[74] If one focuses on these differences, it might be doubtful that constitutional pluralism in the EU can be linked to global constitutionalism for international society.

3.2.1.2 Distinctions between EU law and international law   However, the unique features of EU law are not decisive in entirely distinguishing EU law from international law.[75] In particular, because of recent phenomena and changes in the field of EU law as well as the development of international law, the differences between EU law and international law have become more blurred than before.

3.2.1.2.1. From the perspectives of EU law   On the side of EU law, the following points are worth mentioning. The first point is the aforesaid constitutional tension between EU law and national constitutions, which has impaired the plausibility of supranational discourse on EU law by the ECJ. As a consequence of such tension, EU law has partly lost a ground for why it is considered to be of a sui generis nature.[76] The second point is the adoption of legal measures for the sake of solving the sovereign debt crisis from 2009. These measures have added new elements to the distinctions between EU law and international law. One of the conspicuous features concerning those measures is the combination of EU law instruments with international law instruments. A very typical example is the Treaty on Stability, Coordination and Governance (TSCG)

(Oxford: Hart Publishing, 2012), pp. 12–19. However, some argue that EU law is still a subsystem of international law (Bruno de Witte, 'EU law: is it international law?', in Catherine Barnard and Steve Peers (eds.), *European Union Law* (Oxford: Oxford University Press, 2014), pp. 174–195) or that the separation of EU law from international law is doubtful (Trevor C. Hartley, *Constitutional Problems of the European Union* (Oxford: Hart Publishing,1999), pp. 138–139).

[73] Weiler (n. 1), pp. 296–297.
[74] Lenaerts and Van Nuffel (n. 24), pp. 16–19; Weiler (n. 1), p. 295.
[75] Takao Suami, 'EU law, EEA law and international law: the myth of supranational law and its implications for international law', in The EFTA Court (ed.) (n. 61), pp. 529, 535–540.
[76] Suami (n. 75), pp. 536–537.

concluded in 2012.[77] Remarkably, the TSCG is complicatedly intertwined with EU law. Namely, the EU Treaties are complemented by the TSCG, and it is surprising that the TSCG is complemented by EU law, too (Article 5 (1)). Due to such mutual complementarity, in fact, the TSCG and EU law constitute one united body of law, so the jurisdiction of the ECJ totally covers the TSCG (Article 8).[78] The TSCG arrangement demonstrates a high level of interdependence between EU law and international law, and it further raises reasonable doubt about the complete separation in nature between them. The third point is the changeable distance between EU law and European Economic Area (EEA) law. At the outset, the EEA was considered to be an ordinary international organisation, because the EEA Agreement did not intend to transfer legislative and judicial powers to supranational institutions.[79] According to this view, EEA law must essentially differ from EU law, because EEA law is identified with international law. However, the initial understanding of EEA law has been modified to some extent, and, as of today, both the EU courts and the European Free Trade Association (EFTA) Court have expressed their recognition that EEA law is akin to EU law.[80] The affinity between EU law and EEA law is empirically

[77] In order to maintain the financial stability of the eurozone, the TSCG intends to foster budgetary discipline and to improve the governance of the eurozone (Art. 1 (1)). Originally, this aim was supposed to be achieved through the treaty amendments. However, after the veto exercised by two member states, the EU member states changed their mind and decided to rely upon an intergovernmental agreement, namely the TSCG (Kaarlo Tuori and Klaus Tuori, *The Eurozone Crisis: A Constitutional Analysis*, (Cambridge: Cambridge University Press, 2014), pp. 109–110 and 171–180). This is why the incorporation of the TSCG's provisions into the EU Treaties is legally expected within five years (Arts. 16 and 10).

[78] Suami (n. 75), pp. 537–538.

[79] Preamble of Protocol 35 on the implementation of EEA Rules. In its opinion, the ECJ observed in 1991 that unlike the EEC Treaty, which was a constitutional charter, the EEA Agreement was an international treaty, without the transfer of sovereign rights to an international organisation, which merely created rights and obligations between the contracting parties (Opinion 1/91, *Draft Treaty on the Establishment of a European Economic Area* (n. 71), paras. 20–21). The EFTA Court has also treated EEA law differently from EU law from the beginning (Case E-4/01, *Karlsson v. Iceland*, 30 May 2002, para. 28; Case E-1/07, *Criminal Proceedings against A*, 3 October 2007, paras. 40–41; Suami (n. 75), pp. 532–533).

[80] Although the ECJ has not formally overruled its initial understanding, both the CFI (currently the General Court) and the ECJ have taken the view that EEA law is closer to EU law than ordinary international law when considering similarities between EU law and EEA law in terms of their aims, scopes, institutions and substantive provisions (Case T-115/94, *Opel Austria v. Council*, [1997] ECR II-39, paras. 107–108; Case C-431/11, *UK v. Council*, 26 September 2013, para. 50; Suami (n. 75), pp. 533–534). In addition to the

supported by the practical application of EEA law. Unlike legally binding rulings by the ECJ, the EFTA Court's opinions are of an advisory nature and legally non-binding. Nevertheless, it is reported that the actual effectiveness of the EFTA Court's advisory opinions is comparable to that of the ECJ's rulings.[81] This is because despite the lack of binding effect, most advisory opinions are properly followed by the national courts of the EFTA countries.[82] These examinations on the relationship between EU law and EEA law are enough to raise a doubt about the strict distinction between EU law and international law as a whole.

3.2.1.2.2. From the perspectives of international law   On the side of international law, it is noteworthy that international law itself has developed over the last several decades after the 1960s in the direction of EU law. This development has made the discussion on this issue more complicated. In the 1960s, the contrasts between EU law and international law were evident. In those days, EU law established the principle of direct effect, by which EU law became able to confer legal rights to be protected before national courts upon individuals.[83] By means of this principle, not only the member states but also individuals have become a subject of EU law. In contrast to EU law, international law concentrated on the relationships between sovereign states at that time. In the 1960s, international law paid much less attention to non-state actors than today. However, international law extended its scope afterwards. By reason of: (1) the progress of human rights treaties, (2) the spread of investment treaties providing investor–state dispute settlement (ISDS), (3) the

EU courts, while being still aware of the differences between EEA and EU law, the EFTA Court has also distinguished EEA law from international law in a classical sense (Case E-9/97, *Erla María Sveinbjörnsssssdóttir v. Iceland*, 10 December 1998, paras. 57–59; Suami (n. 75), pp. 534).

[81] Maria E. Méndez-Pinedo, *EC and EEA Law: A Comparative Study of the Effectiveness of European Law* (Groningen: Europa Law Publishing, 2009), pp. 150 and 170–171.

[82] For example, the Supreme Court of Iceland stated that advisory opinions should be in principle followed (Méndez-Pinedo (n. 81), p. 181). It is reported that following the EFTA Court's opinion in the *Sigmarsson* case (Case E-3/11, *Sigmarsson v. the Central Bank of Iceland*, 14 December 2011), the plaintiff withdrew the case before the judgment of the national court (Dóra Guðmundsdóttir, 'Case E-3/11 Sigmarsson v. The Central Bank of Iceland, Judgment of the EFTA Court of 14 December 2011, [2012] 1 CMLR 50 "not so fast!"' (2012) 49 *Common Market Law Review* 2019–2038, at 2037).

[83] Pierre Pescatore, 'The doctrine of "direct effect": an infant disease of Community law' (1983) 8 *European Law Review* 155–177; Ilan Sebba, 'The doctrine of "direct effect": a malignant disease of Community law' (1995) 22 *Legal Issues of Economic Integration* 35–58; Sacha Prechal, 'Does direct effect still matter?' (2000) 37 *Common Market Law Review* 1047–1069.

emergence of international criminal courts and (4) the activation of non-state actors such as non-governmental organisations (NGOs) in international organisations, international law has become applicable to individuals such as natural persons and multinational corporations at present. The specific nature of EU law has to be perceived by using international law as a yardstick. However, the position of the yardstick itself has come closer to EU law to some extent, at least.[84]

3.2.1.2.3. Lack of compulsory enforcement   Finally, as regards their legal enforcement, both EU law and international law share one common feature. Namely, it must be noted that EU law cannot be enforced in the same manner as national law is enforced. In the case of national law, national law enforcement authorities are generally able to compel any party in default to comply with the sentence of national courts. EU law is also enforced by national institutions as well as EU institutions, but once the national authorities do not observe EU law, EU authorities will face difficulties to actually ensure compliance with EU law. As a matter of course, the non-observance of EU law is unlawful under EU law. A member state which has breached EU law must be subject to infringement proceedings before the CJEU (TFEU Articles 258 and 259). However, the CJEU's judgment finding an infringement is declaratory in nature, and even if the member state concerned is ordered to make a penalty payment due to its failure to comply with a judgment by the CJEU, it is not certain how the EU institutions will be able to force the member state to make a payment (TFEU Article 260).[85] Therefore, complying with the judgment has to ultimately rely upon voluntary acts of that member state.[86] In sum, although most European law scholars do not stress this point, the lack of there being a compelling power is a common feature between EU law and international law including EEA

[84] Suami (n. 75), p. 536.
[85] In case a national authority refuses to make a payment which is ordered by a national court, compulsory enforcement against the property of the state is possible in many countries. This is different from a case of penalty payments ordered by the CJEU. However, the finding of infringement constitutes a ground of liability claim against the member state under the principle of state liability established by the Francovich ruling (Joined Cases C-6 and C-9/90, *Francovich and Others* [1991] ECR I-5357, para. 35).
[86] According to the Annual Report for 2014, at the end of 2014, there existed seven cases where the member states concerned had not complied with the judgments of infringements, despite the rulings on penalty payments under Art. 260 (2) of TFEU (European Commission, Monitoring the Application of Union Law, 2014 Annual Report, COM (2015) 329, at 16). However, it is not clear from the report whether or not they had paid such payments.

law.[87] Accordingly, in terms of its enforcement, EU law is closer to international law than national law.

It can be concluded from this analysis that the distinction between the two legal orders is not absolute and unconditional, but it is a matter of degree in one sense.[88] In other words, whether or not EU law is considered part of international law, it is possible to examine both legal orders in a common framework. If so, the experiences of EU law including constitutional pluralism must be meaningful for not only Europe but also East Asia.

3.2.2   Contributions from EU law to global constitutionalism

Since EU law still has many things in common with international law, the experiences of EU law are able to offer valuable suggestions to other regions. To put it differently, international law can bring in the fruit of the progress of EU law for its further development. It is probable that the integration of EU law into international law will affect what international law ought to be. The evolution of global constitutionalism with the participation of constitutional pluralism confirms the dynamics of this interaction. Which aspects of EU law can be useful for other regions including East Asia? This is the next question to be answered from a viewpoint of global constitutionalism.

3.2.2.1   Constitutionalism beyond states   The most substantial importance for global constitutionalism is that the progress of EU law has clearly opened up to the rest of the world a possibility that the application of constitutionalism is feasible in the sphere beyond states.[89]

Constitutionalism is a concept with different meanings, but it was previously discussed only within the sphere of nation states. Constitutionalism in the states is associated with national law-making

[87] Takao Suami, 'EU-ho to kokusai-ho: tagentekina hochitsujyokan to EU-hochitsujyo no seishitsu' (EU law and international law: 'pluralistic perspectives on legal order' and 'nature of EU legal order'), in Koji Fukuda (ed.), *Tagenkasuru EU Gabanansu* (Multipolarization of EU Governance) (Tokyo: Waseda University Press, 2011), pp. 7, 26–28.
[88] Suami (n. 75), pp. 535–538 and 539–540.
[89] Ernst-Ulrich Petersmann, 'State sovereignty, popular sovereignty and individual sovereignty: from constitutional nationalism to multilevel constitutionalism in international economic law?', in Wenhua Shan, Penelope Simons and Dalvinder Singh (eds.), *Redefining Sovereignty in International Economic Law* (Oxford: Hart Publishing, 2008), pp. 27, 58.

authority that is derived from national sovereignty.[90] The national authority that is the supreme authority of the land is a full-fledged authority without limitation, and it is empowered to provide legitimacy with national laws. The same type of authority does not exist for international society. However, in the case of the EU, a number of competences (or powers) that belong to national sovereignty have been transferred from the member states to the EU.[91] The principle of conferral of competences suggests that EU competences are derivative from its member states (TEU Article 5 (1) and (2)), but this origin of EU competences does not make the application of constitutionalism at the EU level unnecessary or redundant. This is because, as long as transferred competences are exercised pursuant to the EU Treaties, national constitutionalism can no longer directly control their exercise. It is true that there is a difference in nature between national authority and EU authority, because unlike national competences, for example, EU competences are not sufficiently supported by a compelling power, but the idea of constitutionalism has been playing an important role in the EU. All things considered, the EU law experiences demonstrate that: first, the existence of a single exclusive authority is not a prerequisite for the application of constitutionalism, and second, constitutionalism can be argued in a pluralistic environment where multiple authorities at the same or different level coexist and work together. Hence, East Asian scholars must be made aware of these significances of the EU law experiences.[92]

3.2.2.2 The Potential to Transform Sovereignty The idea of constitutionalism beyond states is grounded on the present situation of state sovereignty in the EU. National constitutionalism is based on national constitutions that are closely related to state sovereignty. State sovereignty is also fundamental to international law and has been much

---

[90] Michel Troper, 'Sovereignty', in Michel Rosenfeld and András Sajó (eds.), *The Oxford Handbook of Comparative Constitutional Law* (Oxford: Oxford University Press, 2012), pp. 350, 355 and 362–363.

[91] Ibid., pp. 357–359.

[92] Some Japanese scholars approve of the usefulness of global constitutionalism, although they take a careful approach to it (Masami Maruyama, 'Kokuren anzenhosho rijikai niokeru rikkensyugi no kanosei to kadai' (The prospects of constitutionalism in the United Nations Security Council) (2012) 111 *Kokusaiho Gaiko Zassi* (*The Journal of International Law and Policy*) 20–46; Kazuyori Ito, 'Kokusaikeizaiho niokeru kihankozo no tokushitsu to sono dotai' (The normative structure and its dynamics in international economic law: an analysis from the perspective of constitutionalization) (2012) 111 *Kokusaiho Gaiko Zassi* (*The Journal of International Law and Policy*) 47–73).

discussed by a number of scholars. This is because 'sovereignty' gives a legal ground to national authority both internally and externally, and it has been traditionally understood as being absolute, permanent and indivisible.[93] While the concept of sovereignty is referred to less than before by international lawyers,[94] this concept still has very strong currency in East Asian countries as well as developing countries in the Global South. Sovereignty continues to be an issue in international law, and it is clear that the development of both EU and EU law is one of the incidents which has inspired the reconsideration of the classical concept of sovereignty.[95]

In the field of EU law, the question of whether or not state sovereignty of the member states has been transformed has not been solved yet. On the one hand, some scholars understand that the member states have partly lost their sovereignty on the assumption that sovereignty is divisible.[96] On the other hand, focusing on '*Kompetenz-Kompetenz*', meaning the competence to determine one's own competences, which is a core element of sovereignty, other scholars argue that the EU member states still hold absolute perfect sovereignty, irrespective of the transfer of certain sovereign powers to the EU.[97] The discussion of this question is

[93] Lassa Oppenheim, *International Law: A Treatise*, 8th ed. (London: Longmans, 1955), pp. 12–123 (edited by Hersch Lauterpacht); Troper (n. 90), pp. 354–362.

[94] Collin Warbrick, 'States and recognition', in Malcolm D. Evans (ed.), *International Law*, 2nd ed. (Oxford: Oxford University Press, 2006), pp. 217, 219. Instead of or in addition to sovereignty, many frequently use 'jurisdiction' which refers to particular aspects of the general legal competences (such as rights, liberties and powers) constituting sovereignty (James Crawford, *Brownlie's Principles of Public International Law*, 8th ed. (Oxford: Oxford University Press, 2012), pp. 204–206 and 456; Shaw (n. 67), pp. 645–647; Martin Dixon, *Textbook on International Law*, 7th ed. (Oxford: Oxford University Press, 2013), pp. 148–181).

[95] William Maley, 'Trust, legitimacy and the sharing of sovereignty', in Trudy Jacobsen, Charles Sampford and Ramesh Thakur (eds.), *Re-Envisioning Sovereignty: The End of Westphalia* (Aldershot: Ashgate, 2008), pp. 287, 296; Paul Keal, 'Indigenous sovereignty', in Jacobsen, Sampford and Thakur (eds.) (ibid.), pp. 315, 326; Petersmann (n. 89), pp. 27, 58–60.

[96] Jean-Voctor Louis, *The Community Legal Order*, 3rd ed. (Luxembourg: Office for Official Publications of the European Communities, 1995), p. 13; MacCormick (n. 32), pp. 131–133, 141–142.

[97] Daniela Obradovic, 'Community law and the doctrine of divisible sovereignty' (1993) 20 *Legal Issues of Economic Integration* 1–20, at 10–14; Hartley (n. 72), pp. 179–181; Martin Loughlin, 'Ten tenets of sovereignty', in Walker (ed.) (n. 32), pp. 55, 81–83; Cezary Mik, 'State sovereignty and European integration: public international law, EU law and constitutional law in the Polish context', in Walker (ed.) (n. 32), pp. 367, 390–393; René Barents, *The Autonomy of Community Law* (The Hague: Kluwer Law International, 2004), pp. 37–39 and 218–221; Troper (n. 90), pp. 357–359, 361–362.

still open, and both of the present positions are not entirely exempt from criticism.[98] Constitutional pluralists perceive the existence of constitutional authority at the EU level, although EU authority is not exactly the same as national authority in terms of its substance.[99] As a consequence, some of them are in favour of acknowledging the transformation of state sovereignty in the EU.[100]

Provided that the classical conception of sovereignty can be modified and that the new conception of sovereignty can be in existence at the transnational level, the reconceptualisation of sovereignty would be useful to the justification of global constitutionalism. But the transformation of classical sovereignty is not necessarily a prerequisite for global constitutionalism. This is because global constitutionalism is grounded on the autonomous principles of constitutionalism, which can be constructed independently of sovereignty at the national or international level.[101] Accordingly, global constitutionalism does not need to be

[98] First, with regard to the former position, it is criticised that the transferred powers are essentially featured as policymaking competences and do not include competences for compulsory enforcement within the member states. According to critics, sovereignty is an inclusive concept covering both policymaking and its implementation. Second, with regard to the latter position, critics argue that even if being so essential to sovereignty, 'Kompetenz-Kompetenz' is not equal to sovereignty itself. The fundamental feature of the latter position lies in emphasising a distinction between sovereignty and transferred powers. As national constitutional courts presuppose in their judgments (*Brunner v. European Union Treaty* (n. 27), paras. 39–45; French Constitutional Council, Décision no 2007–560 DC (n. 28), para. 9), however, sovereignty is not separable from a substantial amount of policymaking powers (Takao Suami, 'EU/EC hochitsujyo to Lisbon Jyoyaku' (EU/EC legal order and Lisbon Treaty), in Koji Fukuda (ed.), *EU Ohsyu Togo Kenkyu, Lisbon Jyoyaku igo no Ohsyu Gabanansu* (*EU and European Integration Research: European Governance after Lisbon Treaty*) (Tokyo: Seibundo, 2009), pp. 76, 80–82, 87–91).

[99] Walker asserts the transformation of derivative authority into original authority (Neil Walker, 'Late sovereignty in the European Union', in Walker (ed.) (n. 32), pp. 3, 21); Maduro explains that constitutional pluralism recognises 'the legitimacy of the EU constitutional claim' as well as that of national constitutional claims (Maduro (n. 33), p. 76); Mattias Kumm, 'The moral point of constitutional pluralism: defining the domain of legitimate institutional civil disobedience and conscientious objection', in Dickson and Eleftheriadis (eds.) (n. 61), pp. 216, 234–238; Jürgen Habermas, 'The crisis of the European Union in the light of a constitutionalization of international law' (2012) 23 *European Journal of International Law* 335–348, at 342–343.

[100] MacCormick argues that a member state no longer remains 'in the full classical sense a sovereign state', both externally and internally (MacCormick (n. 32), p. 141).

[101] According to Kumm, in the case of global constitutionalism, the authority of constitution does not rest on popular sovereignty but on 'its authorization by the formal, jurisdictional, procedural, and substantive principles' (Kumm (n. 20), pp. 267–269, 272–290); O'Donoghue also specifies constitutionalism as 'norms of constitutionalism'

necessarily involved in sovereignty issues. This is a point of difference between constitutional pluralism in EU law and global constitutionalism. As explained in the previous section, constitutional pluralism proceeds on the premise of constitutional authority that is based upon pooled sovereign powers at the EU level, but global constitutionalism does not share such a premise. However, this does not mean that global constitutionalism has no interest in sovereignty issues at all. On the contrary, the overcoming of state sovereignty is inherent in the idea of global constitutionalism that is ultimately founded on individuals. Global constitutionalism is likely to be an idea which challenges traditional state sovereignty and tries to replace or transform it.[102] It is somewhat difficult to discuss global constitutionalism on the assumption of the traditional conception of sovereignty, although it is not impossible. In this context, examining sovereignty debate in EU law is thought provoking for global constitutionalism. Legal practice in the EU deviates from the all-or-nothing status of state sovereignty, and it makes the traditional conception of state sovereignty doubtful. In any case, EU law is good evidence which empirically reveals any modifications to the absoluteness of sovereignty. For that reason, EU law experiences contribute much to the justification of global constitutionalism.

3.2.3   The relevance of European legal experiences

How EU law experiences in the EU affect global constitutionalism varies according to the situation. In particular, two situations must be distinguished. The first situation is 'international organisations', and the second one is 'domestic settings'.

3.2.3.1   Global constitutionalism and international organisations   As the EU indicates, international organisations may have constitutional

---

that establish the relationship between the actors with a system (Aoife O'Donoghue, 'International constitutionalism and the state' (2013) 11 *International Journal of Constitutional Law* 1021–1045, at 1032; Dunhoff and Trachtman, 'A functional approach to international constitutionalization', in Dunoff and Trachtman (eds.), *Ruling the World?* (n. 3), pp. 9–10, 19–22.

[102] For example, Anne Peters discussed the replacement of state sovereignty with humanity (Peters, 'Are we moving towards constitutionalization' (n. 8), pp. 120–121 and 129–130) and the transformation of traditional state sovereignty into humanised state sovereignty (Peters, 'Humanity as the A and Ω of sovereignty' (n. 8), at 514–522). Both she and Mattias Kumm rejected the idea of sovereignty as ultimate authority (Peters (n. 5), at 587; Mattias Kumm, 'Constitutionalism and the cosmopolitan state' (2013) *NYU School of Law, Public Law Research Paper No. 13–68 1–28*, at 7); Kleinlein (n. 4), at 415.

authority, and several international organisations such as the UN and the WTO are also regarded as having similar authority.[103] This is a reason why global constitutionalism chiefly targets international organisations.[104] When one reflects on the recent expansive role of international organisations, the necessity of applying constitutional principles to the exercise of their powers is obvious for many actors in the current international society. It is probable that even East Asians do not raise an objection to this necessity. This is because the necessity was clearly revealed by a series of targeted-sanction cases. In the *Kadi I* judgment, the ECJ communicated a clear message that any UN procedures to impose targeted sanctions should keenly require innovations to protect interests of individuals from the viewpoint of the rule of law, due process and judicial review.[105]

In response to that judgment, the UN Security Council has already brought about significant procedural improvements in the UN sanction regime, including the introduction of the Ombudsperson and the reinforcement of its powers, although they are not fully sufficient to meet human rights requirements.[106] Clearly, the ECJ's *Kadi I* judgment inspired a reform of the UN procedures for targeted sanctions, and the Security Council's reaction suggests that constitutional principles are not only shared by the international society as a whole but also actually serve a function of determining a course of action in this UN reform. In sum, as this interaction between the ECJ and the Security Council shows, EU law is able to offer international organisations useful suggestions to control their powers under constitutional principles. As regards the application of global constitutionalism to international organisations, the EU law experiences including constitutional pluralism can be a good reference point because of the relative affinity between the EU and other organisations.

---

[103] John H. Jackson, 'Sovereignty: outdated concept or new approaches', in Shan, Simons and Singh (eds.) (n. 89), pp. 3–25; Peters (n. 5), at 595–596.

[104] Peters (n. 6), pp. 266–269; Kleinlein (n. 4), at 403–404.

[105] Joined Cases C-402/05 P and C-415/05 P, *Kadi I* (n. 46), paras. 321–326. In addition to the ECJ, the ECtHR also made full judicial review of national measures on the basis of the UN measures in the light of the ECHR (*Nada v. Switzerland* (Application No. 10593/089) [GC], 12 September 2012; *Al-Dulmi and Montana Management Inc. v. Switzerland* (Application No. 5809/08), 26 November 2013).

[106] Larrisa J. van den Herik, 'Peripheral hegemony in the quest to ensure Security Council accountability for its individualized UN sanction regimes' (2014) 19 *Journal of Conflict and Security Law* 427–449, at 438–444; Security Council Resolution 1904, S/RES/1904 (2009); Security Council Resolution 1989, S/RES/1989 (2011); Joined Cases C-584/10 P, C-593/10 P and C-595/10 P, *Kadi II* (n. 46), para. 133.

3.2.3.2   Global constitutionalism and domestic settings   Unlike with international organisations, the application of constitutional principles to domestic affairs is more problematic.

International law mainly controlled interstate relationships in the past, but it has now become more relevant to the domestic policies of states through the process of having responded to various worldwide problems.[107] In addition, there has been an expansion of international law enforcement on the initiative of individuals. Namely, the direct application of international law before national courts has become a general trend in international society.[108] As a result of an increase in the level of mutual communication between national and international law, their interdependence has deepened to a phase which has never been achieved before. By reason of such growing interdependence, global constitutionalism also recognises that national and international law are actually co-constitutive and interdependent, forming an integrative whole, and then it aims at overcoming a rigorous divide between international law and national law.[109] Therefore, national law, part of it at least, has come within the range of global constitutionalism. To be concrete, global constitutionalism has to get involved in domestic conditions surrounding individuals, and if any domestic conditions are harmful to individuals, transnational constitutionalism will intervene in the specific domestic affairs for the purpose of compensating for any insufficiency in the respective domestic constitutionalism.[110] This means that constitutional principles shared by international society have to penetrate the shield of national borders. According to a common view, however, the status of international law in a national legal order is a matter to be determined by national law.[111] Besides that, even in cases where national courts acknowledge the direct applicability of international law, it is not rare that these courts are reluctant to find violations of international law.[112] Being subject

---

[107] Anne-Marie Slaughter and William Burke-White, 'The future of international law is domestic (or, the European way of law)', in Janne Nijman and André Nollkaemper (eds.), *New Perspectives on the Divide between National and International Law* (Oxford: Oxford University Press, 2007), pp. 110, 111–116.

[108] Anne Peters, 'Membership in the global constitutional community', in Klabbers, Peters and Ulfstein (eds.) (n. 7), pp. 153, 165–166.

[109] Kumm (n. 102), at 7–23; Peters (n. 5), at 580, 591–592.

[110] Peters (n. 5), at 610.

[111] Anne Peters, 'The globalization of state constitutions', in Nijman and Nollkaemper (eds.) (n. 107), pp. 251, 260–266; Crawford (n. 94), pp. 55–59.

[112] The practice of Japanese courts is an example in point (Yuji Iwasawa, *International Law Human Rights and Japanese Law: The Impact of International Law on Japanese Law* (Oxford: Clarendon, 1998), pp. 288–306).

to these limitations, global constitutionalism must elucidate how constitutional principles can affect what national law should be and can ensure the compatibility between national law and international law as much as possible. In this respect, the legal experiences in the EU are also helpful to the entire international society.

An important point to be discussed here is the need to establish a system in which individuals can take an initiative in invoking international law before national courts. The history of EU law demonstrates that the driving force behind the continuous progress of EU law was supplied by individuals. A major cause of the success of EU law is the development of the EU case law, by which individuals can become principal actors of the EU legal order as much as both EU institutions and the member states. In this context, it must be pointed out that the famous *Van Gend en Loos* ruling took note of 'the vigilance of individuals concerned to protect their rights'.[113] As this ruling openly declares, within domestic settings, individuals have great potential to play a role as accelerators of international law, as long as it concerns their interests.[114] Assuming that international law embodying constitutional principles confers on individuals more rights than those of national law, it will be quite natural for individuals to try to invoke international rights at all possible forums.[115] As a consequence, national public institutions, in particular national courts, will have to be under pressure to reconsider existing domestic standards. In sum, individual claims might trigger and establish a virtuous cycle towards the amelioration of people's conditions. Individual participation is consistent with the idea of individual-based international law, because inasmuch as individuals are recognised as international actors, they must be given a space for their energetic activity within international society.[116]

---

[113] Case 26/62, *Van Gend en Loos* (n. 71), 13.

[114] Luis Cabrera, 'Diversity and cosmopolitan democracy: avoiding global democratic relativism' (2015) 4 *Global Constitutionalism* 18–48, at 18–19.

[115] Cabrera presents an Indian minority suffering caste discrimination as evidence (Cabrera (n. 114), at 39–42). Iwasawa also explains the rapid growth of Japanese NGOs' interest in the Japanese government's reports under the International Covenant on Civil and Political Rights (the ICCPR) and mentions a number of Japanese courts' cases in which individuals invoked the ICCPR (Iwasawa (n. 112), pp. 9–11, 51–53).

[116] Needless to say, external pressure with domestic conditions of individuals usually causes serious tension with national authorities. Such tension may have an adverse effect of harming constitutional principles at a worldwide level. In order to escape from this problem, equal participation of all stakeholders in the norm-formation process must be emphasised. It is also important to consider to what extent the discourse of global constitutionalism will permeate the entire international society.

3.3   European experiences in dispute

3.3.1   Constitutional principles as a point of divergence

Another aspect of the European legal experiences is their non-universality or their European particularity. Which elements of the EU law experiences are specific to Europe and might misguide global constitutionalism? This is the next question to be answered. It is likely that examining this question will be useful to save global constitutionalism from falling into the pitfall of unconscious Eurocentrism.

Global constitutionalism is intrinsically a value-oriented idea and grounded upon sharing universal constitutional principles which are inspired by domestic constitutionalism mainly in Western countries.[117] If these principles were not widely shared in the present international society, global constitutionalism would not be feasible throughout the world. Hence, whether or not constitutional principles can be discerned at a worldwide level is a point of divergence between 'global constitutionalism' and 'legal pluralism'. Nico Krisch is probably a leading advocate of the latter. His stark criticism against global constitutionalism is based upon the assumption that the normative elements of constitutionalism cannot be reconciled with the diverse reality of international society.[118] Besides him, not a few East Asians are sceptical of sharing a commitment to the same constitutional principles in the current international climate.[119]

3.3.2   Descriptive and normative ideas

In order to examine this issue more closely, it is necessary to take note of the fact that as stated before, global constitutionalism consists of both descriptive and normative dimensions. The two dimensions are intertwined with each other and inseparable. The normative dimension of global constitutionalism intends to narrow any gap between the reality and the ideal. This supposes that the present state of affairs in the world may change in the future under the influence of global constitutionalism. For example, if East Asian countries confront severe human rights

---

[117] Rainer Wahl, 'In defence of "constitution"', in Petra Dobner and Martin Loughlin (eds.), *The Twilight of Constitutionalism?* (Oxford: Oxford University Press, 2010), pp. 220, 229–232.

[118] He assumes that global law ('post-national law' in his term) is 'a frame comprised of different orders and their norms', which never reaches 'one integrated legal order for the globe' (Nico Krisch, *Beyond Constitutionalism: The Pluralistic Structure of Postnational Law* (Oxford; New York: Oxford University Press, 2010), p. 12).

[119] Xue (n. 59), at 17.

violations resulting from targeted sanctions by the UN, as the EU did in
the *Kadi* cases,[120] some law reforms following global constitutionalism
will be likely to ensue in East Asia. Accordingly, divergences between
existing conditions and ideal conditions do not constitute effective
criticism against global constitutionalism, because the former conditions should not be considered as being perpetually unchangeable.
Therefore, the point to be examined must be whether it is really
impossible to narrow the gap between the present state of affairs and
the ideal conditions. Generally speaking, we cannot predict or prove
that it will be impossible to narrow the existing gap,[121] but we can only
reflect about the likelihood of such a reduction.

3.3.3   A common commitment to constitutional principles

An outright attack upon global constitutionalism entails an overall denial
of constitutionalism in international society. However, constitutional
elements have already become deeply rooted in international society.
Pluralism criticises global constitutionalism for the reason that there is
diversity of existing principles (such as human rights, the rule of law and
democracy) among countries or regions. Diversity is real, but as the
following section will reveal, first, pluralism's emphasis on diversity is
too extreme, and, second, such diversity does not justify the rejection of
global constitutionalism in every situation.

3.3.3.1   A commitment to constitutional values   Regarding the first
point, in addition to *jus cogens*, most countries in the world currently share

---

[120] In November 2014, the Japanese legislature enacted a law for the purpose of freezing
assets of terrorists on the basis of the UN Security Council's Resolutions (*Kokusai-Rengo
Anzenhoshorijikai-ketsugi Dai 1267 Go-to wo fumae Wagakuni ga jittsushisuru Kokusai-
Teroristo no Zaisan no Toketsu-to nikansuru Tokubetsu-Sochi-Ho* [Special Measure Law
on the Freezing Assets of International Terrorists on the Basis of the United Nations
Security Council's Resolution No. 1267 and Others], Law No. 124 of 2014).

[121] Unlike the case in Europe, human rights had been considered a domestic issue in Asia
until recently. However, in 2009, the Association of Southeast Asian Nations (ASEAN)
members agreed to set up the ASEAN Intergovernmental Commission on Human
Rights (Cha-Am Hua Hin Declaration on the Intergovernmental Commission on
Human Rights, 23 October 2009), and in 2012, they also adopted the ASEAN Human
Rights Declaration (Phnom Penh Statement on the Adoption of the ASEAN Human
Rights Declaration, 18 November 2012). The ASEAN human rights system is the fourth
regional system for the protection of human rights and has already contributed to the
progress of human rights in South-East Asia (Gerard Clarke, 'The evolving ASEAN
human rights system: the ASEAN Human Rights Declaration of 2012' (2012) 11
Northwestern Journal of International Human Rights 1–27).

the same commitment to constitutional principles by having concluded a number of international law instruments. In the field of human rights, in particular, international law has already succeeded in building up a great deal of common assets for the entire international society. Many worldwide or regional human rights treaties were signed and ratified by nearly all countries since the Universal Declaration of Human Rights of 1948, and some human rights have already become regarded as customary international law.[122] Of course, the mere fact that almost all countries have become parties of these treaties might be insufficient to overcome the objection to their universality.[123] It is certain that the idea of human rights originated in European history and culture, and is still a European-influenced idea.[124] It is also true that state practices of some illiberal countries show the tension between the universalism of human rights and the relativism of cultural, historical and political traditions.[125] Even in Asia, however, most countries have agreed to the protection of human rights by means of their domestic constitutions as well as their signed and ratified international treaties.[126] Nowadays, all states do not officially deny and ignore the protection of human rights in their public statements. Even after taking account of unfavourable matters to the commitment sharing, it can be inferred that the endorsement of human rights has become universally accepted because of the remarkable developments in international human rights law as well as positive changes in domestic constitutions.[127] The fact should not be

[122] Shaw (n. 67), pp. 265–344. The United Nations is an international organisation which rests on respect for human rights. Namely, the UN Charter refers to respect for both human rights and fundamental freedoms (Art. 1 (3) and Art. 55), and the Universal Declaration of Human Rights expresses a common understanding of the peoples of the world. As of April 2016, the ICCPR was ratified by 168 states, and the International Covenant on Economic, Social and Cultural Rights (ICESCR) was ratified by 164 states. In addition, a standard range of human rights always constitute a part of regional human rights conventions such as the CIS Convention on Human Rights and Fundamental Freedoms, the Inter-American Convention on Human Rights, the Banjul Charter on Human and Peoples' Rights and the Arab Charter on Human Rights.
[123] Allen Buchanan, 'The legitimacy of international law', in Besson and Tasioulas (eds.) (n. 21), pp. 79, 95–96.
[124] Schwöbel (n. 13), pp. 118–122.
[125] Kumm (n. 20), pp. 316–317.
[126] Wen-Chen Chang, Li-ann Thio, Kevin Y. L. Tan and Jiunn-Rong Yeh, *Constitutionalism in Asia: Cases and Materials* (Oxford: Hart Publishing, 2014), pp. 78–79. Not only the ASEAN but also China changed its traditional relative approach to human rights and has accepted their universality (Congyan Cai, 'New great powers and international law in the 21st century' (2013) 24 *European Journal of International Law* 755–795, at 793–794).
[127] Peters (n. 5), at 601; Wen-Chen Chang and Jiunn-Rong Yeh, 'Internationalization of constitutional law', in Rosenfeld and Sajó (eds.) (n. 90), pp. 1165, 1167–1169 and 1182–1183.

158   TAKAO SUAMI

underestimated that certain constitutional principles have already become international public assets in the sense of constituting a sound foundation for the globalised world.[128] Needless to say, the idea of global constitutionalism is duly backed up by this fact.

3.3.3.2 A weak point inherent in pluralism

Regarding the second point, the main question is whether or not one can accept international society without any guidance by constitutional principles. This question can be rephrased as: Which is more suitable to a globalised world: (1) 'pure and radical pluralism' or (2) 'desirable degree of pluralism'? As Krisch rightly fears, a non-pluralistic and hierarchical type of global constitutionalism tends to pose a high risk of exacerbating conflicts of incommensurable constitutional ideas by unilaterally imposing hegemonic ideas on the minority.[129] In terms of controlling such a risk, pluralism generally has substantial advantages, because it is based upon mutual respect among various countries or regions. This is a reason why East Asian sceptics of global constitutionalism tend to empathise with pluralism. However, one has to realise that 'pure and radical pluralism', which rules out any normative claims, cannot avoid entailing various other risks.

At least three risks flow from 'pure and radical pluralism'. First, that type of pluralism is likely to cause anarchy and disorder in international society. In the case of international society which is based upon such pluralism, since asymmetry of influence among different national legal orders would exist, the legal orders of powerful states could have dominant effects on those of other states, and normative values of powerless minorities might be threatened by hegemonic values.[130] Second, as a consequence of there being tolerance for different opinions, 'pure pluralism' may pose a risk of unconditionally supporting oppressive and autocratic governments. In order to escape from such a risk, pluralism might need to be saved from sliding into 'mere relativism' by receiving the assistance of constitutional principles. Mere relativism is not

---

[128] Janne Nijman and André Nollkaemper, 'Beyond the divide', in Nijman and Nollkaemper (eds.) (n. 107), pp. 341, 342–344; Peters (n. 111), p. 307.

[129] Krisch (n. 118), pp. 23, 35–38, 67–68 and 81–85.

[130] Turkuler Isiksel, 'Global legal pluralism as fact and norm' (2013) 2 *Global Constitutionalism* 160–195, at 172–190; Nicolás Carrillo-Santarelli and Carlos Espósito, 'The protection of humanitarian legal goods by national judges' (2012) 23 *European Journal of International Law* 67–96, at 91–94; Marcelo Neves, *Transconstitutionalism*, translated by Kevin Mundy (Oxford; Portland, OR: Hart Publishing, 2013), pp. 175–176.

desirable for international society, because it cannot provide any criteria to help solve normative conflicts in a globalised world.[131] Third, pluralism looks value-neutral at a glance, but one-sided stress on diversity might fall into a pitfall of Eurocentrism. In the present world, each national legal order still can enjoy a fair degree of its own autonomy, but on the other hand, it needs to have links with other legal orders for the sake of cooperating together in solving transnational problems.[132] Effective international cooperation is feasible only on the condition that all actors participating in such cooperation share certain basic rules. This is because common rules will make it possible for each actor to expect how other actors will behave for their cooperation, provided that all actors observe these rules. Accordingly, as long as international actors assume the sharing of constitutional principles, they are likely to be involved in mutual dialogues to clarify what those principles exactly mean. In other words, in the framework of constitutionalism, each actor is usually encouraged to participate in dialogues to confirm whether or not its understanding is the same as the understanding of the other actors. In contrast, it is hard for the motivation for such a dialogue to arise from the application of 'pure pluralism'. Pluralism is based on the idea of mutual respect between the actors involved. Therefore, the actors under 'pure pluralism' virtually tend to lose interest in entertaining dialogues with actors from a region or country that has different ideas from their own and to confine themselves in their local ideas.[133] This means that each actor including Europe will lose an opportunity to reconsider its understanding of constitutional principles.

In conclusion, since most countries have already attained a certain common understanding of constitutional principles, the total rejection of their universality cannot be justified and, if anything, is not desirable for global governance, even though those commonly accepted principles are still surrounded by vagueness and obscurity concerning their exact meaning.

3.3.3.3 The establishment of specific standards and interpretations on the basis of constitutional principles

What is a remaining point to be examined? The remaining point flows from vagueness of constitutional principles. In other words, the problem does not exist in the level of

---

[131] Isiksel (n. 130), at 179–186; Douglas-Scott (n. 62), p. 447; Cabrera (n. 114), at 27–28.
[132] Neves (n. 130), pp. 23–26.
[133] Ibid., pp. 31–32.

the constitutional principle but in the level of shaping more specific norms embodying the commitment to constitutional principles.[134]

Sharing constitutional principles to a certain extent is a great achievement for international society. However, this does not mean the end of the story and, if anything, opens fierce battles about the actual application of those principles. Constitutional principles are abstractly defined in most cases and allow various understandings and different interpretations, although they have fixed thought patterns in the present international society.[135] In order to apply constitutional principles to an individual factual situation, therefore, one has to establish specific norms that implement the principles and define what these constitutional principles being applied actually mean. Judicial interpretation of individual human rights is included in the category of such specific norms. As any agreed principle leaves large room for interpretation, it is not easy to reach a consensus on what it exactly means in relation to a specified situation.[136] The distinction of the two levels, namely principles and norms, can be easily found in the field of human rights. Due to many international treaties on human rights adopted in the framework of the UN, a worldwide consensus on the types of human rights to be protected exists. National practices are usually monitored by expert committees which have been established under respective human rights treaties, but their interpretations are neither legally binding nor enforceable, although their importance is widely accepted.[137]

[134] Ibid., p. 161; Peters (n. 5), at 601.
[135] There is almost consensus on the kinds of human rights to be protected (e.g. civil and political rights, social rights and so on), but the understanding of them is not uniform throughout the world. For example, the Japanese understanding of human rights as well as the rule of law is not the same as the European understanding of them (Takao Suami, 'Rule of law and human rights in the context of the EU-Japan relationship: are both the EU and Japan really sharing the same values?', in Dimitri Vanoverbeke, Jeroen Maesschalck, David Nelken and Stephan Parmentier (eds.), *Changing Role of Law in Japan* (Cheltenham; Northampton: Edward Elgar, 2014), pp. 247–266). Furthermore, there is disagreement on the substance of each kind of human right. For example, the Indonesian Constitutional Court is criticised for its flexible interpretation of prohibition against retrospective prosecution (Chang et al. (n. 126), pp. 299–305).
[136] Douglas-Scott carefully analyzes how difficult it is to achieve a consensus on the substance of constitutional values, especially justice in the context of the EU (Douglas-Scott (n. 62), pp. 412–447).
[137] Expert committees hold two types of monitoring systems, namely country reporting, under which contracting states are obliged to periodically submit reports on their measures to an expert committee for its review, and individual complaint, under which the expert committee is given competence to review complaints from individuals, on condition that the state concerned has accepted the system of individual complaints.

As a consequence, a uniform application of treaty provisions has not been accomplished yet, and remarkable divergence on their implementation still remains in international society.[138] This reality suggests that the main question at present is how to develop specific legal norms in order to apply constitutional principles to each individual situation.

In this respect, it is worth mentioning once again that Europe is more advanced than other regions, because Europe has succeeded in developing regional norms because of its highly sophisticated regional system that can ensure a uniform enforcement of constitutional principles. In Europe, three regional courts (the ECJ and the CJEU, the European Court of Human Rights (ECtHR) and the EFTA Court) have been jointly engaged in developing European standards. While these courts have established the relationship of mutual influence, the ECtHR has been playing the most prominent role among them in setting European standards. The influence of the ECtHR's case law is not limited to Europe. Since there is an overlap in substance between the ECHR and other human rights treaties, as a matter of fact, the ECtHR's case law has become the most important source of inspiration for the interpretation of human rights at the global level.[139] It seems that European standards actually exert special influence on the formation of global norms on human rights.[140] Inasmuch as European standards are shaped through the judicial process in which about fifty countries are involved, they can be generally closer to universal standards than those of any other regions. Despite their preponderance, however, European standards cannot automatically be equal to universal ones, and they still remain regional rules, as long as non-European interests have not been represented in the

All nine human rights UN Conventions have country reporting systems, but only seven out of nine have the system of individual complaints (Shaw (n. 67), pp. 311–335; Crawford (n. 94), pp. 565–567 and 572–574).

[138] For example, the death penalty has been a thorny issue between the EU and Japan for a long period of time (Paul Bacon, 'EU-Japan relations: civilian power and the domestication/localization of human rights', in Paul Bacon, Hartmut Mayer and Hidetoshi Nakamura (eds.), *The European Union and Japan: A New Chapter in Civilian Power Cooperation?* (Farnham; Burlington: Ashgate, 2015), pp. 185–200).

[139] Georg Nolte and Helmut Philipp Aust, 'European exceptionalism?' (2013) 2 *Global Constitutionalism* 407–436, at 427; Kaoru Obata, 'The European human rights system beyond Europe: interaction with Asia' (2015) 23 *Journal für Rechtspolitik* 36–43, at 38, 41–42.

[140] For example, Harpaz contends that 'the adoption of common human rights standards based upon the Strasbourg jurisprudence can assist the EU in its external activities' (Harpaz (n. 63), at 139).

formative process.[141] Thus, the setting up of a system for the formation of globally applicable norms has to be further examined. Due to the limited space allotted for this chapter, only some suggestions for the development of globally applicable norms follow in terms of both substance and procedures.

3.3.4 The path to common legal norms

3.3.4.1 Derogation from global common norms From a substantial point of view, drawing out common norms is not easy at the global level. An optimistic view insists that 'there are important forces militating towards greater conversion in human rights in the future',[142] but there is no guarantee that most disparities between global and domestic norms will disappear in the foreseeable future. On the other hand, even if global common norms are fortunately established, any uniform enforcement of the same standards cannot be easily attained, as long as international law rests upon national implementation.[143] The *Kadi* saga suggests that the highest court in each jurisdiction is likely to function as a safeguard against undue interference with the essential core of national standards.[144] Without cooperation of national institutions, any global standards cannot be properly implemented in the domestic context. This means that global common norms cannot be exactly the same as domestic norms in terms of nature. Namely, even if global norms use the exact same wordings or contents as domestic norms, as the doctrine of the margin of appreciation has shown, the application of global norms will be likely to allow for a broader range of exceptions legitimately claimed by

[141] Even among European scholars, some are cautious that universal norms are dominated by Western standards (Schwöbel (n. 13), pp. 99–100 and 106).

[142] Joel P. Trachtman, *The Future of International Law: Global Government* (Cambridge: Cambridge University Press, 2013), p. 119.

[143] The insufficiency of enforcement is indicated by the fact that the effectiveness of international monitoring by the UN system still remains a problem. As the Japan Federation of Bar Association criticised an uncooperative attitude of the Japanese government towards treaty bodies (Japan Federation of Bar Association, Written Information Submitted for the Summary of the Human Rights Situation in Japan to be Prepared by the United Nations Office of High Commissioner for Human Rights, 8 February 2008), the Japanese government has not followed all recommendations given by universal periodic reviews (A/HRC/8/44/Add.1, 25 August 2008; A/HRC/22/14/Add.1, 8 March 2013). As regards the ICCPR, furthermore, it did not follow many observations by the UN Human Rights Committee (The UN Human Rights Committee, Concluding Observations on the Sixth Periodic Report of Japan, adopted on 23 July 2014). Even in Europe, reactions to the ECHR and the decisions of the ECtHR are not uniform but diverse country by country (Neves (n. 130), pp. 87–91).

[144] Kumm (n. 99), at 220 and 232–242.

each state. That is because special local conditions must be taken into account.[145] Besides, in the case of global norms, having detailed norms with no latitude of deviation does not necessarily improve constitutional conditions at the domestic level; due to the lack of effective enforcement, high standards of international law tend to rather reduce actual levels of compliance in the domestic setting.[146] To be sure, how far such derogation is permissible is always a difficult normative issue.[147] The permission of derogation continually contains a risk of freezing and justifying the status quo. In order to escape from such a pitfall, the derogation must always be combined with a mechanism which functions so that it can constantly raise the level of regional or domestic standards.

3.3.4.2 Equal opportunity for all states and peoples From the procedural point of view, the formative process must observe the principle of equal opportunity for all states and peoples. As regards a value-oriented idea of international law, one has to be always careful of the danger that a dominant country or region will control what such values mean.[148] Therefore, it is an important issue how global common norms will be established. The principle of equal opportunity is inherent in global constitutionalism itself, since constitutionalism rests on the principles of equality, democracy and transparency. In accordance with this principle, global common norms must be built up on the basis of input from all potentially affected actors including non-state actors.[149] The legitimacy of specific legal norms depends upon to what extent equal participation of all affected actors has been effectuated.

---

[145] The doctrine of the margin of appreciation in the ECtHR indicates the necessity of allowing discretion by each jurisdiction (Andrew Legg, *The Margin of Appreciation in International Human Rights Law: Deference and Proportionality* (Oxford: Oxford University Press, 2012), pp. 3–6).

[146] Joost Pauwelyn, *Optimal Protection of International Law: Navigating between European Absolutism and American Voluntarism* (Cambridge: Cambridge University Press, 2008), pp. 187–197.

[147] In this context, one has to pay attention to the external policy of the EU about human rights. Recently, the EU has applied a very active human rights policy on the basis of European standards to its external relation with the third countries (Council, EU Annual Report on Human Rights and Democracy in the World in 2012, 21 October 2013), but its suitability to global governance is a bit doubtful; Nicholas Hachez and Jan Wouters, 'Promoting the rule of law: a benchmarks approach' (2013) 105 *Leuven Centre for Global Governance Studies Working Paper* 1–27.

[148] Kleinlein (n. 4), at 401–402.

[149] Cohen, 'Sovereignty in the context of globalization' (n. 21), pp. 276 and 278; Schwöbel (n. 13), pp. 152–158.

From the East Asian point of view, equality between regions or countries is a major concern, and any norms based upon only one particular region cannot be procedurally legitimate. Equal participation has to be pursued at the following two settings for the time being.

The first setting is the United Nations. The UN institutions have greatly contributed to the harmonisation of the principles and norms of human rights and must continue to play such a role in the foreseeable future. The system of the Human Rights Council established in the 2006 reform takes due account of equal participation in several respects including geographical distribution of its membership, an interactive dialogue between the Council and the country concerned and the participation of non-state stakeholders.[150] That explains that this reform can be affirmatively evaluated from the perspective of equal participation. Likewise, every aspect of the UN system should be continuously reconsidered so that equal participation will be further improved.

The second setting is interaction among various judicial tribunals at the same or different levels, namely national, regional and international levels. Vertical and horizontal interaction among various courts including those in illiberal countries is expected to gradually promote the harmonisation of their norms.[151] Dialogues on constitutional principles have already begun among courts in many jurisdictions and suggest the potential of complementing the imperfections of the current international system in terms of shaping global common norms.[152] Through such dialogues, domestic judges are also able to exert legal influence beyond their jurisdictions.[153] In Europe, reciprocal communication among a variety of courts at the different levels functions well, but courts in other regions have not taken part in such dialogues to the full extent yet.[154] Since regional courts and national courts in Europe are

---

[150] UN General Assembly, Resolution 60/251, A/RES/60/251 (2006); UN Human Rights Council, Resolution 5/1, Institution-Building of the United Nations Human Rights Council, A/HRC/RES/5/1 (2007).

[151] Neves (n. 130), p. 116.

[152] Carrillo-Santarelli and Espósito (n. 130), at 71–74; Eyal Benvenisti and George W. Downs, 'National courts, domestic democracy, and the evolution of international law' (2009) 20 *European Journal of International Law* 59–72, at 65–68; Hans Petter Graver, 'The immoral choice: how judges participate in the transformation of rule of law to legal evil', in The EFTA Court (ed.) (n. 61), pp. 63, 77–80; Neves (n. 130), pp. 106–118.

[153] Carrillo-Santarelli and Espósito (n. 130), at 68.

[154] According to a former judge of the Japanese Supreme Court, that court referred to foreign case law and/or international human rights treaties only in five judgments within its history of sixty-six years (Tokuji Izumi, '*Gurobaru-syakai no nakano Nihon no Saiko-Saibansho to sono kadai: saibankan no kokusaiteki taiwa*' (Japanese Supreme

institutionally linked by preliminary ruling procedures of both the EU and the EEA,[155] it may be questionable to what extent the dialogues by non-European courts, which are not institutionally linked to each other, will be successful in pinpointing global common norms.[156] However, as shown by the European experiences, the forms of intercommunication for judicial dialogues vary. It is noteworthy that these experiences demonstrate the usefulness of holding informal dialogues which take place outside institutionalised procedures.[157] Given the practical difficulties of reaching a political consensus on specific norms at the global level, therefore, it should be noted that national courts in all regions must be actors in the dynamic process of international law-making, although its effectiveness should not be overestimated at present.

4 Conclusion

European legal scholars are naturally familiar with and affected by European legal experiences. That is not the case with non-European scholars. However, besides Europeans, everybody including East Asians must accept that the European integration is an unprecedented legal experiment for the foundation of transnational constitutionalism. Thus, its more than sixty years' history with regional integration is replete with fruitful suggestions which could be valuable for the whole international society. The significance of European legal experiences for global constitutionalism has the following two distinct aspects.

In the first place, although East Asian international lawyers have not fully perceived it, constitutional pluralism in EU law is very valuable for studying a cognitive framework about ongoing changes in the present world. It is rather difficult to understand the logical structure of global

Court in the Global Society and Its Problems: International Judicial Dialogue) (2014) 25 *Kokusai Jinken* (*Human Rights International*) 13–17, at 14–15. In order to prevent judicial dialogue from being dominated by Western courts, non-Western courts have to make efforts to actively participate in such dialogues, because only participating courts can exert some influence on the standard setting at the global level (Kokott and Dittert (n. 61), pp. 51–52).

[155] Kokott and Dittert (n. 61), pp. 44–52; Eyal Benvenisti and George W. Downs, 'National courts, domestic democracy, and the evolution of international law: a rejoinder to Nikolaos Lavranons, Jacob Katz Cogan and Tom Ginsburg' (2010) 20 *European Journal of International Law* 1027–1030, at 1030.

[156] Jacob Katz Cogan, 'National courts, domestic democracy, and the evolution of international law: a reply to Eyal Benvenisti and George Downs' (2010) 20 *European Journal of International Law* 1013–1020, at 1015–1020.

[157] Kokott and Dittert (n. 61), pp. 44–48.

constitutionalism without thoroughly understanding constitutional pluralism. The progress of EU law hints that on the one hand, international society needs to share constitutional values and principles in order to prevent the falling apart of the world but that, on the other hand, it has to be wary of the imposition of specific regional norms on other regions without limitation. With a view to meeting these two requests at the same time, global constitutionalism must be reconciled with pluralism. Hence it follows that constitutional pluralism has constituted the fundamental basis of global constitutionalism. The pluralistic approach in global constitutionalism is the most desirable and feasible one for the current diversified international society.

In the second place, the usefulness of European experiences is more complex and delicate concerning the substance of constitutional principles which underlie global constitutionalism than European international lawyers expect it to be. With a view to fulfilling their missions, constitutional principles cannot remain abstract and have to be transformed into more concrete legal norms. In this context, it must be stressed that European interpretation should not be automatically identified with universal interpretation. European interpretation might turn out to be identical to universal interpretation in the end, but there is no assurance that consistency will always be maintained, as long as European interpretation has been made without taking due account of diverse interpretations in other regions. In order for any interpretation to obtain universal legitimacy, those affected by that interpretation, namely all states, regions and individuals, must have an opportunity to participate or be represented within any procedures, leading to such interpretation. It is unfortunate that the state of affairs in the present international society has not sufficiently met this requirement yet.

Global constitutionalism includes enormous potential to reform the current international system, and it may have positive impacts upon global governance in several ways. In particular, global constitutionalism is able to improve the management of international organisations, give necessary guidance to the national interpretation of constitutional principles and offer normative benchmarks to evaluate behaviours of national governments. It is relatively easy to underscore the advantages of global constitutionalism, while it is considerably difficult to find any clear-cut solutions to rescue global constitutionalism from the existing sceptical atmosphere accompanying it in East Asia. In order to overcome such scepticism, global constitutionalists would have to insist on constitutional reform of the international system in varied respects, so that more non-European perspectives could be put into the international mechanism of universal norm formation, in accordance with the principle of equality. The main targets of reform will be the reorganisation of the law-making process within or outside international organisations and the intensification of international judicial dialogues for the moment.

Global constitutionalism has been mostly constructed on the basis of European resources. Hence it enjoys partial legitimacy only from a procedural point of view. The future of global constitutionalism really depends upon how it will succeed in incorporating non-Western perspectives with Western ones. The first step in this direction is commonsensical, namely arranging for more communication between Europe and other regions including East Asia through all sorts of channels. European contributions to the progress of constitutionalism beyond states must be highly appreciated by the entire international society. If we succeed in rethinking and reconstructing global constitutionalism from a new viewpoint which will contain East Asian perspectives, it will become a more mature legal theory, and the global society will greatly benefit from its development.

5

On the History and Theory of Global Constitutionalism

MATTIAS KUMM

1 Contemporary challenges to global constitutionalism

Modern constitutionalism has its political origins in the eighteenth-century American and French revolutions. Even though the connection between the national and the international was a much discussed topic in eighteenth-century political thought, international jurists did not discuss international law in constitutionalist terms until the twentieth century. A first wave of constitutionalist writing took place in the interwar period until after World War II, when the emergence of the Cold War put an end to it. A second wave was initiated in the 1990s and 2000s after the end of the Cold War, this time more sustained and leading to a greater depth and breadth of writing.[1]

Constitutionalist narratives are very much part and parcel of the history of Western legal and political thought and have been connected to periods of Western hegemony. What reasons do we have to believe that the global constitutionalist universalist project is different from its other Western ideological predecessors with universalist pretensions, such as Christianity or 'Western civilisation', masking particular interests and cultural practices as universal to justify hegemony? Can global constitutionalism be sufficiently civilisationally and culturally inclusive? Can it remain relevant when Western hegemony is arguably receding and the balance of power is shifting in favour of other regions, most notably Asia?

---

[1] See Anthony F. Lang and Antje Wiener (eds.), *Handbook on Global Constitutionalism* (London: Edward Elgar, 2017); see also Anne Peters, 'Global constitutionalism', in Michael T. Gibbon (ed.), *The Encyclopedia of Political Thought* (Malden, MA: Wiley Blackwell, 2015), pp. 1–4. For an example of the breadth and depth of writing, see also the material published in *Global Constitutionalism*, a major Cambridge University Press journal published since 2012.

To engage some of these questions, the following will provide some basic ideas towards an affirmative genealogy of global constitutionalism. The idea of an affirmative genealogy is best explained by reference to two related but different ideas: critical genealogies and progress narratives. Critical genealogies use historical analysis to trace the emergence and use of concepts as a strategy of power, as exemplified in the work of Nietzsche or Foucault. They have a delegitimising thrust. Affirmative genealogies, on the other hand, illuminate the plausibility of the normative claims that are made in the context of the emergence and use of certain concepts.[2] Affirmative genealogies are distinct from progress narratives, in that they neither imply that progress over time is historically inevitable or linear nor suggest that the relevant concepts and ideas are themselves not potentially abused or hypocritically applied. Notwithstanding their affirmative character, affirmative genealogies are more attuned to the complexities, frailties and ambivalence of progress, without giving up on the idea of the progressive clarification and realisation of normative ideals across time and space.

In what follows the first section will provide some conceptual clarifications and historical contextualisation of the idea of global constitutionalism, building on but expanding and deepening the description provided in the Introduction of this book.[3] The second section will provide thumbnail sketches of some central historical events and issues for the history of constitutionalism as it relates to Asia. The conclusion summarises how these histories tend to strengthen the grounds for embracing the universalist claims underlying constitutionalist ideals. Global constitutionalism can be civilisationally and culturally inclusive, notwithstanding its origins. And it may well remain relevant even if Western hegemony is receding and the balance of power is shifting in favour of Asia.

2 Clarifying the issue: what is global constitutionalism?

2.1 Global constitutionalism as a jurisprudential approach

Global constitutionalism is not a political project to establish a world state under a global constitution. If one insists on the conceptual

---

[2] Here I only partially follow Hans Joas, *The Sacredness of the Person* (Washington, DC: Georgetown University Press, 2013), chapter 4, whose general positioning of the idea of an affirmative genealogy between Kant and Nietzsche, and, in modern forms, Habermas and Foucault, I share, without seeking to rely on the somewhat convoluted ideas of Ernst Tröltsch.

[3] See Introduction, Section 2.

distinction between law and politics, as one should,[4] it qualifies as a distinctly legal project. As a legal project it is not an attempt to describe existing international legal structures as equivalents or analogues to domestic constitutional regimes, suggesting that the international legal domain is somehow fundamentally like the state domain. In fact, global constitutionalism is not preoccupied with the concept of the state at all, even though it recognises the central role that states play both in people's lives and in international law.

Instead, global constitutionalism is best described as a jurisprudential approach: it provides a cognitive frame,[5] or mindset,[6] for understanding and engaging the world of law. A jurisprudential approach is less than a fully worked-out theory. There is a place for competing theories of distinct legal issues or areas of the law within a jurisprudential approach.[7] Furthermore, whereas not every lawyer will have a full-fledged theory of the law or particular subparts of it, all lawyers have a cognitive frame or mindset with which they engage legal materials, not only global constitutionalists. Legal materials do not in and of themselves solve legal problems. Questions arise how to identify materials that are properly legal, whether they are applicable, how they are to be interpreted, how conflicts between them ought to be resolved, etc. Here a cognitive frame or mindset provides, first, the resources to construct a distinctively legal order out of inchoate materials, second, relatively concrete ideas about what types of arguments count as plausible and convincing arguments in various contexts and, third, a considerable degree of internal coherence and determinacy. Most lawyers are socialised into adopting a particular cognitive frame or mindset. That is why they often believe that they have no theory and that what they do is simply what you do when you are a lawyer. But once cognitive frames or mindsets operating in law are elevated to consciousness and become the subject matter for explicit reflection and argument, they take the form of jurisprudential accounts.

[4] Of course, establishing a certain kind of law is the result of a political decision, and a commitment to the rule of law can be described as a political commitment, but legal reasoning and legal decision making rightly understood follows its own logic.
[5] See Mattias Kumm, 'The cosmopolitan turn in constitutionalism', in Jeffrey L. Dunoff and Joel P. Trachtman (eds.), *Ruling the World? Constitutionalism, International Law, and Global Governance* (Cambridge: Cambridge University Press, 2009), pp. 258–325.
[6] See Martti Koskenniemi, 'Constitutionalism as a mindset: reflections on Kantian themes about international law and globalization' (2007) 8 *Theoretical Inquiries in Law* 9–36.
[7] This accounts at least in part for the differences between global constitutionalists such as Anne Peters, Geir Ulfstein, Miguel Maduro, Jan Klabbers, Yoon Jin Shin, Daniel Halberstam, others and myself.

In that sense a jurisprudential account is the reflexive form of professional consciousness. Competing jurisprudential accounts typically have
considerable overlaps in what they identify as a legally relevant fact and
a legally relevant argument, so that in legal practice there will be many
occasions where underlying jurisprudential disagreement will be of no
practical relevance. But when there is disagreement among well-
informed, high-level lawyers on a particular issue – think about disagree-
ments among International Court of Justice (ICJ) or Permanent Court of
International Justice (PCIJ) judges, or judges on the Inter-American
Human Rights Court of the European Court of Human Rights
(ECtHR) – then that disagreement will often be a function of the underlying jurisprudential approach embraced by the judge.

In international law the contemporary[8] mainstream[9] competitors of
global constitutionalism as a jurisprudential approach are either *will-
based* (*voluntarist*) or *conventionalist positivist* jurisprudential accounts.
A will-based account is one that insists that ultimately all law binding on
a state is one that the state must have consented to. If you are
a voluntarist, then you believe that treaty law is the paradigmatic form
of international law, customary international law reflects the idea of
implicit consent and general principles of law are a relatively insignificant
catch-all category dealing with trivial or otherwise uncontroversial propositions of law. A conventionalist account seeks to tie all law to conventions. A conventionalist believes that customary international law is
the paradigmatic form of law, with treaties playing an important role in
the formation of customary international law while retaining an independent transactional role due to the customary principle *pacta sunt
servanda*, whereas general principles play a residual role largely subsumed by custom. A global constitutionalist account insists that certain

---

[8] Historically the precursor to international law – the *jus publicum Europaeum* – was
conceived either within the Christian scholastic natural law tradition (from Vittoria and
Suarez to Grotius) or, in the nineteenth century, in civilisational, historicist or naturalist
terms; see Martti Koskiennemi, *The Gentle Civilizer of Nations: The Rise and Fall of
International Law 1870–1960* (Cambridge: Cambridge University Press, 2001).

[9] What makes these accounts mainstream is that they all take seriously the idea of an
internal point of view relating to the law. Various 'critical' approaches, such as Marxism,
postcolonialism, feminism, etc., engage international law from an external point of view,
reflecting, for example, on how law reifies pre-existing power structures along lines of
geography, class or gender. An interesting third kind of approach, that is neither fully
external nor internal, are poststructural theories such as those developed by
David Kennedy, *International Legal Structures* (Baden-Baden: Nomos, 1987) and
Martti Koskenniemi, *From Apology to Utopia: The Structure of International Legal
Argument* (Cambridge: Cambridge University Press, 1989).

moral principles are constitutive of international law and that the content
of these principles is in part more concretely shaped by conventions that
settle reasonable disagreement about its meaning. Multilateral treaties
are both a way to establish custom and of normative significance because
of the moral significance of the self-determination-enhancing possibility
of transactional relations between states within a general public law
framework. Note how all three approaches recognise treaties, customary
law and general principles as a source of law. More generally in practice
most legal issues are not sensitive to differences of underlying jurisprudential approaches. There is much qualified lawyers are able to agree on,
simply by virtue of being qualified lawyers. But competing jurisprudential approaches are to a large extent the reason for there being different
positions in debates about doctrinal details relating to the sources of law
and a wide range of other basic doctrinal issues. Take the example of *jus
cogens*. The idea that there is such a thing as norms enjoying *jus cogens*
status is nowadays undisputed, as are certain paradigm examples of such
norms, such as the prohibition of genocide. Because this concept and its
core instantiations are part and parcel of what states have consented to, is
conventionally accepted and justified as a matter of principle, there is
basic agreement on this. But voluntarists, conventionalists and constitutionalists are likely to disagree not just about what norms qualify as *jus
cogens* but also about how to identify them. To take a stylised rendition of
an extreme example: when the European Court of First Instance in an
obiter dictum in the first *Kadi* decision claimed that all clear and serious
violations of an abstract human right, including the right to property or
access to a court, qualify as a *jus cogens* violation,[10] neither voluntarists
nor conventionalists could conceivably be persuaded, because there was
very little evidence supporting such a claim from either point of view. But
constitutionalists have reasons to take seriously such a claim. If human
rights are constitutive general principles of the global order, then the
claim that any act or agreement violating those principles in a clear and
serious way is null and void appears perfectly plausible. This serves as an
example not only of how different jurisprudential approaches and the
mindsets they produce have a different understanding of the moral
grounds of international law but of how this different understanding
has implications for the interpretation of law.[11] Here it must suffice to

[10] See Case T-306/01, *Yusuf and Al-Barakaat Int'l Found. v. Council and Comm'n*, 2005
E.C.R. II-03649, paras. 343–345.
[11] On these issues I follow Ronald Dworkin, *A Matter of Principle* (Oxford: Clarendon,
1985).

have defined global constitutionalism as a distinctive jurisprudential approach competing with other jurisprudential approaches in international law and to have made plausible the idea that jurisprudential approaches are not only of theoretical interest but at the heart of much of what is interesting and controversial in legal practice.

The next section will attempt to provide a better understanding of global constitutionalism as a jurisprudential approach, starting with the basic ideas and constitutive principles of international law as they were established in the twentieth century. As will become clear, at the heart of a global constitutionalist account of international law are certain principles drawn from the eighteenth-century tradition of the American and French revolutions as constitutive for the constructive understanding, interpretation and progressive development of international law. Note how the various parts of the account provided may on occasion deviate from conventional emphases and understandings of international law and may in part be controversial. That should not be surprising: The particular emphasis and understanding the account puts forward interprets historical shifts in light of a constitutionalist mindset and may be in tension with voluntarist and conventionalist accounts. But as will hopefully become clear, the historical facts lend themselves to such an interpretation. Or, to put it more strongly: a constitutionalist reading presents the most plausible interpretation of the transformation of international law in the twentieth century.

2.2   Global constitutionalism: basic principles

Between the end of World War I and the end of World War II, international law went through fundamental transformations.[12] Between the establishment of the League of Nations and of the United Nations, resulting from the shocks of World War I and World War II, the legal and political world had been radically reconstituted as a matter of principle. Under the leadership of the United States, allies and other state representatives effectively acted as revolutionary agents of the international community to establish the foundations for a new legal and political world ultimately grounded in principles that had previously

---

[12] Of course, describing the whole period between 1918 and 1945 as one of transformation does not imply that the transformation was a twenty-seven-year gradual process. World War II and its end in particular can be characterised either as a rupture or as an acceleration and dynamisation of the transformative process.

been alien to international law: these were constitutionalist principles, genealogically connected to basic normative commitments of the eighteenth-century American and French revolutions, highly contested throughout the nineteenth and early twentieth centuries in most European states, but set to gain hegemonic status with the victory of the Allies after World War II and fully achieving that status after the end of the Cold War. The commitments of the rule of law, democracy and human rights would become central also to international law. To be sure, there were also structural continuities in international law: both before 1918 and after 1945 states remain the central actors of the international system. And the mechanisms through which the shift was brought about were treaties formally consented to by states. As in the aftermath of any other revolution many areas of the law were not directly and immediately effected. But that basic structural Westphalian continuity covers up more than it reveals. There are three basic structural features of the new world order that justify speaking of a revolutionary shift and connecting that shift to constitutionalism.

First, the introduction into international law of the idea of *self-determination as a general principle*[13] in 1945 ultimately brought about the end of empires and led to the *genuine universalisation of statehood* for the first time. The subjects of international law were no longer European sovereigns, who competed to divide up the world between them using rules of international law to structure the 'great game' of competitive empire building. Nor was the issue merely to gradually expand the circle of subjects to include other powers depending on the degree to which they were recognised as *civilised* by established Western powers. Instead, self-determination established as a general principle in the UN Charter gradually led to the full universalisation of statehood as the process of *decolonisation* took its course starting in the 1940s but gathering steam in the 1950s and 1960s and helped abolish the primary forms of international law-enabled domination. There were 51 original member states of the United Nations. Today, there are 193 members of the United Nations

---

[13] To cabin in its transformative potential and reflect British and French sensibilities, the principle was originally described by Western international scholars as a 'political principle', until, partly as an impatient reaction to this downgrading, it was revitalised as a 'right to self-determination' in Art. 1 of the ICCPR and ICESCR in 1966. The principle was originally introduced in the Treaty of Versailles as a more limited principle effectively governing only the dismantling of empires and the resolution of territorial conflict of those on the losing side of World War I. After World War II, such cabining in would prove to be untenable.

as formally equal sovereigns. Much of that shift is connected to the end of empires and the realisation of the principle of self-determination.

Second, the idea of statehood itself was radically reconceived. Internally it was tied to its function to respect, protect and fulfil human rights, echoing the normative commitments of the great eighteenth-century revolutions in the United States and France. States after 1945 were legally bound to comply with human rights as general principles of law referred to in the UN Charter as a general idea and worked out and concretised in the UN Declaration of Human Rights in 1948 and multilateral treaties such as the International Covenant on Civil and Political Rights (ICCPR) and International Covenant on Economic, Social and Cultural Rights (ICESCR) negotiated in the 1960s. Whereas empire-ending decolonisation concerned the external dimension of self-determination and legally delegitimised certain forms of domination by foreign powers, the internal dimension concerned the structure of government institutions and the status of the individual. Once decolonisation had been effectively achieved by the 1970s, human rights came into their own ever more powerfully as a widely embraced lingua franca for the critique and reform of state practices.

The state itself now was understood not merely as an effective power configuration over territory and people but as an institutional framework within which those governed by it would practise self-determination, both individually and collectively. The task of public authorities was now to respect, protect and fulfil the human rights of those it was governing. Furthermore, government structures themselves had to meet requirements that reflected this commitment. To be sure, it was up to citizens to determine the concrete structure of the institutions that would govern them. But respecting human rights also implies the establishment of a government legitimised by free and fair periodic elections[14] and an independent judiciary, in short, the basic features of a liberal constitutional democracy.[15] Ultimately the

---

[14] See Art. 21, Universal Declaration of Human Rights, and Art. 25, ICCPR.

[15] This has been the focus of scholarly interest only after the end of the Cold War; see T. Franck, 'The emerging right to democratic governance' (1992) 86 *American Journal of International Law* 46. This position is not uncontested, although the critique is rarely based on careful legal analysis but more general policy concerns about a lacking international consensus, fostering military intervention and risking a new imperialism. For an extensive discussion see Susan Marks, *The Riddle of All Constitutions: International Law, Democracy and the Critique of Ideology* (Oxford: Oxford University Press, 2000).

point of the state was to serve as an instrument for persons as a basic unit of normative concern and not the other way around. Persons were now reconceived as self-determining agents endowed with human dignity.

Third, the issues central to the interpretation and progressive development of the law concern the understanding of human rights and the adequate institutionalisation of their protection. What kind of individual remedies should be available under international law? Should there be regional or even universal human rights or constitutional courts? If so, what level of deference should be granted to national political processes? Should the international community, acting through the United Nations under chapter VII, have the authority to prevent serious and persistent violations of human rights? And if a permanent member of the Security Council casts a veto, under what circumstances if any could states nonetheless intervene as part of their responsibility to protect? These are some of the questions that over time became central to international law after its constitutionalist turn.

This piercing of the veil of sovereignty and radical changing of the understanding of what is essentially within the jurisdiction of a state to determine for itself were brought about for two reasons: in part for the obvious reason that because the German Fascist regime and some of its allies had committed atrocities against its own population to such an extent that it seemed important for international law to delegitimise human rights–violating behaviour by states, instead of turning a blind eye and describing such behaviour as a sovereign act of state about the substance of which international law has nothing to say. Such agnosticism would ultimately implicate international law and undermine its legitimacy. But perhaps more important was the idea that the internal structure of the state and how it related to its citizens had implications for how it would conduct its foreign policy. Whereas Kant was the first to argue[16] that what he called 'republics' – essentially liberal constitutional democracies – would not go to war against one another,[17] Roosevelt shared the belief that 'making the world safe for democracy' and ensuring 'freedom from fear' meant that international law had to establish basic

---

[16] I. Kant, *Towards a Perpetual Peace*.

[17] A claim substantiated by considerable empirical evidence; see Michael Doyle, 'Kant, liberal legacies and foreign affairs' (1983) 12 *Philosophy and Public Affairs* 205–235. For a useful review of the various permutations of the 'Democratic Peace' debate, see Steven Pinker, *The Better Angels of Our Nature: Why Violence Has Declined* (London: Penguin, 2011), pp. 278–294.

standards for legitimate government.[18] It was of central importance to ensure that individual persons were no longer conceived as subject citizens serving as a resource for competitive power-mongering states, which mobilise their subjects with reference to the dignity, pride and glory of the nation and its superior culture and power to build empires and raise their status. This was important to prevent nationalist ideologies, whether of a fascist or merely authoritarian bent, from continuing to serve as a basis for domination either internally or externally.

But the idea of statehood was also changed more generally in its relationship to the 'outside'. States were conceived as an integral part of a larger international community, whose authority was not derived from the authority of each individual state. Fundamentally, the international community was in authority and could restrict the freedom of states whether an individual state consented to these restrictions or not, both on the grounds of general principles of law – some of them protected as *jus cogens* – and on the grounds of customary international law. Sovereignty was no longer a right not to be subject to restrictions without first having consented to them. Sovereignty was better understood as focused on membership and participation in a larger global community of principle.[19] The legal structure of this shift will be described later. The question is how such a shift is connected to constitutionalism. Fundamentally there are two reasons why such a shift is required by constitutionalist commitments. The first is a commitment to non-domination. If self-determination within a framework of equal sovereign states is the principled starting point for imagining international order, then powerful states should not be able to dominate others, irrespective of whether they have consented to such a restriction or not. Here the prohibition of the use of force and the duty to settle disputes peacefully are paradigmatic. More generally the idea of the rule of law as applicable also to the relationship between states is grounded in this idea, with the concrete rules of law themselves to be interpreted in a way that reflects a commitment to non-domination and sovereign equality. Second, the limited capacity of states to secure global public goods and welfare needed to be overcome. The international community needed to develop

---

[18] See Roosevelt's State of the Union Address of 6 January 1941 discussing the foundational significance of the 'four freedoms' for the global order that the United States would work towards.

[19] See, for example, Abram Chayes and Antonia H. Chayes, *The New Sovereignty: Compliance with International Regulatory Agreements* (Cambridge, MA; London: Harvard University Press, 1995).

a legal and institutional infrastructure that would enable humanity to act collectively to address these issues. Self-determination is not a practice that takes place within the territorial confines of the state. Opportunities are provided and restrictions imposed also by the wider global environment. Those too are not simply to be taken as a natural fact about the world but to be made the subject matter for collective shaping through collective action. This is the background understanding with which constitutionalists make sense of the following legal shifts of general structural significance.

First, states were no longer authorised to go to war to secure their rights under international law. Restating the commitment first entered into by most states in the Kellogg-Briand Pact in 1928,[20] the UN Charter in Article 2 section 4 prohibited the use of force in all cases except when a state was being subjected to an armed attack[21] or when the state was acting within authorisation of the UN Security Council under chapter VII. States that believed their rights to be infringed by another state were under an obligation to settle disputes peacefully. Until the issue was brought to a court or tribunal a party thinking of itself as aggrieved could take certain countermeasures, subject to procedural and substantive constraints, to force the violating side to resume compliant behaviour. But the state would not be permitted to seek legal redress by way of force. Even though the basic idea here was that *the rule of law was to replace the law of force*, and courts and tribunals had a significant role to play after 1945 and significantly proliferated after 1990, the jurisdiction of any court over any dispute is still generally believed to require the consent of states. But notwithstanding this continuous violation of the basic principle of *nemo iudex ins sua causa* central to the rule of law – because asking for consent amounts to making the accused be one's own judge[22] – violations of the prohibition of the use of force could lead to charges of 'crimes of aggression', which in principle could be subjected to criminal sanctions.[23] Similarly serious and systemic violations of humanitarian law or human rights law could be subjected to criminal

---

[20] For an account that highlights the significance of that pact, see Oona A. Hathaway and Scott Shapiro, *The Internationalists: How a Radical Plan to Outlaw War Remade the World* (New York: Simon & Schuster, 2017).
[21] See Art. 51, UN Charter.
[22] Deficiencies lamented by luminaries such as Hans Kelsen and Hersch Lauterpacht after World War II.
[23] I will forego the complicated issues relating to either universal jurisdiction or the jurisdictional complexities of the ICC provisions in this regard.

persecution as war crimes or crimes against humanity, even if the person responsible for these actions was a state official acting under orders or even if the person was the head of state oneself. *Respondeat superior* was no longer recognised as a valid defence, and the immunity of heads of state or ministers in office no longer provided protection. In that sense since 1945,[24] it is simply wrong to say that states have the monopoly of power, if we mean by that the ultimate authority to determine how and when individuals may use force against other individuals.[25] The core of the norms over which the International Criminal Court (ICC) now has jurisdiction is furthermore protected as *jus cogens*. The norms cannot be changed by the opposing will of a state, no matter how powerful.

Second, a preoccupation of the constitutionalist tradition of the eighteenth century was not just to constrain power but to create the preconditions for collective empowerment. Collective self-determination on the level of the state has its limits and is unable to secure a wide range of global public goods central to global welfare. In international law some degree of collective empowerment would occur through innovative re-engineering of the jurisgenerative process as well as through the creation of administrative capacities over time. The core idea here is to overcome the restrictions connected to consensus requirements characteristic of treaty making. On the more conventional side the International Law Commission, a body of highly regarded state-appointed legal experts established under the auspices of the UN, produces reports that either by themselves or by serving as a basis for multilateral treaty making play a central role to not only codify but progressively develop new international law across a wide range of fields.[26] More innovatively a new understanding of customary international law has evolved, which limits the amount of time needed for binding custom to form[27] and reinterprets

---

[24] If not already since the Nuremberg and Tokyo trials, at least since the ICC became operational in July 2002.

[25] Of course, that does not mean that state officials often get away with illegal use of force amounting to wars of aggression or war crimes or crimes against humanity, but this is no different from criminals within the national context often getting away with serious crimes. If that fact was never in and of itself sufficient to undermine the claim that the state has the monopoly of the use of force, then the same must appropriately apply to the claims of international law.

[26] These range from the Law of Treaties to rules relating to the Responsibility of States for Wrongful Acts.

[27] Think of 'pressure-cooked' or 'instant' international law; see the discussion in Federal Republic of Germany/Netherlands, *North Sea Continental Shelf* Judgments [1969] ICJ Rep 3 (20 February 1969).

what counts as state practice or how much state practice and opinion *iuris* is needed.[28] This has facilitated the emergence of new binding norms through strengthening the effective role of the UN General Assembly which enacts Resolutions that, although not binding in themselves, become a central part of a decentralised quasi-legislative process of generating customary international law. Finally, over time, a new plethora of international institutions grounded in multilateral treaties from the General Agreement on Tariffs and Trade (GATT, later the WTO), the World Bank and the International Monetary Fund (IMF) have created an infrastructure for administratively managing certain aspects of the global commons with a focus on the global economy. Today, international institutions have wide-ranging roles in administrative rule making.[29] Moreover, international organisations interact with domestic actors to produce practices described and critically analysed by the field of global administrative law.[30] From a global constitutionalist view these shifts are interpreted as having the general point to build the institutional and legal infrastructure to empower humanity to collectively shape the world through legal regulation, ensuring non-domination and enhancing welfare.

2.3   The real and the ideal within the law: on the critical and transformative potential of constitutionalism

If law is constituted by basic principles that together establish an ideal of constitutionalist legality, then the teleology of a legal system imagined in this way is geared towards the full realisation of these principles. But the actual positive rules and institutions might be in tension with these basic principles or realise them only in a limited, incomplete way. There may be significant tensions between the legally prescribed, principled ideal and the actual institutional and rule-bound practices in positive existence. Such a situation is one in which the concrete legal rules and institutions, although legally valid, are legally deficient. Note how this puts lawyers in a position to criticise existing positive law from the perspective of legal principle, that is, a perspective that is internal to the law. Constitutionalism,

[28] See Brian D. Lepard, *Customary International Law: A New Theory with Practical Applications* (Cambridge; New York: Cambridge University Press, 2010).

[29] José Alvarez, *International Organizations as Law-Makers* (Oxford: Oxford University Press, 2005).

[30] Benedict Kingsbury, Nico Krisch and Richard B. Stewart, 'The emergence of global administrative law' (2005) 68 *Law and Contemporary Problems* 15–62.

then, allows for a critical normative assessment of existing legal rules and institutions from a perspective that is internal to the law.

The international legal order that emerged after 1945 was reconstituted by the core principles described earlier. They were enshrined in legal documents such as the UN Charter. But the institutionalisation and concretisation of these principles was left to be completed over time.

To take the example of human rights, even if it would be correct to claim that after 1945 states were legally required to respect human rights, the requirement was left radically underspecified both in substantive terms and in terms of the availability of remedies in case of violation.[31] The legal project of a commitment to human rights began as a legally articulated promise, rather than an effectively institutionalised reality. And even though there has been a considerable evolution in the field of human rights concerning both the definition of the primary norms and the establishment of the institutions and doctrines enforcing them – primarily but not only regionally rather than universally – a great deal of deficiencies remain.

Similarly the idea of criminalising violations of the use of force that violated prohibitions of wars of aggression, war crimes, crimes against humanity or genocide was established in the Nuremberg and Tokyo trials. But these trials themselves were highly imperfect instantiations of the new principles. Only the vanquished were on trial, not the victors. Neither issues relating to the firebombing of Axis cities, from Dresden to Tokyo, nor the removal of Germans from Poland and Czechoslovakia nor the use of nuclear weapons in Hiroshima and Nagasaki were subjected to legal scrutiny by criminal courts. The courts were not constituted by way of impartial and independent procedures but by the victors. But notwithstanding these serious structural deficits, which are perfectly correctly criticised, it would be wrong to simply decry these faults as an indication that this was just a hypocritical form of dispensing victor's justice. A better way to understand these events is to think of them as part of a path to gradually institutionalise new principles under real-world conditions. It would take further steps after the end of the Cold War, first as ad hoc projects to establish UN tribunals with jurisdictions over specific conflicts in Yugoslavia and Sierra Leone by way of UN Security Council Resolutions, before a general court would be established by the

---

[31] Samuel Moyn's thesis that human rights law came in existence only in 1977 is a gross exaggeration, but he was correct to have pointed out a major shift in the wider political and cultural reception of human rights that occurred in the late 1970s; see his *The Last Utopia: Human Rights in History* (Cambridge, MA: Harvard University Press, 2010).

Statute of Rome in the form of the ICC. And even that Statute, in particular but not only with regard to its limited jurisdiction for crimes of aggression, is subject to plausible and continuing legal critique.

If constitutionalism thus allows for taking a critical perspective on existing legal institutions and doctrines that is internal to the law, the flip side of constitutionalism's critical potential is its potentially transformative character.[32] Both are a function of the possible tension between the ideal and the real within the law. A constitutional transformation occurs when through either interpretation or progressive development the significance of these basic legal principles becomes an argument to reinterpret existing rules or reform existing institutions in structurally transformative ways to make them more compliant with the underlying legal principles that legitimise them.

If an existing legal practice can be criticised in light of its grounding principles and, conversely, that practice may at times be transformed to make it more compliant with underlying principles, then the way to get from criticism to transformation is (1) by way of legal interpretation, (2) by progressive development of the law by law appliers (notably courts) or (3) by law reform by 'political' law-making actors. Once basic principles have been brought to bear to criticise an actual legal proposition as incompatible with the principles underlying it, these are the three ways to ensure that positive rules and practices are more closely aligned with their legitimising principles. In all three cases the underlying principles assume a regulative function, the point of which is to bring actual legal practice more in line with its principled foundations. When it comes to legal interpretation, principles provide objective teleological arguments in favour of interpreting the law in one way rather than another, when an issue is disputed. We speak of progressive development of the law when principled challenges to settled understandings of the law lead to new settlements that are more aligned with underlying principles. The normative limits of admissible progressive development of the law are reached whenever there are reasonable alternative ways of interpreting a principle with regard to an issue that is appropriately addressed by political actors.[33] When that is the

---

[32] For the debate on transformative constitutionalism, see Michaela Hailbronner, 'Transformative constitutionalism: not only in the global south' (2017) 65 *American Journal of Comparative Law* 527–565.

[33] Of course, this formulation covers up a can of worms. For a classical critical treatment of the related distinction between judicial and non-judicial (political) disputes, see Hersch Lauterpacht, *The Function of Law in the International Community* (Oxford: Clarendon, 1933).

case, reform – requiring some kind of political endorsement – becomes necessary to legitimise a choice between reasonable alternatives and validate the particular solution the law is to embrace. Even though more would need to be said, the teleological character of the law does not imply that law, conceived in constitutionalist terms, does not have the resources to uphold the institutionally central distinction between legal interpretation and progressive development of the law on the one hand and political reform on the other.

3   Some ideas on an affirmative genealogy of global constitutionalism with particular attention to the Asian context

The history of constitutionalism is not studied appropriately simply as part of the history of ideas or of the history of certain formal legal institutions and doctrines. It should be studied as part of an actual legal and political practice in the variety of contexts it touches. A history of global constitutionalism would focus not just on how constitutional ideas were invented, interpreted, developed and justified over time but also on how, why and by whom they were resisted. It should focus not just on the successes it helped bring about, in terms of either individual and collective emancipation from domination, economic prosperity and general welfare or cultural and civilisational flourishing, but also on its ambivalences, failures and hypocrisies. A history of global constitutionalism could not plausibly be a simple progress narrative. But the question is whether a greater familiarity with the history of constitutionalism and its contestations might lead to an understanding of it that would make more plausible its normative claims and its potential, notwithstanding all of this. The question is whether a genealogy of constitutionalism, as it has spread both horizontally across political communities and states worldwide and vertically to capture the imagination of statespersons, entrepreneurs and jurists shaping the international legal order, may affirm it, rather than discredit it. In other words, the question is whether the history of global constitutionalism might lend itself to an affirmative genealogy. To the extent that it could, it would have to address a variety of concerns, perhaps the most important of which is the concern that global constitutionalism and its commitment to human rights, democracy and the rule of law are just the latest reincarnation of the West's attempt to cover up its imperial ambitions and particular interests by dressing them up as a universalist ideology. What Christianity was from the sixteenth to the eighteenth century and what 'civilisation' became in the nineteenth and early twentieth centuries were resurrected after World War II, this time as constitutionalist ideology.

3.1   The new constitutionalist world order and 'the West'

Perhaps the best way to make plausible the idea of an affirmative genealogy is to face head-on the most obvious series of concerns or the most serious concerns that appear to give credence to this scepticism. It is true that constitutionalism originated in the heartland of 'the West': in the American and French revolutions in the eighteenth century. It is also true that the modern global constitutionalist project is deeply connected to the Roosevelt and Truman administrations seeking to shape a new world order after World War II. The United States was the revolutionary agent in this regard, putting its considerable war-proven power and diplomatic clout to work to achieve its aim. Here it much suffices to briefly recount three examples.

The first two concern the role of the United States in establishing new constitutions for the main Axis powers. These were effectively ordered to establish some version of a liberal constitutional democracy after the Axis powers surrendered unconditionally. The genealogies of neither the German Constitution nor the Japanese Constitution reflected the commitment to 'We the People' freely deciding on how to govern themselves.

In the case of Germany the leadership was reluctant, because, they claimed, there was no people that could give itself a constitution: the eastern parts of Germany were occupied, after all, by Soviet forces, and the new constitution could be applicable only in the Western-occupied territories. They were told to get on with it nonetheless, and all the representatives from the various states could do to express their discontent was to refuse the new document the name of a constitution. They called it the Basic Law instead, and the Allied powers signed off on it after assuring themselves that the document met their requirements. Only after that was the document ratified by state parliaments.

The story of the Japanese Constitution is even more unsubtle.[34] After having been told to amend and modernise the Meiji Constitution by General MacArthur as the Supreme Commander of Allied Powers (SCAP), the reluctant government established a research committee to study whether an amendment of the constitution was necessary.

[34] The following draws on Shigenori Matsui, *The Constitution of Japan: A Contextual Analysis* (Oxford: Hart, 2011), pp. 4–20.

The committee concluded that amendments to the Meiji Constitution were indeed necessary but that they were relatively minor. When the draft amendments were published, the SCAP was frustrated by their conservative content and had his staff members draft a new constitution within eight days. While that constitution left intact the emperor as head of state, it abolished the feudal system, established the principle of popular sovereignty, required the renunciation of war and prohibited the maintenance of armed forces. The government was then pressured to adopt the draft and moved it through the ratification process.

The genealogy of the UN Charter is not entirely dissimilar. Even though the Charter was adopted by fifty nations at the San Francisco Conference in 1945, the decisions on the basic structure and principles had already been made sometime from the Atlantic Charter, in which Roosevelt arm-wrestled Churchill to sign off on common principles, over the Tehran and Yalta conferences to the Dumbarton Oaks Conference. Much of the preparatory work was done by various parts of the US Roosevelt administration. The UN would not exist in anything like its present form were it not for the leading role of the United States. Axis powers were excluded as enemy states from the negotiations and would not become members until 1956 in the case of Japan and 1973 in the case of the divided Germany. There were 51 states who were the original signatories of the UN Charter in 1945. Today, there are 193 states. The difference is to the greatest extent connected to peoples successfully claiming self-determination against their colonisers and empires disintegrating.

What is clear is that in all of these cases the spread of constitutionalism was part of a distinctly American-dominated project. What is less clear is what it teaches us about constitutionalism's universalist posture in its relationship to the West and the rest of the world. This is not only the case because of the logical gap between a genealogical critique and challenges to the validity of a claim. It is also because this genealogy itself is not without its interesting ambivalences and complexities.

The idea of 'the West' is a complicated notion in the history of constitutionalism. A closer examination quickly makes clear that the connection between constitutionalism and the West is attenuated, at best. Germany as a major European power in the first half of the twentieth century appears to share more traits with Japan, a major Asian power, than with the United States and is treated in much the same way as Japan was by the Allies: as a country in need to be re-educated and weaned off its nationalist militaristic culture. More generally, Germany, much like Japan, both in the early twentieth century during World War I under the kaiser and under National Socialism, adopted ideologies which had nothing to do with constitutionalism. On the contrary, the German nationalist, culturally supremacist 'ideas of 1914' propagated when the war began were self-consciously embraced as a distinct alternative to what were described as the materialist, individualist and ultimately existentially shallow ideas of '1789', which were claimed to be incompatible with German culture.[35] Going further west in Europe to France, the German Nazis found willing collaborators in the conservative authoritarian Vichy regime. In France the ideas of the French Revolution had produced deep divisions and a series of counter-revolutions throughout the nineteenth century, as conservative authoritarians sought to connect the idea of France as a nation not to the principles of the revolution but to its Catholic faith and both the aesthetic superiority of the simple life in the French countryside (*la France profonde*) as well as the aesthetic splendour created by its nobility. Cross off the idea of the aesthetic splendour of the nobility, and you get something close to the populist vision of France that Marine Le Pen is peddling today. Even Britain's role in this context is not simple. World War II was Britain's 'finest hour', as it provided a bulwark against the Nazis. But, of course, Britain itself was a global empire structured internally by a class system in which hereditary privilege remained of central importance, with the working class invited to feel nationally elevated by imagining their miserable plight to be connected to the 'white man's burden' to help bring civilisation to the rest of the world by way of managing an empire in which the sun did not set. The recognition of the principle of self-determination by Churchill was a price he had to pay to secure the desperately needed support of the United States against Hitler. Roosevelt had made it quite clear that he was not willing to invest American blood and treasure to defend and uphold the British Empire.

In 1945 constitutionalisation of the world was an American-led project, not a Western one, because constitutionalism had not taken a deep hold among major powers in Europe before the end of World War II, notwithstanding a century-old history of political and ideological struggles. And its most intrusive actions and attempts at re-education were not aimed at hapless backward people but Germany and Japan, the highly civilised barbarians that had unleashed World War II in Europe and Asia.

---

[35] See Thomas Mann's elaborations on German culture and liberal constitutional democracy in his *Reflections of a Nonpolitical Man* (New York: F. Ungar, 1918).

The constitutional moment of 1945 brings a decisive break between the old European colonial order established before World War I and the post–World War II order. The end of World War II saw the most aggressive imperial powers of their time put into place. At the same time as the idea of self-determination, the prohibition of the use of force and human rights, a set of normative principles were established that also delegitimised the older European empires such as those of Britain and France, even though the process of decolonisation would still require time and national struggle. In that sense the constitutional moment of 1945 was also a high point of anti-imperialism.

3.2 Anti-imperialism as imperialism? The battle of Tsushima as a constitutional moment

Of course, anti-imperialism can itself turn into imperialism very quickly. When the Japanese navy defeated the Russian navy in the battle of Tsushima in 1905, this was widely celebrated by subjugated people of the world as proof that the Western imperial powers could be defeated. For many non-white peoples this seemed to mock Western racial hierarchies and the presumption to 'civilise' the supposedly 'backward' countries in Asia.[36] It made a deep impression on future leaders of liberation struggles and projects of national modernisation, from Mohandas Gandhi, then an unknown lawyer in South Africa, to Mustafa Kemal, later known as Atatürk, then a young Ottoman soldier in Damascus, to Jehawahral Nehru, later the first Indian prime minister, to Sun Yat-sen, later the first president and founder of the Chinese Republic.[37] But even though it is correct to understand this as a moment in which established Western imperial powers and their racial presumptions were undermined in a way that gave hope to and wakened from their lethargy a wide range of subjugated peoples across Asia, it was not an anti-imperialist moment. Ultimately the battle of Tsushima was a battle in a war between two competing imperial powers over who would control Manchuria and Korea: Russia, as an established European power, or Japan, a regional upstart seeking its own place in the sun after having gone through a process of radical modernisation following the Meiji Restoration. What that battle and Japan's subsequent further rise

---

[36] Pankraj Mishra, *From the Ruins of Empire: The Revolt against the West and the Remaking of Asia* (London: Penguin, 2012), p. 3.
[37] Ibid., pp. 1–6.

illustrated was merely that empire and racially and culturally presump-
tuous domination were not something that Europeans or the West could
effectively maintain a monopoly over. If the battle of Tsushima was the
beginning of an Asian awakening and the 'opening chords of the reces-
sional of the West',[38] then it left open the possibility that an awoken Asia
would simply replicate the worst of what the West had to offer.
Imperialism based on presumption of racial or cultural superiority, too,
this suggested, is a Western ideology with potentially global appeal.

To be sure, it was widely believed that Japan's success had something to
do with its constitution.[39] Conversely Russia's weakness was associated
with its ossified autocratic structure. In that sense the battle of Tsushima
was also a constitutional moment. The possibilities to gain self-respect and
constitutional government, so it seemed, go together. It helped fuel a series
of popular constitutional revolutions against autocracies not only in Asia
but also in Russia. Students from all over Asia flocked to Japan to study its
constitution. But the 1889 Meiji Constitution, like its Prussian nineteenth-
century counterpart, which it was developed from, was constitutional only
in form and remained deeply wedded to autocratic government and
hereditary legitimacy. The emperor was the sovereign, his power derived
from religious authority, and he had the status of a living god; the Diet was
weak, and individual rights were benevolent grants of the emperor. Unlike
the case with the post-war constitutional transformations, the Meiji
Constitution shared little more than formalities with constitutionalism.

3.3   An Asian embrace of and contributions to global constitutionalism?

The failure of the battle of Tsushima as an anti-imperialist global constitutional moment teaches something important: defeating imperial
powers alone is insufficient to guarantee the victors anti-imperial bona
fides. If that is so, does the United States qualify as an imperial power in
the morally relevant sense after World War II, given its forceful role to
establish and maintain the post-war order? There may have been
a significant shift between the European variations of empire and the
new global constitutionalist order the United States was instrumental in
bringing about. But the fact that the new legal order has a different
normative structure does not in and of itself ensure that this new normative structure is not just a new manifestation of imperialism.

[38] Ibid., p. 6.
[39] Ibid.

Of course, it is also not enough to simply claim that the establishment of constitutionalism can never be imperial because it simply is the correct legal and political ideology. This was the kind of argument with which all imperial projects were justified and is thus insufficient. But what exactly is required to be able to reject the argument that global constitutionalism is just the latest false universalism foisted upon the world, this time by the United States as the dominant imperial power emerging from World War II?

If constitutionalism is effectively imposed on a particular nation or the world, as it was on Germany and Japan after World War II and as it arguably was on the whole of the world by way of the UN Charter, then it becomes decisive whether those subjected to the order generally embrace its basic principles over time, make it their own, engage with it, participate within it and, if they deem necessary, modify aspects of it as they deem fit. One of the decisive features of constitutionalism is that it legally authorises and highlights such participatory engagement and rejects the lethargic attitude of mere subjects as unworthy of the office of citizenship.

3.3.1   The German Basic Law

The German Basic Law has over the decades not only become a central point of reference in the everyday political and legal debates, with the Constitutional Court recognised as a highly influential and respected institution. Over time the constitution has also become a central factor for German national identity and pride, even though that does not mean that Germans feel constrained to amend it as they deem appropriate.[40] In Germany the idea of constitutional patriotism has real resonance and widespread, even if not universal, support. The claim that the constitution should be understood as an imperial imposition has no contemporary resonance whatsoever.

3.3.2   The Japanese Constitution

In Japan the constitution appears to also be widely regarded as successful and enjoys widespread support. Yet there are two striking features that a scholar of comparative constitutional law cannot help but notice and that are of interest here. On the one hand courts have refused to play the active role that they play in most established liberal constitutional democracies, even though they have the formal powers

---

[40] The German Constitution has been amended by fifty-four amendment laws amending 109 articles in its first sixty years until 2009.

to do so.[41] Furthermore, the constitution has not been amended once, even though there are obvious reasons for doing so. In its famous Art. 9 the constitution renounces not only the right to wage war but also the right to maintain armed forces. Assuming that Japan maintains the right to defend itself as guaranteed under Art. 51 of the UN Charter, as appears to be the dominant view among Japanese scholars, that provision would imply that Japan is denied the right to maintain the military means to do so. Of course, in practice Japan maintains one of the most sophisticated militaries in the world in the form of its Self Defense Forces. This status quo is problematic not only because it undermines the authority of the constitution opening it up to charges of hypocrisy. It also undermines the potentially strong role that Japan appears to in principle be willing to play as a militarily active contributor to missions authorised under chapter VII of the UN Charter. The reasons for both the resistance to more engaged judicial review and to amending the constitution are surely complex, and this is not the place to discuss them in depth. But could it be at least in part because there is a degree of cultural recalcitrance against the legalist spirit that comes with constitutionalism, once the constitution is taken seriously as containing operative norms which guide and constrain political actors? Is it simply because the discrepancy between what the constitution requires and what is done in practice does not matter, because fundamentally, the constitution should not be taken too seriously as a legally operative constraining text but more as a symbol for the new post-war Japan? Could it, perhaps more audaciously, be because if previously the person of the emperor was sacred, it must now be the constitutional text whose role is primarily imagined to be symbolic? Is it because Japanese citizens and politicians don't trust themselves to change anything in the constitution, because they imagine this to be a slippery slope leading inevitably into a new authoritarian, perhaps even militaristic, regime? The new constitution may stand for the new post–World War II Japan, pacifist and prosperous, that as such is a success and enjoys widespread support. It is less obvious that, given these features, constitutionalism as a legal and political practice has developed deep roots in Japan, even though, of course, more would have to be said. What that suggests is that acceptance of constitutions and of liberal constitutional democracy can, in practice, mean a variety of things and does not imply that all core

---

[41] Matsui (n. 34), pp. 140–151.

normative commitments will in fact be effectively institutionalised. Acceptance of something originally foreign will always involve cultural adaptation, but it may also mean partial subversion and the subtle rejection of some facets of what is claimed to be accepted. But even if an account along these lines were to do justice to the Japanese experience with constitutionalism, it suggests that claims that the constitution is not legitimate and that it symbolises the ongoing domination of Japan by the United States are implausible.

3.3.3   Global constitutionalism and its many authors

The global order, as it emerged after World War II, was not simply a product of Western minds, shaped by Western traditions and imposed by powerful Western statespersons. It was the result of a process which included the successful struggle of subjugated colonised nations against imperial oppression. And once the basic post–World War II order was established political struggles and contestation over the meaning of its core principles involved a wide variety of actors. The following can provide only some very cursory glimpses to illustrate that point.

When US President Wilson insisted on establishing the legal principle of self-determination in the Treaty of Versailles that ended World War I, it was applied merely as a principle governing territorial claims relating to defeated powers. It was not applied to territorial claims that the defeated European powers had against the victors, and it was certainly not to apply to territories belonging to the British and French empires outside of Europe. Yet it was as the Treaty of Versailles was negotiated and as later on state delegates were to be seated at the newly established League of Nations that non-European actors made their claims in the name of self-determination and called out the hypocrisy of the European powers, after the atrocities of World War I claims of a superior European civilisation seemed spurious at best. When Gandhi was asked what he thought of Western civilisation he quipped that he thought it would be a good idea, a sentiment that had considerable resonance after World War I. More generally representatives of Egypt, India and other countries claimed they were *civilisations*, thereby implicitly rejecting the presumptions of the existing powers to have the authority to determine which of the relevant actors met relevant 'civilisational' requirements. Pressure mounted to give up the requirement of 'civilisation' in order to be recognised as a state. Thus, the universalisation of statehood, without a civilisational adage, is an achievement that is a result of a political struggle in which those colonised and subjugated appeared as central actors and ultimately overcame their merely passive status.[42]

Another example of an Asian country playing an active, constitutionally progressive role pushing for the development of international law, even if in that specific context not immediately successfully, was India in the context of its intervention in East Pakistan in 1971.[43] It brought humanitarian intervention onto the agenda of the UN Security Council as a subject for discussion and as a potential ground to authorise the use of force, when it wanted to intervene in East Pakistan. The Pakistani government was effectively engaged in a genocide against Bengalis there, which ultimately left at least 500,000 Bengalis dead. Besides addressing the humanitarian concerns, India sought to stop the considerable flow of Bengali refugees across its borders. Since this was in the middle of the Cold War and Pakistan was an ally of the West and India was not, the substantive position that India put forward had no chance of being accepted in the UN Security Council. But its position would find support much later, after the Cold War was over. It is today generally accepted that the mandate to secure international peace and security under chapter VII of the UN Charter also includes the possibility to authorise all necessary measures to secure the rights of individuals against serious and systematic human rights violations, irrespective of whether those violations have little or no tangible physical effect outside of a state's borders.

Furthermore, the role of successive Japanese and other Asian governments and civil society actors to help bring about an elimination of nuclear weapons deserves to be mentioned. For the past twenty-four years Japan has introduced a resolution to bring about the elimination of nuclear weapons before the General Assembly, which generally passes with very widespread support. The issue is also of legal constitutional rather than just political relevance, because any use or threat of use of weapons is arguably in violation of basic principles of humanitarian law.[44] Nuclear weapons may well be described as the original sin of the

---

[42] For a description of this evolution, see Arnulf Becker Lorca, *Mestizo International Law: A Global Intellectual History of 1842–1933* (Cambridge: Cambridge University Press, 2014).

[43] For a book-length treatment of the issues focusing on the roles of Nixon and Kissinger seeking to preclude Indian intervention, see Gary Bass, *Blood Telegrams: Nixon, Kissinger, and a Forgotten Genocide* (New York: Alfred A. Knopf, 2013); see also his 'The Indian way of humanitarian intervention' (2015) 40 *Yale Law Review* 227–294.

[44] When the ICJ had an opportunity to adjudicate the issue it effectively avoided it by way of a highly unusual *non licet* decision, thus leaving the issue open (ICJ, *Legality of the Threat or Use of Nuclear Weapons*, Advisory Opinion, ICJ Reports 1996, 226; see also ICJ,

post–World War II constitutionalist order, the way that slavery was the original sin of the eighteenth-century US constitutional project: a core feature of the newly established constitutionalist order, which is fundamentally incompatible with commitments underlying it. In July of 2017 122 countries, excluding the United States and practically all European Union countries but including Bangladesh, Malaysia, Indonesia, Thailand and Vietnam, adopted the Treaty on the Prohibition of Nuclear Weapons. It remains to be seen whether the treaty will prove to be an effective step towards the elimination of nuclear weapons by building pressure on nuclear powers.[45] But what this issue too makes clear is that the divide between the different sides has little to do with regional geography or culture. It has a great deal to do with geostrategic considerations, ambitions of hegemony, insecurities and the old drama of principle seeking to constrain and guide power. And in this drama Asian and Western actors find themselves on both sides of the divide.

3.3.4   Global Constitutionalism and the challenge posed by China

China today appears to be a country unwilling to embrace a constitutionalism domestically that has very little to do with intrinsic features of its culture, traditions and history and a great deal to do with highly path-contingent options and preferences taken by the existing party elite and, more recently, by Xi Jinping more specifically. These are decisions that have a great deal to do with real failures of liberal constitutional democracy elsewhere, suggesting that China might do better to explore other options. What that means for China's relationship to global constitutionalism in international law, however, remains ambivalent.

Much like Japan, China embraced radical reform and modern constitutional government as a result of its humiliations when confronted with other powers: first in the Opium Wars in the middle of the nineteenth century, which, beyond the unequal treaties imposed on it, led to the loss of Hong Kong to the British, then – in the eyes of the Chinese perhaps even more humiliatingly – in the defeat in the first Sino–Japanese war of

---

Obligations Concerning Negotiations Relating to Cessation of the Nuclear Arms Race and to Nuclear Disarmament (Marshall Islands v. India), Judgment of 5 October 2016, relating to duty of nuclear powers to make a good-faith effort to work towards the elimination of nuclear weapons under the Non-Proliferation Treaty).

[45] Four of the eight current nuclear powers are Asian: China, India, Pakistan and North Korea.

1894–1895.[46] Note how that humiliation was not simply the result of China being disrespected as an equal by others effectively establishing themselves as superior. The pain was sharpened by imperial China imagining itself as the centre of the world, with other nations and peoples relating to the centre through complicated rituals of submission and trading privileges.[47] When the British first established unequal treaties with China, it was not even clear to the Chinese government that it was unequal in any sense relevant to its moral universe. Sure, British citizens would be subject to consular jurisdiction and not imperial jurisdiction, but in ancient China jurisdiction was generally personal and not territorial. And if the Chinese were not granted consular jurisdiction over their citizens in Britain on a reciprocal basis, then that made perfect sense: Chinese subjects were generally not allowed to and had no reasons to travel elsewhere anyway, whereas, of course, there were good reasons for others to come to China to show reverence and learn from the superior Chinese culture and hope to gain from trade with it. But the losses against Japan hurt: after all how could a tiny island long dependent on the Chinese language and culture defeat an empire many times its size? The military defeat against Japan prepared the ground for the end of the Quing Dynasty and the birth of China as a constitutional republic in 1911, with Sun Yat-sen as its first president. Even though the specifics of the constitution needed, of course, to be adapted to special Chinese circumstances, unlike the Meiji Constitution of 1889, the Chinese Constitution reflected a genuine commitment to constitutionalist principles. Because of foreign occupations, the remaining powerful role of warlords and the divisions between nationalists and Communists the country was in permanent turmoil, until in 1949 Mao Tse Tung was able to unify mainland China under Communist rule and establish the People's Republic of China with his nationalist rival Chian Kai-shek holding on to Taiwan. Even though Chian Kai-shek's Kuo-Ming Tang governed in Taiwan by way of martial law for the first decades, by the late 1980s Taiwan not only was enjoying considerable economic success but gradually developed into a modern liberal constitutional democracy. In mainland China, too, after the death of Mao Tse Tung, who had to

---

[46] For a history of China's encounter with and embrace of international law, see Rune Svarverud, *International Law as World Order in Late Imperial China: Translation, Reception and Discourse 1847–1911* (Leiden; Boston: Brill, 2007); see also Chi-Hua Tang, 'China-Europe', in Bardo Fassbender and Anne Peters (eds.), *The Oxford Handbook of the History of International Law* (Oxford: Oxford University Press, 2012), pp. 701–723.

[47] Svarverud (n. 46), pp. 8–15.

be prodded by Stalin to believe that having a formal constitution was a good idea because it might help legitimise the regime and stabilise it,[48] with a turn towards markets under Deng Xiaoping there would be a new Chinese Constitution enacted in 1982. That constitution generally shared the core hallmarks of a modern constitution, guaranteeing democracy, human rights and the rule of law. But it did insist on the political monopoly of the Communist Party. And as in all Communist countries, its role remained negligible in political life. Instead, important shifts in power and political orientation would at best be reflected in the Communist Party's statutes, not the constitution. Similarly, what mattered were not parliamentary bodies or court decisions but decisions by the party Congresses. If the situation in China today is different from the situation in other countries that had embraced Communism but then went on to establish liberal constitutional democracies, it is because of the way the Chinese leadership handled the potentially transformative moments in 1989, when major student demonstrations in Beijing threatened the stability of the regime. Unlike the East German Communist Party elite facing the same issues that year, the Chinese government decided to clamp down. Nonetheless, even among those who favoured the clampdown there were those who embraced the idea that China would eventually develop into a liberal constitutional democracy. They just did not think that China was quite ready to take that step yet. Not surprisingly throughout the 1990s and 2000s, Chinese scholars at universities openly discussed the possibilities and implications of when and how China would eventually join the constitutionalist world.[49] Whereas academic debates and publications were tolerated, it was not, however, possible to publish open political calls to establish a liberal constitutional democracy, as 303 intellectuals did in 2008, when they published Charter 08 on the occasion of the 60th anniversary of the UN Declaration of Human Rights and the 100th anniversary of the Chinese Constitution as well as the 10th anniversary of China signing the International Covenant on Civil and Political Rights. But short of public political advocacy for liberal constitutional democracy putting the Communist Party and its political monopoly on power under

---

[48] Qianfan Zhang, *The Constitution of China: A Contextual Analysis* (Oxford: Hart, 2012), p. 43.

[49] See, for example, Li Buyun, 'Constitutionalism and China', originally published in 1993 and republished in Yu Keping (ed.), *Democracy and the Rule of Law in China* (Leiden; Boston: Brill, 2010), pp. 197–230.

immediate threat, much was permitted.[50] That only changed after Xi Jinping took power in 2012. These debates within the universities have effectively been put to rest by more severe party guidelines on what should and should not be discussed in political and legal seminars and by the threat of sanctions. What is clear looking at Chinese recent history, as well as the experience in Taiwan and current events in Hong Kong, is that claims that somehow China's culture and tradition make it uniquely unsuitable for embracing liberal constitutional democracy are difficult to sustain.

Leadership's decision to choose an anti-constitutionalist course after 2012 and to instead emphasise, consolidate and expand party control is likely to have many reasons. But among those reasons is no doubt the perceived failure of liberal constitutional democracies to deliver what they promise and to reflect a plausible model for best civilisational practice in the contemporary world. On the one hand the example of Russia taught China that it did well not to engage in regime change itself, when it was confronted with a serious challenge in 1989. After all Russia not only lost its position as a superpower in the international system, its economy also suffered a severe downturn, and the standard of living declined significantly for a large part of the population in the decade after the introduction of Western reforms. Furthermore, India, the world's largest democracy since its independence, has been developing at a much slower pace than China. For a traveller comparing life in the city of Mumbai with life in the city of Shanghai by the second decade of the twenty-first century, the superiority of liberal constitutional democracy as a developmental economic model is less than obvious. Finally was it not the case that the European Union and the United States – those supposed models of constitutionalist commitments – were engaging in strangely irrational actions to respond to the challenges posed by terrorism, getting bogged down in useless and illegal wars, struggling with a serious financial crisis, and, after providing lacklustre economic growth for a decade, now suffering from capture by political movements, parties and individuals which seemed to accelerate self-destructive tendencies? Was it really plausible that the Chinese Communist Party could not do better than that? Could it not reinvent itself as a quasi-meritocratic

---

[50] Perhaps typical for expressing moderately progressive sensibilities of this time was Yu Keping, *Democracy Is a Good Thing: Essays on Politics, Society and Culture in Contemporary China* (Washington, DC: Brookings, 2009), advocating an incremental building-block approach to democratic evolution in China, focused first on civil society, local government, intra-party democracy and strengthening the rule of law.

organisation recruiting talent to technocratically govern the country, merging the idea of a Leninist avant-garde party with Confucian ideas of bureaucratic merit, thus ensuring further growth and stability and perhaps, in the long term, global pre-eminence?[51]

It was no doubt also the thirty years of successful growth that made the Communist Party leadership confident about what it might be able to do, just at a moment when liberal constitutional democracy seemed weak. Note that this may well turn out to be a judgment to regret. Liberal constitutional democracies also seemed weak and decadent when a wide variety of Fascist and Communist forces appeared to have all the vitality necessary to conquer the future in the 1930s. And the achievement of the Communist Party to date is more ambivalent than the official narrative suggests. Even after nearly forty years of growth the standard of living of the average Chinese on the mainland is still not as high as that of the average Chinese in Taiwan or Hong Kong, let alone the average South Korean or Japanese. Instead of standing in awe one might just as well ask: Why so little so late? Why did it take China so long for it to regain a position that it had lost in the eighteenth and nineteenth centuries? Not implausibly the historical role of the Chinese Communist Party, which includes responsibility for the disastrous Maoist policies and human suffering connected to 'the Great Leap Forward' and the 'Cultural Revolution', has not just been to cure China from its century of humiliation. Even though it is difficult to know whether and how China's economic developmental situation would have improved earlier under a different, more genuinely democratic and liberal constitutional regime, it would be wrong to exclude the possibility that the monopoly of power enjoyed by the Communist Party may have been a contributory cause for its comparatively late recovery.

4 Conclusion

The series of historical sketches in this chapter have exemplified some basic ideas towards an affirmative genealogy of global constitutionalism and yielded a number of insights. Historically, the link between 'the West' and global constitutionalism is significantly more attenuated than it is often portrayed to be. On the one hand constitutionalist ideas have been

---

[51] For an understanding along those lines see Daniel A. Bell, *The China Model: Political Meritocracy and the Limits of Democracy* (Princeton, NJ: Princeton University Press, 2015).

and continue to be, at various times, in various jurisdictions, subject to rejection and contestation in the West, both fundamentally and with regard to specific manifestations. The West is no more closely associated with constitutionalism than with competing ideas. Various forms of authoritarian nationalist ideologies, celebrating national culture, ethnicity, religion and tradition, fascist or communist ideologies, or empire, are no less Western than constitutionalism and have been as influential globally as, if not more influential than, constitutionalism. On the other hand, constitutionalist ideas have been embraced by Asian actors against European states (embraced by the colonised and brought to bear against colonisers, unmasking their hypocrisy) to liberate themselves and throw off the yoke of imperial domination. With the appropriation of these ideas by non-Western actors, their meaning could sometimes be altered and progressively reformed. Universal categories and their meaning have often been shaped by encounters and conflict and not simply dictated by one side. Furthermore, constitutionalist ideas have been used by those dominated within Asian states against their respective oppressors. They have been and continue to be embraced and invoked against local and national elites in non-Western contexts who defend their privileges and established practices of domination with reference to sovereignty, culture and tradition. Those elites, in turn, replicating well-established patterns practised in the West, rely on concepts of sovereignty, nationalism and culture to declare those who invoke rights and constitutionalist ideas as inauthentic, corrupt and the fifth column of the – foreign – enemy. Anti-constitutionalist actors have often served, in their respective contexts, as apologists for the ideology of self-serving regional or national elites in the name of national culture and tradition, providing them with intellectual cover against challenges made by those they govern, challenges often made in the name of human rights, democracy and the rule of law. These are phenomena that critical postcolonial sensibilities tend to obfuscate rather than illuminate, furthering the reification and essentialisation of the idea of civilisational or cultural difference, rather than focusing on ongoing relationships of domination within cultures and civilisations and on coalitions of domination and resistance across cultures and civilisations.

There is no guarantee that constitutionalism will remain relevant in the future, not globally, not in Asia and not even in the West. But constitutionalism may well remain relevant even if Western hegemony is receding and the balance of power is shifting in favour of Asia. What matters is that a sufficiently powerful coalition of actors embrace it, in

Asia, in South America, in Africa and in the West. Whether that will be the case in the midterm appears to be an open question. And if constitutionalism won't remain relevant, because various anti-constitutionalist powers become hegemonic forces successfully shaping the world in their image, then it would be wrong to assume that the reason for its demise is its insufficient civilisational and cultural inclusiveness. The reason for its demise might just be the complacency or ignorance of those who did not defend it appropriately and the ambition and ruthlessness of those who stand to profit from it.

Asia, in South America, in Africa and in the West. Whether that will be the case in the midterm appears to be an open question. And if constitutionalism won't remain relevant, because various anti-constitutionalist powers become hegemonic forces successfully shaping the world in their image, then it would be wrong to assume that the reason for its demise is its insufficient civilisational and cultural inclusiveness. The reason for its demise might just be the complacency or ignorance of those who did not defend it appropriately and the ambition and ruthlessness of those who stand to profit from it.

PART II

Pursuit of Common Values

Human Rights and the Rule of Law from East Asian Perspectives

6

Are We Talking the Same Language?

The Sociohistorical Context of Global Constitutionalism in East Asia as Seen from Japan's Experiences

DIMITRI VANOVERBEKE

1 Introduction

Global constitutionalism aims at fostering a legitimate international legal order to promote the well-being of people through inter alia the rule of law, a separation of powers, fundamental rights protection and democracy.[1] Global constitutionalism will, however, encounter severe difficulties when proposed as a model for East Asia.[2] Associations will immediately be made with past Western imperialism,[3] present-day American hegemony or Eurocentrism and will lead to its rejection out of hand as yet another tool for the West's domination of the East. Indeed, despite the 'double nature'[4] of international legal norms, being '*both* an instrument of power and an obstacle to its exercise',[5] many East Asian states tend to highlight the former, and most are reluctant to embrace transnational legal norms including the idea of global constitutionalism.

One reason for this reluctance can be found in negative historical experiences with the treaty systems forcibly imposed by Western powers

---

[1] Anne Peters, 'Global constitutionalism', in Michael T. Gibbons (ed.), *The Encyclopedia of Political Thought*, 1st ed. (Maiden, MA: John Wiley & Sons, Ltd., 2015), pp. 1–2.

[2] East Asia as a regional concept differs according to the context in which the concept is used. References to 'East Asia' in this chapter include Japan, China, the Korean Peninsula, Taiwan and the eleven South-East Asian nations (the ten ASEAN countries in addition to Timor Leste). See also Thomas J. Pempel, *Remapping East Asia: The Construction of a Region* (Ithaca, NY: Cornell University Press, 2005).

[3] Graham Hassall and Cheryl Saunders, *Asia-Pacific Constitutional Systems* (Cambridge: Cambridge University Press, 2006).

[4] Nico Krisch, 'International law in times of hegemony: unequal power and the shaping of the international legal order' (2005) 16 *European Journal of International Law* 369–408, at 371.

[5] Ibid.

on East Asian nations. Far-reaching stipulations, ranging from extraterritoriality to full control of political and economic life amounting to de facto colonisation and outright colonisation, were recorded in most nations belonging to the East Asian region.[6] Many so-called unequal treaties were signed between Western powers and East Asian states in the nineteenth century, such as the Treaty of Nanjing (1842), the Treaty of Wanghia (1844) and the Treaty of Tianjin (1858). These treaties were unequal in several ways: they were imposed at gunpoint; they were designed to protect the economic and political interests of Britain and other imperial powers, including extraterritoriality and restrictions on tariffs on foreign trade; they were not reciprocal; and they were very difficult to undo.[7] Historical experiences with international law in the nineteenth century have had a long-lasting impact on East Asian states, and they shape the way that these states approach international law and global constitutionalism today.

That is, however, only one side of the story. East Asia may be a fertile ground for global constitutionalism when we consider that the essence of the concept is an ongoing and continuous process of research and debate on global constitutional norms. Japan offers a good example of how the dynamics of constitutionalism developed over a long period and what impact this made on society.

This development started as early as the drafting of the Meiji Constitution (1889) in the 1880s. Japan's then leadership sought a new tool to restrict democracy by codifying strong control of the people by the nation and avoiding limits on government in the name of 'We the People'.[8] At the same time, however, a debate on constitutionalism was – maybe unwittingly – set in motion and resulted in unexpected consequences. A societywide debate enhanced the demand for and the legitimacy of the law and planted the seeds of what can be called an early stage of public debate on democracy, the rule of law and constitutionalism. To translate into Japanese new and oft-called 'Western' concepts in

---

[6] So-called unequal treaties were signed with various East Asian nations in the nineteenth century and were the basis of a negative perception of international law as an instrument to regulate bilateral relations. See Michael R. Auslin, *Negotiating with Imperialism: The Unequal Treaties and the Culture of Japanese Diplomacy* (Cambridge, MA: Harvard University Press, 2009); Richard S. Horowitz, 'International law and state transformation in China, Siam, and the Ottoman Empire during the nineteenth century' (2004) 15 *Journal of World History* 445–486.

[7] Horowitz, ibid., at 455.

[8] Martin Loughlin, 'What is constitutionalisation?', in Martin Loughlin and Petra Dobner (eds.), *The Twilight of Constitutionalism?* (New York: Oxford University Press, 2010), p.52.

nineteenth-century Japan such as law, rights and constitutionalism was no easy task, not least due to the existence of the then very hierarchical relation between state and citizen. Nevertheless, the language was rapidly developed, and vigorous debate at various societal levels ensued. The debate included a critical civil society addressing civil rights and liberties as well as triggering bottom-up dynamics integral to modern constitutionalism, and it set the stage for future experiences with constitutionalism. In addition, Japan's second and current constitution (1947) offers important insights into how constitutionalism is approached in the country that first bridged law from Europe and legal practice in East Asia. In the aftermath of World War II, public debate that took place during drafting of the constitution and after its entry into force was important for the dynamics of democracy of a new Japan. It had a two-fold positive effect of economic development and regional peace building and therefore became essential to the state's legitimacy – both domestically and internationally. Is then constitutionalism really foreign to East Asia?

Recent developments in regional cooperation in East Asia suggest a negative answer to that question. There are certainly promising signs not only at the level of nation states but also regionally (in East Asia) of a potential for global constitutionalism. We observe of late vibrant dynamics of non-state networks (industry, NGOs, civil society, etc.), public debate and movements towards state-induced institutional reforms that foster the rule of law and enhance the prominence of constitutional norms in East Asia. Multinationals and subcontractors, East Asian non-governmental organisations (NGOs) and civil society organisations have proliferated and demand predictability and stability through standards and regulations. States in the region seek more opportunities for economic development and cannot remain insensitive to these demands, which also result in a spillover to domestic law and policy. In order to understand how the debate on global constitutionalism – currently prominent in Europe – is perceived in East Asia, it is imperative to undertake empirical studies 'that situate the emergence of global constitutional quality in the long durée of social processes in international history'.[9] The East Asian historical and contemporary social context can offer us the clues necessary to assess the validity of the argument that the debate on global constitutionalism is foreign to East Asia.

[9] Thomas Müller, 'Global constitutionalism in historical perspective: towards refined tools for international constitutional histories' (2014) 3 *Global Constitutionalism* 71–107, at 72.

2   East Asia's first experience with constitutionalism: the Meiji Constitution of 1889

At the onset of the twentieth century, Nitobe Inazō, a prominent Japanese diplomat and scholar, claimed that constitutionalism is not about national values but about an effective organisation of the citizen–state relationship. Constitutionalism includes an 'attitude, a frame of mind, the philosophy of striving toward some form of political legitimacy, typified by respect for a constitution'.[10] Realising Nitobe's statement was exactly what the Japanese drafters of the constitution in the nineteenth century – the Meiji Constitution of 1889 – aimed at. Society was in turmoil with growing and at times violent political opposition as well as with upheavals by labour and poor tenant farmers.[11] How to maintain the social fabric by the new regime and which symbols to use were the main questions that had to be addressed. Constitutionalism was one answer. Many political leaders and constitutional architects were convinced that constitutionalism was about forging a national identity. Such a predominant identity, as noted by Michel Rosenfeld, is in the United States, for example, captured by the phrase 'We the People'.[12] In nineteenth-century Japan, a core constitutional identity was considered a prerequisite to the rulers accepting a modern constitution. The prevailing identity revolved around the emperor who – so it was presented to the people – benevolently offered in 1889 the constitution to the people, who remained his subjects.

The Meiji leadership largely understood law in general and legal codes in particular as tools for the state for the coercive control of the citizens and as a *conditio sine qua non* for international recognition. This was clear, for example, in the fact that establishing legal codes in nineteenth-century Japan was not in the jurisdiction of the Ministry of Justice but the Ministry of Foreign Affairs.[13] The primary purpose of Japan's first modern constitution therefore was not so much nation building as nation preservation. To gain international recognition, however, Japan had to

[10] Jan Klabbers, 'Setting the scene', in Jan Klabbers, Anne Peters and Geir Ulfstein (eds.), *The Constitutionalization of International Law* (Oxford: Oxford University Press, 2009), p. 10.
[11] Dimitri Vanoverbeke, *Community and State in the Japanese Farm Village: Farm Tenancy Conciliation, 1924–1938* (Leuven: Leuven University Press, 2004).
[12] Michel Rosenfeld, 'Modern constitutionalism as interplay between identity and diversity: an introduction' (1992) 14 *Cardozo Law Review* 497–532.
[13] Takekazu Ogura, *The History of Land Legislation* (土地立法の史的考察), (Tokyo: Nōgyō hyōronsha, 1951), pp. 184–185.

answer to the requirements of modern constitutionalism that, apart from the symbolic purpose of nation building, included the instrumental purpose of defining the structure of the office of government.[14] Loughlin explains that 'the instrumental aspect, which expresses the principle of legality, looks primarily to the future, whereas the symbolic, drawing on custom and myth and expressing the principle of legitimacy, primarily makes an appeal to the past'.[15] Symbolism in the Meiji Constitution obviously revolved around the emperor, and that symbol was closely tied to the concept of a 'sacred' national territory protected by him.[16] This was a very rational choice of the Meiji leadership: national unity was lacking up to 1868 in a Japan that consisted of more than 260 quasi-independent fiefs, and international pressure threatened the independence of the nation from the 1850s on. Indeed, there was a prioritisation of the symbolic function (i.e. nation building) over the instrumental function (i.e. defining the structure of government) in Japan's first experience with constitutionalism. The unexpected consequence of constitutionalism in Meiji Japan was that the process of drafting and implementing the constitution triggered a wide debate on government, and this debate became a stepping stone for the development of a vigorous civil society and engendered sociopolitical activity beneficial for the modernisation and democratisation of the country.

From the very beginning of modernity in the years after the Meiji Restoration of 1868, the leaders of a 'new' Japan learned about constitutionalism and considered this a means to prove to the international powers that Japan was modern and therefore entitled to independence as a nation state. Immediately after 1868, missions to the United States and Europe were dispatched to learn about Western constitutions among other institutions that were deemed to make modernity work.[17] One of the most remarkable was undoubtedly the so-called Iwakura mission, which involved the entire government for more than a year and a half as well as all the important nations at the time (1871–1873).[18] This mission was also concerned about the development of constitutionalism in

[14] Loughlin, 'What is constitutionalisation?' (n. 8), p. 52.
[15] Ibid.
[16] Donald Keene, *Emperor of Japan: Meiji and His World, 1852–1912* (New York: Columbia University Press, 2013).
[17] See, for example, Takeharu Okubo, *The Quest for Civilization: Encounters with Dutch Jurisprudence, Political Economy, and Statistics at the Dawn of Modern Japan* (Leiden: Global Oriental, 2014).
[18] Ian Nish, *The Iwakura Mission to America and Europe: A New Assessment* (London: Routledge, 2008).

Europe and interested in the concept as a possible transplant given the government's aim of modernising the country. Research on and translation of various constitutions in the world were paving the way for constitutionalism.[19] What was Japan's real interest in European constitutions? This can best be seen in the preface to one of the earliest translations (1875) of a leading European constitution, the 1831 constitution of Belgium:

> Belgium is the newest of the European nations. It is a small nation that is well-organised. It is remarkable because it can do great things thanks to unity. The reason why this is possible is the constitution that according to its observers is an example of perfection. Despite the fact that Belgium is only composed of eight provinces and has not more than five million inhabitants, it has a sound political system and does not find unity in a common religion but in liberty for its people. Moreover, it does not strive for hegemony, as it is located between the Great Powers. Yet it is successful in maintaining independence and not surprisingly, as indicated in its national flag, it is a nation strong in unity.[20]

Maintaining independence was indeed the primary aim of embracing constitutionalism in nineteenth-century Japan. Soon after, the Senate authored the first official constitutional draft in modern Japan. The Senate referred to the British, American and French constitutional systems and based specific articles on the Prussian, Austrian, Dutch, Belgian, Italian, Spanish and Portuguese constitutions. There seems to have been a genuine desire in the Senate to draft a constitution to establish a form of rule that was shared between the citizen and the emperor and that was considered the most effective way of establishing peace and unity in the new nation where identity was associated with the fief more than with the nation. The Senate's first draft in 1876 was based on the English Bill of Rights and on the Belgian Constitution of that time. The emperor was 'sacred and inviolable', possessing the 'power of administration'.[21] At the same time, the draft stipulated that

---

[19] George M. Beckmann, *The Making of the Meiji Constitution: The Oligarchs and the Constitutional Development of Japan, 1868–1891* (Ann Arbor, MI: University of Kansas Press, 1957).

[20] Kowashi Inoue, *The Constitutions of Monarchies*, Vol. 2 (王国建国法. 下), translation of E. Laferrière's *Constitutions d'Europe et d'Amérique* (Paris: Cotillon, Libraire du Conseil d'Etat, [1875] 1869), final two pages. For the digital version, see http://dl.ndl.go.jp/info:ndljp/pid/788895.

[21] Toshiyoshi Miyazawa, 'On the constitutional proposal by the Genrō-in' (元老院 の 憲法草案 に つ い て) (1941) 55 *Kokka Gakkai Zasshi* (国家学会雑誌) (*The Journal of the Association of Political and Social Science*) 435–467.

the emperor had to swear loyalty to the constitution before the two houses. Legislative power was divided between the emperor and the parliament. It was further stated that the ministers were appointed and dismissed by the emperor but that they had to take an oath of loyalty to the constitution and could be impeached by the Senate. The Lower House was to have the sole right of approving the budget. Governmental leaders at the time considered these proposals too liberal, because they 'did not at all take into account the specific Japanese context and [were] a mere copy of the European constitutions'.[22] The leaders feared that such a constitution would bring no stability and rejected it at once.

At the same time, i.e. in the mid-1870s, several 'intellectuals, urbanites, and villagers began to voice their own demands for "freedom and popular rights"'.[23] By the decade's end, hundreds of such organisations convened regularly and discussed inter alia constitutionalism. One participant, 'a farmer from Chiba, published a stinging criticism of the government's gradual approach to constitutionalism in a leading Tokyo newspaper, and he called upon the ordinary men and women of Japan to come together in a petition movement designed to force the Meiji oligarchs to institute representative government'.[24] Many non-governmental groups were involved in the civil rights movement of the 1870s and 1880s, and they produced their own draft constitutions. Among them there was a draft prepared by Ueki Emori, the leader of 'an association that functioned both as a self-help society for former samurai and as a vehicle for promoting liberal political thought'.[25] In his 'Constitutional Proposal for Japan'[26] of August 1881, he included clear limits on the power of the monarch as well as universal suffrage and human rights protection. Ueki's draft also provided for a federal system and judicial review, which gave it a uniquely progressive content.[27]

Pressure on the government mounted, and to prevent upheaval and stagnation in the country, the process of constitution drafting had to be

---

[22] Kazuhiro Takii and David Noble, *The Meiji Constitution: The Japanese Experience of the West and the Shaping of the Modern State* (Tokyo: International House of Japan, 2007), p. xii. See also Miyazawa (n. 21).

[23] James L. McClain, *A Modern History of Japan* (New York; London: WW Norton and Co., 2002), p. 189.

[24] Ibid., p. 190.

[25] Ibid.

[26] Saburo Ienaga, Shozo Matsunaga and Eiichi Emura, *The Constitutional Concepts in Early Meiji Japan* (明治前期の憲法構想) (Tokyo: Fukumura Shuppan, 2005), pp. 385–397.

[27] Ibid.

brought to an end.[28] The Constitutional Drafting Committee was created
in autumn 1886 and consisted of long-time allies of Prime Minister Ito
Hirobumi. German constitutional scholars wielded considerable influence over the final shape. From the wide variety of constitutions that were
consulted as inspiration in drafting the Meiji Constitution, the Prussian
Constitution of 1850 was the most important, both as to the number of
articles that were modelled after it and as to how the relation between the
head of state and the citizens was construed.[29] Many other constitutions
made a small contribution to the final content of the Meiji Constitution
(e.g. the Portuguese Constitution of 1826 and the Italian Constitution of
1848). Some constitutions contributed in a substantial way to the Meiji
Constitution (e.g. the Dutch Constitution of 1848, the Austrian
Constitution of 1867 and various French constitutions).[30]

The idea of creating a new nation with a strong unity, identity,
domestic stability and order was the main legacy of European constitutionalism in Meiji Japan, hence the prioritisation of the symbolic purpose
of the constitution. This is evident in Prime Minister Ito Hirobumi's
address on 18 June 1888 to the Privy Council, the most powerful institution in imperial Japan, which had to give final approval to the draft
constitution before it could be submitted to the parliament.[31] Ito started
by pointing out that 'constitutional politics have played no role in the
history of East Asian nations and therefore Japan will be embarking on
a totally new path of which it is unclear whether it will be beneficial for
our nation'.[32] He noted further that in Europe too, constitutionalism was
a recent development but that there 'it germinated in history unlike Japan

[28] Stephen Vlastos, 'Opposition movements in early Meiji, 1868-1885', in Marius B. Jansen (ed.), *The Cambridge History of Japan, Volume Five: The Nineteenth Century* (New York: Cambridge University Press, 1989), pp. 367–431.
[29] Kowashi Inoue, 'Understanding the Constitution (unfinished manuscript)' (憲法資料・未完初稿), in Hirobumi Ito (ed.), *Documents on the Constitution*, Vol. 2 (憲法資料・中巻) (Tokyo: Kenpō Shiryō Kankōkai Zohan, 1934), pp. 53–206. There are seventy-six articles in the Meiji Constitution. Inoue's notes on the sources for each article indicate that forty draft articles drew to some extent on the Belgian Constitution.
[30] Hiroshi Ono, 'The reception by Japan in the 19th century of the Magna Carta' (19世紀後半日本におけるマグナ・カルタの継受) (2015) *Japan Legal History Association* (法制史学会), Proceedings of the 67th plenary symposium: '800 years of the Magna Carta: beyond the discourse of the myth of the Magna Carta', pp. 67–78.
[31] Ito Hirobumi, Address to the Privy Council Committee for the Establishment of a Constitution (枢密院憲法制定会議) on 18 June 1888, National Archives of Japan (国立公文書館), Government, Documents of the Privy Council, Draft of the Meiji Constitution, documents from 18 June to 13 July 1888 (reference code A03033488000), available online: http://www.jacar.go.jp/.
[32] Ibid.

where [constitutionalism] is a totally new thing'.[33] In his address, Ito contrasted the European constitutions with their restrictions on the powers of monarchs with the draft of the Meiji Constitution, which did not place any restrictions on power of the emperor. Ito emphasized the nation-building function of constitutionalism, explaining that 'today, in view of establishing a constitution, first we have to establish a main *axis* [機軸] without which politics would be entrusted to the arbitrariness of the people resulting in a loss of the unifying power of politics in a nation worthy of that name'[34] (my emphasis). According to Ito,

> the central axis of the European nations as reflected in their constitutions can be found in religion as the central axis that unifies the minds of the people. In Japan the power of religion is weak and cannot be considered an axis of the nation. Buddhism has brought prosperity to all the people by connecting them, but this is weaker than the Shintoism entrusted to us by our ancestors. Therefore, the only possible unifying axis in Japan is the emperor. Because of this, the main significance of the draft [Meiji] constitution is that it is made out of respect for the monarch.[35]

The first constitution in modern Japan came into effect on 29 November 1890 and had unexpected consequences.[36] Aside from the aforementioned awakening of civil society and public debate on the constitution, elections were organised, and the parliament became operative and resulted in vigorous political debate and often even in conflict between the members of parliament and government. Remarkable in this respect was Article 71 of the Meiji Constitution, which was to confine the power of the parliament. It stipulated that if the parliament did not approve the budget proposal for the next fiscal year, the amounts in the budget of the previous year would automatically apply. This proved to be a means of providing power to the people's representatives.[37] Indeed, inflation and the need for capital

---

[33] Ibid.

[34] Ibid.

[35] Ibid.

[36] Nikolas Rose and Peter Miller, 'Political power beyond the state: problematics of government' (1992) 43 *British Journal of Sociology* 173–205 at 190–191; see also Sharon Asiskovitch, 'Digging their own graves: unexpected consequences of institutional design and welfare state changes' (2009) 43 *Social Policy & Administration* 226–244.

[37] The Constitution of the Empire of Japan (1889), Art. 71: 'when the Imperial Diet has not voted on the Budget, or when the Budget has not been brought into actual existence, the Government shall carry out the Budget of the preceding year'. See also Csaba Gergely Tamás, 'The birth of the parliamentary democracy in Japan: an historical approach' (2012) 17 *Zeitschrift für Japanisches Recht* 146–167.

to develop infrastructure and the military were of such a high order that the budget of the previous year was always highly inadequate and the government needed to compromise with the parliamentarians to make sure that its budget would enable it to implement its policies. These developments gradually engrained the idea of constitutionalism and resulted in its clear ownership by the Japanese people. This was despite the fact that when the constitutional debate was launched, this idea seemed very remote, European and difficult to imagine taking hold in Japan.

Evidence that constitutionalism did take hold in Japan can be seen at the turn of the twentieth century, which brought the emergence of party politics and the development of cities and middle-class society.[38] An impressive number of debates on the protection of constitutionalism took place in this period.[39] This is evidenced, for example, in the number of newspaper articles related to the protection of constitutional politics (憲政擁護) in a leading Japanese newspaper (*Asahi Shinbun*). In 1913, no fewer than 1,084 articles on constitutionalism were published in it. That year, a prominent constitutional scholar – Minobe Tatsukichi – argued that constitutionalism included constitutional restraints on the prerogatives of the head of state – in the case of Japan, of course, the emperor. Minobe also stressed the importance of educating the citizens 'so that they might participate, preserve their rights, and resist despotism of bureaucratic government'.[40] Other scholars criticized his argument vehemently and 'emphasized the Emperor as sovereign, the constitution as his imperial gift, and the historical and moral nature of the state. The people must be educated so that they might develop a strong natural spirit'.[41] These opposing arguments are reflective of the debate on constitutionalism in early twentieth-century Japan and illustrate how a public discussion on legal rights and constitutionalism can be triggered by the constitution. This discussion between two radically opposing camps continued until the start of World War II and left its legacy on Japan's turn to democracy, human rights and the rule of law after 1945.

[38] Richard Sims, *Japanese Political History since the Meiji Restoration, 1868–2000* (London: Palgrave Macmillan, 2001). See also Ta'ichiro Mitani, *The Formation of Party Politics in Japan: The Development of Political Leadership by Hara Kei* (増補日本政党政治の形成: 原敬の政治指導の展開) (Tokyo: Tokyo University Press, 1995).

[39] Yukio Ozaki and Marius B. Jansen, *The Autobiography of Ozaki Yukio: The Struggle for Constitutional Government in Japan* (Princeton, NJ: Princeton University Press, 2001).

[40] Carol Gluck, *Japan's Modern Myths: Ideology in the Late Meiji Period* (Princeton, NJ: Princeton University Press, 1985), p. 241.

[41] Ibid.

3   Post–World War II constitutionalism in Japan and East Asia

World War II's end heralded a new era in the history of constitutionalism in East Asia. Not only the norms of constitutions but also requirements regarding the quality of the norms emerged after 1945, as exemplified by the Charter of the United Nations that was signed in that year.[42] The new Japanese Constitution of 1947 introduced limited government, and despite the fact that it was drafted by the occupation forces – and was therefore labelled by some 'imposed constitutionalism'[43] – the content and the way that authority was construed to determine its meaning resulted in a document for which the people of Japan were the main source or the constituent power that was vested in the people. Moreover, in view of the bitter experiences with Japan, its neighbours were also stakeholders in this new stage of constitutionalism.

As soon as the war ended, the occupation forces announced that they would ensure that a new constitution for Japan would become the cornerstone of a new democratic state, far removed from the spirit of imperialism and militarism in the Meiji Constitution of 1890. Proposals for constitutional reforms soon started to be published. Constitutional drafts by individual lawyers[44] and informal groups of stakeholders as well as by organisations (such as political parties and the Japan Lawyers Association in June 1946) included many progressive provisions and

[42] Thomas Müller, 'Global constitutionalism in historical perspective: towards refined tools for international constitutional histories' (2014) 3 *Global Constitutionalism* 71–107.

[43] This is nowadays to be heard in the discourse of some prominent members of the ruling Liberal Democratic Party of Japan (LDP). In an interview in the newspaper *Nishi Nihon Shinbun* of 28 April 2015, a prominent LDP member of parliament commented that 'it is an historical fact that the Constitution was made under influence of the GHQ. We should be courageous and revise it.' On the concept of imposed constitutions, see Noah Feldman, 'Imposed constitutionalism' (2005) 37 *Connecticut Law Review* 857–889.

[44] Proposals included those of the liberal lawyer Fuse Tatsuji (published in December 1945), Okabayashi Tatsuo (published on 16 May 1946) and organisations such as the Constitutional Research Group (published in November 1945) as well as the draft constitution made by the Japan Communist Party and published on 19 June 1946 and the proposal prepared by the Japan Lawyers Association in June 1946. Fuse Tatsuji (1880–1953) was a leading advocate for universal suffrage. He also was very active in the nationwide Rice Riots of 1918 defending the farmers and later in the defence of the heavily discriminated-against Korean community in pre-war Japan. He also played an important role in assisting tenant farmers in their struggle against the paternalistic and parasitical landlords in the 1920s and 1930s. After Japan's defeat in World War II, he continued to promote citizen rights. Okabayashi Tatsuo (1904–1990) was a lawyer and, from 1932, a member of the Communist Party. Okabayashi remained a leading lawyer of the Communist Party in Japan in the post-war era too. He was a principal lawyer in landmark cases such as the Matsukawa Derailment Incident of 1949.

often were the reflection of insights that had been acquired over a long period of time starting well before World War II. A new wave of constitutionalism from within the country arose and, together with the occupation, pressured the government and legislators to move ahead with establishing restricted government and guarantees for liberties for the people aiming at the transformation of Japan into a genuine democracy. Constitutionalism was alive and well in Japanese society in the aftermath of World War II.

Nonetheless, a new constitution would not have been possible without the occupation forces. The new Japanese prime minister in October 1945 did not consider the constitution a priority. The country was in ruins, and economic recovery was more important, he and his administration stressed. Two days after his appointment, however, the Supreme Commander of the Allied Powers (SCAP), General Douglas MacArthur, summoned the prime minister and ordered five major reforms to foster the transformation of Japan into a stable democracy. Utmost priority was to be on drafting a new constitution.[45] On 13 October 1945, the Constitutional Problems Investigation Committee was established, headed by Matsumoto Jōji, a specialist in commercial law and former minister of commerce and industry. This committee soon produced a draft that was a minor revision of the Meiji Constitution (the emperor retained sovereignty).[46] The Matsumoto draft was leaked to the press in February 1946 and upset readers because of the gap between the people's wishes and the Japanese authorities' failure to depart from the past structure of the imperial nation state.[47]

On 3 February 1946, the General Headquarters (GHQ) ordered its Government Section (GS) to draft a new constitution for Japan. Remarkably, the commission entrusted with the secret task managed to submit its work to the SCAP on 10 February 1946. Three days later, the Japanese authorities accepted this draft and ordered its swift publication and discussion by the Japanese leaders in the subsequent months. In the words of a prominent member of the occupation forces:

> It was the most dramatic period of the institution, when its members had just completed, in strict seclusion and secrecy, the draft of a revised Japanese constitution after it had become evident that the Japanese

[45] Tatsuo Satō, *The History of Drafting the Japanese Constitution*, Vol. 1 (日本憲法成立史) (Tokyo: Yūhikaku, 1962), p. 484. See also Ray A. Moore and Donald L. Robinson, *Partners for Democracy: Crafting the New Japanese State under MacArthur* (Oxford; Tokyo: Oxford University Press, 2002), p. 51.
[46] Ibid.
[47] Satō (n. 45), p. 484.

Government needed guidance and assistance to produce a document that would embody the essentials of democratic government.[48]

Many articles in the draft that would become the Constitution of Japan on 3 May 1947 provided for extensive rights such as the revision of criminal procedure rights and the duties for the government aiming to 'ensure that vulnerable members of society could live with dignity'.[49] The end result was a progressive text that included equality for all people, equal education and many more stipulations that were entrenched in the constitution. Post–World War II Japan construed democracy, human rights and the rule of law as the core of this constitution for a new democratic Japan.[50] Accepting the Constitution of Japan of 1947 was said to be the price that Japan had to pay for World War II. However, the debate that paralleled the drafting process, its implementation by the courts after it went into effect and the fact that it was never amended contradict the labels 'foreign constitution' and 'imposed constitution'. Constitutionalism was genuinely embraced in Japan. The Japanese Constitution can be rightly called one of the most effective initiatives taken by the occupiers after World War II. It also fulfilled a symbolic function: this time, it was not primarily aimed at nation building but more at international peace building. Attention here is mainly directed to the first and the ninth article. The first article stipulates that all power emanates from the people. (Article 1: 'The Emperor shall be the symbol of the State and of the unity of the people, deriving his position from the will of the people with whom resides sovereign power.') Moreover, the symbolic function of peace building by means of Article 9 – the so-called pacifism clause – can hardly be

---

[48] Alfred C. Oppler, *Legal Reform in Occupied Japan: A Participant Looks Back* (Princeton, NJ: Princeton University Press, 1976), p. 20. See Report of Government Section, Supreme Commander of the Allied Powers, *Political Reorientation of Japan, September 1945 to September 1948* (Washington, DC: Government Printing Office), two volumes, p. 790.

[49] Sylvia Brown Hamano, 'Incomplete revolutions and not so alien transplants: the Japanese Constitution and human rights' (1999) 1 *University of Pennsylvania Journal of Constitutional Law* 415–490, at 432.

[50] At this period, it became clear that the SCAP and the Japanese leadership would steer constitutionalism after 1947 in a more legal-positivist direction. The Supreme Court's independence was established, and its judges would have the ultimate authority in determining the constitution's meaning. Japan moved towards what Loughlin defines as 'an analytical logic, in which the judiciary, through a forensic technique of textual interpretation, assert final and exclusive authority to resolve the Constitution's meaning'. Loughlin, 'What is constitutionalisation?' (n. 8), p. 59.

overestimated: it embodies an aim that goes beyond the borders of Japan, namely of restoring trust and long-term peace in East Asia.[51]

Chapter II, Renunciation of War, Constitution of Japan, Article 9:

> Aspiring sincerely to an international peace based on justice and order, the Japanese people forever renounce war as a sovereign right of the nation and the threat or use of force as means of settling international disputes.
>
> In order to accomplish the aim of the preceding paragraph, land, sea, and air forces, as well as other war potential, will never be maintained. The right of belligerency of the state will not be recognized.

This article in the 1947 Constitution was an essential stepping stone to Japan's rapidly becoming the world's second largest economy. Japan did prioritise investments in its civil economy over investments in military-related affairs, and it used the constitution as a shield against mounting pressure by the United States – Japan's new ally – for Japan to reinvest in defence in the wake of the coming Cold War.

Gradually, trust could be restored between Japan and its neighbours, and the state's focus could be redirected to economic development. The way that the state guided economic growth would be commended by many prominent analysts explaining the underlying reason for the so-called Japanese Miracle, i.e. the rapid economic growth after World War II.[52] The constitution certainly played a remarkable role in the positive development of today's Japanese society. Constitutionalism in Japan was no different from that in other nations as it was, per Yasuo Hasebe, 'providing a framework for fair and impartial social cooperation between people with various, incompatible and sometimes even incommensurable worldviews and cultures'.[53] Nonetheless, the discourse gradually changed. The centrality of the language of law gave way to framing with cultural claims of how different Japan was from other societies.[54]

---

[51] Kenneth L. Port, 'Article 9 of the Japanese Constitution and the rule of law' (2005) 13 *Cardozo Journal of International & Comparative Law* 127–160, at 127.

[52] Chalmers Johnson, *MITI and the Japanese Miracle: The Growth of Industrial Policy: 1925–1975* (Stanford, CA: Stanford University Press, 1982). See also David Bennett Friedman, *The Misunderstood Miracle: Industrial Development and Political Change in Japan* (Ithaca, NY: Cornell University Press, 1988).

[53] Albert Hung-Yee Cheng, Jong-Sup Chong, Yasuo Hasebe, Cheryl Saunders, Kevin Yl Tan and Jiunn-Rong Yeh, 'Asian constitutionalism at crossroads: new challenges and opportunities' (2010) 5 *National Taiwan University Law Review* 181–200, at 185.

[54] Tamotsu Aoki, *The Changes in the Theories on the Japanese Culture: Culture and Identity in Postwar Japan* (「日本文化論」の変容―戦後日本の文化とアイデンティティ) (Tokyo: Chūō Kōronsha, 1990).

This occurred particularly in the wake of Japan's rapid economic development after the Korean War and the search in- and outside Japan for the causes of the 'economic miracle'. These messages were reflected in literature on the specificity of Japanese society – labelled *nihonjinron* (日本人論) or 'theory on the Japanese' – many of which became bestsellers in Japan. This literature defined the way the people in- and outside the country thought about stereotypical differences between Japan and its main point of reference, namely the United States. A widely acclaimed article from 1964, 'The Discovery of the Japanese Social Structure',[55] paved the way for a widely supported image of cultural uniqueness, which was followed in 1967 by the bestseller *Human Relationship in a Vertical Society: A Theory of a Homogenous Society.*[56] The author argued that homogenous groups were the core of Japanese society. Many publications in the same vein followed, and some were translated into English. The political and bureaucratic leaders supported the general image in those publications. For example, Amaya Naohiro, a former high-level bureaucrat of the Ministry of International Trade and Industry, commented in an article on the antimonopoly law in Japan that 'today, as in the old days, the basic unit of Japanese society is not "atomistic" individuals, but "molecule-like" groups . . . The fundamental ethic which supports a group has been "harmony"'.[57] Positive messages by political leaders to the Japanese public were frequent. To choose another example, Prime Minister Ohira proclaimed at the end of the 1970s that 'culture would take the place of economics and the rationalistic urbanisation and materialistic civilisation of Western style modernisation would be replaced by the Japanese-style welfare state'.[58] The same type of discourse prevailed in the field of Japanese law.[59]

[55] Chie Nakane, 'The discovery of the Japanese social structure' (日本的社会構造の発見) (1964) 79 *Chūō Kōron* 48–85, at 43.
[56] Chie Nakane, *Human Relations in a Vertically Structured Society: The Theory of a Homogenous Society* (タテ社会の人間関係―単一社会の理論) (Tokyo: Kōdansha Gendaishinsho, 1967).
[57] Naohiro Amaya, 'The ethics of harmony and the logics of the antimonopoly law: what antitrust policy for Japanese society?' (和の倫理と独禁法の論理―日本社会において独禁政策はどうあるべきか?) (1980) 58 *Bungei Shunju* 176–193, at 183. In Frank K. Upham (ed.), *Law and Social Change in Postwar Japan*, translated by Frank Upham (Cambridge, MA: Harvard University Press, 1989), p. 206.
[58] *Asahi Shinbun*, 25 January 1979. Cited by Carol Gluck, 'The past in the present', in Andrew Gordon (ed.), *Postwar Japan as History* (Berkeley, CA: University of California Press, 1993), p. 72.
[59] Yoshiyuki Noda, *Introduction au droit Japonais (Introduction to Japanese Law)* (Paris: Dalloz, 1966).

Tokyo University's Kawashima Takeyoshi wrote in 1963 that 'the specific social attitudes towards disputes are reflected in the judicial process. Japanese not only hesitate to resort to a lawsuit but are also quite ready to settle an action already instituted through conciliatory processes during the course of litigation.'[60] It was easy to understand Kawashima's explanation of a cultural uniqueness of legal thinking in Japan in the context of the broader discourse that prevailed in- and outside Japan. At the same time, it was indeed more advantageous to settle through conciliation processes due to the availability of mediators, the speed of mediation and the relatively low cost. It was in the state's interest to maintain this perception of a gap between Western law and specific cultural practices, as they were also at the base of the idea of the 'imposed constitution'. The perception certainly allowed leadership (i.e. government, civil servants, etc.) to continue to actually control society and more precisely economic developments in a way that became known as 'soft authoritarianism',[61] in which the 'technocratic elite [directed] the course of industrial development by mobilizing domestic resources'.[62] This was what Chalmers Johnson termed the 'developmental state'.[63]

4 The next stage: is global constitutionalism possible in East Asia?

As said, constitutionalism in post-war Japan developed in combination with the 'developmental state'.[64] This prominent example of '"hybrid regimes", which combine democratic and authoritarian elements',[65] is to

[60] Takeyoshi Kawashima, 'Dispute resolution in contemporary Japan', in Arthur Taylor von Mehren (ed.), *Law in Japan: The Legal Order in a Changing Society* (Cambridge, MA: Harvard University Press, 1963), pp. 41–59.
[61] Chalmers Johnson, 'Political institutions and economic performance: the government-business relationship in Japan, South Korea, and Taiwan', in Frederic C. Deyo (ed.), *The Political Economy of the New Asian Industrialism* (Ithaca, NY: Cornell University Press, 1987), p. 136.
[62] Mark Beeson 'Democracy, development, and authoritarianism', in Mark Beeson and Richard Stubbs (eds.), *Routledge Handbook of Asian Regionalism* (London: Routledge, 2012), p. 241; see also Daniel H. Foote, 'The benevolent paternalism of Japanese criminal justice' (1992) 80 *California Law Review* 317–390. On the relationship between the state and citizens, see also Tessa Morris-Suzuki, *The Technological Transformation of Japan: From the Seventeenth to the Twenty-First Century* (Cambridge: Cambridge University Press, 1994).
[63] Chalmers A. Johnson, *Japan, Who Governs? The Rise of the Developmental State* (New York: WW Norton & Company, 1995).
[64] Ibid.
[65] Beeson, 'Democracy, development, and authoritarianism' (n. 62), p. 242.

be found not only in Japan but also elsewhere in East Asia. In their search for economic development and stability since the late 1960s, many states in East Asia embarked on institution building and constitutionalism.[66] According to some authors, this process did not always show the same characteristics as did constitutionalism in Europe. Yeh and Chang, for example, argue that 'what is really shared between East Asian constitutionalism and standard (Western) constitutionalism is a very thin understanding of the liberal constitutional foundation upon which state, society and individuals are defined in one aspect in terms of state-centred institutions and rights guarantees'.[67] The primary aim of constitutionalism remains the same, but the citizen–state relation is perceived quite differently than in European nations. Coleman and Maogoto explain that 'both Eastern and Western perceptions of sovereignty evolved as a response to chaos, and the desire to find order and stability in what were very violent and uncertain environments'.[68] This is true not only for China, Japan and Korea in North-East Asia but also for the nations of South-East Asia. East Asia in the twentieth century suffered various destructive wars, and many nations also struggled with the aftermath of colonisation. Empowered elites wanted clarity as to new territorial arrangements.[69] The reaction of that elite in East Asia, Preston argues, was 'state-making, nation-building and development'.[70] In East Asia, 'the crisis gave aspirant replacement elites their chance and they took it; they seized control of particular parts of the territories of disintegrating state-empires and turned them into states pursuing nation-building'.[71] This could be accomplished only on condition of economic and political stability, when, per Preuss, 'the multitude had to become

---

[66] Justin Blount and Tom Ginsburg, 'Participation in constitutional design: Asian exceptionalism', in Rosalind Dixon and Tom Ginsburg (eds.), *Comparative Constitutional Law in Asia* (Cheltenham: Edward Elgar, 2014), pp. 23–46.

[67] Jiunn-Rong Yeh and Wen-Chen Chang, 'The emergence of East Asia constitutionalism: features in comparison' (2011) *National University of Singapore, Asian Law Institute, Working Paper Series No. 006* 32.

[68] Andrew Coleman and Jackson Nyamuya Maogoto write that the key difference between the two is that in the West the empire 'failed . . . In the East, the Empire won, and the concept of Eastphalian sovereignty was absolute, particularly in its internal dimension'. Andrew Coleman and Jackson Nyamuya Maogoto. '"Westphalian" meets "Eastphalian" sovereignty: China in a globalized world' (2013) 3 *Asian Journal of International Law* 237–269.

[69] Peter Preston, 'The shift to the modern world in East Asia: war, memory and regional identity', in Beeson and Stubbs (eds.), *Routledge Handbook of Asian Regionalism* (n. 62), p. 37.

[70] Ibid., p. 39.

[71] Ibid., p. 41.

a collective entity which embodied the unity of the multitude'.[72] Japan played for various reasons an important role as an example in this process of nation building. It had been the first nation established in the region, it had been successful in economic growth and it was a partner with or at least an important factor to reckon with for many East Asian nations in their endeavours for economic development. In their quest for independence and aim at preserving peace, a certain degree of hybridity (authoritarianism combined with the rule of law) was deemed necessary and resulted in serious consideration of legal codes, the rule of law and an opening to constitutionalism.

Today, the process of regional cooperation in East Asia that relates to law is the development of international production networks (IPNs). These IPNs have been a significant integrative force in the development of the East Asian regional economy.[73] This represents, according to Christopher Dent, the main pattern of regional cooperation in East Asia. Cooperation is no longer restricted to IPNs but spills over to other spheres such as popular culture, civil society and law. Yet the most dynamic and far-reaching processes of cooperation do not centre on the state. East Asia is the platform for modes of regional cooperation – labelled 'regionalisation' – characterised by 'societal-driven, bottom-up process'.[74] Regional cooperation, whether related to trade or to other interactions beyond borders, triggers, however, a discussion on processes and standards. This was no different in East Asia. In the region, the IPNs' increasing importance, internal economic development and the need to forge alliances (such as in Europe, often referred to in East Asia as 'fortress Europe') have an important impact. Also, in the region, China is growing more powerful and assertive.

The Association of Southeast Asian Nations (ASEAN) is an important institution in this respect. It was established in 1967 in response to increasing regional tension due to the Vietnam War. ASEAN was first aimed at peace preservation and then from the mid-1970s developed gradually into an association for economic development. ASEAN includes ten member states (Brunei, Cambodia, Indonesia, Laos, Malaysia, Myanmar, the Philippines, Singapore, Thailand and Vietnam). In the aftermath of the Cold War and the Asian financial crisis of 1997–1998, ASEAN had to reorient itself and prove its political

---

[72] Ulrich K. Preuss, 'Disconnecting constitutions from statehood', in Loughlin and Dobner (eds.), *The Twilight of Constitutionalism?* (n. 8), p. 35.

[73] Christopher M. Dent, *East Asian Regionalism*, 2nd ed. (London: Routledge, 2016), p. 40.

[74] Ibid., p. 7.

relevance to avoid becoming obsolete at a time when Japan and China became the main contenders for leadership over East Asia.[75] This proved no easy task, as ASEAN adheres rigorously to its own modus operandi, the so-called ASEAN Way. This way consists of an emphasis on informal rules, decision making exclusively by consensus, conflict avoidance rather than conflict resolution and absolute non-interference.[76] It is considered a more effective path to regional cooperation than the transnationalism of the EU. Remarkably, in 2007, ASEAN took an important first step towards formalising regional cooperation through the promulgation of the ASEAN Charter. The ASEAN Charter is also an important first step in a possible debate on global constitutionalism, as it promotes legal norms: its preamble proclaims respect for 'the principles of democracy, the rule of law and good governance, respect for and protection of human rights and fundamental freedoms'.[77]

The gradual turn towards formal cooperation and an increased prominence of legal framing can be seen in Article 14 of the Charter, which stipulates the establishment of the ASEAN Human Rights Body.[78] Following Article 14, the ASEAN Intergovernmental Commission on Human Rights (AICHR) was launched on 23 October 2009 to 'promote and protect human rights and fundamental freedoms of the peoples of ASEAN'.[79] AICHR working groups began drafting an ASEAN Human Rights Declaration (AHRD) in 2011. This too was a remarkable move towards promoting fundamental legal norms with validity beyond a single nation state. The drafting process involved consultation with civil society organisations.[80] The AHRD was adopted by ASEAN's heads

---

[75] See Beeson and Stubbs (eds.), *Routledge Handbook of Asian Regionalism* (n. 62).

[76] Amitav Acharya, 'Human rights and regional order: ASEAN and human rights management in post-Cold War Southeast Asia' (1995) *Human Rights and International Relations in the Asia-Pacific* 167–182. The ASEAN Way can be called an international regime because it fits the definition of international regimes by Stephen Krasner, i.e. 'regimes can be defined as sets of implicit or explicit principles, norms, rules, and decision-making procedures around which actors' expectations converge in a given area of international relations'. Stephen D. Krasner, *International Regimes* (Ithaca, NY: Cornell University Press, 1983), p. 8.

[77] The ASEAN Charter (http://www.asean.org/wp-content/uploads/images/archive/publications/ASEAN-Charter.pdf).

[78] Mathew Davies, 'Explaining the Vientiane Action Programme: ASEAN and the institutionalisation of human rights' (2013) 26 *The Pacific Review* 385–406, at 386.

[79] AICHR–ASEAN Intergovernmental Commission on Human Rights (http://aichr.org). Also: Yuval Ginbar, 'Human rights in ASEAN: setting sail or treading water?' (2010) 10 *Human Rights Law Review* 504–518.

[80] See Katherine G. Southwick, 'Bumpy road to the ASEAN Human Rights Declaration' (2013) 197 Asia Pacific Bulletin 1–2, at 1.

of state in Phnom Penh on 18 November 2012, emphasising in its preamble 'human rights cooperation' between the ASEAN nations but without any mention of specific mechanisms or commitments for the protection of human rights.[81] The AHRD affirms that the UN Declaration of Human Rights is universal. Besides civil and political rights, it also refers to economic, social and cultural rights, the right to development and the right to peace.

In parallel to these developments, the ASEAN Committee on the Rights of Migrant Workers (ACMW) and the ASEAN Commission on Women and Children (ACWC) were established in 2007 and 2010, respectively. Together with AICHR and the AHRD, the ACMW and the ACWC could become the stepping stones of a debate on fundamental legal norms for South-East Asia. Nonetheless, scepticism about the prospects of the debate remains warranted, as the restrictions in the recently established human rights instruments are manifold. ASEAN's first human rights institutions did not foresee any compliance or enforcement procedures, as these would threaten the sacrosanct ASEAN approach of non-interference in domestic matters; remedies are possible only at the national level. How to overcome this approach that stems out of historical experiences is a major concern for the global constitutionalism debate.

Obviously, the preceding developments illustrate the strong prevalence of the state in formal regional mechanisms for the protection of human rights, but this exists parallel to important bottom-up dynamics involving stakeholders in a vibrant economic, cultural and civil society environment. It is therefore the case – in a similar way to what we see in Japan nationally – that a hybrid structure of state and citizen is shaping the policy debates. In that structure, we see potential for the global constitutionalism debate in East Asia as 'an increasing range of public life is being subjected to the discipline of the norms of liberal-legal constitutionalism'.[82] The global constitutionalism debate is therefore not foreign to East Asia and can contribute in an important way – repeating Yasuo Hasebe's statement – to providing 'a framework for fair and impartial social cooperation between people with various, incompatible and sometimes even incommensurable worldviews and cultures'.[83]

---

[81] ASEAN Human Rights Declaration, 19 November 2012, Phnom Penh, www.asean.org /storage/images/ASEAN_RTK_2014/6_AHRD_Booklet.pdf.

[82] Loughlin, 'What is constitutionalisation?' (n. 8), p. 61.

[83] Albert Hung-Yee Cheng et al. (n. 53), at 185.

5 Conclusion

Despite the association in East Asia of the debate about global constitutionalism with historical experiences of constitutionalism, a bottom-up dynamic led by intellectuals and other members of civil society launched a process that results in the development of the idea of constitutionalism.

True, the first constitution of East Asia, Japan's Meiji Constitution of 1889, was a tool for the government to control the people in the emperor's name, but the debate on constitutionalism engrained the idea deeply in the public discourse and impacted policies directly and indirectly. After 1945, the occupation forces drafted a new constitution for Japan, which promoted democracy and individual rights as the pillars of post-war Japan. This led to a resilient constitution with the people of Japan as the main source of the constituent power. The outcome resulted from a continuous debate that existed in Japanese society well before the end of World War II and that continues to play an important role in the dynamics of today's Japanese society. The constitution was embraced by the Japanese people, and this was helpful in stimulating rapid economic growth.

The first steps of a gradual process can also be observed in East Asia of late, according to which formal institution building and mechanisms for the promotion and protection of norms beyond the nation states are being established. As in the Japanese experience, this process is highly influenced by the historical experiences of the South-East Asian nations. It is also reflective of a gap between citizens and the state. Nonetheless, recent developments of more formal institutions and a turn toward the rule of law prove that a bottom-up movement can, when the time is ripe, result in opening a window of opportunity. The ongoing processes that can be observed in South-East Asia are promising for the debate on global constitutionalism in East Asia, but the debate as it develops in East Asia is premised on an awareness of historical experiences and of cultural framing that impacts the relation between citizens and state in the way they understand the debate.

Aside from the legacy of history, it is a bottom-up perspective on the development of legal norms that will offer insights as to the viability of the global constitutionalism debate for East Asia.[84] The intellectual framework of global constitutionalism can contribute to establishing

---

[84] In the global constitutionalism debate related to East Asia, therefore, a discussion that concerns not only transnational global norms but also private actors' inclusion in the process of juridification will be important. Lars Chr. Blichner and Anders Molander, 'Mapping juridification' (2008) 14 *European Law Journal* 36–54.

a common platform to link regionalism with regionalisation – i.e. to bridge state and society.[85] It can also help powerful states to enhance their influence beyond political allies and beyond their national borders as well as help less powerful states in their economic development, because they will be able to rely on the norms of global constitutionalism in their domestic and global organisation and operations. Finally, it can acknowledge diversity and foster inclusion of all communities in a rapidly changing context by providing a platform and framework for dialogue. If global constitutionalism is more a debate on global legitimacy than a debate on ideology, it should offer possibilities for East Asia.[86]

[85] Anne Peters, 'The merits of global constitutionalism' (2009) 16 *Indiana Journal of Global Legal Studies* 397–411.

[86] See, for example, Peter J. Katzenstein, *A World of Regions: Asia and Europe in the American Imperium* (Ithaca, NY: Cornell University Press, 2005).

7

Chinese Perspectives on the Rule of Law

Prospects and Challenges for Global Constitutionalism

MATTHIEU BURNAY

1 Introduction

The beginning of the twenty-first century marked the return of the rule of law to the top of the agenda of states as well as regional and international organisations. Although the rule of law finds its origins in European legal traditions – one often relates it to the English rule of law, German *Rechtsstaat* and French *Etat de Droit* – it has become a principle at the very heart of many constitutions worldwide. It functions as an ideal, meaning that the society should be ruled by the law and that the ruler him- or herself should be subservient to the law. It constitutes therefore the ultimate protection against arbitrariness and abuses of power. Emblematically, the United Nations General Assembly (UNGA) adopted by consensus the High-Level Declaration on the Rule of Law at the National and International Levels (the Declaration) in September 2012.[1] While the Declaration constitutes a milestone on the rocky path towards a consensus on the rule of law at the national and international levels, the Declaration does acknowledge the diversity in understandings of the rule of law, as it points to the 'broad diversity of national experiences in the area of the rule of law'.[2] The rule of law is, in other words, recognised as a home-grown concept whose definition and content vary by state depending on the legal culture, constitutional tradition as well as economic, social and political system at hand. This innovative approach negates the universal character of the rule of law and recognises the existence of a multiplicity of rule of law experiences across legal cultures and traditions. Being one of 'the trinitarian mantra of the constitutionalist

---

[1] UNGA, Declaration of the High-Level Meeting of the General Assembly on the Rule of Law at the National and International Levels, A/67/L.1, 2012, adopted by consensus.
[2] Ibid., para. 10.

faith',[3] the rule of law acts as both a condition and a mutually reinforcing driver of constitutionalism: 'as the highest law of the state, constitutions contain the laws that must prevail if the RoL is to be achieved'.[4] Recognition of rule of law diversity across legal systems is therefore necessary for a critical understanding of the prospects for the emergence of a consensus on global constitutionalism and the constitutionalisation of international law.

Against this background, the present chapter aims to analyse the Chinese perspective on the rule of law. The People's Republic of China (PRC) has re-emerged as a central actor in global governance, and understanding the development of the 'socialist rule of law with Chinese characteristics' is necessary to understanding the prospects for China's contribution to global constitutionalism and the constitutionalisation of international law.

Within traditional Chinese society, rule of law as a concept for social governance in the term's modern sense never attained the same prestige and importance as it did in Europe or the United States. Apart from a first failed attempt to embrace some kind of rule of law during the republican era (1911–1949), only very recently did the rule of law emerge atop China's political agenda. It was, in fact, in the midst of the opening-up and reforms policies (1979–) that China started a process that brought back, to a certain extent, the principle of legality to the heart of Chinese society and its governance model. This reform of the legal system aimed to restore social, economic and political stability[5] in a country that had been deeply harmed by a decade of Cultural Revolution[6] as well as to create the cohesion and openness required to attract foreign investments and contribute to China's socio-economic development. The reform of the legal system furthermore engendered a dynamic in which the law has become progressively

[3] Mattias Kumm, Anthony F. Lang Jr., James Tully and Antje Wiener, 'How large is the world of global constitutionalism?' (2014) 3 *Global Constitutionalism* 1–8, at 3.
[4] Tom Ginsburg and Mila Versteeg, 'Constitutional correlates of the rule of law', in Maurice Adams, Anne Meuwese and Ernst Hirsch Ballin (eds.), *Constitutionalism and the Rule of Law: Bridging Idealism and Realism* (Cambridge: Cambridge University Press, 2017), p. 506.
[5] Political stability became ensured by a greater institutionalisation of the political system and decision-making process. See, for instance, David Sg Goodman, 'The transition to the post-revolutionary era' (1988) 10 *Third World Quarterly* 111–128, at 112.
[6] Benjamin Liebman, 'Assessing China's legal reforms' (2009) 23 *Columbia Journal of Asian Law* 17–33, at 23.

perceived as enabling citizens to enhance their rights, particularly in voluntary private agreements.

In order to understand the prospects of China contributing to the reflection on global constitutionalism and the constitutionalisation of international law, this chapter begins by analysing the three main drivers of the growing 'legalisation' of the Chinese society during the opening-up and reforms era. It then briefly refers to the recent emphasis put by the Chinese Communist Party (CCP) on the socialist rule of law with Chinese characteristics in its rhetoric and policy-making. Finally, the chapter critically assesses the main challenges for the Chinese legal system from a rule of law point of view. It argues that China's 'multiple-speeds legal system' contains some attributes of a rule of law system, while remaining continuously influenced by China's one-party system. It uses therefore the distinction between 'formal' and 'substantive' versions of the rule of law or rather between 'thin' and 'thick' versions of the rule of law.[7] While 'thin' rule of law is limited to a minimalist version of the rule of law and includes the basic conditions for a legal system, 'thick' versions of the rule of law include 'elements of political morality'[8] and therefore also look at the substantial quality of the legal rules. Typically, Western liberal-democratic rule of law traditions recognise the interdependence between human rights, democracy and the rule of law.[9] This chapter concludes that the challenge for the CCP is to give enough guarantees for the development of a rule of law that leaves enough scope for the reinforcement of the principle of legality within China, while not challenging its own monopoly on the political power. In such a context, the prospects for China's contribution to global constitutionalism and the constitutionalisation of international law can only appear limited.

---

[7] See generally Paul Craig, 'Formal and substantive conceptions of the rule of law: an analytical framework', in Richard Bellamy (ed.), *The Rule of Law and the Separation of Powers* (Aldershot: Ashgate, 2005), pp. 95–115; Brian Tamanaha, *On the Rule of Law: History, Politics, Theory* (Cambridge: Cambridge University Press, 2004), p. 190; and Randall Peerenboom (ed.), *Asian Discourses of Rule of Law: Theories and Implementation of Rule of Law in Twelve Asian Countries, France and the US* (London: Routledge, 2004), p. 508.

[8] Randall Peerenboom, 'The X-files: past and present portrayals of China's alien "legal system"' (2003) 2 *Washington University Global Law Studies Review* 37–95, at 58.

[9] See, for example, Statement by José Manuel Barroso on 'The European Union and the rule of law' at the UNGA High-Level Meeting on the Rule of Law, United Nations, 24 September 2012.

2   A modern legal system as an instrument of reforms and opening up

From a legal point of view, the opening-up and reforms policy initiated by Deng Xiaoping – and pursued by the next three generations of Chinese leaders – has arguably had three main consequences that have all contributed to the growing 'legalisation' of Chinese society. These include the proliferation of laws and growing institutionalisation of the legislative process; the strengthening of legal capacity through training and professionalisation of the judicial function; and the growing legal awareness of Chinese citizens as well as their growing recourse to litigation.

Since the beginning of the opening-up and reforms policy, the PRC has enacted a huge number of laws in a dynamic best described as 'legal proliferation'. The gradual opening of China to the rest of the world along with China's fast economic growth required tackling issues and situations with complex legal implications. The overall purpose of these new laws has been to strengthen the legal capacity of the country. Three important caveats must be added at this stage.

First, the quantitative evolution of legislation unfortunately does not equate with a qualitative evolution. Chinese laws and regulations are, in comparison with those of well-developed legal systems in Europe and the United States, particularly vague and abstract, and they generally leave a great scope for interpretation.[10] The 'zones of lawlessness' that remain in the Chinese legal system can prove useful for the state, as they provide a 'space of flexibility to cope with unforeseen circumstances'.[11] Second, the various fields of law have not been developed at the same speed. More than half of the 130 laws adopted between 1979 and 1993 related to economics and administration.[12] Although the disequilibrium is not as significant today, laws and regulations in the field of private law have clearly remained the priority during the period of opening-up and reforms policy. Third, the institutionalisation of law-making does not imply that all the institutions involved have the same influence on the construction of the Chinese legal system. For example, the Standing Committee of the National People's Congress retains a much greater

---

[10] Liebman (n. 6), at 30. In his views, the lack of specificities in Chinese legislation would explain the necessary flexibility in China's legal reforms.

[11] Flora Sapio, *Sovereign Power and the Law in China* (Leiden: Brill, 2010), p. 4.

[12] He Weifang, *In the Name of Justice: Striving for the Rule of Law in China* (Washington, DC: Brookings Institution Press, 2012), p. XXXVIII.

influence than the National People's Congress (NPC), which meets only once a year. The importance of the Standing Committee of the National People's Congress is best demonstrated by its legislating 'in an *ultra vires* fashion' when it enacts laws that normally fall under the exclusive competence of the NPC[13] per Article 7 of the Legislation Law.[14]

In parallel to the regulatory and legal proliferation process, China has simultaneously strengthened its legal and judicial capacity through the creation of modern institutions. These include the legislature, a comprehensive court system as well as administrative and enforcement agencies. The reform of legal education and the professionalisation of the judiciary appear here as two important drivers in the legal and judicial capacity building. Although almost all law schools were closed during the Cultural Revolution and most judges did not dispose of the necessary technical knowledge, legal education has been truly strengthened during the period of opening up and reforms.[15] From having been a totally underdeveloped field of studies, law curriculums are now established in the main Chinese universities and have become a very popular major. The greater demand for legal studies has in turn led to the improvement of the training and technical knowledge of legal practitioners.[16] This improvement has also been favoured by the establishment of highly competitive examinations to obtain the positions of lawyers, judges and prosecutors.[17]

Nonetheless, the full professionalisation of the judiciary remains problematic. The absence of a professional legal tradition 'weakens the development of legal ethical rules essential to a healthy legal

---

[13] Jianfu Chen, 'Sources of law and law-making', in *Chinese Law: Context and Transformation* (Leiden: Martinus Nijhoff Publishers, 2008), p. 182; Stanley B. Lubman (ed.), *The Evolution of Law Reform in China: An Uncertain Path* (Cheltenham: Edward Elgar, 2012), p. 216.

[14] Legislation Law of the People's Republic of China, adopted at the Third Session of the Ninth National People's Congress on 15 March 2000 and promulgated by Order No. 31 of the president of the People's Republic of China on 15 March 2000.

[15] For a comprehensive set of statistics on legal education in China, see Guanghua Yu, *The Roles of Law and Politics in China's Development* (Singapore: Springer, 2014), pp. 53–59.

[16] See Weifang He, 'China's legal profession: the nascence and growing pains of a professionalized legal class' (2005) 19 *Columbia Journal of Asian Law* 138–51, at 145. See also generally Wang Zhenmin, 'Legal education in China' (2002) 36 *The International Lawyer* 1203–1212; Jean Pierre Cabestan, Qinglan Li, Sun Ping and Yves Dolais, 'The renaissance of the legal profession in China', in Mireille Delmas-Marty and Pierre-Etienne Will (eds.), *China, Democracy and Law: A Historical and Contemporary Approach* (Leiden: Brill, 2013), pp. 705–740.

[17] Jingwen Zhu, 'China law development report 2012: professionalization of China's legal workers' (2013) 8 *Frontiers of Law in China* 857–861, at 858.

profession'.[18] The Ministry of Justice has recently called on its local branches to promote professional legal ethics among lawyers. In this campaign, the ministry also emphasised the role of lawyers 'to safeguard social peace' – understand the absence of contestation.[19] In addition, foreign lawyers are still not allowed direct access to the Chinese judiciary, which obviously impedes the development of a fully open judicial system.[20] Finally, the legal education that was very promising in the 1990s appears to be facing a crisis today, with a very large number of law graduates seriously struggling to find a job. 'Shifts in the broader political wind' and reflection upon 'the new official line regarding law and legal institutions' also constitute new difficulties related to legal education in China.[21]

During the reforms and opening-up era, the public awareness and trust that law and the judicial system can act as privileged instruments to resolve disputes have grown. There were 440,000 cases accepted by People's Courts of First Instance in 1978 and more than five million in 1996.[22] The increasing use of formal litigation also changed the overall perspective of Chinese citizens vis-à-vis judicial proceedings. To say that legal consciousness is now high in China would be an oversimplification; it is arguable that Chinese citizens are more aware of their rights. Mary E. Gallagher still talks of an 'informed disenchantment' to describe plaintiffs' perception of the Chinese legal system. In her words, 'engagement with the law may leave one with a better sense of one's rights but with reduced belief in the law as a capable protector of those rights'.[23] Lack of trust in the system and its related legitimacy remains the first impediment to formal litigation's recognition as the primary channel to protect citizens' rights. A further impediment originates in a recent setback

[18] He (n. 16), 146.
[19] 'Chinese lawyers asked to promote the rule of law', *Global Times*, 4 June 2014, available at http://www.globaltimes.cn/content/863876.shtml.
[20] See Andrew Godwin, 'The professional "tug of war": the regulation of foreign lawyers in China, business scope issues and some suggestions for reform' (2009) 33 *Melbourne University Law Review* 132–162. Godwin argues that a distinction must be made between the 'strict letter of the law' and 'the liberal interpretation and enforcement of the law' that regulate what foreign lawyers are authorised to do in China (at 132).
[21] Carl F. Minzner, 'The rise and fall of Chinese legal education' (2013) 13 *Fordham International Law Journal* 334–395, at 336.
[22] Jingwen Zhu, 'Data analysis of flow of litigation into different channels in China' (2009) 30 *Social Sciences in China* 100–118, at 100.
[23] Mary E. Gallagher, 'Mobilizing the law in China: "informed disenchantment" and the development of legal consciousness' (2006) 40 *Law and Society Review* 783–816, at 809–810.

against formal litigation, with the CCP organising a mass campaign promoting mediation in preference to formal litigation. This policy change was originally anchored in an interpretation of China's Supreme Court in 2007 that called for the rate of cases solved through mediation within Chinese courts to be increased.[24] In the opinion of Wang Shengjun, former president of China's Supreme Court, mediation should even take priority in civil disputes.[25]

3   China's recent emphasis on the rule of law

As late as in 1999, the rule of law became a constitutional principle with the inclusion of a new paragraph in Article 5 of the PRC Constitution. The amendment read as follows: 'the People's Republic of China governs the country according to law and makes it a socialist country under rule of law'.[26] The Law on Legislation that was promulgated a year later to harmonise and strengthen the Chinese legal system also refers to the building of a 'Socialist Country under the Rule of Law' without actually defining it.[27]

In the last two decades, the Chinese government has increasingly referred to the rule of law. The emphasis on the rule of law recently became even more frequent, as exemplified by the theme chosen for the 2014 Fourth Plenum of the CCP, namely Governing the Nation in Accord with the Law (*yifa zhiguo*). During the Plenum, the socialist rule of law was presented as the main solution to China's main

---

[24] Several Opinions of the SPC on Further Displaying the Positive Roles of Litigation Mediation in Building of a Harmonious Socialist Society (最高人民法院关于进一步发挥诉讼调解在构建社会主义和谐社会中积极作用的若干意见), dated 1 March 2007, in Knut B. Pissler, 'Mediation in China: threat to the rule of law?', in Klaus J. Hopt and Felix Steffek (eds.), *Mediation: Principles and Regulations in Comparative Perspective* (Oxford: Oxford University Press, 2013), p. 964.

[25] See Wang Shengjun, 'Chinese Chief Justice stresses priority of mediation over court rulings in civil cases', Xinhua News Agency, available at http://www.gov.cn/english/2011–05/30/content_1873796.htm.

[26] Amendment to the Constitution of the People's Republic of China, adopted at the Second Session of the Ninth National People's Congress and promulgated for implementation by the announcement of the National People's Congress on 15 March 1999.

[27] Art. 1 of the Law on Legislation reads as follows: 'This Law is enacted in accordance with the Constitution with a view to standardizing legislation, establishing a sound legislative system of the State, establishing and improving the socialist legal system with Chinese characteristics, safeguarding and developing socialist democracy, promoting the government of the country according to law and building a socialist country under the rule of law.' Legislation Law of the PRC, adopted at the Third Session of the Ninth National People's Congress on 15 March 2000 and promulgated by Order No. 31 of the president of the People's Republic of China on 15 March 2000.

challenges. The role that has been assigned to the rule of law as both an objective and an instrument to tackle some of China's main economic, social and political challenges is most evident in an editorial of Xinhua News Agency that was published right before the Plenum. It argued: 'All the pains currently suffered by the Chinese economy – ranging from overcapacity, real estate bubbles, risks of local government debts and shadow banks, to restricted growth in non-public sectors and insufficient innovation – could find their roots in excessive administrative interference, corruption and unfair competition, all of which are the result of the lack of rule of law.'[28]

In a context where democratic and human rights values are increasingly portrayed as external values imposed by Western forces, the socialist rule of law with Chinese characteristics appears useful to support the legitimacy and sustainability of the CCP ruling. In a communiqué on 'the Current State of the Ideological Sphere' that was circulated within the Party by its General Office – a document better known as 'Document 9' – the Party opposed the promotion of 'Western Constitutional Democracy' and 'universal values' to the promotion of socialist values as defined within China's Constitution and political doctrine.[29] Per Document 9, the socialist rule of law with Chinese characteristics can appear as a useful principle to frame China's policies and reforms. Unlike democracy and human rights, the rule of law does not, in fact, have a strong connotation anchored in constraining international rules (e.g. Universal Declaration on Human Rights) or ideologies (e.g. liberal democracy). It leaves much scope for interpretation and can be more easily presented as a home-grown concept. Nevertheless, major uncertainties remain regarding the actual implementation of the conclusions of the Plenum and regarding the prospects for maintaining the rule of law on the CCP policy agenda in the future. China's legal system continues to face numerous challenges from a rule of law perspective. Some of these will be elaborated in the next section.

4   Challenges to the rule of law in China

Despite all the major developments in the Chinese legal system since the start of the opening-up and reforms era, many shortcomings that cast

[28] Wang Cong, 'Xinhua insight: CPC convenes first plenum on "rule of law" in reform, anti-graft drive', Xinhua News Agency, available at http://news.xinhuanet.com/english/indepth/2014–10/20/c_133729667.htm.
[29] Document 9: A Chinafile Translation, Chinafile.org, 8 November 2013, available at http://www.chinafile.com/document-9-chinafiletranslation.

considerable doubt on China's past and present progress towards a full-fledged rule of law system cannot but be pointed to.[30] Three elements highlight the genuine shortcomings of the Chinese legal system from a rule of law perspective. These include the lack of constitutionalism, shortcomings in law implementation/law enforcement as well as the recent authoritarian tendency to 'turn against law'.

4.1   The constitution as a 'sleeping beauty' (Ji Weidong)

The current Chinese Constitution was enacted in 1982 and was subsequently revised in 1988, 1993, 1999 and 2004.[31] The new text mirrors the Chinese government's willingness to depart from the conception of a state in perpetual revolution and its intention to build up a modern and more stable society. The constitution is not only a socialist constitution that provides 'barometers of the state's policies and values and reflect[s] the current social condition'.[32] It is also a document with political values that enables 'judges, activist lawyers, and Chinese citizens to use the courts as a mechanism for constitutional litigation, and by scholars to push for what is usually referred to as "judicialization of the constitution"'.[33]

While the constitution exists and is often referred to by Chinese leaders,[34] the absence of constitutionalism can be asserted as a main shortcoming of the Chinese legal system.[35] It implies that the constitution is not the supreme source of power and legitimacy. In practice, the

---

[30] Carothers argues that 'rewriting constitutions, laws, and regulations is the easy part. Far-reaching institutional reform, also necessary, is arduous and slow.' Thomas Carothers, 'The rule of law revival' (1998) 77 *Foreign Affairs* 95–106, at 95–96.

[31] Constitution of the People's Republic of China, adopted at the Fifth Session of the Fifth National People's Congress, promulgated for implementation by the proclamation of the National People's Congress on 4 December 1982 and amended subsequently in 1988, 1993, 1999 and 2004.

[32] Ann Kent, 'Waiting for rights: China's human rights and China's Constitutions' (1991) 13 *Human Rights Quarterly* 170–201, at 182; Thomas E. Kellogg, 'Constitutionalism with Chinese characteristics? Constitutional development and civil litigation in China' (2009) 7 *International Journal of Constitutional Law* 215–246, at 217.

[33] Kellogg, ibid., at 218.

[34] On the occasion of the thirtieth anniversary of the 1982 Constitution, President Xi Jinping stated that 'to fully implement the Constitution needs to be the sole task and the basic work in building a socialist nation ruled by law'. As quoted in Zhao Yinan, 'Uphold Constitution, Xi says', *China Daily*, 5 December 2012, available at http://usa.chinadaily.com.cn/china/2012–12/05/content_15985894.htm.

[35] Qianfan Zhang, 'A constitution without constitutionalism: the paths of constitutional development in China' (2010) 8 *International Constitutionalism* 950–76, at 951.

absence of constitutionalism is best demonstrated by the absence of a truly independent mechanism to interpret, enforce or review the constitution and by the impossibility of invoking and protecting constitutional rights in Chinese courts.[36] In an apparent attempt to render the constitution litigable, the Supreme People's Court (SPC) made a direct reference to a constitutional right in a judicial interpretation in 2001. The notorious *Qi Yuling* case was then concluded by the Higher People's Court of Shandong Province applying this innovative judicial interpretation.[37] In that case, Qi Yuling was denied her right to access education – a right protected by Article 46 of the constitution[38] – because another person, Chen Xiaoqi, had attended university using her name and identity. In its interpretation, the SPC stated that 'given the facts in this case, we believe that, by means of infringing on Qi Yuling's right to select and use her own name, Chen Xiaoqi et al. have violated her fundamental constitutional right to education and have caused actual damages. Therefore, Chen Xiaoqi et al. should bear corresponding civil liability.'[39] The Higher People's Court ruled, in agreement with the SPC interpretation, that Qi Yuling should be awarded compensation 'for the direct and indirect economic loss and mental injury arising from the infringement of the right to education'.[40] Despite the great hopes and positive reactions in response to this first attempt at judicial review, the SPC cancelled its own decision in a notice in 2008.[41] No real explanations were given, but this sudden change made it clear that the *Qi Yuling* case was 'an outlier, not a trendsetter' on the rocky path towards constitutionalism in China.[42]

[36] On the challenge of constitutionalism in China, see Stéphanie Balme and Michael W. Dowdle (eds.), *Building Constitutionalism in China* (New York: Palgrave Macmillan, 2009).
[37] *Qi Yuling v. Chen Xiaoqi et al.*: Dispute over Infringement of a Citizen's Basic Right to Receive Education Protected by Constitution, Higher People's Court of Shandong Province, 2001, available at http://www.lawinfochina.com/display.aspx?lib=case&; id=124.
[38] Art. 46 reads as follows: 'Citizens of the People's Republic of China have the duty as well as the right to receive education' (§1). 'The state promotes the all-round development of children and young people, morally, intellectually and physically' (§2).
[39] *Qi Yuling v. Chen Xiaoqi et al.* (n. 37); Judicial interpretation by the Supreme People's Court (2006) 39 *Chinese Education and Society* 58.
[40] *Qi Yuling v. Chen Xiaoqi et al.* (n. 37).
[41] Supreme People's Court Decision on Abolishing Some Judicial Interpretations (the Seventh Batch), issued before the end of 2008, 18 December 2008.
[42] Donald Clarke, 'Supreme People's Court withdraws Qi Yuling interpretation', *Chinese Law Prof Blog*, 12 January 2009, available at http://lawprofessors.typepad.com/china_law_prof_blog/2009/01/supreme-peoples.html.

This quite negative picture should not overshadow the important role of the constitution in setting agendas and raising constitutional awareness. Constitutionalism should be perceived as a process that crystallises and testifies to the progresses and setbacks of the Chinese legal system. The paradox is that despite its reluctance to go in the direction of constitutionalism, China has sought to constitutionalise very important issues. The constitutional reform of 2004 introduced significant new rights in the Chinese Constitution, including the protection of human rights (Const. Article 33) and property rights (Const. Article 13). The Chinese government has thereby created 'its own nightmare'[43] by introducing new clauses in its constitution that people now keep invoking. Despite the continuous pressure and setbacks, Chinese citizens have not forsaken the constitutional argument, and they continue to put into action their constitutional awareness: 'They have continued to constitutionalize a broad range of political-legal disputes and advance increasingly sophisticated constitutional arguments concurrently through litigation, petitions, review proposals, academic and popular literature, media commentary, and other forums.'[44] An interesting recent example of constitutional (and rule of law) activism is an editorial that was published jointly by thirteen Chinese newspapers. The editorial denounced the well-known *Hukou* system – the household registration system – and asked for it to be reformed significantly in agreement with the constitution. The editorial read as follows:

> The Constitution stipulates that the citizens of the People's Republic of China are all equal before the law, that the nation respects and protects human rights, and that the citizens' personal freedoms will not be infringed upon. Freedom of movement is an inseparable component of human rights and personal freedom; it is a basic right that the Constitution bestowed the people. However, the current household registration policy has created unequal statuses among urban residents and between urban residents and peasants, constraining the Chinese citizens' freedom of movement. All laws and administrative and local regulations must not contradict the Constitution – this is the legal basis for accelerating the current reforms of the household registration system.[45]

[43] Jerome Cohen referred to the creation by the CCP of 'its own nightmare' when referring to the significant changes in the Chinese legal system that inform and sometimes even encourage pressure for further reforms.
[44] Keith Hand, 'Resolving constitutional disputes in contemporary China' (2011) 7 *University of Pennsylvania East Asia Law Review* 51–160, at 57.
[45] For the original text of the editorial and a translation, see Donald Clarke, 'The famous Hukou editorial', *Chinese Law Prof Blog*, 26 March 210, available at http://lawprofessors.typepad.com/china_law_prof_blog/2.010/03/the-famous-hukou-editorial.html.

4.2 Law implementation and law enforcement

Even if the Chinese legal system has become increasingly comprehensive through the opening-up and reforms policy, a gap remains between the text of the law and the implementation of the law in China. Following Roscoe Pound's distinction between the 'law in the books' and the 'law in action',[46] a legal system needs to see its legislation properly implemented all over the country and enforced by the competent judicial and administrative authorities for it to be considered truly effective. In order to understand and explain the significance of the law implementation/ enforcement shortcomings, reference is usually made to China's environmental law.

As the leading emitter of greenhouse gases worldwide, China is only gradually endorsing a more active role for itself in the global climate regime, and it still refuses to endorse any binding commitments such as emission reduction targets.[47] While China is very often criticised (like the United States) for its reluctance to abide by specific emission reduction targets under an international treaty, China's central government has developed a panoply of environmental laws (i.e. the Environmental Protection Law[48]) and regulations covering a wide range of issues that include water pollution,[49] the protection of the marine environment[50] and atmospheric pollution.[51] All these provisions mirror the growing recognition of the need to fight against pollution, especially as China will be very vulnerable to the effects of rising temperatures. The main challenges of Chinese environmental law do not therefore come from the 'law in the books' as much as from the 'law in action', the central government having great difficulty in combating non-compliance and weak

---

[46] Roscoe Pound, 'Law in books and law in action' (1910) 44 *American Law Review* 12–36.
[47] David Belis and Simon Schunz, 'China, the European Union and global environmental governance: the case of climate change', in Hans Bruyninckx, Qi Ye, Nguyen Quang Thuan and David Belis, *The Governance of Climate Relations between Europe and Asia: Evidence from China and Vietnam as Key Emerging Economies* (Cheltenham; Northampton, MA: Edward Elgar, 2013), p. 56.
[48] The Environmental Protection Law of the People's Republic of China, adopted on 26 December 1989, as revised at the Eighth Meeting of the Standing Committee of the Twelfth National People's Congress of the People's Republic of China on 24 April 2014.
[49] Water Pollution Prevention and Control Law of the People's Republic of China, adopted on 11 May 1984, revised subsequently on 15 May 1996 and 28 February 2008.
[50] Marine Environment Protection Law of the People's Republic of China, adopted on 23 August 1982, revised subsequently on 25 December 1999 and 28 December 2013.
[51] Law of the People's Republic of China on the Prevention and Control of Atmospheric Pollution, adopted on 5 September 1987, revised subsequently on 29 August 1995 and 29 April 2000.

enforcement.[52] In the words of Wang Jin, head of the All-China Lawyers' Association's Environmental and Resources Law Committee, 'laws without regulation, troops without power, duties without action: in the final assessment, this is the current state of environmental law in China'.[53] Three main and mutually reinforcing causes for this weak implementation/enforcement of China's environmental laws can be identified: the strong decentralisation of decision making, the absence of incentives for local governments to comply with the rules enacted at the central level as well as corruption.

China's strongly decentralised governance[54] makes it difficult for the central authority to know what is happening locally, to combat local officials' reluctance to implement the law as well as to pressure local courts to enforce it in practice. In addition, the interests of central authorities and local stakeholders might be at cross purposes. As emphasised by Benjamin Van Rooij, local stakeholders (i.e. companies, workers, courts, state representatives) might not share the same concern for environmental protection, which leads to 'local protectionism'.[55] For many companies, increasing profits remains the main motive for their activities. Party representatives and government officials often prioritise economic growth and social stability over other issues, environmental issues included. Finally, citizens might be sometimes attracted by short-term economic gains – e.g. in the form of financial compensation – instead of advocating for the protection of the environment and ultimately their own health.[56] This 'compensation trap'[57] opens major opportunities for corruption, which is the third explanation for the weak implementation/enforcement of China's environmental laws.

---

[52] Benjamin Van Rooij, 'Implementation of Chinese environmental law: regular enforcement and political campaigns' (2006) 37 *Development and Change* 57–74, at 58.

[53] Wang Jin, 'China's green laws are useless', *China Dialogue*, 23 September 2010, available at https://www.chinadialogue.net/article/show/single/en/38.31–China-s-green-laws-are-useless-.

[54] See generally Alfred M. Wu, 'How does decentralized governance work? Evidence from China' (2013) 22 *Journal of Contemporary China* 379–393.

[55] Van Rooij (n. 52), at 61.

[56] Anna Lora Wainwright, Yiyun Zhang, Yunmei Wu and Benjamin Van Rooij, 'Learning to live with pollution: the making of environmental subjects in a Chinese industrialized village' (2012) 68 *The China Journal* 106–124, at 123.

[57] Benjamin Van Rooij, Anna Lora Wainwright, Yunmei Wu and Yiyun Zhang, 'The compensation trap: the limits of community-based pollution regulation in China' (2012) 29 *Pace Environmental Law Review* 701–745, at 701.

4.3 'China's turn against law': an analysis of recent challenges to the rule of law in China

In a 2010 speech, Jiang Ping, former president of China University of Political Science and Law, referred to the current 'full retreat' of the rule of law in China.[58] Updated analysis of the latest developments in the Chinese legal system leads us to confirm the recent significant setbacks in terms of legal development towards a rule of law system in China. Carl F. Minzner goes so far as to talk of 'China's turn against law'[59] to describe and explain recent developments, which include efforts against any type of rule of law–related activism as well as the initiation of political campaigns against the rule of law. 'A new narrative has emerged which views litigation as a pathology to be cured, and law as cold and unresponsive to human needs.'[60]

On the one hand, the recent emphasis on the rule of law in the discourses of the CCP is contrasted by a real crackdown on lawyers and civil society activists currently occurring in China. Proponents of 'universal values' such as the rule of law, human rights and constitutionalism have become the targets of what has become well known as the '709 Crackdown'. According to a Hong Kong–based non-governmental organisation (NGO), China Human Rights Lawyers Concern Group, more than 320 lawyers and citizens have so far been the victims of the ongoing crackdown.[61] Illegal detention, torture, food deprivation, forced medication and disappearance are all different forms of the 'new torture' exacted on a part of China's civil society.[62]

On the other hand, the overall tendency of the Chinese government to 'turn against the law' has been promoted through important political campaigns that utilise the media as a bridge between the government, the Party and the Chinese citizens.[63] In the legal field, a model judge

---

[58] Donald Clarke, 'Jiang Ping: China's rule of law is in full retreat', *China Law Prof Blog*, 2 March 2010, available at http://lawprofessors.typepad.com/china_law_prof_blog/2010/03/jiang-ping-chinas-rule-of-law-is-in-fullretreat.html.

[59] Carl F. Minzner, 'China's turn against law' (2011) 59 *American Journal of Comparative Law* 935–984, at 935.

[60] Ibid., at 936.

[61] China Human Rights Lawyers Concern Group, '['709 Crackdown'] Latest data and development of cases as of 17 October 2017', available at http://www.chrlawyers.hk/en/content/%E2%80%98709-crackdown%E2%80%99-latest-data-and-development-cases-1800-17-october-2017.

[62] Eva Pils, 'A new torture in China', China Policy Institute Analysis, 10 August 2017, available at https://cpianalysis.org/2017/08/10/a-new-torture-in-china/

[63] On media's role in sustaining power in China, see Daniela Stockmann and Mary E. Gallagher, 'Remote control: how the media sustain authoritarian rule in China' (2011) 44 *Comparative Political Studies* 436–467.

campaign testifies to China's changing perspective on law, judicial proceedings and the judicial system. This campaign attracted national scrutiny and led to the award of 'National Model Judge' to Judge Chen Yanping in 2010. Being a proponent of a 'world without litigation',[64] she has been praised for ruling 3,100 cases without any appeal, for striving for the Confucian ideal of a world without litigation and for favouring the development of a 'harmonious society'.[65]

The suppression of contestation through the oppression of organised or individual activism along with the promotion of a 'world without litigation' through mass campaigns shares the same concern for a stable society that does not challenge the established order. In that regard, law is being perceived as an unreliable instrument and the judicial system as a potential challenge to the Party's rule.

5   The rule of law in China: towards a 'multiple-speeds legal system'?

With all these developments in mind, this chapter argues that China's legal system can be characterised as a 'multiple-speeds legal system' in which respect for the rule of law varies depending on the rules' impact on the legal, political, economic and social stability of the country. As Donald Clarke observed,

> China's legal system is about the effective functioning of government, so when the system changes it does so to help government function better. This does not mean the system cannot also develop to accommodate better issues arising between citizens who have little connection to the government – but it does that on the side. The fundamental characteristics of the system stem from its statist orientation.[66]

The current rhetoric of Xi Jinping on 'Governing the Nation in Accord with the Law' defends the idea that the rule of law and the rule of the Party through law have the same meaning: they both testify to 'the necessity for party to rule over the nation and through the conduit of

---

[64] Ou Qinping, *Sanwu faguan yuan tianxia wusong* (The 'Three No's Judge' seeks world without litigation), 18 January 2010, available at http://cpc.people.com.cn/GB/64093/64104/10788439.html; in Minzner (n. 59).
[65] Minzner (n. 59), at 950.
[66] David Clarke, 'China's jasmine crackdown and the legal system', *East Asia Forum*, 26 May 2011, available at http://www.eastasiaforum.org/2011/05/26/china-s-jasmine-crackdown-and-the-legal-system/.

law and legal institutions'.[67] In practice, a distinction should be made between the implementation of the rule of law as serving and protecting socio-economic relations and the rule of law as a principle to restrain public authorities' power.[68] While tremendous progress has been made as regards the former, enormous challenges persist as regards the latter. This trend has particularly been obvious of late in the numerous crack-downs against judicial independence and civil society activists. In such a 'multiple-speeds legal system' that is constrained by the supremacy of the CCP power, the 'law-stability paradox'[69] seems to explain how exactly the socialist rule of law with Chinese characteristics develops. It rules out 'thick' rule of law theories and challenges 'thin' rule of law theories accordingly.

On the one hand, the law-stability paradox explains why China is unlikely to develop a legal system that does not incorporate basic components of a 'thin' rule of law such as the principle of legality and some correlated principles (i.e. transparency, publicity, non-retroactivity, stability). It is broadly acknowledged in China that strengthening the principle of legality is a prerequisite to social and political stability as well as to economic growth. On the other hand, the law-stability paradox also explains why law and judicial institutions can pose a threat for the CCP as well. These can challenge stability in a society that is far from harmonious. The potential threat from the rule of law explains why the Chinese government rejects 'thick' versions of the rule of law and is keen to make a clear distinction between the rule of law, democracy and human rights. Its purpose is to construct a 'Socialist Rule of law' in which 'Western legal norms are explicitly rejected'.[70] In that context, even the development of a 'thin' rule of law remains a challenge, as the Party can still easily negate legality and some corollary principles (i.e. access to justice, transparency). The supremacy of the CCP explains both the development and the limitations of a 'thin' rule of law in China. Only through an 'identity change' of the CCP could the rule of law be implemented in all areas of law in China.[71]

[67] Susan Trevaskes, 'Weaponising the Rule of Law in China', in Flora Sapio, Susan Trevaskes, Sarah Biddulph and Elisa Nesossi (eds), *Justice: The China Experience* (Cambridge: Cambridge University Press, 2017), p. 114.
[68] Pitman B. Potter, 'Legal reform in China: institutions, culture, and selective adaptation' (2004) 29 *Law and Social Inquiry* 465–495.
[69] Liebman (n. 6), at 31.
[70] Minzner (n. 59), 952.
[71] Lance L. P. Gore, 'The political limits to judicial reform in China' (2014) 2 *The Chinese Journal of Comparative Law* 213–232, at 232.

From the perspective of the law-stability paradox, the Chinese leadership seems to be now facing a central challenge in constructing the socialist rule of law with Chinese characteristics'. China must reform its legal system in a way that gives sufficient guarantees in terms of rule of law in order to further anchor China in the dynamics of globalisation and to ensure the long-term sustainability of its economic growth. In addition, the government needs to provide sufficient guarantees for the protection of individual rights in a context where the CCP's legitimacy depends on its ability to persuade the people of its qualification to reform the country and to contribute to the improvement of their well-being.[72] Demands for the enhancement of individual rights – which include social, economic, cultural as well as civil and political rights – are increasingly pressing and can hardly be neglected by a leadership that is under permanent scrutiny from media and people. The difficulty in developing the rule of law in a way that reinforces the two aforementioned objectives lies in the fact that all these reforms have to be achieved while avoiding the CCP's supremacy being questioned. The challenge for the CCP is therefore to give up enough but not too much in terms of commitment to the rule of law.

6   The rule of law in China and the debate on global constitutionalism

China's contribution to the development of the rule of law informs the debate on global constitutionalism and suggests three different ways how China might participate in the constitutionalisation of international law.

First, global constitutionalism provides for a modification of sovereignty by constitutional processes and values to organise the functioning and justify the legitimacy of the international order. Constitutional principles would therefore enable the strengthening of global governance in terms of fairness, justice and effectiveness.[73] The analysis of constitutionalism – or lack of constitutionalism – in China demonstrates that constitutionalism remains a disputed principle within the Chinese legal system. The CCP's supremacy remains the main source of legitimacy and effectiveness within China's legal and political order. In the same spirit,

---

[72] Maria Bondes and Sandra Heep, 'Conceptualizing the relationship between persuasion and legitimacy: official framing in the case of the Chinese Communist Party' (2013) 18 *Journal of Chinese Political Science* 317–334, at 331.

[73] Anne Peters, 'The merits of global constitutionalism' (2009) 16 *Indiana Journal of Global Legal Studies* 397–411, at 400.

China continues to emphasise sovereignty in its external relations and to promote the principle of non-intervention. Against the idea that 'the principle of sovereignty is being ousted from its position as a *Letztbegründung* (first principle) of international law',[74] China continues to support a state-centric view on sovereignty and is likely to oppose attempts 'to constrain, discipline, or regulate difference'[75] between legal systems through the constitutionalisation of international law.

Second, the rule of law, human rights and democracy represent 'the trinitarian mantra of the constitutionalist faith'.[76] Global constitutionalism refers to the relationship between these three principles, which are, generally speaking, considered interdependent and reinforcing of each other within constitutionalist discourses.[77] Along the same line, the 2012 High-Level Declaration on the Rule of Law at the National and International Levels presented the rule of law, human rights and democracy as being 'interlinked and mutually reinforcing'.[78] The Declaration therefore endorses a substantive (or 'thick') understanding of the rule of law that incorporates 'elements of political morality'.[79] China's experience with the rule of law demonstrates the CCP's will to disentangle the rule of law from human rights and democracy in order to consider the development of the rule of law within China in its own right. The question remains whether the growing Chinese support for a 'thin' rule of law can transform into a support for a 'thin' global constitutionalism. 'Thin' global constitutionalism might not, in fact, offer a consensus strong enough to reconcile differences with a common – transnational – identity that is constitutionalism's ultimate purpose.[80]

Third, both the constitutionalisation of international law and the fragmentation of international law testify to the actual diversity/

[74] Ibid., at 398.
[75] Matthew Craven, 'Unity, diversity and the fragmentation of international law' (2003) 14 *Finnish Yearbook of International Law* 3–31, at 33.
[76] Kumm et al. (n. 3), at 3.
[77] See, for instance, Statement by José Manuel Barroso at the General Assembly High-Level Meeting on the Rule of Law on 'The European Union and the rule of law', United Nations, 24 September 2012.
[78] Ibid., para. 5.
[79] Peerenboom (n. 8), at 58. Contrary to this view, Quénivet argues that the United Nations approach to the rule of law endorses a formal – a 'thin' – understanding of the rule of law. Noëlle Quénivet, 'The United Nations' legal obligations in terms of rule of law in peacebuilding operations' (2007) 11 *International Peacekeeping: The Yearbook of International Peace Operations* 203–227, at 227.
[80] Michel Rosenfeld, 'Is global constitutionalism meaningful or desirable?' (2014) 25 *European Journal of International Law* 177–199, at 181.

pluralism within the international legal order. The idea of 'fragmented constitutionalism' departs from the perspective of constitutionalism as a 'totality' and recognises the diversity within and between legal orders.[81] The Chinese perspective on the rule of law testifies in the same sense to China's attachment to the 'broad diversity of national experiences in the area of the rule of law'.[82] China is likely to remain cautious about the idea of global constitutionalism, as the current fragmentation of international law allows China to pursue its self-contradictory practice in the different international forums.[83] At the same time as it is developing a 'multiple-speeds legal system', China has become a 'responsible stakeholder' in certain fields of international law and not in others. China's good compliance records in the World Trade Organization's dispute settlement mechanism contrast, for example, with China's reluctance to support the development of international criminal justice by reinforcing the International Criminal Court. 'While there is a great willingness by China to accept international adjudication in economic and technical areas, there is still a reluctance to do so in certain fields, including military activities, sovereignty disputes, and more significantly, human rights.'[84]

7 Conclusion

The enhancement of the rule of law has become an important motto and driver of China's development model. This emphasis is based on the successful contribution of the restored legal system with its complex legislature and improved legal capacity to the transformation of China into a dynamic economy and unified country. In contrast with the Western liberal-democratic perspective on the rule of law, China tends to reject the idea that the rule of law, democracy and human rights are interdependent values. The challenges to the rule of law are still numerous. Although one should never forget that China had to reconstruct its entire legal system in 1976 following the Cultural Revolution, a decade in

---

[81] Anne Peters, 'Constitutional fragments: on the interaction of constitutionalization and fragmentation in international law' (2015), *Centre for Global Constitutionalism, University of St. Andrews, Working Paper No. 2* 22.

[82] UN General Assembly, Resolution on the Rule of Law at the National and International Levels, A/RES/66/102, 12 September 2012, para. 10.

[83] Ge Chen, 'Piercing the veil of state sovereignty: how China's censorship regime into fragmented international law can lead to a butterfly effect' (2014) 3 *Global Constitutionalism* 31–70, at 34.

[84] Dan Zhu, 'China, the International Criminal Court, and international adjudication' (2014) 61 *Netherlands International Law Review* 43–67, at 65–66.

which all legal aspects of China's governance system were annihilated, one should look very critically at current Chinese legal practice and emphasise the CCP's instrumentalisation of the rule of law. This instrumental perspective explains why the Chinese legal system is evolving at multiple speeds and gets closer to or farther from the rule of law depending on the Party's strategic interests. Far from being accomplished, the rule of law is nevertheless a useful benchmark to assess the evolution of the Chinese legal system as well as a common ground for discussions between China and its international partners.

In this sense, China's potential contribution to the debate on global constitutionalism and the constitutionalisation of international law remains uncertain. On the one hand, China's pragmatic 'multiple-speeds legal system' could leave the door open for the constitutionalisation of certain aspects of international law. As demonstrated by the 2004 constitutional reform and the agenda-setting power of the Chinese Constitution, China has not completely renounced the constitutional argument. On the other hand, China is likely to remain suspicious about the overall idea of global constitutionalism. Just as China opposes the idea of constitutionalism as an obstacle to CCP one-party rule internally, it will probably consider the overall idea of global constitutionalism to be a constraint on and threat to China's national sovereignty.

8

Cosmopolitanising Rights Practice

The Case of South Korea

1 Introduction

Constitutional rights practices in South Korea are increasingly acquiring cosmopolitan features, and this local development has rich implications for global constitutionalism.[1] Constitutional rights actors – including the constitutional court and rights-bearing individuals – are engaging with the global in dynamic ways, prompting tensions, struggles and new developments in conventional constitutional rights review. Cosmopolitanising features of constitutional rights practices in this less-researched jurisdiction are highlighted in this chapter by exploring (1) the interaction of constitutional law with international human rights law in rights adjudication – the diverse modes of engagement between the two levels of law and the implications of the varied practices and present struggles (Section 2); (2) the Korean Constitutional Court's changing attitude towards comparative constitutional law and foreign rights practices as well as the evaluation

* Assistant Professor, Seoul National University School of Law.
1 'Global constitutionalism' in this chapter is intended to mean more than the popular topic of 'constitutionalisation of international law' or constitutionalism *beyond* states, which typically draws on, either descriptively or prescriptively, constitutional dimensions of international law or international organisations such as the United Nations and World Trade Organization (WTO). Among many on global constitutionalism with this focus, see Anne Peters, 'The merits of global constitutionalism' (2009) 16 *Indiana Journal of Global Legal Studies* 397–411; Jan Klabbers, Anne Peters and Geir Ulfstein, *The Constitutionalization of International Law* (Oxford; New York: Oxford University Press, 2009); Christine E. J. Schwöbel, *Global Constitutionalism in International Legal Perspective* (Leiden: Martinus Nijhoff Publishers, 2011). Global constitutionalism broadly understood embraces conceptualisation, operation and realisation of constitutional values and principles (1) *beyond*, (2) *across* and (3) *within* states. The present chapter focuses on the practice of global constitutionalism emerging *within* a state, with local constitutional actors at the domestic level engaging with the global in diverse ways and evolving into cosmopolitan actors of human rights and constitutional jurisprudence.

of these changes in light of the Court's evolving self-identity vis-à-vis the wider world (Section 3); and (3) the encounter of (Asian) tradition and culture with constitutional rights and principles as well as the merits of constitutional rights review in resolving tensions between rights and tradition (Section 4). The Court's transnational activities outside the courtroom are also examined, especially its leadership role in building a regional network for human rights and constitutional jurisprudence in Asia. To gain greater insight into the practice of the Court, its president, justices, assistant judges and researchers were interviewed by the author.

Individual rights-holders are also integral players in South Korea's cosmopolitanising rights practice. The mutually empowering relationship between global-minded individuals and the constitutional court is illuminated in Section 5. This work concludes that the overall development in South Korea exemplifies a practice of bottom-up and locally grown global constitutionalism emerging outside the European region. It provides a counterweight to the oft-levelled charges that global constitutionalism is an elitist and primarily Eurocentric enterprise. It suggests that the story of Korea may offer a promising perspective from which to understand and advance global constitutionalism as a truly global project.

2   Engagement with international human rights law

The creation of the Constitutional Court of Korea (the Korean Constitutional Court) was a key element of the historic amendment of the South Korean Constitution in 1987, the momentous year that Korea achieved democratisation, led by a citizens' nationwide movement and ending the three decades of military dictatorship.[2] Since it began operating in September 1988, the Constitutional Court has played an active role in rights adjudication. As of December 2016, the Court has received 30,591 applications and has decided 10,897 cases on the merits.[3] The cases brought to the Court have increased gradually – 362 cases in 1990, 1,060 cases in 2001, 1,720 cases in 2010 and 1,951 cases in 2016. Among the 2,992 cases the Court decided on the merits regarding the

---

[2] For English-language literature surveying the history and system of constitutional courts in Asia, including South Korea, see, e.g., Tom Ginsburg, *Judicial Review in New Democracies: Constitutional Courts in Asian Cases* (Cambridge: Cambridge University Press, 2003).
[3] The statistics on court cases are regularly updated on the Court's English-language website: http://english.ccourt.go.kr/cckhome/eng/decisions/caseLoadStatic/caseLoadStatic.do.

constitutionality of specific domestic laws, the Court has invalidated 653 laws as unconstitutional, either in whole or in part. Among the 7,866 cases decided on the merits concerning government actions, the Court has found 769 such actions unconstitutional.

Developing rights discourses and practices in individual states is particularly important in Asia, partly because Asia has no regional human rights adjudication system. Constitutional courts and equivalent bodies in Asia are often the only venue for ordinary citizens and non-citizens to contest and vindicate their rights. Accordingly, individuals in South Korea have sought to use the Constitutional Court as a platform to invoke and apply international human rights norms. The Constitutional Court has gradually become a site where international human rights law and constitutional law squarely meet. This section examines how constitutional law interacts with international human rights law during rights contestation and adjudication, as exemplified by the practice of the Korean Constitutional Court.[4]

2.1   Legal framework and the conventional theory

Like many other states' constitutions, the Constitution of the Republic of Korea (the South Korean Constitution) mentions the domestic legal status of international law, but it does so in a relatively abstract manner. Article 6 paragraph 1 provides: 'Treaties duly concluded and promulgated under the Constitution and the generally recognized rule of international law shall have the same effect as the *domestic law* of the Republic of Korea' (emphasis added). A traditional but still prevalent view among constitutional and international law scholars in South Korea reads the term 'domestic law' in this provision to mean *statutes*, one of the five levels of domestic law in Korea – the constitution, statutes, enforcement decrees (issued by the president), enforcement regulations (issued by

---

[4] Introductory comparative research on Korean and Taiwanese constitutional court cases has been conducted by Wen-Chen Chang, 'The convergence of constitutions and international human rights: Taiwan and South Korea in comparison' (2011) 36 *North Carolina Journal of International Law* 593–624. Broader discussions include Vicki Jackson, *Constitutional Engagement in a Transnational Era* (Oxford: Oxford University Press, 2013); Mattias Kumm, 'Democratic constitutionalism encounters international law: terms of engagement', in Sujit Choudhry (ed.), *The Migration of Constitutional Ideas* (Cambridge: Cambridge University Press, 2006), pp. 256–293; Stephen Gardbaum, 'Human rights and international constitutionalism', in Jeffrey L. Dunoff and Joel P. Trachtman (eds.), *Ruling the World? Constitutionalism, International Law, and Global Governance* (Cambridge; New York: Cambridge University Press, 2009), pp. 233–257.

a relevant ministry) and local ordinances. Most Korean scholars consider that both international treaties and customary international law have equal status as statutes and that international human rights law (IHRL) does not differ from other kinds of international law in its domestic legal status.[5] These scholars rely on national sovereignty, consent-based international treaty systems, the supremacy and autonomy of the national constitution and comparison with domestic law-making (noting that IHRL cannot have a constitution-like status since its adoption does not follow a process equivalent to constitutional amendment). These scholars also interpret the constitution literally, pointing out that the text of the South Korean Constitution does not distinguish IHRL from other types of international law.[6] This position, if taken to its logical conclusion, implies that IHRL, along with other international treaties, may not serve as a standard for constitutional review, since its legal status is not superior to statutes. For the same reason, it becomes contestable whether IHRL can even serve as a reference point for constitutional interpretation. Only a handful of scholars in South Korea take a different position, viewing IHRL either as located between the constitution and statutes or as having a quasi-constitutional status.

2.2   Cases

The Korean Constitutional Court's view of the legal status and effect of IHRL has not been unambiguous. However, its practice over the years indicates that the Court has departed from the conventional theory just described.

In the *Foreign Industrial Trainees* case, a few migrant workers, represented by a group of human rights lawyers, challenged the national foreign labour system. Until this case, simple skilled migrant workers had not been treated as 'workers' in a legal sense but as 'industrial trainees', and they had been denied the equal protection of labour rights

[5] Many of these scholars regard some treaties as having an even lower status than statutes, especially those ratified without the legislative branch's consent.

[6] These scholars also invoke the South Korean Constitution Addenda Article 5 (which provides that 'acts, decrees, ordinances and treaties in force at the time this Constitution enters into force, shall remain valid unless they are contrary to this Constitution'), arguing that it establishes the supremacy of the constitution over international law. A persuasive counterargument can, however, be made that it does not preclude the possibility that international law can have a status equivalent to, though not overriding, the constitution. Indeed, this provision can be deemed to acknowledge the possibility of a pluralist legal system with IHRL and constitutional law as equal parts.

and full application of the Labour Standards Act. In 2007, the Korean Constitutional Court held that the foreign trainee system was as a whole unconstitutional, being a violation of the right to equality of these migrant workers.[7] In its reasoning, the Court referred to provisions of the International Covenant on Economic, Social and Cultural Rights (ICESCR), including the principle of non-discrimination (Art. 2) and the enjoyment of just and favourable working conditions (Art. 7), as important in interpreting the equality clause of the constitution. The Court specified that 'the provisions of this Covenant should be taken into account when interpreting our Constitution'.

In addition, the Court frequently cites international human rights documents that do not have binding effect (*soft law*) as resources to consider in constitutional interpretation. In the *'Comfort Women'* case decided in 2011,[8] the Court cited a report by the Special Rapporteur on violence against women Radhika Coomaraswamy ('Report on the mission to the Democratic People's Republic of Korea, the Republic of Korea and Japan on the issue of military sexual slavery in wartime', adopted by the UN Commission on Human Rights in 1996) and the 1998 report by Gay J. McDougall, Special Rapporteur on systematic rape, sexual slavery and slavery-like practices during armed conflict (on the issue of 'comfort women' in Korea and Japan). The Court cited these reports in determining the significance of the infringement of victims' rights and the unconstitutionality of the Korean government's inaction in resolving this issue. The practice of citing non-binding international human rights documents began earlier in a variety of cases. In the *Teachers' Union* case in 1991, the Court discussed the relevance of the International Labour Organization (ILO)/United Nations Educational, Scientific and Cultural Organisation (UNESCO) Recommendation Concerning the Status of Teachers (1966) in deciding on the constitutionality of prohibiting private school teachers from forming and joining a labour union.[9] In a 1992 case, a detainee challenged the actions of investigators at the National Security Agency who attended, listened in on and documented conversations at a meeting between his counsel and him. The Court found this conduct unconstitutional, citing the Body of Principles for the Protection of All Persons under Any Form of Detention or Imprisonment adopted by the UN General Assembly in 1988.[10]

---

[7] Constitutional Court of Korea, 2004 Hun-Ma 670 (30 August 2007).
[8] Constitutional Court of Korea, 2006 Hun-Ma 788 (30 August 2011).
[9] Constitutional Court of Korea, 89 Hun-Ga 106 (22 July 1991).
[10] Constitutional Court of Korea, 91 Hun-Ma 111 (28 January 1992).

Another case was brought against a prison officer who kept a defendant handcuffed and tied up with a rope around his upper body during the investigation procedure at a prosecutor's office. The Court found the officer's action unconstitutional, citing the UN Standard Minimum Rules for the Treatment of Prisoners.[11] In a challenge to a law mandating employers to employ people with disabilities, the Court held the law constitutional, consulting the ILO Recommendation (No. 99) Vocational Rehabilitation (Disabled) Recommendation of 1955.[12]

There are several cases in which the Court has engaged with international human rights law more directly. In *Conscientious Objectors*,[13] Jehovah's Witnesses challenged the Military Service Act, which punishes anyone refusing to do obligatory military service with up to three years' imprisonment. The Court explicitly reviewed whether this domestic law violated international human rights law. The Court first referred to Article 6 paragraph 1 of the Constitution ('Treaties duly concluded and promulgated under the Constitution and the generally recognized rule of international law shall have the same effect as the domestic law of the Republic of Korea') and found that this provision declares the *constitutional principle of respecting international law*. The Court then proceeded with a substantive review of whether international human rights law requires states to recognise the right to conscientious objection and answered in the negative. The majority opinion examined Article 18 of the International Covenant on Civil and Political Rights (ICCPR), which South Korea joined in 1990, and noted that the Covenant does not specifically mention conscientious objection in its provision on the rights to thought, conscience and religion. The Court detailed the interpretations by the UN Human Rights Committee and the earlier Commission on Human Rights that Article 18 of the ICCPR includes the right to conscientious objection as well as these bodies' recommendations that member states recognise this right and adopt a system of alternative service for conscientious objectors. However, the Court held that these interpretations 'are only recommendations, not having binding effect'. The majority also found that the right to conscientious objection cannot be considered customary international law either, though several states, European included, recognise this right.

---

[11] Constitutional Court of Korea, 2001 Hun-Ma 728 (26 May 2005).
[12] Constitutional Court of Korea, 2001 Hun-Ba 96 (24 July 2003).
[13] Constitutional Court of Korea, 2008 Hun-Ga 22 (30 August 2011).

The Court concluded that there is currently no international law guaranteeing the right to conscientious objection, such that South Korea's criminal punishment of conscientious objectors does not violate the constitutional requirement to respect international law under Article 6. In their dissent, two justices cited the UN bodies' recommendations along with other countries' established practices in holding that the law is unconstitutional as a violation of the right to conscience.

The ICCPR has been taken as a direct standard of constitutional review along with relevant constitutional provisions (including Article 6 and provisions on fundamental rights) in less prominent cases as well. In a case brought against the criminal law penalising collective refusal to work by employees, the Court reviewed whether the law violated the ICCPR Article 8 right against forced labour and found that it did not.[14] Asked whether a domestic law punishing the issuance of a bounced check with wilful negligence was constitutional, the Court reviewed whether the law violated ICCPR Article 11 ('No one shall be imprisoned merely on the ground of inability to fulfil a contractual obligation') and answered in the negative.[15]

The preceding examples show how the Court engages with IHRL in constitutional rights review. The Court has yet to articulate the exact status of IHRL in the domestic legal order of South Korea. Its actual practice suggests, however, that the Court regards IHRL differently from other types of international law. As illustrated, the Court sometimes takes IHRL as an important reference for interpreting constitutional provisions. In these cases, non-binding international documents are also frequently consulted. In other cases, the Court directly adopts IHRL, usually major human rights covenants such as the ICCPR, as a standard for constitutional review. The Court then tends to use Article 6 paragraph 1 of the Constitution as a link, reading it as embodying a more general constitutional principle of respecting international law. Through this reasoning IHRL is elevated from a resource of reference to a standard of review. IHRL's status is contrasted with the Court's attitude towards other types of treaties. The Court has repeatedly made it clear that international treaties that are not human rights treaties have the same effect as domestic statutes. Thus, they can be only an object of

---

[14] Constitutional Court of Korea, 97 Hun-Ba 23 (16 July 1998).
[15] Constitutional Court of Korea, 2009 Hun-Ba 267 (28 July 2011); 99 Hun-Ga 13 (26 April 2001).

a constitutionality test and not a standard for constitutional review of other domestic law or state actions. The Court has reviewed the constitutional validity of such treaties in numerous cases.[16]

2.3 An emerging cosmopolitan idea and practice of human rights

As the preceding cases demonstrate, the actual practice of the Korean Constitutional Court deviates significantly from the conventional doctrinal view. The Court has not articulated the precise legal status and effect of IHRL vis-à-vis the constitution, but it is clear from its practice that the Court treats IHRL as different in kind from other international law. While the current court practices are not completely clear or coherent, IHRL apparently functions either as an important reference point for constitutional rights interpretation or as a direct standard of constitutional review, whereas other types of treaties have only been constitutionally reviewed for their validity. The *Conscientious Objectors* case supports the view that IHRL to which South Korea has committed itself holds presumptive authority in relation to domestic law and constitutional interpretation.[17] The Court in this case took great pains to prove that there is no IHRL obligation on states to recognise a specific right to conscientious objection. If the Court had found that international law indeed provides for this right, it might have decided the case differently. In *Foreign Industrial Trainees*, the Court's engagement was weaker, but it did closely consult the ICESCR's relevant provisions as a reference point, noting that the Covenant's mandates need to be considered when interpreting the constitution. What on one hand makes the Court take this unconventional position, which 'Big C constitutionalists'[18] might claim is incoherent or even unconstitutional? Why on the other hand has it not

[16] The international treaties whose constitutionality the Court has reviewed include the Marrakesh Agreement Establishing the World Trade Organization; Articles of Agreement of the International Monetary Fund; Agreement of Fisheries between the Government of the Republic of Korea and the Government of Japan; and Asia-Pacific Regional Convention on the Recognition of Qualifications in Higher Education.

[17] For discussion of the presumptive authority of international law, see, e.g., Başak Çalı, *The Authority of International Law: Obedience, Respect, and Rebuttal* (Oxford: Oxford University Press, 2015); Mattias Kumm, 'The legitimacy of international law: a constitutionalist framework of analysis' (2004) 15 *European Journal of International Law* 907–931.

[18] These conventional scholars' position aligns with the 'Big C constitutionalist' view elaborated by Mattias Kumm, 'The cosmopolitan turn in constitutionalism: an integrated conception of public law' (2013) 20 *Indiana Journal of Global Legal Studies* 605–628.

pronounced more clearly on the relation between international and constitutional law as well as on the exact difference between IHRL and other international law? The Court's current mode of engagement with IHRL reflects the conflicts, confusion and struggle that the Court has experienced: while the Court is fully aware of the conventional theoretical position, it also recognises the significance and distinctiveness of IHRL in comparison to other essentially consent-based treaties.

Current court practice implies an emerging *cosmopolitan* idea and practice of rights and marks a departure from the *nationalist constitutionalist* tradition. It signals that the Court recognises that rights should be understood and adjudicated in the intertwined normative set of international and national law and that rights bear both universality and locality, which can be realised only through the organic operation of IHRL and the constitution.[19] Through this idea and practice developing around the Court's rights adjudication, IHRL is attaining a constitution-like status, even in the absence of theoretical articulation or sophistication in Korean public law scholarship. The Court justices made a breakthrough in linking IHRL and the constitution by taking a broad interpretation of Article 6 and finding the underlying constitutional principle of respecting international law. This interpretative stretch has enabled the Court to substantively review the constitutional validity of domestic law and state actions in light of international human rights norms, while maintaining the framework of constitutional review. By approaching international and constitutional law in an integrated manner, the justices avoid the questions of what the precise hierarchal status of IHRL in the Korean constitutional order is and whether the Court can take IHRL as a free-standing standard of rights review. Despite the lack of a clear constitutional text addressing IHRL's status, the Court, by developing its practice, has incorporated IHRL into constitutional

---

[19] For discussion on the cosmopolitan understanding of constitutionalism in relation to international law, see Mattias Kumm, 'The cosmopolitan turn in constitutionalism: on the relationship between constitutionalism in and beyond the state', in Dunoff and Trachtman (eds.) (n. 4), pp. 263–264 ('Cosmopolitan constitutionalism establishes an integrative basic conceptual framework for a general theory of public law that integrates national and international law.'); Kumm (n. 18), at 611–612 (emphasising 'the deep interdependencies between national and international law' and noting, 'International law is neither derivative, nor is it autonomous. National and international law are co-constitutive and form an integrative whole.'). See also Jackson (n. 4) (analysing three modes towards 'the transnational' and describing the mode of 'convergence'); Vlad F. Perju, 'Cosmopolitanism in constitutional law' (2013) 35 *Cardozo Law Review* 711–768.

review of the justifiability of domestic law and state actions.[20] Putting aside the possible charge of theoretical imperfection, this layered effort represents the Court's understanding of the universality of human rights and its normative progress towards a cosmopolitan form of rights practice that contextualises the rights' universality through domestic constitutional review. The current practice of the Korean Constitutional Court, including its departure from the conventional doctrinal view and its struggle and attempt to accommodate IHRL as a substantive standard of review along with the constitution, suggests that the two levels of law can operate in harmony without their being placed in a unitary hierarchy.[21]

The fact that the Court has begun to take IHRL as a direct standard of constitutional review, not merely as a point of reference, is a notable step forward, especially when compared to other well-known models. The South African Constitution requires the court only to *consider* international law when interpreting its bill of rights.[22] The German Constitutional Court held that the European Convention on Human Rights (ECHR) as interpreted by the European Court of Human Rights must be *taken into account* when the court decides on relevant rights.[23]

---

[20] Some states adopt constitutional provisions stipulating more concretely the effect of international law in general or of certain kinds of international law. For example, see the Dutch Constitution Art. 94 specifying that 'statutory regulations in force within the Kingdom shall not be applicable if such application is in conflict with provisions of treaties or of resolutions by international institutions that are binding on all persons' and the Constitution of Argentina Sec. 75 para. 22 listing several international human rights treaties with constitutional supremacy.

[21] This practice hints at a model of pluralist operation of international and constitutional law in rights adjudication. Research on pluralist legal systems has been concentrated on the European context, focusing on Europe's supranational regimes and the regimes' relation to individual states' legal orders. To mention a few, Matej Avbelj and Jan Komárek (eds.), *Constitutional Pluralism in the European Union and Beyond* (Oxford; Portland, OR: Hart Publishing, 2012); Neil Walker, 'The idea of constitutional pluralism' (2002) 65 *Modern Law Review* 317–359; Miguel Maduro, 'Courts and pluralism: essay on a theory of judicial adjudication in the context of legal and constitutional pluralism', in Dunoff and Trachtman (eds.) (n. 4), pp. 356–380. See also Alec Stone Sweet, 'A cosmopolitan legal order: constitutional pluralism and rights adjudication in Europe' (2012) 1 *Global Constitutionalism* 53–90.

[22] The Constitution of South Africa, Art. 39: (1) When interpreting the Bill of Rights, a court, tribunal or forum (a) must promote the values that underlie an open and democratic society based on human dignity, equality and freedom; (b) must consider international law; and (c) may consider foreign law.

[23] *Görgülü v. Germany* (2004), 2 BvR 1481/04. See Kumm (n. 4), pp. 280–281; Christian Tomuschat, 'The effects of the judgments of the European Court of Human Rights according to the German Constitutional Court' (2010) 11 *German Law Journal* 513–526.

Nonetheless, there are limitations in Korean practice that might undermine the progressiveness shown by the Korean Constitutional Court. First, it remains debatable whether the Court always feels obliged to engage with IHRL. The Court typically draws on IHRL when applicants or their lawyers invoke the mandates of IHRL as a ground for their constitutional claims. It is the Court's duty to discuss IHRL when it is part of the claim; if not, an explicit engagement with IHRL still seems discretionary. One might argue that the Korean approach in this regard is closer to the US Supreme Court's (engaging irregularly with international law) than to the German, which takes engagement as obligatory. However, the German 'duty to consider' model concerns the relation between the national constitution and the ECHR, the regional human rights regime with which individual member states have a tighter affiliation, rather than IHRL. Another controversial point is the Korean Constitutional Court's attitude towards soft IHRL. In *Conscientious Objectors*, the majority discussed and dismissed as non-binding the Human Rights Committee's recommendations to the Korean government, while the dissent took them seriously. Lastly, since most constitutional rights claims invoke IHRL along with constitutional provisions, it is unclear how the Court would respond if a rights claim were to invoke IHRL as the sole basis for challenging the validity of domestic law or government actions.

Despite its limitations, incoherence and vagueness, the Korean Constitutional Court's overall practice of engaging with IHRL reflects the Court's growing cosmopolitan ideas of rights. The very existence of conflicts and confusion evidences the emergence of new ideas and practices on a constitutional scene that had previously been the exclusive domain of the Big C constitutionalists. The Court did not tie itself to the traditional dogmatic theory and is developing a dynamic and transnationalising rights practice that leans towards pluralist, rights-based, cosmopolitan constitutionalism. Through this engagement, the Court's identity and role exceed a domestic constitutional court's. While based in a specific jurisdiction in Asia, the Court is growing into an important player in the cosmopolitan project of concretising and contextualising universal human rights.

3   Engagement with foreign rights practices

3.1   Trajectory of development

The attitude taken towards foreign rights practice in constitutional review is another indicator of domestic constitutional actors' visions of themselves and their constitutions in relation to others around the globe.[24] This section discusses a gradual change observed in the mode of the Korean Constitutional Court's engagement with foreign law.

In its earlier years, the Court relied predominantly on German practice. It regarded Germany as the most persuasive reference point on a variety of issues: the initial design of the constitutional court system; the basic structure of constitutional rights review centred on the proportionality principle; detailed theories of reasoning and sentencing; individual cases decided by the German Constitutional Court; even technical rules for operating the system. As it modernised its domestic law, Korea joined the continental/civil law family. Under the influence of the colonial history, modern Korean law drew heavily on Japanese law, which had earlier absorbed much German law. The First Constitution of Korea, promulgated in 1948, took the Weimar Constitution as its primary model. Most of the leading first-generation constitutional law scholars in Korea studied for doctoral degrees in Germany and were influential in founding the constitutional court system in the late 1980s and theories of constitutional review in the early years. Similarities in civil law systems also made the German law cases more accessible and comprehensible. Apart from this historical background, many judges and scholars in Korea (as in many other countries) have considered the German Constitutional Court system and its theories of constitutional review to be an advanced role model in general. The systematic features of German constitutional review and its organised structure of reasoning also made the German model easier to comprehend and assimilate. The early years of the Court's foreign law engagement can be characterised as ones of 'predominant dependence on Germany'. In addition to German, US law and cases have been regularly consulted and cited on the assumption of their being generally advanced, especially when a specific legal doctrine has originated from US case law. Japanese law has been frequently cited as well, but mainly because several Korean domestic laws followed Japanese law, and reference was made mostly for statutory interpretation, not constitutional interpretation.

---

[24] For general and comparative discussion on this matter, see, e.g., Sujit Choudhry (ed.), *The Migration of Constitutional Ideas* (Cambridge: Cambridge University Press, 2006); Anne-Marie Slaughter, 'Judicial globalization' (2000) 40 *Virginia Journal of International Law* 1103–1124; Gábor Halmai, 'The use of foreign law in constitutional interpretation', in Michel Rosenfeld and András Sajó (eds.), *The Oxford Handbook of Comparative Constitutional Law* (Oxford: Oxford University Press, 2012), pp. 1328–1347.

As its own decisions have accumulated, the Court has become less dependent on these select states and openly interested in understanding worldwide trends as well as specific practices in numerous other countries. It is now an established and routinised practice for the Court to conduct comparative research involving a variety of states and regions. Extensive, in-depth research on foreign rights practices is conducted by a company of nearly seventy young research judges at the Court. They are hired either directly from the Judicial Training and Research Institute, a two-year mandatory national training institution for those who have passed the national judicial examination, or from among experienced judges and lawyers. The majority of research judges are appointed in their twenties or thirties, fluent in one or two foreign languages, and work full-time at the Court in a permanent capacity. Recently, the Court has begun to hire researchers other than judges who have expertise in less-researched jurisdictions. The main duty of these research judges is to produce a substantive research report for each pending case. An integral part of this report is research on related foreign and international law. The Constitutional Court justices consult these reports and consider them seriously during their deliberation and adjudication. Most justices, usually in their fifties or early sixties, have been educated only in Korea and have served in ordinary courts or in the prosecutor's office for decades before being appointed to the Constitutional Court. As ordinary court judges and prosecutors, and as law students before that, most had little exposure to transnational dimensions of law and little occasion to doubt a nationalist approach to the constitution. They often undergo transformation while serving at the Constitutional Court, and in that, their collaboration with young judges and researchers plays a critical role. The justices gradually gain transnational insights, as reflected in their judgments. In recent decisions, the Court has often devoted a separate section to the 'law of other states' and discussed specific foreign law and a global trend on related topics. While US Supreme Court cases such as *Roper*[25] and *Lawrence*[26] have been treated as pioneering and have enflamed debates on citing foreign law for constitutional review, and South Africa's *Death Penalty* case[27] has been widely praised as a paradigmatic example of trans-judicial dialogues,[28] such practice constitutes routine for the Korean Constitutional Court.

[25] *Roper v. Simmons*, 543 US 551 (2005).
[26] *Lawrence v. Texas*, 539 US 558 (2003).
[27] *S v. Makwanyane and Another*, CCT 3/94 (1995).
[28] E.g. Anne-Marie Slaughter, 'A global community of courts' (2003) 44 *Harvard International Law Journal* 191–219, at 195.

Reference to foreign law by the Court is made in a serious manner. The research judges' reports not only discuss constitutional law cases of other states but also provide detailed introductions to the foreign legal systems, supplemented by academic literature. The research judges interviewed by the author agreed that their comparative research genuinely seeks answers and has real effects on the Court's deliberation and decision making. This effective role of foreign rights practices stands in contrast to ex post facto justification, result-driven decoration or 'cherry picking' – a criticism typically levelled against referring to foreign law in constitutional review.[29]

In a further step in this direction, the Court launched the Constitutional Research Institute in 2011, a research institute undertaking extensive studies of constitutional law from longer-term academic and comparative perspectives.[30] Institute researchers, mostly scholars with law degrees from abroad, conduct wide-ranging research about constitutions and constitutional courts around the world and in-depth comparative research about topics both general and specific (e.g. the proportionality principle, social and economic rights, equality, constitutional rights of non-citizens, national reunification, freedom of expression, the rights of sexual minorities, the rights of refugees and constitutional problems of antiterrorism legislation). On its website, the Institute uploads its research work and up-to-date information about other states' constitutional practices, including their constitutional review system, recent constitutional news and decisions in various jurisdictions, important foreign legislation and various topics of comparative constitutional study.

Since comparative research is conducted routinely and systematically, cases citing foreign law are common. A few examples may be mentioned here by way of illustration. In January 2014, the Court found the Public Official Election Law unconstitutional for disenfranchising prison inmates and those with suspended sentences. In the opinion's subsection entitled 'law of other states', the Court surveyed related legislation in Australia, Canada, Germany, Israel, Italy, Japan, South Africa, Sweden and the United States.[31] It also discussed decisions by the US Supreme Court, the Supreme Court of Canada, the Constitutional Court of South

---

[29] See, e.g., Jeremy Waldron, 'Partly Laws Common to All Mankind': Foreign Law in American Courts (New Haven, CT; London: Yale University Press, 2012), pp. 171–186.

[30] The English-language website of the Institute is at: http://ri.ccourt.go.kr/eng/ccourt/main/index.jsp.

[31] Constitutional Court of Korea, 2012 Hun-Ma 409 (28 January 2014).

Africa, the High Court of Australia, the Constitutional Council of France and the European Court of Human Rights.[32] This comparative discussion served as an important ground for the Court's finding the domestic election law unconstitutional. In the *Adultery* case delivered in 2015,[33] the Court began its reasoning by observing that 'it is a global trend to decriminalize adultery' and went on to cite the abolition of adultery crimes in Argentina, Austria, Denmark, France, Germany, Japan, Spain, Sweden and Switzerland. After conducting a proportionality review, the Court invalidated the criminal law that punished an adulterer with imprisonment as violating the right to privacy and sexual self-determination. In the 2010 *Death Penalty* case,[34] the Court mentioned that as of 2008, 105 states retained the death penalty system (36 of whom had not executed anyone in the last thirty years) and that 92 states had abolished capital punishment. The absence of a dominant global trend provided an additional justification for the Court's decision that retaining a death penalty system does not violate the constitutional right to life.[35] In 2014, the Court held that the law mandating military service for male citizens only was constitutional, noting that among more than 70 states with conscription, few impose it on women. Cases from Latin America and Asia have been appearing more frequently in recent Court decisions.[36]

Comparative research conducted by research judges is not limited to high-profile cases. Constitutional review of a variety of cases is complemented by study of foreign law and practice. Examples include cases concerning the term and retirement age of judges, stock market exchange regulation, restriction on outdoor advertisements, health insurance regulation, drugstore licenses, tax law on married couples, automobile taxation, defamation against public figures, limitation on voting age

---

[32] The research judge's report for this case made mention of related practices in forty-two European countries (discussed in the ECtHR *Scoppola v. Italy* case) and included a chart categorising practices in various countries (along with a detailed explanation of each category citing foreign court decisions), as well as UN Human Rights Committee comments and recommendations, and the Venice Commission guidelines on the subject submitted to the Council of Europe.

[33] Constitutional Court of Korea, 2011 Hung-Ga 31 (26 February 2015).

[34] Constitutional Court of Korea, 2008 Hun-Ga 23 (25 February 2010).

[35] Constitutional Court of Korea, 2011 Hun-Ma 825 (27 February 2014).

[36] For example, in the *Crime of Contempt* case, the dissenting opinion cited related practices of Chile, Costa Rica, Honduras and Guatemala. Constitutional Court of Korea, 2012 Hun-Ba 37 (27 January 2013). The Court increasingly cites the practice of Taiwan, China and other Asian countries in addition to Japan.

and voting time, collection of DNA information and a duty to report in advance plans to assemble (among many others).

3.2   Transnational activities beyond the courtroom

The global vision of the Korean Constitutional Court is also apparent in its lively transnational activities outside the courtroom. The Court has made clear its ambitions to solidify a leadership position in Asia and to become a significant constituent of the global community of constitutional jurisprudence and human rights. South Korea is one of very few Asian states holding a regular membership seat on the Venice Commission.[37] Justice Il-Won Kang of the Korean Constitutional Court has served as co-president of the Joint Council on Constitutional Justice of the Commission since 2014 and was elected as a member of the Bureau in December 2015 for a two-year term. He has also been active on the Commission as an individual member, e.g. participating in the project of the Draft Law on Introduction of Changes and Amendments to the Constitution of the Kyrgyz Republic and submitting an amicus curiae brief on Moldova's Law on Professional Integrity Testing in 2014. News about Korean constitutional law and practice is regularly updated on the Commission's website. In an interview with the author, Justice Kang explained that 'Korea is expected to play a unique role in the Venice Commission, especially in bridging traditional democracies in Western Europe and emerging democracies in Asia. After listening to my comments on their constitutional amendment plan, Kyrgyz members of parliament stated, "It feels like we finally saw the light after a long tunnel. Your down-to-earth comments based on Korea's recent experience of democratization give us clearer vision and hope than the advice by delegates from Europe, which feels too far away from us".'
In September and October 2014, South Korea hosted the 3rd Congress of the World Conference on Constitutional Justice, attended by the heads of constitutional courts, supreme courts and equivalent organisations from almost 100 countries, with the theme of 'Constitutional Justice and Social Integration'. In June 2018, Korea hosted a World Congress of the International Association of Constitutional Law.

Park Han-Chul, Court president until January 2017, has been enthusiastic about creating 'the Asian Court of Human Rights' and hosting it in South Korea. Under his leadership, the Korean Constitutional Court has

[37] Kazakhstan and Kyrgyzstan are also members of the Commission.

led a preliminary effort to establish a network among Asian constitutional courts and their judges. In 2012, the Court hosted the Inaugural Congress of the Association of Asian Constitutional Courts and Equivalent Institutions (AACC), with the theme of 'Present and Future of Constitutional Justice in Asia'. The AACC currently comprises constitutional adjudication bodies from sixteen Asian countries, including Afghanistan, Azerbaijan, Indonesia, Kazakhstan, Kyrgyzstan, Malaysia, Mongolia, Myanmar, Pakistan, the Philippines, Russia, South Korea, Tajikistan, Thailand, Turkey and Uzbekistan. In 2016, the AACC board of members agreed that South Korea will host the association's permanent Research Secretariat.[38]

The Court has been very active in hosting various international symposiums on constitutional jurisprudence and in inviting constitutional judges and scholars from abroad as short- or mid-term visitors. In addition, it regularly sends its research judges to parallel institutions or universities around the world to conduct research for extended periods. The Court's English-language website provides a detailed introduction to the Court system and practice, updated news on its various transnational activities and a searchable database of its important decisions and publications, fully translated into English.[39]

3.3 Transforming self-identity from local to cosmopolitan

A survey of the Court's engagement with foreign law over the last three decades of practice along with its recent transnational activities shows how the self-image of this local constitutional actor has evolved into a global one. Unlike in the United States, engaging with foreign law is not widely seen as a threat to democratic constitutionalism in South Korea;[40] indeed, it is conducted as a way of expressing and enhancing the *transnationalising self* of constitutional actors. For the Korean Constitutional Court, referring to foreign constitutional practice has gradually evolved from a way of 'catching up' with a handful of role-model countries.

---

[38] http://english.ccourt.go.kr/cckhome/eng/introduction/news/newsDetail.do. After heated negotiations with Indonesia, another enthusiastic partner in the region, it was decided that South Korea and Indonesia will jointly host the Secretariat, with Korea hosting a research part and Indonesia an administrative.

[39] For the Court's English-language database, see http://english.ccourt.go.kr/cckhome/eng/decisions/casesearch/caseSearch.do.

[40] See, e.g., Norman Dorsen, 'The relevance of foreign legal materials in U.S. constitutional cases: a conversation between Justice Antonin Scalia and Justice Stephen Breyer' (2005) 3 *International Journal of Constitutional Law* 519–541.

It now means conducting extensive comparative research as part of an effort to make more sound and persuasive judgments for the parties involved and for a global audience. The Court's transnational aspirations go even further: to play a 'standard-setting' role in Asia and to contribute to the global project of promoting constitutionalism across borders. This long-term development in South Korea is a story of the birth and growth of a local constitutional actor attaining a cosmopolitan self-understanding as it is exposed to and engages with the wider world of rights jurisprudence and constitutionalism.[41]

The former and current Court justices interviewed by the author agreed that the fundamental reason for referring to foreign rights practices lies in the universality of human rights and the common concerns of states about legitimate restrictions of rights and that this engagement is made possible through a mutually comprehensible language of constitutional reasoning across jurisdictions.[42] The Korean judges' view supports the argument that regular reference to foreign rights practices does not necessarily threaten the autonomy of a domestic constitution or a constitutional adjudication body but that it can be an expression of and an effort to become a larger self. The Korean Constitutional Court has transformed itself from being a follower and importer in its early jurisprudence, dependent on a few reference countries, to being a regional leader and an autonomous and influential participant in global constitutional dialogues. This development has been achieved through active and continuous transnational engagement.

Nonetheless, limitations are also present. A careful look at the flow of cross-jurisdiction dialogues raises the question whether the flow is in fact composed of *two-way* communications that contribute to mutual fertilisation or whether it is largely limited to judicial borrowing from one region to another.[43] Concerns exist about geographical imbalance. There

---

[41] See Slaughter (n. 28), at 192 (discussing an emerging global community of courts based on 'the self-awareness of the national and international judges who play a part'). See also Jeremy Waldron, 'Foreign law and the modern Ius Gentium' (2005) 119 *Harvard Law Review* 129–147.

[42] These judges' remarks confirm scholars' account of factors and reasons for consulting rights jurisprudence in other jurisdictions. See, e.g., Christopher McCrudden, 'A common law of human rights? Transnational judicial conversations on constitutional rights' (2000) 20 *Oxford Journal of Legal Studies* 499–532, at 527–529 (discussing possible reasons why human rights cases entail greater use of foreign law than other cases); Anne-Marie Slaughter, 'A typology of transjudicial communication' (1994) 29 *University of Richmond Law Review* 99–137.

[43] This concern is partly addressed in Slaughter (n. 42).

are abundant cases in which Western democracies cite each other's rights practice.[44] Asian courts frequently cite European and Anglo-American cases, but rarely is it the other way around. Asian courts cite Western cases much more frequently than they refer to other Asian countries' practices. Some cases raise the suspicion that the Korean Constitutional Court can be selective in citing foreign law. In the 2012 *Abortion* case,[45] the research judge prepared a report detailing abortion law in Austria, China, France, Germany, Ireland, Italy, Mexico, the Netherlands, Spain, the United Kingdom and the United States. In a 4:4 decision, the Court found that the domestic criminal law punishing those involved in abortion (including women and doctors) was still constitutional. The court opinion affirming it did not mention foreign practices that are generally more open to abortion under certain conditions. The dissenting judges did cite foreign law to support their position.

Despite such limitations, which are also common in many other jurisdictions, the overall practices of the Korean Constitutional Court put it among the most active constitutional actors in Asia and beyond in terms of transnational engagement and cosmopolitan identity. Change is also underway in the communication flows. As mentioned, the Korean Constitutional Court has begun to cite the practice of Latin American and Asian states. The Taiwan Constitutional Court occasionally cites Korean examples. The Korean Constitutional Court increasingly receives requests from other states and international bodies for English translations of or background information on its recent decisions. Its vigorous transnational activities of late and its intensifying efforts in comparative study and global communication have raised the expectation that greater mutual and substantive rights dialogues will occur between the West and Asia and among Asian jurisdictions in the years to come.

4 Tradition and rights reasoned through constitutional review

Another dimension of constitutional rights actors' cosmopolitanising identity and practice is how traditions are treated in the constitutional

---

[44] See Cheryl Saunders, 'The use and misuse of comparative constitutional law' (2006) 13 *Indiana Journal of Global Legal Studies* 37–76 (discussing practice among common law jurisdiction); Halmai (n. 24), at 1331–1334 (discussing earlier US practice); McCrudden (n. 42), at 517–523 (discussing relevant factors such as the type of political regime in which the foreign court is situated; pedagogical impulse; perceived audience; and the existence of common alliances).

[45] Constitutional Court of Korea, 2010 Hun-Ba 402 (23 August 2012).

framework. It is doubtful that 'Asian values' could serve to justify denying human rights to any extent.[46] The ways that tradition or national culture comes into constitutional rights practice are subtler and more varied. This section examines the cases in which domestic laws rooted in traditional values have been challenged by citizens as oppressing their constitutional rights, while tradition has been asserted by other groups as a justification for restricting rights. These cases illustrate how the conflict between traditional values (under the influence of the Confucian history in East Asia) and constitutional rights and principles – adopted with Korea's independence and modernisation since 1945 – has been exposed, deliberated and addressed through and within the framework of constitutional review.

4.1   Cases

If one had to pick the single most transformative decision made by the Korean Constitutional Court so far, a good candidate would be *Household Head System* (*hojuje*) from 2005.[47] The household head system had been a foundation of Korean family law since its inception, representing and reproducing traditional social and family structures based on a type of male supremacy rooted in the Confucian tradition. Under this system, every Korean citizen was registered as a member of a 'household', a basic unit of the society. A 'household' comprised a 'house head', the eldest male in a family, and his subordinated family members, including his mother, wife and children. The family law made a female citizen belong to her father when she was born, to her husband when she married and then to her son when her husband died; in contrast, a male citizen was free to create his own household and serve as a head when he married. This institutionalised patriarchal family system was unique among modern democracies. Along with legislative efforts to abolish *hojuje*, a nationwide coalition of women's rights and civil rights groups brought a constitutional challenge before the Korean Constitutional Court.

After a series of open hearings and deliberation, the Court found that the family law was unconstitutional as it violated individuals' dignity and gender equality in the family under Article 36 paragraph 1 of the

[46] See generally Daniel A. Bell, *East Meets West: Human Rights and Democracy in East Asia* (Princeton, NJ: Princeton University Press, 2000); Amartya Sen, *Human Rights and Asian Values* (New York: Carnegie Council on Ethics and International Affairs, 1997).
[47] Constitutional Court of Korea, 2001 Hun-Ga 9 (3 February 2005).

constitution. The majority opinion dealt with the relation between tradition and constitutional principles. Its reasoning started with holding that

> if the Constitution sustains a neutral position toward a family life and system, it might be desirable to respect a traditional family system unless it goes against other constitutional provisions. However, if the Constitution adopts certain values and principles with respect to a family life and system, especially in the period of political and social transformation [i.e. upon adoption of the First Constitution in 1948], then those constitutional values and principles should be the supreme norm.

It also held that 'the role of family law is not limited to reflecting social reality. . . . It should confirm and disseminate the constitutional principle.' The Court then discussed the relation between tradition and a democratic family system. It pointed to Article 9 of the constitution: 'The State shall strive to sustain and develop the cultural heritage and to enhance national culture' and to Article 36 paragraph 1: 'Marriage and family life shall be entered into and sustained on the basis of individual dignity and equality of the sexes, and the State shall do everything in its power to achieve that goal', and it emphasised the importance of a harmonised interpretation of these two constitutional principles. The Court found that Article 36 paragraph 1 indicates a constitutional resolve to no longer acknowledge a long-standing patriarchal family order in the society. The Court articulated that the tradition mentioned in Article 9 is a concept with both historical and contemporary aspects, embracing the present as well as the past, and thus that it should be valid and reasonable according to today's standards. If a traditional order goes against constitutional values and principles, including individual dignity and gender equality, then it cannot be constitutionally justified under Article 9. The Court proceeded to find that the household head system is unconstitutional as it violates gender equality and individual dignity.

In contrast, the dissenting opinion of two justices emphasised a constitutional duty to sustain and promote traditional culture, including the family system, which reflects 'our unique and rational patrilineal tradition'. Evaluating the household head system with the proportionality test, the dissent argued that preserving a patrilineal family order can be a legitimate government purpose, given the state's duty to uphold traditions under Article 9. These justices found that the household head system met the necessity and the narrow balancing requirements: the wife-belongs-to-husband family practice has been taken for granted for a long time in a patrilineal society; this reality has not changed much until today; and this family system does not bring about substantively discriminatory effects against women.

After the Court's decision in *Household Head System*, an entirely new, digitalised and individualised citizen registration system was developed and began to operate in South Korea. Every Korean citizen is now registered as an individual, neither as a household head nor as a member subject to a head.

Another transformative case concerns family law as well. Marriage between citizens who have the same family name and origin had long been prohibited by law. This prohibition was based on the tradition of an agricultural society with an extended family system, combined with the Confucian and patriarchal social order. Under the law, about four million people with the family name Kim and the same regional origin but without any close family ties were not allowed to marry each other. In 1997, the Court found this law unconstitutional in violation of human dignity and the right to pursue happiness as well as the gender equality principle under the constitution.[48] The Court emphasised that tradition and social order themselves change over time and that the law's basis was no longer a tradition protected under Article 9. The Court also noted that this type of prohibition had been abolished in China, where it originated, as early as the 1930s. The Court did not proceed with the proportionality test, finding that preserving an outdated social order cannot be a legitimate government purpose in restricting constitutional rights. In contrast, two dissenting justices took the position that citizens' constitutional rights and equality are protected within the tradition. They considered that the preservation of the social order by enforcing a traditional marriage custom was a legitimate reason for the state to restrict rights and equality and that the extent to which it restricted rights under this law was not excessive.

The Confusion tradition and ethics appear in the criminal (procedural) law as well. The Korean Criminal Procedure Law prohibits a person from suing one's parents/grandparents or parents-/grandparents-in-law for criminal charges.[49] This prohibition is rooted in the traditional Confucian ethics of *hyo*, a filial duty to one's parents. In a decision in 2011, five justices found the law unconstitutional, but the Court could not reach the six votes required to invalidate any law or

---

[48] Constitutional Court of Korea, 95 Hun-Ga 6 (16 July 1997).

[49] Crimes of sexual and domestic violence are exempted from this prohibition under Korean law.

government action in Korea.[50] Reviewing the provision under the proportionality principle, the five justices found that depriving a crime victim of the right to sue his/her offender so as to preserve a family value based on the Confucian tradition (the purpose of which they deemed legitimate) violates the equality right of those whose lineal ascendants are their criminal offenders. The other four justices regarded this law as constitutional, reasoning that a crime victim's right to sue is not a constitutional right but a mere legal right under criminal procedure law; that the legislature therefore holds broad discretion to regulate this right while taking into account the nation's own judicial culture, ethics and tradition; that Confucian traditions and ethics remain valid today, especially for the relationship between direct ascendants and descendants; that in this relationship, traditional culture and ethics should be more decisive than legal regulation; that among the ethics, respect for one's parents has been considered as the supreme moral value; and that the law embodying this value has a rational basis for discrimination.

4.2 Implications

The preceding cases illustrate how traditions encounter constitutional rights. The constitutional review process serves to expose, deliberate and resolve conflicts and tensions between individual rights and traditional values or orders of society embedded in the law. The dynamics are more complex than a dichotomous confrontation between universal human rights and cultural relativism.[51] Traditions are contested within a constitutional framework through the rights reasoning process with the language of constitutional rights and principles.[52] Restrictive laws rooted in traditions need stronger justification than the assertion that the law supports traditional values or conventional social order.[53] Rights-based constitutionalism deconsecrates traditions and requires them to be

[50] Constitutional Court of Korea, 2008 Hun-Ba 56 (24 February 2011).
[51] For general discussion on the subject, see, e.g., Jack Donnelly, 'Cultural relativism and universal human rights' (1984) 6 *Human Rights Quarterly* 400–419. See also James Tully, *Strange Multiplicity: Constitutionalism in an Age of Diversity* (Cambridge: Cambridge University Press, 1995) for discussion of accommodating cultural diversity in modern constitutionalism.
[52] See Mattias Kumm, 'Comment: contesting the management of difference: transnational human rights, religion and the European Court of Human Rights' Lautsi decision', in Kolja Raube and Anika Sattler (eds.), *Difference and Democracy: Exploring Potentials in Europe and Beyond* (Frankfurt: Campus Verlag, 2011), pp. 245–259.
[53] Ibid., pp. 252–254.

justified in constitutional terms when they restrict rights, equality or other constitutional principles.[54]

The constitutional dynamics between rights and traditions are more complex in the Korean context since its constitution provides for succeeding and developing traditions as a constitutional duty of the state (Article 9). In the first two cases, the Constitutional Court addressed this tension by interpreting traditions in the contemporary context – excluding oppressive and outdated customs from the definition of tradition to be upheld under Article 9. Finding that preserving a patriarchal social order cannot serve as a legitimate purpose in restricting rights and equality, the Court did not have to proceed further with the proportionality test.[55] In contrast, the dissenting justices regarded that maintaining a traditional family order can serve as a legitimate purpose for restricting rights, backing up their position with the Article 9 duty. However, their proportionality reviews lack detailed and thorough reasoning. In the last case, five of the nine justices also tried to address the tension through proportionality reasoning. While these justices deemed upholding a filial duty to one's parents as a legitimate purpose of law, they found the law unconstitutional because it restricted rights excessively. The other four refused to review the law under the proportionality test, emphasising the legislature's discretion in regulating this type of issue.

These cases exemplify the ways that tension and conflict between rights and traditions are deliberated and reasoned in constitutional review. The majority opinions in each case make clear that a tradition or custom that does not uphold today's constitutional values and principles cannot serve to justify a restriction on rights and equality. Even if some traditional values have continuing merits for contemporary society (such as *hyo* in the last case), the law based on these values needs to be justified through a further balancing test. The court practices also demonstrate the emancipatory potential of constitutional rights contestation and adjudication for the individuals whose rights and equality have been denied in the name of tradition and national culture.

---

[54] Ibid.

[55] See Mattias Kumm, 'Political liberalism and the structure of rights: on the place and limits of the proportionality requirement', in George Pavlakos (ed.), *Law, Rights and Discourse: The Legal Philosophy of Robert Alexy* (Oxford; Portland, OR: Hart Publishing, 2007), pp. 142–148. Regarding a general structure of the proportionality test, see, e.g., Robert Alexy, *A Theory of Constitutional Rights* (Oxford; New York: Oxford University Press, 2009); Matthias Klatt and Moritz Meister, *The Constitutional Structure of Proportionality* (Oxford: Oxford University Press, 2012).

As locality and specificity are reasoned through constitutional terms, a rights-based constitutional practice attains a cosmopolitan character with a capacity to accommodate both the locality of contexts and the universality of rights norms.

5 Assessment: bottom-up and locally grown global constitutionalism

Popular scepticism about global constitutionalism partly stems from the worry that it is an essentially elitist idea based predominantly on the European experience.[56] Both the charge of elitism and the charge of Eurocentrism raise concerns about a top-down approach to constitutionalism. This section revisits the Korean rights practices discussed so far, reflecting on whether the Korean example provides grounds for alleviating these concerns.

5.1   Individual empowerment: disproving elitism

The previous sections examined the emerging practice of global constitutionalism (GC) in South Korea, focusing on the Constitutional Court as a key actor. However, the primary intended beneficiaries of GC are not the courts or states but every rights-bearing *individual*. GC aims to realise human rights, democracy and the rule of law for the sake of individuals across borders of states and levels of law. As discussed in the previous section, rights-based constitutionalism can be emancipatory for individuals, and this potential entails multiple dimensions of empowerment. Individual citizens and non-citizens are empowered by the adoption of the constitutional list of rights and an effectively functioning mechanism to contest these rights, challenging unreasonable or oppressive laws and government actions.[57] International human rights norms and other

---

[56] For discussion of the elitist charge against global constitutionalism, see, e.g., Anne Peters, 'Compensatory constitutionalism: the function and potential of fundamental international norms and structures' (2006) 19 *Leiden Journal of International Law* 579–610, at 609; McCrudden (n. 42), at 531–532; Kumm (n. 19), p. 314. See also Philip Allott, 'The emerging international aristocracy' (2003) 35 *New York University Journal of International Law and Politics* 309–337.

[57] See Mattias Kumm, 'The idea of Socratic contestation and the right to justification: the point of rights-based proportionality review' (2010) 4 *Law & Ethics of Human Rights* 140–175, at 168 (pointing out that the right to contest in constitutional review settings is at least as empowering as the right to vote). See also Rainer Forst, *The Right to Justification* (New York: Columbia University Press, 2012).

jurisdictions' rights practices further empower these individuals by providing them with additional grounds to demand justification for state actions that deviate from global norms or practice. This transnational rights practice encourages the individual to grow into a cosmopolitan rights-bearer acting locally with a global mindset. Thus, through the constitutional rights review system, individuals are empowered not only as beneficiaries of GC but also as its key actors. Recall the claimants in the cases discussed so far: women subordinated to men under the household head system; 'comfort women' ignored by both Japanese and Korean governments; migrant workers abused by the discriminatory foreign labour system; disenfranchised prisoners and convicts; and incarcerated conscientious objectors, among numerous others who have been oppressed, discriminated against and marginalised by laws about which they had very little say. Through the constitutional rights review system, these rights-bearing individuals are empowered to bring a case, require justifications and engage in rights debates. They often provoke transformative outcomes towards a more free, equal and just society. Through empowerment, these individuals become the drivers and developers of *bottom-up global constitutionalism*.[58] The cosmopolitanising rights practice led by empowered ordinary citizens and non-citizens provides powerful grounds for challenging the charge that GC is an *elitist* enterprise.[59]

Individuals are not the only group empowered and mobilised by the cosmopolitanising system of constitutional rights review. The Korean example demonstrates how the Court and the individual can mobilise and empower each other. In many cases, the Court is informed of relevant international human rights norms and foreign practices by individual applicants. Increasingly, their lawyers and non-governmental organisations

---

[58] See Wen-Chen Chang, 'An isolated nation with global-minded citizens: bottom-up transnational constitutionalism in Taiwan' (2009) 4 *National Taiwan University Law Review* 203–235. More generally, Boaventura de Sousa Santos and César A. Rodríguez-Garavito (eds.), *Law and Globalization from Below: Towards a Cosmopolitan Legality* (New York: Cambridge University Press, 2005). See also James Tully et al., 'Editorial: introducing global integral constitutionalism' (2016) 5 *Global Constitutionalism* 1–15 (discussing the concept and the bottom-up practice of eco-social constitutionalism).

[59] E.g. McCrudden (n. 42), at 531–532 (pointing out that 'in the judicial interpretation and application of human rights principles, the voices of the historically disadvantaged and marginalized are the voices least often heard, nationally and internationally. . . . Ignoring the problem of participation whilst at the same time appearing to engage in a closed dialogue with other judges at the supranational level, may weaken the protection of human rights rather than reinforcing it.').

(NGOs) research intensively and invoke international and foreign human rights law as grounds for the constitutional claims. The rights practice by globally motivated private actors drives the Court to respond to their transnational rights claims when deliberating and writing its decisions. Court justices regularly ask research judges to conduct further research into relevant international norms and foreign practices in addition to those invoked by applicants. The Court also has its own transnational aspirations of playing a leadership role in Asia and beyond. The Court's global engagement further mobilises individuals, lawyers and civil society to engage in transnational human rights practices more earnestly, which again informs the Court and advances its practice. Thus, multiple aspects of bottom-up GC practices are developing in and through the constitutional rights review system: from individual rights-holders to the Constitutional Court; from young research judges to senior justices; and from the local to the transnational.

5.2 Locally grown global constitutionalism practice: challenging Eurocentrism

Cosmopolitanising rights practice in South Korea, facilitated by bottom-up participation of global-minded individuals and the transnational ambitions of the Constitutional Court, exemplifies a locally grown practice of global constitutionalism. It provides an empirical challenge to the charge that GC is inherently Eurocentric and to some extent imperialist.[60] Although the judges and justices of the Korean Constitutional Court and individual applicants and lawyers have little knowledge about or exposure to GC scholarship, they are the key actors advancing locally grown GC ideas and practice. The phenomenon has been initiated and has developed not through top-down preaching by European elite lawyers or scholars but through local actors' transnational self-awareness and justice-seeking efforts.

It is also important to recognise the diversity among states and their various actors in East Asia. For a state like South Korea – a nation

---

[60] See, e.g., Anne Peters, 'Global constitutionalism', in Michael T. Gibbons (ed.), *The Encyclopedia of Political Thought* (Chichester; Malden: Wiley-Blackwell, 2014), pp. 1484–1486; Christine E. J. Schwöbel, 'The political economy of global constitutionalism', in Anthony F. Lang, Jr. and Antje Wiener (eds.), *Handbook on Global Constitutionalism* (Cheltenham; Northampton: Edward Elgar Publishers, 2017). See also Nico Krisch, *Beyond Constitutionalism: The Pluralist Structure of Postnational Law* (Oxford; New York: Oxford University Press, 2010).

internally democratised and economically developed in recent decades
and a mid-level player in terms of external political and military power –
actively engaging with the global community and expressing its high-
standard human rights practice through an advanced judicial system can
constitute a national effort to enhance its global reputation and success.
This tendency is especially conspicuous as regards Taiwan: like South
Korea, it is relatively well democratised and economically developed.
However, the nation is significantly restrained by Chinese political pressure. Actively engaging in transnational practices and being recognised
as an advocate of human rights are part of its national strategy for
international survival.[61] In contrast, regional heavyweights Japan and
China do not seem particularly motivated by the promise of GC. As for
the various actors, measuring and comparing people's enthusiasm about
the core substance of GC in each jurisdiction would be difficult. It is
relatively clear, however, that in South Korea and Taiwan, citizens'
demands for human rights and democracy with global sensitivity work
largely in harmony with national constitutional bodies' transnational
aspirations. The examples of South Korea and Taiwan provide evidence
to counter the charges of European parochialism or imperialism levelled
against GC. They also point to the pitfalls in overgeneralising about East
Asia and conceiving of it as a homogeneous region.[62]

5.3   Towards truly global global constitutionalism

The rights practice in South Korea examined from multiple angles in this
chapter exemplifies a practice of bottom-up global constitutionalism that
has developed locally, outside of Europe. This development reflects and
furthers cosmopolitanising ideas about rights, self and the world held by
local constitutional actors – the constitutional court with transnational
aspirations and the global-minded rights-holding individuals. Their
active engagements with international and foreign human rights law

---

[61] See Chang (n. 58); David S. Law and Mila Versteeg, 'The evolution and ideology of global
constitutionalism' (2011) 99 *California Law Review* 1163–1258, at 1178.

[62] It is doubtful whether diverse manifestations in different East Asian states would allow
a categorisation such as 'East Asian constitutionalism'. An initial, cautious attempt with
a comparative approach was made by Jiunn-Rong Yeh and Wen-Chen Chang,
'The emergence of East Asian constitutionalism: features in comparison' (2011) 59
The American Journal of Comparative Law 805–839. See Sen (n. 46), pp. 13–14
('The temptation to see Asia as one unit reveals, in fact, a distinctly Eurocentric perspec-
tive. East Asia itself has much diversity, and there are many variations between Japan and
China and Korea and other parts of East Asia.').

facilitate more comprehensive, concrete and sound understanding and realisation of human rights. Cosmopolitanising ideas of rights and self are also embedded in the constitutional rights practice of rethinking tradition and national culture in constitutional terms, thereby taking seriously the locality as well as the universality of rights. Current tensions and struggles show the transformation and widening of the rights practice underway. The example of South Korea provides a perspective from which to comprehend and advance global constitutionalism beyond elitist and Eurocentric concerns. This story suggests workable ways to realise global constitutionalism as a truly global project: empowering ordinary rights-bearing individuals not only as the project's primary beneficiaries but also as its key actors through active participation in rights contestation transnationally; mobilising local rights adjudication bodies to engage seriously with global jurisprudence of rights and other constitutional values; and facilitating dynamic interactions among local constitutional actors in and across jurisdictions to further the cosmopolitan ideas of rights and justice. The promise of global constitutionalism can be better achieved through these bottom-up and locally developing cosmopolitan rights practices. The case of South Korea thus points to a brighter future of global constitutionalism.

PART III

Horizontal Interactions

Trade, Environment and Development

9

Global Constitutionalism

The Social Dimension

ANNE PETERS*

1 Introduction

In the streets of Tunis in 2010, the vegetable vendor Mohamed Bouazizi torched himself. His death sparked the Arab 'spring', a bloody revolt which transformed the Middle East and North Africa (MENA) region. The Parliament of the EU later awarded the Sakharov prize for freedom of thought to Bouazizi and four other persons. However, all those who had committed suicide did not pursue any specific political or ideological programme – they were small entrepreneurs protesting against the withdrawal of vending licenses, the arbitrary confiscation of scales and repeated fines. Put differently: these 'martyrs' had demanded legal security for their capital and protection against expropriation.[1]

A second example is the Syrian uprising of 2011 which led to an ongoing transnational war that has so far caused around half a million deaths and millions of refugees. The uprising had been triggered by a combination of factors including 'growing poverty caused by rapid economic liberalization and the cancellation of state subsidies after 2005, a growing rural–urban divide, widespread corruption, rising unemployment, the effects of a severe drought between 2006 and 2010 and a lack of political freedom'.[2]

---

* The author thanks Steven Ratner and Takao Suami for helpful critique and suggestions on the draft. She also thanks all participants of the Max Planck research seminar, notably Elif Askin, Franz Ebert, Raffaela Kunz and Milan Tahraoui for valuable input, and the student research assistants for their outstanding support.
[1] Hernando de Soto, *The Facts Are In: The Arab Spring Is a Massive Economic Revolution* (Tunis: Cérès éditions, 2013).
[2] Francesca de Châtel, 'The role of drought and climate change in the Syrian uprising: untangling the triggers of the Revolution' (2014) 50 *Middle Eastern Studies* 521–535, at 521.

278 ANNE PETERS

Both incidents illustrate the frequent confluence of material and ideational deprivation, of poverty and bondage. Indeed, rulers in all times and places have harmed people over which they held some power by oppressing them (curtailing their freedom) and by plundering them (directly or indirectly depriving them of their means of subsistence).[3] Concomitantly, political opposition demanding reforms and social unrest up to revolt and revolution usually react against both harms: not only against deprivations of freedom such as censorship and discrimination but also against the denial of basic social needs of parts of the population, caused by governmental neglect, excessive or arbitrary taxation and wealth accumulation of the governors and their clients.

The interdependence and interaction of the ideational and material conditions of life are aptly captured in the phrase 'development as freedom' by Amartya Sen.[4] This interaction has led national constitutionalism to embrace the social question. In a climate of globalisation fatigue, it is high time that global constitutionalism[5] does the same. In doing so, it can build on and push further post-neo-liberal expressions in current international law.

In order to formulate and justify the quest for a global *social* constitutionalism, we first need to clarify what the 'social' means in this context. The concept of the 'social' has its origin in the Latin word *socius* which means companion or ally.[6] 'Social' is present in terms such as 'socialism',[7] in the International Covenant on Economic, *Social* and Cultural Rights (ICESCR), in the European *Social* Charter[8] and in the concept of

---

[3] Mathias Risse, 'Do we owe the global poor assistance or rectification?' (2005) 19 *Ethics and International Affairs* 9–18, at 17 speaks of 'authoritarian predators'.

[4] Amartya Sen, *Development as Freedom* (Oxford: Oxford University Press, 1999). See in detail Section 9.

[5] See for the concept of global constitutionalism Anne Peters, Takao Suami, Dimitri Vanoverbeke and Mattias Kumm, 'Global Constitutionalism from European and East Asian Perspectives: An Introduction', in this volume.

[6] Consider also the following uses of the word: man/woman as a social being, social capital, social skills, social justice, social politics, the social state. Related and derivative terms are, for example, society, sociology, socialisation.

[7] Cf. Michael Newman, *Socialism: A Very Short Introduction* (Oxford: Oxford University Press, 2005), p. 2, mentioning as 'the most fundamental characteristic of socialism ... its commitment to the creation of an egalitarian society'.

[8] Revised Version of 3 May 1996 (ETS No. 163). Thereby the member states of the Council of Europe 'agreed to secure to their populations the social rights specified therein in order to improve their standard of living and their social well-being', and for 'facilitating their economic and social progress', as the Charter's preamble puts it.

'corporate *social* responsibility' (CSR). Social policies range from social assistance, social security and social insurance schemes over a labour market policy to an education policy. This chapter does not focus on 'social' in the broad sense of everything connected to a collective or group, to a *society* – as the opposite of private or individual. ('Social' in that broad sense figures, e.g., in Jean-Jacques Rousseau's '*contrat social*', in the mentioning of a 'social and international order' in Article 28 of the Universal Declaration of Human Rights (UDHR) and in the concept of the 'pressing social need' in the case law of the Strasbourg Human Rights Court.[9]) Rather, the chapter understands by 'social' an attribute of laws, policies and institutions which seeks to improve the material living conditions of humans and mitigate poverty and inequality of wealth and income.

The chapter shows that the social question, thus understood, has always been to some extent shaped by factors outside the nation state (Section 2). It reviews the traditional social impetus of international law (Section 3), and it highlights that high hyper-globalisation and global supply chains have exacerbated and globalised the social question and have thus raised new types of critique and brought new expectations to international law (Section 4). The chapter then highlights and pulls together important trends in our post-2015 international legal order as forming an overall 'more social' international law (Sections 5–7). The important interim finding is that this new body of law is characterised by its cross-border social responsibility for individuals (Section 8). It is then submitted that this 'more social' and individual-focused international law can be well understood and developed further within a framework of global constitutionalism (Section 9). The most important reason for absorbing the social question is to mitigate the neo-liberal tilt of global constitutionalism. Only the full integration of the social question, understood as a global question, into the programme of global constitutionalism will be able to rescue that programme from becoming reduced to a much-loathed 'new constitutionalism', denounced as a political project to deepen the power of capital and to extend a 'market civilisation' in which the transnational investor is the principal political subject and in which the social is kept out and down.[10] With

---

[9] When Scelle in his *Précis* defined international law as '*droit intersocial*', he relied on the broad notion (Georges Scelle, *Précis de droit des gens: Principes et systématique*, Vol. I: Introduction, le milieu intersocial (Paris: Sirey, 1932), p. 27).

[10] See in detail Section 9.1.

such a renovation from within, global constitutionalism can form part of a fresh 'post-neo-liberal imagination'[11] of international law (Section 10).

2 External forces acting on the national social question

The facts and policies of the 'social' have never been a purely domestic matter. Social policies on the local or national scale have always been co-shaped by outside factors and actors, both by interventions from one state into another and by international institutions.[12] Medical aid, education and other 'benefits of civilization' were, since the beginning of the colonial conquest, in the heart of the activities of European powers and European societal actors (churches, chartered companies and the like) in the non-European regions. From the eighteenth until well into the twentieth century, European proselytism, imperialism, colonialism, physical violence and abuse, and the destruction of local culture were intimately bound up with and justified by the claim that such interventions sought to bring social improvements and to raise the standards of living in the retarded, backward, underdeveloped regions.

Law-making on the labour conditions and social security of workers started only after the industrialisation in Europe. The first piece of legislation was the British factory legislation (starting with the establishment of a factory inspectorate in 1833). States which have made social policies a part of their national and constitutional identity are called welfare states or *social* states.[13] It is important for our analysis that such building of social states in twentieth-century Europe was intimately linked to events *outside* those nation states. It was therefore no purely domestic development – quite to the contrary. It was, firstly, a reaction by Western European governments to appease and console the labour movements which protested against competition by cheap labour in the colonies and were prone to be 'contaminated' by the Russian Revolution. Secondly, the rise of the welfare state was probably

---

[11] Andrew Lang, *World Trade Law after Neo-Liberalism: Re-Imagining the Global Economic Order* (Oxford: Oxford University Press, 2011), p. 343.

[12] See on the international social law and governance activities, Section 3.

[13] See for an excellent exposition of three complementary welfare (social) state conceptions David Garland, *The Welfare State: A Very Short Introduction* (Oxford: Oxford University Press, 2016), pp. 7–8. For Garland, the welfare state is 'designed to steer the capitalist juggernaut along a more socially acceptable course. At its core is a set of social protections, superimposed upon capitalist economic processes, designed to modify and moralize the market economy.' (Ibid., p. 9.)

facilitated by war. In Germany, important steps were taken after the German–French war of 1870, and further leaps were made after World Wars I and II, respectively. The usual explanation for this path is that the surge of nationalism and national solidarity created by war helped to secure the acceptance needed for the introduction of solidarity and insurance-based schemes by law. The war-driven logic would also explain why the United States, which never had to fight a war against a foreign enemy on its territory, so far had not built up a full-fledged welfare state.[14]

In today's globalised economy, the domestic social and labour standards within a given state are de iure or de facto co-determined to some extent by the behaviour of mobile capital and labour, by other states and by international organisations and other institutions of global governance.[15] The mobility of capital holders has resulted in states competing to have production facilities sited on their territory. If one country attempts to improve social standards, e.g. with regard to labour safety, it fears that the affected sectors or branches of industry might escape strict regulations by relocating.[16] The anticipation of such relocation to cheap and low-standard countries incites policymakers, anxious to maintain tax revenues and jobs, to lower taxes. This in turn reduces the states' means which could finance social projects. The anxiety is also an incentive for freezing labour standards because compliance with high standards normally renders the production process more costly. When individual countries in this way try to keep or regain economically significant industrial sectors by supplying an attractively permissive legal environment, there is a danger of a downward spiral of

[14] Stein Kuhnle and Anne Ander, 'The emergence of the Western welfare state', in Francis G. Castles, Stephan Leibfried, Jane Lewis, Herbert Obinger and Christopher Pierson (eds.), *The Oxford Handbook of the Welfare State* (Oxford: Oxford University Press, 2010), pp. 61–80 and 79–80 with further references.
[15] The effects of capital and labour mobility on social standards and other features of the social state are very complex, and it is difficult to establish causalities. For a nuanced explanation of the coexistence of both welfare cuts and expansion of welfare spending under conditions of capital and labour mobility, see Alexander Hicks and Christopher Zorn, 'Economic globalization, the macro economy, and reversals of welfare: expansion in affluent democracies, 1978–94' (2005) 59 *International Organization* 631–662. See also Jagdish Bhagwati, *In Defense of Globalization* (New York: Oxford University Press, 2004), pp. 67, 71–72, 98–102, 122–134 refuting the assertions of an increase of the global welfare gap, the increase of child labour and the lowering of labour protection standards and salaries due to globalisation.
[16] Anne Peters, 'The competition between legal orders' (2014) 3 *International Law Research* 45–65.

standards.[17] The 'race to the bottom'[18] is a widespread idea among voters and lawmakers counting on those voters. For example, the new General Comment No. 24 on State Obligations under the International Covenant on Economic, Social and Cultural Rights in the Context of Business Activities, adopted by the Committee on Economic, Social and Cultural Rights (CESCR), finds that 'lowering the rates of corporate taxes with a sole view to attracting investors encourages a race to the bottom that ultimately undermines the ability of all States to mobilise resources domestically to realise Covenant rights. As such, this practice is inconsistent with the duties of the States Parties to the Covenant.'[19]

The side effects of interstate competition for market participants may be beneficial or pernicious for different groups of persons. Workers in high-standard states may be (or believe to be) menaced by unemployment when production facilities are moved to low-standard production states. This is, for example, the current situation in many regions of the United States where factories have been shut down and the companies moved to China or Mexico. Industrialised states and labour unions often shun the persistence of low social standards in states which seek to become or remain attractive as production sites (e.g. China as the 'world's factory') as 'social dumping'.[20] One as yet embryonic legal strategy is the insertion of so-called social clauses or CSR clauses into trade and investment agreements.[21] Such clauses commit the parties in more or less hortatory language to observe core labour principles or specific enumer-

---

[17] See for an analysis of the downward spiral in the field of social standards and taxes Ramesh Mishra, *Globalization and the Welfare State* (London: Edward Elgar, 1999), pp. 41 and 50–51.

[18] 'Race to laxity' (US Supreme Court, *Ligget Co. v. Lee* (288 US 517, 558–559 (1933)).

[19] UN Committee on Economic, Social and Cultural Rights (CESCR), General Comment No. 24 on State Obligations under the International Covenant on Economic, Social and Cultural Rights in the Context of Business Activities of 23 June 2017 (UN Doc. E/C.12/GC/24), para. 37.

[20] The European Commission described social dumping as a situation where foreign service providers can undercut local service providers because their labour standards are lower (European Observatory of Working Life, 'Social dumping' (19 May 2016), www.eurofound.europa.eu/observatories/eurwork/industrial-relations-dictionary/social-dumping-0).

[21] See Rafael Peels, Elizabeth Echeverria Manrique, Jonas Aissi and Anselm Schneider, *ILO Research Paper No. 13: Corporate Social Responsibility in International Trade and Investment Agreements: Implications for States, Business, and Workers* (Geneva: International Labour Office, 2016).

ated labour standards.[22] The objective is to prevent goods produced under substandard conditions from benefitting from trade liberalisation. But what some states see as social dumping others consider to be a legitimate competitive advantage. The question is, then, at what point the competition becomes unfair.

That question must remain open at this point. What matters for this chapter is simply that interstate competition or the perception – independent of the reality of this competition as an empirical fact – has been and continues to be a relevant factor in the political and legal process leading to social laws and standards.

3   Traditional international social law

Since its beginnings, international law has been a *'droit international libéral-providence'*.[23] It has worked and is working on the dual agenda of promoting both *freedom* and *prosperity*.[24] And of course international relations and the rules accompanying and framing them have always been driven by the economic interests of influential players. Intercourse between political communities and their members (both peaceful and violent) has usually turned around trade, around the exploitation of natural resources or manpower and around competition over these factors. The first international treaties concerned – besides peace – trade and settlement for economic enterprise.[25] In that sense, someone being rich or poor has always partly been influenced by international rules and by the international political order, and this influence has been crescent.

---

[22] See, e.g., Art. 6 of the Agreement Between the United States of America and the Hashemite Kingdom of Jordan on the Establishment of a Free Trade Area of 24 October 2000; chapter 16: 'Labor' of the Dominican Republic–Central America Free Trade Agreement of 5 August 2004; chapter 18: 'Labour' of the Australia–United States Free Trade Agreement of 18 May 2008. See also Art. 19(2)–19(3) of the so-far aborted Trans-Pacific Partnership, signed on 4 February 2016 by Australia, Brunei, Canada, Chile, Japan, Malaysia, Mexico, New Zealand, Peru, Singapore and Vietnam (not in force); Art. 3(2)–3(3) of the EU–Vietnam Free Trade Agreement, signed on 2 December 2015 (not in force).

[23] Emmanuelle Jouannet, *Le droit international libéral-providence: une histoire du droit international* (Brussels: Bruylant, 2011).

[24] UN General Assembly, Resolution 70/1 on Transforming Our World: The 2030 Agenda for Sustainable Development of 25 September 2015 (UN Doc. A/RES/70/1), preamble, the first sentences: 'This Agenda is a plan of action for people, planet and *prosperity*. It also seeks to strengthen universal peace in larger *freedom*' (emphases added).

[25] See, e.g., the US–Prussian Treaty of Amity and Commerce of 9 July/10 September 1785 (http://avalon.law.yale.edu/18th_century/prus1785.asp).

In the twentieth century, a flurry of activities of international organisations and other intergovernmental bodies (COPs, soft organisations, interstate conferences) has impacted the domestic social sphere and domestic social law-making.[26] The 'social question' which began to occupy the governments of industrialising states near the end of the nineteenth century was almost immediately taken up in the then emerging forms of interstate cooperation (congresses, administrative unions and later international organisations). For example, a Superior Health Council was set up in Constantinople in 1839 to deal with diseases such as cholera.[27]

The actual take-off was after World War I with the foundation of the League of Nations and the International Labour Organization (ILO) in 1919.[28] A driving force of the foundation of the ILO was the fear in many Western states (of governments and entrepreneurs alike) of the movement of the 'Socialist International' and of a spillover of the Bolshevik revolution of 1917 from Russia to other states. The insertion of Part XIII ('Labour') in the Treaty of Versailles and the subsequent adoption of international labour conventions sought to buy off the revolutionaries.[29] This was the same motivation as the one propelling domestic labour law reform, exemplified by Bismarck's undercutting of the German socialist movement by introducing laws

---

[26] See for an excellent analysis Klaus Armingeon, 'Intergovernmental organizations', in Francis G. Castles, Stephan Leibfried, Jane Lewis, Herbert Obinger and Christopher Pierson (eds.), *The Oxford Handbook of the Welfare State* (Oxford: Oxford University Press, 2010), pp. 306–317.

[27] The Council was established by the '*Règlement organique du Conseil de santé à Constaninople pour les provencances de mer*' (signed 10 June 1839), in Friedrich Wilhelm August Murhard (ed.), *Martens Nouveau recueil*, Vol. XVI (Goettingen: Dieterich, 1842), 2nd part, pp. 920–926.

[28] The areas of 'improvement' listed in the ILO preamble are 'the regulation of the hours of work, including the establishment of a maximum working day and week, the regulation of the labour supply, the prevention of unemployment, the provision of an adequate living wage, the protection of the worker against sickness, disease and injury arising out of his employment, the protection of children, young persons and women, provision for old age and injury, protection of the interests of workers when employed in countries other than their own, recognition of the principle of equal remuneration for work of equal value, recognition of the principle of freedom of association, the organisation of vocational and technical education and other measures'. They seem as relevant today as they were in 1919.

[29] James Thomson Shotwell, 'The International Labor Organization as an alternative to violent revolution' (1933) 166 *The Annals of the American Academy of Political and Social Science* 18–25.

on the social security of workers,[30] preceded by the prohibition of the German Social Democrat Party.[31]

The ILO was from its foundation 'animated by a powerful sense of its mission and mandate to effect social reform through law'.[32] The ILO sought to tackle the social question, 'understood as a realm of disorder located between the economy and the state and associated with multiple interlinked problems connected to a large, underemployed proletariat', and reflected the commitment to the 'liberal ideals of progressive social reform' that had emerged in the United States and Europe since World War I.[33] By 1944 and with the adoption of the Philadelphia Declaration, 'the ILO's initial narrow focus on setting labour standards had given way to a complete worldview in which the achievement of human rights, development, industrialization, and trade were all inextricably bound together'.[34] Guy Fiti Sinclair concludes that 'the "social" has remained an important justification for (and object of) intervention by both international law and development', but also calls for 'caution in too quickly advocating a return to "the social" as a strategy for the renewal of either international law or development'.[35]

The League of Nations' work in social matters 'remains one of the League's lasting successes'.[36] The two social policy priorities of the League were the trafficking in women and children and in drugs (opium). The League's work led to the ratification, by League members and non-members, of numerous conventions, ranging from the 1921 International Convention for the Suppression of the Traffic in Women and Children to the 1939 Convention for the Suppression of the Illicit Traffic in Dangerous Drugs. These instruments and resolutions by League organs established a plethora of international commissions or committees,[37] in whose work also non-member states actively participated.

---

[30] The German chancellor was the driving force for the German laws on sickness insurance of workers, on the insurance against work accidents and on the insurance against invalidity and old age (statutes adopted between 1883 and 1889).

[31] (Nr. 1271) *Gesetz gegen die gemeingefährlichen Bestrebungen der Sozialdemokratie* of 21 October 1878, *Reichs-Gesetzblatt*, No. 34, pp. 351–358.

[32] Guy Fiti Sinclair, 'International social reform and the invention of development' (2018) 20 *Journal of the History of International Law* 145–197.

[33] Ibid., 155.

[34] Ibid., 195.

[35] Ibid., 196 and 197.

[36] Christian J. Tams, 'League of Nations', in Rüdiger Wolfrum (ed.), *Max Planck Encyclopaedia of Public International Law* (Oxford: Oxford University Press, 2006), para. 37.

[37] For example, an Advisory Committee on the Traffic in Women and Children, renamed Advisory Committee on Traffic in Women and Protection of Children (established in 1923), an Information Centre for Questions Regarding Child Welfare (established in

After World War II, the promotion of 'social progress' and of 'better standards of life in larger freedom' was one of the overarching aspirations of the newly founded world organisation, as laid out in the preamble to the UN Charter (and repeated verbatim in the preamble to the Universal Declaration of Human Rights of 1948). The social dimension is mentioned in the Charter in one row after preventing war, 'faith' in human rights and respect for international law. The UN Charter's preamble then continues with the promise 'to employ international machinery for the promotion of the economic and social advancement of all peoples'.

Article 1 of the UN Charter on Purposes and Principles lays down, as the third cluster of purposes, 'to achieve international cooperation in solving international problems of a ... social character'. To achieve this objective, the Charter devotes an entire chapter (chapter IX) to 'international economic and social cooperation'.[38] Also, the Charter establishes a principal organ, the Economic and Social Council (ECOSOC; regulated in another full chapter, chapter X) to deal with these matters.[39] Social cooperation, social progress and social problems thus figure more prominently in the UN Charter than human rights.[40] Human rights protection did not – unlike the 'social' question – earn an entire chapter of the Charter, nor did its drafters think this matter warranted a principal organ in the organisation.[41]

Mention must also be made of the entire branch of the international law of development (*droit international du développement*) which was drawn up in the 1970s in the context of decolonisation, mostly by French authors.[42] It was matched by the proposal coming from the developing

---

1934), a Conference of Central Authorities of Eastern Countries on the traffic in women and children (Bandoeng, Java; established in 1937) and the like.

[38] The chapter's opening provision, Art. 55, stipulates that 'the United Nations shall promote a) higher standards of living, and conditions of economic and social progress and development; b) solutions of international economic, social, health, and related problems ...'.

[39] The ECOSOC's main mandate is to 'make or initiate studies and reports with respect to international ... social matters' and to 'make recommendations with respect to such matters to the General Assembly, to the Members of the United Nations, and to the specialized agencies concerned' (Art. 62(1)).

[40] Human rights are mentioned, besides in the preamble, only in Art. 1(3), Art. 55 lit. c) and Art. 68 of the UN Charter.

[41] The Human Rights Commission (dissolved in 2006) was established only as a subsidiary organ of the ECOSOC (cf. Art. 68 of the UN Charter). The UN Human Rights Council was created in 2006 as a subsidiary organ of the General Assembly (Art. 22 of the UN Charter).

[42] See for new accounts Philipp Dann, Stefan Kadelbach and Markus Kaltenborn, *Entwicklung und Recht, eine systematische Einführung* (Baden-Baden: Nomos, 2014); Kerry Rittich, 'Theorizing international law and development', in Anne Orford and Florian Hofmann (eds.), *The Oxford Handbook of the Theory of International Law* (Oxford: Oxford University Press, 2016), pp. 820–843.

states to create a New International Economic Order (NIEO) which would significantly depart from the extant economic order so as to accommodate better the interests of the Global South.[43] Both transformative legal strategies more or less failed.

The international institutions can in principle influence national social politics both through deliberate social politics (as done, e.g., by the ILO) and indirectly through rules and measures in other policy fields which have repercussions on national social politics and on the social human rights of populations of targeted states. The international, explicitly 'social' governance modes are typically soft, ranging from information gathering and dissemination over adopting guidelines and recommendations to rarer instances of standard setting or distributing money. Often, the relevant organisations only diffuse ideas. For example, the Organisation for Economic Co-operation and Development (OECD) report entitled 'The welfare state in crisis' published in 1981 was probably 'seminal in setting the negative tone towards the welfare state'.[44] As a counterweight, the ILO has since the second half of the 1990s spread the concepts of 'decent work'[45] and 'fair globalisation'.[46] In contrast, international measures indirectly affecting domestic social policies are stronger, especially when they are shaped and enforced by full-fledged international dispute settlement mechanisms such as in international trade and investment. We may retain that the improvement of social conditions through law has been a constant theme of global governance. The twentieth century had indeed developed a 'social law of nations'.[47]

[43] Unsurprisingly, the NIEO meets renewed interest today. See Tony Anghie, 'Legal aspects of the New International Economic Order' (2015) 6 Humanity 145–158; Umut Öszu, '"In the interests of mankind as a whole": Mohammed Bedjaoui's New International Economic Order' (2015) 6 Humanity 129–143; Margot Salomon, 'From NIEO to now and the unfinished story of economic justice' (2013) 62 International and Comparative Law Quarterly 31–54; Ingo Venzke, 'Possibilities of the past: histories of the NIEO and the travails of critique' (2018) 20 Journal of the History of International Law (forthcoming in issue 3).
[44] Rune Ervik, Nanna Kildal and Even Nilssen, 'Introduction', in Rune Ervik, Nanna Kildal and Even Nilssen (eds.), The Role of International Organizations in Social Policies: Ideas, Actors and Impact (Cheltenham: Edward Elgar, 2009), pp. 1–19, p. 3.
[45] Seminal: 'Decent work', Report of the Director-General (Juan Somavia), International Labour Conference, 87th Session (Geneva 1999). See in scholarship Nausheen Nizami and Narayan Prasad, Decent Work: Concept, Theory and Measurement (Singapore: Springer, 2017).
[46] ILO, Declaration on Social Justice for a Fair Globalization, adopted by the International Labour Conference at its 97th Session, Geneva, 10 June 2008.
[47] Alain Pellet, Le droit international du développement, 2nd ed. (Paris: Presses Universitaires de France, 1987), p. 4: 'le droit social des nations'.

4 Globalisation fatigue and post-Washington consensus

The body of international social law has proved woefully inadequate. The international law of development has been dismissed as a 'stillborn' law and a 'formidable illusion',[48] because it did not seem to contribute to the development of any country. Most importantly for our analysis, the social law of nations has not been able to cushion the social hardships brought about by globalisation, 'essentially neoliberalism writ large'.[49]

'Neo-liberalism' is the pejorative label for the ideology and policy model that emphasises the value of free market competition, hence for ideas developed by twentieth-century economic liberals, applied from the 1979s onwards to reform Latin American countries and then, in another wave, in Eastern Europe after the breakdown of the socialist state economies after 1989.[50] 'Neo-liberalism' is also a label given to the international economic and legal setting on the basis of the 'Washington Consensus' of 1990,[51] resulting from the establishment of the World Trade Organization (WTO) with its package of liberal trade agreements in 1994 and the surge of international investment agreements.

Ulrich Beck had in 1990 written that 'the premises of the welfare state ... melt under the withering sun of globalization'.[52] This diagnosis and expectation had triggered an anti- or alter-globalisation movement fuelled by social concerns.[53] The plans and ideas for 'alternative globalisation' have consistently been formulated under the banner of the 'social'. For example, the most important alternative

---

[48] Maurice Kamto, 'Requiem pour le droit international de développement', in Stéphane Doume-Bille, Habib Gherari and Rahim Kherad (eds.), *Mélanges en l' honneur de Madjid Benchikh* (Paris: Pedone, 2010), pp. 494–507, p. 494 (my translation).

[49] Mishra (n. 17), p. 114.

[50] See for nuanced discussions of the critical standard narrative of neo-liberalism Clive Barnett, 'Publics and markets: what's wrong with neoliberalism', in Susan J. Smith, Sallie A. Marston, Rachel Pain and John Paul Jones (eds.), *The Sage Handbook of Social Geographies*, Vol. III (Thousand Oaks, CA: Sage, 2010), pp. 269–296; Thomas Biebericher, *Neoliberalismus zur Einführung*, 2nd ed. (Hamburg: Junius, 2015).

[51] The term was coined by a US economist as a description and later became a prescription. John Williamson, 'What Washington means by policy reform', in John Williamson (ed.), *Latin American Adjustment: How Much Has Happened?* (Washington, DC: Institute for International Economics, 1990).

[52] Ulrich Beck, *What Is Globalization?*, translated by Patrick Camiller from the German original *Was ist Globalisierung?* (1997) (Cambridge: Polity Press, 2000), p. 1.

[53] Geoffrey Pleyers, *Alter-Globalization: Becoming Actors in a Global Age* (Cambridge: Polity Press, 2010). Emblematic events were the protests against the 1999 WTO ministerial conference in Seattle, the demonstrations against the G8 summit of 2007 in Heiligendamm (Germany) and the 'Occupy Wall Street' movement of 2011.

civil society platform is the World *Social* Forum, first held at Porto Alegre (Brazil) in 2001, last in Montreal in 2016. Today, more than fifteen years after the Washington Consensus, the persistent reality of transboundary capital mobility and global supply chains[54] combined with more information about the living conditions in other parts of the world contributes to a new mindset, both on the side of the poor and on the side of the rich.[55] We perceive more clearly than we did some decades ago the harm done by globalisation in ecological, cultural and social terms.

With all due caution against the demonisation of neo-liberalism, it is obvious that the Washington Consensus has not delivered the promise of welfare for all through trickle-down effects realised through the market. Large groups of persons (mainly in the Global South but also in the North) have only marginally or not at all benefitted from global trade and investment. On top of not benefitting, many have become victims of technical and demographic change and of pollution, and have lost their homes and jobs. Both victims (or perceived victims) and sympathetic observers are nowadays at least as bothered by the wealth disparities inside states and across the globe as by political oppression. All this has given rise to the 'groundswell of discontent' with globalisation, as the managing director of the International Monetary Fund, Christine Lagarde, put it.[56] That discontent has been to some extent absorbed by the political establishment – if only to 'smoothe out the edges of modern capitalist development'.[57] The rough and maybe purely strategical accommodation of the global social question by various global governance institutions has even led to a petering out of the alter-globalisation movements.[58]

---

[54] See for the importance of this new intra-firm phenomenon for global labour conditions General Conference of the International Labour Organization, Resolution Concerning Decent Work in Global Supply Chains, adopted by the 105th Session of the General Conference of the International Labour Organization (10 June 2016).

[55] Pankaj Mishra, *Age of Anger: A History of the Present* (New York: Farrar, Straus and Giroux, 2017), p. 346.

[56] Christine Lagarde, 'Making globalisation work for all', Sylvia Ostry Lecture, Toronto, 13 September 2016.

[57] Janine Brodie, 'Globalization and the social question', in Marjorie Cohen (ed.), *Governing under Stress: Middle Powers and the Challenge of Globalization* (London: Zed Books, 2004), pp. 12–32, p. 17.

[58] The best-known anti-globalisation association, Attac (founded in France in 1998), is dissolved, and the street violence in Hamburg at the occasion of the G20 summit in 2017 was senseless criminality devoid of political content.

Awareness of the dark sides of globalisation[59] not only has changed the political tides but has also triggered new scholarly trends. The search for a post-neo-liberalism and a 'post–Washington Consensus'[60] as an intellectual framework is ongoing. Philosophers have attacked the global political and legal order as conveying and perpetuating a fundamental structural social injustice against populations of the Global South.[61] Economists have uncovered the profound unfairness of capital accumulation protected by our financial system.[62] Sociologists are asking for a 'new social settlement' under conditions of globalisation.[63]

The debates on poverty, inequality, and social exclusion as global concerns accompany the timid expressions of a 'more social', and more individualised international legal framework which is in the making (Sections 5–8). The crucial difference between the 'old' inter-state international law of solidarity and development and the new 'more social' law is its attention to individuals across state boundaries, as we will see.

5   Agenda 2030 and beyond

The marker of the new 'more social law' is Agenda 2030, adopted by the UN General Assembly in 2015.[64] Agenda 2030 has been qualified by non-

---

[59] Jochen von Bernstorff, 'International law and global justice: on recent inquiries into the dark side of economic globalization' (2015) 26 *European Journal of International Law* 279–293.

[60] Joseph Eugene Stiglitz, 'More instruments and broader goals: moving toward the post-Washington Consensus', in *WIDER Annual Lectures* 2 (Helsinki: The United Nations University/World Institute for Development Economic Research, 1998). According to Kerry Rittich, the international law and governance of development embraced 'the social dimension' – in the sense of the post–Washington Consensus – already in 1999. The turn in the World Bank is epitomised by its then president's discussion draft: James D. Wolfensohn, A Proposal for a Comprehensive Development Framework of 21 January 1999 (see Kerry Rittich, 'The future of law and development: second generation reforms and the incorporation of the social' (2004/2005) 26 *Michigan Journal of International Law* 199–234, at 200).

[61] Thomas Pogge concretely addresses the relevant legal questions. See most recently Thomas Pogge and Krishen Mehta (eds.), *Global Tax Fairness* (Oxford: Oxford University Press, 2016).

[62] Thomas Piketty, *Le capital au XXIième siècle* (Paris: Seuil, 2013).

[63] Brodie (n. 57), pp. 12 and 24.

[64] Agenda 2030 (n. 24). Agenda 2030 covers the fifteen-year period (2015 to 2030) in continuation of the Millennium Declaration of 2000 which had set goals (the MDGs) to reach before 2015.

governmental organisation (NGO) observers and scholars as 'historic'[65] and as a 'change of paradigm'.[66] The following sections draw attention to the building blocks of the 'more social' and cross-border individual-targeted international law.

5.1   The international law against poverty

The emergence of an international law against poverty around the turn of the millennium[67] was a response to the failure of classical international development law. The World Bank has espoused the fight against poverty as its major new cause and has to some extent supplanted its traditional focus on development, now understood as *human* development and good governance. In this policy, the needs of the individual are the ultimate normative reference point. Related to this, poverty has been recognised as a human rights topic by the UN Human Rights Council.[68] The 'eradication of extreme poverty and hunger' had been set as Millennium Development Goal (MDG) No. 1 by the UN General Assembly in the year 2000.[69] The bar has even been set higher in Agenda 2030, adopted as a follow-up to the Millennium Declaration in 2015. Sustainable Development Goal (SDG) No. 1 is to 'end poverty in all

---

[65] Jens Martens and Wolfgang Obenland, *Die 2030-Agenda: Globale Zukunftsziele für nachhaltige Entwicklung* (Bonn: Global Policy Forum, 2016), p. 5; Esuna Dugrova, 'Social inclusion, poverty eradication and the 2030 Agenda for Sustainable Development', in United Nations Research Institute for Social Development (UNRISD) Working Paper 2015–14 (Geneva: United Nations Research Institute for Social Development, October 2015), p. 5.

[66] Martens and Obenland (n. 65), p. 9.

[67] Key legal literature is Lucy Williams (ed.), *International Poverty Law: An Emerging Discourse* (London: Zed Books, 2006); Margot E. Salomon, *Global Responsibility for Human Rights: World Poverty and the Development of International Law* (Oxford: Oxford University Press, 2007); Krista Nadakavukaren Schefer (ed.), *Poverty and the International Economic Legal System* (Cambridge: Cambridge University Press, 2013). Seminal from a philosophical perspective: Thomas Pogge, *World Poverty and Human Rights: Cosmopolitan Responsibilities and Reforms*, 2nd ed. (Cambridge: Polity Press, 2008).

[68] See, e.g., UN Human Rights Council, Guiding Principles on Extreme Poverty and Human Rights of 18 July 2012 (UN Doc. A/HRC/21/39), endorsed by the UN Human Rights Council (UN Doc. A/HRC/RES/21/11 of 18 October 2012). See for a recent document UN Human Rights Council, Report of the Special Rapporteur on Extreme Poverty and Human Rights of 22 March 2017 (UN Doc. A/HRC/35/26).

[69] The MDGs were developed out of the UN Millennium Declaration of the UN General Assembly of 8 September 2000 (UN Doc. A/RES/55/2). 'Development and poverty eradication' was one of the eight sections of this declaration.

its forms everywhere'.[70] Overall, the United Nations and the World Bank have celebrated progress on the front of poverty reduction.[71]

The emergence of an international anti-poverty law is 'a crucial contemporary development'.[72] The displacement of the policy objective from trying to develop countries to combating poverty encapsulates a two-fold shift: firstly, it downsizes the ambition. Combating poverty sounds like a more modest goal than reforming a country and revamping an economy. Secondly, targeting poverty facially deflects the focus from macroeconomics and legal and political institutions to the individual and his or her needs. The individualist turn seeks to harness socio-economic rights as a vehicle and tool for combating poverty.[73]

Both shifts make an anti-poverty policy at least prima facie 'much less revolutionary' than the old development paradigm.[74] This might allow the approach to bridge the North–South divide in international politics and to garner consensus in various ideological camps. But opponents have disqualified the human rights–based approach to development and poverty as an 'uncritical acceptance of status quo',[75] a verdict to which we will turn at the end of the chapter.[76]

Also, what has been touted as a success by the World Bank has been called into question by critical analysts. Notably Thomas Pogge has

[70] The detailed formulation is: '1.1: By 2030, *eradicate extreme* poverty for all people everywhere, currently measured as people living on less than $1.25 a day. 1.2: By 2030, *reduce at least by half* the proportion of men, women and children of all ages living in *poverty* in all its dimensions according to national definitions.' The Agenda 2030 Declaration states in para. 1: 'We recognize that *eradicating poverty* in all its forms and dimensions, including extreme poverty, *is the greatest global challenge* and an indispensable requirement for sustainable development' (emphases added). The preamble of the 2030 Declaration begins with exactly the same wording. See also Declaration para. 24: 'We are committed to ending poverty in all its forms and dimensions, including by eradicating extreme poverty by 2030. All people must enjoy a basic standard of living, *including through social protection systems*' (emphasis added).
[71] The World Bank website states that 'there has been marked progress on reducing poverty over the past decades. The world attained the first Millennium Development Goal target – to cut the 1990 poverty rate in half by 2015 – five years ahead of schedule, in 2010' (www.worldbank.org/en/topic/poverty/overview#1).
[72] Emmanuelle Jouannet, 'How to depart from the existing dire condition of development', in Antonio Cassese (ed.), *Realizing Utopia: The Future of International Law* (Oxford: Oxford University Press, 2012), pp. 392–417, p. 401.
[73] Paradigmatically, David Bilchitz, *Poverty and Fundamental Rights* (Oxford: Oxford University Press, 2007) (with a focus on South Africa).
[74] Ibid., p. 407.
[75] Lucy Williams, 'Towards an emerging international poverty law', in Williams (ed.), *International Poverty Law* (n. 67), pp. 1–13, p. 12.
[76] See Section 10.

relentlessly uncovered flaws in the World Bank's definitions, measurements and other data on poverty.[77] Pogge went as far as criticising the MDG of eradicating poverty as a 'cruel joke upon the poor: the celebration of a vast crime against humanity'.[78] However, Pogge's views are themselves highly contested, and despite shortcomings or even manipulation of the facts and figures having taken place, a modicum of success in reducing poverty seems to be real (although the number of people living in extreme poverty globally remains unacceptably high). It is unclear though how much if at all international law and institutions contributed to lifting people out of poverty worldwide, notably in Asia.

5.2   The international law against inequality

Another target of (international) social law is, next to poverty, the inequality of wealth and income, across the globe. Anti-discrimination law has been an entry point for combatting material inequality but has so far not provided strong leverage. Article 26 of the International Covenant on Civil and Political Rights (ICCPR) guarantees 'equal protection of the law' but not equality of wealth or income. Article 2(2) of the ICESCR and Article 2(1) of the ICCPR contain ancillary prohibitions against discrimination which apply only in connection with the exercise or enjoyment of a right under the covenants. Also, discrimination can come into play only if there is unequal treatment on the basis of a suspect classification. Both human rights covenants prohibit discrimination on the basis of 'other status'. Poverty has traditionally not been considered as suspect a classification as race or gender, but the Committee on Economic, Social and Cultural Rights (CESCR) has included economic status to form a 'status' in terms of the ICESCR and has held that individuals and groups must not be 'arbitrarily treated on account of belonging to a certain economic or social group'.[79]

So international law has begun to respond, firstly, to the widely shared perception that *within* most countries, the cleavage between rich and poor is not decreasing but – if anything – increasing. It is also mostly

---

[77] Thomas Pogge, *Poverty, Human Rights and the Global Order: Framing the Post-2015 Agenda* (Bergen: Comparative Research Programme on Poverty, 2012).

[78] Ibid., p. 23.

[79] CESCR, General Comment No. 20, Non-Discrimination in Economic, Social and Cultural Rights (Art. 2, para. 2, of the International Covenant on Economic, Social and Cultural Rights), of 2 July 2009 (UN Doc E/C.12/GC/20), para. 35.

assumed that this 'growing gap' – to use the words of a recent OECD report[80] – is at least in part due to economic globalisation.[81]

The second issue of concern is material inequality *among* countries. On this point, it is acknowledged that during an overall growth period (global economic expansion) in the second half of the twentieth century, the wealth gap between rich and poor countries increased. However, according to the World Bank, the 'intercountry income differences diminished over the MDG-monitoring period', i.e. since 2000.[82] The two different reference points – inequality among states and inequality among individuals – are to some extent linked, because individuals in a poor state will generally be poorer as well.

A new way of looking at global inequality in times of globalisation has been suggested by the World Bank economist Branko Milanovic.[83] According to Milanovic's famous elephant graph, the last twenty-year period of intense economic globalisation (1998–2008) has produced two big winners, namely poorer people in emerging countries and super-rich individuals from developed states (mostly the United States). The biggest losers are poor and working-class people in rich states. The real income of the latter stagnated over this twenty-year period.[84] To put it simply, the current constellation, during a period of intense economic globalisation accompanied by repeated financial crises, is roughly one of a convergence of wealth (decreasing inequality) among states but accompanied by

---

[80] The report mentions 'the growing gap between lower-income households – the bottom 40 percent of the distribution – and the rest of the population' in OECD, *In It Together: Why Less Inequality Benefits All* (Paris: OECD Publishing, 2015), executive summary, p. 15. The same report states that 'in several emerging economies, particularly in Latin America, income inequality has narrowed, but income gaps remain generally higher than in OECD countries' (ibid.).

[81] See for the OECD world: OECD, 'Income distribution', OECD Social and Welfare Statistics (database) (2016) (http://dx.doi.org/10.1787/data-00654-en). Among the OECD members, Chile is the most unequal state (Palma ratio 2.85). See for the BRICS states UNDP Human Development Report (http://hdr.undp.org/en/composite/IHDI–e). Here, South Africa is the most unequal state (Palma ratio 8.0). Greece, a state intensely affected by an internationally concerted austerity programme, has a Palma ratio of 1.4 (See for the Palma ratio n. 86.)

[82] World Bank Group, Global Monitoring Report 2015/2016: Development Goals in an Era of Demographic Change (2016), p. 127.

[83] I report his findings on the basis of a good explanation by Anthea Roberts, 'Being charged by an elephant: a story of globalization and inequality', *EJIL talk!*, 19 April 2017, relying on Branko Milanovic, *Global Inequality: A New Approach for the Age of Globalization* (Cambridge, MA: Harvard University Press, 2016). The elephant graph is in Milanovic, p. 11.

[84] Roberts (n. 83).

growing material inequality of individuals within states and by a loss or stagnation of income of the poorer groups in rich states.[85]

Just as with poverty, the definition and the measurement of inequality are difficult to achieve in economic and scientific terms[86] and controversial in ideological terms. And while the desirability to rectify gross inequality of wealth and income is recognised probably by all political actors, the amount of equalisation and of course the political and legal strategies to realise it are highly disputed. But against the background of reasonable and unreasonable disagreement about facts and figures, the trend of international law is visible. Notably *inter-individual* inequality has been recently acknowledged as an issue for international law and governance. So much has been recognised not only by the United Nations[87] but also by the World Bank and by the OECD[88] and of course by humanitarian NGOs. For example, a new Oxfam Report highlights that eight individuals own as much as half the population of the globe.[89]

In his foreword to the first issue of a new World Bank series of studies on poverty, the World Bank president writes: 'Today we face a powerful threat to progress around the world: Inequality. High income inequality is hardly new in human history. But today, inequality is constraining national economies and destabilising global collaboration in ways that put humanity's most critical achievements and aspirations at risk.'[90] Therefore, the World Bank considers that material 'inequalities are associated with high financial cost, affect economic growth, and generate social and political burdens and barriers. But levelling the playing field is

[85] I will argue on the basis of these assertions without being able to verify the accuracy of these statistics myself.

[86] Since 2011, income inequality is mostly measured by the Palma ratio. Palma is the ratio of the richest 10% of the population's share of gross national income divided by the poorest 40%'s share (José Gabriel Palma, 'Homogeneous middles vs. heterogeneous tails, and the end of the "Inverted-U": the share of the rich is what it's all about', Cambridge Working Papers in Economics (CWPE) 1111, January 2011).

[87] UN Department of Economic and Social Affairs, Inequality Matters: Report on the World Social Situation (UN Doc. ST/ESA/345) (New York: United Nations Publications, 2013).

[88] See OECD, *Focus on Inequality and Growth – Does Income Inequality Hurt Economic Growth?* (2014); OECD, *In It Together: Why Less Inequality Benefits All* (Paris: OECD Publishing, 2015).

[89] See Deborah Herdoon, *An Economy for the 99%: It's Time to Build a Human Economy That Benefits Everyone, Not Just the Privileged Few* (Oxford: Oxfam, 2017). See also Oxfam, *The Cost of Inequality: How Wealth and Income Extremes Hurt Us All* (Oxford: Oxfam, 2013); Oxfam, *Wealth: Having It All and Wanting More*, Oxfam Issue Briefing (Oxford: Oxfam, 2015).

[90] Jim Jon Kim, 'Foreword', in World Bank, *Poverty and Shared Prosperity 2016: Taking on Inequality* (Washington, DC: The World Bank Group, 2016), p. 1.

also an issue of fairness and justice that resonates across societies on its own merits. These substantive considerations highlight the importance of directing attention to the problem of inequality.'[91]

Along the same line, the 2030 Agenda for Sustainable Development has formulated the mitigation of the inequality of wealth and income among individuals as an official development goal.[92] In the Agenda 2030 Declaration, the heads of state and government and high representatives 'resolve, between now and 2030, to end poverty and hunger everywhere; to *combat inequalities within and among countries*'.[93] The Declaration also says that 'inclusive and sustainable economic growth ... will only be possible' if wealth is shared and *income inequality is addressed*'.[94] Accordingly, Goal 10 of Agenda 2030 itself is to 'reduce inequality within and among countries'.[95] Point 10.1 seeks to, 'by 2030, progressively achieve and sustain income growth of the bottom 40 percent of *the population* at a higher rate than the national average'. Agenda 2030 thus sets a goal of global redistribution. It implicitly refers to the Palma ratio[96] by mentioning the bottom 40 per cent. But Goal 10 does not state to which 'population' it refers: to the different populations within different nation states or to a cross-country comparison? The heading of the goal points to both reference groups. In order to reduce interstate and intra-state inequality, Goal 10.4 is to 'adopt policies, especially *fiscal, wage and social protection policies*, and progressively achieve greater equality'.

The formulation of an explicit goal to reduce inequality has been called 'one of the most remarkable' results of the SDG negotiations.[97] But it has also been said that Agenda 2030's concrete formulation is 'completely insufficient' for substantially reducing the inequality of income.[98] Pogge and Sengupta speak of a 'grotesque lack of ambition in its primary Target 10.1'.[99]

---

[91] Ibid., p. 2. The writings of the World Bank president are most likely not apt to contribute as such to the formation of hard or even soft legal rules, but they manifest a policy orientation of the bank.

[92] Agenda 2030 (n. 24).

[93] Ibid., Declaration, para. 3.

[94] Ibid., Declaration, para. 27 (emphasis added).

[95] Ibid., Goal 2.3, which is to 'double the agricultural productivity and incomes of small-scale food producers'.

[96] See for the Palma ratio n. 86.

[97] Martens and Obenland (n. 65), p. 83.

[98] Ibid., p. 84.

[99] Thomas Pogge and Mitu Sengupta, 'The Sustainable Development Goals (SDGS) as drafted: nice idea, poor execution' (2015) 24 *Washington International Law Journal* 751–587, at 581.

It remains to be seen whether Agenda 2030 marks a step towards formulating (and potentially also implementing) some international rules and standards that should guide social policies which would be addressed to individual human beings as potential beneficiaries. The 'fiscal, wage and social protection policies' mentioned in Agenda 2030 might comprise redistributive taxation, minimum wages or insurance schemes for health, old age or unemployment.

The focus of international (soft) law on intra-state and transboundary inequality *among individuals* is novel. Granted, the problem of inter-individual equality is mainly an issue for domestic policies such as taxation and welfare. But the stagnation of the bottom incomes in rich states combined with climbing middle incomes in developing states are likely to have destabilising effects in the rich states of the West and have in fact already triggered protectionism and opposition against trade and investment agreements.[100] Cross-border material inequality of individuals' living standards is therefore a proper focus of international law. International law has in fact very tentatively started to address it, albeit without formulating hard and clear legal duties.

6   The extension of international social rights

Social rights have been intensely codified in the post–World War II international and regional legal orders (beginning with the Universal Declaration of Human Rights of 1948,[101] the ICESCR of 1966 and various other human rights instruments[102]), notably in Europe (in the European Social Charter of 1961 (revised in 1996) and the EU Charter of Fundamental Rights of 2000). For easy reading, I will call 'social rights' the set of rights basically codified in the ICESCR (including the so-called economic and cultural rights). The enjoyment of these rights (e.g. rights to housing, education and health) is almost always undermined or rendered next to impossible in conditions of poverty and gross material inequality.

---

[100] Cf. Roberts (n. 83), at 2.

[101] The UDHR notably contains the right to social security (Art. 22), a right to work (Art. 23), food, housing and medical care (Art. 25) and education (Art. 26).

[102] The modern human rights instruments such as the Convention on the Rights of the Child, the Migrant Workers' Convention and the Convention on the Rights of Persons with Disabilities contain numerous rights previously called second-generation rights. Also, a quintessential first-generation right such as the right to life has the function of a social right when it is construed as encompassing a legal entitlement to the satisfaction of basic human needs such as shelter and food.

The practical significance of international social rights was initially very limited. Although the interdependence between civil rights on the one hand and social rights on the other hand had already explicitly been acknowledged in the UDHR,[103] the quality of social rights as 'true' human rights was drawn into question by the West during the entire phase of the Cold War. The juridical-doctrinal structure of those rights was not well elaborated due to the paucity of case law and of legal scholarship. Social rights were under-enforced because domestic courts feared to trod into the political reserves of parliaments and shied away from applying social rights; on the UN level, only state reporting was available. In 2014 still, it was diagnosed that social rights 'play[ed] no noteworthy role in the regulation of the global economy' and had 'not yet established themselves as "global social rights"'.[104]

All this has changed quite dramatically in the last decades as will be shown in this section. I see the rise of international and European social rights connected to increased awareness about the negative consequences of economic globalisation, to the heightened sensitivity to global social justice and most recently to the indignation about the adverse social impacts of the financial crises. In fact, the social rights–based approach to global governance is now depicted as the contrast programme to 'rights-flouting neoliberalism'.[105] Taken together with an increased reliance on rights litigation as weapons for bringing about societal transformation, these social concerns – which all possess a transboundary dimension – have motivated the both practical and academic activation of international social rights.[106]

6.1 Extension ratione materiae: radiation into all international law

The first dimension of the activation and operationalisation of international social rights is their radiation[107] into all subfields of international

[103] Art. 22 of the UDHR states that some degree of 'realization of economic, social and cultural rights' is 'indispensable' for human 'dignity and the free development of [human] personality'.
[104] Michael Krennerich, 'Social security: just as much a human right in developing countries and emerging markets' (2014) 47 Verfassung und Recht in Übersee 105–123, at 123.
[105] Aiofe Nolan, 'Introduction', in Aiofe Nolan (ed.), Economic and Social Rights after the Global Financial Crisis (Cambridge: Cambridge University Press, 2014), pp. 1–20, p. 6.
[106] Seminal: Sarah Fredman, Human Rights Transformed: Positive Rights and Positive Duties (Oxford: Oxford University Press, 2008).
[107] Theodor Meron, The Humanization of International Law (Leiden: Martinus Nijhoff, 2006), p. XV.

law that are relevant for the global social question. The imbuement with rights has left deep marks in the international law of development,[108] international labour law,[109] international trade law (including procurement law, international subsidies law and the law of trade-related aspects of intellectual property),[110] international investment law,[111] finance law (including the issues of World Bank conditionalities, the memorandums of understanding on austerity measures and sovereign debt workouts),[112] the international law of natural disasters,[113] refugee and migrant law,[114] and finally anti-corruption law.[115] The seeping of rights into these regimes, their 'righting',[116] is not limited to the subgroup of international human rights which I here call 'social rights' but concerns human rights more generally. For the purposes of this chapter, I am interested only in social rights (such as the right to education, health or social security).

Depending on the issue area and on the concrete problems at hand, human rights, notably social rights, function now either as a reinforcement of the regime's overall objectives (e.g. in the law of migration) or rather as a counterpoint (e.g. in trade law), and sometimes as both. The deep structural importance of the righting of regimes cannot be

[108] Seminal: Philip Alston and Mary Robinson (eds.), *Human Rights and Development: Towards Mutual Reinforcement* (Oxford: Oxford University Press, 2005).

[109] Seminal: Philip Alston (ed.), *Labour Rights as Human Rights* (Oxford: Oxford University Press, 2005).

[110] Seminal: Thomas Cottier, Joost Pauwelyn and Elisabeth Bürgi (eds.), *Human Rights and International Trade* (Oxford: Oxford University Press, 2005).

[111] Seminal: Pierre-Marie Dupuy, Ernst-Ulrich Petersmann and Francesco Francioni (eds.), *Human Rights in International Investment Law and Arbitration* (Oxford: Oxford University Press, 2009).

[112] Seminal: Daniel Bradlow, 'The World Bank, the IMF, and human rights' (1996) 6 *Transnational Law and Contemporary Problems* 47–90.

[113] See Art. 2 of the ILC Draft articles on the protection of persons in the event of disasters, 2016 (UN Doc. A/71/10; *Yearbook of the International Law Commission*, 2016, Vol. II, part two).

[114] Ruth RubioMarín (ed.), *Human Rights and Immigration*, Collected Courses of the Academy of European Law (Oxford: Oxford University Press, 2014).

[115] Martine Boersma, *Corruption: A Violation of Human Rights and a Crime under International Law?* (Cambridge: Intersentia, 2012); Anne Peters, 'Korruption und Menschenrechte' (2016) 71 *Juristen-Zeitung* 217–296.

[116] The term 'righting' was coined by Karen Knop and applied in a critical spirit to the law of occupation by Ayeal Gross (Aeyal Gross, *The Writing on the Wall: Rethinking the International Law of Occupation* (Cambridge: Cambridge University Press, 2017), chapter 5). Other authors have used the term 'rightsification' (John Gershman and Jonathan Morduch, 'Credit is not a right', in Tom Sorell and Luis Cabrera (eds.), *Microfinance, Rights and Global Justice* (Cambridge: Cambridge University Press, 2015), pp. 14–26, 21).

overestimated. In development law, for example, it constitutes a 'reversal of perspective from classic international development law' as an interstate law respectful of state sovereignty and neutral towards the political regime towards a law 'built around the central figure of the individual, his rights, and his basic needs'.[117]

Indeed, the human rights–based approach to development (called HRBA) is probably the most telling example of the imbuement of a legal field with human rights. The HRBA appeared in the 1990s as a political slogan in the development policies of some countries and made its entry into the World Bank in 2001 with a keynote speech by then Human Rights Commissioner Mary Robinson. Here, Robinson explained the 'rights-based approach' as a 'conceptual framework for the purpose of human development that is normatively based on international human rights standards and operationally directed to promoting and protecting human rights. The rights-based approach integrates the norms, standards and principles of the international human rights system into the plans, policies, and processes of development.'[118]

The main benefits of recognising rights (to health, to education and so on) in the law of development are seen in the fact that this allows one to assess the performance of development work in relation to universally agreed standards and that the HRBA draws attention to the most discriminated against and to the excluded.[119] Importantly, 'there is no space in human rights for a trickle-down approach to the achievement of minimum essential levels of rights or ensuring access to basic services. From a human rights perspective, recovery must start with the most vulnerable and disadvantaged, who are rights holders rather than burdensome or passive recipients of charity'.[120] Finally, the human rights perspective requires states to debate fiscal options openly, with transparency and participation of affected groups.[121] Overall, the new focus on rights seeks to lend higher legitimacy to development law (feeding on the prestige of

[117] Jouannet (n. 72), pp. 398–399.
[118] Mary Robinson, *A Voice for Human Rights* (Philadelphia: University of Pennsylvania Press, 2006), pp. 299–307: 'Bridging the gap between human rights and development: from normative principle to operational relevance', World Bank Presidential Lecture, Washington, DC, 3 December 2001.
[119] Mary Robinson, 'What rights can add to good development practice', in Philip Alston and Mary Robinson (eds.), *Human Rights and Development: Towards Mutual Reinforcement* (Oxford: Oxford University Press 2005), pp. 25–41.
[120] Magdalena Sepúlveda Carmona, 'Alternatives to austerity: a human rights framework for economic recovery', in Nolan (ed.), *Economic and Social Rights* (n. 105), pp. 23–56, p. 42.
[121] Ibid., p. 47.

human rights). It also has the effect of legalising the field more (because it is oriented at human rights as *legal* standards).

But exactly this individualisation and legalisation is not unequivocally beneficial or progressive. The imbuement of the various regimes with human rights considerations has been criticised as an inappropriate or even strategical deflection from institutional and structural root causes of underdevelopment, poverty and material inequality. It might unduly divert from the macroeconomic analysis.[122] Along this line of reasoning, the introduction of the individual communications mechanism to enforce the ICESCR[123] appears counterproductive. This critique often mingles with an overall scepticism against a supposedly too 'liberal' international law. For example, the redesign of the international law of development towards 'human development' including its concentration on combating poverty can be seen in a negative light as a 'neo-liberal' move of the World Bank.[124]

Importantly, the principal value of the infiltration of the entire international legal order with human rights does not lie in those rights' independent enforceability as isolated legal entitlements, although one practical consequence is that specific rules and decisions in the mentioned legal fields have now also come under the scrutiny of domestic and international human rights–monitoring institutions. Besides and probably more importantly, the oozing of human rights (notably social rights) into the various branches of international law has created the obligation for all other (non-human-rights-specific) law-applying institutions to interpret 'their' regimes' rules and principles in the light of international social rights.[125] This interpretative approach might even encompass the presumption that a specific rule of international law, e.g. the UN member states' obligation to carry out a Security Council resolution (Article 25 of the UN Charter), is not intended to force an actor to disregard or even encroach upon social rights.

---

[122] See for this argument, Mary Dowell-Jones, *Contextualising the International Covenant on Economic, Social and Cultural Rights: Assessing the Economic Deficit* (Leiden: Nijhoff, 2004).

[123] With the optional protocol (n. 132).

[124] Jouannet (n. 72), p. 407.

[125] See, e.g., Eritrea–Ethiopia Claims Commission (EECC), Final Award: Eritrea's Damages Claims, 17 August 2009, Reports of International Arbitral Awards, Vol. XXVI, pp. 505–630, paras. 18–22. The EECC here interprets the international law on post-war reparations in the light of international social rights and refers to the General Comments of the CESCR as 'guides to action'. The author thanks Gustavo Prieto for this reference.

6.2   *Extension* ratione loci: *extraterritorial application*

International social rights have received a further boost through the efforts to expand their territorial scope. Since around the turn of the millennium, the extraterritorial application of international economic, social and cultural (ESC) rights has been discussed intensely,[126] coinciding with the emergence of the human rights–based approach to development. In 2011, a group of scholars and activists adopted the Maastricht Principles on Extraterritorial Obligations of States in the Area of Economic, Social and Cultural Rights.[127] The fight of scholars and NGOs for an extraterritorial application of international social rights complements the focus on social justice among states. While critics had near the end of the twentieth century deplored the 'global misdistribution of power and wealth … as a lack of justice between States' and have called for an interstate North–South redistribution, now '*individuals* and groups increasingly express their grievances against foreign states in direct terms'.[128]

The political starting point of this new movement is the claim that, due to global interdependence, the legal, political and administrative actions of states in the fields of trade or any other area of the economy increasingly have negative repercussions on the social rights of people situated outside their territory. Importantly, the core issue is not state conduct (e.g. police or military action) outside state borders but rather the extraterritorial effects of measures adopted inside the state. This includes the state's regulation of business actors domiciled inside its territory but whose activities may have an adverse impact on social rights enjoyed by persons outside this territory.[129] Trade laws, import restrictions,

---

[126] Seminal: International Council on Human Rights Policy, *Duties Sans Frontières: Human Rights and Global Social Justice* (Versoix: International Council on Human Rights Policy, 2003); Fons Coomans and Menno Kamminga (eds.), *Extraterritorial Application of Human Rights Treaties* (Antwerp: Intersentia, 2004).

[127] Maastricht Principles of 28 September 2011. Text with commentary by some of the forty signatory authors of the principles in Olivier De Schutter, Asbjørn Eide, Ashfaq Khalfan, Marcos Orellana, Margot Salomon and Ian Seiderman, 'Commentary to the Maastricht Principles on Extraterritorial Obligations of States in the Area of Economic, Social and Cultural Rights' (2012) 14 *Human Rights Quarterly* 1084–1169.

[128] Wouter Vandenhole, 'Extraterritorial human rights obligations' (2013) 5 *Journal européen des droits de l'homme* 804–835, at 809 (emphasis added).

[129] See CESCR, General Comment No. 24 (n. 19), part C on the extraterritorial obligations of states. The General Comment notably postulates that 'extraterritorial obligations arise when a State Party may influence situations located outside its territory, consistent with the limits imposed by international law, by controlling the activities of corporations domiciled in its territory and/or jurisdiction, and thus may contribute to the effective enjoyment of economic, social and cultural rights outside its national territory' (ibid., para. 28).

export subsidies for agricultural products and the refusal to award development aid potentially affect the housing, food and work of persons situated in other states and thus possibly also their related *rights*.

Given the fact that in a globalised economy, many acts and omissions of governance in state A might have some repercussion on the well-being of the citizens/residents of state B, we need criteria which determine the threshold above which extraterritorial human rights–based obligations of state A are triggered in the first place.[130] This threshold might be discussed in terms of 'jurisdiction'. Unlike the treaties on political and civil rights, such as the ICCPR and the European Convention on Human Rights (ECHR), the ICESCR does not explicitly limit the human rights obligations of the state parties to their territory or sphere of jurisdiction.[131] In contrast, Article 2 of the optional protocol to the ICESCR[132] allows for individual communications only against the state which has 'jurisdiction' over the person or group.

However, the criterion of 'control' which has emerged from the case law under the ECHR and the ICCPR as the main element of 'jurisdiction' hardly fits in constellations of mere extraterritorial effects of intraterritorial state action. It does not make sense to look for 'control' of the US legislator awarding a rice subsidy to domestic farmers which harms African farmers.[133] The US Congress will never 'control' the African farmers. So *if* we deem social human rights obligations based on extraterritorial effects of intraterritorial state conduct appropriate in principle, we must identify a different threshold (be it called jurisdictional link or not) triggering state duties towards claimants of social human rights.[134]

---

[130] Beyond this minimal threshold, in each concrete situation, an *interference* (to use the term established for rights under the ECHR) by a concrete violator with the social right of a concrete person in question could and would still have to be determined.

[131] Neither does Art. 4 ('General Obligations') of the Convention on the Rights of Persons with Disabilities (CRPD) of 13 December 2006 contain a jurisdictional clause. This convention lays down all kinds of rights, including numerous social rights, for persons with disabilities.

[132] UN General Assembly, Resolution 67/117 adopted on 10 December 2008 (UN Doc. A/63/117); entry into force on 5 May 2013; forty-five signatures and twenty-two ratifications as of August 2017.

[133] The understanding of jurisdiction as 'control' makes sense only for extraterritorial (physical) conduct, e.g. when the British army detains a terror suspect in Iraq.

[134] The parallel question of a threshold arises for democratic decision making. If all who are affected by political decisions of one state should be morally entitled to participate in decision making, this would require to enfranchise far too many 'extraterritorial' individuals. A fair and more feasible threshold might be to include only those 'probably affected' (Robert Goodin, 'Enfranchising all affected interests' (2007) 35 *Philosophy & Public Affairs*, 40–68; Robert Goodin, 'Enfranchising all subjected, worldwide' (2016) 8

In the ongoing debate on the extraterritorial applicability of social rights, two main views have emerged. One group of authors and the human rights–monitoring bodies explicitly or implicitly espouse a *facticist* view.[135] They claim that state A is saddled with some social rights obligations as soon as A's actions or omissions *in fact* impinge on the social rights of persons situated in state B. The follow-up questions (which degree of factual connection is needed and whether the concept of jurisdiction should be used here) will be examined later. Other scholars espouse a narrower and more normative conception of jurisdiction. They demand, on top of state A's factual capacity to influence the social rights situation of persons in state B, an additional normative relationship between state A and those persons to trigger state A's human rights duties. One variant is the claim that a state's obligation to respect, protect and fulfil (social) human rights is a corollary to the state's *political authority* over the persons in question.[136]

The better arguments speak in favour of a facticist conceptualisation of extraterritorial social rights obligations. The main reason is that the division of labour known within domestic legal orders, namely that human rights law is designed to react against harms emanating from the public authority while tort law and criminal law provide remedies against harms stemming from private action, does not work in the transnational sphere. Because there is no international tort law or criminal law available against the brute exercise of transnational naked power or violence (be it physical or economic), the restriction of the application of human rights law to relationships of (political)

International Theory 365–389). Granting those who did not participate in making a decision-which turns out to affect them-rights (and remedy) is often seen as a way for compensating their disenfranchisement.

[135] The 2011 Maastricht Principles (n. 127) seem to give an exceedingly broad facticist meaning to the concept of jurisdiction.

[136] See (not specifically for social rights) Samantha Besson, 'The extraterritoriality of the European Convention on Human Rights: why human rights depend on jurisdiction and what jurisdiction amounts to' (2012) 25 *Leiden Journal of International Law* 857–884. According to Besson, jurisdiction 'also includes a normative dimension by reference to the imposition of reasons for action on its subjects and the corresponding appeal for compliance (e.g. through giving instructions)' (at 865); see along that line Aravind Ganesh, 'The European Union's human rights obligations towards distant strangers' (2016) 37 *Michigan Journal of International Law* 475–538; Nehal Bhuta, 'The frontiers of extraterritoriality: human rights as global law', in Nehal Bhuta (ed.), *The Frontiers of Human Rights: Extraterritoriality and Its Challenges* (Oxford: Oxford University Press, 2016), pp. 1–19. One might say that this approach treats jurisdiction as a proxy for state sovereignty.

authority would leave victims of 'unpolitical' exercises of power without any remedy.

Having determined that extraterritorial obligations to honour social human rights can be triggered on account of a factual link between state A's action or inaction and detrimental impacts on the social rights of persons outside its boundaries, numerous follow-up questions emerge. The link required seems to be a matter of degree. The intensity of the link could co-determine the intensity of state A's extraterritorial human rights obligations.[137] These obligations can be grouped in the three dimensions of respect, protect and fulfil. Notably, under international law as it stands, extraterritorial human rights obligations *to fulfil* are so far not accepted.

The factual link (jurisdiction) is only a threshold which determines that social rights might come into play. In order to identify actual violations of social rights, further conditions would have to be satisfied. However, in the real world, this hardly ever seems to be possible. A harmful policy would have to fall into the scope *ratione personae* on the rights-holders' side, i.e. would have to affect determinate groups of victims. Then, the material scope of the rights would have to be determined. Which kind of duties do the dimensions of respect, protect and (possibly) fulfil comprise exactly? Duties to regulate, to take human rights into account or even to compensate?

Next, the problem of causality comes into play. Where numerous intervening actions of many different people lie between a cotton subsidy for US farmers and the hunger of an Indian family which used to live on the income of its own cotton farm which shut down, it is highly doubtful whether it can be said that the US subsidy caused the encroachment of those Indian children's right to food in a legal sense.

Another question is the maximum range of admissible measures. Where a jurisdictional and causal nexus between one state's policies and violations of social rights in another state can indeed be established, this would only mean that some remedial measures might be required as a matter of human rights law, while further, interventionist measures might on the contrary be prohibited by the victim state's sovereignty protected by the principle of non-intervention.

---

[137] See notably Cedric Ryngaert, 'Jurisdiction: towards a reasonableness test', in Malcom Langford, Wouter Vandenhole, Martin Scheinin and Willem van Genugten (eds.), *Global Justice, State Duties: The Extraterritorial Scope of Economic, Social and Cultural Rights in International Law* (Cambridge: Cambridge University Press, 2013), pp. 192–211.

Further thorny questions relate to the allocation of the human rights–based obligations among the territorial state in which victims find themselves (normally states of the Global South) and between the outsider states (normally states of the North). Here, the principle of subsidiarity suggests a primary obligation of the territorial state.[138] This would at the same time imply that the obligations would in principle shift to (some) outsider states forming the international community to the extent that the territorial state is *incapable* of fulfilling its primary obligations.[139]

The next question is whether obligations also shift to outsider states when the territorial state is able but merely *unwilling* to properly respect, protect and fulfil the social human rights of its inhabitants. Another question then is which obligations fall on which outsider states precisely, that is, according to which principles the presumable obligations can be defined, limited and allocated among various states.

To conclude, in times of economic globalisation, every state is somehow connected to the populations and business activity in other states. Governmental action or inaction may produce detrimental social and economic effects on the other side of the globe. But the result can be neither an unbounded responsibility for every harm by every state nor – formulated in human rights language – unbounded state obligations to honour the (social) human rights of every person on the globe. The crucial question is therefore the 'boundary problem' (Mathias Risse).[140] 'This boundary problem is an intrinsic feature of attempts to assess what follows from the idea of common humanity.' In the end, 'the question of how much, and precisely what, is owed in virtue of our common humanity will remain rather intractable'.[141]

---

[138] See, e.g., Committee on the Rights of the Child, General Comment No. 16 on State Obligations Regarding the Impact of the Business Sector on Children's Rights of 15 March 2013 (UN Doc. CRC/C/GC/16), para. 42 on the 'primary' obligations of host states of business. The obligations of outsider states might be seen as 'dormant' as long as the territorial state lives up to its obligations.

[139] Comisión Interamericana de Derechos Humanos, *Pueblos indígenas, comunidades afrodescendientes y recursos naturales: protección de derechos humanos en el contexto de actividades de extracción, explotación y desarrollo* (OEA/Ser.L/V/II, Doc. 47/15, of 31 December 2015), para. 79. The territorial state's incapacity also triggers its duty to seek assistance from other states (cf. Maastricht Principles (n. 127), principle 34; ILC draft articles for disaster relief (n. 113), Art. 11).

[140] Mathias Risse, *On Global Justice* (Princeton, NJ: Princeton University Press, 2012), pp. 81 and 302. See also n. 134.

[141] Ibid., p. 81.

6.3   *Extension* ratione personae

Besides the expansion of the territorial scope of international social rights, another recent development is the extension of the duty-bearers beyond states.

6.3.1   International organisations as obligors

Social human rights obligations have, firstly, been extended to international organisations. A number of situations, involving different organisations, have stimulated this trend.

One constellation involves international financial institutions which directly or indirectly finance state policies or development projects which affect social rights of the populations, e.g. the right to housing affected by resettlements and evacuations to build new infrastructure.[142] And when the lending or other forms of financial support to states or their banks are conditioned on privatisation requirements or on other austerity prescriptions (budget cuts, downsizing the bureaucracy, etc.), this may have serious impacts on the social services in the borrowing states, ranging from housing schemes over the health care and education systems to pensions and other social security benefits.

A new scenario is the restructuring of sovereign foreign debt in which international organisations are involved (besides foreign states and private entities as creditors). A prominent instance was the credit and bail-out arrangement between the Troika (IMF, European Commission and European Central Bank) and various EU member states, notably Greece, which led to cutbacks of social spending.

Against this background, especially the World Bank and the IMF have been the main targets of attacks by the globalisation critics, even more than the states themselves, and have been blamed, often in a summarial fashion, for creating and perpetuating economic and social injustice.[143] Although the reproach tends to overstate the actual power and means which international bodies have at their disposal, the idea that the

---

[142] Seminal: Sigrun I. Skogly, *The Human Rights Obligations of the World Bank and the International Monetary Fund* (London: Cavendish Publishing Limited, 2001); Mac Darrow, *Between Light and Shadow: The World Bank, the International Monetary Fund and International Human Rights Law* (Oxford: Hart, 2003). See more recently Willem van Genugten, *The World Bank Group, the IMF and Human Rights* (Cambridge: Intersentia, 2015).

[143] Joseph Eugene Stiglitz, *Globalization and Its Discontents* (New York: W.W. Norton, 2002); Jean Ziegler, *Les nouveaux maîtres du monde et ceux qui leur résistent* (Paris: Fayard, 2002).

organisations themselves should in principle be held accountable for negative social effects to which they contribute is valuable.

The World Bank's new Environmental and Social Framework Setting is attentive to social impacts of its investment project financing.[144] In this political document, the bank does not assume an *own* human rights obligation.[145] But the bank commits itself to conduct a '*due diligence* of proposed projects' which covers the 'environmental and *social risks and impacts* related to the project'.[146]

Another example is the contamination of the population of Haiti with cholera by UN peacekeepers which prima facie encroached on the cholera victims' right to health. Besides, the right to health is also affected by restrictions of access to medicine caused by the protection of intellectual property and patents through the Trade-Related Aspects of Intellectual Property Rights (TRIPS) Agreement, and this has raised the question of the human rights obligations of the WTO.[147] Early discussions arose with regard to economic sanctions.[148] Notably the comprehensive boycott imposed on Iraq by the Security Council from 1991 to 2003 had detrimental social impacts (ranging from undernourishment over lack of medical service to infant mortality due to lack of clean water).[149]

With regard to all these constellations, a host of specific legal questions have emerged. The starting point of any reflection is the International

---

[144] World Bank, Environmental and Social Framework Setting, Environmental and Social Standards for Investment Project Financing of 4 August 2016. This new framework is applicable only to investment project financing (not to lending). It comprises a World Bank policy and the Environmental and Social Standards (ESS), to be respected by the borrowers. For purposes of this chapter, ESS 2 (Labor and Working Conditions) and ESS 4 (Community Health and Safety) seem most pertinent.

[145] Ibid., 'A vision for sustainable development', p. 5, para. 3: 'The World Bank's activities *support* the realization of human rights expressed in the Universal Declaration of Human Rights. Through the projects it finances, and in a manner consistent with its Articles of Agreement, the World Bank seeks to avoid adverse impacts and will continue to *support its member countries* as they strive to progressively achieve *their* human rights commitments' (footnote omitted, emphases added).

[146] Ibid., p. 9, in detail points 30–35 of the World Bank policy.

[147] Holger Hestermeyer, *The WTO and Human Rights: The Case of Patents and Access to Medicine* (Oxford: Oxford University Press, 2007), pp. 99–102 (with a 'presumption' of human rights obligations of the WTO).

[148] See CESCR, General Comment No. 8 on the Relationship between Economic Sanctions and Respect for Economic, Social and Cultural Rights of 12 December 1997 (UN Doc. E/C.12/1997/8), paras. 11–14.

[149] See, e.g., UNICEF/IRAQ, Situation Analysis of Children and Women in Iraq, 30 April 1998, at p. 1: 'Situations such as Iraq's where the capacity of the state to exercise its responsibilities for social welfare have been subjected to serious constraints over the past seven years because of economic sanctions'.

Court of Justice's (ICJ) statement that international organisations are international legal persons which are, generally speaking, 'bound by any obligations incumbent upon [them] under general rules of international law'.[150] But this dictum leaves open *which* obligations are 'incumbent' on the organisations.[151] Human rights, domestic and international, have been invented and designed as a protection against states on account of their specific power resources with a potential to violate human dignity. So the preliminary question of principle is whether the activities of international organisations have become similar to that of states and also similarly dangerous for the enjoyment of human rights which would allow or even require to turn the human rights shield also against them.

Prevailing doctrine and practice meanwhile confirm that international organisations are susceptible to be bound by international human rights.[152] Nevertheless, the differences between states and organisations might suggest modifications in the intensity of bindingness and the scope and type of human rights obligations whose details are still unclear. International organisations are not party to the human rights treaties (and cannot even accede to them). Recent case law therefore assumes human rights obligations of international organisations qua customary law[153] – which raises the question which social human rights have attained this legal status.[154]

Moreover, international organisations depend on states as members and implementers of the organisations' measures. Therefore, the question of the assignment or attribution of primary obligations (and of the

---

[150] ICJ, Interpretation of the Agreement of 25 March 1951 between the WHO and Egypt, Advisory Opinion, ICJ Rep. 1980, 72, para. 37.

[151] See for a general discussion, Kristina Daugirdas, 'How and why international law binds international organizations' (2016) 57 *Harvard Journal of International law* 325–381.

[152] One group of scholars explains this with the help of a qualification of the power exercised by the organizations as 'international public authority' (Armin von Bogdandy, Matthias Goldmann and Ingo Venzke, 'From public international to international public law: translating world public opinion into international public authority' (2017) 28 *European Journal of International Law* 115–145).

[153] International Criminal Tribunal for Rwanda, *Prosecutor v. Rwamakuba*, Case No. ICTR-98-44C-T, decision on appropriate remedy, 31 Jan 2007, para. 48.

[154] For example, the then general counsel to the IMF squarely denied the bindingness of social human rights for the IMF, mainly by denying their status as general international law. François Gianviti, 'Economic, social and cultural human rights and the International Monetary Fund' (undated working paper), para. 56 at p. 43; the working paper is referred to in CESCR, Report on the 25th, 26th and 27th Session 2001 of 2 June 2002 (UN Doc. E/C.12/2001/17), p. 145.

international responsibility for breaches) arises. Generally speaking, because the organisations normally act in conjunction with states or through states, the former's obligations are arguably mostly subsidiary or complementary to the involved states' obligations.

A related question is how the sphere of human rights responsibility can be demarcated in the first place, given that organisations do not have any (chiefly territorial) 'jurisdiction' which normally determines the human rights obligations of states.[155] Arguably, the jurisdiction of organisations, for purposes of their human rights obligations, is defined functionally (not in terms of territory) by their founding document. This then raises the question whether the protection of human rights can be part of their mandate even if not explicitly mentioned in their constituent treaty. At this point, it can be argued that the constituent treaty must always be interpreted in light of the relevant and applicable member states' obligations (Article 31(3) lit. c of the Vienna Convention on the Law of Treaties (VCLT)) – which would include the human rights obligations. This interpretation moreover suggests that the protection of human rights (in some form) can be an implied power of a given organisation.

The next issue is the substance of potential social human rights obligations. Many scholars and some practitioners agree that organisations are – as a minimum – saddled with obligations *to respect* (social) human rights. For example, the independent expert's Guiding Principles on Foreign Debt and Human Rights of 2011, welcomed by the UN Human Rights Council in 2012, postulate that 'international financial organizations and private corporations have an obligation to respect international human rights. This implies a duty to refrain from formulating, adopting, funding and implementing policies and programmes which directly or indirectly contravene the enjoyment of human rights.'[156] In addition, obligations of international organisations to protect human rights are conceivable.[157] For example, specifically with regard to lending conditionalities it has been argued that the financial organisations are obliged not to pressure the borrowing state into

[155] Cf. Art. 1 of the ECHR.
[156] UN Human Rights Council, Report of the Independent Expert [Cephas Lumnias] on the Effects of Foreign Debt and Other Related International Financial Obligations of States on the Full Enjoyment of All Human Rights, Particularly Economic, Social and Cultural Rights, Annex: Guiding Principles on Foreign Debt and Human Rights of 10 April 2011 (UN Doc. A/HRC/20/23), para. 9 (footnote omitted).
[157] Mac Darrow, 'World Bank and International Monetary Fund', in David Forsythe (ed.), *Encyclopedia of Human Rights*, Vol. V (Oxford: Oxford University Press, 2009), pp. 373–381, p. 378.

neglecting its own social human rights obligations.[158] This could be understood as a specific obligation to protect incumbent on the organisation. In the context of financing, lending and debts, specific obligations of the international financial institutions 'to take into account'[159] or to 'pay consideration'[160] to human rights have been postulated. In contrast, it is generally assumed that international organisations are not obliged to fulfil human rights. For example, the World Bank does not seem to be obliged to furnish housing to populations transferred by projects.

Further questions are the potential justifications of curtailments of human rights. On which public interest objectives can an organisation rely? Obviously, the contractual limitations clauses such as Article 4 of the ICESCR which allows for limitations of the international ESC rights only when 'determined by law [and] only in so far as this may be compatible with the nature of these rights and solely for the purpose of promoting the general welfare in a democratic society' cannot be applied formally to the organisations. Which legal bases are needed, how does the principle of proportionality come to bear and which society is the reference-point? Further problems relate to remedies and reparation. Must the immunity of organisations be limited or waived in order to allow for redress granted by domestic courts?

None of these questions has as yet been fully resolved. What matters for this chapter is that social human rights have steeply gained relevance as a legal argument in the quest for accountability of international organisations. This means that – in the academic debates – the

---

[158] Markus Krajewski, 'Human rights and austerity programmes', in Thomas Cottier, Rosa M. Lastra, Christian Tietje (eds.) and Lucia Satragno (ass. ed.), *The Rule of Law in Monetary Affairs* (Cambridge: Cambridge University Press, 2014), pp. 490–518; Matthias Goldmann, 'Human rights and sovereign debt workouts', in Juan Pablo Bohoslavsky and Jernej Letnar Cernic (eds.), *Making Sovereign Financing and Human Rights Work* (Oxford: Hart, 2014), pp. 79–100, at p. 93. See also Andreas Fischer-Lescano, 'Human rights in times of austerity policy: the EU institutions and the conclusion of Memoranda of Understanding', legal opinion commissioned by the Chamber of Labour (Vienna, 2014), at 20.

[159] Robert Dañino, 'The legal aspects of the World Bank's work on human rights' (2006) 8 *Development Outreach* 30–32, at 31. The author was senior vice president and general counsel of the World Bank from 2003 to 2006. See also CESCR, General Comment No. 15 on the Right to Water of 20 January 2003 (UN Doc. E/C.12/2002/11), para. 60.

[160] Juan Pablo Bohoslavsky and Jernej Letnar Cernic, 'Placing human rights at the centre of sovereign financing', in Juan Pablo Bohoslavsky and Jernej Letnar Cernic (eds.), *Making Sovereign Financing and Human Rights Work* (Oxford: Hart, 2014), pp. 2–14, p. 2.

legal sphere of application of social human rights has been much expanded, although the actual practice of the organisations themselves and the views pronounced by their officials and legal advisers do not fully follow.

6.3.2 Business as obligor

The next potential obligor of (social) human rights are business actors. For the purposes of this chapter it is worth recalling that the debate is conducted under the heading of corporate *social* responsibility (CSR). This label is adequate because what is at issue are social problems (such as the creation of jobs or environmental damage) and mostly social rights (ranging from health at the workplace over various labour rights to the right to water as affected, e.g., by infrastructure privatisation). Generally speaking, current human rights norms do not impose hard legal obligations on private economic actors directly under international law to respect, promote or fulfil international human rights. Only those human rights belonging to the small number of peremptory norms (e.g. the right not to be discriminated against on account of one's race) seem to be opposable to private actors, due to the absolute character of these norms.[161] Against this background, there is a tendency to reign in business actors, visible in international soft law documents and in the case law.

In 2011, the UN Human Rights Council adopted the Guiding Principles on Business and Human Rights ('Ruggie Principles').[162] The principles are divided into three pillars: firstly, they require that states meet their duty to protect; secondly, they define corporate responsibility; and thirdly, they require states and business actors to provide effective remedies, i.e. complaint mechanisms. The Council of Europe

---

[161] IACtHR, Juridical Condition and Rights of the Undocumented Migrants, Series A No. 18, Advisory Opinion OC 18–03 of 17 September 2003, p. 113, holding No. 5: 'That the fundamental principle of equality and non-discrimination, which is of a *peremptory nature*, entails obligations erga omnes of protection that bind all States and *generate effects with regard to third parties, including individuals*' (emphases added). The absolute, non-derogatory quality of the obligation in substance is usually viewed as implying that the obligation must therefore also be respected by everyone.

[162] UN Human Rights Council, Report of the Special Representative of the Secretary-General on the Issue of Human Rights and Transnational Corporations and Other Business Enterprises (John Ruggie), with Guiding Principles in the Annex (UN Doc. A/HRC/17/31 of 21 March 2011), adopted by the UN Human Rights Council (UN Doc. A/HRC/RES/17/4 of 6 July 2011).

has called on its member states to implement the Ruggie Framework which it qualifies as the 'current globally agreed baseline' in the matter of business and human rights.[163]

Within the Ruggie Framework, corporate 'responsibility' does not mean responsibility in the sense of the law of international responsibility, i.e. the secondary obligations arising from a violation of international law. Rather, it is linked to the idea of CSR in corporate practice. It appears to be a code for attenuated standards of conduct that have a political/moral/social basis rather than a legal basis. The corporate responsibility set out in Ruggie Principles 11–24 means that business enterprises – irrespective of positive law – must 'respect' the core internationally recognised human rights and the ILO workers' rights.[164] To implement their responsibility, enterprises should carry out human rights due diligence.[165] Finally, under the third pillar, which is in practical terms crucial, enterprises should provide for remediation for human rights violations that they have caused or to which they have contributed, or they should contribute to the search for such remediation.[166] The UN Human Rights Council recently fleshed out that third pillar.[167] The Guidance to Improve Corporate Accountability and Access to Judicial Remedy for Business-Related Human Rights Abuse co-constitutes and confirms the trend to tackle a 'diagonal' social concern

---

[163] Council of Europe, Recommendation CM/Rec. (2016) 3 of the Committee of Ministers to member states on human rights and business, adopted by the Committee of Ministers on 2 March 2016 at the 1,249th Meeting of the Ministers' Deputies, with Appendix on the Implementation of the UN Guiding Principles on Business and Human Rights, Appendix I a 1.

[164] Relevant human rights encompass at least the International Bill of Human Rights and the ILO Declaration of Fundamental Principles and Rights at Work of 1998 (ibid., Principle 12).

[165] See later text with ns. 207–211.

[166] Ruggie Principles (n. 162), Principle 22 ('remediation').

[167] See High Commissioner for Human Rights, Report on Improving Accountability and Access to Remedy for Victims of Business-Related Human Rights Abuse, with Annex: Guidance to Improve Corporate Accountability and Access to Judicial Remedy for Business-Related Human Rights Abuse (UN Doc. A/HRC/32/19 of 10 May 2016), with a companion document: High Commissioner for Human Rights, Improving Accountability and Access to Remedy for Victims of Business-Related Human Rights Abuse: Explanatory Notes for Guidance (UN Doc. A/HRC/32/19/Add.1 of 12 May 2016). The explanatory notes contain a Model Terms of Reference for a review of the coverage and effectiveness of laws relevant to business-related human rights abuses (para. 5). This work was welcomed by the UN Human Rights Council, Business and Human Rights: Improving Accountability and Access to Remedy (UN Doc. A/HRC/RES/32/10 of 15 July 2016).

ANNE PETERS

(i.e. a matter of concern between one state and an alien individual) in cross-border cases.[168]

The issue of transnational social obligations of business actors has been only sparingly addressed from the perspective of international investment law.[169] In the practice of investor–state arbitration, international law has rarely been applied by arbitral tribunals as a barrier to investor activity.[170] It seems no coincidence that the first investment arbitration award which postulates direct human rights obligations of an investor under international law concerned a big social issue, namely a public water service. In a dispute arising out of water privatisation in the Argentinian province of Buenos Aires, an International Centre for Settlement of Investment Disputes (ICSID) Tribunal for the first time examined a (social) human rights–based counterclaim filed by a host state on its merits (*Urbaser v. Argentina*, 2016).[171] The right to water is a social right, spelled out by the CESCR in its General Comment No. 15, mainly derived from the rights to food and health, as codified in the ICESCR.[172] The tribunal ultimately rejected this counterclaim as well but made some important statements on the corporation's human rights obligations.

Authors and states demanding that business should be bound by international human rights (which would include the social rights in the spotlight of this chapter) *de lege ferenda* regularly postulate that the potential power of these actors ultimately poses just as much a threat to human rights and basic rights as that of states, without asking whether that 'private' economic power can be equated with the specific 'public' power of the state.[173] Or the assumption is that, especially in an age of

---

[168] Report: para. 5; see also ibid., paras. 24–28; Guidance: Policy Objective 9: Cooperation in Cross-Border Cases.

[169] See, e.g., Dai Tamada, 'Investor's responsibility toward host-states? Regulation of corruption in investor-state arbitration', in Noemi Gal-Or, Cedric Ryngaert and Math Noortmann (eds.), *Responsibilities of the Non-State Actor in Armed Conflict and the Market Place* (Leiden: Brill, 2015), pp. 203–216.

[170] See on the extant case law on potential investor obligations flowing from various branches of international law Anne Peters, 'The refinement of international law: from fragmentation to regime interaction and politicization' (2017) 15 *International Journal of Constitutional Law* 671–704, at 676–678 with further references.

[171] ICSID, *Urbaser S.A. and Consorcio de Aguas Bilbao Bizkaia, Bilbao Biskaia Ur Partzuergoa v. The Argentine Republic*, ICSID Case No. ARB/07/26, Award of 8 December 2016.

[172] CESCR, General Comment No. 15 on the Right to Water of 20 January 2003 (UN Doc. E/C.12/2002/11).

[173] David Weissbrodt and Muria Kruger, 'Norms on the responsibilities of transnational corporations and other business enterprises with regard to human rights' (2003) 97 *American Journal of International Law* 901–922, at 901.

global supply chains, business actors exercise 'corporate sovereignty'[174] which must be controlled and reined in by concomitant human rights obligations. Such an imposition of human rights obligations on business would be conceptually possible, but it would constitute a paradigm change.[175] Human rights, including social rights, were invented as rights against the state because the state was endowed with specific powers. In a market-based society, economic actors are in a fundamentally different starting position.

But in a world of transnational supply chains, the enterprises operate globally and are able to escape from undesired strict requirements under national law by changing locations. They specifically seek out host states whose national law offers cheap conditions of production. These states of convenience do not necessarily live up to international benchmarks; their national regulation is typically lax and/or is not fully enforced. Therefore, and rightly so, the social expectation has developed in recent decades that enterprises bear a more extensive responsibility for the welfare of their employees and, alongside the state, for the common good – in short, a corporate *social* responsibility.

However, this corporate social responsibility should not translate in a simple imposition of human (social) rights obligations on transnationally operating enterprises, notably because states might shirk their responsibility. If reformed international human rights bodies were to deal with human rights violations by enterprises as well, some states would presumably seize the opportunity to divert attention away from themselves.[176]

It follows that simply expanding the binding nature of state-tailored human rights into the sphere of transnational business is not normatively desirable without modifications. It is more promising, and more tailored to the qualitative difference between states and enterprises, to strengthen the *indirect* imposition of the obligation to respect human rights on enterprises by intensifying the duties of the state to protect, as demanded by the Ruggie Principles. So far, states are bound to discharge their duty

[174] Joshua Barkan, *Corporate Sovereignty: Law and Government under Capitalism* (Minneapolis, MN: University of Minnesota Press, 2013); Daniel J. H. Greenwood, 'The semi-sovereign corporation', in James Charles Smith (ed.), *Property and Sovereignty: Legal and Cultural Perspectives* (Farnham: Ashgate, 2013), pp. 267–294.
[175] Therefore, a formal legal act would be necessary to realise such a change. Mere progressive interpretation of the extant law would be illegitimate because it would not satisfy the international and constitutional principle of legality.
[176] See in this sense also John Ruggie, 'Business and human rights' (2007) 101 *American Journal of International Law* 819–840, at 826.

to protect through national action plans (NAPs) which aim to translate the UN principles into practical action at national level.[177] To conclude, the emerging tools for holding business actors to account need to be further strengthened so as to shape a tighter web of both national and international *social* law (composed of labour law, social rights and environmental law) which would realise the social responsibility of business.

6.4 The enforcement of social rights

Since around the turn of the millennium, domestic, international and notably European courts and other monitoring bodies have begun to adjudicate on social rights. Notably the constitutional courts of South Africa[178] and India[179] have issued judgments on constitutional social rights, interpreted in the light of international and foreign law.[180] This new body of case law is revolutionary for two reasons. Firstly, it is transforming social rights from rather programmatic provisions into operational entitlements. Secondly, the case law has the potential to transnationalise these rights, because the courts and committees can enter into a judicial dialogue and are likely to align the guarantees to each other. Also, the invocation of rights is not reserved to nationals of the attacked states and potentially not even to persons under the

---

[177] See, e.g., the German National Action Plan ('Nationaler Aktionsplan: Umsetzung der VN-Leitprinzipien für Wirtschaft und Menschenrechte 2016–2020') of 21 December 2016.

[178] Constitutional Court of South Africa, *Government of the Republic of South Africa and Others v. Grootboom and Others* (CCT11/00) [2000] ZACC 19; 2001 (1) SA 46; 2000 (11) BCLR 1169 (4 October 2000) – on housing, with reference to Art. 11 of the ICESCR; *Mazibuko and Others v. City of Johannesburg and Others* (Centre on Housing Rights and Evictions as Amicus Curiae), 8 October 2009, Case CCT 39/09, 2010 (39) BCLR 239 (CC) – on water services to indigent households, with reference to the ICESCR; *Governing Body of the Juma Musjid Primary School & Others v. Essay N.O. and Others* (CCT 29/10) [2011] ZACC 13; 2011 (8) BCLR 761 (CC) (11 April 2011) – on the right to education, with reference to various international instruments. See in scholarship Sandra Liebenberg, *Socio-Economic Rights: Adjudication under a Transformative Constitution* (Claremont: Juta, 2010); Bilchitz (n. 73).

[179] Until 2009, out of the total forty-six cases in which the court referred to international human rights norms, 35% involved economic, social and cultural rights (alone or alongside the civil and political rights). Rajat Rana, 'Could domestic courts enforce international human rights norms? An empirical study of the enforcement of human rights norms by the Indian Supreme Court since 1997' (2009) 49 *Indian Journal of International Law* 533–575 with further references.

[180] See the remarkable analysis by Katharine G. Young, *Constituting Economic and Social Rights* (Oxford: Oxford University Press, 2012).

jurisdiction of the respective state. Their extraterritorial applicability is an issue which awaits further clarification (see Section 6.2).

On the European regional level, the European Court of Human Rights has acknowledged and built up social rights under the ECHR.[181] The court repeats that 'the right to ... any social benefit in a particular amount is not included as such among the rights and freedoms guaranteed by the Convention'.[182] But it has under narrow conditions protected social benefits (e.g. a disability pension) under the heading of property.[183] Also, the European Court of Human Rights (ECtHR) has employed the ECHR's prohibition on discrimination (Article 14 of the ECHR, in conjunction with other guarantees) as a vehicle of social equalisation, in matters such as pensions or employment benefits: *if* a contracting state has legislated on such welfare benefits, then its laws must be designed and applied without discrimination.[184] The court also derived social rights directly from ECHR provisions, notably a social minimum standard from Article 3 of the ECHR. For especially vulnerable persons (e.g. asylum seekers), the prohibition of inhumane treatment exceptionally generates entitlements to decent housing and a minimum of food and medical aid if these persons otherwise have no opportunity to lead a life in dignity.[185]

This evolution, brought about through judicial activism, to some extent revises the original set-up of human rights protection in Europe, with the ECHR on the one hand and the European Social Charter[186] on

---

[181] See for a full discussion of the case law transforming the ECHR into a social rights instrument ECtHR, *Konstantin Markin v. Russia*, Grand Chamber Judgment of 22 March 2012, Application No. 30078/06, pp. 51–57 (partly concurring, partly dissenting opinion of Judge Pinto de Albuquerque).

[182] ECtHR, *Béláné Nagy v. Hungary*, Judgment of 10 February 2015, Application No. 53080/13, para. 35. Leading case ECtHR, *Teteriny v. Russia*, Judgment of 30 June 2005, Application No. 11931/03, para. 46.

[183] See ECtHR, *Ásmundsson v. Iceland*, Judgment of 30 March 2005, Application No. 60669/00, qualifying changes to a disability pension law which led to a total loss of pensions for the applicant as a disproportionate and discriminatory interference with his right to enjoy his possessions and thus as a violation of Art. 1 of Protocol 1 to the ECHR.

[184] See recently ECtHR, *Aldeguer Tomàs v. Spain*, Judgment of 14 September 2016, No. 35214/09 (discrimination on account of sexual orientation in the calculation of a survivor's pension of a homosexual couple); ECtHR, *Di Trizio v. Switzerland*, Judgment of 2 February 2016, Application No. 7186/09 (gender discrimination in the calculation of a disability allowance as a violation). The leading case is ECtHR, *Stec et al. v. UK*, Grand Chamber Judgment of 12 April 2006, Application Nos. 65731/01 and 65900/01.

[185] ECtHR, *M.S.S. v. Belgium and Greece*, Grand Chamber Judgment of 21 January 2011, Application No. 30696/09, paras. 205–264.

[186] ETS No. 163. The revised social charter is in force since 1 July 1999.

the other hand. The European Social Charter is not endowed with a court but allows only for collective and individual complaints to a committee. But also the European Social Committee has responded to social crisis and has, for example, found a violation of Article 12 of the European Social Charter (right to social security) through Greece's modification of its pensions schemes as part of its austerity programme.[187] The judicial 'loading' of the ECHR with social entitlements has a tangible impact on the social security systems in the European *espace conventionnel*.

At least as important, the operationalisation of economic and social rights in Europe has been boosted by the European Charter of Fundamental Rights (CFR) of 2000. The CFR contains a Title IV 'Solidarity' (Articles 27–38). The CFR's strong social dimension is further manifest in its Title III 'Equality' (Articles 20–26). The fundamental right not to suffer discrimination (Article 21 of the CFR) prohibits, inter alia, any discrimination on the basis of 'social origin' and 'property'. This provision lends itself to be used for dismantling unfair *material* inequality (of wealth, of income, of educational opportunities and the like). The entry into force of the Lisbon Treaty in 2009 brought the CFR under the jurisdiction of the Court of Justice of the EU (CJEU).[188] The CJEU has now developed a case law on fundamental social rights.[189] It does not consider all social provisions of the CFR to be directly applicable in the sense of conferring on individuals actual rights which they may invoke before an agency or court. Also, the CJEU mostly applies the CFR provisions in conjunction with specific EU social legislation. A host of social benefits and rights are not only owed to EU citizens but must also be granted to third-country nationals.[190]

---

[187] European Committee of Social Rights (ECSR), *Federation of Employed Pensioners of Greece (IKA-ETAM) v. Greece*, Decision of 7 December 2012, Complaint No. 76/2012.

[188] Arts. 6(2), 19(1) and 51 of the Treaty on European Union (TEU).

[189] See, e.g., on workers' right to a paid annual leave, Art. 31(2) of the CFR: Case C-316/13, CJEU, Judgment of 26 March 2015 in *Gérard Fenoll v. Centre d'aide par le travail «La Jouvene», Association de parents et d'amis de personnes handicapées mentales (APEI) d'Avignon*; Case C-396/13, CJEU, Judgment of 12 February 2015 in *Sähköalojen ammattiliitto ry v. Elektrobudowa Spółka Akcyjna*. See on parental leave, Art. 33(2) of the CFR: Case C-222/14, CJEU, Judgment of 16 July 2015 in *Konstantinos Maïstrellis v. Ypourgos Dikaiosynis*.

[190] See, e.g., on housing benefits for low-income tenants under Art. 34 of the CFR (and under Council Directive 2003/109/EC of 25 November 2003 concerning the status of third-country nationals who are long-term residents, OJ 2004 L 16, p. 44): Case C-571/10, CJEU, Judgment of 24 April 2012 in *Kamberaj v. Istituto per l'Edilizia sociale della Provincia autonoma di Bolzano (IPES) et al.*

On the universal level, and in response to financial crises, the human rights bodies have developed criteria which states should meet so as to avoid breaching social human rights through their austerity measures.[191] The first optional protocol to the ICESCR allows – since 2013 – individual communications about violations of the social covenant rights to the Committee on Economic, Social and Cultural Rights (CESCR).[192] The individual communications procedure bears some resemblance to judicial proceedings. So far twenty-two states have ratified the protocol and have thereby subjected themselves to the mechanism.[193]

The judicial and quasi-judicial enforcement of social rights, unconceivable only a decade ago, can be seen as a form of *individualisation* of global and regional social governance. This individualisation is accompanied by a different, to some extent antagonist, trend that will be discussed next.

7 Social impact assessment and due diligence

Beside the aforementioned employment of social rights as justiciable entitlements stands their non-individualised function as a background grid for practices and procedures which seek to prevent cross-border social harm.[194] These tools are known as *social impact assessment*,[195]

---

[191] See for four requirements on adjustment policies to avoid a breach of the ICESCR by member states the Letter of Chairperson of the CESCR (Ariranga G. Pillay), Letter to State Parties (on human rights and austerity measures) of 16 May 2012 (UN Doc. CESCR/48th/SP/MAB/SW) at p. 2. The UN Human Rights Office of the High Commissioner (2013), 'Report on austerity measures and economic and social rights' mentions six 'human rights compliance criteria': the existence of a legitimate objective in public interest ('a compelling State interest'), proportionality, prohibition of retrogression (high threshold of justification), non-discrimination ('vulnerability'), minimum level/core content and participation (see esp. p. 12).

[192] See n. 132.

[193] The first decision was CESCR, Communication No. 2/2014 against Spain of 17 June 2015 (UN Doc E/C.12/55/D/2/2014): violation of the right to housing through enforcement of a mortgage.

[194] Walker specifically mentions the increasing focus on social rights as one of the factors which incited the establishment of human rights impact assessment (Simon Walker, *The Future of Human Rights Impact Assessments of Trade Agreements* (Antwerp: Intersentia, 2009), p. 5).

[195] Frank Vanclay and Ana Maria Esteves (eds.), *New Directions in Social Impact Assessment* (Cheltenham: Edward Elgar, 2011). Social impact assessments were invented in the 1950s, alongside environmental impact assessment. Human rights impact assessment has grown out of these and inversely influenced the former older tools. It seems therefore warranted to deal with both social and (social) human rights impact assessments in a summarial fashion.

human rights impact assessments[196] and *(social) human rights due diligence.*[197] Another tool is social and human rights mainstreaming which I will leave aside.[198] All these tools are not sharply defined and may overlap. They comprise steps of reflection, deliberation or discussion which must be documented and accompanied by procedural safeguards. For example, one step is to *take into account* the social interests and social rights of potentially adversely affected communities (and to document this).[199] Accompanying procedural elements are to allow spokespersons of those communities to *participate* in the deliberations and then to *communicate* the results of decision making to them.

Social impact assessment includes 'the processes of analysing, monitoring and managing the intended and unintended social consequences, both positive and negative, of planned interventions (policies, programs, plans, projects) and any social change processes invoked by those

---

[196] See for key literature Walker (n. 194); Nordic Trust Fund, *Study on Human Rights Impact Assessments: A Review of the Literature, Differences and Other Forms of Assessments and Relevance for Development* (Commissioned by the Nordic Trust Fund; The World Bank, 2013).

[197] See for a comparative legal study on regulatory techniques of states to ensure business due diligence in the fields of environment protection, workplace safety, anti-money laundering and other legal areas, and their possible transfer to human rights, Olivier de Schutter, Anita Ramasastry, Mark Taylor and Robert Thompson, Human Rights Due Diligence: The Role of States (2012), updated by Mark Taylor, Human Rights Due Diligence: The Role of States (2013 Progress Report).

[198] The UN began its policy of human rights mainstreaming with UN General Assembly, Report of the UN Secretary General on Renewing the United Nations: A Programme for Reform of 14 July 1997 (UN Doc. A/51/950). Without using the term 'mainstreaming', the report defined as a 'major task' for the UN 'to enhance its human rights programme and fully integrate it into the broad range of the Organization's activities' (ibid., para. 79). Created in 2009, the UN Development Group's Human Rights Working Group (UNDG-HRWG) advances human rights mainstreaming efforts within the UN development system. See, e.g., UNDG, Mainstreaming Human Rights in Development (New York 2013). See for the EU the Joint Communication by the European Commission and the High Representative of the European Union for Foreign Affairs and Security Policy, Action Plan on Human Rights and Democracy (2015–2019), 10897/15, Brussels, 20 July 2015, esp. at p. 2. See, in scholarship, Gerd Oberleitner, 'A decade of mainstreaming human rights in the UN: achievements, failures, challenges' (2008) 30 *Netherlands Quarterly of Human Rights* 359–390.

[199] Cf. in the area of environmental law Art. 10 of the ILC Draft Articles on Prevention of Transboundary Harm from Hazardous Activities of 2001 (UN Doc. A/56/10); *Yearbook of the International Law Commission*, 2001, Vol. II, part two: 'Factors involved in an equitable balance of interests: In order to achieve an equitable balance of interests as referred to in paragraph 2 of article 9, the States concerned shall take into account all relevant factors and circumstances'.

interventions. Its primary purpose is to bring about a more sustainable and equitable biophysical and human environment.'[200] The usual steps of a social impact analysis are screening, scoping, evidence gathering, analysis, conclusions and recommendations, and finally an evaluation mechanism.[201]

The deliberative and procedural tools have evolved both in the purely domestic context (such as in regulatory impact analyses) and in the transboundary and international sphere, and the ideas and practices on both levels of governance have mutually influenced each other. The said tools are meanwhile applied by various actors – by states, by international organisations[202] and by business actors[203] – as a component of their national, transnational and international activities.

7.1   Soft legal obligations

No hard-and-fast, specific international legal obligation exists which would compel states, international organisations or business actors to go through the said procedures for preventing and mitigating transboundary social harm. I will in the following limit myself to identifying potential responsibilities of states (as opposed to international organisations and business actors[204]). A more *general* deliberative and procedural obligation in that direction might be derived from the trustee-like facet of sovereignty in its feature as an 'other-regarding'

---

[200] International Association for Impact Assessment (IAIA), International Principles for Social Impact Assessments, Special Publications Series No. 2, May 2003, p. 4.

[201] See, e.g., UN special rapporteur on the right to food (Olivier de Schutter), Guiding Principles on Human Rights Impact Assessments of Trade and Investment Agreements of 19 December 2011 (UN Doc. A/HRC/19/59/Add.5), 'VI. Key steps in preparing a human rights impact assessment', Principle 7; similarly, Nordic Trust Fund 2013 (n. 196), p. XII.

[202] The World Bank and UN Environment Programme (UNEP) were the front-runners in integrating social impact assessments into their development projects. In EU law-making, impact analyses are a regular part of its regulatory process. See Commission staff working document, Better Regulation Guidelines, COM (2015) 215 final, SWD (2015) 110 final (2015), chapter III.

[203] See, e.g., Désirée Abrahams (IBLF) and Yann Wyss (IFC), Guide to Human Rights Impact Assessment and Management, the International Business Leaders Forum (IBLF) and the International Finance Corporation (IFC), in association with the UN Global Compact 2010.

[204] Even accepting that business actors are – under the law as it stands – not directly bound by international human rights obligations (see Section 6.3.2, pp. 312–316), they could still be saddled with an obligation to conduct an impact assessment.

sovereignty[205] or from a presumed principle of 'solidarity'[206] as potential legal bases for such tools.

7.1.1 Due diligence

Due diligence procedures have their roots on the one hand in domestic law and in corporate practices to shield corporations from liability[207] and on the other hand in international law, originating in state responsibility and environmental law and from there percolating into human rights law.[208] Here three different strands of law and legal politics have met: the states' international law–based obligations to regulate private actors (and the ensuing state responsibility for failing to regulate), the idea of corporate social responsibility and the increased attention to social rights.[209] The confluence of these three strands has made due diligence the ideal legal umbrella to reign in business in order to prevent human rights violations caused by transnational business activity. In fact, the UN Human Rights Council's Framework on Business and Human Rights and the Ruggie Principles of 2011 spell out due diligence 'responsibilities' of *business actors* while at the same time implying that the *states'* overall obligation to protect human rights includes the specific duty to enact proper regulation which exactly defines those due diligence procedures.[210] The International Law Association (ILA) rightly points out that thus 'the Framework cleverly (though potentially misleadingly)

---

[205] Eyal Benvenisti, 'Sovereigns as trustees of humanity: on the accountability of states to foreign stakeholders' (2013) 107 *American Journal of International Law* 295–333, esp. at 301 and 314–318.

[206] Postulating an obligation to take into account the interests *of other states* on the basis of a principle of solidarity: Rüdiger Wolfrum 'Solidarity amongst states: an emerging structural principle of international law', in Pierre-Marie Dupuy et al. (eds.), *Common Values in International Law: Essays in Honour of Christian Tomuschat* (Kehl: Engel, 2006), pp. 1087–1101, p. 1087.

[207] Due diligence procedures have been initially designed by national regulators as a tool to foster private actors' compliance with the laws on workplace safety, environmental protection and criminal law provisions on bribery and money laundering. By performing and reporting on certain due diligence procedures, business can avoid civil and criminal liability.

[208] See generally Joanna Kulesza, *Due Diligence in International Law* (Leiden: Brill, 2016).

[209] A recent ILA report stresses that human rights due diligence is mainly associated with social and economic rights as an element of the states' obligation of progressive implementation, Art. 2 of the ICESCR (ILA Study Group on Due Diligence in International Law, First Report, Tim Stephans (rapporteur) and Duncan French (chair), 7 March 2014, p. 14).

[210] Principle 15 of the Ruggie Principles (n. 162). Details are fleshed out in Principles 17–21. See, in this sense, also CESCR, General Comment No. 24 (n. 19), para. 16.

aims to use a terminology that is familiar to both human rights law and business management practices'.[211]

7.1.2   Impact assessments

Impact assessments have so far been tentatively legalised under international law but rarely made legally mandatory. Environmental impact assessments are required by general international law. According to the ICJ, the obligation to conduct an environmental impact assessment is triggered when a proposed industrial activity (e.g. building a plant) 'may have a significant adverse impact in a transboundary context, in particular, on a shared resource'. The omission to conduct an *ex ante* assessment violates *'the duty of vigilance and prevention'*.[212]

The case law on human rights impact assessments by states is scarce. The ECtHR ruled that a 'governmental decision-making process concerning complex issues of environmental and economic policy must in the first place involve *appropriate investigations and studies* so that the effects of activities that might damage the environment and infringe individuals' rights may be predicted and evaluated in advance'.[213] The ECtHR here appears to find that the ECHR contains an obligation to conduct an ex ante human rights impact assessment as one step in environmental law-making. Also, the European Committee of Social Rights (ECSR) considered that, as a part of the contracting states' obligation to give full effects to the rights codified in the European Social Charter, 'States Parties must be *particularly mindful of the impact* that their choices will have for groups with heightened vulnerabilities as well as for other persons affected'.[214] This statement might be read as a treaty-based obligation to conduct a social rights impact assessment in a situation where – as the ECSR says – 'the achievement of one of the rights in question is exceptionally complex and particularly expensive to resolve'.[215]

Moreover, several quasi-normative frameworks call for human rights impact assessments. In 2011, the special rapporteur on the right to food

---

[211] ILA First Report (n. 209), p. 15.
[212] ICJ, *Case Concerning Pulp Mills on the River Uruguay (Argentina v. Uruguay)*, Judgment of 20 April 2010, para. 204.
[213] ECtHR, *Giacomelli v. Italy*, Judgment of 2 November 2006, Application No. 59909/00, para. 83.
[214] ECSR, *International Association Autism Europe (IAAE) v. France*, decision on the merits of 7 November 2003, Complaint No. 13/2002, para. 53 (emphasis added).
[215] Ibid.

presented Guiding Principles on Human Rights Impact Assessments of Trade and Investment Agreements.[216] In the same year, the NGO/expert-authored Maastricht Principles called for an assessment of transboundary impacts on the enjoyment of social human rights for any type of state action with potential extraterritorial effects.[217] Also the UN Human Rights Council's Guiding Principles on Extreme Poverty and Human Rights of 2012 postulate a state obligation to conduct an assessment of the extraterritorial impacts of laws, policies and practices on the enjoyment of human rights by persons living in poverty beyond its borders.[218]

Similarly, although the World Bank is not explicitly obliged under its founding document to conduct social impact analyses or human rights due diligence before financing a development project, the bank's current Environmental and Social Standards (ESS) prescribe them both for the borrower and foresee a gap analysis by the bank itself.[219]

7.1.3   Social impact analysis before the conclusion of trade agreements

Specifically in the constellation of treaty making, not only the UN Human Rights Council (as mentioned)[220] but also the UN ESC Rights Committee[221] and the Council of Europe[222] assert that states parties of human rights treaties are obliged to perform a human rights impact assessment before the conclusion of trade and investment agreements by virtue of their pre-existing human rights obligations.

The legal explanations are the rule that states should avoid subsequent treaties that impose obligations inconsistent with pre-existing agreements (cf. Article 26 and 30 of the VCLT), the right of citizens to take part in the conduct of public affairs (Article 25 lit. a) of the ICCPR, the legal obligation of all UN member states to cooperate in human rights

---

[216] Guiding Principles on Human Rights Impact Assessments (n. 201), Principle 1.

[217] Maastricht Principles (n. 127), Principle 14 ('Impact assessment and prevention').

[218] UN Doc. A/HRC/21/39 of 18 July 2012, para. 92, endorsed by UN Human Rights Council (UN Doc. A/HRC/RES/21/11 of 18 October 2012).

[219] See World Bank Policy and the Environmental and Social Standards of 2016 (n. 144), ESS 1: 'Environmental and Social Due Diligence'.

[220] See UN Guiding Principles on Human Rights Impact Assessments (n. 201), introduction and para. 6.

[221] CESCR, General Comment No. 24 (n. 19), para. 13.

[222] Council of Europe, Recommendation CM/Rec. (2016) 3 of the Committee of Ministers to Member States on Human Rights and Business, adopted by the Committee of Ministers on 2 March 2016 at the 1,249th Meeting of the Ministers' Deputies with Appendix on the Implementation of the UN Guiding Principles on Business and Human Rights, Appendix para. 23.

matters (Article 55 lit. c) in conjunction with Article 56 of the UN Charter and the (theoretical) prevalence of this Charter-based obligation of cooperation over potentially conflicting trade agreements under Article 103 of the UN Charter. Finally, some human rights (including, e.g., the right not to be starved by the state in a cruel and inhumane way) possibly belong to the corpus of *jus cogens* which cannot be contracted away; countervailing international treaties will be null and void (Article 53 of the VCLT).[223]

Finally, legal obligations concerning the 'if' must be distinguished from legal obligations about the 'how'. Even where a state is free to decide *whether* to perform due diligence or an impact assessment, there are legal obligations about the modalities. So *when* a state autonomously decides to prescribe social impact assessments in its treaty-making procedures or imposes social due diligence in its own domestic law on business actors (e.g. as a precondition for receiving an export subsidy), or when the World Bank makes a Poverty and Social Impact Analysis precondition for a development policy or investment loan to a borrower state, then all these actors must – arguably – draw on the established sets of principles governing these procedures and must respect the internationally recognised modalities of using the tools.

7.2   Unresolved legal questions

The questions are when (at which threshold) the aforementioned soft or hard obligations to conduct social impact assessments (including notably a social human rights impact assessment) or due diligence is triggered and – concomitantly – how far the assessment must go and how intense it must be.

Obviously, any assessment must cover social impacts. But what is a social impact? According to the International Association for Impact Assessment,

> social impacts include all the issues associated with a planned intervention (i.e. a project) that affect or concern people, whether directly or indirectly. Specifically, a social impact is considered to be something that is experienced or felt in either a perceptual (cognitive) or a corporeal (bodily, physical) sense, at any level, for example at the level of an individual person, an economic unit (family/household), a social group (circle of

---

[223] See the commentary to Principle 1 of the UN Human Rights Council, Guiding Principles on Human Rights Impact Assessments (n. 201).

friends), a workplace (a company or government agency), or by community/society generally'[224]

Because ultimately all consequences of any measure or project may be seen as a social impact and because these impacts are nowadays to some extent transnational, the actual performance of the social impact assessment must be limited in order to retain any meaning.

It seems difficult to conceptualise the threshold with the help of the concept of jurisdiction known from international human rights law.[225] Jurisdiction seems irrelevant for identifying and delimiting the scope of the obligation. The reason is that the purpose of impact assessments and due diligence is not to identify human rights violations and to sanction them but rather to prevent both future human rights violations and other 'human rights stresses'.[226] But their rationale to prevent and mitigate adverse social impacts does require a regulatory and institutional capacity to design a political measure for avoiding or mitigating harm and to implement enhancement or compensatory measures. It would make no sense to ask an actor to perform due diligence and assess social impacts whose prevention or mitigation is outside its reach.

The threshold question has arisen with regard to environmental impact assessments,[227] but the attempt to translate these concepts to the area of social conditions including social rights raises additional questions. At what point can we identify a 'serious' or 'significant' adverse transboundary social impact? We might quote the International Law Commission (ILC), stating that the human social condition 'does not correspond to political boundaries. In carrying out lawful activities within their own territories, States have impacts on each other. These

---

[224] Frank Vanclay et al., Social Impact Assessment: Guidance for Assessing and Managing the Social Impacts of Projects, International Association for Impact Assessment, April 2015. The International Association for Impact Assessment, an academic/business/civil society entity, has been qualified as a leading authority on best practices of impact assessment. The association concedes that 'almost anything can potentially be a social impact so long as it is valued by or important to a specific group of people' (ibid.).

[225] See Section 6.2 text with ns. 130–136, pp. 303–304.

[226] Cf. Gauthier De Beco, 'Human rights impact assessments' (2012) 27 Netherlands Quarterly of Human Rights 139–166, at 156; Walker (n. 194) p. 93. Also, impact assessments and due diligence by business actors cannot rely on any jurisdictional criterion, because business does not have a 'jurisdiction'.

[227] ILC, Draft Articles on Prevention of Transboundary Harm from Hazardous Activities, with commentaries, Yearbook of the International Law Commission, 2011, Vol. II, part two, Art. 2, para. 4.

mutual impacts, so long as they have not reached the level of "signifi-cant", are considered tolerable.'[228]

The identification of negative social impacts presupposes that causal-ities can be established. We can meaningfully speak of an adverse impact of a given policy or legal measure on the social situation of a person sitting in a different state only if the measure is indeed apt to cause such impact. Due to overriding, intervening and confluent multiple contribu-tions of many actors, and due to the geographical and temporal distance between state A's action and effects in state B, it may be exceedingly difficult if not impossible to establish causality in its usual legal sense of *conditio sine qua non.*

A further question is to whom these deliberative and procedural obligations would be owed: to one or more states, to the international community as a whole or to the potentially affected non-nationals? Under the law of international state responsibility, it seems plausible to qualify the aforementioned obligations as obligations *erga omnes,*[229] and this regime does not rule out additional beneficiaries of the primary duties.

To conclude, the preventive and mitigating tools sketched out here (impact assessments and due diligence) have their origins mainly in environmental law but seem particularly relevant to address problems raised by the cross-border social consequences of state action. They are an entry point for the decentralised implementation of a global social constitution (see Section 9).

8   Interim conclusion: the emerging cross-border social responsibility for human beings

None of the reported legal phenomena and trends has appeared out of the blue. Concepts of *mission civilisatrice,* solidarity, development, coopera-tion and protection have been endorsed in international law and scholar-ship from the beginnings of the discipline, often with Eurocentric, paternalist and racist overtones. But in the moment of a new global awareness about the fallouts generated by ruthless neo-liberal globalisa-tion, the aforementioned elements reflect the spirit of post-neo-liberal governance. Importantly, they manifest the recognition not only of

---

[228] ILC, Draft Articles on Prevention of Transboundary Harm from Hazardous Activities, with commentaries, *Yearbook of the International Law Commission,* 2011, Vol. II, part two, Art. 2, para. 5.

[229] Cf. ILC Art. 42 lit. b of the Articles on State Responsibility.

interstate obligations or 'solidarity' (as notably in the classic international law of development) but of additional, albeit weakly legalised responsibilities[230] for the material welfare of individuals independent of the latter's nationality and place of residence, in the form of a *cross-border social responsibility for human beings.*

What I have described as a rise of social rights comprises two seemingly contradictory features. On the one hand, the rights' function as entitlements is being sharpened (notably through the new enforcement practices). On the other hand, social rights form a mere background noise when they are used as a guideline for the interpretation of hard rules in trade and investment. The dilution of social rights is most obvious in the new tools of social human rights impact assessment and due diligence. However, both functions of rights (as enforceable entitlements and as mere interpretative guidelines) can coexist without cancelling each other out.[231]

The legal contours of impact assessments and due diligence as tools to prevent and mitigate cross-border social harm are very hazy. It is not clear whether the practices will develop further into actual deliberative and procedural obligations of states and international organisations whose violation would be sanctionable. But independently of the problems of threshold, causality, creditors and sanctions, it is legally relevant that these tools are based on a *shift of perspective.* These practices build on the expectation that the decision makers espouse an inclusive perspective which transcends the boundaries of the nation state. While under the rules of domestic democracy, decision makers are in political and legal terms accountable only to the citizens who elected them, the espousal of this broader perspective leads them to take into account the interest of other states and their citizens. This does not mean that they owe specific outputs but that they are saddled with specific deliberative and procedural responsibilities.

The main legal component of the cross-border social responsibility for human beings is an international law–based obligation to properly *integrate* consideration for material needs of humans in other states into domestic decision making in all relevant fields of law and politics.

---

[230] 'Responsibility' is here used in the sense of a 'soft' duty or obligation, as in the concept of 'responsibility to protect' (R2P).

[231] The constitutionalist perspective, which will be explained in the next section, helps in assessing this issue because much of constitutional law writing deals with the dual function of rights both as structural features of a constitution and as individual entitlements.

In narrow constellations, the cross-border social responsibility may even amount to states' legal obligations to respect, protect and fulfil social human rights outside their territory. *Mutatis mutandis*, such a cross-border social responsibility to respect social rights, to employ due diligence and to conduct social rights impact assessments is accepted for international organisations and corporate actors, as well.

The motivations for assuming the cross-border social responsibility vary and depend on actor and context. The traditional nationalist competition-based policy objectives were to level the playing field for states, to protect domestic workers from a downward spiral, to prevent the scooping out of the social state and to lower the incentive for undesired inflowing labour migration by improving the living conditions in the emigrants' countries of origin. These continue to play an important role. With the increasing global capital and migrant flows, and with budgetary difficulties of national economies, these traditional nation-centred rationales even gain currency.

On the other hand, universalist considerations float, too: states and other global players acknowledge that the sovereign states' trade, financial and other policies produce negative externalities which might warrant some counteraction, they recognise international entitlements flowing from human rights and they may subscribe to cosmopolitan accounts of global social justice. Taken as a whole, the social thickening of international law in the form of cross-border social responsibility for humans has a constitutional significance and should therefore be approached in a constitutionalist mindset, as I will argue in the next section.

9   The global social question from a constitutionalist perspective

This section demonstrates the added value of analysing the global social question and the emerging instruments of a more social international law from the perspective of global constitutionalism. A number of considerations support my broad claim that the body of international guidelines, rules and practices directed at mitigating poverty and inequality in a cross-border fashion, not only in interstate relations but addressed to 'extraterritorial' individuals in a cross-border fashion (as canvassed in Sections 5–8), are an important dimension of global constitutional law and a proper focus of global constitutionalism.

Employing a constitutionalist approach to the aforementioned legal elements is, firstly, a shorthand for acknowledging and pulling together those hard and soft principles and procedures under the heading of a 'global social constitution'. Secondly, this approach comprises the call for conceptualising and fleshing out in more detail a 'social global constitutionalism'. Ultimately, the fusion of the social with the constitutional should prove beneficial for both facets, for the social dimension and for constitutionalism: on the one hand, global constitutionalism supports the social dimension of international law by acknowledging the social question as a constitutional (and that means as a fundamental and serious) concern. Thus, a constitutional framing favours the development of a 'more social' international law as sketched out earlier and furnishes arguments in defence and promotion of this trend. On the other hand, the absorption of the social dimension will remove a blind spot and can prevent global constitutionalism from falling out of step with hyper-globalisation as will be discussed in the following section.

9.1   Socialising compensatory constitutionalism

The principal argument for the reformulation of a more social global constitutionalism is the need to escape what has been condemned as the 'new constitutionalism of disciplinary neo-liberalism'.[232] The background is that in the current post-national constellation, the traditional constitutional functions, such as the guarantee of the rule of law and the protection of human rights, have to some degree escaped the confines of the nation state and thereby also the umbrella of the domestic constitutions. In order to preserve or regain the constitutional achievements, compensatory[233] or complementary[234] constitutional instruments and strategies, namely international guarantees of the rule of law and of human rights, have been installed. Taken together with the national constitutional law, this arrangement manifests a 'global' constitutionalism because it encompasses both the international and the domestic levels of regulation.

---

[232] Stephen Gill and A. Claire Cutler, 'New constitutionalism and world order: general introduction', in Stephen Gill and A. Claire Cutler (eds.), *New Constitutionalism and World Order* (Cambridge: Cambridge University Press, 2014), pp. 1–21, p. 5.

[233] Anne Peters, 'Compensatory constitutionalism: the function and potential of fundamental international norms and structures' (2006) 19 *Leiden Journal of International Law* 579–610.

[234] Jeffrey Dunoff and Joel Trachtman, 'A functional approach to international constitutionalization', in Jeffrey Dunoff and Joel Trachtman (eds.), *Ruling the World? Constitutionalism, International Law, and Global Governance* (Cambridge: Cambridge University Press, 2009), pp. 3–35, pp. 14–18.

But what has been celebrated as beneficial compensatory constitutionalism by some has been condemned by others as an utterly one-sided 'new constitutionalism'. The concept of 'new constitutionalism' was coined by Stephen Gill as part of a critical theory and is explained as the legal form of neo-liberalism[235] or – more starkly – as 'a principal institutional component of neo-liberal hegemony'.[236] The label of constitutionalism is used in this body for the *constitution-like agreements* which regulate global and regional capitalism, trump the decisions of national bodies, are binding for an indefinite future, are difficult to amend, and define a new set of negative freedom from democratic intervention'.[237]

From the critical perspective, the 'new' values of constitutionalism are mostly inspired by private corporate actors.

> New constitutionalism is not simply a set of neutral laws and mechanisms of regulation and governance associated with contemporary capitalism but also reflects a specific complex of dominant forms of political agency, as well as a set of actors, practices and forces in political and civil society – particularly large corporations. These practices have as a goal ... the "locking in" of neoliberal frameworks of accumulation, with American geopolitical power as its ultimate guarantor.[238]

New constitutionalism is, in short, seen as a *conscious project* 'to insulate the economy and private power from any potential for democratization of control'.[239] Importantly, 'the new constitutionalism of the post-1980s period entails not only a rolling back of possible restrictions on capitalist property rights, but the rolling forward of the new international juridical framework that systematically privileges the discretionary rights of capital on a world scale'.[240]

This critique has the merit of highlighting that contemporary global governance consists primarily in effective rules (which are managed by

---

[235] Stephen Gill, 'Globalisation, market civilization, and disciplinary neoliberalism' (1995) 24 *Millennium: Journal of International Studies* 399–423, at 412.
[236] Dries Lesage, Mattias Vermeiren and Sacha Dierckx, 'New constitutionalism, international taxation and crisis', in Gill and Cutler (eds.), *New Constitutionalism and World Order* (n. 232), pp. 197–210, p. 197.
[237] Janine Brodie (n. 57), p. 20 (emphasis added); also David Schneiderman, *Constitutionalization Economic Globalization: Investment Rules and Democracy's Promise* (Cambridge: Cambridge University Press, 2008), esp. pp. 3–4.
[238] Gill and Cutler, 'New Constitutionalism and World Order' (n. 232), p. 4.
[239] Ibid., p. 11.
[240] Neil Brenner, Jamie Peck and Nik Theodore, 'New constitutionalism and variegated neoliberalization', in Gill and Cutler (eds.), *New Constitutionalism and World Order* (n. 232), pp. 126–142, p. 127.

well-functioning organisations) on free trade, capital mobility and investor rights. In marked contrast, multilateral agreements regulating harmful tax competition or labour, social and environmental standards are much weaker, and these issue areas largely lack international organisations or bodies. Put differently, there is indeed a mismatch between global markets on which global capital moves, coupled with global rules that secure and protect them (market-enabling regimes such as WTO and investment protection agreements, each accompanied by robust dispute settlement mechanisms), and the national rules embedding markets and constraining market forces (market-constraining regimes) which would realise the social protection and security of the weaker market participants.

Applying the theories of classical fiscal federalism to the transnational sphere, Adam Harmes has analysed this mismatch as a deliberate neo-liberal plot which ensures that the lower-level (national) policies designed to redistribute wealth and correct market failures will be constrained by the outmigration of firms.[241] The value of this analysis is to read together the successful 'zoning up' of capital and market facilitation as a nefarious combination with the 'keeping down' of the social regulation. The real or perceived policy competition which makes national governments hesitant to levy the taxes they need in order to fund social programmes and to raise steep redistributive taxes functions as an effective factual (and according to the body of critical literature even intentional) constraint on social policies (see also Section 2).

However, it is not self-evident, as the critical camp implies, that the mismatch results from a conspiracy of politicians in a neo-liberal mindset captured by transnational corporations. The mismatch between the strong global market-*enabling* regimes and the weak or absent global market-*restraining* regimes might also be owed to democratic preferences of citizens who lack transnational solidarity.

Finally, the mismatch could be theoretically remedied by moves in two directions: either by bringing the economy back down (on a national level) or by 'bringing up' the social and redistributive policies. The first option would require the reimposition of capital and exchange controls and a termination of free trade agreements.

---

[241] Adam Harmes, 'New constitutionalism and multilevel governance', in Gill and Cutler (eds.), *New Constitutionalism and World Order* (n. 232), pp. 143–157, pp. 148 and 156.

But despite recent postures of economic protectionism this option does not seem promising.[242] Taking trade law as an example, it has been pointed out that the dominant 'post-neo-liberal' reaction to the WTO's legitimacy crisis, namely deference to national regulation, is insufficient because it 'radically underestimates the extent to which a state's regulatory choices are already structured, constrained, and constituted by international economic forces'. The quest for preserving the members' autonomy is illusory 'precisely because such autonomy is itself illusory in contemporary conditions'.[243] In that sense, TINA ('there is no alternative') is a true statement. There is no alternative to accommodating the mobility of capital.

But this does *not* mean that the harmonisation and implementation of decent social protection are outright impossible. One reason is that, ironically, social protection has been threatened as much by the success of neo-liberal politics (resulting in cutbacks of social spending) as by neo-liberalism's failures (financial crises which led to austerity). Therefore, a renewed, more socialised neo-liberal globalism may well 'depend on the revival of robust social regimes'.[244]

The social policy development in a globalising era would have to be a double movement, in the form of both rolling back excesses of neo-liberalism and rolling out new policies of social spending, which will be characteristically experimental and uneven. For example, the UN special rapporteur on extreme poverty and human rights recently suggested a global basic income scheme.[245] Or, the legitimacy crisis of international trade law could be overcome by reformulating a legitimising collective purpose.[246] Both scholarly and political work could focus more 'on the substantive outcomes of international economic law' and overcome the current divorce of the authority to take trade policy decisions from the responsibility for their social consequences.[247] International law scholars could (and should) direct 'analytical attention to the *distribution and*

---

[242] Chang-Tai Hsieh, Nicholas Li, Ralph Ossa and Mu-Jeung Yang, 'Accounting for the new gains from trade liberalization' (2017) *University of Zurich Department of Economics: Working Paper No. 249*; Jaebin Ahn, Era Dabla-Norris, Romain Duval, Bingjie Hu and Lamin Njie, 'Reassessing the productivity gains from trade liberalization' (2016) *International Monetary Fund Working Paper No. 16/77*.

[243] Lang (n. 11), p. 344.

[244] Janine Brodie, 'New constitutionalism, neo-liberalism and social policy', in Gill and Cutler (eds.), *New Constitutionalism and World Order* (n. 232), p. 249.

[245] Human Rights Council, Report of the Special Rapporteur on Extreme Poverty and Human Rights (Philip Alston) of 22 March 2017 (UN Doc. A/HRC/35/26).

[246] Lang (n. 11), p. 347.

[247] Ibid., p. 352.

social consequences of particular legal rules and interpretative choices [in trade law], focusing on those consequences which at present remained largely unacknowledged'.[248]

Experts on social law and governance have pointed out that 'if ultra-nationalism and protectionism, as a backlash against unregulated globalization, are to be avoided, then some form of action on social protection ... is needed to complement and to "save" economic internationalization. National responses need to be supplemented with action at the transnational level to establish and safeguard social standards.'[249] Scholars have called for 'new "constitutions" of the social' and for 'a socially buffered global capitalism [which] must occur outside the timeworn boundaries of the national state'.[250] The objectives of governance would need to move 'beyond the short-term calculations of economic efficiency, quarterly profits, and capital mobility to embrace the meaning of human well-being and security in a globalizing era'.[251] A global social constitutionalism is an adequate intellectual framework for such an enterprise.

9.2 Facilitating interdisciplinary debate

The second argument in favour of analysing both the social problems of the globalised world and the social trends in international law in a constitutionalist vocabulary is the interdisciplinary connecting power of the framework of global constitutionalism. It is exactly this vocabulary which can reach out to the global distributive justice debate. Cross-border moral obligations of citizens of affluent countries to assist the poor (however distant) have been discussed already since the 1970s,[252] and a broad philosophical debate on what is now called global justice[253] sprang up. 'Global *economic* injustice' is currently the second 'most prominent global justice issue'.[254]

---

[248] Ibid. (emphasis added).

[249] Mishra (n. 17), pp. 114–115.

[250] Brodie (n. 57), pp. 12 and 24; Brodie (n. 244), p. 254.

[251] Brodie (n. 57), p. 27.

[252] Seminal: Peter Singer, 'Famine, affluence, and morality' (1972) 1 *Philosophy and Public Affairs* 229–243; Peter K. Unger, *Living High and Letting Die: Our Illusion of Innocence* (New York: Oxford University Press, 1996).

[253] The term 'global justice' was to my knowledge coined by Thomas Pogge in 'Priorities of global justice' (2001) 32 *Metaphilosophy* 6–24.

[254] Gillian Brock, 'Global justice', in Edward N. Zalta (ed.), *The Stanford Encyclopedia of Philosophy* (Winter 2016 Edition), available at https://plato.stanford.edu/archives/

While recently some legal scholars have positively engaged with the philosophers' arguments,[255] the legal and philosophical reflections on global social justice have remained basically disconnected, not the least because the two disciplines speak of different kinds of obligations (moral and legal). At this point, the vocabulary of global constitutionalism can furnish the 'missing link',[256] because its terms have both precise legal meanings and strong political and philosophical connotations. In modesty, global constitutionalism seems able to offer a common framework for an interdisciplinary discourse on global social law, social politics and social justice. At the least, legal analysis can offer a positivist answer to the philosophical core question whether (social) justice is at all conceivable beyond the nation state.[257] To the extent that legal rules exist, the answer is yes.

9.3   Overcoming regime fragmentation

The next benefit of a constitutionalist language for describing, analysing and evaluating the global social question and the related legal developments is its defragmenting effect. International legal analysis of poverty and material inequality is crucially shaped by the absence of a unified institution for addressing global economic inequalities in a comprehensive fashion. This has made international legal scholarship think about distributive justice only in a 'piecemeal manner'.[258]

Global constitutionalism can of course not provide a magic formula to glue together and to straighten out the internal contradictions and conflicts arising from the interplay of highly complex international legal regimes ranging from international trade law over foreign investment

win2016/entries/justice-global/ (ranging second after philosophical reflection on the proper use of military force).

[255] Robert Howse and Ruti Teitel, 'Global justice, poverty, and the international economic order', in Samantha Besson and John Tasioulas (eds.), *Philosophy of International Law* (Oxford: Oxford University Press, 2010), pp. 437–452; Chios Carmody, Frank J. Garcia and John Linarelli (eds.), *Global Justice and International Economic Law: Opportunities and Prospects* (New York: Cambridge University Press, 2012); Steven Ratner, *The Thin Justice of International Law: A Moral Reckoning of the Law of Nations* (Oxford: Oxford University Press, 2015); Yossi Dahan, Hanna Lerner and Faina Milman-Sivan (eds.), *Global Justice and International Labour Rights* (Cambridge: Cambridge University Press, 2016).

[256] Ratner (n. 255), p. 27. See also ibid., p. 19: 'dialogue of the (near-)deaf'.

[257] See for negative responses Thomas Nagel, 'The problem of global justice' (2005) 33 *Philosophy and Public Affairs*, 113–147; David Miller, 'National responsibility and global justice' (2008) 11 *Critical Review of International Social and Political Philosophy* 383–399.

[258] Ratner (n. 255), p. 28.

protection law to international tax law. But global constitutionalism does provide a specific lens through which to see the legal issues.

Once we postulate that the policy goals to reduce poverty and to mitigate transboundary wealth disparities are not only politics as usual but – due to their fundamental importance for realising the core mission of international law – endowed with a constitutional significance (as forming part of global constitutional law), we accept the proposition that secondary law adopted within these regimes, reform proposals and law application should always pay special attention to the impacts of any measure on poverty and inequality, and must to that end be conducted with a side view to the law produced by other international institutions, too. In a similar fashion as the concept of sustainable development, the concept of social constitutionalism might do the job of sharpening our alertness for mutual repercussions, necessary trade-offs or synergies among the rule of law and rights on the one hand and the rules and principles of development, trade and investment on the other hand.

9.4 Acknowledging the social principle as a shared constitutional heritage

The next consideration which militates in favour of highlighting the ongoing social thickening of international law as a core element of global constitutionalism and which suggests encouraging the continuation of this trajectory as part of a constitutionalist aspiration is the historical pedigree of this union. The social question has been central to the constitutionalist enterprise in many nation states.

All components of constitutionalism are interdependent and moreover depend on a minimum of material well-being and absence of gross material inequality. This connection is the deeper reason why – as legal comparison shows – many modern (post–World War II and post-1990 constitutions) in Europe and beyond refer to social objectives, social justice, social solidarity and/or social rights.[259] Of course, these constitutional provisions tell us almost nothing about the real amount of social security and justice which exists in a given state. But the proclamations manifest a global consensus that the welfare dimension is – however

---

[259] See for examples of welfare state proclamations outside Europe Art. 25 of the Constitution of Japan of 3 November 1946; Art. 1 of the Constitution of Colombia of 6 July 1991. The preamble of the Constitution of South Africa of 18 May 1996 promises to 'establish a society based on . . . social justice'. The promotion of social justice is also an explicit telos and raison d'être of the EU (see Art. 3(3) of the TEU).

defined and implemented it is in practice – a 'signet of modern statehood'.[260]

The international community is constituted first of all by states, and it is therefore governed by principles endorsed by the individual members which thus form a shared constitutional heritage. The social principle is part of this heritage. It is therefore unsurprising that analysts of the UN Millennium Declaration have proposed to incorporate the MDGs in national constitutions, thereby 'constitutionalizing the MDGs'.[261]

Naturally, the black letter law provisions in state constitutions have been predominantly understood as addressing the 'domestic' social question within nation states. However, social problems and the political and legal responses have throughout the twentieth century been to some extent influenced by factors beyond the states' confines (see Section 2). Also, the constitutional texts which express an aspiration of social solidarity and security are normally textually open. Against this background, it does not seem warranted to declare these benchmarks *a limine* inapplicable to the global social question.[262] If anything, the importance ascribed by traditional constitutionalism to the social question has grown in the era of globalisation fallouts. This warrants the analysis of that question, and of international law's responses, within a constitutionalist framing.

9.5   Mitigating Eurocentrism

A further asset of integrating the social dimension deeper into the framework of global constitutionalism is its potential to mitigate the Eurocentrism of the global constitutionalist discourse. It might be objected that the focus on social laws and policies risks to reinforce the European bias of global constitutionalism, because these measures presuppose well-financed and well-functioning bureaucracies and because in fact full-fledged welfare states exist mainly in Europe.

Although this is of course true, the de-Europeanising thrust of the idea of a global social constitutionalism lies in its cross-border focus. The objective of global social constitutionalism is not to protect, from

---

[260] Fabian Wittreck, Art. 20, in Horst Dreier, *Grundgesetz Kommentar*, 3rd ed., Vol. II (Tübingen: Mohr Siebeck, 2015), Art. 20, para. 20 (my translation).
[261] Yash Pal Ghai and Jill Cottrell, *The Millennium Declaration, Rights and Constitutions* (Oxford: Oxford University Press, 2011), p. 70.
[262] Cf. Charles R. Beitz, 'Does global inequality matter?' (2001) 32 *Metaphilosophy* 95–112, at 99.

a national perspective and within national confines, the well-being and social security of citizens of nation states. Rather, the objective of global social constitutionalism is to integrate the concern for a minimum well-being and social security of 'extraterritorial' persons into the law and decision-making processes of nation states, to the extent that the former groups are substantially affected by the latter's law-making and decision making.

Besides this fundamental cross-border orientation, the idea of a global social constitution also promotes social security within states as a universal aspiration. While the social state has been invented in Europe, its rationale is not tied to any particular cultural feature of Europe. Rather, the need for a governance of social security has emerged with industrialisation. With due caution against simplistic modernisation narratives it seems fair to say that wherever urbanisation and industrialisation (including of the agricultural sector) go on, wherever people cease to live on subsistence-based and family-owned farming, wherever the demographic composition of societies changes and wherever kin- and village-based social security practices erode or end, the need for a more formalised, 'official' social security scheme arises.[263] With the ongoing transformation of societies all over the world, having more legalised social security measures is becoming a global necessity.

Notably a basic 'social market model' as developed in Europe is similarly (even if within a different configuration of values and institutions) applied by East Asian capitalism.[264] Ramesh Mishra insists that 'the importance of this basic social market approach as a model for connecting the economic with the social cannot be overstated'.[265] To this we might add the social market model's potential to connect different cultures of the world. Integrating the social dimension into the constitutionalist discourse seems to accommodate better than a purely 'liberal' (or 'neo-liberal') constitutionalism both the living conditions and value judgments of large populations worldwide. It is thus apt to form a bridge between European and East Asian understandings of what must form part of international constitutional law.

---

[263] Krennerich (n. 104).

[264] This is 'quite different from the individualistic, hyper-liberal version associated with Anglo-Saxon economies' (Mishra (n. 17), p. 114).

[265] Ibid.

9.6   Mitigating a measure mentality

Another benefit of framing social matters as a constitutional question is its aptitude to mitigate the current 'measure mentality'. In international law and governance, a turn to indicators has taken place.[266] 'Governance by indicators'[267] means that normative objectives and aspirations are no longer mainly formulated as rules and principles but predominantly as (seemingly) objective and measurable quantitative goals and targets. The turn to indicators has begun in the area of development studies and practice, and has spilled over to human rights[268] and to the rule of law.[269] The focus on indicators is laudable to the extent that it renders operational the lofty goals and thereby helps to track noncompliance and secure accountability. On the other hand, an exclusive focus on numbers risks marginalising factors and concerns which are not quantifiable and difficult to measure.

Obsession with measurement can backfire and be exploited by critics of specific rules and principles. For example, an Asian representative in the Agenda 2030 process said that the rule of law should not obtain any place in Agenda 2030 because it is not measurable: 'Rule of law at the national level is in essence a matter of internal affairs. There is no "one size-fits-all" model for rule of law and it is hardly goal-able and properly measured.'[270]

But even within the measurement-paradigm, this objection does not fully hold. Indicators for assessing the rule of law performance have been

[266] See Jim Parsons, 'Developing clusters of indicators: an alternative approach to measuring the provision of justice' (2011) 3 *Hague Journal on the Rule of Law* 170–280.
[267] Kevin E. Davis, Angelina Fisher, Benedict Kingsbury and Sally Engle Merry (eds.), *Governance by Indicators: Global Powers through Quantification and Rankings* (Oxford: Oxford University Press, 2012).
[268] Todd Landmann and Edzia Carvalho, *Measuring Human Rights* (London: Routledge, 2010); United Nations, Office of the Human Rights Commissioner (UNHCR), *Human Rights Indicators: A Guide to Measurement and Implementation* (United Nations, 2012); Malcolm Langford and Sakiko Fikuda-Parr, 'The turn to metrics' (2012) 30 *Nordic Journal of Human Rights* 222–238.
[269] The World Justice Project Rule of Law Index measures performance using forty-four indicators across eight primary rule of law factors (World Justice Project, WJP Rule of Law Index 2016, https://worldjusticeproject.org/our-work/wjp-rule-law-index/wjp-rule-law-index-2016). See, for an assessment, Tom Ginsburg, 'Pitfalls of measuring the rule of law' (2011) 3 *Hague Journal on the Rule of Law* 269–280.
[270] Statement by Dr Endah Murniningtyas, Deputy Minister for Natural Resources and Environment of the National Development Planning Agency, Indonesia, on behalf of China, Indonesia and Kazakhstan, Eighth Meeting of the OWG on SDGs, 3–7 February 2014.

recently developed and applied by the US-based international NGO World Justice Project.[271] Whatever one thinks of the usefulness of a rule of law indicator called 'order and security', it is agreed that a total takeover of measurement and the elimination of law from the structure of governance (domestic and global) would unnecessarily empty the toolbox and undercut the ideational and transformative potential of legal norms as inspired by political and moral beliefs.[272]

The exercise of judgment about the *normative* dimension of governance and the practice of contestation and accountabilisation will be revitalised by analysing transnational social concerns not only through numbers and indicators but also in the vocabulary of law. The use of the high-key language of constitutional law is apt to bolster this approach.

9.7   Feedback loops between the social condition and constitutional institutions

The final and crucial argument in favour of framing the global social question in constitutionalist terms is its potential to explain and use productively the interaction between the social (material) situation of human beings and the quality of the governance institutions which affect their lives. Social welfare and social equality of a population are determined not only by economic growth but also by regulation of the economy, including social and labour laws and constitutional principles and procedures, co-shaped by international law and institutions. The constitutionalist perspective generally underlines the importance of institutions and also the significance of the interaction between legal institutions and the economy. While this perspective is of course not the only one doing this job, it does it well, because constitutionalism is an umbrella concept which pays attention to the interplay of the various components of a constitution (or of constitutional law).

9.7.1   The rule of law – development nexus

The interdependence between liberal constitutional principles (such as the rule of law including the protection of civil rights and democracy) and the social dimension of law and governance is often expressed in terms of rule of law and development.

---

[271]   See the World Justice Project Rule of Law Index (2016) (n. 269).
[272]   Cf. AnnJanette Rosga and Margaret L. Satterwaithe, 'The trust in indicators: measuring human rights' (2009) 27 *Berkeley Journal of International Law* 253–315, at 315.

In the UN General Assembly's 2012 Rule of Law Declaration, the UN member states declare themselves 'convinced that the rule of law and development are strongly interrelated and mutually reinforcing, that the advancement of the rule of law at the national and international levels is essential for sustained and inclusive economic realization of all human rights and fundamental freedoms, including the right to development' and 'recognize the importance of fair, stable and predictable legal frameworks for generating inclusive, sustainable and equitable development, economic growth and employment, generating investment and facilitating entrepreneurship'.[273]

The interdependence between the liberal dimension of governance (its rule of law face) and its social dimension is also brought to the fore by the UN Agenda 2030. Agenda 2030 deals with development but embraces a strong rule of law component: 'The new Agenda recognizes the need to build peaceful, just and inclusive societies that provide equal access to justice and that are based on *respect for human rights (including the right to development), on effective rule of law and good governance* at all levels and on transparent, effective and accountable institutions.'[274] This passage and the rule of law goal (Goal 16) had been controversial, one of the 'hottest topics' in the adoption process leading to Agenda 2030.[275] The outcome has been called a 'sea change'[276] in the area of law and development. Goal 16 is to 'promote peaceful and inclusive societies for sustainable development, provide access to justice for all and build effective, accountable and inclusive institutions at all levels'. More specifically, Sub-Goal 16.3 is to 'promote the rule of law at the national and international levels and ensure equal access to justice for all'. The explanation of this goal is that the adopting heads of states have acknowledged that respect for the rule of law and access to justice will help to realise the development objectives.[277] Agenda 2030 also acknowledges a positive link between development and democratic decision making by mentioning 'the essential role of national parliaments through their enactment of legislation and adoption of budgets and their role in ensuring accountability for the effective implementation of our commitments'.[278]

---

[273] UN General Assembly, Resolution 67/97 on the Rule of Law at the National and International Level of 14 December 2012 (UN Doc A 67/97), paras. 7 and 8.

[274] Agenda 2030 (n. 24), para. 35 (emphases added).

[275] Irene Khan, 'Shifting the paradigm: the rule of law and the Agenda 2030 for Sustainable Development' (2016) 7 *The World Bank Legal Review* 221–238, at 221.

[276] Ibid., at 238.

[277] See Agenda 2030 (n. 24), para. 35.

[278] Agenda 2030 (n. 24), para. 45.

The seminal scholarship which has been absorbed by policymakers is the work by Nobel Prize laureate Amartya Sen. Sen has highlighted how material (economic) factors co-determine what he calls 'capabilities'[279] and how poverty reduces freedom. In *Development as Freedom*, published in 1999, Sen placed side by side the political and the economic 'sources of un-freedom', namely 'poverty as well as tyranny, poor economic opportunities as well as systematic social deprivation, neglect of public facilities as well as intolerance or over-activity or repressive states'.[280] The other side of the coin is that political freedoms are instrumental in pushing governments to satisfy material needs:

> The rulers have the incentive to listen to what people want if they have to face the criticism and seek their support in elections. . . . Political and civil rights give people the opportunity to draw attention forcefully to general needs, and to demand appropriate public action. Government response to the acute suffering of people often depends on the pressure that is put on the government, and this is with the exercise of political rights (voting, criticising, protesting, and so on) can make a real difference.[281]

Overall, Amartya Sen and the texts adopted by the UN General Assembly rightly suppose both a positive and a negative feedback between the social and the liberal constitutional sphere. Social injustice and insecurity will undermine the liberal achievements, while concomitantly, the liberal-democratic framework is a side condition and potentially a *conditio sine qua non* for successfully tackling the social question. The foundational role of the social principle can be expressed as an *effet utile* argument: the absence of absolute poverty and also the absence of gross inequality in wealth and income are necessary to give full effect to the 'liberal' constitutional trinity (rule of law, human rights and democracy): Humans must satisfy their basic needs in order to be able to enjoy civil and political human rights and to engage as democratic citizens.

Simultaneously, the inverse relationship is believed to be at work: respect for political and civil rights and ordered and due processes can be instrumental for lifting people out of poverty and for contributing to the approximation of living conditions and material opportunities not only within states but across the globe. Put differently, civil and political human rights and democracy (the latter being in turn interlinked with

---

[279] I leave aside the specific implications of the 'capabilities' approach here. See Amartya Sen, 'Human rights and capabilities' (2005) 6 *Journal of Human Development* 151–166.
[280] Sen (n. 4), p. 3.
[281] Ibid., pp. 150–152.

and constituted by free speech, free media and free elections) function as 'developers'.

To conclude, important scholarship and recent political rhetoric at the UN level believe in a positive feedback loop and co-constitutiveness between liberties, democracy and prosperity. This co-constitutiveness warrants the inclusion of the social in the global constitutionalist programme. The global constitutionalist approach usefully directs attention to the positive feedback loop and brings the international law-based guarantees of human rights in the picture which pervade and shape the domestic constitutional guarantees.

9.7.2 The peace–social justice nexus

The importance of social stability, social security and inter-individual social equality for maintaining interstate *peace* (a genuinely international constitutional principle) has been routinely highlighted in formal international legal documents of the twentieth century. Already after World War I, the Western fear of the uprising of the proletariat and of a world revolution had been mixed with the sentiment that the 'social question' had contributed to the outbreak of the Great War. The preamble of part XIII of the Treaty of Versailles, which was the ILO Constitution, stated that 'universal peace . . . can be established only if it is based upon social justice'. The preamble went on to say that 'conditions of labour exist involving such injustice, hardship, and privation to large numbers of people as to produce unrest so great that the peace and harmony of the world are imperilled'. It then cited 'the sentiments of justice and humanity as well as . . . the desire to secure the permanent peace of the world' as the high contracting parties' motive for establishing an international organisation of labour.[282]

Along a similar vein, after World War II, the drafters of the UN Charter professed the belief that 'conditions of stability and well-being . . . are necessary for peaceful and friendly relations among nations', as Article 55, the opening article of chapter IX on 'international economic and social cooperation', formulates it. A random example of a contemporary international document acknowledging the relationship between peace and social development is the 2009 secretary general report on implementing the responsibility to protect: 'Chronic

---

[282] Preamble of the Constitution of the ILO, part XIII of the Treaty of Versailles (Treaty of Peace with Germany, signed 28 June 1919), publ. in (1919) 13 *American Journal of International Law Suppl.* 151–386.

underdevelopment does not, in and of itself, cause strains among different ethnic, religious or cultural communities. But it can exacerbate the competition for scarce resources and severely limit the capacity of the State, civil society, and regional and sub regional organisations to resolve domestic tensions peacefully and fully.'[283] Agenda 2030, too, endorses the peace–social justice nexus in the language of 'development': 'Sustainable development cannot be realized without peace and security; and peace and security will be at risk without sustainable development.'[284]

To sum up, modern international lawmakers have constantly evoked this connection and have claimed that interstate peace depends on intrastate social peace. This steady political belief of treaty makers throughout the twentieth century is borne out by the facts as will be shown.

9.7.3   Empirical findings

Research in political economy has – roughly speaking – found correlations or even mutually positive influences between economic growth on the one hand and rule of law/political freedoms/democracy on the other hand.[285] Morton Halperin and others have demonstrated 'how democracies promote prosperity'.[286] Their results confirm a prior study, published in 2000, which also found that – roughly speaking – democratic governance improves human well-being[287] and – inversely – that democracy functions better on a wealthy basis.[288]

More recent empirical research nuances the findings reported in this chapter. The correlation between a robust rule of law (measured by

[283] UN General Assembly, Report of the Secretary-General on Implementing the Responsibility to Protect of 12 January 2009 (UN Doc A/63/677), para. 43.

[284] Agenda 2030 (n. 24), para. 35 (emphases added).

[285] Janine Aron, *Growth and Institutions: A Review of the Evidence*, World Bank Research Observer (New York: Oxford University Press, 2000), pp. 99–135; Daniel Kaufmann, 'Human rights and governance: the empirical challenge', in Philip Alston and Mary Robinson, (eds.), *Human Rights and Development* (Oxford: Oxford University Press, 2005), pp. 352–402. See on the positive correlation between economic growth and judicial independence Stefan Voigt, Jerg Gutmann and Lars Peter Feld, 'Economic growth and judicial independence, a dozen years on: cross-country evidence using an updated set of indicators' (2015) 38 *European Journal of Political Economy* 197–211.

[286] Morton H. Halperin, Joseph T. Siegle and Michael M. Weinstein, *The Democracy Advantage: How Democracies Promote Prosperity and Peace*, rev. ed. (London: Routledge, 2010).

[287] Adam Przewoski, Michael Alvarez, José Antonio Cheibub and Fernando Limoni, *Democracy and Development: Political Institutions and Well-Being in the World, 1950–1990* (Cambridge: Cambridge University Press, 2000), p. 12.

[288] Ibid., pp. 269 and 273.

indicators) and economic growth (which is generally taken to signal more welfare of the population) that has been animating the rule of law–guided and human rights–driven approach to development seems to be stronger for those states which already have good institutions and are rich.[289] These differentiated findings to some extent undermine the assumption of a positive feedback loop between the liberal constitutional principles including democracy and the social dimension and suggest that a search for additional factors is needed. For example, with regard to China, it has been claimed that a specific, 'cadre' type of administration has facilitated development despite the persistence of corruption and 'bad government' in terms of the usual indicators.[290] Another new study finds 'that equality is a pivotal factor that determines whether democratic institutions have a positive and lasting effect on institutional quality'.[291]

Overall, empirical research on the links between the various elements of constitutionalism on the one hand and economic performance of societies on the other hand is ongoing and will surely be further refined. So far, the results lend support to the claim that constitutionalism should protect not only the (property) rights of the wealthier world market participants (as argued in the debate on the constitutionalisation of the WTO) but also the interests of poor members of society who mainly act as a labour force rather than as capital holders.

Integrating the social dimension into global constitutionalism aligns with the ongoing recalibration of the development discourse. Traditionally, development theory and practice have fully believed in the economic 'science'. But this focus has been rightly criticised for its neglect of the disastrous environmental consequences. Additionally, this 'science' has proven incapable of predicting or mitigating the recent financial and economic crises.[292] We therefore need a complement to

---

[289] Aslı Ozpolat, Gulsum Gunbala Guven, Ferda Nakipoglu Ozsoy and Ayse Bahar, 'Does rule of law affect economic growth positively?' (2016) 7 *Research in World Economy* 107–117; Saima Nawaz, 'Growth effects of institutions: a disaggregated analysis' (2015) 45 *Economic Modelling* 118–126, at 123.

[290] Bo Rothstein, 'The Chinese paradox of high growth and low quality of government: the cadre organization meets Max Weber' (2015) 28 *Governance: An International Journal of Policy, Administration, and Institutions* 533–548.

[291] Rainer Kotschya and Uwe Sunde, 'Democracy, inequality, and institutional quality' (2017) 91 *European Economic Review* 209–228, at 225.

[292] See critically Gilbert Rist, *The History of Development: From Western Origins to Global Faith*, 4th ed. (London: Zed Books, 2014), esp. pp. 277–280 on the 'exhaustion of the economic paradigm'. Rist however warns against any 'new development programme claiming universal validity' and would probably consider constitutionalism to be just that.

the one-sided and outworn economic paradigm. Global constitutionalism can furnish such a complement. The lens of a global *social* constitutionalism follows up on the concept of sustainable development and allows us to embrace the interconnectedness and the both positive and negative feedback loops between economic performance and the realisation of the rule of law, human rights and democracy better than the usual focus on a purely 'liberal' (or 'neo-liberal') global constitutionalism.

10 Conclusion: towards a global social constitutionalism

'There is a strong risk that when confronted with the challenge of addressing economic insecurity the human rights system will proceed in zombie mode. It will keep marching straight ahead on the path mapped out long ago, even as the lifeblood drains out of the enterprise.'[293] With these words, the current special rapporteur on extreme poverty and human rights of the UN, Philip Alston, asked for new thinking on social rights. This quest is applicable not only to international human rights law but to the entire international legal framework and to global constitutionalism as a mindset. Both international law and its scholarly analysis must respond to the global social question if they want to remain alive and relevant for contributing to an urgently needed global social settlement at a historical juncture in which the damage done by neo-liberal globalisation has become obvious.

To this end, this chapter has, first, highlighted and pulled together a number of new legal phenomena under the heading of the social. The emergence of an international anti-poverty regime, the reinvigoration of international law's concern for material inequality among individuals across countries, the rise of social rights (manifest in the human rights–based approaches to all relevant subfields of international law, in the idea of 'human development', in the social rights' actual application in constellations of financial crises, in the pressure towards their extraterritorial application and in those rights' opposability to international organisations and business) and finally new standard procedures such as social human rights due diligence and social impact assessments have all reinforced, extended and operationalised those international regimes which address the social condition of humans in a transboundary fashion (Sections 5–7). Keeping in mind that international law has always had a welfarist orientation, these trends do intensify and reinvigorate the

[293] Human Rights Council, Report (n. 245), para. 7.

social dimension of international law markedly and notably display a thrust towards the individual, including towards the 'extraterritorial' individual. So the crucial novel feature of this 'more social' international law is the leitmotiv of a *cross-border social responsibility of states* (and to a limited extent also of international organisations and business) to cater to *individuals* (Section 8).

Second, the chapter has argued that these trends towards a more social international law can be well understood, explained and assessed from the perspective of global constitutionalism (Section 9). This intellectual framework captures the extant legal trends and notably the cross-border social responsibility for individuals particularly well because constitutionalism is premised, as a post-Kantian framework, on a moral and legal *normative individualism.*[294] The idea here is that politics and law ultimately should be guided and justified by the concerns, interests and rights of individuals.[295]

The social dimension of the international legal order has been neglected in the debate on global constitutionalism which so far has focused on the trinity of rule of law, human rights and democracy. But the positive and negative feedback loops between the realisation of classical liberal goals on the one hand and the guarantee of minimally acceptable material living conditions on the other hand make it impossible to satisfy the classic constitutional quests without simultaneously addressing the social question. And in an interconnected world characterised by global flows of information and digital hyper-connectivity, global supply chains, intense global trade, foreign investment and migration, both the social question and the constitutional question have gone global in the sense that the principles, institutions and procedures developed within nation states cannot fulfil their functions without extension to international and foreign actors.

The fusion of the social and the constitutionalist programme to form an agenda of *global social constitutionalism* has the benefit of upgrading the social concern to the level of importance it deserves and is apt to rescue global constitutionalism from Eurocentrism and blindness towards the collateral damage of economic globalisation. In addition,

---

[294] Fernando Tesón, *A Philosophy of International Law* (Boulder, CO: Westview Press, 1998), p. 27; Dietmar von der Pfordten, 'Normativer Individualismus und das Recht' (2005) 60 *JuristenZeitung* 1069–1080, at 1069.

[295] That paradigm does not deny that humans live socially (i.e. in communities), that their identity is constituted in part by those communities, that persons act jointly and that they have and should have collective goals.

this conceptualisation has the merit of contributing to the defragmentation of international law and of counterbalancing a potentially one-sided focus on governance indicators. Finally, integration of the social dimension into global constitutionalism will facilitate trans-disciplinary connections by bridging the intellectual gap between the legal framework and discourse on the one hand and the philosophical debate on global justice on the other hand.

The recent emergence of the 'more social' international law which espouses a cross-border responsibility for individuals does not comprise the establishment of central institutions comparable to welfare state bureaucracies. No universal agency of social affairs with an own budget and enforcement powers exists. The UN Economic and Social Council (ECOSOC; chapter X of the UN Charter, Articles 61–72) comes closest to such an agency but has no money to distribute. The absence of a central (democratic) lawmaker, of a central budget and of a centralised enforcement branch makes it impossible to design and implement 'Bismarckian' insurance schemes and to define and successfully levy 'Beveridgean' progressive taxes which could deploy redistributive effects and which would finance social measures ranging from schools to hospitals. So the structure of social governance remains decentralised and horizontal, with various state and non-state actors forming a network of social governance bodies. This form of governance without enforcement powers is of course typical for international law. But while rule making, rule application and to some extent also adjudication do function in a decentralised fashion, it is hard to see how such a system could ever manage money flows and contribute to redistributing money.

Moreover, even the modest unfolding of the social dimension of international law – without any global top-down scheme of redistribution – at first sight sits ill with an equally tangible backlash in other, more traditional areas of international law. Classic core jobs of international law such as preventing military conflict, guaranteeing stable territorial boundaries and providing for interstate dispute settlement are currently badly fulfilled. This seeming dissonance between open critique amounting to noncompliance in the areas of international military security and territorial issues on the one hand and heightened demands for international social rules on the other hand is no real internal contradiction. The quest for social rules reacts to production, trade and labour conditions which are heavily affected by ongoing economic globalisation. The symbolic topics such as sovereignty and non-intervention, motivating, e.g., national resistance against the prosecution of high politicians before the International Criminal Court, are merely verbally detached from economic interdependence by the political discussants. In reality, populist rhetorics insisting on state sovereignty, on territorial integrity and on national identity are a typical reaction to the anxiety (of governments and their voters alike) caused by economic globalisation. For this reason, the coexistence of social reinforcement with political backlash may even be unexceptional.

In fact, the historical experience is that international social rules have thrived in periods in which progress in the field of 'high politics' was limited. For example, the League of Nations' social politics was successful independently of the organisation's failure in guaranteeing world peace.[296] The current political and economic constellation might even be conducive to the further development of a global social order, because the imbalance between the strong international regimes protecting property (WTO and investment treaties) and the relative weakness of international regimes on human rights, labour and environment has become more visible than ever.[297] It is therefore possible that, against the background of massive critique of neo-liberalism, the trend of reinforcing the social dimension of international law will continue.

The ongoing socialisation of international law and its framing within a global social constitutionalism as proposed here are purely incremental and reformist approaches and lack a revolutionary impetus. Some sceptics will deplore this as a deflection from the necessity – felt by many – both to attack the basic structures of capitalism and to call into question the extant international economic order as a whole. Radical critics point out that the 'root causes'[298] of underdevelopment lie elsewhere than what the World Bank reports suggest, that poverty is being 'created'[299] by interested international actors and that material inequality is not the result of adverse circumstances and bad domestic politics but a 'planned misery'.[300] From this standpoint, deprivation is planned and perpetuated

---

[296] Patricia Clavin and Jens-Wilhelm Wessel, 'Transnationalism and the League of Nations: understanding the work of its economic and financial organisation' (2005) 14 *Contemporary European History* 465–492. See for the key contemporary document Société des Nations, *Le développement de la collaboration internationale dans le domaine économique et social* ('Bruce Report') of 22 August 1939 (LoN Doc. No. A.23.1939).

[297] See the discussion on 'new constitutionalism' in Section 9.1 (pp. 331–334).

[298] Susan Marks, 'Human rights and root causes' (2011) 74 *Modern Law Review* 57–78.

[299] Jason Beckett, 'Creating poverty', in Orford and Hofmann (eds.) (n. 42), pp. 985–1010.

[300] Rodolfo Walsh, a legendary investigative journalist, thus qualified the application of 'Chicago School neo-liberalism' by the Argentinian military government, as recounted in Naomi Klein, *The Shock Doctrine: The Rise of Disaster Capitalism* (London: Penguin,

by the powerful designers and exploiters of international law (politicians in the affluent states in collusion with global capital). This boils down to the perspective that international law is not more than the superstructure of the global material conditions of production.[301] From this standpoint, any attempt to 'socialise' a fundamentally liberal international order is insufficient and counterproductive because it will perpetuate fundamental global social injustice.

I concede to this critique that the reformist, 'more social' constitutionalism carries a risk of realising two evils at once, namely to scale down social rights from individual entitlements into structural norms *and* to deflect from the root causes of social misery by individualising social problems and neglecting the macroeconomic and macro-political analysis. However, we should also remember that both international legal experiments on the governance of the global social question at the extreme ends of the political spectrum have not fared well. Neither the basically human rights–free NIEO of the 1970s[302] nor the neo-liberalism of the 1990s have contributed much to global social justice. Against this historical experience, a reform strategy with international social rights (notably the right not to live in abject poverty) as its centrepiece is worth trying.

To conclude, global constitutionalism should move further towards embracing the social dimension. This can and should be done – analytically – by acknowledging that the extant bits and pieces of international social law already do form part of the body of international constitutional law and – normatively – by developing legal arguments, processes and strategies to strengthen the social aspiration, as a matter of constitutional justice. The study of inter- and transnational social law standards and entitlements through the lens of global constitutionalism conveys the added value of cross-fertilisation and interaction with the liberal constitutional principles and thus works against playing those dimensions out against each other in a false competition. The traditional trinity of global constitutionalism can and should be extended to cover a fourth aspect, a social limb.

2007), pp. 95–96. Marks (n. 298) at 75 considers global capitalism as a 'planned misery' 'that belongs with the logic of particular socio-economic arrangements'.

[301] B. S. Chimni, 'Marxism and international law: a contemporary analysis' (1999) 34 *Economic and Political Weekly* 337–349; China Miéville, *Between Equal Rights: A Marxist Theory of International Law* (Leiden: Brill, 2005).

[302] See n. 43.

10

Development Issues in the Discourse of Global Constitutionalism

HYUCK-SOO YOO

If it is true that not only peace, but also prosperity, is indivisible, then one can understand that, with regard to welfare provisions, a law is needed which proceeds from the conception of 'one world'. . . . The international community is not merely one of peace; it must needs be a welfare community, concerned with the welfare of any one of its members. The world community is bound to become a welfare community, just as the nation state became a welfare state.

Bernard V. A. Röling, *International Law in an Expanded World* (Amsterdam: Djambatan N.V., 1960), pp. IX, 83

1 Introduction: development issues and global constitutionalism

According to World Bank estimates, 10.7 per cent of the world's population in 2013 lived on less than US$1.90 a day, down from 35 per cent in 1990. Nearly 1.1 billion people have escaped extreme poverty since 1990. In 2013, 767 million people lived on less than US$1.90 a day, down from 1.85 billion in 1990. The recent reduction in extreme poverty has been mainly driven by East Asia and the Pacific (71 million fewer poor) – notably China and Indonesia – and South Asia (37 million fewer poor) – notably India.[1] In contrast, global inequality – the inequality among all citizens worldwide, regardless of country of residence – has increased from the Industrial Revolution through the 1980s. It is wider today than it was in the 1820s. In particular, the share of income going to the top 1 per cent has increased in many countries for which information is available. Inequality remains unacceptably high.[2]

---

[1] World Bank Group, Understanding Poverty, http://www.worldbank.org/en/topic/poverty/overview#1.
[2] World Bank Group, Taking on Equality, 2016, https://openknowledge.worldbank.org/bitstream/handle/10986/25078/9781464809583.pdf#page=89.

To eliminate, or even to reduce, poverty and inequality between countries and among citizens worldwide would be a tremendous challenge for international society.[3] These goals are part of an international development agenda that has been one of the topical issues in the international community. Since this and like problems are a matter not only of the achievement of economic growth but also of (re)distribution and welfare, the agenda is concerned with justice, especially distributive justice. The agenda also needs to be dealt with centrally and effectively and with a strong feeling of solidarity among peoples of the whole world, especially in developed countries.[4] In international society, however, there is no central government or even effective global governance and only very weak solidarity among the world's peoples.

How has the discourse of global constitutionalism addressed poverty and inequality among countries and peoples together with international development issues? Do global constitutionalism's shared principles and values include the correction of the big gap between haves and have-nots in international society?

According to Anne Peters, global constitutionalism is both descriptive and normative as an intellectual framework. Global constitutionalism first redescribes (reconstructs) some features and functions of international law as forming constitutional bits and pieces, as fulfilling constitutionalist functions and as reflecting constitutionalist principles.[5] Oliver Diggelmann and Tilmann Altwicker argue that the debate on global constitutionalism should be seen as an attempt to contribute to reshaping the international reality by changing our knowledge of the international world.[6] If so, to what extent can we, having a new epistemological standpoint and understanding, reconstruct some international legal

---

[3] In this chapter, 'international society' denotes a society of states based on the definition of Hedley Bull, *The Anarchical Society: A Study of Order in World Politics*, 2nd ed. (West Sussex: Columbia University Press; New York, Chichester, 1995), p. 13. 'International community' denotes an international society in which 'there exists a more or less extended set of common interests of international society or of humankind'. Christian Tomuschat, 'International law: ensuring the survival of mankind on the eve of a new century' (1999) 281 *Recueil des Cours* 9–438, at 78.

[4] The usefulness of the dichotomy of developed/developing countries as an analytical concept has almost vanished today, and we use these terms interchangeably with affluent/poor countries. (Further see later in the chapter.)

[5] Anne Peters, 'What about "global constitutionalism": crisis or consolidation?', lecture at Waseda University, 14 October 2016 (on file with the author).

[6] Oliver Diggelmann and Tilmann Altwicker, 'Is there something like a constitution of international law? A critical analysis of the debate on world constitutionalism' (2008) 63–3 *ZaöRV* 650.

features and functions to improve an underdeveloped and miserable situation in developing countries and a structural gap in the economies of developed countries?

The global constitutionalist discourse suggests that certain basic values (rule of law, human rights and democracy, maybe free trade[7]) have acquired universal acceptance, as manifested in the ratification of relevant multilateral treaties.[8] Three more constitutional principles were added in the twentieth century: welfare, social security and ecological sustainability.[9] Global constitutionalism is said to be more than a mere claim that a political order or system is 'constituted'. Constitutionalisation, as a process inspired by constitutionalist thought, entails something other than legalisation. A constitutional order also needs to be legitimate.[10]

This chapter will discuss how the discourse of global constitutionalism addresses and embraces the issue of international development. It comprises four sections including this introduction. Section 2 gives a brief review of the issue in international society from 1945 to today. Section 3 considers how the discourse of global constitutionalism has dealt with the issue of development and the problems of inequalities, poverty and (re)distribution among countries and peoples in the world. Finally, the chapter will offer some prospects and a conclusion about international development discourse in the international community as a whole.

2   A short history of the development question in international society after World War II

The concept of development, as currently construed, is essentially a post–World War II phenomenon.[11] The emergence of the issue of international development was above all due to American hegemony. The concept and paradigm of international development have been, however, changed many times, with changes of idea, objective and practice.

---

[7] Jan Klabbers, 'Setting the scene', in Jan Klabbers, Anne Peters and Geir Ulfstein (eds.), *The Constitutionalization of International Law* (Oxford: Oxford University Press, 2009), pp. 16, 26; Erika de Wet, 'The international constitutional order' (2006) 55 *International and Comparative Law Quarterly* 51–76, at 62.

[8] Klabbers, 'Setting the scene' (n. 7), p. 16. Rule of law, human rights and democracy are what Mattias Kumm calls the trinity of contemporary principles of constitutionalism.

[9] Peters (n. 5).

[10] Klabbers, 'Setting the scene' (n. 7), p. 43.

[11] Ruth E. Gordon and Jon H. Sylvester, 'Deconstructing development' (2004) 22 *Wisconsin International Law Journal* 1–98, at 9.

When we consider development issues in international relations since 1945, two periods before and after the 1980s should be variously differentiated. The 1980s, the 'lost decade for development', was a significant turning point in the history of international development. We will describe this history in three phases, according to the dominant economic idea, concept of development and weight of external and internal dimension of development. The first phase was the 'era of development' (1945–1970s), after intervened the 'lost decade for development' (1980–1990); the second was the neo-liberalism period (1980s–1990s); and the third has been the post-neo-liberalism period (2000s–).

2.1   First phase: the 'era of development' (1945–1970s)

2.1.1   Two specific historical conditions of the 'era of development'

The period from World War II to the 1970s, called the 'era of development', is the product of a couple of specific historical conditions in international relations after 1945. The one is *Pax Americana*; the other is the linkage between the Cold War and the North–South divide.

According to David Williams,[12] international development emerged as a mechanism for global ordering in an era when the legitimacy of colonial rule was declining. It provided a means for trying to shape, manage and control social, economic and political processes in an era of formal sovereignty. US President Truman's inaugural address on 20 January 1949 opened a new 'era of development'.

> We must embark on a bold new program for making the benefits of our scientific advances and industrial progress available for the improvement and growth of *underdeveloped* areas. The old imperialism – exploitation for foreign profit – has no place in our plans. What we envisage is a program of development based on the concepts of democratic fair dealing. (emphasis added) (https://trumanlibrary.org/whistlestop/50yr_archive/inagural20jan1949.htm)

From his address, we can infer two aspects of development issues. First, Truman created the 'underdeveloped world', and 'development' meant to

---

[12] David Williams, 'Development, intervention, and international order' (2013) 39 *Review of International Studies* 1213–1231, at 1215.

escape from the undignified condition of 'underdevelopment'.[13] Second, from then on a new game had started to be followed, a pursuit of the stage that 'the others' had succeeded in reaching – the unilinear model of 'development'.

At the same time, international development was a weapon in the Cold War. Many US policymakers thought that the lack of development in Third World countries would provide a breeding ground for communism. Indeed, foreign aid and other forms of assistance were explicitly used in the fight against communism. The subtitle of W. Rustow's *The Stages of Economic Growth*, which introduced the very important concept of 'take-off' for development, was 'a non-communist manifesto'.[14]

The Cold War competition between the United States and USSR symbolised the linkage between the Cold War and the North–South divide.[15] Superpower competition in foreign aid gave developing countries not only resources and protection but also bargaining power. Countries in the South took a neutral stance to the superpowers, in the 'non-alignment' movement, so that many benefited from military and financial support from one or the other, sometimes from both. The end of the Cold War meant the dissolution of the linkage between the Cold War and North–South divide, especially the disappearance of benefits from superpower competition.

2.1.1.1 The concept of development as economic growth based on embedded liberalism
This is the period when 'the embedded liberalism compromise' dominated major countries.[16] According to the compromise, every government can intervene in its own economy, following post-war multilateral regimes. Many developing countries as members of the General Agreement on Tariffs and Trade (GATT) pursued import substitution policies, protecting domestic infant industries legally. The focus was an external dimension of international development, namely the character and content of the international economic order.

---

[13] Gustavo Esteva, 'Development', in Wolfgang Sachs (ed.), *The Development Dictionary: A Guide to Knowledge as Power* (London: Zed Books Ltd., 2007), pp. 6–7.

[14] Walt W. Rostow, *The Stages of Economic Growth: A Non-Communist Manifesto*, 2nd ed. (Cambridge: Cambridge University Press, 1971).

[15] Mitsuru Yamamoto, 'Reisen Shuketsu to Nambokumondai no Saiteigi' (The end of Cold War and redefinition of North–South divide) (1993) 400 *Kokusai Mondai* 45–57.

[16] John Gerard Ruggie, 'International regimes, transactions, and change: embedded liberalism in the postwar economic order', in Stephen D. Krasner (ed.), *International Regimes* (Ithaca, NY: Cornell University Press, 1983), p. 209.

In the 1950s and 1960s, development primarily meant 'a rise in the levels of living of the common people', and it was often equated with economic growth.[17] The main strands in the thinking about development economics emphasised capital formation as the most important factor, sought to correct this emphasis by stressing the importance of human capital later and revived interest in trade as the engine of growth.[18] Central to all development theories was the belief that the Third World should follow in the West's footsteps. Development began as a quest for 'modernity', and all societies purportedly pass through distinct phases as they modernise. As Rostow's five stages development theory explains, all societies traverse the fixed and unilinear path. 'Development means "modernisation".'[19] Perhaps another part of its appeal was its apparent optimism, for it represents a belief in 'progress'.[20]

2.1.1.2 The challenge of NIEO and its failure
Under favourable historical conditions, developing countries had challenged the existing international economic order and sought to reshape international law. During the 1960s, developing countries grew dissatisfied with the working of the international economic system in general and of international trade rules in particular. The existing economic order appeared to work well for the developed countries but poorly for the developing countries. A New International Economic Order (NIEO) and 'international development law' as a new discipline were advocated by mainly French scholars of international law during the 1960s and 1970s.[21]

The NIEO agenda, as articulated in the Charter of the Rights and Duties of States, included subjecting private foreign capital to the domestic laws of Third World host countries, full and effective participation in world governance, special trade preferences, stabilising export prices for commodities exported by Southern countries, debt forgiveness or rescheduling, as well as technology transfer. The Charter also recognised explicitly the sovereign right to nationalise foreign property and to

[17] Heinz W. Arndt, *Economic Development: The History of an Idea* (Chicago, IL: University of Chicago Press, 1987) pp. 50–51.
[18] Ibid., pp. 54–87.
[19] David Kennedy, 'The "rule of law", political choices, and development common sense', in David Trubek and Alvaro Santos (eds.), *New Law and Economic Development: A Critical Approach* (New York: Cambridge University Press, 2006), p. 98.
[20] Gordon and Sylvester (n. 11), at 15–17.
[21] The pioneer work is Michel Virally, 'Vers un droit international du developpement' (1965) *Annuaire Français de Droit International* 3–12; Maurice Flory, *Droit international du development* (Paris: PUF, 1977).

determine what compensation should be paid, and it confirmed the right of host governments to supervise transnational corporations operating within their jurisdictions. The Charter further mandated that industrialised countries cooperate to improve the living standards and general welfare in developing countries.[22]

As a matter of normative status, the general acceptance by the international community of the principle of permanent sovereignty over natural resources (PSNR) was almost the only success of developing countries in shaping the changing rules of the international order. It might be an example of the 'law of protection', as Röling noted.[23] The preamble of UNGA Resolution 1803 (XVII) deems PSNR a basic constituent of the right to self-determination; all states have the inalienable right to freely dispose of their natural wealth and resources in accordance with their national interests. PSNR was motivated by developing states' concern that the orthodox international law on foreign investment undermined the effective exercise of their economic sovereignty by favouring the interests of capital-exporting states and corporations and by enabling those foreign actors to constrain host government policy options.[24]

The failure to establish a NIEO has been attributed in part to developing countries' failure to present a unified platform and an agreed set of concrete objectives. The central reason was the fact that industrialised states did not want any such thing. They were unwilling to enter into genuine global negotiations and were then, as now, unwilling to see rules created that did not serve their economic interests well, especially when these rules were to be consolidated into an obligation to assist developing countries and peoples.[25]

2.1.2 Second phase: neo-liberalism period (1980s–1990s)

2.1.2.1 The Third World debt crisis and the 'lost decade' for 'development' (1980–1990) The change of world political and economic structure in the 1980s had serious consequences for North–South relations. The 1980s are often termed the 'lost decade' for developing countries.

---

[22] The Charter of Rights and Duties of States, GA Res. 3281(xxix), UN GAOR, 29th Sess., Supp. No. 31 (1974) 50.

[23] Bernard V. A. Röling, *International Law in an Expanded World* (Amsterdam: Djambatan N.V., 1960), p. 63.

[24] Margot E. Solomon, 'From NIEO to now and the unfinishable story of economic justice' (2013) 62 *International and Comparative Law Quarterly* 31–54, at 39.

[25] Ibid., at 46.

Diverse structural factors were behind this shift.[26] Chief among them was the Third World debt crisis. Most analysts trace the roots of the Third World debt crisis to the oil shock of the early and mid-1970s, when sharply rising oil prices simultaneously impoverished oil-importing Third World countries and flooded international financial markets with oil profits in need of investment.[27] 'Petro-dollars' also flowed into poor, often politically unstable Third World countries. As interest rates rose thereafter, Third World countries that were unable to raise sufficient export revenues acquired huge debts.

The Third World debt crisis in the 1980s also led the International Monetary Fund (IMF) and World Bank to strengthen their position and power vis-à-vis the Third World. Most IMF activity was directed towards industrialised nations until the oil crisis in the early 1970s. As newly established Euro-Markets were flooded with 'petro-dollars', creditworthy industrialised states avoided the IMF and ran to Euro-Markets. The IMF found itself lending almost exclusively to Third World countries. By the mid-1980s, the World Bank had also begun to grant loans to developing countries for adjustment purposes. Both the IMF and World Bank lending have always been conditional on the debtor nation's promise to correct inappropriate public policies.[28]

During the 'lost decade', the Third World countries lost their unity as a block with the common purpose of fighting against countries in the North and divided into subgroups, namely rich oil-producing countries, advanced developing countries with newly industrialised economies (NIEs), least developed countries (LDCs) and the rest of developing countries. Diversification of strategy and particularisation of interests of the Third World countries decreased Southern countries' solidarity as a historical group with shared colonial experience and economic backwardness. One may say that the Third World as a political expression and the developing country as an economic expression have lost their substantial meanings.[29]

2.1.2.2   From embedded liberalism to neo-liberalism   The post-war consensus known as 'the compromise of embedded liberalism' was swept away by a new set of economic ideas about development.

---

[26] Hyuck-Soo Yoo, 'WTO to Tojokoku: Tojokoku no "taiseinaika" no keii to igi (tyu)' (The WTO and developing countries: the history and meaning of integration of developing countries in the WTO regime (2)) (1998) *Boeki to Kanzei* 64–87, at 79.

[27] Gordon and Sylvester (n. 11), at 39.

[28] Kennedy (n. 19), p. 130.

[29] Yoo (n. 26), at 75.

These ideas came to be termed 'neo-liberalism' between the mid-1970s and mid-1980s. The 1990s brought the collapse of the Soviet Union and the end of the Cold War, making neo-liberalism hegemonic as a mode of development policy discourse.[30] The 'Washington Consensus' became the new orthodoxy.

The basics of neo-liberal development policy are well known.[31] Within economics, the lead passed 'from macroeconomics to microeconomics'. An economy is no longer imagined primarily as an input-output production cycle to manage the relationship among economic aggregates; it is now an imagined 'market' in which individual economic actors transact with one another, responding to price signals and thereby allocating resources to their most productive use. Government is there less to manage the economy than to support the market. 'Getting distribution right' has been displaced by 'getting prices right'. The neo-liberal economics do not differentiate between countries in terms of economic development. At the same time, the development policy agenda at the international level shifted away from the United Nations to the IMF, GATT and World Bank.

2.1.2.3 Integration of developing countries in LIEO ('Taiseinaika')
The arrival of the era of neo-liberalism resulted in the integration of the South in the neo-liberal international economic order dominated by the North, led by the United States.[32] Neo-liberal economists often explicitly rejected the claim that the economic conditions of developing countries required a different kind of economics.[33] Developing countries could no longer but follow liberal prescriptions to develop their economy.

From then on, they were to give up some discretion that they had enjoyed during the 'era of development'. There was a consensus under embedded liberalism about modest government intervention in the

---

[30] 'Neo-liberalism' is defined as 'a theory of political economic practices that proposes that human well-being can be best advanced by liberating individual entrepreneurial freedoms and skills within an institutional framework characterized by strong private property rights, free markets, and free trade'. David Harvey, *A Brief History of Neoliberalism* (Oxford: Oxford University Press, 2005), p. 2.

[31] David Kennedy summarises this shift concisely and accurately (n. 19), pp. 129 ff.

[32] Hyuck-Soo Yoo, 'WTO to Tojokoku – Tojokoku no "taiseinaika" no keii to igi (ge-1)' (The WTO and developing countries: the history and meaning of integration of developing countries in the WTO regime (3)) (2000) *Boeki to Kanzei* 49–73, at 72 f.

[33] David Williams, *International Development and Global Politics: History, Theory and Practice* (Abingdon: Routledge, 2012), p. 112.

economy.[34] The GATT regime gave developing country members some room to use tools with trade distortion and protection measures. Almost all developing countries employed the export-led policy and import substitution policy to protect their infant industry virtually without time limits.

With the failure of the South's challenge and the triumph of neo-liberalism, the focus of development discourse shifted from the external to the internal aspect of development. Countries' underdevelopment should not be attributed to the character of the international economic order and the existing international law. Instead, the question should be asked: 'Why are other countries successes, but you are not?' Countries were told to look at their economic efficiency, the degree of political reform, good governance and so on. Development is essentially a matter of 'self-help'. The past discretion of developing members to use tools with trade distortion and protection measures was almost completely taken away or limited in the World Trade Organization (WTO) regime.[35]

2.1.3 Third phase: post-neo-liberalism period (2000s–)

2.1.3.1 The appearance of the holistic view of development During the 1990s, disappointment with neo-liberalism increased,[36] opening space for new thinking. The United Nations Development Programme (UNDP) had issued the first Human Development Report in 1990, which introduced a new approach for advancing human well-being. Human development – or the human development approach – is about expanding the richness of human life, rather than simply the richness of the economy where human beings live. 'Human development' consists of elements that directly 'enhance human abilities' (such as a long and healthy life, knowledge and a decent standard of living) and those that create 'conditions for human development' (such as participation in political and community life, environmental sustainability, human security and rights, and gender equality).

The holistic view of development triumphed and won popular support when the 1998 Nobel laureate Amartya Sen advocated 'development as freedom'. Development is 'a process of expanding the real freedoms that

---

[34] Kennedy (n. 19), p. 98.
[35] Yoo (n. 32), at 69.
[36] Peter Muchlinski, 'Multinational enterprises and international economic law: contesting regulatory agendas over the last twenty years' (2011) 21 *Nihon Kokusaikeizaiho Gakkai Nenpo* 53–92, at 67.

people enjoy'. Substantive freedom in enriching human life is the primary end and principal means of development. In particular, political freedom has the position of both a constitutive freedom and an instrumental freedom in Sen's concept of development.[37] It was why Sen had especially emphasised the virtues of democracy, which enriches citizens' lives.[38]

The focal point for development policy was increasingly provided not by economics but by ideas from literatures of political science, political economy, ethics, social theory and law. Human rights and the rule of law became substantive definitions of development. One should promote human rights, not to facilitate development, but as development. The rule of law is no longer a development tool; it is itself a development objective. Increasingly law – understood as a combination of human rights, courts, property rights, formalisation of entitlements, prosecution of corruption and public order – defined development.[39]

The holistic view, though noble in its aspirations, presents some difficulties. These are reflected in the criticism raised by Bhupinder Chimni that Sen fails to address adequately the social constraints on the realisation of the holistic goals of development ('development as freedom').[40] There are also economic constraints: in order to promote non-economic values, such as the rule of law, a society needs trained legal professionals, an efficient court system and a reliable enforcement mechanism, all of which require in turn considerable economic and technical resources. Access to a clean and safe environment and to education also require economic resources. Without economic development, which enables a developing country to secure the economic resources necessary to promote non-economic values, their effective promotion as constituent elements of development may not be realistic.[41] This explains why many places in poverty that have failed to achieve economic development have also failed to meet social development goals.

---

[37] Amartya Sen, *Development as Freedom* (Oxford: Oxford University Press,1999).
[38] Amartya Sen, 'Democracy as a universal value' (1999) 10 *Journal of Democracy* 3–17, at 10.
[39] Kennedy (n. 19), p. 157.
[40] Bhupinder Chimni, 'The Sen conception of development and contemporary international law discourse: some parallels' (2008) 1 *The Law and Development Review* 2–22.
[41] In fact, history shows that newly industrialising economies in Asia had sacrificed political freedom for fast economic development (the 'liberal trade-off').

2.1.3.2 Current dimensions of development issues in international society The paradigm of development has been shifted in three ways. First, the development dimension has shifted from the question of international economic order and external conditions of development to the question of the developing state's internal structure and policy. Second, the idea of development has changed from embedded liberalism to neoliberalism, though the latter now faces severe criticism. Third, the concept of development has been expanded from an economic to a more holistic one. The focal point for development policy has been increasingly provided less by economics alone than by ideas from literatures of political science, political economy, ethics, social theory and law.

Yong-Sik Lee suggests that the economic environment faced today by many developed countries may justify the extension of the concept of development to the developed countries that have created substantial income gaps among citizens and regions in relative economic backwardness.[42] Lee advocates a new analytical paradigm, 'given that the structural issues in the economies of developed countries today are not only cyclical economic issues that were once considered as normal and resemble the chronic problems of the developing world'.[43]

If the concept of development were extended to developed countries, its implications would be huge. Originally development meant escaping from the undignified condition called 'underdevelopment' with the assistance of the more advanced and catching up and becoming modern and developed like the West. The goal of development has been to achieve the level of industrialised countries, based on the unilinear model of evolution. New analytical approaches by Lee will force a revision of the conventional wisdom about the development paradigm.

Robert Zoellick's statements express vividly the contemporary situation of the issues of development.[44] 'Economics, in particular development economics, must broaden the scope of the questions that it

---

[42] Yong-Sik Lee, 'General theory of law and development' (2017) 50 *Cornell International Law Journal* (forthcoming) 19. Available at the Social Science Research Network (SSRN): https://ssrn.com/abstract=2951317. Mika Tsutsumi describes a collapse of the middle class and a deterioration of US society's economic situation in her bestseller series *Hinkondaikoku* (Great Poor Country) (Tokyo: Iwanami syoten, 2008).

[43] Ibid., p. 21. Chimni notes that 'in thus moving away from the "traditional" understanding of development as growth or industrialization Sen makes the concept of development relevant to advanced industrialized countries as well'. Chimni (n. 40), p. 5.

[44] Robert B. Zoellick, News & Broadcast – Democratizing Development Economics, as prepared for delivery, Georgetown University, 29 September 2010.

asks – thereby also becoming more relevant to today's challenges. It must help policymakers facing complex, multi-faceted problems.' 'The flow of knowledge is no longer North to South, West to East, rich to poor.' 'This is no longer about the Washington Consensus.' 'The record of development has shown that one size won't fit all.'

3 Global constitutionalism and development: descriptive and normative aspects

As shown, the paradigm of international development has changed since World War II, especially since the 1980s. First, the concept and contents of development have been broadened, and the coverage of subjects has been expanded. In addition, the dimension of development has been shifted from an external to an internal one. Finally, development is no longer a problem of only developing countries; it is becoming the problem of the whole world, including developed countries.

How has the discourse of global constitutionalism addressed and embraced the issues of development and the problem of inequalities, poverty and (re)distribution among countries and peoples in the world? We do not deny that global constitutionalism as the intellectual framework could be a useful heuristic tool and a carrier of a normative agenda. When we consider the problem of development in the international order through the lens of global constitutionalism, however, we should be cautious about the unique character of international development, which is different from other international legal areas.

First, the development problem is fundamentally related to the dimension of solidarity and ((re)distributive) justice, which are very weak aspects of the international legal order. Second, a core element of global constitutionalism is to check and constrain the abuse of public authority with a separation of powers[45] to limit government power and discretion. To develop successfully, however, a state and nation need not only strong and efficient government with somewhat broad discretion and competence (at least early on) but also effective global governance at the international level. Third and no less important, though the contemporary international law has been based on the state value, the holistic view of development relates to both the state value and human/individual value.[46]

---

[45] Klabbers, 'Setting the scene' (n. 7), p. 9.
[46] Bull (n. 3), chapter 4.

This section explores the possibility and limits of global constitutionalism when it addresses and embraces the development question in terms of positive and normative aspects.

3.1   The present state of international law in the area of international development: constitution-like elements in international law?

A starting point is to describe the current features of international law in the international development area. What kinds of principles and rules compose international development law? Are there any features and functions of international law in the area of international development that form constitutional bits and pieces, to the extent of constitutionalisation? Peters defines global (or international) constitutionalisation as 'the continuing process of the emergence, creation and identification of constitution-like elements in the international legal order'.[47] How much can we identify constitution-like elements in the development area of the international legal order?

3.1.1   The gap between the promising goals of development and the poor and weak positive international law in the development area

A characteristic of the normative state of international law in the area of international development is a big gap between the level of goals and objectives of development and the level of individual and concrete rules to achieve it.[48]

As the 2030 Agenda for Sustainable Development notes, it is easy to identify many international documents that declare the development and progress of developing countries as the common goals and/or objectives of the international community. The fourth trade principle for development in the Final Act and Report of the First United Nations Conference on Trade and Development (1964) advocated that 'economic development and social progress should be the common concerns of the whole international community'.[49] Article 17 of the Charter of Economic Rights

[47]   Anne Peters, 'Compensatory constitutionalism: the function and potential of fundamental international norms and structures' (2006) 19 Leiden Journal of International Law 579–610, at 582.

[48]   Takatoshi Morikawa, 'Kaihatsu kyoryoku to Kokusaiho' (Development cooperation and international law) in Takatoshi Morikawa, Tatsuhiko Ikeda and Osamu Koike (eds.), Kaihatsu kyoryoku no Ho to Seiji (Law and Politics of Development Cooperation) (Tokyo: Kokusai kyoryoku syultupankai, 2004), p. 204.

[49]   http://unctad.org/en/Docs/econf46d141vol1_en.pdf, p. 20.

and Obligations of States (1974) provides that 'international co-operation for development in [sic] the shared goal and common duty of all States'. Broadening and changing the goals and objectives, almost the same sentences have been repeated in nearly every international instrument and conference since.

In contrast, when we look for the concrete principles and rules of international law in the area of international development, we find that very few norms give rights to developing countries and impose obligations to develop countries in order to implement the goals and objectives of international development. Developed countries addressed this issue and promised repeatedly to do something for the development and progress of developing countries, and many international institutions and mechanisms for development have until now functioned for the development of the developing world. Developed countries have, however, been very cautious in yielding something to developing countries and accepting any duty to do something. We can agree that the existing international laws and mechanisms about development are not enough and that hard laws are very few. These norms and mechanisms depend usually on the benevolence and discretion of developed countries. In addition, there is still no customary law in this area. Even the concepts of sustainable development have not yet acquired the status of customary law.[50]

3.1.2 The positive international laws relating international development in the main areas

Let us look briefly at the existing international laws relating to international development in the main areas.

3.1.2.1 International trade law
Trade is the pioneering area for applying special rules in favour of developing countries. Most international legal rules apply uniformly to all countries on the principle of sovereign equality. The GATT and WTO have been also based on the principle of non-discrimination and reciprocity in relations among member countries. The principle of non-discrimination is expressed as the most-favoured-nation obligation (Article 1 of the GATT), and reciprocity is an integral part of the GATT and WTO, though not expressly stipulated anywhere in the GATT/WTO.

Since the 1960s, differential rules have been employed in the GATT. Part IV was incorporated as a soft norm in 1966. Article 36 paragraph 8

---

[50] De Wet (n. 7), at 62.

laid down a principle of non-reciprocity in negotiating the reduction of tariffs and other barriers to the trade of less developed contracting parties. The introduction in 1971 of the General System of Preferences (GSP) also prescribed differential rules in terms of deviating from the most-favoured-nation obligation. A principle of non-reciprocity, the GSP and a couple of preferential treatments (e.g. Article 18) together are said to compose a 'duality of norms'.

The GATT's differential rules were succeeded by the WTO's. The WTO agreements contain numerous provisions that accord special and differential treatment (S&DT) to developing countries and LDCs. Although the S&DT provisions in the WTO took on a more positive nature than in the GATT, those provisions' purpose is to make developing country members implement treaty obligations equally with some grace periods rather than to correct their unequal status and for them to achieve substantial equality with developed countries.[51]

3.1.2.2 Investment When developing countries had challenged the existing international economic order in the 1950s and 1960s, the top priority was the right to regulate and supervise foreign investment and transnational corporations within their jurisdiction in accordance with national laws and regulations and with national objectives and priorities. In addition, developing countries wanted to nationalise, expropriate or transfer ownership of foreign property, in which case 'appropriate compensation' should be paid by the state adopting such measures (taking account of its relevant laws and regulations as well as all circumstances that the state considers pertinent).

Indeed, the UNGA Resolution about PSNR and Article 2 of the Charter of Economic Rights and Obligations of States (1974) stipulate 'appropriate compensation' in the case of nationalisation and expropriation. However, the United States has consistently advocated the 'Hull Formula' (which provides 'full' compensation, that is, 'adequate, prompt and effective') and has reserved its position in the aforementioned resolutions. Later, developed countries launched a counter-attack and concluded many bilateral investment treaties (BITs) that include the Hull Formula. BITs amount now to more than 3,000. With the rebirth of the International Centre for Settlement of Investment Disputes (ICSID) after the 1980s, investment arbitrations have prospered and generated an investment case law system.

[51] Yoo (n. 32), p. 59.

On the one hand, the problem of compensation has been today shelved at the level of general international law; on the other hand, international investment faces a new era regulated by the huge number of BITs and the investment arbitration case law under the neo-liberalism ideology.[52]

3.1.2.3 Environment

The environment is now the area that provides the most representative consideration of the specific situation of developing countries. Differential rules in favour of developing countries are prevalent in recent multilateral environmental treaties. The most important rule concerns the concept of 'common but differentiated responsibilities'. Under it, developed country parties should take the lead and bear a greater share of the burden in combating climate change and its adverse effects.

Besides the concept of 'common but differentiated responsibilities' as a general one, three categories of differential rules in favour of developing countries can be seen in multilateral environmental treaties.[53] First, certain treaties assign more lenient substantive obligations to developing countries. (For example, the Kyoto Protocol obligates developed countries and those with economies in transition to reduce their greenhouse gas emissions but not developing countries.) Second, certain treaties require developed parties to provide financial assistance to developing countries (e.g. Article 10 of the Montreal Protocol on Substances that Deplete the Ozone Layer, Article 11(2)(b), etc.). Finally, some environmental agreements explicitly link compliance of developing countries with financial assistance by developed countries.

3.1.2.4 Right to development

The emergence of the right to development means that development and human rights have an explicit linkage to each other. Usually the right to development is said to belong to human rights of the third generation. Karel Vasek, who coined the term 'solidarity rights', included 'the right to development' among the latter.[54]

After the Declaration on the Right to Development (UNGA Resolution, 4 December 1986), many international documents called

---

[52] Hyuck-Soo Yoo, 'Kokusai Toshi ni kansuru Ho' (International investment law) (2003) 279 *Hogaku Kyositu* (*Lecture pour le futur*) 111–128.

[53] Moshe Hirsch, 'Developing countries', in Rüdiger Wolfrum (ed.), *Max Planck Encyclopedia of Public International Law*, Vol. III (Oxford: Oxford University Press, 2012), p. 75.

[54] Naomi Roht-Arriaza and Sara C. Aminzadeh, 'Solidarity rights (development, peace, environment, humanitarian assistance)', in ibid., Vol. IX, p. 279.

for the fulfilment of the right to development (Rio Declaration on Environment and Development) or reaffirmed the right to development as a universal and inalienable right and as integral to fundamental human rights (paragraph 10, the Vienna Declaration and Programme of Action 1993; Millennium Declaration 2000).

Nonetheless, the right to development per se has never been included in any binding legal instruments.[55] Many uncertainties about the right to development also remain. Who is the subject of the right – individuals or states? What is the right to development – an inalienable right and integral to fundamental human rights or the bundle of human rights to development? Finally, though the legal character of the right to development has been debated, claiming that the right to development is already a human right as positive law is difficult.[56]

In sum, a couple of principles and rules of international law exist concerning international development. There also exists some uncertainty, and almost all of these principles and rules are soft law, even when they bestow benefits on developing countries and impose duties on developed countries.

3.1.3 Can we redescribe existing international law of development as forming constitutional bits and pieces?

Given the present state of the international law of development as described, to what extent can we identify international principles and rules as constitutionalist elements? Or how can global constitutionalism redescribe and reconstruct some features and functions of international law in the area of development to form constitutional bits and pieces?

In the 1960s and 1970s, the 'international development law' discipline advocated by French scholars tried to 'reread' the whole corpus of international law in the light of development goals. The scholars dealt with a new legal reality, namely economic inequality among states and a deficient independence of developing countries in international society.[57] Traditional international law was based on the principle of the formal sovereign equality of states, whose relations were governed by

---

[55] Ibid., p. 280.

[56] Alhagi Marong, 'Development, right to, international protection', in Wolfrum (ed.) (n. 53), Vol. III, p. 88.

[57] Peter Slinn, 'Differing approaches to the relationship between international law and the law of development', in Francis G. Snyder and Peter Slinn (eds.), *International Law of Development: Comparative Perspectives* (Abingdon: Professional Books, 1987), p. 28.

strict reciprocity and consent. The 'rereading' of the traditional principle of sovereign equality has been successful in establishing the principle of positive discrimination in favour of developing states.[58] 'The notion of compensatory inequality' and 'the principle of differentiation (duality of norms)' are exemplars of positive discrimination.

International development law as an academic discipline has declined rapidly since the 1980s, with the defeat of the NIEO and the victory of neo-liberalism. Although it introduced the economic factor and level of development into the legal analysis and evaluation of interstate relations,[59] the aim of 'international development law' must be more daring and involve a deeper and more radical transformation than a revision or an adjustment of existing rules. The role thereby of differential rules in the GATT/WTO has changed from correcting unequal status of developing country members and finally achieving substantial equality with developed countries towards allowing them to implement treaty obligations equally with some grace periods.

Can global constitutionalism therefore redescribe and reconstruct international law in the area of development and provide international principles and rules as constitutionalist elements? Another reason for the failure of international development law is said to be its emphasis on territorial sovereignty of developing countries and its ignoring the role of people in developing countries as the final stakeholder of development.[60] It is therefore possible that the global constitutionalism approach could complement the weakness of the international development law discipline and contribute to the improvement of the discourse about the normative state of international development.

Peters offers a couple of examples of redescribing existing international law. She suggests that from the constitutionalist perspective, sovereignty will be redescribed as 'popular sovereignty' and as responsibility, placing humans, not states, at the centre of the international order. In addition, while the traditional focus on 'diplomatic' negotiations as a mode of law-making paid no attention to the involvement of the public,

---

[58] Flory emphasises that the 'International Law of Development is not neutral in content, since it implies purposiveness and even a result'. Maurice Flory, 'A north-south legal dialogue: the International Law of Development', in ibid., p. 11.

[59] Ahmed Mahiou, 'Development, international law of', in Wolfrum (ed.) (n. 53), Vol. III, p. 81.

[60] Satoshi Kotera, 'Kaihatsu no Kokusaiho no Yukue: Aratana "Shin Kokusai Keizai Chitsujo" he Mukete' (The future of international law of development: toward a new 'New International Economic Order') (2014) 120 *Hogakusinpo* (Chuo Law Review) 261–290, at 275.

a constitutionalist perspective, using terms such as 'participation' and 'transparency', allows us to see a problem here. Finally, the international human rights covenants can be qualified not merely as international treaties but as constitutional instruments that reinforce constitutional constraints on states.[61]

In the general course of 1999,[62] Tomuschat suggests that the international legal order had entered a third stage in which international law provides a comprehensive blueprint for social life. International law intrudes into matters previously shielded from outside interference. Human rights, democracy and good governance are depicted as three main developments in this stage. Central concepts of good governance are accountability, transparency and the rule of law. The constitutionalist 'trinity' (human rights, rule of law and democracy[63]) coincides exactly with Tomuschat's proposition. In that sense, Peters's redescription can reinforce and complement the internal governance of developing countries, in terms of the administration of development.[64]

We can now identify not only conventional principles and rules of international development (such as differential rules, sustainable development, common but differentiated responsibility) but also new principles (such as rule of law, good governance, democratic accountability). Global constitutionalism scholars use these principles and rules as constitutionalist elements in the international dimension of the world as well as in the internal dimension of states.

3.1.4   Can it be a thick version of the 'constitutional order'?

Like the international development law discipline, global constitutionalism can be a heuristic tool and an attractive intellectual framework to identify shortcomings of international law, and it can be the carrier of a normative agenda.[65] Its redescription and reconstruction have nonetheless their own limitations. The decisive reason that the demand of the NIEO and the international development law discipline that it engendered had failed is that developed countries did not want the

---

[61] Peters (n. 47), at 2.
[62] Tomuschat (n. 3), at 63.
[63] Anne Peters, 'Global constitutionalism: crisis or consolidation?', Waseda University Open Lecture Series No. 7 (2016), p. 5.
[64] Sen defines development as freedom and democracy as a universal value, and he emphasises the *constructive* role of democracy in the formation of values and in the understanding of needs, rights and duties. Sen (n. 38), at 3.
[65] Anne Peters has especially emphasised this. 'The merits of global constitutionalism' (2009) 16 *Indiana Journal of Global Legal Studies* 397–411, at 405.

NIEO.[66] Developed countries still do not want to change the present international economic order based on neo-liberal ideology, regardless of many criticisms from various sides. If we want to change the present situation, we need a constitutional order for the international community in a strong sense instead of a bundle of principles and institutions comprised together.[67] De Wet envisages a 'constitutional order' in which 'the different national, regional and functional (sectoral) constitutional regimes form the building blocks of international community ("international polity") that is underpinned by a core value system common to all communities and embedded in a variety of legal structures for its enforcement'.[68] If we imagine such a constitutional order from the viewpoint of international development, it must be a community in which every member considers distributive justice as a core value and is obliged to cooperate to achieve it, based on the strong feeling of solidarity.[69]

According to Bull, distributive justice comes about by the decision of the whole society in view of its common good or interest. However, world politics in the present era is principally a process of conflict and cooperation among states having only the most rudimentary sense of the common good of the world as a whole, and the dominant idea is of 'commutative' rather than 'distributive' justice. In addition, today's international order, which is mainly based on the idea of interstate justice, is quite inhospitable to projects of the realisation of 'cosmopolitan or human justice'.[70] As Crawford explains, classical international law's relationship to distributive justice was indirect, if it existed at all. This law was primarily concerned with allocating territory, power and rights. An ostensible example of distributive justice was the rights accorded to landlocked and 'geographically disadvantaged' states under the law of the sea; in practice, these did not amount to

---

[66] Solomon (n. 24), at 46. Also see Ha-Joon Chang, *Kicking Away the Ladder: Development Strategy in Historical Perspective* (London: Anthem Press, 2002).

[67] Klabbers argues that there is more to constitutionalism and constitutionalisation than merely the claim that a political order or system is somehow 'constituted'. Klabbers, 'Setting the scene' (n. 7), p. 8.

[68] De Wet (n. 7), at 53.

[69] Klabbers notes that 'the international community might be a precondition or, on the contrary, the result of the constitutionalization of the international legal order'. Klabbers, 'Setting the scene' (n. 7), p. 153.

[70] Bull (n. 3), p. 80. Governments, he says, enter into a 'conspiracy of silence' to give priority to the coexistence between them rather than to the rights and duties of their respective citizens.

much.[71] Alston notes correctly that the question of international distributive justice 'seems to be curious anathema to the vast majority of
international law scholars and practitioners'.[72]

Global constitutionalism scholars presuppose that the international
community is a legal community or that the constitutionalisation of the
international legal order will lead to it being so. It is not evident, however,
in what way justice is addressed in the discourse of global constitutionalism. Klabbers et al. argue their purpose is not to find a way of guaranteeing global justice.[73] In his general course, Tomuschat recognises some
values as universal, as a thick version of constitutionalism, but distributive justice is not among them.[74] Peters addresses solidarity in the context
of democracy, though not distributive justice directly. She argues that
solidarity between states as a legal principle forms part of the global
constitutional order. Further, global solidarity as a form of social reaction
to social inequality and as a precondition of democratic mechanisms is,
and will remain, thin.[75] Peters states that while 'an international principle
of solidarity is arguably inherent in some regimes', 'solidarity is no
overarching general legal principle from which concrete legal obligations
could be deduced'.[76] Campanelli adds that solidarity seems inherent in
specific contexts of international law, such as sustainable development,
humanitarian assistance and human rights.[77]

Although solidarity is one of the most interesting testaments to the
transformation of international law into 'a value based international legal
order',[78] the constitutionalisation of the international legal order is still
ongoing. We should note that unfortunately little constitutionalisation in

[71] James Crawford, *Chance, Order, Change: The Course of International Law, General Course on Public International Law* (The Hague: Brill, 2014), p. 469.
[72] Philip Alston, 'Remarks on Professor B.S. Chimni's a just world under law: a view from the south' (2007) 22 *American University International Law Review* 221–236, at 230 (cited by Chimni (n. 40), at 18). Chimni states that mainstream international law scholars do not seriously engage with the idea of global justice. The creation of a just world is not seen as the task of international law. In the absence of some form of global sovereignty, the Rawlsian principles of justice and any other theory of distributive justice that anticipate some form of a global state are not applicable.
[73] Klabbers, 'Setting the scene' (n. 7), p. 4.
[74] Tomuschat (n. 3), at 80.
[75] Klabbers, Peters and Ulfstein (eds.), *The Constitutionalization of International Law* (n. 7), pp. 311. Peters maintains that if there is potential for global solidarity, it is in quality no different from national solidarity.
[76] Ibid.
[77] Danio Campanelli, 'Solidarity, principle of', in Wolfrum (ed.) (n. 53), Vol. IX, p. 291.
[78] Ibid.

the areas of inequality, reduction of poverty and development has been achieved to date. International law has proven incapable of being a starting place for reordering the international economic system and for sharing economic power with the Third World.[79] Peters argues that the 'international legal order is in the process of shifting from an order based on "Westphalian sovereignty" to a "hybrid" or "dualistic" world order, based on (modified) state sovereignty and the autonomy or self-determination of the individual'.[80] However, as Crawford observes,[81] Peters might be somewhat optimistic from the perspective of international development law.

3.2 Prospect and conclusion

More than fifty years ago, Röling argued that a clear parallel can be drawn between the sociological development of the international and national communities. There has been a gradual democratisation of the legal community and an accompanying change in the aims and content of the law internationally and nationally.[82]

On the national level, the aims and content of the law have changed in roughly three stages. From a law of liberty for the powerful and wealthy individual and the formal legal equality of the nineteenth century it has changed to a law of (social) protection, which shields the weak by restricting and supplementing the law of liberty. The third stage is a law of welfare based on solidarity and fraternity, which provides for the social-economic responsibility of the state and community for all its members.

In the case of the international community, reform of the existing law, which does not offer adequate protection for the poor and weak nations, has been more difficult and has changed in a different way, due to the lack of a world legislator. After decolonisation and the abolition of European international law, an international law of protection has been sought, with national sovereignty and national independence being emphasised. Röling aptly noted that the emphasis on national sovereignty is partly a transitional phenomenon that must be experienced but that will pass.[83] The principle of PSNR is an example of an international law of protection. Röling tried to discern the direction for the welfare world community from the UN Charter

---

[79] Gordon and Sylvester (n. 11), at 71.
[80] Peters (n. 47). at 587.
[81] Crawford (n. 71), p. 451.
[82] Röling (n. 23), p. 56.
[83] Ibid., p. 77.

per se, Resolutions and Declarations, though these offer only vague and weak principles.[84]

Röling's expectation has been so far fulfilled to a very limited degree. Nonetheless, as Andrew Hurrell argues,[85] the normative structure of international society has significantly moved towards greater solidarity, and a global order has been slowly emerging. We think that though 'lingering half-formed at the edge of our field of vision',[86] international society has started to capture, name and also promote 'constitutionalisation as a sort of leitmotif'[87] slowly but surely. If we want to fulfil Röling's expectation more and to move beyond 'just a bundle of values embodied by a miscellany of rudimentary structures',[88] we should change our past paradigm of international development and the reduction of poverty and inequality.

First, it makes little sense, given a holistic notion of development that does not differentiate developed from developing countries, to think in terms of the dichotomy between traditional/classical international development law and modern/new international development law.[89] International development law as an academic discipline has completed its historical mission with the failure of NIEO and the victory of neo-liberalism. Similarly, the value of the dichotomy of developed/developing countries as an analytical concept has almost vanished today, though these expressions will be used for a while out of force of habit.[90] The issue of international development should be shifted from the development of underdeveloped areas in particular to the serious, intolerable disparity among members of the international community in general. Put another way, international development is not only about the problems of 'less

---

[84] Ibid., pp. 87.

[85] Andrew Hurrell, 'Order and justice: what is at stake?', in Rosemary Foot, John Lewis Gaddis and Andrew Hurrell (eds.), Order and Justice in International Relations (Oxford: Oxford University Press, 2003) pp. 39 ff. Hurrell raises four dimensions of change.

[86] Crawford (n. 71), p. 467.

[87] Bardo Fassbender, 'The meaning of international constitutional law', in Nicholas Tsagourias (ed.), Transnational Constitutionalism (Cambridge: Cambridge University Press, 2007), p. 309.

[88] Crawford (n. 71), p. 466.

[89] Daniel D. Bradlow, 'Differing conceptions of development and the content of international development law', in Asif H. Qureshi and Xuan Gao (eds.), Volume V International Development Law (London: Routledge, 2010), p. 1; Emmanuelle Tourme-Jouannet, What Is a Fair International Society? International Law between Development and Recognition (Oxford: Hart Publishing, 2013).

[90] In fact, the dichotomy remains in international legal textbooks and documents and will be used from now on. It should be, however, emphasised that the dichotomy's value and usefulness have been substantially lost, so it is better to use more value-free distinctions, such as affluent countries, middle- and low-income countries and poor countries, in the future.

developed countries'; it is also about the problem of the big gap of development and poverty and the existence of inequality in the whole international community. From now on, international development law will be incorporated into international economic law and international social/welfare law at large.[91]

The international community and developed countries should prioritise caring for zones of turmoil in the world where innocent peoples suffer cruelly under failed states and rogue regimes. In addition, the international community should be concerned about citizens and regions of relative economic backwardness regardless of a country's degree of development. It must work to suppress the recent emergence of right-wing nationalism and xenophobia in developed countries.

Second, the excessive swing of the pendulum to the internal dimension of development should be checked. A developing country's internal governance and domestic structure and policy are, of course, very important for its development, especially economic growth. There are also a range of domestic factors, from inadequate economic policies through corruption to geography, that may help to account for the current state of inequality. Nonetheless, it does not follow from the existence of local variations that these must be the only causally relevant factors and that external factors are irrelevant.[92] Recognising a state's domestic duties to address poverty and development failures does not preclude a full investigation into the ways in which the international economic order and international actors can be deeply implicated in the deprivation suffered by almost half the global population.[93]

What then is a feasible alternative design of the global economic order, feasible alternative paths of globalisation under which today's imbalance among countries would have been largely avoided? A lack of space prevents me from going into more detail about imaginable global economic orders beyond making three points.

First, this order should strive to deal with structural and multifactorial causes of the gap, poverty and violence among nations and areas, based on the idea of 'structural violence' advocated by Johan Galtung.[94] Next, it

---

[91] See Anne Peters, 'Global Constitutionalism: The Social Dimension', Chapter 9 in this book.

[92] Thomas Pogge, 'Divided against itself: aspiration and reality of international law', in James Crawford and Martti Koskenniemi (eds.), *The Cambridge Companion to International Law* (Cambridge: Cambridge University Press, 2012), p. 373.

[93] Solomon (n. 24), at 32–33.

[94] Johan Galtung, 'Violence, peace and peace research' (1969) 6 *Journal of Peace Research* 167–191.

should have a couple of tools ready to help the poor. The first type of tool is to give them some policy discretion in domestic reform and to give improved market access to affluent countries. The second type is international distribution. The poor will be accorded greater opportunity to compete and greater aid in doing so.[95] The possible compatibility between economic efficiency and social justice and other human values will be accordingly enhanced in this order.[96] The third point, which is the most difficult but no less important for that, concerns the global market system. Karl Polanyi warned seventy years ago that the market system violently distorts our views of humankind and society and that these distorted views were proving a main obstacle to the solution of our civilisation's problems.[97] These include the development issue. The existing international economic order based on neo-liberalism has proven shortcomings. We cannot, however, return to the period of embedded liberalism, since globalisation is deeper today. How can the global economic order benefit from the functioning global market, and how can it reconcile market value with non-market value?

In that sense, global constitutionalism can be understood as an effort to deal with a new reality of international community and developed countries. It does, as the many criticisms attest, have its limitations as a discourse of international law, especially regarding international development. Nonetheless, it has also considerable potential to confront new reality and to solve problems of the international community of the twenty-first century. The aim of this chapter has been to complement, not criticise, global constitutionalism.

[95] Joel P. Trachtman, 'Legal aspects of a poverty agenda at the WTO: trade law and "global Apartheid"', (2003) 6 *Journal of International Economic Law* 3–21.

[96] Tourme-Jouannet proposes reforming the existing international economic order with a view to introducing a new NIEO, i.e. a legal and economic order compatible with establishing international social justice. This order is a liberal social version that is economically efficient and socially equitable. It addresses the inequitable character of the 'system', not just particular rules; it uses fairness as equity, as a general principle for creating or revising the legal norm; and it effects the ultimate transition from the old classical liberal interstate law to an international law centred on the human being. Tourme-Jouannet (n. 89), p. 85. Although we agree with the idea that international order should be economically efficient and socially equitable, we do not think that a new NIEO and new international development law are necessary.

[97] Esteva (n. 13), p. 19.

11

A New Idea for Constructing the Global Legal Mechanism of the Right to Development

XIGEN WANG[*]

1 Introduction

Development is one of the most important themes in the world today.[1] The right to development emerged in the process of examining the problems of development and the values of human rights. Due to the persistence of the international community, a global legal document, the Declaration on the Right to Development,[2] was adopted by the General Assembly of the United Nations (UN) in 1986, making the right to development an essential component of modern human rights.[3] The right to development has been, however, criticised since its birth in 1972 for its challenge to first-generation human rights, which concern civil and political rights, and to second-generation human rights, which

[*] Xigen Wang, Doctor of Law, President of the Human Rights Institute at Wuhan University (The National Human Rights Base), Changjiang Distinguished Professor, the national leading scholar in philosophy and social sciences granted by the State Council of China. Upon invitation by the United Nations, Wang serves as the high-level consultant on the right to development. Wang has participated in the drafting of the standards of the right to development and related activities of the UN several times since 2007. Wang has published more than fifty papers and six monographs on the right to development. Wang was the advanced visiting scholar at Harvard and Columbia Law Schools from 2007 to 2008 as well as a part-time professor at the School of Law of Erasmus University Rotterdam. (Addresses: fxywxg@whu.edu.cn; School of Law, Wuhan University, China. Zip code: 430072.) Many thanks are due to Song Dingbonan, who is now a PhD candidate at the School of Law of Wuhan University and a visiting scholar at the School of Law of Erasmus University Rotterdam. Her research focuses on human rights and the rule of law. Ms. Song contributed much to the editing of this article's text, literature research, data collection and discussion of viewpoints.
[1] The 2005 World Summit declared that 'peace and security, development and human rights are the pillars of the United Nations system'. 2005 World Summit Outcome, 24 October 2005, UN Doc. A/RES/60/1.
[2] Declaration on the Right to Development, 4 December 1986, UN Doc. A/RES/41/128.
[3] Kéba M' Baye, 'Le droit au développement comme un droit de l'home' (1972) 2–3 *Human Rights Journal* 505–534.

concern economic, social and cultural rights.[4] The UN Open-Ended Working Group on the Right to Development[5] and its controlling organ – the high-level task force on the implementation of the right to development[6] – have achieved much and have devoted enormous enthusiasm and hard work to realising the right to development. Nonetheless, the right to development rests on the soft basis of moral conscience, such as alms for the poor, and lacks normative protection and the legal force of hard law. The legal mechanism of the right to development has yet to be established. The root cause is the failure to conduct rational communication on the methodologies, philosophical basis and practice of the rule of law. Consequently, it is nearly impossible to seek common ground while respecting differences. This chapter will reveal from the perspective of jurisprudence the problems about choice of concepts, content updating and the normative route of the global legal mechanism of the right to development against the background of globalisation.

2   The deficiency of the existing construction mode of the legal mechanism of the right to development

The completely different attitudes towards the practice of the right to development originate in different opinions about the relationship between human rights and development. It is still impossible to decide which opinion in the international academic and practical domains is right. The seven main approaches include: the holistic approach, the

---

[4] The division of human rights into three generations was proposed by the Czech jurist Karel Vasak in 1979. The first-generation human rights deal essentially with liberty and participation in political life. They are 'negative' rights that 'require the state do nothing to interfere with individual liberties, and correspond roughly to the civil and political rights'. The second-generation human rights are related to equality and 'require positive action by the state to be implemented, as is the case with most social, economic and cultural rights'. Karel Vasak, 'A 30-year struggle; the sustained efforts to give force of law to the Universal Declaration of Human Rights' (1977) 11 *The UNESCO Courier: a window open on the world* 28–29. As for the third-generation human rights, they are the 'collective' human rights, which include the right to development, the right to peace and the right to national self-determination. Wang Xigen, *Fazhishehui de jibenrenquan-fazhanquanfalvzhiduyanjiu* (*The One of Basic Human Rights in Society with Rule of Law: A Study on Legal System of the Right to Development*) (Beijing: Chinese People's Public Security University Press, 2002).
[5] Cf. Commission on Human Rights Resolution 1998/72, 22 April 1998, UN Doc. E/CN.4/1998/72 (1998) and Economic and Social Council Decision 1998/269, 30 July 1998, UN Doc. E/DEC/1998/269.
[6] Cf. Commission on Human Rights Resolution 2004/7: The Right to Development, 13 April 2004, UN Doc. E/CN.4/RES/2004/7. Adopted by forty-nine votes to three. See chapter VII, E/2004/23-E/CN.4/2004/127.

human rights–based approach, the social justice approach, the capabilities approach, the right to development approach, the responsibilities approach and the human rights education approach.[7] Although their emphases are not identical, they can be described by two theoretical models from the global perspective and on the basis of human rights: the view of rights-based development and the view of the right to development.

The rights-based development is the more common theory. According to it, the international community considers development and human rights together, which affirms that development should be pursued in a 'human rights way' or that human rights must 'be integrated into sustainable human development'.[8] It is, however, merely the abbreviation of 'the human rights approach to development assistance'[9] and focuses on 'the relationship between development co-operation, the Universal Declaration on Human Rights[10] and international human rights instruments'.[11] The main components of rights-based development include that it is 'based on international human rights standards and directed to promotion and protection of human rights'; that it will in essence 'integrate the norms, standards and principles of the international human rights system into the plans, policies and processes of development'; and that it will 'express linkage to rights, accountability, empowerment, participation and non-discrimination and attention to vulnerable groups' as the essential factors.[12]

The view of rights-based development is practically rational to an extent. For example, it can be helpful regarding issues such as assistance to developing countries, poverty reduction and mitigation of debt crises. Although a 'rights-based development' has been adopted by the UN

[7] Stephen P. Marks, 'The human rights framework for development: seven approaches', in Archna Negi, Arjun K. Sengupta and Basu Mushumi (eds.), *Reflections on the Right to Development* (New Delhi: Sage Publications, 2005), pp. 23–60.

[8] Marks, ibid., pp. 23–60.

[9] The Human Rights Council of Australia Inc., *The Rights Way to Development: A Human Rights Approach to Development Assistance* (Marrickville: Human Rights Council of Australia Inc., 1995). See also André Frankovits and Patrick Earle, *The Rights Way to Development: Manual for a Human Rights Approach to Development Assistance.* (Marrickville: Human Rights Council of Australia Inc., 1998).

[10] Universal Declaration of Human Rights, 10 December 1948, UN Doc. A/RES/3/217 A.

[11] Organisation for Economic Co-operation and Development (OECD), *The Development Dimension: Integrating Human Rights into Development-Donor Approaches, Experiences and Challenge* (Paris: OECD Publishing, 2006), p. 19.

[12] United Nations Office of the High Commissioner for Human Rights, 'What is a rights-based approach to development?', available at www.unicef.org/tdad/unicefcrba.doc.

Office of the High Commissioner for Human Rights (OHCHR),[13] this view is not intended to replace the right to development.[14] Because the rights-based approach still mirrors the traditional view of human rights in reality, it does not treat development as the content of human rights and does not admit that the right to development is a human right, let alone establish the right to development in the basic statute of the human rights system. The right to development is considered just a tool. Consequently, this approach will not only be harmful to the overall construction of the legal mechanism of the right to development but could also negate the right to development ultimately and revert to the traditional view of human rights.

Analysed from the background, the rights-based development is a measure adopted by the developed countries and related international organisations to assist underdeveloped countries and areas to resolve North–South issues. The rights-based development, combining development assistance with basic human rights (e.g. the right to food, the right to water, the right to sanitation, the right to housing and the right to education), aims to implement development assistance strictly within the range of the existing international human rights conventions and documents rather than to establish a new legal mechanism for the protection of the right to development.

In terms of ontology, the view of rights-based development has been dressed in the clothes of modern development, even 'postmodern' development,[15] but it is hardly 'the emperor's new clothes'. The legal

---

[13] See OHCHR, *Frequently Asked Questions on a Human Rights-Based Approach to Development Cooperation* (New York; Geneva: OHCHR, 2006), UN Doc. HR/PUB/06/8.

[14] See OHCHR, *Frequently Asked Questions on the Right to Development* (Geneva: OHCHR, 2016), UN Doc. Fact Sheet No. 37.

[15] The essence of postmodernism lies in the following four features: the surface/depth, the whole/fragment, the margin/centre and the macro/micro. Human rights guided by postmodernism, which can be called the 'postmodern human rights', will be characteristic of the feature 'surface', and human rights will be viewed in terms of practical social relations rather than only in ontological depth. The postmodern human rights can better meet people's demands for human rights. The postmodern human rights are the collective human rights featuring differentiation rather than the modern individual human rights emphasising generalisation and abstraction, so the suppression of the 'whole' to the 'fragment' can be avoided. The postmodern human rights emphasise the human rights of marginal groups and urge special care for them, whereas the modern human rights ignore their demands for universal value as an excuse. Meanwhile, the postmodern human rights will be 'micro' human rights. The postmodern human rights will pay close attention to the human rights of the groups that are submerged, obscured and ignored in the grand narratives of modernism and furthermore concern the micro rights in economic, political, cultural and social relationships. The postmodern human rights will provide the

philosophical basis is still the individualist concept of human rights from the classic natural law school; its core concern is with the traditional human rights employed by citizens to fight against the authorities, which is a sharp contrast to the optimisation of the relationship model of modern human society.

In terms of methodology, the rights-based development is not a model of equal interaction and communication based on autonomy of the will. The giver and the recipient of the assistance are not equal, and it is difficult for them to communicate with each other. The interaction just stays in the realm of 'commerce'.[16] Therefore, the rights-based development cannot restore the life world or realise social justice. Methodologically, it is not a 'consensus' paradigm based on common perspectives introduced by dialogue and negotiation. The classic or the refined individualist conception of human rights is the root cause of the inevitably historical and practical deficiency of rights-based development.

If the view of rights-based development is allowed to expand without limit, the relationship between development and human rights will be reduced to the view that evaluates development assistance by human rights standards. Assistance will be given to those who conform to the human rights standards of the assistance giver or the donor, whereas those who fail to meet such standards will have no chance to receive the assistance. Therefore, the view of rights-based development has strong instrumental colour, and the benefit of the value of such instrumental human rights to development is greatly inferior to the value of the right to development.

Of course, this chapter is not intended to negate the relevance of and inseparability between the civil and political rights and the right to development; it expects that the right to development can be treated as a relatively independent kind of human rights based on valuing the interdependence of various human rights, just as the Declaration on the Right to Development provided. If the right to development can be

---

subjects with more detailed and more comprehensive human rights. In short, the perspective of postmodernism will help us deconstruct the problems of polarisation and the growing gap between the rich and the poor in modern society.

[16] For Habermas, the concept of 'communicative action' refers to 'the interaction of at least two subjects capable of speech and action who establish interpersonal relations (whether by verbal or by extra-verbal means). The actors seek to reach an understanding about the action situation and their plans of action in order to coordinate their actions by way of agreement.' See Jürgen Habermas, *The Theory of Communicative Action: Reason and the Rationalization of Society*, Vol. 1 (Boston, MA: Beacon Press, 1984), p. 86.

fully subsumed in the civil and political rights and the economic, social and cultural rights in the two covenants,[17] the right to development will have no reason to exist, which would be wholly unacceptable according to the Declaration. Therefore, the development is not only a kind of measure but also a form of human rights. Development is not just a means of achieving human rights but itself is a kind of substantive human rights.

3 The optimisation of the global legal mechanism ideas of the right to development

Therefore, the choice of human rights ideas is crucial for constructing the global legal mechanism of the right to development. As for how to choose the idea with the optimum value, my opinion is that a fundamental transformation from the view of rights-based development to the view of the right to development must be realised. The global legal mechanism of the right to development must be constructed following the idea of the right to development rather than of rights-based development. To achieve this transformation, the problem of methodology should be first solved. The methodology of radicalism, which refers to antagonism and confrontation, should be changed into a methodology that takes both antagonism and cooperation into account. Seeking value consensus and resource reorganisation in the interaction and communication of plural human rights cultures is based on the communicative rationality of mankind and social solidarity. The communicative rationality of the right to development lies not only in the fact that it will help the subjects in the position of poverty and marginalisation get the equal opportunities to development but also in the fact that it can help deal with the 'legitimacy crisis'[18] of developed subjects, by mitigating and even deconstructing the international political and economic relations of tension and confrontation and prevent the 'colonisation of life world'.[19] In the complicated global world, where the shared life and universal knowledge

---

[17] Namely the International Covenant on Economic, Social and Cultural Rights, New York, 16 December 1966, entry into force 3 January 1976, UN Doc. A/6316 (1966); 993 UNTS 3; 6 ILM 368 (1967); and the International Covenant on Civil and Political Rights, New York, 16 December 1966, entry into force 23 March 1976, UN Doc. A/6316 (1966); 999 UNTS 171; 6 ILM 368 (1967).

[18] Jürgen Habermas, *Hefahuaweiji* (*Legitimation Crisis*), translated by Cao Weidong and Liu Beicheng (Shanghai: Shanghai People's Publishing House, 2000).

[19] Jürgen Habermas, *The Theory of Communicative Action: System and Life World: A Critique of Functionalist Reason*, Vol. 2 (Boston, MA: Beacon Press, 1987), pp. 301–308.

are gradually weakening, if 'complexes of interaction cannot be stabilised simply on the basis of the reciprocal influence that success-oriented actors exert on one another, then in the final analysis society must be integrated through communicative action'.[20] It requires the construction of a global public realm and the cultivation of the ability to criticise, communicate and create the 'value', the prerequisites for which are public participation, free debate as well as rational interaction and communication. The right to development, with human justice and equality of opportunity for development as its core, is seeking the fundamental leap forward from formal rationality to substantial rationality led by equal communication.

With communicative rationality as the theoretical starting point, the optimisation of the legal mechanism idea of the right to development focuses on integrating the following five aspects. First, from the perspective of subject, it is necessary to realise the communication of the individual and the collective. The right to development is put forward as a kind of collective human right of a certain people and country, especially the developing country. After repeated communication and development, the individuality and the relevance for the individual and the collective of the right to development have been generally accepted. The Declaration on the Right to Development clearly confirms that 'the entire population and all individuals' share the right to development. At the international level, the state, as the bearer of the right to development, is both an individual subject and a collective subject. At the national level, the state as the collective is obligated to ensure that the right to development of each citizen as the single individual is realised. Second, from the objective perspective, it is necessary to realise the communication of anthropocentrism and cosmo-centrism. Development, as the objective of the right to development, has exceeded the pure paradigms of economic growth. It demands bilateral communication in the human-to-human dimension and the human-to-objective-world dimension, and it should be guided by the scientific outlook on development, which is comprehensive, coordinated and sustainable. Third, from the perspective of content, the integration of the classic human rights with the modern human rights is needed. As the Declaration on the Right to Development provides, the right to development is the right on 'the economic, social, cultural and political

[20] Jürgen Habermas, *Between Facts and Norms*, Vol. II (Cambridge: Polity Press, 1996), p. 26.

development',[21] and 'equal attention and urgent consideration should be given to the implementation, promotion and protection of civil, political, economic, social and cultural rights'.[22] The development does not focus on the civil and political rights alone but on the economic, social and cultural rights as well. More important is to integrate them organically into an undivided whole so that they will be raised to a higher level. The all-round development of people can be thereby realised within the process of differentiation and integration of the rights to economic, social, political and cultural development. Fourth, from the perspective of process, it is necessary to integrate the three available action models, which are 'participate in', 'contribute to' and 'enjoy' economic, social, cultural and political development. The right to development, with the equal opportunity to participate in development as the starting point and the development rules and fairness of process as the medium, is committed to substantial justice, which refers to sharing the result of development fairly: it finally unites the fairness of starting point, process and result. As Article 1 of the Declaration on the Right to Development points out, what the right to development aims at is to 'participate in, contribute to, and enjoy development'. Fifth, from the perspectives of time and space, it is necessary to achieve the communication of the centre and the margin. The process of modernisation is interpreted as the polarisation of the centre and the margin. The fragmentation of the marginal subject is the greatest obstacle to realising the right to development and the direct cause of the birth of the right to development. The fundamental premise behind the effort to eliminate the adverse effect of modernisation on realising the right to development is the fact that the marginal subject struggles for equal discourse power to overturn the central subject's discourse hegemony.

Put otherwise, the right to development shall go beyond the pure individual-oriented view or community-oriented view of human rights and unleash the power of tolerance, rationality and harmony from the tense relationship between traditional human rights theory and modern human rights theory. The right to development is supposed to construct

---

[21] Art. 1 of the Declaration on the Right to Development provides that 'the right to development is an inalienable human right by virtue of which every human person and all peoples are entitled to participate in, contribute to, and enjoy economic, social, cultural and political development, in which all human rights and fundamental freedoms can be fully realized'.

[22] Art. 6 of the Declaration on the Right to Development provides that 'all human rights and fundamental freedoms are indivisible and interdependent; equal attention and urgent consideration should be given to the implementation, promotion and protection of civil, political, economic, social and cultural rights'.

a brand-new framework and platform for the innovation of norms and the reconstruction of the global legal mechanism of the right to development and for the choice of the legal strategy of the right to development. This framework and platform will be no longer limited by the existing international human rights documents.

4   The expansion and refinement of the Declaration on the Right to Development

Since the right to development is a new type of human rights and the influence of legal nature and legal effect hierarchy is negative, the Declaration on the Right to Development has certain historical limitations and practical defects. 'The declaration is predicted to be a great guiding force for the human rights strategy in the future. However, as a legal document, it has a great weakness.'[23] 'The right to development is, in fact, in a process of conceptualisation and operationalisation.' The Declaration was an important step but not the final outcome.[24] The analysis about the deficiency of the right to development and the Declaration on the Right to Development focuses only on the weakness of the legal effect; suggestions for the improvement of the idea and content are lacking. In order to maintain their vitality, I believe that the right to development and the relative legal documents should be refined and expanded in the following respects.

First, the people-oriented development principle should be established. The people-oriented development principle should be introduced and accorded the primary place among all principles on the theoretical basis of the global legal mechanism of the right to development. Analysed historically, the view of development developed from the view of God-oriented development in medieval times to the view of matter-oriented development in recent times and finally to the view of people-oriented development in modern times. Among them, only the view of people-oriented development is the scientific one that conforms to the general law.

---

[23] Asbjørn Eide, 'National sovereignty and international efforts to realize human rights', in Asbjørn Eide and Bernt Hagtvet (eds.), *Human Rights in Perspective: A Global Assessment* (Oxford: Blackwell, 1992), pp. 12–13.

[24] Øyvind W. Thiis, 'Norwegian development assistance and the right to development', in Jaqueline Smith, Lalaine Sadiwa and Peter Baehr (eds.), *Human Rights in Developing Countries Yearbook 1996* (The Hague: Kluwer Law International, 1996), pp. 18–36.

Second, a new concept of 'the right to sustainable development' should be extracted. Article 1 of the Declaration on the Right to Development is a type of rights on the 'economic, social, cultural and political development' and also emphasises the 'inalienable right to full sovereignty over all their natural wealth and resources'.[25] The concept of development has not been, however, raised to the level of 'sustainable development', because the concept of sustainable development has not been realised by the ordinary people and had not become a part of the United Nations system as a conception when the Declaration was adopted. Even if the conception was put forward, it was always realised as an obligation or duty instead of a right. Humankind was always considered as the destroyer of sustainable development rather than as its beneficiary. The results are two-fold: humankind is to be held accountable and cannot enjoy sustainable development at all, and the investigation into responsibility will become a mere formality if no one makes a claim that the right to sustainable development has been violated. Instead, sustainable development should be considered as a right instead of as just a duty, and the concept of the right to sustainable development should be introduced. The 'economic, social, cultural and political development' in Article 1 of the Declaration on the Right to Development can be revised to the 'economic, social, cultural and political development and the sustainable development of man and nature'. Of course, there is the possibility of adopting a new term of 'the right to sustainable development', and 'there is no need to formally tamper with the revision of the text of the resolution'.[26] Key to reaching consensus is that research on the right to sustainable development be intensified to prove scientifically the subject, the object, the content, the relation mode between the rights and obligations of the right to sustainable development as well as constituent factors of the legal norms. In the meantime, the right to sustainable development should be expressly provided in the following global legal norms of the right to development.[27]

[25] Art. 2 of the Declaration on the Right to Development provides that 'the human right to development also implies the full realization of the right of peoples to self-determination, which includes, subject to the relevant provisions of both International Covenants on Human Rights, the exercise of their inalienable right to full sovereignty over all their natural wealth and resources'.

[26] The Legal Nature of the Right to Development and Enhancement of Its Binding Nature, 16 February 2004, UN Doc. E/CN. 4/Sub. 2/2004/16.

[27] See Wang Xigen, 'On the right to sustainable development: foundation in legal philosophy and legislative proposals', in Stephen P. Marks (ed.), Implementing the Right to Development: The Role of International Law (Geneva: Friedrich-Ebert-Stiftung, Geneva Office, 2008), pp. 39–46.

Third, the new concept of 'the right to regional development' should be established.[28] The right to development is a unity of individual human rights and collective human rights. From the perspective of collective human rights, the subject is the state or the people, which is embodied in Article 2 and Article 5 of the Declaration on the Right to Development.[29] Unbalanced regional development within a state can, however, be an obstacle. Just as between states in the international community, there are great differences between developed and underdeveloped regions within states. The advancement of underdeveloped regions is a major measure towards realising the right to development. It is therefore necessary to introduce the concept of 'the right to regional development' at state level and to have it confirmed by legislation. Although the concept of 'region' refers to a certain geographic space, the subject of the right to regional development is the people who live in it, especially those in the poor and fragile areas. Their demand for the realisation of the right to development is more urgent than that of people living in the developed areas. Policies and rules should regulate the right to development of those living in the underdeveloped areas, and programs for external investment, assistance, cooperation and capacity building should be adopted for the sake of their right to development.

Fourth, the sub-forms of the right to development should be further specified. The right to development as maternal rights can be divided into five sub-forms: the right to economic development, the right to social development, the right to cultural development, the right to political development and the right to sustainable development. Those sub-forms should be expressly formulated to make their denotation and

---

[28] See Wang Kangmin and Wang Xigen, 'Lun quyu fazhanquan he falinian de gengxin' (On the right to regional development and the renewal of legal ideas) (2009–2011) *Political Science and Law* 2–9; Lv Ning and Wang Xigen, 'Quyu fazhanquan falv zhidu de jiben yuanze' (The basic principles of legal system of the right to regional development) (2010–2012) *Journal of South-Central University for Nationalities (Humanities and Social Sciences)* 122–126; Wang Xigen and Peng Jianjun, 'Lun quyu fazhanquan de benzhi shuxing he falv shijian' (On the essential attributes and legal practices of the right to regional development) (2009–2011) *Journal of South-Central University for Nationalities (Humanities and Social Sciences)* 102–107.

[29] Art. 5 of the Declaration on the Right to Development provides that 'States shall take resolute steps to eliminate the massive and flagrant violations of the human rights of peoples and human beings affected by situations such as those resulting from apartheid, all forms of racism and racial discrimination, colonialism, foreign domination and occupation, aggression, foreign interference and threats against national sovereignty, national unity and territorial integrity, threats of war and refusal to recognize the fundamental right of peoples to self-determination'.

388XIGEN WANG

connotation clear and to make the protection of the right to development more operational. Specification can also help correct the misunderstanding that the right to development is only a hodgepodge of various human rights and avoid the mistake that it can be simply replaced with human rights in the two Conventions on Human Rights.

5 The construction of the legal mechanism of the right to development

There are two opposing propositions on how to construct a global legal mechanism of the right to development. The conservative proposition holds that the legal protection of the right to development can be based only on soft law with little legally binding force (e.g. declarations, resolutions and statements). Trying to legally compel the developed subject to assume legal obligations towards the less developed subject is unreasonable and unrealistic. As the working paper of the Economic and Social Council recalls: 'it has already been amply demonstrated that there are strong differences of opinion among legal luminaries as to whether the right to development can be placed within a legally binding framework. The view that human rights instruments address the obligations of a State to its citizens and not obligations between States seems to be in ascendancy.'[30] The other proposition, radicalism, requires that an 'international legal standard of a binding nature' and 'concept document' on the right to development with binding force[31] be established. In particular, it calls for the adoption of 'an international convention on the right to development'[32] to ensure through legal enforcement that the right to development is realised.

Despite different explanations of the legal effect of the right to development,[33] Resolution 41/128 has undoubtedly so far 'utilised the

[30] Florizelle O'Connor, Working Paper on the Right to Development, 23 February 2005, UN Doc. E/CN. 4/Sub. 2/2005/23.
[31] Commission on Human Rights Resolution 2003/83: The Right to Development, 25 August 2003, UN Doc. E/CN.4/RES/2003/83. It was adopted by a vote of forty-seven in favour and three against, with three abstentions.
[32] Report of the High-Level Task Force on the Implementation of the Right to Development in its Fourth Session, 31 January 2008, UN Doc. A/HRC/8/W G.2/TF/2.
[33] 'The General Assembly's resolution on the right to development, resolution 41/128, like all other such declarations or resolutions, belongs within what some international lawyers regard as a space somewhere just above "soft law" – legal principles, norms and standards adopted at international diplomatic conferences. This comes below "hard law" – "treaty law", customary international law and general principles of international law.' (See para. 38 of The Legal Nature of the Right to Development and Enhancement of Its Binding Nature, 16 February 2004, UN Doc. E/CN. 4/Sub. 2/2004/16.)

mechanism of an independent expert and the less formalised, indirect mainstreaming methods', and 'this is certainly not adequate'.[34] Both of the aforementioned propositions have a realistic basis. The conservative is built on the classic theory of legal effect and legal source. It focuses on the legal effect understood from the perspective of the preventive function of law, whereas the radical focuses on the legal effect understood from the perspective of legal consequence, remedy and the responsibility system for the right to development. The main difference between them is whether the basis of the legal mechanism of the right to development lies in the existing soft law or in hard law about to be created. My opinion is that neither proposition should be simply refuted by the other in the choice of the construction of the legal mechanism of the right to development. A new strategic system, the 'legal strategic system of the right to development', should be established based on Article 10 of the Declaration on the Right to Development.[35] It should be guided by the principle of the world's harmonious development and should comprehensively and systematically design the protection of the right to development. Such a strategic system can be a 'dual-track system'.

The first track refers to the selection of the mechanism. The construction of the legal mechanism of the right to development should not only reflect contemporary reality, but it should also make provision for the future: it might thereby achieve the two-way interaction between the realistic legal framework and future development requirements and between the developed and underdeveloped countries. To this end, the legal mechanism of the right to development should be bifurcated into a hard law mechanism and a soft law mechanism. The soft law mechanism includes the dialogue mechanism, assistance mechanism and empowerment mechanism, while the hard law mechanism includes the mechanism of declaring on legal effect, regulatory mechanism, monitoring mechanism, assessment mechanism and remedy mechanism. The judicial mechanism and quasi-judicial mechanism on the right to development should be established and remedies provided when rights and obligations in legal norms cannot be fully realised, so as to

---

[34] See para. 48 of The Legal Nature of the Right to Development and Enhancement of Its Binding Nature, 16 February 2004, UN Doc. E/CN. 4/Sub. 2/2004/16.

[35] Art. 10 of the Declaration on the Right to Development points out: 'Steps should be taken to ensure the full exercise and progressive enhancement of the right to development, including the formulation, adoption and implementation of policy, legislative and other measures at the national and international levels.' The Declaration on the Right to Development, 4 December 1986, UN Doc. A/RES/41/128.

construct a last line of defence for the realisation of the right to development.

The second track refers to the path dependence. In the process of constructing the legal mechanism of the right to development, the UN General Assembly has been deeply vexed that: 'it is the translation of the resolution into a treaty form, the introduction of judicial or quasi-judicial complaints or communications procedures or the introduction of sanctions for defaulters that would necessitate further indication of consent by States'. That will be, without a doubt, difficult to achieve.[36] I propose an effective, alternative method to solve the problem: the right to development should not be simply replaced with the civil and political rights or the economic, social and cultural rights, nor should the inseparability of the right to development and such rights be renounced. In light of these circumstances, the 'walking on two legs' method, which is based on the interaction – not substitution – of the right to development and other human rights, should be adopted on the path to achieve the rule of law of the right to development. On the one hand, the existing hard law norms provided for in international human rights conventions should be fully and skilfully utilised to make a link to the right to development. The right to development would be endowed with legal force by gradually becoming part of the existing conventions and would be enforced based on such hard law norms. For example, the right to choose independently a development path in the Declaration on the Right to Development can be linked to the first article of the two covenants on human rights.[37]

---

[36] See para. 49 of The Legal Nature of the Right to Development and Enhancement of Its Binding Nature, 16 February 2004, UN Doc. E/CN. 4/Sub. 2/2004/16.

[37] Art. 1 of the International Covenant on Civil and Political Rights provides that '1. All peoples have the right of self-determination. By virtue of that right they freely determine their political status and freely pursue their economic, social and cultural development. 2. All peoples may, for their own ends, freely dispose of their natural wealth and resources without prejudice to any obligations arising out of international economic co-operation, based upon the principle of mutual benefit, and international law. In no case may a people be deprived of its own means of subsistence. 3. The States Parties to the present Covenant, including those having responsibility for the administration of Non-Self-Governing and Trust Territories, shall promote the realization of the right of self-determination, and shall respect that right, in conformity with the provisions of the Charter of the United Nations.' Art. 1 of the International Covenant on Economic, Social and Cultural Rights provides that '1. All peoples have the right of self-determination. By virtue of that right they freely determine their political status and freely pursue their economic, social and cultural development. 2. All peoples may, for their own ends, freely dispose of their natural wealth and resources without prejudice to any obligations arising out of international economic co-operation, based upon the principle of mutual benefit, and

The right to free participation in development, the right to equal development of women and the right to equal development of minorities can be linked to Article 25, Article 3 and Article 27,[38] respectively, in the International Covenant on Civil and Political Rights.[39] The effect will, of course, be limited due to the differences between the right to development and the existing conventions. On the other hand, seeing that the aforementioned method cannot fully realise the right to development and is even just an expediency, a special legal norm system on the right to development beyond the human rights conventions should be established under proper conditions. A specific and legally enforceable convention on the right to development should be, in other words, adopted.

Although the road to realise the right to development is still long, we should not give up in the face of obstacles, nor should we always give in to reality. Consider how great and insurmountable the hardships and challenges seemed between the publication of the first international convention by the World Conference on Human Rights in 1948 and the two covenants' publication in 1966. We can believe instead that all the efforts made by the Working Group on the Right to Development, the Expert Group on the Right to Development and the people yearning for peace and development will converge in a bright future for the right to development.

international law. In no case may a people be deprived of its own means of subsistence. 3. The States Parties to the present Covenant, including those having responsibility for the administration of Non-Self-Governing and Trust Territories, shall promote the realization of the right of self-determination, and shall respect that right, in conformity with the provisions of the Charter of the United Nations.'

[38] Art. 25 of the International Covenant on Civil and Political Rights points out that 'nothing in the present Covenant shall be interpreted as impairing the inherent right of all peoples to enjoy and utilize fully and freely their natural wealth and resources'. Art. 3 of the International Covenant on Civil and Political Rights provides that 'the States Parties to the present Covenant undertake to ensure the equal right of men and women to the enjoyment of all economic, social and cultural rights set forth in the present Covenant'. Art. 27 provides that '1. The present Covenant shall enter into force three months after the date of the deposit with the Secretary-General of the United Nations of the thirty-fifth instrument of ratification or instrument of accession. 2. For each State ratifying the present Covenant or acceding to it after the deposit of the thirty-fifth instrument of ratification or instrument of accession, the present Covenant shall enter into force three months after the date of the deposit of its own instrument of ratification or instrument of accession.'

[39] I put forward this train of thought more than ten years ago and wrote it down in my monograph *Fazhishehui de jibenrenquan-fazhanquanfalvzhiduyanjiu* (*The One of Basic Human Rights in Society with Rule of Law: A Study on Legal System of the Right to Development*) (Beijing: Chinese People's Public Security University Press, 2002), chapter 7.

12

Fair Is Foul, and Foul Is Fair

The Mixed Character of Constitutionalism in the Global Economic Governance

KAZUYORI ITO

1 Introduction

Today's international economic law, particularly in the field of international trade and investment, has substantially reinforced its regulatory framework through multilateral and bilateral treaties. The Agreement on the World Trade Organization (WTO), among others, imposes detailed discipline on the matters previously reserved to the jurisdiction of national governments. The application and interpretation of the WTO Agreement are also systematically controlled by the dispute settlement system, which exercises de facto compulsory jurisdiction. Given these developments, some theorists even talk of the 'constitutionalisation' of the WTO regime. They argue that it has become an autonomous normative scheme that has virtually displaced the decentralised regulatory powers of national authorities and that it fulfils thereby several constitutional functions (such as the rule of law, the protection of the rights of individuals and the coordination of value conflicts). In the field of international investment law, a major part of norms is provided only in the form of bilateral agreements. Nevertheless, the autonomous and integral character of these norms has been considerably enhanced, primarily because their interpretations are judicially standardised in the process of arbitration. Based on this fact, the constitutionalisation of international investment law has come to be discussed as well.

Should we, however, consider that powers are being irreversibly concentrated in international bodies to the degree that the proponents of the idea of constitutionalisation assume? In point of fact, the integral nature of the WTO regime is being partly eroded by, for instance, the continued non-compliance with WTO rulings in a few disputes, the emergence of non-trade issues and the rise of regionalism. Likewise, the autonomous development of international investment law is being challenged by some states' efforts to elaborate treaty language more precisely or to issue an interpretative declaration for the purposes of limiting arbitrators' discretion.

The present chapter focuses on the increased tensions between these centripetal and centrifugal forces in international economic norms and argues that the concept of constitutionalisation itself should be reformulated. As will be discussed later, we could use the term 'global constitutionalism' to refer to the situation where the relevant international bodies are required to legitimate their extensive authority in relation to other polities by balancing a variety of integrating and decentralising elements appropriately. Such an understanding would offer a reshaped criterion for evaluating the relationship between the international legal discipline and national sovereign authorities.

2 'Constitutionalisation' discourse in international trade and investment law

2.1 Developments in international trade law

The remarkable growth of the legal discipline advanced under the WTO Agreement was one reason why theorists of international relations developed the concept of 'legalisation'. In measuring the degree of legalisation, theorists usually employ three indices: obligation, precision and delegation.[1] A concern thereby is the extent to which the autonomous regulatory power of states has been transferred to international organisations. As the transfer of power proceeds, the regime assumes the character of 'objective legal order', where individual states can no longer exert their subjective influence over the administration of international norms. Has the WTO acquired an objective nature in this sense? If so, how does it relate to the idea of constitutionalism?

---

[1] 'Obligation' means that states or other actors are bound by a rule or commitment. 'Precision' means that rules unambiguously define the conduct they require, authorise or proscribe. 'Delegation' means that third parties have been granted authority to implement, interpret and apply the rules; to resolve disputes; and (possibly) to make further rules. See Kenneth W. Abbott, Robert O. Keohane, Andrew Moravcsik, Anne-Marie Slaughter and Duncan Snidal, 'The concept of legalization' (2000) 54 *International Organization* 401–419.

2.1.1   Evolutions in the normative character
of substantive obligations

The General Agreement on Tariffs and Trade (GATT) of 1947, initially created as a temporary substitute for the doomed Charter of the International Trade Organization (ITO), was equipped with quite rough principles about trade in goods, which left many issues unregulated or imprecisely regulated. In contrast, the WTO Agreement, which came into force in 1995, contains much more detailed disciplines than its predecessor, particularly as regards trade remedies law addressing safeguard, anti-dumping and anti-subsidy measures. It also extends its regulatory scope into new frontiers such as trade in services, trade-related investment measures and intellectual property protection, making the regime more comprehensive. As a result, the ability of individual member states to manipulate rules or abuse the vagueness of law has substantially decreased.

The objective nature of international trade norms can be partly traced back to some key features of the original GATT system. The reciprocal exchange of market access concessions, one of the GATT's core achievements, is usually a deal between specific states, with a subjective and contractual nature. Meanwhile, those beneficial conditions created in bilateral terms are also to be made available to every other member state via the most-favoured-nation (MFN) clause. Hence the GATT scheme has promoted, at least potentially, trade opportunities for all contracting parties – a common interest that transcends the scope of subjective gains.

Having achieved significant tariff reductions by the end of the 1960s, the GATT contracting parties turned to regulating non-tariff measures with a trade-distorting effect. Since apparently neutral product standards such as safety or environmental requirements may work against goods from specific countries, there was a need to introduce some constraints on state regulatory discretion. This need led to the adoption of several 'codes', i.e. optional agreements, during the Tokyo Round negotiation (1973–1979) and their development as an integral part of the WTO regime, as typified by the Agreement on Technical Barriers to Trade (TBT). Rules of this kind require each government to provide domestically for an unbiased legal setting for producers from all countries. By implication, non-compliance with these rules affects legal interests of member states as a whole.

If the WTO obligations have such a collective character and not just a reciprocal one, a subset of the member states cannot denounce or modify any WTO norms only between themselves without going through the proper amendment process. Article 41(1)(b) of the Vienna Convention on the Law of Treaties provides that some of the parties to a multilateral treaty may modify the treaty as between themselves alone, if: (1) the modification does not affect the enjoyment by the other parties of their treaty rights; and (2) it is not incompatible with the effective execution of the object and purpose of the treaty as a whole. These conditions could be met only when the treaty in question consists of rights and obligations that are reducible into bilateral elements. For its part, the primary virtue of WTO law does not lie in a guarantee of material trade flows currently existing between any two countries but in the protection of overall expectations for future trade opportunities.[2] To the extent that the WTO pursues this sort of systemic stability and predictability in international trade, its norms cannot be split into bilateral elements, nor can they be modified freely between some of the parties alone.[3] Accordingly, a measure infringing WTO law would not be legitimised on the grounds that the state at issue had joined an accord that tolerates such a measure. This rule consolidates further the objective nature of the WTO discipline.

2.1.2   Judicialisation of the dispute settlement

As the substantive rules of the WTO/GATT have developed their objective nature, the dispute settlement mechanism created under the WTO Agreement has been gradually judicialised as well. Originally, the GATT obligations were a compilation of the tariff reductions obtained through reciprocal deals, whose effectiveness was founded on the equivalence of interests exchanged among the contracting parties. For this reason, the essence of a dispute under the dispute settlement procedure in Article 23

[2] This idea has been unequivocally set forth in several dispute settlement decisions. See, e.g., *European Economic Community – Payments and Subsidies Paid to Processors and Producers of Oilseeds and Related Animal Feed Proteins*, Report of the Panel, 25 January 1990, BISD 37S/86, para. 150; WTO, *Japan – Taxes on Alcoholic Beverages*, Report of the Appellate Body of 4 October 1996, WT/DS8/AB/R, p. 16. For an analogous argument, see Chios C. Carmody, 'WTO obligations as collective' (2006) 17 *European Journal of International Law* 419–443.
[3] According to Malte Jordan, the WTO Agreement has taken on the character of public law due to its emphasis on the protection of systemic predictability in international economic relations, and therefore it cannot be modified between specific states. See Malte Jordan, *Sanktionsmöglichkeiten im WTO-Streitbeilegungsverfahren* (Berlin: Duncker & Humblot, 2005), p. 69. For an opposing view, see Joost Pauwelyn, 'A typology of multilateral treaty obligations: are WTO obligations bilateral or collective in nature?' (2003) 14 *European Journal of International Law* 907–951.

of the GATT was whether any benefit of a party had been 'nullified or impaired'. That the nullification of benefits was caused by the failure of another party to carry out its obligations was not necessarily required for a complaint to be submitted. Given that the principal goal of dispute settlement was to rectify the disequilibrium in benefits produced between some parties, the arbiters were expected to present a solution based on a compromise mutually acceptable to the disputing parties, rather than a rigorous judicial ruling. That is why the dispute settlement process in the GATT's early years is often characterised as an extension of a diplomatic negotiation.

The situation started to change thereafter. Where at first the body handling a dispute took the form of a 'working group' composed of, among others, officials from the disputing parties, later, it was replaced by a 'panel' whose members were appointed in a personal capacity. Increasingly, those panels took on the nature of judicial proceedings that primarily make factual findings and apply relevant rules in an objective way based on arguments submitted by the claimant and respondent. From the late 1980s, there have been several cases in which one of the disputing parties refused to adopt the panel's ruling as a GATT decision – a fact that paradoxically indicates that the dispute settlement process had come closer to a judicial review, out of the hands of the states concerned.

The establishment of the WTO took away even the member states' power to block the adoption of panels' rulings. The Dispute Settlement Understanding (DSU), a component of the WTO Agreement, stipulates that a panel report shall be adopted unless the member states decide otherwise by consensus, making the adoption of reports virtually inevitable. Additionally, the DSU established the Appellate Body, a standing organ that is to hear appeals from panel cases, particularly regarding the legal interpretations of panels. These new features introduced by the DSU have encouraged the prompt accumulation of precedents and the formation of a case law system, which requires adjudicators to settle varied disputes not ad hoc but in line with consistent judicial doctrines.

Due to this progressive judicialisation, the dispute settlement mechanism has turned its interest towards the issue of whether any breach of obligations objectively exists, rather than whether certain subjective benefits of a party are nullified or impaired. Already in the later period of the GATT, the nullification or impairment of benefits began to be measured not by the real decline in trade volume but by the prejudice to the general expectations for trade opportunities created by the GATT norms.[4] The nullification of benefits is hereby almost identical to the breach of obligations. Subsequently, a provision was placed in the DSU that states 'in cases where there is an infringement of the obligations assumed under a covered agreement, the action is considered *prima facie* to constitute a case of nullification or impairment' (Article 3(8)). A rebuttal to the 'presumption' that an actual breach of obligations constitutes a case of nullification or impairment has yet to be sustained in practice.

As the element of remedying subjective damage has been attenuated to the utmost, standing to bring claims under the DSU came to be very extensively permitted. In the *EC – Bananas* case, the Appellate Body found that a complainant need not demonstrate its own 'legal interest' to bring a claim, because a member state is expected to decide autonomously whether any such action would be fruitful.[5] This amounts to the extension of standing even to a state suffering indirect or potential damage. So seen, the WTO norms can constitute obligations *erga omnes partes* as is formulated in Article 48(1)(a) of Draft Articles on Responsibility of States for Internationally Wrongful Acts.[6]

Finally, an attempt to settle a dispute by relying on a self-help measure, typified by Section 301 of the US Trade Act of 1974, is clearly prohibited under WTO law. The DSU does not allow a member state to make a unilateral determination that a violation has occurred (Article 23(2) (a)), and it requires states to obtain an authorisation from the WTO before suspending concessions or other obligations in response to the failure of the member concerned to implement the rulings adopted in the WTO (Article 23(2)(c)). Accordingly, a retaliatory measure suspending

---

[4] For instance, in the *US – Superfund* case of 1987, though the United States argued that the challenged tax differential between domestic and foreign products was so small that its trade effects were minimal or nil and that it did not nullify or impair benefits accruing to the claimants, the panel observed that 'the impact of a measure inconsistent with the General Agreement is not relevant for a determination of nullification or impairment'. See *United States – Taxes on Petroleum and Certain Imported Substances*, Report of the Panel, 17 June 1987, BISD 34S/136, paras. 5.1.4–5.1.5.

[5] WTO, *European Communities – Regime for the Importation, Sale and Distribution of Bananas*, Report of the Appellate Body of 9 September 1997, WT/DS27/AB/R, paras. 132–135. This tolerant attitude was accounted for by the recognition that, 'with the increased interdependence of the global economy ... Members have a greater stake in enforcing WTO rules than in the past since any deviation from the negotiated balance of rights and obligations is more likely than ever to affect them, directly or indirectly' (ibid., para. 136).

[6] Put otherwise, WTO law permits each member to rely on an '*actio popularis*'. See Mitsuo Matsushita, Thomas J. Schoenbaum and Petros C. Mavroidis, *The World Trade Organization: Law, Practice, and Policy*, 2nd ed. (Oxford: Oxford University Press, 2006), p. 114.

concessions or other obligations under the WTO Agreement can assume the character of an organised sanction even though the measure is actually implemented by an individual member state.[7] It must be distinguished from a 'countermeasure,' which is in international law a means of unilaterally invoking the responsibility of another state.[8]

2.1.3 'Constitutionalisation' theories of the WTO

Given these both substantive and procedural developments in international trade norms, some theorists have come to discuss the 'constitutionalisation' of WTO law, evidently as a concept that represents the ultimate stage of legalisation. There are naturally several strands in the argument, reflecting various constitutional functions. Those often emphasised will be summarised as follows.

First, theorists note the structural evolution of legal order. The WTO Agreement has produced much clearer and well-organised substantive norms as primary rules and has introduced effective instruments of adjudication as secondary rules, jointly inducing states to shift from power-oriented to rule-oriented behaviour.[9] The vagueness of law

---

[7] Jordan (n. 3), pp. 27–29; Steve Charnovitz, 'Rethinking WTO trade sanctions' (2001) 95 *American Journal of International Law* 791–832, at 803–808. The core element of sanctions lies in the exclusion of a self-judgment by an individual actor in responding to unlawful acts. An authoritative organ is to determine not only the existence of a violation but also the measure to be taken in response to that violation. See Charles Leben, 'Les contremesures inter-étatiques et les réactions à l'illicite dans la société international' (1982) 28 *Annuaire Français de Droit International* 9–77, at 30.

[8] Some theorists characterise a measure suspending concessions or other obligations under the WTO Agreement as a countermeasure (see, e.g., Petros C. Mavroidis, 'Remedies in the WTO legal system: between a rock and a hard place' (2000) 11 *European Journal of International Law* 763–813, at 800; Joost Pauwelyn, 'Enforcement and countermeasures in the WTO: rules are rules – toward a more collective approach' (2000) 94 *American Journal of International Law* 335–347). A defining feature, however, of a countermeasure is that the determinations on the existence of an unlawful act and the necessity to take a measure in response are predominantly reserved to the self-judgment of an individual state (Denis Alland, *Justice privée et ordre juridique international: étude théorique des contre-mesures en droit international public* (Paris: Éditions A. Pedone, 1994), pp. 102–103). Abi-Saab argues that if both the existence of an unlawful act and the content of a responding measure are determined by the competent international organ, the latter ceases to be a countermeasure and qualifies as a sanction. See Georges Abi-Saab, 'Cours général de droit international public' (1987) 207 *Recueil des cours de l'Académie de droit international* 9–463, at 299–300.

[9] See, e.g., John H. Jackson, 'The WTO "constitution" and proposed reforms: seven "mantras" revisited' (2001) 4 *Journal of International Economic Law* 67–78; David Palmeter, 'The WTO as a legal system' (2000) 24 *Fordham International Law Journal* 444–480, at 467–478.

under the GATT, which was a source of various arbitrary acts of states, has been largely cured by the extension of treaty norms to cover most crucial matters in international trade. To put it simply, what is stressed here is the extent to which the 'completeness' of law has been approximated.

Second, the function of guaranteeing fundamental rights is given attention. It is argued that WTO law directly ensures freedom of international commerce for private actors just like the protection of human rights does in a national constitution.[10] The treaty norms are expected to work as a 'precommitment,' which would prevent governments from yielding to the temptation of protectionist policies that are detrimental to free trade. This can justify recognising the direct effect of the WTO Agreement in domestic litigation for private actors' benefit.[11]

Third, a constitutional function is attributed to the capacity to reconcile diverse values. Due to WTO law's enhanced comprehensiveness, it is alleged that it can coordinate autonomously the value of free trade with other policy objectives.[12] Even if the policy preference differs from state to state, WTO law is expected to provide proper accommodation, which would eventually elaborate an integrated value order among countries.[13]

Fourth, the existence of an independent judicial organ that can maintain the legal order is regarded as an element of constitutionalism. As noted before, WTO law controls the response to an unlawful act exclusively through the judicial mechanism and prohibits any decentralised reaction to disputes. The interpretation of the WTO Agreement is detached from the intentions of governments and delegated to the legal profession, which has fostered the discipline's autonomous evolution.[14] It is further argued that this judicial evolution of norms even extends to matters of governing structure such as the allocation of powers or the

---

[10] Ernst-Ulrich Petersmann, 'Human rights and international economic law in the 21st century: the need to clarify their interrelationships' (2001) 4 *Journal of International Economic Law* 3–39; Markus Krajewski, *Verfassungsperspektiven und Legitimation des Rechts der Welthandelsorganisation (WTO)* (Berlin: Duncker & Humblot, 2001), pp. 186–188.

[11] Petersmann (n. 10), at 33–34.

[12] Thomas Cottier, 'Limits to international trade: the constitutional challenge' (2000) 94 *American Society of International Law Proceedings* 220–222, at 220–221.

[13] Peter M. Gerhart, 'The two constitutional visions of the World Trade Organization' (2003) 24 *University of Pennsylvania Journal of International Economic Law* 1–75.

[14] Alec Stone Sweet, 'Constitutionalism, legal pluralism, and international regimes' (2009) 16 *Indiana Journal of Global Legal Studies* 621–645, at 639–644.

methodologies of judicial review, often accompanied by reference to related doctrines developed under domestic constitutional regimes.[15]

As is evident from these descriptions, many theorists consider that the concept of constitutionalisation stands at the very end of a continuum of legalisation and that WTO law has reached that extreme because it has taken on an autonomous normative structure unfettered by the decentralised regulatory powers of national authorities. Accordingly, what lies at the core of the theories of constitutionalisation examined here are aspirations for the rule of law on the international level.

From this perspective, international constitutionalism will work almost identically as national constitutions, since both are basically expected to constrain the exercise of sovereign political power. The fundamental value to be pursued here would be the protection of liberty and reasonable expectations of private actors operating in the civil domain, including that beyond borders. This could be equivalent to the Kantian ideal of a cosmopolitan constitutional order for the world civil society, where the notion of constitutionalism should be extended to the sphere of external sovereignty.

2.2 Developments in international investment law

States once had a wide discretion to set their own legal standards on the treatment of alien assets. This was partly due to developing countries' rejection of the idea that international law contains certain common rules on the protection of alien assets. In the 1980s, however, most developing countries began to seek capital from abroad and to conclude bilateral treaties with developed countries that mutually guarantee the protection of foreign investment. While these treaties have significantly 'denationalised' standards regarding alien assets, such norms are alleged to have retained their subjective nature, because almost all the treaties were concluded bilaterally. Nevertheless, there is an argument to be made that even if these treaties are bilateral in their form, their substantive norms are so converged as to make them a de facto multilateral regime.[16] If this is the case, we might be able to consider that international investment law has now taken on a sufficiently objective and integrated nature.

---

[15] Deborah Z. Cass, 'The "constitutionalization" of international trade law: judicial norm-generation as the engine of constitutional development in international trade' (2001) 12 *European Journal of International Law* 39–75.

[16] Stephan W. Schill, *The Multilateralization of International Investment Law* (Cambridge: Cambridge University Press, 2009), chapter 1.

2.2.1   Standardisation of substantive norms

There are more than 2,000 bilateral investment treaties (BITs) in force, and not every BIT has been drafted 'from scratch'. Major capital-exporting countries have their own 'model' BITs, which have quite often served as a template for negotiating specific treaties. Moreover, one can observe a close textual resemblance among model BITs, which is probably a function of their usually being rooted in a few draft articles formerly prepared for the conclusion of multilateral conventions.[17] The convergence of the normative content of BITs has been accelerated through the constant mutual observation of what other states do in drafting their BITs.[18]

In addition, MFN clauses, which are regularly included in BITs, have a significant effect in levelling differences in the treatment of foreign investment. Under the MFN clause, states are generally precluded from creating exclusively privileged bilateral relations and thereby are embedded in the multilateral context. 'General' MFN clauses in any multilateral treaties such as the GATT have a levelling effect that extends to all the contracting parties at once, whereas MFN clauses in BITs can equalise treatment only between those states that have individually con-cluded a BIT with the host state. However, since a BIT can potentially come into being between any two countries, each government must formulate every single BIT keeping in mind its relations with all other countries. An MFN clause thus makes it difficult for the government to differentiate autonomously the substance of BIT norms by country.

Another factor that promotes the de facto multilateralisation of BITs is the notion of 'investor' as a qualification for protection. Most BITs require only that the corporate 'investor' be 'established' in one party. Therefore, even if there is no BIT between a company's home state and the host state of its investment, the company can still enjoy protection under a treaty by channelling its investment through an affiliate estab-lished in the third country that has concluded a BIT with the host state.[19]

---

[17] Important among these are the 1959 Abs-Shawcross Draft Convention on Investment Abroad and the 1967 OECD Draft Convention on the Protection of Foreign Property.

[18] One may term this as 'serial multilateralism' instead of conventional 'conference multi-lateralism.' See Jeswald W. Salacuse, 'The emerging global regime for investment' (2010) 51 *Harvard International Law Journal* 427–473, at 465.

[19] This affiliate company can be a mere shell if the relevant BIT defines an 'investor' based on formal 'establishment' alone and does not contain any additional conditions. See International Centre for Settlement of Investment Disputes (ICSID), *Tokios Tokelés v. Ukraine*, ICSID Case No. ARB/02/18, Decision on Jurisdiction of 29 April 2004, paras. 19, 27–29.

In other words, if a state has concluded at least one BIT with a broad definition of investor, it must expect that, in practice, investors from around the world will take advantage of the legal protection specifically offered under the BIT. As the scope of BITs can be universalised like this, states will find it hard to control whom they should provide with legal protection.

2.2.2   How have arbitrations influenced the evolution of norms?

Countries in the South formerly insisted that foreign investment disputes be settled through the host state's local remedies, which are often susceptible to the influence of the state authorities. Modern investment treaties regularly bypass the local remedies of the host state and grant foreign investors the right to bring a case against the host state directly to an independent arbitral tribunal (usually referred to as the investor–state dispute settlement (ISDS) mechanism). Characteristic of this mechanism is the host state's general and prospective consent to arbitration expressed in each investment treaty, which allows arbitral tribunals to handle any investment-related disputes occurring in the future. This amounts to a form of compulsory jurisdiction of arbitral tribunals, concurrent with a loss of state control over the choice of cases to be adjudicated. The influence of states on the arbitral process is further curtailed through the well-established approach that the applicable law in investment arbitrations should be primarily the relevant investment treaty itself and not the host state's statutes.[20]

It is the governments that determine the text of investment treaties, and therefore states are still able to formulate the applicable rules. Nonetheless, substantive norms contained in these treaties have been generally written in very ambiguous language, such as the requirement to accord foreign investors 'fair and equitable' treatment. Arbitral tribunals have naturally assumed a gap-filling function and have produced an elaborate body of jurisprudence, sometimes reaching beyond the original intent of states. It should also be noted that the law has been advanced by arbitrators appointed in a private capacity, not by judges serving as public officials. The field of international investment law is thus characterised by a cycle of norm creation virtually removed from state control: arbitrations begin solely with the submission of disputes by foreign investors,

---

[20] ICSID, *Wena Hotels Ltd. v. Arab Republic of Egypt*, ICSID Case No. ARB/98/4, Decision on Annulment of 5 February 2002, para. 41.

and norms evolve through constructive interpretations derived from the legal expertise of arbitrators. From this perspective, a surge in recourse to investment arbitration and the consequent accumulation of arbitral awards have not only denationalised investment-related disputes but have also fostered an 'autonomous' legal process, where international discipline grows in its own right regardless of states' intent.

2.2.3 'Constitutionalisation' of international investment law

Building upon these novel features, some theorists have tried to apply the concept of constitutionalisation to the field of international investment law. As in the case of the WTO, these arguments basically seek to reinforce the international rule of law, i.e. to restrain states' sovereign discretion through international norms with enhanced autonomous character, thereby ensuring private actors a free and predictable business environment.[21]

On this view, one could find a constitutional element in the fact that modern BITs are effectively multilateralised rather than merely contractual or reciprocal.[22] Others put greater emphasis on the introduction of the private right of action, which has not been realised in the WTO, and argue that the rights of private actors are more directly protected in international investment law.[23] A further argument tackles the problem that the enhanced protection of foreign investment could erode the regulatory autonomy of states to pursue public policy objectives (e.g. concerning the environment, health, human rights) and attributes a constitutional function to arbitrators' ability to balance conflicting

---

[21] David Schneiderman, *Constitutionalizing Economic Globalization: Investment Rules and Democracy's Promise* (Cambridge: Cambridge University Press, 2008), p. 4. He notes that the investment rules regime 'has as its object the placing of legal limits on the authority of government, isolating economic from political power, and assigning to investment interests the highest possible protection. ... The ensemble of rules and institutions is a form of precommitment strategy that binds future generations. ... Like constitutions, they are difficult to amend, include binding enforcement mechanisms together with judicial review, and oftentimes are drawn from the language of national constitutions.'

[22] Consequently, the principles of investment protection have been interpreted in an objective manner rather than in deference to the subjective intent of states. See Schill (n. 16), pp. 372–373.

[23] Ernst-Ulrich Petersmann, 'Introduction and summary: "administration of justice" in international investment law and adjudication?', in Pierre-Marie Dupuy, Francesco Francioni and Ernst-Ulrich Petersmann (eds.), *Human Rights in International Investment Law and Arbitration* (Oxford; New York: Oxford University Press, 2009), p. 10; Alec Stone Sweet and Florian Grisel, 'Transnational investment arbitration: from delegation to constitutionalization?', in Dupuy, Francioni and Petersmann (eds.), ibid., pp. 126–127.

values.[24] This would correspond to the theory of constitutionalisation in the context of the WTO that focuses on the function of coordinating diverse values in a unified manner.

In sum, a variety of constitutionalisation theories in international investment law commonly take the properties of national constitutionalism as an ideal and expect the international norms to share the same function. To this extent, the notion of constitutionality among international trade and investment lawyers is very similar.

3 Reframing constitutionalism in the context of global governance

3.1 Mixed character of constitutionalism

3.1.1 Legitimacy crisis entailed in the reinforcement of international norms

This section is intended to examine whether and, if so, to what extent these 'constitutionalisation' arguments are plausible. There seems to be nothing wrong with the concept of international constitutionalism that they advocate, just as the fundamental ideals of constitutionalism developed in the domestic context are hardly questionable. Is it then a simple truism that the international society is encouraged to evolve following the blueprint presented by the international constitutionalists and not vice versa?

On the one hand, the reinforced legal and institutional structures of the WTO and BITs can undoubtedly enhance several constitutional values. They can prevent states from exercising their power arbitrarily against private actors. The judicialisation and compulsory jurisdiction of the dispute settlement system have improved the individuals' right to free trade and the foreign investors' right to property. Opportunistic behaviour of governments is clearly diminished, and the rule of law is enhanced. It is undeniable that the WTO Agreement and investment treaties have made an important contribution to the fulfilment of constitutional ideals in a certain sphere of the global society.

On the other hand, the same laws and institutions may sometimes disturb, or detract from, the realisation of other constitutional values. WTO law has been criticised for not giving enough consideration to non-

---

[24] Suzanne A. Spears, 'The quest for policy space in a new generation of international investment agreements' (2010) 13 *Journal of International Economic Law* 1038–1075, at 1072; Schill (n. 16), pp. 375–378.

trade issues (e.g. environmental protection, public health, food safety and human rights), reflecting the WTO legal system's bias towards free trade. Investment treaties have also caused disputes that involve tensions between an investor's rights and the host state's legitimate interest in regulating for the public good. From this perspective, ensuring economic freedom for some may harm the rights of others, such as the right to safe food, medicine and a clean environment. In addition, global institutions' second-guessing of judgments made by democratically accountable political branches may detract from the value of popular self-governance at the national level.

A treaty regime can obviously work alongside national constitutions to facilitate the realisation of specific values that coincide with the treaty's objective. As a consequence, however, it will also affect negatively the attainment of other values external to the treaty. This is because values always risk clashing, contradicting each other,[25] and thus cannot be realised to their fullest extent at the same time. As Isaiah Berlin puts it, 'we are faced with choices between ends equally ultimate, and claims equally absolute, the realisation of some of which must inevitably involve the sacrifice of others'.[26] Moreover, if values are equally absolute and incommensurable, we cannot formulate a unified priority among them that could accommodate the conflict.

We must therefore recognise that WTO law and investment treaties have a mixed effect on the constitutional values seen in their totality. If, as the constitutionalisation theories prefer, these treaty norms continue to evolve towards an autonomous legal order detached from the subjective goals of individual states, there is a risk of injuring the constitutional rights or liberties of people who give weight to values other than economic freedom.

3.1.2 Partialised public authorities in the global society

Such a mixed character of constitutionalism is of course not a feature unique to global governance. In the context of national constitutionalism, various constitutional ideals cannot be realised without conflict among them. Nonetheless, national societies can make decisions that address conflicts of constitutional values legitimately through the comprehensive mechanism of democratic politics. As the modern state monopolises public power on a territorial basis, it is competent to handle

---

[25] Victor M. Muñiz-Fraticelli, *The Structure of Pluralism: On the Authority of Associations* (Oxford: Oxford University Press, 2014), p. 15.

[26] Isaiah Berlin, 'Two concepts of liberty', in Henry Hardy and Roger Hausheer (eds.), *The Proper Study of Mankind* (London: Farrar, Strauss, Giroux, 1997), p. 239.

any kind of societal values developed in that territory and is expected to determine from a holistic perspective which should be prioritised.

In the last few decades, however, many different public authorities of state have dispersed into multilateral, regional and transnational bodies. Norms created by these bodies now cover wide-ranging areas traditionally left to national law and impact individuals' basic interests without respecting national legitimation channels.[27] Although actors involved in such rule making have their own constituencies that may hold them accountable through delegation mechanisms, these constituencies do not necessarily coincide with all the persons actually affected by the decisions.[28] It is difficult for a public debate that could influence the rule making, an essential element of democratic legitimacy, to take place there.[29]

To make matters worse, the public authorities on the international level appear in a fragmented manner, as they are constituted on a function-by-function basis. Many are dominated by those who have highly specialised knowledge and technologies and who work for what is in their parochial interest – almost certainly not in the interest of the wider public.[30] This generates the risk of injuring some critical values lying outside these functional regimes, since decisions taken within them often have a cross-sectional impact.[31]

---

[27] Samantha Besson, 'Ubi ius, ibi civitas: a republican account of the international community', in Samantha Besson and José L. Martí (eds.), *Legal Republicanism: National and International Perspective* (Oxford: Oxford University Press, 2009), p. 215. Accordingly, as von Bogdandy and Venzke put it, 'any conception of public authority which continues to include only national authority fails to grasp the extent to which international institutions influence political self-determination and social interactions'. See Armin von Bogdandy and Ingo Venzke, *In Whose Name? A Public Law Theory of International Adjudication*, translated by Thomas Dunlap (Oxford: Oxford University Press, 2014), p. 113.

[28] Tim Corthaut, Bruno Demeyere, Nicholas Hachez and Jan Wouters, 'Operationalizing accountability in respect of informal international lawmaking mechanisms', in Joost Pauwelyn, Ramses A. Wessel and Jan Wouters (eds.), *Informal International Lawmaking* (Oxford: Oxford University Press, 2012), p. 315.

[29] Von Bogdandy and Venzke (n. 27), p. 122.

[30] John S. Dryzek, *Foundations and Frontiers of Deliberative Governance* (Oxford: Oxford University Press, 2010), p. 122. See also Gunther Teubner, *Constitutional Fragments: Societal Constitutionalism and Globalization*, translated by Gareth Norbury (Oxford: Oxford University Press, 2012); Peter M. Haas, 'Introduction: epistemic communities and international policy coordination' (1992) 46 *International Organization* 1–35, at 3; Kalypso Nicolaïdis and Joyce L. Tong, 'Diversity or cacophony? The continuing debate over new sources of international law' (2004) 25 *Michigan Journal of International Law* 1349–1375.

[31] Thomas Kleinlein, 'Judicial lawmaking by judicial restraint? The potential of balancing in international economic law', in Armin von Bogdandy and Ingo Venzke (eds.),

Conflict among constitutional values therefore becomes more evident where public authorities are largely dispersed into globalised but fragmented polities. If a given polity attempts to realise one of the constitutional norms better, other constitutional norms might be countervailed in another polity. Although these polities may sometimes be mutually supportive and can share common constitutional norms, tensions and incompatibility are more likely to come about. The crucial fact is that in a global context, all the polities including states are incomplete and imperfect in terms of protecting constitutional values and human liberty.

If this is indeed true, both the universalistic conception and relativistic (or statist) conceptions of constitutionalism should be rejected because they assume the complete constitutional legitimacy of either international institutions or national sovereign authorities. On the one hand, the statist approach, which seeks to re-establish popular democracy by resisting the intrusion of external norms into the nation state's constitutional space, disregards some positive aspects derived from the development of global institutions.[32] For example, international norms can promote values that are difficult to fulfil through the efforts of individual states (e.g. stopping climate change, reducing poverty, combatting terrorism and stabilising currency). On the other hand, existing constitutionalisation theories in international trade and investment law are also misconceived. National sovereignty could be sometimes a source of legitimate value judgments rather than of trouble. From the perspective of global legal pluralism, as Jean Cohen puts it, 'the constitutionalisation of the global political system is neither a feasible nor a desirable response to the new forms of global power, for it would threaten the diversity, autonomy, and legitimacy of competing normative and political orders'.[33] If the ever-increasing power of international bodies is taken seriously, the need is to control in a constitutional manner the exercise of power by the international regulators.

This last point will lead us to seek a reformulated notion of constitutional legitimacy rather than to dismiss the idea of constitutionalism from global economic governance altogether.

International Judicial Lawmaking: On Public Authority and Democratic Legitimation in Global Governance (Heidelberg: Springer, 2012), p. 255.

[32] Oren Perez and Daphne Barak-Erez, 'The administrative state goes global', in Michael A. Helfand (ed.), *Negotiating State and Non-State Law: The Challenge of Global and Local Legal Pluralism* (New York: Cambridge University Press, 2015), p. 165.

[33] Jean L. Cohen, *Globalization and Sovereignty: Rethinking Legality, Legitimacy, and Constitutionalism* (Cambridge: Cambridge University Press, 2012), p. 22.

3.2   How to secure the constitutional legitimacy

3.2.1   Criteria for assessing the legitimacy

If the conflict among values is inevitable, no polity could make a decision that would be absolutely correct in constitutional terms. However, a decision that has negative effects on certain constitutional values can still be considered as reasonable or justifiable when certain conditions are met, namely when all those affected by the decision are given a chance to have an input into the decision-making process and those voices are treated as on a par with each other. What underlies these conditions is the notion of autonomy or self-determination: this ultimately justifies the exercise of public authority. A privilege can be accorded to these conditions without contradicting the tenets of pluralism, since they form a proto-value that ensures fair political process when clashes of normal values are addressed.[34]

This idea of political self-government is inherently related to the defence of liberty, particularly understood in republican terms. It corresponds typically to the absence of domination: one is dominated by others when one's freedom to choose between certain options is reduced by their control over that choice, i.e. by the imposition of an alien will.[35] In order to realise this liberty, citizens should enjoy equal access to power or equally effective political influence. As soon as some citizens have greater political influence than others, they are more capable of imposing their desires, beliefs or preferences than others and thus are more likely to dominate others.[36] Non-domination is secured by treating each person as worthy of equal concern and respect as an autonomous source of reasons and information about their collective life.[37] To put it another way, decision makers are obligated to 'listen to the other side' (*audi alterem partem*)[38] and to show equal concern and respect to all relevant views.

---

[34]   This idea is also captured in the concept of 'the right to have rights', namely 'the status of being a citizen that permits participation in an ongoing reflexive and constitutive political process'. See James Bohman, 'Cosmopolitan republicanism and the rule of law', in Besson and Martí (eds.), *Legal Republicanism* (n. 27), p. 63.

[35]   Philip Pettit, 'Law and liberty', in Besson and Martí (eds.), *Legal Republicanism* (n. 27), p. 42.

[36]   Samantha Besson and José L. Martí, 'Law and republicanism: mapping the issues', in Besson and Martí (eds.), *Legal Republicanism* (n. 27), p. 18.

[37]   Richard Bellamy, 'The republic of reasons: public reasoning, depoliticization, and non-domination', in Besson and Martí (eds.), *Legal Republicanism* (n. 27), p. 105.

[38]   Philip Pettit, *Republicanism: A Theory of Freedom and Government* (Oxford; New York: Oxford University Press, 1997), p. 189.

To this end, decisions should not be legitimated based on voting or other formal thresholds alone; they should be considered legitimate only when based on good reasons. This reflects the spirit of deliberative democracy, a form of government in which public decisions are justified through free and equal citizens giving one another reasons that are mutually acceptable and generally accessible.[39] Admittedly, attaining consensus may still be difficult even when the deliberative process operates effectively, since any public decision can harm certain societal values. Decisions short of consensus may, however, be *justified* when those who are negatively affected and who disagree with the ultimate outcome itself still accept the grounds of such decisions as reasonable. In this regard, the goal of deliberation does not lie in achieving consensus but in producing meta-consensus that the legitimacy of public decisions depends on the quality of reasons presented.[40]

Obviously, a decision made with an attitude that insists on a partial value and that does not go beyond narrow self-interest would be hardly regarded as reasonable.[41] Rational deliberation requires that each actor not only try to persuade others but also be *open to persuasion*.[42] As Clarissa Hayward notes, 'the deliberative model assumes, in particular, that people's perceptions of what it is that serves their good can ... change in response to the reasoned exchange of opinions and arguments'.[43] During political decision making, we should accordingly recognise heterogeneity and interpretative conflict as a resource and not

---

[39] Pettit (n. 35), p. 55. For another explanation, 'the basic proposition of deliberative theory is that any claim to legitimacy must justify itself in an intersubjective discourse'. See Christoph Möllers, *The Three Branches: A Comparative Model of Separation of Powers* (Oxford: Oxford University Press, 2013), p. 60.

[40] According to Dryzek, 'meta-consensus can refer to agreement on the legitimacy of contested values, on the validity of disputed judgments, on the acceptability and structure of competing preferences, and on the applicability of contested discourses'. See Dryzek (n. 30), p. 15.

[41] Ian Johnstone, *The Power of Deliberation: International Law, Politics and Organizations* (New York: Oxford University Press, 2011), p. 16.

[42] Ibid., p. 14.

[43] Clarissa Hayward, 'Making interest: on representation and democratic legitimacy', in Ian Shapiro, Susan C. Stokes, Elisabeth J. Wood and Alexander S. Kirshner (eds.), *Political Representation* (Cambridge; New York: Cambridge University Press, 2009), p. 119. Hayward adds that 'deliberative democrats are right to underscore that interests are not fixed or static: that much of what happens in democratic politics is not simply a matter of *responding to* people's interests and preferences ... but also of *shaping* what it is that people want and/or what it is that serves their good' (ibid., p. 121, emphasis in the original text).

as an obstacle to deliberative problem solving.[44] After all, if the principle of non-domination is taken seriously, ensuring the *contestability* of all public decisions will be the most important guideline in designing deliberative institutions.[45]

Based on the preceding discussion, we can now describe the proper concept of global constitutionalism today. Assuming no polity in the global society can promote its own constitutional values without impairing another's, global constitutionalism should not so much aim to protect specific values, as is often argued, as it should rather aim to provide guarantees to safeguard the political process. Decisions affecting groups of people should be, at the very least, taken after those groups have been consulted and provided with a chance to persuade.[46] If global constitutionalism seeks to enhance human liberty and autonomy in the global legal arena, it should be careful not to narrow its ambition to the promotion of specific values attainable through the development of specialised international norms; it should concern itself with the issue of autonomy and self-determination of people in the broader society, an issue often disregarded in international legal affairs.

As noted, constitutionalisation theories in international economic law tend to emphasise the international rule of law. The norms that fall in the scope of 'law' here are, however, limited to those that protect certain parochial values. In addition, such values are largely rooted in the Western neo-liberal market economies, where the idea of 'fair competition' prevails over government intervention in the market. While these values have now spread into non-Western areas and have undoubtedly stimulated economic growth, they have also come into conflict with several values common in these areas. If that is the case, the constitutional character of a global economic institution should be assessed according to the extent that it grants equal and serious consideration to inputs from different areas of the world, particularly when these seem incompatible with that institution's essential values.

[44] Johnstone (n. 41), p. 25.
[45] Iseult Honohan, 'Republicans, rights, and constitutions: is judicial review compatible with republican self-government?', in Besson and Martí (eds.), *Legal Republicanism* (n. 27), p. 91.
[46] Jan Klabbers, 'The right to be taken seriously: self-determination in international law' (2006) 28 *Human Rights Quarterly* 186–206, at 203.

3.2.2   Ways to reach reasonable decisions

How then can global institutions seeking to realise the idea of deliberative democracy actually create a context for reasonable deliberation? Some of the methods and principles to be followed will be discussed here.

In order to account for possible negative externalities and the external interests of the global community, decision making should first of all be transparent and accessible to relevant parties in civil society as well as to affected administrators. To that end, institutions must facilitate information distribution to permit inclusive, informed contestation of their current terms of accountability.[47] This form of accountability is analogous to that provided by domestic administrative law (the requirements of hearings, transparency, notice and reason giving, perhaps with judicial review).[48] Administrative procedure could on many occasions offer a forum for the deliberative exchange of views regarding the content of a sector-specific rule. In this context, the 'global administrative law' project attains its plausibility.[49] Its emphasis on greater transparency, accountability and enhanced procedural fairness suggests that decisions made within a transnational regime would be more legitimate.[50]

Second, the coordination among the distinct autonomous, at times competitive yet interrelated, legal orders should proceed through non-hierarchical dialogue and mutual accommodation.[51] Interrelations between global polities including states should specifically (1) seek moderate normative consistencies instead of hierarchical integrity of law; (2) generate norms through friction, mutual observation and reflection between partial legal orders; and (3) respond to collisions of norms in a decentralised manner.[52] From this perspective, if global polities aim to interact with each other on an equal footing, they must show proper

---

[47] Allen Buchanan, *Human Rights, Legitimacy, and the Use of Force* (Oxford; New York: Oxford University Press, 2010), pp. 123–124.

[48] Johnstone (n. 41), p. 30.

[49] See, e.g., Benedict Kingsbury, Nico Krisch and Richard B. Stewart, 'The emergence of global administrative law' (2005) 68 *Law and Contemporary Problems* 15–61; Gordon Anthony, Jean-Bernard Auby, John Morison and Tom Zwart (eds.), *Values in Global Administrative Law* (Oxford: Hart Publishing, 2011). See also Richard B. Stewart, 'Remedying disregard in global regulatory governance: accountability, participation, and responsiveness' (2014) 108 *American Journal of International Law* 211–270.

[50] Friedrich Kratochwil, *The Status of Law in World Society: Meditations on the Role and Rule of Law* (Cambridge: Cambridge University Press, 2014), p. 180.

[51] Cohen (n. 33), p. 70.

[52] Andreas Fischer-Lescano and Gunther Teubner, *Regime-Kollisionen: Zur Fragmentierung des globalen Rechts* (Frankfurt am Main: Suhrkamp, 2006), p. 62.

KAZUYORI ITO

deference to each other, as expressed, for example, in the principle of subsidiarity. Subsidiarity doctrines force decision makers to enquire whether there is another authority better positioned to decide an issue.[53] At the same time, the equal standing of polities will also require each polity to be involved in mutual monitoring of constitutional legitimacy. A polity is thereby to refuse to treat another polity's decision as reasonably acceptable if the decision's harm to the deliberative values is sufficiently serious. This constitutes a form of *conditional* deference, where a decision of a public authority is justified *as long as* it is consistent with autonomy and self-determination of citizens. The sense of being monitored might induce each polity to explain and justify decisions in a way comprehensible to others.

Third, judicial organs should be recognised as active participants in the process of deliberation. Judicial opinions are accordingly expected to be written in the form of presenting public reasons and to be conscious of the equal standing of polities, which requires them to be properly deferential. Again, however, such deference should be made contingent upon the fulfilment by the respective decision maker of minimum due process requirements, which would guarantee the inclusion and consideration of external interests.[54] The adjudicating bodies should therefore develop international standards of adequate consideration and afford more deference to domestic or international regulators that honour them.[55] To the extent that multiple judicial organs in the global society are conducive to the reasoned exchange of views, their legitimacy will be enhanced.

As seen, the relationship between global polities including states should be recognised as neither hierarchical nor isolated. Such a 'non-edged' structure of world order might hardly seem to be constitutional according to either the universalistic or statist conception of constitutionalism. If,

---

[53] Paul S. Berman, 'Non-state lawmaking through the lens of global legal pluralism', in Michael A. Helfand (ed.), *Negotiating State and Non-State Law: The Challenge of Global and Local Legal Pluralism* (New York: Cambridge University Press, 2015), p. 30. Mattias Kumm offers another explanation: 'at its core, the principle of subsidiarity requires any infringements of the autonomy of the local level by means of preemptive norms enacted on the higher level to be justified by good reasons'. See Matthias Kumm, 'Constitutional democracy encounters international law: terms of engagement', in Sujit Choudhry (ed.), *The Migration of Constitutional Ideas* (Cambridge: Cambridge University Press, 2007), p. 264.

[54] Michael Ioannidis, 'A procedural approach to the legitimacy of international adjudication: developing standards of participation in WTO law', in von Bogdandy and Venzke (eds.) (n. 31), p. 246.

[55] Ibid., p. 249.

however, we take autonomy and self-determination of people seriously, decision making based on the sense of parity among polities would be the essential criterion of constitutional politics. With this concept of global constitutionalism in mind, the next section will assess anew the constitutional legitimacy of some practices adopted under the WTO Agreement and investment treaties.

4 Assessing the constitutional legitimacy of economic governance regimes

4.1 Aspects of constitutional significance in international trade law

4.1.1 Necessity test in the general exception clause

Article 20 of the GATT is an exception clause that can serve to justify trade restrictions otherwise amounting to a violation of the GATT. Under it, a contracting party may adopt a trade-restrictive measure in order to protect non-trade values such as public morals or human health, provided that the measure is 'necessary' to achieve the objective intended. In assessing whether the measure is necessary or not, the WTO judicial body tends to weigh and balance a series of factors. It recognises, however, each party's prerogative to determine what objectives should be sought in its jurisdiction. For the Appellate Body:

> The fundamental principle is the right that WTO Members have to determine the level of protection that they consider appropriate in a given context. Another key element of the analysis of the necessity . . . is the contribution it brings to the achievement of its objective. A contribution exists when there is a genuine relationship of ends and means between the objective pursued and the measure at issue.[56]

The principal task of the WTO judicial body is not to second-guess the substantive value assessment undertaken domestically but to determine whether the measure is supported by coherent reasoning and positive causality and is in this sense objectively justifiable.[57] If it is found, for example, that an alternative measure would achieve the same end and be less restrictive of trade, the member state will be required to replace its

---

[56] WTO, *Brazil – Measures Affecting Imports of Retreaded Tyres*, Report of the Appellate Body of 3 December 2007, WT/DS332/AB/R, para. 210.

[57] For this formulation, see WTO, *United States – Continued Suspension of Obligations in the EC – Hormones Dispute*, Report of the Appellate Body of 16 October 2008, WT/DS320/AB/R, para. 590.

measure[58] – an ordering that is by no means hierarchical but is based on reasonableness.

Article 20 contains another requirement that 'such measures are not applied in a manner which would constitute a means of arbitrary or unjustifiable discrimination between countries where the same conditions prevail'. Arbitrary discrimination has been considered to exist when a measure does not respect the principles of due process (such as transparency, opportunity to be heard, reason giving and procedure for review); in this situation, the parties concerned cannot be certain whether their respective views are treated in a fair and just manner.[59] The WTO judicial body will consider a trade restriction to be acceptable as long as the decision-making authority guarantees foreign interests a chance to present their own reasons in domestic procedures. The development of such a standard of review should not be understood as deference to national sovereignty as such but as deference to procedurally legitimate decision making.[60]

The way in which Article 20 is applied shows the growing practice of conditional deference in the exercise of judicial power reinforced under the WTO. This will enhance, rather than diminish, the constitutional legitimacy attached to the judicial mechanism, provided we agree with the deliberative concept of constitutionalism.

4.1.2   International standards developed in other institutions

Procedural conditions requiring transparency, participation and deliberativeness are also directed to international bodies that produce norms relevant to WTO law, such as international standards. Article 2.4 of the TBT Agreement provides that member states shall use relevant international standards as a basis for formulating their own technical regulations to trade. While the TBT Agreement does not explain what qualifies as 'relevant' international standards, the TBT Committee, which is responsible for the agreement's implementation, adopted a decision in 2000 entitled Principles for the Development of International Standards.[61]

---

[58] As an illustration, see WTO, *China – Measures Affecting Trading Rights and Distribution Services for Certain Publications and Audiovisual Entertainment Products*, Report of the Panel of 12 August 2009, WT/DS363/R, paras. 7.887–7.909.

[59] WTO, *United States – Import Prohibition of Certain Shrimp and Shrimp Products*, Report of the Appellate Body of 12 October 1998, WT/DS320/AB/R, paras. 180–181.

[60] Ioannidis (n. 54), p. 247.

[61] Committee on Technical Barriers to Trade, Decision of the Committee on Principles for the Development of International Standards, Guides and Recommendations with relation to Articles 2, 5 and Annex 3 of the Agreement, G/TBT/9, Annex 4, 13 November 2000.

This decision specifies six principles that should be respected during international standard setting: (1) transparency, (2) openness, (3) impartiality and consensus, (4) effectiveness and relevance, (5) coherence and (6) development dimension. These can be read as requiring that more input from a wider set of interests be provided in the international standardisation community.[62]

The Appellate Body later found that the decision constitutes a 'subsequent agreement between the parties' in the meaning of Article 31(3)(a) of the Vienna Convention on the Law of Treaties and that it shall be taken into account when interpreting the TBT Agreement.[63] In fact, in the US-Tuna II case, the Appellate Body refused to treat the Agreement on the International Dolphin Conservation Program (AIDCP) as a source of 'relevant' international standards because its membership is not 'open on a non-discriminatory basis to relevant bodies of at least all WTO Members' as required by the TBT Committee decision.[64] Further, the Appellate Body affirmed the general imperative that international standardising bodies ensure transparency and representative participation without privileging any particular interests in developing international standards.[65] It is on the condition that such principles are duly respected and meaningful opportunities for deliberation are afforded that the WTO judicial body could opt for greater deference to the decisions made by international standard setters. This style of cross-institutional review would follow a middle way between uncritical endorsement and categorical rejection[66] and for that reason could be held as constitutionally plausible.

4.1.3 Non-compliance with judicial decisions

There have been several cases where member states refused to comply with WTO rulings. As noted, the DSU allows a complaining party to suspend concessions or other obligations in response to the failure of

[62] Panagiotis Delimatsis, '"Relevant International Standards" and "Recognised Standardisation Bodies" under the TBT Agreement', in Panagiotis Delimatsis (ed.), The Law, Economics and Politics of International Standardisation (Cambridge: Cambridge University Press, 2015), p. 131.
[63] WTO, United States – Measures Concerning the Importation, Marketing and Sale of Tuna and Tuna Products, Report of the Appellate Body of 16 May 2012, WT/DS381/AB/R, paras. 371–372.
[64] The AIDCP standard of tuna-fishing technique has been agreed by only a dozen countries, and if other countries wish to join, the existing parties to the AIDCP must decide to invite them by consensus (ibid., paras. 398–399).
[65] Ibid., paras. 379, 384.
[66] Von Bogdandy and Venzke (n. 27), p. 204.

a defendant party to implement a judicial decision (Article 22(1)). At the same time, Article 22(4) stipulates that the level of the suspension of concessions shall be equivalent to the level of the nullification or impairment. This provision is expected to work as a restraint on the escalation of disputes,[67] based on the recognition that the suspension of concessions shall be temporary and be applied only until the challenged measure has been removed (Article 22(8)). That said, the equivalence rule has occasionally caused both the challenged and retaliatory measures to exist simultaneously for a long time due to the lack of pressure exerted by the suspension of concessions. Particularly when the infringing measure protects a value of vital importance in the defendant's society, the government will seek to maintain the measure despite the cost of the 'equivalent' retaliation from trade partners.

This kind of wilful non-compliance with international rulings appears to be nothing but an unconstitutional phenomenon. From another perspective, however, non-compliance could be considered a reaction to the excessive intrusion of international discipline into the vital values of national society. In this situation, the defendant party might even try to create a novel equilibrium of rights and obligations distinct from the lawful solution indicated in the judicial decision. To cite one case, the European Union has maintained an import ban on beef products made using growth hormones, even after the ban was judged to be inconsistent with WTO law and the United States suspended concessions on EU products. The sides eventually agreed that the EU can maintain the import ban if it offers a duty-free quota on beef products made without using hormones, while the United States shall terminate its retaliatory measure after three years.[68]

---

[67] Robert E. Hudec, 'Broadening the scope of remedies in WTO dispute settlement', in Friedl Weiss (ed.), *Improving WTO Dispute Settlement Procedures* (London: Cameron May, 2000), pp. 389–390.

[68] WTO, *European Communities – Measures Concerning Meat and Meat Products (Hormones)*, Joint Communication from the European Communities and the United States of 30 September 2009, WT/DS26/28. For other cases in which disputing parties arrived at mutually agreed solutions without the challenged measures being brought into conformity with WTO law, see WTO, *European Communities – Regime for the Importation of Bananas*, Geneva Agreement on Trade in Bananas of 15 December 2009, WT/L/784; WTO, *United States – Subsidies on Upland Cotton*, Notification of a Mutually Agreed Solution of 23 October 2014, WT/DS267/46; WTO, *United States – Final Countervailing Duty Determination with Respect to Certain Softwood Lumber from Canada*, Notification of Mutually Agreed Solution of 16 November 2006, WT/DS257/26; WTO, *United States – Section 110(5) of the US Copyright Act*, Notification of a Mutually Satisfactory Temporary Arrangement of 26 June 2003, WT/DS160/23.

Under such circumstances, non-compliance could be arguably characterised as an objection or a challenge to the reasonableness of the legal
opinions expressed by the WTO judicial body, though not all the
instances of non-compliance have such a character. A latent option of
non-compliance could be used as a means of conditional deference by
states to international adjudicators.

4.2 Aspects of constitutional significance in international investment law

4.2.1 Proportionality analysis and the host state's regulatory autonomy

In the field of international investment law, arbitral tribunals are increasingly involved in proportionality analysis, particularly in disputes that
involve tensions between an investor's rights and the host state's legitimate interest in regulating for the public good. In domestic constitutional law, proportionality analysis has been commonly used to mediate
the conflict between private autonomy and the public good.[69]
In investment case law, proportionality analysis is often referred to in
order to distinguish between indirect expropriation that requires compensation and regulation that is non-compensable. Most tribunals do not
consider solely the effects of the host state's regulatory measure but also
the object and purpose of the measure, which must then be balanced
relative to its effects.[70] According to one arbitral award:

> After establishing that regulatory actions and measures will not be initially
> excluded from the definition of expropriatory acts, in addition to the
> negative financial impact of such actions or measures, the Arbitral
> Tribunal will consider, *in order to determine if they are to be characterised*
> *as expropriatory, whether such actions or measures are proportional to the*
> *public interest presumably protected thereby and to the protection legally*

---

[69] According to German legal doctrine, proportionality analysis demands a four-step
evaluation of the impugned measure: first, the measure must pursue a legitimate
aim; second, it must be suitable or effective for the achievement of the stated objective;
third, it must be necessary, which means that no less restrictive or less intrusive alternative is available; fourth, it must be appropriate for the achievement of the aim. See
Ahron Barak, *Proportionality: Constitutional Rights and Their Limitations*, translated by
Doron Kalir (New York: Cambridge University Press, 2012); Matthias Klatt and
Moritz Meister, *The Constitutional Structure of Proportionality* (Oxford: Oxford
University Press, 2012).

[70] Kleinlein (n. 31), p. 268.

granted to investments, taking into account that the significance of such impact has a key role upon deciding the proportionality.[71]

Proportionality analysis has been also used to assess whether a regulatory measure is consistent with the 'fair and equitable treatment' standard. In the *Total* case, the tribunal said, 'the circumstances and reasons (importance and urgency of the public need pursued) for carrying out a change impacting negatively on a foreign investor's operations on the one hand, and the seriousness of the prejudice caused on the other hand, compared in the light of a standard of reasonableness and proportionality are relevant'.[72]

It may seem that proportionality analysis, which compares competing values rather directly, could be more intrusive than the WTO's necessity test.[73] In practice, arbitral tribunals relying on proportionality analysis have not so much engaged in substantive balancing of ends and means as they have examined whether state authorities can offer reasonable and coherent explanations for the challenged measure. We should not understand balancing under proportionality analysis in utilitarian or consequentialist terms[74] but as a matter of assessing the relative strength of reasons.[75] It is thus an essential ingredient of rational balancing that each regulatory action provides for a transparent procedure of argumentation

---

[71] ICSID, *Técnicas Medioambientales Tecmed, S.A. v. United Mexican States,* ICSID Case No. ARB (AF)/00/2, Award of 29 May 2003, para. 122 (emphasis added). For other arbitral awards that rely on proportionality analysis in determining whether indirect expropriation exists, see ICSID, *LG&E Energy Corp., LG&E Capital Corp., and LG&E International, Inc. v. Argentine Republic,* ICSID Case No. ARB/02/1, Decision on Liability of 3 October 2006, paras. 194–195; ICSID, *Azurix Corp. v. The Argentine Republic,* ICSID Case No. ARB/01/12, Award of 14 July 2006, paras. 311–312, 322; ICSID, *Occidental Petroleum Corporation and Occidental Exploration and Production Company v. The Republic of Ecuador,* ICSID Case No. ARB/06/11, Award of 5 October 2012, para. 450.

[72] ICSID, *Total S.A. v. The Argentine Republic,* ICSID Case No. ARB/04/01, Decision on Liability of 27 December 2010, para. 123. See also ICSID, *EDF (Services) Limited v. Romania,* ICSID Case No. ARB/05/13, Award of 8 October 2009, paras. 292–293; ICSID, *AES Summit Generation Limited and AES-Tisza ErömüKft v. The Republic of Hungary,* ICSID Case No. ARB/07/22, Award of 23 September 2010, para. 10.3.9.

[73] It is argued that proportionality sensu stricto demands a weighing and balancing of competing interests with the possible consequence that a measure may be found illegal because it imposes an undue disadvantage even if no alternative was available that could have achieved the stated objective to the same extent. See Ingo Venzke, 'Making general exceptions: the spell of precedents in developing Article XX GATT into standards for domestic regulatory policy', in von Bogdandy and Venzke (eds.) (n. 31), p. 203.

[74] Kai Möller, *The Global Model of Constitutional Rights* (Oxford: Oxford University Press, 2012), p. 134.

[75] Ibid., p. 139.

and an adequate reason for decision.[76] In sum, arbitral tribunals have used proportionality analysis to require states to ensure deliberative decision making that does not exclude inputs from foreign investors.[77]

4.2.2 Standards created in other fields

When it comes to the horizontal relationship between investment treaties and treaties in other fields, there have been some noteworthy cases where arbitral tribunals referred to the standards established by certain non-investment treaties in order to examine whether the host state accorded 'fair and equitable treatment' to foreign investors.

For instance, in the *Chemtura v. Canada* case, a US company challenged a Canadian regulatory measure that prohibits the use or sale of pesticides containing lindane. In its rebuttal, Canada stressed that this chemical substance had raised serious concerns at the international level, as exemplified by the Aarhus Protocol on Persistent Organic Pollutants of 1998 (restricting the use of lindane and requiring a reassessment of lindane) and the Stockholm Convention on Persistent Organic Pollutants (including lindane among the chemicals designated for elimination in 2009).[78] The arbitral tribunal observed that the Canadian authority had introduced the measure in pursuance of its mandate and the country's international obligations,[79] and it concluded that Canada acted in conformity with the obligation to secure fair and equitable treatment.

In the *Philip Morris v. Uruguay* case, a Uruguayan presidential decree that requires 80 per cent of the surface of cigarette packages to be covered by health warnings was challenged as impairing the claimant's right to use its legally protected trademarks and thereby reducing the value of its investment. The arbitral tribunal found that the principle of large health warnings is internationally accepted, because the World Health Organization (WHO) Framework Convention on Tobacco Control (FCTC) provides in Article 11(1)(b)(iv) that health warnings on cigarette packages 'should be 50% or more of the principal display areas but shall

---

[76] Kleinlein (n. 31), pp. 285–286.

[77] The tribunal in the *Tecmed* case notably stated that 'it should be also considered that the foreign investor has a reduced or nil participation in the taking of the decisions that affect it, partly because the investors are not entitled to exercise political rights reserved to the nationals of the State'. See ICSID, *Técnicas Medioambientales Tecmed, S.A. v. United Mexican States* (n. 71), para. 122.

[78] *Chemtura Corporation v. Government of Canada*, Arbitration under UNCITRAL Rules, Award of 2 August 2010, paras. 135–136.

[79] Ibid., paras. 138–143.

be no less than 30% of the principal display areas'.[80] The arbitral tribunal deemed the decree to be a reasonable measure issued in good faith to implement an obligation assumed by Uruguay under the FCTC and its adoption not to be a breach of the standard of fair and equitable treatment.[81]

Apparently, relying on outside treaties as a criterion for evaluating legality is a proper way to treat investment protection and other societal values on an equal footing. Unquestioning acceptance of norms and standards created under external institutions would, however, be more detrimental than beneficial to the enhancement of deliberative legitimacy. Deference should be *conditional* on how far the standard-setting process in an outside regime is transparent, participatory, objective and intercultural – factors that indicate whether decisions are based on good reasons. Because the arbitral awards mentioned do not consider these factors, coming close instead to an attitude of simple deference, they are not yet fully justifiable in constitutional terms.

5   Conclusion

If one understands international and national constitutionalism in a functionally analogous manner, as constitutionalisation theories in international economic law often do, the development of any treaty regime (or of its judicial organ in particular) would be surely welcome. A pluralist insight reveals, however, that the advancement of certain societal values would inevitably involve the sacrifice of others and that there could be no unified order of priority capable of accommodating the conflict. On this assumption, constitutionalism associated solely with the evolution of a specific treaty regime would effectively entail a mixed impact on the global society as a whole: what is fair can be foul, depending on one's standpoint.

Nevertheless, decisions of each polity could be universally justified if all those affected by the decisions were granted a chance to have an input in the decision-making process rather than being required simply to accept the results. Although value conflicts themselves would never disappear, decisions achieved with equal concern and respect for all relevant views are most likely to ensure that each person has the

---

[80] ICSID, *Philip Morris Brands Sàrl, Philip Morris Products S.A. and Abal Hermanos S.A. v. Oriental Republic of Uruguay*, ICSID Case No. ARB/10/7, Award of 8 July 2016, para. 412.

[81] Ibid., para. 420.

opportunity for self-determination, which constitutes a fundamental element of human liberty. Global polities should therefore not so much seek to prioritise their own specific values as they should focus on the issue of autonomy of people in the broader society and deliberate on whether their exercise of power is based on good reasons. In this regard, an exchange of views across sectoral, cultural and generational lines would be of primary importance for enhancing the reasonableness of decisions. If we attempt to entrench these ideas of political legitimacy among decision makers and participants in global polities, the concept of global constitutionalism, as it is (re)formulated in this chapter, would be not just useful; it would be indispensable.

13

Conceptualising Global Environmental Constitutionalism in a Regional Context

Perspectives from Asia and Europe

LOUIS J. KOTZÉ[*]

1 Introduction

Global environmental quality has been steadily deteriorating as a result of expanding drivers of socioecological change including, among others, industrialisation, population growth, expansion of neo-liberal consumer-oriented economies and growth-without-limits developmental paradigms embedded in political leitmotifs such as 'sustainable development' and 'green economy'. The United Nations Environment Programme (UNEP) in its *Global Environmental Outlook 5* confirms that anthropogenic drivers of environmental change are 'growing, evolving and combining at such an accelerating pace, at such a large scale and with such widespread reach that they are exerting unprecedented pressure on the environment'.[1] The result is an impending, and in some instances very real, socioecological crisis that is characterised by inter- and intra-species injustices with an inter-generational and intra-generational temporal dimension that places unprecedented strain on the Earth system and its constituents.[2]

[*] Research Professor, Faculty of Law, North-West University, South Africa and Visiting Professor of Environmental Law, University of Lincoln, United Kingdom. This chapter builds on the propositions offered in Louis J. Kotzé, Global Environmental Constitutionalism in the Anthropocene (Oxford: Hart Publishing/Bloomsbury Publishing, 2016). I am particularly indebted to Anne Peters for her extensive comments on earlier versions of this chapter, as well as to George Radics for his views on regional environmental governance in ASEAN. The generous funding by the Alexander von Humboldt Foundation that made this research possible is greatly acknowledged. All views and errors are my own.
[1] United Nations Environment Programme (UNEP), *Global Environment Outlook: Environment for the Future We Want* (GEO 5) (Nairobi: UNEP, 2012), p. 23, available at www.unep.org/geo/geo5.asp.
[2] Jonas Ebbesson, 'The rule of law in governance of complex socio-ecological changes' (2010) 20 *Global Environmental Change* 414–422.

Several metaphors have recently evolved through which the world is trying both to come to terms with the extent of this human-induced crisis and to craft the most appropriate regulatory responses to counter the crisis and its multifarious socioecological exigencies. The most current of these is the term 'Anthropocene', which emphasises the central role of mankind as a major driving force in modifying the biosphere, while suggesting that the Earth is rapidly moving into a critically unstable state with the Earth system gradually becoming less predictable, non-stationary and less harmonious as a result of the global human imprint on the biosphere.[3] Through the lens of the Anthropocene, humanity has become a geological agent in much the same way as a volcano or meteor, able to change the Earth and its system and possibly even to cause another mass extinction.[4]

While having little, if any, normative characteristics itself, the metaphor of the Anthropocene could have significant normative implications for our regulatory institutions through which we seek to maintain an ordered coexistence.[5] For present purposes, law, as a normative institution, specifically is deeply implicated in the systems that are causing the global socioecological crisis,[6] with the Anthropocene metaphor exposing the historic and continuing inability of law to mediate, and in some instances its proneness actively to perpetuate, a multitude of anthropogenic causes and consequences. These include, among others, the enclosure of the commons through property laws; the dispossession of indigenous peoples under colonial laws; continuing corporate neocolonial practices and resulting ecological exploitation through laws promoting industrialisation and economic growth; and deepening asymmetrically distributed patterns of socioecological advantage and disadvantage that prevail in society and that are actively maintained by the law.[7] At the same time, however, law is also central (among other

---

[3] Louis J. Kotzé, 'Rethinking global environmental law and governance in the Anthropocene' (2014) 33 *Journal of Energy and Natural Resources Law* 121–156.
[4] Mike Hodson and Simon Marvin, 'Urbanism in the Anthropocene: ecological urbanism or premium ecological enclaves?' (2010) 14 *City* 299–313.
[5] See for a comprehensive critique on the role and potential of environmental law and governance in the Anthropocene Louis J. Kotzé (ed.), *Environmental Law and Governance for the Anthropocene* (Oxford: Hart Publishing; Bloomsbury Publishing, 2017).
[6] Nicholas Robinson, 'Fundamental principles of law for the Anthropocene?' (2014) 44 *Environmental Policy and Law* 13–27, at 13.
[7] See further Anna Grear, 'Deconstructing Anthropos: a critical legal reflection on "Anthropocentric" law and Anthropocene "humanity"' (2015) 26.3 *Law and Critique* 225–249.

regulatory institutions) to counter the causes of the Anthropocene, including devising ways to adapt to the Anthropocene's new socioecological reality, as the burgeoning body of global climate adaptation laws aptly suggests.[8]

When confronting the role of law in causing, perpetuating and addressing the socioecological crisis, one must also interrogate the issue of constitutionalism which is central to law. In the words of Richard Albert:

> Constitutionalism is ubiquitous. It informs how states behave in the international order, how governments treat their constituents, how communities order themselves, how groups relate to individuals, and how citizens interact with each other. Constitutionalism compels and constrains all dimensions of our everyday lives in ways large and small that we often do not fully appreciate, perhaps because constitutions take many forms that we do not generally associate with constitutionalism. Yet whether in the arts, sports, trade, entertainment, politics, or war, constitutionalism is both the point of departure and the port of call.[9]

The core thesis of this chapter is that the Anthropocene's deepening global socioecological crisis underlines the urgent need to revisit the potential of constitutionalism in achieving some of the global regulatory interventionist outcomes that would be necessary to maintain an ordered coexistence and to improve socioecological security.[10] More specifically, there is a case to be made in support of globalising environmental constitutionalism, which requires exploring the extent to which environmental constitutionalism manifests in the global regulatory space. In pursuing this thesis, the chapter specifically aims to highlight how global environmental constitutionalism currently manifests in a regional environmental law and governance setting in the European Union (EU) and the Association of Southeast Asian Nations (ASEAN). The EU and ASEAN are both regional governance institutions, but they are also very

---

[8] See, among many others, J. B. Ruhl, 'General design principles for resilience and adaptive capacity in legal systems – with applications to climate change adaptation' (2010) 89 *North Carolina Law Review* 1373–1404.

[9] Richard Albert, 'The cult of constitutionalism' (2012) 39 *Florida State University Law Review* 373–416, at 374.

[10] Socioecological security is the latest all-encompassing manifestation of an understanding of security that moves beyond state security, human security and environmental security by explicating the relationship between the environmental system and the security of human and natural capital. See, among others, Irene Petrosillo, Nicola Zaccarelli, Teodoro Semeraro and Giovanni Zurlini, 'The effectiveness of different conservation policies on the security of natural capital' (2009) 89 *Landscape and Urban Planning* 49–56.

different in terms of the power they exert on member states, their competencies, enforcement capacity and effectiveness, among other factors. While the comparison therefore might seem counter-intuitive, I hope to provide a perspective on the potentially different manifestations of global environmental constitutionalism in a comparable, but different, regional setting. I also hope to provide common ground for global constitutionalism and environmental law discourses to bridge the separated discursive tracks that these two areas of interest have hitherto followed.

For this purpose, in Section 2, I briefly describe the terms 'constitution', 'constitutionalism' and 'global constitutionalism'. Because the principal referent of global constitutionalism from which it departs is the nation state, Section 3 focuses on the emerging 'environmental constitutionalism' paradigm as determined from a domestic perspective, including various motivations behind its development and a discussion of some of the formal and substantive elements of domestic environmental constitutionalism offered by the constitutions of countries in the EU and ASEAN regions.[11] Section 4 elaborates on the regional manifestation of global environmental constitutionalism by comparing some of the formal and substantive environmental constitutionalism arrangements that exist in the governance regimes of the EU and ASEAN.

2 Constitutions, constitutionalism and global constitutionalism

While constitutional language has become an integral part of our political and legal systems, indeed of society itself, there is a revival of constitutional ideas in what Dunoff terms an 'age of constitutionalism'.[12] This observably pronounced salience is attributed to, among other factors, post–World War II political reconstruction; processes of decolonisation (mostly in Africa and South America); the radical constitutional changes in the former Eastern Bloc countries in the aftermath of the Cold War; the transitions made by post-fascist (Spain, Portugal) and post-apartheid

---

[11] For a detailed discussion of the emergence of environmental constitutionalism in domestic legal orders, see David Boyd, 'Constitutions, human rights, and the environment: national approaches', in Anna Grear and Louis J. Kotzé (eds.), *Research Handbook on Human Rights and the Environment* (Cheltenham: Edward Elgar, 2015), pp. 170–199; and generally, James May and Erin Daly, *Global Environmental Constitutionalism* (Cambridge: Cambridge University Press, 2015).

[12] Jeffrey L. Dunoff, 'Constitutional conceits: the WTO's "constitution" and the discipline of international law' (2006) 17 *European Journal of International Law* 647–675, at 648.

(South Africa) regimes towards the formation of market-based economies and liberal-democratic constitutional orders; the response to globalisation; related calls for the constitutionalisation of international
organisations and their corresponding treaty regimes; and the emergence
of regional governance institutions and regimes.[13] It is generally believed
that constitutional language embodies the notion of progress in that it is
perceived to foster progressive social orderings that are characterised by
the 'creation and maintenance of a dichotomy between right and wrong,
good and evil, civilized and uncivilized nations'.[14]

From a purely formalistic point of view, a constitution is seen as the act
and/or the norms that constitute a political body and the structure and/or
characteristics that define a constituted political body:[15] 'Constitutions
constitute a political entity as a legal entity, organize it, limit political
power, offer political and moral guidelines, justify governance, and contribute to integration.'[16] Or as Peters states: a 'constitution (in
a normative sense) is the sum of basic (materially most important) legal
norms which comprehensively regulate the social and political life of
a polity',[17] providing, among other items, the foundation of a legal order,
the establishment of the *trias politica* of the state (including the executive,
legislative and judicial powers) and the basis for legitimate government.[18]
As part of their formalistic constitutive functions, constitutions are concerned with the results and the act of constituting authority and power.
They derive their authority from a constituent power (*pouvoir constituant originaire*); they provide the principal authority for a state to make
subsequent rules such as legislation; they regulate the allocation of

[13] Jeffrey L. Dunoff, 'Why constitutionalism now? Text, context and the historical contin-
gency of ideas' (2004/2005) 1 *Journal of International Law and International Relations*
191–211, at 192; Morly Frishman and Sam Muller (eds.), *The Dynamics of
Constitutionalism in the Age of Globalisation* (The Hague: Hague Academic Press,
2010); Martin Loughlin, 'What is constitutionalisation?', in Petra Dobner and
Martin Loughlin (eds.), *The Twilight of Constitutionalism* (Oxford: Oxford University
Press, 2010), p. 60.
[14] George Galindo, 'Constitutionalism forever' (2010) 21 *Finnish Yearbook of International
Law* 137–170, at 144.
[15] Dario Castiglione, 'The political theory of the Constitution' (1996) XLIV *Political Studies*
417–435, at 418.
[16] Karolina Milewicz, 'Emerging patterns of global constitutionalization: toward
a conceptual framework' (2009) 16 *Indiana Journal of Global Legal Studies* 413–436,
at 418.
[17] Anne Peters, 'Compensatory constitutionalism: the function and potential of fundamental international norms and structures' (2006) 19 *Leiden Journal of International Law*
579–610, at 581.
[18] Loughlin, 'What is constitutionalisation?' (n. 13), p. 50.

powers, functions and duties among government agencies; and they define in a vertical sense the power relationship with the governed and, often in a horizontal sense, the power relations between individuals.[19]

To avoid an ontological reality in which a constitution is nothing but the formalisation of political power where law entrenches and perpetuates power instead of constraining it, a constitution is and should be more than a mere observable fact or a shorthand term that describes the formalisation of the power structures of a state.[20] In other words, a constitution cannot only be purely constitutive in a formalistic sense; it must also contain substantive norms that are elevated as higher order law.[21] Constitutions are thought to derive this special elevated status as a fundamental unified norm of a polity from safeguards such as the review functions of courts and the rule of law, and from substantive meta-ethical preconceptions that are notionally embedded in, among other items, natural law, rights, liberty and equality, which all amalgamate to elevate a constitution to the status of superior law.[22] To this end, the idea of constitutionalism goes beyond the simple articulation of formal constitutive rules;[23] it also instils a constitution with its own inherent dignity from which it derives its legitimacy and supreme normative authority.[24]

In addition to articulating the formal and substantive aspects of constitutional notions, the foregoing also suggests that our current understanding of contemporary constitutions and constitutionalism is inherently state bound, tied as this understanding is to state sovereignty, physical borders, a demos and a government. Is it, however, possible to think about constitutionalism in global terms 'beyond the state', as it were? Our insular state-bound perception of constitutionalism is being altered by at least two considerations that at once also foreshadow the extension of the global constitutionalism debate into the environmental domain. First, consequent on states not being able to adequately regulate globalised phenomena beyond their borders, the forces of globalisation

---

[19] Charles Fombad, 'Challenges to constitutionalism and constitutional rights in Africa and the enabling role of political parties: lessons and perspectives from Southern Africa' (2007) 55 *American Journal of Comparative Law* 1–45, at 6.

[20] Giovanni Sartori, 'Constitutionalism: a preliminary discussion' (1962) 56 *American Political Science Review* 853–864, at 857.

[21] Robert Alexy, *A Theory of Constitutional Rights* (Oxford: Oxford University Press, 2002), p. 350.

[22] Castiglione (n. 15), at 420.

[23] Milewicz (n. 16), at 419.

[24] Josef Isensee, 'Staat und Verfassung', in Josef Isensee and Paul Kirchhof (eds.), *Handbuch des Staatsrechts: Verfassungsstaat* (Heidelberg: C.F. Müller, 2014), p. 15.

are creating regulatory gaps and resultant opportunities for global constitutionalism. For example, global environmental issues such as climate change are affecting everyone everywhere with scant regard to physical borders or to the sanctity of state sovereignty. It might be easier or more appropriate to regulate such issues at a global or a regional level in the collective interests of several states around the globe or, regionally, groups of states.[25]

Second, and related to the foregoing point, Schwöbel argues that 'any changes in global social reality are believed to call for new or enhanced regulation',[26] essentially because such changes lead to anxiety about the lack of law in the global regulatory space and the prevalence of disorder as a result. To this end, because constitutionalism is seen as a way to achieve a better and more structured regulatory order, global constitutionalism seeks to identify and advocate for the application of constitutional principles in the global regulatory domain with a view to improving the effectiveness and fairness of a 'chaotic' international legal and governance order.[27] If we accept that the Anthropocene evinces changes in the current global social reality, it is possible to appreciate the appeal of global constitutionalism as a useful framework to better regulate the human–environment interface in a changed global social reality and governance order that are currently being dislodged by the global socio-ecological crisis.

Global constitutionalism could be classified into specific tracks with a view to understanding this concept. First, efforts to seek constitutionalism in the corridors of the global law and governance maze manifest most clearly, and certainly most intuitively, in the arguments of those suggesting that international law and its governance institutions have become, or are becoming, constitutionalised.[28] Some general claims by

---

[25] These non-traditional state entities have all become 'autonomous forms of social orderings which constitutes [sic] their own cognitive spaces on a global scale'. Poul Kjaer, *Constitutionalism in the Global Realm* (London: Routledge, 2014), p. 4.

[26] Christine Schwöbel, 'The appeal of the project of global constitutionalism to public international lawyers' (2012) 13 *German Law Journal* 1–22, at 10.

[27] Anne Peters, 'The merits of global constitutionalism' (2009) 16 *Indiana Journal of Global Legal Studies* 397–411, at 397.

[28] See, for example, Anne Peters, 'Global constitutionalism in a nutshell', in Klaus Dicke, Stephan Hobe, Karl-Ulrich Meyn, Anne Peters, Eibe Riedel, Hans-Joachim Schütz and Christian Tietje (eds.), *Weltinnenrecht: Liber Amicorum Jost Delbrück* (Berlin: Walther Schücking Institut für Internationales Recht, 2005), pp. 535–550; Erika de Wet, 'The international constitutional order' (2006) 55 *International and Comparative Law Quarterly* 51–76; Bardo Fassbender, 'The United Nations Charter as the constitution of the international community' (1998) 36 *Columbia Journal of International Law* 529–619.

the internationalist school around which it fashions its respective visions of global constitutionalism include:[29] there is a global authority organised around the United Nations and its organs with the Charter of the United Nations, 1945, as its global constitution; there is a discernible international community acting as a constituent power; and a normative hierarchy exists which is similar to a domestic bill of rights that contains elevated norms such as human rights and *jus cogens* and *erga omnes* obligations, indicating universal values that supersede multilateral and bilateral normative arrangements and other 'inferior' norms.[30]

A second approach is one that traces constitutionalism in increasingly autonomous clustered regimes of international law that are organised around a specific issue area.[31] A prominent example of where the global constitutionalism debate occurs in this respect is in the area of global trade which consists of a specific regime that is clustered to the extent that it consists of an international organisation, a set of enforceable norms, administrative institutions and enforcement machinery, in this case the World Trade Organization and the many trade-related agreements that have been adopted under its auspices.[32]

A third approach is that of global civil society constitutionalism,[33] which specifically focuses on the emergence of civil 'constitutions' in a global society, including non-state entities such as non-governmental organisations, multinational corporations and epistemic communities. These non-state entities are seen to contribute to global law beyond the state where law has 'in line with the logic of functional differentiation, established itself globally as a unitary social system'.[34]

A fourth approach is that of transnational comparative constitutionalism. Contrary to the internationalist approach, 'global' in this context

---

[29] Ronald MacDonald, 'Fundamental norms in contemporary international law' (1987) 25 *Canadian Yearbook of International Law* 115–149.

[30] Neil Walker, 'Taking constitutionalism beyond the state' (2008) 56 *Political Studies* 519–543, at 535–536.

[31] See for a general discussion Alec Stone Sweet, 'Constitutionalism, legal pluralism, and international regimes' (2009) 16 *Indiana Journal of Global Legal Studies* 621–645.

[32] See for an overview of these agreements and other legal texts www.wto.org/english/docs_e/legal_e/legal_e.htm.

[33] See for a general overview Gunther Teubner, 'Societal constitutionalism: alternatives to state-centred constitutional theory?', in Christian Joerges, Inger-Johanne Sand and Gunther Teubner (eds.), *Transnational Governance and Constitutionalism* (Oxford: Hart Publishing, 2004), pp. 3–28.

[34] Gunther Teubner and Andreas Fischer-Lescano, 'Regime-collisions: the vain search for legal unity in the fragmentation of global law' (2004) 25 *Michigan Journal of International Law* 999–1045, at 1007.

has a strong comparative, cross-jurisdictional and/or transnational focus that is collectively seen as a global amalgamation of variously situated domestic norms around the globe that are less isolated within their domestic jurisdictions than what national borders and state sovereignty might have one believe at first glance.[35]

The final approach, and the specific focus of this chapter, seeks global constitutionalism in a regional governance order such as the EU and ASEAN, which are considered by global constitutionalists neither a sort of superstate, nor a classic international organisation, but rather what Ingolf Pernice calls a regional constitutional federation (*Verfassungsverbund*).[36] Proponents of this approach argue that some form of softer multi-level constitutionalism exists in regional governance regimes, an issue that is further canvassed later in the chapter.[37]

The foregoing discussion points to the potential of global constitutionalism to bring about a 'better' and more structured global law and governance order in that it aims 'to guarantee a political [and socio-juridical] process that brings about sustainable and fair compromises between diverging interests'.[38] Global constitutionalism could do so by restricting the arbitrary rule of global powers through a global or regional type of constitution containing a set of higher order norms; in a related sense 'softening' the sovereignty of states and restricting their unilateral actions through the limits imposed by human rights that are encapsulated in treaties or captured as *jus cogens* norms; enhancing participative governance by non-state actors through the process of global civil society activism; demanding transparency and accountability from those who govern in the global domain; where these are absent, providing normative and other institutional arrangements related to specific issue areas such as the environment; and providing the possibility for transnational, cross-jurisdictional juridical transplantation to occur. The extent to which this is or could be occurring in the regional environmental law

---

[35] Thomas Cottier and Maya Hertig, 'The prospects of 21st century constitutionalism' (2003) 7 *Max Planck Yearbook of United Nations Law* 261–328, at 269–275.

[36] Ingolf Pernice, 'Multilevel constitutionalism in the European Union', Walter Hallenstein Institut Paper 5/02 (2001), available at http://whi-berlin.de/documents/whi-paper0502 .pdf.

[37] See, among other sources, Neil Walker, 'Reframing EU constitutionalism', in Jeffrey Dunoff and Joel Trachtman (eds.), *Ruling the World: Constitutionalism, International Law, and Global Governance* (Cambridge: Cambridge University Press, 2009), pp. 149–176.

[38] Christian Volk, 'Why global constitutionalism does not live up to its promises' (2012) 4 *Goettingen Journal of International Law* 551–573, at 560.

and governance domain is investigated in Section 4. As a precursor to that discussion, the next section reflects more critically on the evolution and meaning of 'environmental constitutionalism' as a specialised form of constitutionalism.

3 Environmental constitutionalism

The revival of constitutionalism is one that is raising 'the intensity of interest in constitutions and constitutionalism considerably . . . [creating] an opportunity for modern notions of constitutionalism to be expanded into new territories and to be tested under new circumstances'.[39] In recent years there has been an evident expansion of notions of constitutionalism into the 'new' territory of environmental law,[40] notably alongside the growing recognition of the need for constitutional provisions as well as structures and processes to embrace environmental care and to extend the power of constitutionalism into the environmental regulatory domain. With reference to the potential of achieving enhanced environmental protection through constitutionalism, while some have called for 'a wider range of options [and] a new paradigm',[41] others suggest that 'the constitutionalism of the future'[42] must as a result of contemporary threats and challenges embrace notions such as human solidarity for the preservation of the planet and its resources and equitable principles in the allocation of scarce resources within and among people and countries.

While it is difficult to determine exactly when the first environmental provision of any kind was incorporated into a constitution (one estimation is that this occurred in 1866 in the Romanian Constitution),[43] Joshua

---

[39] Francois Venter, *Constitutional Comparison: Japan, Germany, Canada and South Africa as Constitutional States* (Cape Town: Juta-Kluwer Law International, 2000), p. 30.

[40] It is generally accepted that environmental law and particularly international environmental law are relatively young legal disciplines that have only really started to develop and to gain autonomy following the United Nations Conference on the Human Environment, held in Stockholm from 5 to 16 June 1972, and its soft law declaration, the Declaration of the United Nations Conference on the Human Environment. See www .unep.org/Documents.Multilingual/Default.asp?documentid=97&articleid=1503.

[41] Brain Gareau, 'Global environmental constitutionalism' (2013) 40 *Boston College Environmental Affairs Law Review* 403–408, at 408.

[42] Bertrand Ramcharan, 'Constitutionalism in an age of globalisation and global threats', in Morly Frishman and Sam Muller (eds.), *The Dynamics of Constitutionalism in the Age of Globalisation* (The Hague: Hague Academic Press, 2010), pp. 18–19.

[43] Zachary Elkins, Tom Ginsburg and James Melton, *Comparative Constitutions Project Characteristics of National Constitutions* (2014), version 2.0, available at http://comparativeconstitutionsproject.org/ccp2015/download-data/.

Gellers indicates that the first environmental right to have found its way into a constitution was in 1974 when Yugoslavia adopted such a right.[44] Significantly, this date corresponds with the United Nations Conference on the Human Environment held in Stockholm in 1972, which is widely considered to be the global political impetus that sparked the exponential growth of international, regional and national environmental law regimes. The Stockholm Declaration states, among other items:

> In the long and tortuous evolution of the human race on this planet a stage has been reached when, through the rapid acceleration of science and technology, man has acquired the power to transform his environment in countless ways and on an unprecedented scale. Both aspects of man's environment, the natural and the man-made, are essential to his well-being and to the enjoyment of basic human rights [and] the right to life itself.[45]

While this statement acknowledges the rights-related aspects associated with the human–environment relationship, a more general question as to context arises: What is the motivation behind the convergence between environmentalism and constitutionalism, and how did this convergence collectively contribute to the way we understand environmental constitutionalism today?

Much of the early conceptual development of environmental constitutionalism can be found in German literature, notably in the work of, among other scholars, Kloepfer, Steinberg and Bosselmann.[46] While this is somewhat generalised, these scholars have vested their strategies for environmental protection and the pursuit of sustainability in the constitutionalism paradigm because they believe: constitutional transformations have proven advantageous for improving regulatory outcomes in other domains such as armed conflict and human rights protection, and they could do the same for the environment; because the state is the main actor in upholding constitutionalism and because it is empowered by a constitution to do so, the state must play the predominant role in

[44] Joshua Gellers, 'Explaining the emergence of constitutional environmental rights: a global quantitative analysis' (2015) 6 *Journal of Human Rights and the Environment* 75–97.
[45] Declaration of the United Nations Conference on the Human Environment, 1972, Preamble, para. 1. See also its Principle 1.
[46] Michael Kloepfer, 'Auf dem Weg zum Umweltstaat', in Michael Kloepfer (ed.), *Umweltstaat: Ladenburger Diskurs* (Berlin: Springer, 1989), pp. 39–78; Rudolf Steinberg, *Der ökologische Verfassungsstaat* (Frankfurt am Main: Suhrkamp, 1998); Klaus Bosselmann, *Im Namen der Natur: Der Weg zum ökologischen Rechtsstaat* (Bern: Scherz, 1992).

safeguarding the natural foundations of all life; politics, laws and societal behaviour generally speaking are not geared towards ecological sustainability, and because a constitution has the power to instigate thorough-going change of a polity and its legal system, there is a reasonable prospect that constitutionalism would be able to do the same in the environmental domain; the present socioecological crisis is so severe that it warrants nothing less than an ecological constitutional moment; and because the envisaged changes to law, politics and societal behaviour might be so drastic in order to ensure more sustainable outcomes, constitutionalism (given its past achievements) is a suitable juridical modicum that is legitimately able to initiate, carry and complete these paradigm-shifting changes in society and its law and governance structures.

My own tentative efforts to understand global environmental constitutionalism in an earlier work required me to look for the essence of environmental constitutionalism from a conceptual point of view.[47] It seemed appropriate to distinguish environmental constitutionalism's formal/constitutive functions (or its 'thin' characteristics) from its prescriptive or substantively constitutional functions (otherwise called its 'thick' characteristics). In line with the general understanding of constitutions and constitutionalism discussed in this chapter, whereas formal environmental constitutionalism relates to constitutional law establishing, defining and organising the main organs of government, its constitution and its powers, substantive environmental constitutionalism relates to constitutions being substantively constitutional, i.e. superior law that is justiciable and entrenched and that expresses a common ideology and higher order environmental protective measures such as through environmental rights.

When applied to the environmental domain and in further pursuit of the formal–substantive metaphor, it is possible to understand formal environmental constitutionalism as a means to determine or at least to guide, at the highest possible level, the ordering, composition and architecture of environmental governance. This would include, among other things, the means and procedures to establish environmental governance powers and institutions, including the power of environmental authorities themselves when they make decisions that affect the environment (for example, their power to evaluate and decide on methods for

---

[47] Louis J. Kotzé, 'Arguing global environmental constitutionalism' (2012) 1 *Transnational Environmental Law* 199–233.

renewable energy generation or mining activities); to establish and steer law-making, conflict resolution and law enforcement processes of the state insofar as they relate to environmental matters; to determine the roles and responsibilities of all the public and private actors involved in environmental governance; and to regulate the vertical interaction between the state and its subjects and the horizontal interaction between the subjects in respect of environmental matters. A domestic example of formal environmental constitutional provisions can be found in the Constitution of Thailand, 1997. Chapter XIV spells out specific provisions which empower local government to ensure environmental protection: 'for the purpose of promoting and maintaining the quality of the environment, a local government organization has powers and duties as provided by the law', which must cater for the management, preservation and exploitation of natural resources and the environment in the area of the locality.[48] Title XI of the Constitution of France, 1958, creates the Economic, Social and Environmental Council which is required to scrutinise, among other items, government bills, draft ordinances, draft decrees and private members' bills dealing with environmental matters.

An environmental constitution in the substantive sense could provide for, among other things, a rights-based approach to environmental governance, including a right to a healthy environment and for the rights of nature, as well as incidental political and socio-economic rights and rights that facilitate participative, representative and transparent environmental governance. Other than rights, substantive environmental constitutionalism provisions could include directive principles or principles of state policy that work to galvanise or compel legislative, judicial and executive activities to protect the environment.[49] These could encompass the many state and non-state duties with respect to environmental protection such as: to ensure inter- and intra-generational equity; to conserve resources; to ensure equitable access to and use of resources; to avoid adverse environmental impacts; to prevent environmental disasters, minimise damage and provide emergency assistance; to compensate for environmental harm; to ensure environmental justice; to ensure access to justice; and to ensure sufficient civil society representation and participation.[50] The German

---

[48] Section 290 of the 1997 Constitution of Thailand.

[49] Erin Daly, 'Constitutional protection for environmental rights: the benefits of environmental process' (2012) 17 *International Journal of Peace Studies* 71–80, at 71.

[50] Edith Brown Weiss, *In Fairness to Future Generations: International Law, Common Patrimony, and Intergenerational Equity* (New York: Transnational, 1989), pp. 50–86.

Constitution's provision on the environment is an example of constitutional environmental duties a government may incur. Article 20(a) states: 'Mindful also of its responsibility toward future generations, the state shall protect the natural foundations of life and animals by legislation and, in accordance with law and justice, by executive and judicial action, all within the framework of the constitutional order.' Article 19 of the Constitution of Laos, 1991, places an individual duty on non-state actors to 'protect the environment and natural resources', whereas Article 390(b) of the Constitution of Myanmar, 2008, provides: 'Every citizen has the duty to assist the Union in carrying out . . . environmental protection.' An example of a higher order constitutional environmental right can be found in the Constitution of Indonesia, 1945, which states in Article 28H(1): 'Each person has a right to a life of well-being in body and mind, to a place to dwell, to enjoy a good and healthy environment, and to receive medical care.' In the European context, the Constitution of France, 1958, provides: 'Everyone has the right to live in a balanced and health-friendly environment.'[51]

4   Global environmental constitutionalism in a regional setting: the example of the EU and ASEAN

Having established some possible formal and substantive manifestations of environmental constitutionalism from a domestic point of view, this section of the chapter turns to a brief discussion of how these formal and substantive aspects manifest globally in the EU and ASEAN.

Regional environmental governance is now a fully recognised manifestation of global environmental governance. It has emerged as a response from regionally grouped states to geographically and politically shared environmental problems and as a means to exert greater influence as a regional collective in global environmental diplomacy, law-making and governance. To this end, regional environmental governance is especially desirable under the following circumstances:

> When the global seems to fail (or, at least, is not an appropriate level to deal with collective action problems) and states simply cannot solve their own environmental problems through unilateral action or where scaling up has the potential to deliver more effective outcomes, then the

---

[51] Art. 1 of the Charter of the Environment.

'goldilocks principle' kicks in; regionalism becomes attractive as it is neither 'too hot' nor 'too cold' but 'just right'.[52]

Other benefits include the potential for regional environmental governance to provide for enhanced commonalities to address a particular environmental challenge; greater familiarity with key actors; the ability to tailor mitigation and adaptation actions to a smaller global constituency; and the ability to focus on ecologically defined regions such as river basins, rather than political-administrative entities.[53]

In a narrow sense, regional environmental governance could be made up of a regional environmental treaty regime that governs a specific environmental aspect or shared resource in a specific region. An example is the body of norms and institutions that has been set up to govern Lake Konstanz that is shared between Germany, Switzerland and Austria.[54] Expansively considered, the regionalist approach to global environmental constitutionalism seeks constitutionalism in broader regional governance orders, especially with respect to their normative and institutional environmental aspects, such as in the EU and ASEAN. The remainder of this chapter focuses on the expansive approach.

4.1 Regional environmental constitutionalism in the EU

The EU, arguably more than any other regional governance organisation, exudes some global constitutional characteristics as a result of its robust and enforceable treaty system and its governance institutions, the central importance of its human rights instruments and the adjudicatory oversight role of the European Court of Human Rights and the European Court of Justice.[55] As a benchmark for regional governance and consequently for the expansive regionalist approach to global environmental constitutionalism described earlier:

---

[52] Lorraine Elliot and Shaun Breslin, 'Researching comparative regional environmental governance: causes, cases and consequences', in Lorraine Elliot and Shaun Breslin (eds.), *Comparative Environmental Regionalism* (London: Routledge, 2011), p. 4.
[53] Jörg Balsiger and Stacy VanDeveer, 'Navigating regional environmental governance' (2012) 12 *Global Environmental Politics* 1–17, at 3.
[54] See for detail www.worldlakes.org/uploads/10_Lake_Constance_27February2006.pdf.
[55] Miguel Maduro, 'How constitutional can the European Union be? The tension between intergovernmentalism and constitutionalism in the European Union', in Joseph Weiler and Christopher Eisgruber (eds.), *Altneuland: The EU Constitution in a Contextual Perspective*, Jean Monnet Working Paper 5/04, available at www.jeanmonnetprogram.org/archive/papers/04/040501-18.pdf.

the EU remains highly significant. This is partly because as the most institutionalized regional organization it provides a solid example of actual regional governance. It is also because the experience of the EU informs policy debates elsewhere over how to emulate the successes and/ or avoid some of the problems of Europe in the construction of regional forms. And it is also because, through contingent aid and 'interregional' partnership arrangements, there is a deliberate and active attempt to promote the EU 'model' of regional governance in other parts of the world.[56]

While the EU does not have a constitution as such (despite failed attempts that started in 2001 to negotiate a Treaty Establishing a Constitution for Europe), it is argued that its treaty system, including the Treaty of Lisbon, 2007, could be regarded as forming some type of collective constitutional structure that supersedes the national constitutional orders of member states,[57] while also determining, constraining and regulating the exercise of power by EU institutions. The possibility of thinking about the EU, its institutions and normative set-up in constitutional terms has been amplified (even before formal negotiations with respect to establishing a constitution for Europe began) by the European Court of Justice's characterisation of the founding treaties of the EU as the 'constitutional Charter of a Community based on the rule of law'.[58] Such deliberate judicial phraseology seems to suggest that the constitutionalisation of the EU is anything but an empty exercise or a matter of semantics.

While commentators have not explicitly addressed the notion of European *environmental* constitutionalism in any systemised or comprehensive way, the EU's global constitutionalism debate is relevant, if underexplored, for the environmental domain, with some questioning whether an 'ever closer ecological union' could be observed in Europe.[59] The focus of this debate is on the environmental aspects of the EU's institutional and normative architecture, and it seeks to find formal and substantive environmental constitutionalism elements in a regional governance entity that

---

[56] Elliot and Breslin, 'Researching comparative regional environmental governance' (n. 52), p. 1.

[57] The supremacy of EU law over member states' law was already confirmed in 1964 by the European Court of Justice in *Flaminio Costa v. ENEL* [1964] ECR 585 (6/64).

[58] Opinion 1/91, Referring to the Draft Treaty on a European Economic Area, ECR 1991 I, 6084; Case 294/83, *Parti écologiste 'Les Verts' v. European Parliament*, ECR 1986, 1339.

[59] Albert Weale, Geoffrey Pridham, Michelle Cini, Dimitrios Konstadakopulos, Martin Porter and Brendan Flynn (eds.), *Environmental Governance in Europe: An Ever Closer Ecological Union?* (Oxford: Oxford University Press, 2000).

438 LOUIS J. KOTZÉ

does not have an explicit *environmental* constitution setting out elaborate environmental provisions. Despite the EU system's absence of such explicit environmental constitutional provisions, it is sufficiently clear by now that the EU is an influential environmental governance actor internally with respect to its member states and externally vis-à-vis the rest of the world, and there are several considerations acting in support of the notion of regional European environmental constitutionalism. These considerations collectively play at the idea of the EU becoming, or being, a relatively strong regional constitutional federation (*Verfassungsverbund*) that also focuses on environmental regulation.

First, the twenty-eight EU member states could increasingly be seen acting as a unified, if still imperfect, collective that acts on behalf of its member states in their environment-related interests.[60] As evidence of its post-state unified regional approach to law and governance, the EU maintains permanent diplomatic missions in various countries across the world, and it is represented as a collective at the United Nations, at the World Trade Organization and in important global networks of influential states such as the G8. In the environmental context, the EU is a party to the United Nations Framework Convention on Climate Change (UNFCCC), its Kyoto Protocol and the recent Paris Agreement of 2015, as are all EU member states in their own right, with the European Commission representing and negotiating on behalf of its member states during Conferences of the Parties.[61] Its representative collectivity is, however, not always absolute or even sufficient during global environmental treaty negotiations, and the European Commission has been criticised for lacking a unified voice and for it being often difficult to determine 'who is talking in the name of the EU, and who is doing it to defend national interests while proclaiming to represent the EU as a whole'.[62]

[60] Used here in the sense to 'denote the repository of interests that transcend those of individual states ... In this conception, the element which distinguishes a "community" from its components is a "higher unity", as it were, the representation and prioritization of common interests as against the egoistic interests of individuals.' To this end, an international community 'needs to have certain interests common to all its members and a certain set of common values, principles and procedures'. For present purposes, such common values, principles and procedures could revolve around the environment. See Bruno Simma and Andreas Paulus, 'The "international community" facing the challenge of globalization' (1998) 9 *European Journal of International Law* 266–277, at 268.

[61] European Commission, *Climate Action*, available at http://ec.europa.eu/clima/policies/international/negotiations/un/index_en.htm.

[62] Rosa Maria Fernandez Martin, 'The European Union and international negotiations on climate change: a limited role to play' (2012) 8 *Journal of Contemporary European Research* 192–209, at 193.

Second, formally the EU derives its environmental governance mandate from its constituting instruments, including the Single European
Act that provides in Article 130(r)(1):

> Action by the Community relating to the environment shall have the
> following objectives: to preserve, protect and improve the quality of the
> environment; to contribute towards protecting human health; [and] to
> ensure prudent and rational utilization of natural resources.

In support of the argument that the EU increasingly acts as a regionalised
collective on behalf of its member states in environmental matters,
Article 130(r)(4) provides: 'The Community shall take action relating
to the environment to the extent to which the objectives referred to in
paragraph 1 [see above] can be attained better at Community level than at
the level of the individual Member States.' A unified and more or less
uniform environmental normative framework is continuously being
created through environmental regulations and directives that the
European Commission issues and according to which member states
are required to align their domestic legal systems.[63] While the foregoing
is an example of formal constitutional provisions that enable regional
governance, from a rule of law perspective, this results in the emergence
of a more predictable, consistent, legitimate and binding regional environmental law and governance framework that also sets out substantive
limitations with respect to the environment and specifically on actions
that might harm the environment. It also suggests that increasingly
environmental protection measures are becoming more unified, influential and coherent across Europe.

Third, in terms of substantive higher order environmental norms,
none of the EU's constituting instruments provide for an explicit environmental right or any other explicit form of higher order environmental
norm. The Charter of Fundamental Rights of the European Union of
2000 does, however, include under its section on solidarity rights an
environmental provision which states: 'A high level of environmental

---

[63] Art. 288 of the Treaty on the Functioning of the European Union, 2007, determines that:
'to exercise the Union's competences, the institutions shall adopt regulations, directives,
decisions, recommendations and opinions. A regulation shall have general application.
It shall be binding in its entirety and directly applicable in all Member States. 26.10.2012
Official EN Journal of the European Union C 326/171 A directive shall be binding, as to
the result to be achieved, upon each Member State to which it is addressed, but shall leave
to the national authorities the choice of form and methods. A decision shall be binding in
its entirety. A decision which specifies those to whom it is addressed shall be binding only
on them. Recommendations and opinions shall have no binding force.'

protection and the improvement of the quality of the environment must be integrated into the policies of the Union and ensured in accordance with the principle of sustainable development.'[64] This provision, which has become binding on all EU member states since 2009, along with all the other provisions of the charter,[65] although relatively weak and devoid of the classic rights jargon, 'may become a benchmark for judicial review by the EU Court of Justice of legislative and executive EU acts as well as national measures implementing EU environmental obligations'.[66]

The Council of Europe's European Convention for the Protection of Human Rights and Fundamental Freedoms of 1950 also does not provide for an explicit environmental right,[67] with environmental entitlements instead being raised and protected through the assertion of other incidental rights.[68] The convention does not apply universally; it remains a geographically delimited (mostly European) transnational regime but one which could nevertheless be 'persuasively characterized as constitutional and consistent with the ideal of constitutionalism',[69] most notably because it entrenches rights protection and rights values at the higher 'constitutional' level in Europe. The European Court of Human Rights is also relatively active in protecting environmental interests such as through the convention's right to privacy (Article 8), as can be seen from its rich jurisprudence on human rights in the environmental context.[70] So too is the European Court of Justice an active participant in developing binding environmental law jurisprudence and providing judicial oversight of compliance with the EU's environmental measures.[71] The extent to which the European Court of Human Rights

---

[64] Art. 37 of the Charter of Fundamental Rights of the European Union.

[65] The Charter has been incorporated as a binding legal text in the Lisbon Treaty of 2007, and as a result it has become binding on all EU member states since 2009.

[66] Jonathan Verschuuren, 'Contribution of the case law of the European Court of Human Rights to sustainable development in Europe', in Werner Scholtz and Jonathan Verschuuren (eds.), *Regional Environmental Law: Transnational Comparative Lessons in Pursuit of Sustainable Development* (Cheltenham: Edward Elgar, 2015), pp. 363–384.

[67] Available at http://www.echr.coe.int/Documents/Convention_ENG.pdf.

[68] Ole Pedersen, 'European environmental human rights and environmental rights: a long time coming?' (2008) 21 *Georgetown International Environmental Law Review* 73–111.

[69] Michel Rosenfeld, 'Is global constitutionalism meaningful or desirable?' (2014) 25 *European Journal of International Law* 177–199, at 193.

[70] See for a summary of environment-related cases the summary of the European Court of Human Rights at www.echr.coe.int/Documents/FS_Environment_ENG.pdf.

[71] See generally Philippe Sands, 'European Community environmental law: legislation, the European Court of Justice and common-interest groups' (1990) 53 *Modern Law Review* 685–698.

and the European Court of Justice have been able to contribute to the development of substantive regional environmental constitutionalism in Europe is suggested by Haas's view that 'in some instances environmental decisions have been elevated above the political level of contending domestic interests'.[72] Also, even though it is not limited to EU member states, the United Nations Economic Commission for Europe Convention on Access to Information, Public Participation in Decision-Making and Access to Justice in Environmental Matters (Aarhus Convention), 1998, embodies the right for a person 'to live in an environment adequate to his or her health and well-being'.[73] In doing so, the convention significantly strengthens the force of substantive regional environmental constitutionalism by allowing communications to be brought before its Compliance Committee by one or more members of the public concerning any party's compliance with the convention.[74] It is accordingly entirely in a position to enforce higher order rights-based provisions aimed at environmental protection, albeit only insofar as procedural issues are concerned.

A fourth consideration that suggests the existence of regional EU environmental constitutionalism is separation of powers. Often described as some sort of federal system similar to that of the United States,[75] and although the distinction is not watertight since the natures of some of its governance functions overlap, the EU has an executive authority in the form of the European Commission and European Union Council (also called the Council of Ministers) that act closely with the European Parliament which is the primary legislative authority. The European Court of Justice serves as its main judicial body.[76] All of these institutions have some sort of environmental protection mandate and competence as explained earlier.

---

[72] Peter Haas, 'Regional environmental governance', in Tanja Börzel and Thomas Risse (eds.), *The Oxford Handbook of Comparative Regionalism* (Oxford: Oxford University Press, 2016), p. 437.

[73] The Aarhus Convention is applicable to EU and non-EU states (if the latter countries ratify it), and its impact could thus be much broader than on the EU region. See among the many publications on the Aarhus Convention Svitlana Kravchenko, 'The Aarhus Convention and innovations in compliance with multilateral environmental agreements' (2007) 18 *Colorado Journal of International Environmental Law and Policy* 1–50.

[74] United Nations Economic Commission for Europe at www.unece.org/env/pp/pubcom .html.

[75] Gerard Conway, 'Recovering a separation of powers in the European Union' (2011) 17 *European Law Journal* 304–322.

[76] Alan Rosas, 'Separation of powers in the European Union' (2007) 41 *International Lawyer* 1033–1046, at 1034.

The foregoing discussion suggests that despite the absence of a European environmental constitution and an explicit substantive environmental right in the EU's more general constituting instruments, the EU as a regional governance body exudes various formal and substantive environmental constitutionalism characteristics that allow it collectively as a regional organisation, and its member states individually, to steer environmental regulatory outcomes in a regional setting through a regional constitution type of arrangement.

4.2 Regional environmental constitutionalism in ASEAN

While the existence of regional environmental constitutionalism is relatively clear in the EU, the same cannot be said of ASEAN. Preceded by an organisation formed in 1961 called the Association of Southeast Asia, ASEAN was originally established in 1967 through the ASEAN Declaration by five countries: Indonesia, Malaysia, the Philippines, Singapore and Thailand. Since then, another five countries have joined this regional governance body: Vietnam, Myanmar, Cambodia, Laos and Brunei. As with the EU, ASEAN was not initially established to address environmental concerns per se but rather to create a more unified and influential regional collective that represents those interests of its member states related to development, culture, politics and regional security. Compared to its EU counterpart, however, ASEAN rather represents a 'light' form of regional governance, mostly because its members states have not surrendered their autonomous sovereignty to that regional body in the same way EU member states have done: in ASEAN 'the notion of sovereignty is valued, and any detraction from it is jealously guarded against'.[77] The non-interventionist approach to regional governance of ASEAN is essentially based on the 'ASEAN Way', which rests on the notions of consultation, consensus, non-confrontation, private and personal diplomacy, and non-interference,[78] as opposed to more deliberate and far-reaching intervention in the affairs of its member states. The prevailing view therefore seems to be: 'Of the world's significant regional organizations, the powers ceded by [ASEAN] members to the

---

[77] Koh Kheng-Lian, 'ASEAN patterns of consensus building in environmental management' (2006) 13 *South African Journal of Environmental Law and Policy* 139–145, at 140.

[78] Lorraine Elliott, 'ASEAN environmental governance: strategies of regionalism in Southeast Asia' (2012) 12 *Global Environmental Politics* 38–57, at 41.

centre are less than within the European Union (EU), the African Union (AU), or the Organization of American States (OAS).'[79]

This 'softer' approach to regional governance is also evident in the environmental domain. The ASEAN Charter of 2007, which could be considered some form of a constitution of ASEAN, introduced for the first time a legal and institutional framework for ASEAN and went well beyond the ASEAN Declaration in formally constituting ASEAN and its regional governance institutions. As far as formal regional environmental constitutionalism is concerned, it establishes environmental protection as one of the principal objectives of ASEAN, albeit couched in terms that pursue global peaceful coexistence, namely 'to ensure that the peoples and Member States of ASEAN live in peace with the world at large in a just, democratic and harmonious environment'.[80] More pertinently, Article 9(1) states as a foundational purpose of ASEAN to 'promote sustainable development so as to ensure the protection of the region's environment, the sustainability of its natural resources, the preservation of its cultural heritage and the high quality of life of its peoples'. The ASEAN Ministerial Meeting on the Environment (AMME) and its ASEAN Senior Officials on the Environment (ASOEN) have been designated as the principal sectoral ministerial bodies to ensure the realisation of this objective, and they are responsible for formal decision making on the environment and for developing environmental policy recommendations and for promoting regional cooperation, respectively.

To date, however, the environmental governance approach of these institutions has been relatively 'soft'. While the EU has developed an impressive regional body of binding environmental law and governance instruments, ASEAN regional environmental governance is rather evident in various non-binding soft law instruments ranging across memoranda of understandings, accords, common positions, declarations, resolutions, environmental programmes and plans of action.[81] In step

---

[79] Simon Chesterman, 'Does ASEAN exist? The Association of Southeast Asian Nations as an international legal person' (2012) 8 *Singapore Year Book of International Law* 199–211, at 200.

[80] Art. 1(4) of the ASEAN Charter.

[81] See for a more detailed recent discussion Ben Boer, 'Introduction to ASEAN regional environmental law', in Werner Scholtz and Jonathan Verschuuren (eds.), *Regional Environmental Law: Transregional Comparative Lessons in Pursuit of Sustainable Development* (Cheltenham: Edward Elgar, 2015), pp. 259–267. The effectiveness of the non-binding nature of these instruments is questioned by some: 'In cases when national and regional legislative and policy initiatives towards environmental protection and sustainability in general and the forging of links between trade/investment and the

with the ASEAN Way, the soft institutionalism approach inherent in the foregoing prefers non-binding agreements, a reliance on national institutions rather than a strong centralised and top-down regional bureaucracy, and a general reluctance to interfere in domestic and regional environmental matters.[82] In contrast to the European approach, 'there appears to be a reluctance on the part of some ASEAN countries to engage in the negotiation of regional binding legal instruments in the environmental field',[83] and to date only four binding environment-related instruments have been created: the Agreement on the Conservation of Nature and Natural Resources, 1985; the Southeast Asian Nuclear-Weapon Free Zone Treaty, 1995; the ASEAN Agreement on Transboundary Haze Pollution, 2002; and the sub-regional Agreement on Cooperation for the Sustainable Development of the Mekong River Basin, 1995.

While the European Commission had explicit legal personality, with the EU only more recently gaining legal personality by virtue of Article 47 of the Treaty on European Union,[84] the ASEAN Declaration of 1967 did not afford this institution any legal personality. As Boer suggests, '[the Declaration] represented an important, but nevertheless informal political arrangement . . . which set the tenor of what became a relatively loose legal approach to the manner in which the organization conducted its affairs for 40 years'.[85] It was only with the adoption of the ASEAN Charter in 2007 that ASEAN obtained legal personality and, accordingly, the potential to more fully engage autonomously and authoritatively in regional governance and law-making.[86] Two major developments that are relevant for the global constitutionalism debate followed suit, namely the establishment of the ASEAN Intergovernmental Commission on Human Rights in 2009 and the adoption by the commission of the ASEAN Human Rights Declaration in 2012. With reference to substantive regional environmental

environment in particular exist and in some cases are even effective, they are more often than not driven by foreign donors.' Jörn Dosch, 'Reconciling trade and environmental protection in ASEAN-China relations: more than political window dressing?' (2011) 2 *Journal of Current Southeast Asian Affairs* 7–29, at 17.

[82] Elliott (n. 78), at 43–44.

[83] Boer (n. 81), p. 263.

[84] Which means the EU has the ability to: conclude and negotiate international agreements in accordance with its external commitments; become a member of international organisations; and join international conventions, such as the European Convention on Human Rights.

[85] Boer (n. 81), p. 253.

[86] Art. 3 of the ASEAN Charter determines that 'ASEAN, as an inter-governmental organisation, is hereby conferred legal personality'.

constitutionalism, under the heading 'Economic, Social and Cultural Rights', the declaration provides an environmental right in the guise of a socio-economic right:

> 28. Every person has the right to an adequate standard of living for himself or herself and his or her family including:
>
> ...
>
> f. The right to a safe, clean and sustainable environment.

In addition, the declaration places a positive obligation on member states to 'adopt meaningful people-oriented and gender responsive development programmes aimed at poverty alleviation, the creation of conditions including the protection and sustainability of the environment for the peoples of ASEAN to enjoy all human rights recognised in this Declaration on an equitable basis'.[87] The intention was that the declaration should at least meet the minimum standards of the Universal Declaration of Human Rights, 1948 (UDHR), but that it should be tweaked to best suit the specific identity of ASEAN countries and to create an 'added value' for the region.[88] While the ASEAN Declaration's environmental provision has been drafted not as a goal in itself (i.e. environmental protection) but rather as a condition for the fulfilment of another more overarching goal (i.e. the achievement of an adequate standard of living), it goes well beyond the scope of the UDHR which does not contain an environmental right provision. Its environmental right provision is also markedly more far-reaching than that of the EU. Laudable as this may be, regrettably, the ASEAN provides for no regional judicial mechanisms such as those of the EU and, perhaps more disappointingly, no judicial institution to oversee the observance and implementation of human rights contained in the ASEAN Human Rights Declaration. The ASEAN Intergovernmental Commission on Human Rights that was created in 2009 does not function as a court; the focus of its mandate is predominantly on the promotion of human rights which 'limits its role to an advisory forum for the ASEAN Secretariat and member states, rather than giving the commission independent enforcement powers'.[89] There is accordingly little opportunity for judicial recognition and safeguarding of whatever superior 'constitutional' claims may flow from the environmental right.

---

[87] Art. 36 of the ASEAN Human Rights Declaration.

[88] Catherine Shanahan Renshaw, 'The ASEAN Human Rights Declaration 2012' (2013) 13 *Human Rights Law Review* 557–579, at 559.

[89] Michelle Staggs Kelsall, 'The New ASEAN Intergovernmental Commission on Human Rights: toothless tiger or tentative first step?' (2009) 90 *Asia Pacific Issues* 1–8, at 2.

Likewise, despite these developments towards a more powerful regional governance body that seeks to emulate normative (rights-based) guarantees provided in international law, there is a view that 'there has been little indication of a willingness to grant any form of independence to the [ASEAN] organization *qua* organization, with active resistance to such a development in the area of human rights'.[90] With respect to the last point of criticism, commentators have pointed to the many deficiencies that accompanied the drafting process of the ASEAN Human Rights Declaration that collectively impact its legitimacy, including, among others: the controversial drafting process was not done by independent experts; the public and non-governmental groups were excluded in the many phases of the drafting process; and there has been a serious lack of transparency and lack of regional consultations during the drafting process.[91]

The foregoing discussion suggests that the EU represents a stronger form of regional environmental governance and associated aspects of global environmental constitutionalism when compared to the ASEAN. Clearly the EU governance set-up more fully embodies the notion of *trias politica*; the prevalence of higher order constitutional norms encapsulated in rights; influential judicial institutions which oversee compliance with the rule of law; a strong, binding normative environmental law framework; and a more deliberate top-down form of regional environmental governance that has been designed to limit the sovereign free will of member states in various areas, including the environment.

That said, with specific reference to ASEAN, Lorraine Elliott indicates there is a view that 'interstate cooperation does not have to follow a European model of formal constitutionalism to be successful in generating transnational governance arrangements across a range of issue areas',[92] an approach which is characterised by altogether more horizontal and networked structures as opposed to the vertical, top-down approach followed in other regional bodies such as the EU. The jury is, however, still out on the effectiveness and future potential of this bottom-up approach, and it seems likely that a greater interventionist approach will have to be followed to fully realise the potential of ASEAN in regional environmental governance. What is encouraging is that ASEAN now provides its member states with a formal and substantive regional

[90] Chesterman (n. 79), at 206.
[91] See, for example, Renshaw (n. 88), at 557–579.
[92] Elliott (n. 78), at 42.

environmental constitutionalism blueprint, notably through the ASEAN Human Rights Declaration and the ASEAN Charter, to realise their full potential in providing more comprehensive regional environmental protection. ASEAN and its member states could progressively do so through the creation of more binding regional environmental treaties and by enforcing these; by fully utilising ASEAN's environmental governance structures that have already been formally constituted; by creating a strong independent regional judiciary; and by building on the rights-based environmental protection provisions in the ASEAN Human Rights Declaration, among other tactics.

5 Conclusion

The global socioecological crisis is one of the most recent and pressing challenges for the state. As a response to this crisis, environmental constitutionalism is a specialised form of constitutionalism that offers a vision of a potentially more contemporary, notionally enlarged, ecologically oriented constitutional state that has progressed beyond the social welfare state and that, through its constitution, has to redefine its traditional role in the larger scheme of governance matters; re-envisage its functions and the role and rule of the law in achieving better environmental care; and revisit the role of traditional constitutional constructs such as rights, democracy and the individualistic nature of liberal constitutionalism for environmental protection. While it is unlikely that the ecological constitutional state exists in a perfect or complete form anywhere in the world, environmental constitutionalism has much going for it and remains an ideal for all states the world over to strive towards.

The contemporary constitutional state is, however, unable on its own to address the global socioecological crisis. The metaphor of the Anthropocene suggests that a truly global effort is necessary that would require of states, as the traditional key referents of constitutionalism, to govern beyond their borders in regulatory spaces beyond the reach of pure state-based normative regulatory interventions. There is considerable potential for states to do so in a regional law and governance setting as the discussion in this chapter illustrated. It is in this sense and for this reason that the need arises for a global constitutional approach to environmental governance beyond the state. The emergence of formal and substantive environment-related constitutional elements in regional governance regimes such as the EU and ASEAN evinces a recent addition to the global constitutionalism agenda. Regional environmental constitutionalism is as yet a normatively and analytically underdeveloped area of this agenda, but it has considerable potential to develop into a coherent and autonomous field of enquiry and normative programme, while simultaneously contributing to extending the potential of constitutionalism to counter the global socioecological crisis.

PART IV

Implementation and Enforcement

Implementation and Enforcement

14

The Emerging Principle of Functional Complementarity for Coordination Among National and International Jurisdictions

Intellectual Hegemony and Heterogeneous World

KAORU OBATA

1 Introduction

The first problem that global constitutionalism faces is its applicability or appropriateness on the universal level.

In this regard, I would like to recognise the relevance of a constitutionalist way of thinking to explain several phenomena in positive international law. Wolfgang Friedmann's law of cooperation[1] can readily account for various legal institutions, as it presupposes general interests of the international community as a whole. Thus, we have a global constitution or a set of constitutions in this layer of international law.[2]

From an East Asian viewpoint, however, it is easy to criticise global constitutionalism if it advocates the comprehensive applicability of one unique constitutional order to the world community. East Asia has a serious problem in proliferating weapons of mass destruction and an imminent threat to peace. The responses by the international community to its problem are different from those to, for example, the Taliban and Al-Qaeda. In the latter case, the United Nations Security Council (UNSC) has also targeted many persons in Europe. It created an Ombudsperson for the Al-Qaeda sanctions,[3] whereas none exists for

---

[1] Wolfgang Friedmann, *The Changing Structure of International Law* (London: Stevens & Sons, 1964), pp. 60–63.

[2] Regarding Friedmann's orientation to stratification, see Kaoru Obata, '"Stratification of international law" as the construction of a world public sphere: the legal project of Wolfgang Friedmann in his later period' (2001) 20 *Yearbook of World Law* (Japanese Association of World Law) 151–176 (in Japanese).

[3] UNSC Resolution 1904 (2009), 17 December 2009, UN Doc. S/RES/1909, paras. 20–21. The Al-Qaeda sanctions regime has also covered ISIL since 2015. See UNSC Resolution 2253, 17 December 2015, UN Doc. S/RES/2253, para. 1.

the sanctions against the Democratic People's Republic of Korea (DPRK) or other countries.[4] This difference might suggest that the DPRK regime is outside the world constitutional order, as this order may well incorporate the due process principle.

International relations in East Asia presuppose antagonistic conflicts of vital interests and are governed by the 'law of power'.[5] It is for such relations that Friedmann formulated the concept 'law of coexistence', because the utmost concern in the region is nuclear war.[6] More seriously, this concern is not shared enough in the international community. A constitutional way of thinking in these conditions would merely deceive, at least if it argues for the universal applicability of one unique constitution in a homogeneous manner. Global constitutionalists should admit to such a limitation.

Keeping in mind this extrinsic criticism, the present chapter treats a basic question intrinsic in a possible global constitutional order, namely whether or not that order works fairly and equitably. I address this question by analysing the concept of functional complementarity. In this connection, I also examine whether or not, and if so how far, the concept is universally applicable and could be regarded as a fundamental principle of a global constitution.

By 'functional complementarity' I do not intend for any similar positive law concepts to be understood along with it, though I keep in mind 'subsidiarity' in the systems of European Union (EU) law[7] and the European Convention on Human Rights (ECHR) as well as complementarity in the system of the International Criminal Court (ICC). Instead, I find a strong tendency common in the aforementioned systems to coordinate exercises of competence by various jurisdictions according to their procedural effectiveness to provide redress. The principle of

---

[4] See, for example, 'Security Council Committee established pursuant to Resolution 1718', available at https://www.un.org/sc/suborg/en/sanctions/1718 (last accessed on 13 August 2017).

[5] Georg Schwarzenberger, *Frontiers of International Law* (London: Stevens, 1962), pp. 25–29.

[6] In a sense, a proto-constitutionalism would be necessary if we were to regard coexistence as essential for humankind. Friedmann might have thought so when he reformulated his friend Schwarzenberger's term 'power' into 'coexistence', particularly after China's emergence as the third pole and the 1962 Cuba crisis. See Wolfgang Friedmann, 'Half a century of international law' (1964) 50 *Virginia Journal of International Law* 1333–1358, at 1347, 1353–1354. Such thinking could be characterised as (proto-)constitutional, which will not however be treated by this chapter.

[7] Article 5(3) of the Treaty on European Union, Official Journal of European Union 2016/C 202/01.

functional complementarity is defined here as such a concept. Attention should be paid to the concept's non-hierarchical character, which excludes any priority a priori of local or national authorities.

Defined as such, the concept of functional complementarity certainly corresponds to current discussions on global constitutionalism. The global constitution does not seem to work in a similar way to modern constitutions of nation states. No clear hierarchy has been established between a global constitution and the laws of the world's component parts. The prediction of certain leading publicists in the twentieth century, e.g. Alfred Verdross[8] and Kisaburo Yokota,[9] has not come true. If the world is integrated in a (set of) constitutional order(s), however, a somehow coherent relationship should be found between the component parts. Functional complementarity, which enables coordination for the sake of effectiveness in implementing shared values, would establish convergence among suborders, maintaining the pluralistic nature of the world.[10]

2   The functional complementarity principle in Europe

2.1   Version upgrade of the concept of subsidiarity in the ECHR system[11]

It is generally accepted that the principle of subsidiarity has long been firmly established as the basis of the ECHR system.[12] The *Belgian*

---

[8] Alfred Verdross, *Die Verfassung der Völkerrechtsgemeinschaft* (Wien: Springer, 1926).

[9] See, among others, Kisaburo Yokota, *International Law: First Part* (Tokyo: Yuhikaku, 1933) (in Japanese). See also Kisaburo Yokota, 'Begriff und Gliederung der Verfassung der Völkerrechtgemeinschaft', in Alfred Verdross, Josef Dobretsberger and Hans Kelsen (eds.), *Gesellschaft, Staat und Recht; Untersuchungen zur reinen Rechtslehre; Festschrift Hans Kelsen zum 50* (Wien: Springer, 1931), p. 390.

[10] See, among others, Nico Krisch, *Beyond Constitutionalism: Pluralist Structure of Post National Law* (Oxford: Oxford University Press, 2010). For various versions of so-called constitutional pluralism, see Keisuke Kondo, 'Constitutional pluralism', in Shotaro Hamamoto and Masao Okitsu (eds.), *A European Order or European Orders* (Tokyo: Keiso Shobo, 2013), pp. 5–29 (in Japanese).

[11] Convention for the Protection of Human Rights and Fundamental Freedoms, Rome, 4 November 1950, in force 3 September 1953, Council of Europe Treaty Series (hereinafter cited as CETS) No. 5. For historical analysis relevant here, see Ed Bates, *The Evolution of the European Convention on Human Rights: From Inception to the Creation of a Permanent Court of Human Rights* (Oxford: Oxford University Press, 2010). See also Kaoru Obata, *The Constitutionalization of European Human Rights Law: A Critical Study in a Process of International Law* (Tokyo: Shinzansha, 2014) (in Japanese).

[12] This understanding was propagated by the seminal article Herbert Petzold, 'The convention and the principle of subsidiarity', in Ronald St. J. MacDonald, Franz Matscher and Herbert Petzold (eds.), *The European System for the Protection of*

Linguistics case (1969)[13] is regarded as the locus classicus, and the *Handyside* case (1976)[14] is frequently quoted in this context. The latter judgment describes 'the machinery of protection established by [the ECHR] [a]s subsidiary to the national systems'.[15] As clearly indicated by *Handyside*, the margin-of-appreciation doctrine[16] was derived from the ECHR's subsidiary nature.

It does not necessarily follow, however, that 'subsidiarity' here is the same notion as the one highlighted after the Cold War. The ECHR system changed radically in 1998 with Protocol No. 11.[17] Before the protocol entered into force, the acceptance of two optional clauses[18] by the state parties concerned had been a prerequisite for judicial determinations by the European Court of Human Rights (ECtHR) on individual applications. The crevasse had to be bridged by the political will of each government, and the ECtHR had no way to do so other than by making itself subsidiary. After 1998, the mandatory jurisdiction of the ECtHR has been automatic for all contracting parties, so the structural gap has been filled. In the current system, the ECtHR is not institutionally required to respect the relevant decisions in national jurisdictions. We may wonder why it still relies on the principle of subsidiarity.

The negative aspect of subsidiarity, which can be defined as restriction of international control, is explained by a practical need to reduce the ECtHR's workload given the exponential increase in applications to it.[19] Even after 1998, the concept is frequently used by the ECtHR to explain its passive attitude to fact finding; to examine whether an application should be declared inadmissible because the applicant would be

Human Rights (Dordrecht; Boston; London: Martinus Nijhoff Publishers, 1993). Petzold was deputy registrar (1975–1990) and registrar (1994–1998) of the ECtHR.

[13] ECtHR, *Certain Aspects of the Laws on the Use of Languages in Education in Belgium* (Merits), Plenary Court Judgment of 23 July 1968, Application Nos. 1474/62; 1677/62; 1691/62; 1769/63; 1994/63; 2126/64s, para. 10 at p. 35.

[14] ECtHR *Handyside v. UK*, Plenary Court Judgment of 7 December 1976, Application No. 5493/72.

[15] Ibid., at para. 48.

[16] See, among other sources, Yutaka Arai, *The Margin of Appreciation Doctrine and Principle of Proportionality in the Jurisprudence of ECHR* (Antwerp: Intersentia, 2002).

[17] Protocol No. 11 to the ECHR, Strasbourg, 11 May 1994, in force on 1 November 1998, CETS No. 155.

[18] Former Articles 25 and 46. The original text of the ECHR is found in 213 United Nations Treaty Series (hereinafter cited as UNTS) 221.

[19] Luzius Wildhaber, 'Address on the "Journée de Réflection" on reform of the convention system' (2000), in Luzius Wildhaber, *The European Court of Human Rights 1998–2006: History, Achievements, Reform* (Kehl: Engel, 2006), pp. 105–112.

disqualified as a victim considering the redress obtained locally; as well as to apply the local remedies rule (Article 35(1) of the ECHR) or the margin of appreciation.

In the 2000s, however, the rate of admissible applications did not drop but slightly increased;[20] the frequent invocation of 'subsidiarity' did not lead to a quantitative reduction of the ECtHR's workload. Almost the only function of 'subsidiarity' was qualitative, enabling the positive adoption of national interpretation rather than the passive acceptance of, or non-intervention in, national process.

The *Kudla* judgment in 2000[21] makes clear that 'subsidiarity' now has an additional meaning. Article 13, which provides for an effective remedy for the violation of a convention right, leads to a general assessment of the national remedial institution.[22] The ECtHR had used it restrictively, and if the court found a violation of Article 6, which provides the right of access to a fair trial, it had categorically denied the possibility of an Article 13 violation. In *Kudla*, the ECtHR invoked the principle of subsidiarity to abandon such previous case law.[23] If a given national remedial institution is found to be ineffective, the international instance should intervene *due to* subsidiarity. Note should be taken of the fact that the ECtHR had always found violations *despite* subsidiarity coupled with the margin-of-appreciation doctrine.

2.2   The ECtHR's doctrine of 'equivalent protection' and the 'Solange' theory

The principle of functional complementary has also led to a substantial suspension of judgment by the court when a given remedial institution is considered particularly effective. In the *Bosphorus* case,[24] an Irish measure

---

[20] See Steven Greer, *The European Convention on Human Rights: Achievements, Problems and Prospects* (Cambridge: Cambridge University Press, 2006), pp. 35, 39.

[21] ECtHR, *Kudla v. Poland*, Grand Chamber Judgment of 26 October 2000, Application No. 30210/96.

[22] For the previous case law on Article 13, see Andrew Drzemczewski and Christos Giakoumopoulos, 'Article 13', in Louis Edmond Petitti, Emmanuel Decaux and Pierre-Henri Imbert (eds.), *La Convention européene des droits de l'homme; Commentaire article par article*, 2nd ed. (Paris: Economica, 1999), pp. 455–456.

[23] ECtHR, *Kudla* (n. 21), para. 152.

[24] ECtHR, *Bosphorus Hava Yollari Turizm ve Ticaret Anonim Sirkreti v. Ireland*, Grand Chamber Judgment of 24 February 2005, Application No. 45036/98.

to implement a European Community (EC) regulation was alleged to violate the right of property under Article 1, ECHR Protocol No. 1.[25]

The ECtHR recognised that a contracting party could transfer some competence to an international organisation that was not a contracting party, but it sought to set some safeguard for this 'deficit of human rights'.[26] The ECtHR found that:

> State action taken in compliance with such legal obligations is justified as long as the relevant organisation is considered to protect fundamental rights, as regards both the substantive guarantees offered and the mechanisms controlling their observance, in a manner which can be considered at least equivalent to that for which the Convention provides.[27]

If equivalent protection is considered to be provided by the organisation, the presumption will be that a state has not departed from the ECHR's requirements when it does no more than implement legal obligations flowing from its membership in the organisation.[28]

As a result of this doctrine of 'equivalent protection', delegation of competence is possible only as far as the delegated jurisdictions can exercise similarly effective control over human rights abuses. The doctrine is reminiscent of the 'Solange' theory[29] first propounded by the German Federal Constitutional Court.[30] Indeed, the theory is an exemplar of the principle that we call 'functional complementarity'. Within the EU legal order, the development of reverse[31] and horizontal[32] versions has been suggested, so that it becomes a general

[25] Protocol No. 1 to the ECHR, Paris, 20 March 1952, in force 18 May 1954, CETS No. 9.
[26] ECtHR, Bosphorus (n. 24), para. 154. The words 'deficit of human rights' are mine.
[27] Ibid., para. 155.
[28] Ibid., para. 156.
[29] For a concise restatement of the theory, see Gráinne de Búrca, 'The ECJ and the international legal order: a re-evaluation', in Gráinne de Búrca and Joseph H. H. Weiler (eds.), The Worlds of the European Constitutionalism (Cambridge: Cambridge University Press, 2012), p. 142.
[30] Solange I, Beschluß v. 29.5.1974, Entscheidungen des Bundesverfassungsgerichts, 37, 271 [1974] 2. Common Market Law Reports 540; Solange II, Beschluß v. 22.10.1986, Entscheidungen des Bundesverfassungsgerichts, 73, 339 [1987] 3. Common Market Law Reports 225.
[31] Armin von Bogdandy, Matthias Rottmann, Carlino Antpôhler, Johanna Dickschen, Simon Hentrei and Maja Smrkolj, 'Reverse Solange: protecting the essence of fundamental rights against EU member states' (2012) 49 Common Market Law Review 489–520. 'Reverse Solange' means putting priority on EU control should member state mechanisms misfunction.
[32] Iris Canor, 'My brother keeper? Horizontal "Solange": "an ever closer distrust among the peoples of Europe"' (2013) 50 Common Market Law Review 383–422.

framework for coordination of actual exercises of shared competences among various jurisdictions.[33]

2.3   Implementation of the principle in European regional law and its functioning

One may wonder whether functional complementarity is still working in the ECHR system. The amendment to the ECHR by Protocol No. 15,[34] which was adopted in 2013, would add a recital to the preamble that contains an express recognition of the 'principle of subsidiarity' together with the concept of 'margin of appreciation' (Article 1, Protocol No. 15). This was an outcome of the Brighton Conference in 2012.[35]

In fact, the process leading to Protocol No. 15 suggests a growing emphasis on the negative aspect of subsidiarity. The 'margin of appreciation' now seems to cover the whole range of rights in the ECHR, not being restricted to rights subject to derogation (Article 15 of the ECHR) or to limitations.[36] It is, however, expressly subject to the ECtHR's 'supervisory jurisdiction'.[37] No such restriction is proposed for the 'principle of subsidiarity'. This would mean that 'subsidiarity' has a positive aspect: it implies not competence or power but *responsibility* to secure

---

[33] Here we may refer to the principle of subsidiarity in EU law. In 1992, Ken Endo drew attention to the fact that it has not only a negative version but also a positive. See Ken Endo, 'The principle of subsidiarity: from Johannes Althusius to Jacques Delors' (1994) 44 *Hokkaido Law Review* 2064–1965, at footnote * at 2063. The former is defined as '*limitation* of the competence of the "higher" organisation in relation to "lower entity"', whereas the latter is defined as '*possibility* or even the obligation of interventions from the higher organisation' (emphasis in original). Ibid., at 2054. Endo argues that both versions are found not only in European political thought but also in the EC, especially under Jacques Delors's presidency. Ibid., at 2008–2000. An elaborated Japanese version of the article is Ken Endo, 'A post-sovereign political concept: potential of the principle of subsidiarity in the European Union' (2003) 945 *Thought (Iwanami Shoten)* 207–228 (in Japanese).

[34] Protocol No. 15 to the ECHR, Strasbourg, 24 June 2013, not yet entered into force, CETS No. 213.

[35] High-Level Conference on the Future of the European Court of Human Rights, *Brighton Declaration*, available at https://rm.coe.int/1680593071 (last accessed on 16 August 2017), para. 12 (b).

[36] The following explanation could be, however, regarded as preserving the original idea of the margin of appreciation: 'the States Parties enjoy a margin of appreciation in how they apply and implement the Convention, depending on the circumstances of the case and the rights and freedoms engaged'. *Explanatory Report to Protocol No. 15 Amending the Convention for the Protection of Human Rights and Fundamental Freedoms*, para. 9. This is a quotation from the *Brighton Declaration*, ibid., para. 11.

[37] See the new last paragraph to be inserted in the ECHR's preamble.

Table 14.1 *Number and Rate of Violations of Articles 6 and 13, ECHR*

Period	English Judgments Finding Violation of		English Judgments on Merits
	Article 6	Article 13	
17.8.2007–16.8.2012	3,603 (53.4)	822 (12.2)	6,743 (100)
17.8.2012–16.8.2017	1,615 (35.6)	612 (13.5)	4,534 (100)

Source: Author's calculation utilising filter function of HUDOC

the rights' (emphasis added), which is mentioned as a direct corollary of the principle.[38]

Functional complementarity is thus still working in the ECtHR system. Judgments finding Article 13 violations increased about twenty-eight times between 1995 and 2005.[39] The increase in relation to Article 6 was seven-fold. This trend has continued, or has even intensified, in the past decade. As Table 14.1 shows, the rate of findings of Article 6 violations has dramatically decreased, while that regarding Article 13 has steadily increased. Thus, it is safe to say that the ECtHR no longer hesitates to declare that national remedial institutions have been ineffective.

Bearing also in mind the development of the '*Solange*' theory in the EU legal order, functional complementarity now may well be characterised as a principle of European regional law. It should be remembered that such a principle was gradually recognised during the ECHR accession of Central and Eastern Europe countries and the EU eastern enlargement. In the same period, the United Kingdom and Nordic countries incorporated the ECHR into their domestic legal orders.[40]

In this context, the statement in 1990 of Rolv Ryssdal, then ECtHR president, deserves extensive quotation:

> [Incorporation] has in fact two advantages: it provides the national court with the possibility of taking into account of the Convention and the Strasbourg case-law to resolve the dispute before it, and at the same time it gives the European organs an opportunity to discover the views of the

---

[38] Ibid.

[39] The statistics are taken from Greer (n. 20), p. 74, table 1.

[40] See, among other sources, Jörg Polakiewicz, 'The status of the convention in national law', in Robert Blackburn and Jörg Polakiewicz (eds.), *The Fundamental Rights in Europe* (New York: Oxford University Press, 2001), p. 36; Ursula Kilkelly, 'Introduction', in Ursula Kilkelly (ed.), *ECHR and Irish Law* (Bristol: Jordans, 2004), pp. lvii–lviii.

national court regarding the interpretation of the Convention and its application to a specific set of circumstances. The dialogue which thus develops between those who are called upon to apply the Convention on the domestic level and those who must do so on the European level is crucial for an effective protection of the rights guaranteed under the Convention.[41]

In 1995, Daniel Tarschys, then secretary general of the Council of Europe, urged the United Kingdom to incorporate the ECHR, arguing that: 'Britain's commitment to Europe is an essential prerequisite . . . for the stability of that wider Europe which we are trying to build.'[42] Both men's statements put great stress on the 'principle of subsidiarity'.

Thus, it is clear that the principle of functional complementarity served to transfer interpretations by national jurisdictions whose institutions have a high reputation to those with a poor reputation mainly through the exercise of international jurisdiction. (See Figure 14.1.)

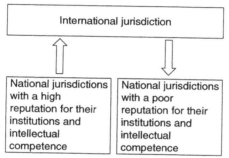

Figure 14.1   Relationships among Jurisdictions According to 'Functional Complementarity'

Experience shows that the relationship is somehow fixed between jurisdictions that exercise upstream influence and those affected by downstream influence. Borrowing Antonio Gramsci's terms,[43] the hegemony for authoritative interpretations emerges and is reproduced from

---

[41] Rolv Ryssdal, Speech, Ceremony for the 40th Anniversary of the European Convention on Human Rights, International Institute of Human Rights Studies, Trieste, 18 December 1990, reproduced in Robert Blackburn, *Towards a Constitutional Bill of Rights for the United Kingdom* (London: Pinter, 1999), p. 258.

[42] Daniel Tarschys, 'The Council of Europe: The Challenge of Enlargement', Speech to the Royal Institute of International Affairs, 15 February 1995, reproduced in ibid., p. 270.

[43] See, among other sources, Robert W. Cox, 'Gramsci, hegemony and international relations: an essay in methods', in Stephan Gills (ed.), *Gramsci, Historical Materialism and International Relations* (Cambridge: Cambridge University Press, 1983), pp. 49–66. Gramsci is still the subject of great attention among Japanese academics.

a small number of particular sites, which are unevenly distributed even within Europe. If a group of lawyers and legal scholars possess such intellectual hegemony, they could command interpretations predominant all over Europe, hollowing out international control over the jurisdictions with which they are affiliated.[44]

3 Universal applicability of the functional subsidiarity principle

3.1 Ambiguity in the law of immunity of international organisations

The ECtHR had considerable opportunity to develop the law relating to the immunity of international organisations. In *Waite and Kennedy v. Germany*,[45] the applicants, who had worked for the European Space Agency (ESA),[46] an international organisation in Darmstadt, Germany, invoked Article 6 of the ECHR (access to court) against German courts' decisions. These had rejected their claims in a labour dispute as inadmissible by virtue of the ESA's jurisdictional immunity.[47] The ECtHR found no Article 6 violation, but its reasoning was not straightforward. The court first recognised that the rule of immunity as applied to the applicants' case had a legitimate objective.[48] As to proportionality, the ECtHR went into the particulars of the case and declared that:

> it would be incompatible with the purpose and object of the [ECHR] . . . if the Contracting States were thereby absolved their responsibility under the [ECHR] in relation to the field of activity covered by such attribution [of competences to international organizations].[49] . . . For the Court, a material factor in determining whether granting ESA immunity from German jurisdiction is permissible under the [ECHR] is whether the

---

[44] The likelihood of this occurring had been crucial for British lawyers in committing to ECHR incorporation. See, among other sources, Lord Bingham, 'The European Convention on Human Rights: Time to Incorporate', 1993, reproduced in Blackburn (n. 41), pp. 1019 ff., p. 1022 f.

[45] ECtHR, *Waite and Kennedy v. Germany*, Grand Chamber Judgment of 19 February 1999, Application No. 26083/94.

[46] Convention for Establishment of a European Space Agency, 30 May 1975, in force on 30 October 1980, 1297 UNTS 186. There are twenty-two current members, all European: Austria, Belgium, Czech Republic, Denmark, Estonia, Finland, France, Germany, Greece, Hungary, Ireland, Italy, Luxembourg, the Netherlands, Norway, Poland, Portugal, Romania, Spain, Sweden, Switzerland and the United Kingdom. See 'Welcome to ESA', available at http://www.esa.int/About_Us/Welcome_to_ESA/What_is_ESA (last accessed on 16 August 2017).

[47] ECtHR, *Waite and Kennedy* (n. 45), paras. 11–28.

[48] Ibid., para. 63.

[49] Ibid., para. 67.

applicants had available to them *reasonable alternative means* to protect effectively their rights under the [ECHR].[50]

The ECtHR then examined various remedies applicable to disputes with the ESA.[51] 'Taking into account in particular the alternative means of legal process available to the applicants',[52] the court concluded that there had been no violation.

The reasoning developed here could be paraphrased as follows: as long as internal procedure provides effective means to address disputes with international organisations, granting immunity to them from national jurisdictions is compatible with the international right of access to tribunals; national courts must otherwise admit cases against international organisations.

Jurisdictional immunity of international organisations is no longer automatic but depends on the effectiveness of available remedies. The international law of human rights serves to coordinate exercises of competences between international organisations and national authorities. Here we see a remarkable effect of the principle of functional complementarity.

This new criterion in the ECtHR case law was found, however, to be totally inapplicable in a recent case before the same court. In *Stichting Mothers of Srebrenica and Others v. the Netherlands*,[53] the application was unanimously declared inadmissible by a Third Section Chamber despite there being no reasonable remedies for the claim against the United Nations (UN).

The case originated in an infamous atrocity known as the 'Srebrenica massacre', which occurred in July 1995. About 8,000 men and boys were killed by the military forces of Republika Srpska and Serbia after the fall of Srebrenica, which had been declared a 'safe area' by the UNSC and where the United Nations Protection Force (UNPROFOR),[54] which consisted nominally of so-called *Dutchbat*, was present.[55] The 'Mothers of Srebrenica' foundation began proceedings in the Dutch courts on behalf of victims' relatives against the state of the Netherlands and the UN. In all instances in the Netherlands, the claims against the state were accepted, but those against the UN were rejected by virtue of that

---

[50] Ibid., para. 68 (emphasis added).
[51] Ibid., paras. 69–70.
[52] Ibid., para. 73.
[53] ECtHR, *Stichting Mothers of Srebrenica and Others*, Decision of 11 June 2013, Application No. 65542/12.
[54] The UNPROFOR is a UN peacekeeping force, established in accordance with UNSC Resolution 743 (1992).
[55] ECtHR, *Mothers of Srebrenica* (n. 53), paras. 15–20.

organisation's jurisdictional immunity.[56] The ECtHR, having confirmed the absence of 'reasonable alternative means' in UN law,[57] fatefully reduced this criterion's significance.

> It does not follow, however, that in the absence of an alternative remedy the recognition of immunity is *ipso facto* constitutive of a violation of the right of access to a court. ... As regards international organisations, this Court's judgments in *Waite and Kennedy* and *Beer and Regan*[58] cannot be interpreted in such absolute terms either.[59]

The question arises as to how the UN in its alleged tort during the peace-related operations could be distinguished from the ESA in labour disputes. The ECtHR itself, though its precise position was ambiguous, relied heavily on the special nature of the UN's related chapter VII function, substantially following the line drawn by the Dutch Supreme Court.[60] The Dutch Appeal Court had made a distinction based on the fact that the UN predated the ECHR system.[61] In addition, the Dutch District Court had invoked the UN's almost universal membership, in contrast to the ESA's limited, European membership.[62]

In sum, the ECtHR has recognised that the principle of functional complementarity is applicable to the relationship between states and international organisations of European or technical nature, whereas it is inapplicable to the UN by virtue of its almost universal membership or unique nature, being equipped with enforcement power amid threats to peace.

[56] Ibid., paras. 54–94.
[57] Ibid., para. 163. For an overview of UN internal remedies, see Helmut Buss, Thomas Fitschen, Thomas Laker, Christian Rohde and Santiago Villalpando (eds.), *Handbook on the Internal Justice System of the United Nations* (Turin: United Nations System Staff College, 2014).
[58] ECtHR, *Beer and Regan v. Germany*, Grand Chamber Judgment of 19 February 1999, Application No. 28934/95. It is a twin of *Waite and Kennedy* as regards both its fact and the reasoning of ECtHR. Judgment in the two cases was delivered on the same day.
[59] ECtHR, *Mothers of Srebrenica* (n. 53), para. 164.
[60] *Mothers of Srebrenica and Others v. the State of Netherlands and UN*, Supreme Court of the Netherlands, Judgment of 13 April 2012 (translation by the International Crime Database), available at http://www.asser.nl/upload/documents/20120905T111510-Supreme%20Court%20Decision%20English%2013%20April%202012.pdf (last accessed on 12 August 2017), paras. 4.3.1–4.3.6.
[61] *Mothers of Srebrenica and Others v. State of the Netherlands and the UN*, Appeal Court in the Hague, Judgment of 30 March 2010 (unofficial translation by the court), available at http://www.haguejusticeportal.net/Docs/Dutch%20cases/Appeals_Judgment_Mothers_Srebrenica_EN.pdf (last accessed on 12 August 2017), para. 5.4.
[62] *Mothers of Srebrenica and Others v. State of the Netherlands and the UN*, District Court in the Hague, Judgment of 10 July 2008, available at https://uitspraken.rechtspraak.nl/inzien document?id=ECLI:NL:RBSGR:2008:BD6796&showbutton=true (last accessed on 12 August 2017), para. 5.24

The Dutch District Court's reasoning illustrates the argument that a transnational constitutional order is still regional, i.e. that there exists a European constitutional law but no global constitution. It certainly reminds us of the peculiar, self-restricting judgment of the European Court of Justice in *Kadi I*.[63]

A far more serious limitation on the principle of functional complementarity may be found in the ECtHR's reasoning. It argued that, as far as acts in UN peace operations are concerned, the exercise of competences could not be coordinated according to the principle. The ECtHR's reasoning suggests that the rule of pluralistic global constitutional law ends where the rule of power starts. To this limited extent, the ECtHR judgment in *Mothers of Srebrenica* should be considered reasonable and significant.

Nevertheless, we should harbour serious reservations about the judgment, beyond its ambiguity. First, it goes in the opposite direction to the *Kadi I* judgment, where remedies are substantially available even against UN sanctions. It is therefore uncertain whether the case law has been settled along the lines of *Mothers of Srebrenica*. Second, the potential redress is *post factum* and does not suspend ongoing operations. Is it appropriate to 'protect' UN peace operations in such an absolute manner? Strong doubt is called for.

In any event, the principle of functional complementarity cannot be automatically applied in the context of UN peace operations. It has a subject matter limitation, especially relating to peace maintenance.

3.2   The 'positive' complementarity and its decline in the ICC system

In order to assess the universal applicability of the notion of functional complementarity, it is more useful to discuss situations in the ICC system. The ICC exercises its jurisdiction based on the principle of complementarity.[64] This principle contrasts with the precedents of the ad hoc international criminal tribunals, whose statutes had provided for primacy of international instances.[65]

[63] Joint Cases C-402/05 P and 415/05 P, *Kadi and Al Barakaat* v. *Council and Commission*, [2008] ECR-I-6351, paras. 286–288. In this Judgment, the ECJ examined the measures against Mr. Kadi only in light of EU law. International obligations was taken into consideration only as a part of EU law.
[64] Tenth paragraph of the preamble and Article 1 of the Rome Statute of the International Criminal Court (Rome Statute). Signed on 17 July 1998, entered into force on 1 July 2002, 2187 UNTS 3.
[65] See Article 9(2) of the Statute of the International Criminal Tribunal for the Former Yugoslavia, updated version, available at http://www.icty.org/x/file/Legal%20Library/

It is necessary to rectify such a dichotomy between the permanent court's complementarity and the ad hoc tribunals' primacy. In originating the word 'complementarity', James Crawford[66] kept in mind the principle of subsidiarity in EU law.[67] He thought it necessary to use another word, because 'it was not appropriate to describe an international criminal court as "subsidiary" to national courts'.[68] Of course, the ICC would not be theoretically subsidiary to national courts even if the latter normally exercise criminal jurisdiction. Note should be taken also of the actual text of the Rome Statute. This leaves no room for further contestation by a national jurisdiction once the ICC itself declares a case to be admissible, through applying the complementarity principle.[69] *Kompetenz-Kompetenz* lies in the ICC, not in national authorities.

It is true that the ICC must normally rely on states' cooperation,[70] at least for the accused to be present at trial.[71] It would be thus understandable if the ICC, particularly the prosecutor, were nervous about obtaining the cooperation of the state where a suspect resides. In order to secure the state's cooperation, the court might be indeed advised not to exercise *Kompetenz-Kompetenz* for a unilateral determination that it has no genuine will to prosecute the suspect.[72]

In this context, the ICC Office of the Prosecutor (ICC-OTP) introduced the notion of 'positive' complementarity.[73] In a landmark document of

---

Statute/statute_sept09_en.pdf (last accessed on 16 August 2017); Article 8 (2) of the Statute of the International Criminal Tribunal for Rwanda, available at http://unictr.unmict .org/sites/unictr.org/files/legal-library/100131_Statute_en_fr_0.pdf   (last   accessed in August 2017).

[66] Crawford was then chairperson of the Working Group on the topic in the International Law Commission. See Report of the International Law Commission, on the work of its 46th session, in *Yearbook of the International Law Commission 1994*, Vol. II (2), paras. 81, 89, at p. 26.

[67] James Crawford, 'The drafting of the Rome Statute', in Philippe Sands (ed.), *From Nuremberg to The Hague: The Future of International Criminal Justice* (Cambridge: Cambridge University Press, 2003), pp. 138–139.

[68] Ibid.

[69] Art. 1 in particular (4) of the Rome Statute.

[70] It is remarkable that there exists no *Kompetenz-Kompetenz* to decide on the matter of compliance with obligations to cooperate with the ICC. See part 9 of the Rome Statute.

[71] Art. 63 of the Rome Statute. See also Art. 61 (2).

[72] Art. 17 (1)(a)(b) and (2) of the Rome Statute.

[73] See, in particular, Luis Moreno-Ocampo, 'A positive approach to complementarity: the impact of the office of the prosecutor', in Carsten Stahn and Mohamed M. ElZeidy (eds.), *The International Criminal Court and Complementarity: From Theory to Practice*, Vol. I (Cambridge: Cambridge University Press, 2011), pp. 21–32.

2003,[74] the ICC-OTP had frequently referred to putting 'an end to impunity'.[75] It was, however, rather the need for national support in investigations in situ[76] and the limited resources of the court[77] that directly led to the central idea of this paper, that is, cooperative relationships or burden sharing with national authorities. On this basis, the ICC-OTP used the term 'positive complementarity' in a paper[78] in 2006. The practice of self-referral is along these lines.[79]

The idea of 'positive complementarity' contrasts with the 'negative'[80] version of complementarity, which presupposes competitive or antagonistic relationships with national jurisdictions.[81] The former thus serves for the coordination of exercises of competence between national jurisdictions and the ICC for the sake of the effective administration of criminal justice. By adopting the notion of 'positive complementarity', the ICC is governed by the concept of functional complementarity. Note should be taken also of the weakness of the ICC's position, because its OTP had admitted from the beginning the need to rely on national authorities.

Nevertheless, strong doubt has been cast on the appropriateness of 'positive complementarity', first from a legal viewpoint. The notion leads to, or presupposes, an interpretation of Article 17(1) of the Rome Statute according to which the national authorities' inaction is an independent and initial criterion for admissibility.[82] The inaction might be motivated

---

[74] Paper on Some Policy Issues before the Office of the Prosecutor, September 2003, available at https://www.legal-tools.org/uploads/tx_ltpdb/030905_policy_paper.pdf (last accessed on 3 August 2017).

[75] Ibid., p. 3 and passim.

[76] Ibid., p. 2.

[77] Ibid., p. 3.

[78] Report on Prosecutorial Strategy, 14 September 2006, available at https://www.icc-cpi.int/NR/rdonlyres/D673DD8C-D427-4547-BC69-2D363E07274B/143708/ProsecutorialStrategy20060914_English.pdf (last accessed on 3 August 2017), p. 4.

[79] Among the ten situations currently under investigation, five have been referred by the government of territorial states. 'Situations under investigation' available at https://www.icc-cpi.int/pages/situations.aspx (last accessed on 16 August 2017).

[80] The term 'negative' in the context of the ICC system is used to mean that the ICC should exercise its jurisdiction without consideration of interactive relationships between the ICC and territorial states. This meaning is totally different from the word used in context of the EU or ECHR system, as explained in the text accompanying n. 19. It should be noted that the notion of 'positive complementarity' in the ICC context clearly illustrates contemporary arguments for functional complementarity.

[81] A concise scheme is found in Pham Thi Thu Huong, 'A changing notion of complementarity under the Rome Statute of the International Criminal Court' (2012) 245 *Nagoya University Journal of Law and Politics* 634–585, at 587.

[82] Paper on Some Policy Issues (n. 74), p. 5. See also *Prosecutor v. Katanga et al.*, ICC Appeal Chamber Judgment of 25 September 2009, para. 78.

by, for example, the wish to secure the ICC's political mobilisation against rebels. This interpretation would, however, be incompatible with the whole structure of Article 17, because the other two paragraphs set out criteria and a way of determining the two main reasons for inadmissibility, i.e. unwillingness and inability.[83]

Positive complementarity has been criticised also from the viewpoint of the proper administration of justice. It not only promotes active cooperation with bona fide states, but it also leads to compromise or politically motivated 'division of labour' with less than bona fide states or with governments having a vital interest in suppressing rebels. It contradicts the central idea of the *proprio motu* prosecutor free from political manipulation.[84]

The supporters of the notion of 'positive complementarity' have frequently alleged that it catalyses the proper administration of criminal justice domestically. A recent detailed study, however, indicates that such effects are yet to occur.[85] Strong doubt would be then cast on the usefulness of the notion.

A lethal blow to 'positive complementarity' may ironically come from recent trends of invoking this notion in the relationship between universal and regional jurisdictions as well. The African Union, which has persistently resisted the arrest and trial of the Sudanese President Omar Al-Bashir, is determined to establish a criminal chamber within the African Court of Justice and Human Rights.[86] It intends to 'keep the ICC out by creating a regime of regional complementarity'.[87]

Although it would mean a radical change in current practice,[88] it would be easy to keep the ICC out with indictments before an African court that would exercise criminal jurisdiction conferred by national authorities, as far as the notion of 'positive complementarity' is taken as

---

[83] William Schabas, 'The rise and fall of complementarity', in Stahn and ElZeidy (eds.) (n. 73), p. 161. More thoroughly developed criticism against (re)interpretations of several provisions of the Rome Statute by the notion of 'positive complementarity' is found in Sarah M. H. Nouwen, *Complementarity in the Line of Fire: The Catalysing Effect of the International Criminal Court in Uganda and Sudan* (Cambridge: Cambridge University Press, 2013), pp. 36–45.

[84] Schabas (n. 83), pp. 161–162.

[85] Nouwen (n. 83), passim, in particular p. 406.

[86] Chancha Bhoke Murungu, 'Towards a criminal chamber in the African Court of Justice and Human Rights' (2011) 9 *Journal of International Criminal Justice* 1067–1088, at 1067–1068.

[87] Rowland J. V. Cole, 'Africa's relationship with the International Criminal Court: more political than legal' (2013) 14 *Melbourne Journal of International Law* 670–698, at 694.

[88] It is well established by the ICC's actual practice, where of the ten situations currently under investigation, nine are in Africa. See 'Situations under investigation' (n. 79).

granted. The ICC would otherwise show deep and constant distrust of a framework created by African countries. Indeed, many specialists in international criminal law consider that 'a genuine prosecution by a lawfully constituted regional tribunal' should make the case inadmissible before the ICC.[89] Any parallel investigation at the universal level would mean an antagonistic attitude towards lower-level jurisdictions, which is incompatible with the notion of 'positive complementarity'.

It is, however, highly unlikely that mainstream scholars interested in a general theory of international law or cosmopolitan constitutionalists would share this view.[90] The only way for them seems to be to revert to a purely negative version of complementarity, thereby enabling cases simultaneously treated by a regional court to be investigated and indicted.

It would presuppose (at least potentially) antagonistic relationships with national or regional authorities. The at times severe tension with universal jurisdictions is an actual and vivid reality, at least as regards Africa or Asia. Against this background, the concept of functional complementarity does not work well.

Another reason for the decline of 'positive complementarity' in the ICC's practice is the special character or the highly limited scope of 'core crimes'[91] that the court treats. This categorisation has its roots in the so-called Nürnberg Principles, which are elaborated well in a text adopted by the International Law Commission in 1950.[92] According to the text, these crimes are punishable as 'crimes under international law' (Principle IV),[93] and their perpetrators are not relieved by 'the fact that internal law does not impose a penalty' for the act (Principle II).

[89] See Miles Jackson, 'Regional complementarity: the Rome Statute and public international law' (2016) 14 *Journal of International Criminal Justice* 1061–1072, at 1062 and articles cited in footnotes 7 and 8 at 1063.
[90] Teresa Reinold, 'Constitutionalization? Whose constitutionalization? Africa's ambivalent engagement with the International Criminal Court' (2012) 10 *International Journal of Constitutional Law* 1076–1105.
[91] Articles 6 (Genocide), 7 (Crimes against Humanity), 8 (War Crimes) and 8 bis (Crimes of Aggression) of the Rome Statute.
[92] Principles of International Law Recognized in the Charter of the Nürnberg Tribunal and in the Judgment of the Tribunal, in *Yearbook of the International Law Commission*, Vol. II (1950), pp. 374–378.
[93] For genocide, which may be regarded as derived from the crime against humanity, see also Art. 1, Convention on the Prevention and Punishment of the Crime of Genocide, adopted on 9 December 1948, in force 12 January 1951, 78 UNTS 277.

It is therefore safe to say that it is the international community as a whole, embodied by the ICC,[94] that is to exercise the original power to punish the 'core crimes' in the Rome Statute.[95] Though it is generally overlooked, states can only exercise derived power for that purpose. It would otherwise be impossible to provide reasonable grounds for the ICC's *Kompetenz-Kompetenz* in any invocation of complementarity or for the Security Council's power to refer the situations absent the territorial or national state's consent.

In theoretical terms, the principle of functional complementarity should be somehow modified when the relevant competences are not evenly distributed. In the relationship between the jurisdiction with original competence and those with only derived competence, the former would ultimately prevail, though certain concessions could be made or respect paid to the latter.

In sum, the reason why 'positive complementarity' has fallen into decline is two-fold. From a legal viewpoint, this type of complementarity tends to put a priority on the jurisdictions at the national level. To tackle the 'core crimes', the jurisdiction at the universal level is allocated original competence, but the national jurisdictions can exercise only derived competences. In this condition, 'positive complementarity' does not work. From a factual viewpoint, a lack of real confidence (among mainstream scholars at least) in African (or Asian) judicial systems seriously affects the idea of hand-in-hand cooperation that the notion of 'positive complementarity' presumes and promotes.

Aside from the theoretical effects in the case of original/derived competences, the principle of functional complementarity has a geographical limit, excluding countries or regions without a reasonably reliable administration of justice.

4　Conclusion

The principle of functional complementarity is established in European regional constitutional law. It is a sufficiently reasonable principle in the

---

[94] The Security Council might be a subsidiary agent to represent it, conferred the power to refer the situations to the prosecutor of the ICC (Art. 13(b) of the Rome Statute).

[95] In this context, it would be reasonable or advisable to recall the observations of Wolfgang Friedmann: 'The organisation of peace differs from that of any other human interest in that it can only be universal.' Friedmann (n. 1), p. 258.

pluralistic world where no hierarchical order exists but certain minimum core values are regarded as shared.

The functioning of the principle is not free from substantial criticism. The sites of intellectual hegemony are unevenly distributed in the world. Hidden inequality based on such hegemony always exists. In the games governed by the new rules of functional complementarity, a more powerful site of intellectual hegemony could easily exercise its power of influence all over the world and be substantially immune from other jurisdictions' control. I have never argued for the abolition of the principle for this reason; instead, I recognise the inevitability of its emergence in this plural and globalised world where competences of numerous jurisdictions could be exercised at the same time and about the same subject matter.

This does not necessarily mean that the principle has a universal scope of application. The intellectual hegemony contained in the principle, however, makes it difficult to recognise such limits, because its fairness would be self-evident within the scope of its application. In fact, when jurisdictions are involved that are not reasonably reliable, the validity of the principle simply disappears. The original or derived character of competence could seriously affect the principle's uniform application. Preservation of the exclusiveness of jurisdiction over the UN's own peace operations is sometimes strongly advocated, which rules out any applicability of the principle.

In sum, though a global constitution may exist, it does not work in a coherent and harmonious manner. Even the pluralistic version of constitutionalism, which presumes validity of the principle of functional complementarity, does not offer any optimism about the union of the world's peoples. We should draw a far more complex picture, abandoning an image of utopia ruled by pre-established harmony. For this very reason, 'boring' demands such as coexistence or avoidance of a nuclear war must prevail over everything.

15

Human Rights NGOs and Global Constitutionalism from a Chinese Academic Perspective

GUIMEI BAI[*]

1 Introduction

For the purposes of this chapter, global constitutionalism may in general be described as a theoretical approach to public international law. Although there are different dimensions or schools of thought among constitutionalist international law scholars, each assumes the existence of an international or global community composed not only of sovereign states but also of non-state actors and individuals or groups of individuals.[1] In this community, non-governmental organisations (NGOs), particularly human rights NGOs (HRNGOs), are playing very important roles in the process of global constitutionalism.

[*] The author would like to extend her sincere thanks to Ms Zhang Yueyao, Mr Wan Yu and Chao Yi for their time and trouble in collecting relevant information and documents. Her heartfelt thanks also go to Mr Zhao Lizhi, who helped revise the English texts and correct and add references, as well as Mr Yota Negishi and Mr Malcolm McLaren, who provided some valuable suggestions on modifications. Last but not least, the author wants to thank Professor Anne Peters from the bottom of her heart for her kind encouragement as well as her generosity in providing the author with significant information and materials. The author herself is responsible for any errors or mistakes in this chapter.

[1] See on different schools Christine E. J. Schwöbel, *Global Constitutionalism in International Legal Perspective* (Leiden; Boston: Martinus Nijhoff Publishers, 2011), p. 13. See, for a different categorisation into three groups, Gao Xiang, 'Tide of constitutionalism in international law and the reference to China' (2010) 23.2 *Journal of Wuhan University of Technology* (Social Science Edition, No. 2, in Chinese) 228. See, for 'compensatory constitutionalism', Anne Peters, 'Conclusions', in Jan Klabbers, Anne Peters and Geir Ulfstein (eds.), *The Constitutionalization of International Law* (New York: Oxford University Press, 2009), p. 347. The expression 'constitutionalist reading' of international law is used by Peters interchangeably with that of 'constitutionalist approach'. Anne Peters, 'The merits of global constitutionalism' (2009) 16 *Indian Journal of Global Legal studies* 404. See Mattias Kumm, 'The legitimacy of international law: a constitutionalist framework of analysis' (2004) 15.5 *The European Journal of International Law* 931.

Common to the various themes of global constitutionalism are the following ideas. First, the sovereignty of the state (as it is the only bearer of political power) should be limited. Second, the rule of law is the best way to limit state sovereignty, and international organisations such as the United Nations seem to be the best mechanism to decentralise state power. Third, there should be a global community with universal values preserved by all community members. Fourth, fundamental principles, *jus cogens* and obligations *erga omnes* promoting the universal values of the global community should be obeyed and confirmed. Fifth, protection of individual rights is not just a means of restraining state power but also the most important manifestation of the legitimacy of state sovereignty.

In trying to clarify and evaluate the role of Chinese human rights NGOs (CHRNGOs) in the context of international constitutionalism or the constitutionalisation of international law, I will not comment on the various approaches of international constitutionalism. I will instead analyse the Chinese government's attitude to those approaches and to the contributions made by CHRNGOs towards the universal goals of peace, development and human rights.

I will pose thereby two questions. First, are there nothing but interests of nation states or interests of individuals and groups; are there, in other words, any common interests or common values in the international community that human beings ('We the People') should strive for? Second, how could CHRNGOs contribute, together with the international community, to the cause of human rights?

This chapter will be divided into four main sections. After this introduction, Section 2 will focus on the current situation in China concerning domestic constitutionalism. Section 3 will deal with CHRNGOs, concentrating on how they started and developed. Subsection 3.2 will analyse the contributions made by CHRNGOs to the implementation of international human rights law. Section 4 will focus on the problems and challenges. Section 5 is the conclusion, proposing some solutions.

2 Current situation in China concerning domestic constitutionalism

Global or international constitutionalism is a rather new concept in China, but it has been one of the most sensitive since about four years ago, when rumours spread about 'Document No. 9' issued by the Communist Party Central Committee in 2013. In order to maintain stability, seven concepts are forbidden to be mentioned in universities (aka the 'seven non-mentions'). These are universal values, freedom of the press, civil society, civil rights, historical mistakes made by the Chinese Communist Party, crony capitalism and judicial independence. At least four of the seven are closely related to constitutionalism. The debate on constitutionalism started at the beginning of the twenty-first century, and though it has experienced several ups and downs, it has never stopped among Chinese university professors (commonly called 'intellectuals'). The most distinguished and influential are Guo Daohui, Jiang Ping and Li Buyun.[2] They represent the moderate group of pro-constitutionalists in China, since they take the middle way between Western constitutionalism and Chinese socialism. For example, Guo emphasised the combination of socialism and constitutionalism, which he identified as 'constitutional socialism' rather than 'socialist constitutionalism'.[3] In his theory, constitutionalism and socialism are both new concepts. His socialism means that the society is supreme rather than the state. He explained that the society is composed of people, and 'people' means every individual. Guo's new constitutionalism is based not only on classic constitutionalism with human rights, democracy and rule of law as core elements but also on the essence of republicanism. The ideas of freedom, equality and brotherhood are parts of his new constitutionalism.[4]

Li Buyun observed that constitutionalism is in the tradition of the Chinese Communist Party led by Mao Zedong, who made an important presentation on New Democratic Constitutionalism at the inaugural meeting of the Association for Promotion of Constitutionalism in Yan'an in 1940. Having reviewed the Party's policies in the past and the present as well as the literature on constitutionalism over the past twenty years, Li concluded that most of the Chinese academy supports the idea of socialist constitutionalism under the leadership of the Party. Li is the first Chinese constitutional law scholar to use the concept of socialist

---

[2] They are courteously called 'three old men of rule of law' (*Fa Zhi San Lao*, in Chinese). See *Salute to the Constitution: Five Talks on Rule of Law* by 'Three Old Men of Rule of Law', available at http://news.ifeng.com/opinion/gaojian/special/fzslwlfz/ (4 December 2014), visited on 3 February 2017. They were interviewed by Phoenix Information TV (*Fenghuang Zixun* TV) on the first Chinese Constitutional Day on 4 December 2014.

[3] Guo Daohui, 'Constitutional socialism as what I identified' (14 October 2011), available at www.aisixiang.com/data/45176.html, visited on 3 February 2017. Li Buyun used the concept of socialist constitutionalism in 'Taking the path of socialist constitutionalism with Chinese character', People's Forum (February 2014), available at http://theory.rmlt .com.cn/2014/0126/223834.shtml, visited on 3 February 2017.

[4] Guo (n. 3).

constitutionalism. In his article 'Constitutionalism and China', which was presented at a seminar in 1993, he defined 'constitutionalism as a political system which regards the realisation of a series of democratic principles and system as its main content, rule of law as its basic guarantee, and the fulfilment of the most extensive human rights as its goal. Under constitutionalism, a country is managed by the constitution which embodies the ideals of modern civilisation.'[5] He reiterated the three core elements in his socialist constitutionalism: 'democracy is the foundation, rule of law is one of the important conditions, and the guarantee of human rights is the goal'.[6]

There is actually no substantive difference among the constitutionalists, though they seem to emphasise different concepts, either constitutionalism or socialism, and Li has even accepted constitutionalism under the leadership of the Party. Their ideas, representing most of the academy of constitutional and administrative law, are essentially in agreement with the spirit of the Party's policy (particularly relating to governance by law and administration by law), and the key points are governing and administrating the country in keeping with the constitution. These popular views are also in line with the core themes mentioned earlier. Despite taking the middle way by keeping some socialist elements and accepting the Party's leadership, they are severely criticised by a few far-left scholars such as Yang Xiaoqing and Wang Zeng.

In Yang's article, published in a Party-sponsored journal, she undertook a comparative study of Western constitutionalism and the people's democratic system in China. Yang thinks that constitutionalism is the basic institutional framework of modern Western politics. Its key elements and ideas are part of capitalism and capitalist dictatorship *rather than* a system of a socialist people's democracy. Her views are based on the following arguments. First, constitutionalism is founded on the market economy of private ownership, while the people's democracy is founded on an economy of multiple ownerships with public ownership as its core. Second, constitutionalism espouses parliamentary politics with a governing party and opposition parties decided through electoral contests, while under

---

[5] See Li Buyun, 'Constitutionalism and China', an article made up of contributions by the author to the Seminar on Constitutionalism and China at Columbia University, New York, from February to May 1993. This article was republished in his essay collection Li Buyun, *Constitutionalism and China*, rev. ed. (Beijing: Law Press, 2006) (in English), p. 2.

[6] Ibid., p. 3. He summarised this idea with sixteen Chinese characters: *ren min min zhu* (people's democracy), *yi fa zhi guo* (governance by law), *ren quan bao zhang* (protection of human rights), *xian fa zhi shang* (constitutional supremacy).

a system of people's democracy, all powers belong to the people, and the people's congress system serves as China's political system. The Chinese Communist Party's leadership was not the result of elections but the achievement of the Chinese democratic revolution. Third, constitutional-ism realises a separation of powers. The legislature, executive branch and judicature are independent of each other. Under a system of people's democracy, legislative and executive powers are combined. Fourth, con-stitutionalism comprises judicial independence, and judicial organs exer-cise judicial review, while under the people's congress system, the National People's Congress and its Standing Committee monitor the implementa-tion of the constitution. Fifth, constitutionalism requires that military forces be mutualised or nationalised, whereas the People's Liberation Army must be completely led by the Party.[7] Yang finds that constitution-alism is a framework developed in the West over hundreds of years and that it fits to capitalist politics, economy, military affairs, culture and diplomacy but does not to socialist countries. In her article, she distinguishes between essential and non-essential elements of constitutionalism. The five ele-ments mentioned earlier are essential, while non-essential ones include market economy, equality before the law, the supremacy of human rights, freedom of press, federalism, freedom of religion (mainly for Christianity), parliamentary control over the budget, human rights without boundaries and armed intervention in internal affairs of other counties.[8]

Yang attacks Western institutionalism for serving power politics and a hegemonic discourse as well as for its fraudulence. At the same time, she criticises the idea of socialist constitutionalism that most of the Chinese academy promotes. Using Marxist theory as a weapon, she accuses Western constitutionalism of being essentially a capitalist liberal democ-racy and a capitalist dictatorship, with the veneer of democracy of the whole people. She criticises socialist constitutionalists for their appeal to Western constitutionalist power politics, for their engagement in a hegemonic discourse and for their concentration on non-essential elements of constitutionalism instead of on the essential ones. Yang concludes that adding 'socialist' before 'market economy' is acceptable because that cannot change China's nature and basic system. Socialist constitutionalism is unacceptable because it does not fit Chinese national conditions.[9]

---

[7] See Yang Xiaoqing, 'The comparison of constitutionalism with the system of people's
     democracy' (2013) 10 *Hongqi Wengao* 4–5.
[8] Ibid.
[9] Ibid.

Similarly, Wang Zeng argues that the concept of constitutionalism is abused by Western scholars. It is 'like the "cold war", "brain wash", "universal value" and "totalitarianism", etc. These concepts may lead people to think about something as a Pavlovian response so that they may follow Western thinking unconsciously or involuntarily and easily fall into the pitfall of Western ideological discourse.' Wang insists that the ethos of Western constitutionalism must be opposed in order to maintain the governance by law and administration by the constitution of Chinese characteristics. His arguments are very much like Yang's.[10]

Xiao Gongqin observed that constitutionalist socialism is one of the ideological trends developed in China in the past twenty years. He identified further trends, namely liberalism in the 1980s, new authoritarianism in the late 1980s and early 1990s, the new left thought in the mid-1990s, as well as cultural conservatism and democratic socialism in the early twenty-first century. Compared to those five approaches or schools, constitutionalist socialism to Xiao is more inclusive and acceptable. Constitutionalist socialism and liberalism focus on democracy, rule of law and constitutionalism, but the former abandoned the latter's plagiarism of the Western pluralist system. Although both constitutionalist socialism and new authoritarianism emphasise a stable order and the recourse to the existing authority to maintain the traditional order, the former tries harder to use the governing Party's language to express its ideas, which makes it more operative and acceptable in the present socialist system. Constitutionalist socialism also shares some values with the new left thought. The two stress equality and justice as well as the concerns of the lower class, focusing thereby on socialism's ultimate concern. However, constitutionalist socialism rejects the utopian cultural romanticism of the new left thought, which wants to revert to a state-plan economy. Compared to democratic socialism, constitutionalist socialism clarifies the special historical background and the original conditions of the Nordic countries. Both concepts seek to combine socialism with democracy.[11] Xiao commented that constitutionalist socialism absorbed some core ideas from other theories, such as new republicanism, new

---

[10] See Wang Zeng, 'Governing the country by law or administration by the Constitution and "constitutionalism" are two very different kettles of fish', *Guangming Daily*, 17 November 2014, p. 3, available at http://epaper.gmw.cn/gmrb/html/2014-11/17/nw .D110000gmrb_20141117_1-03.htm, visited on 15 February 2017.

[11] Xiao Gongqin, 'My comments on constitutionalist socialism', available at http://history .sina.com.cn/his/zl/2013-10-25/175472264.shtml, visited on 3 February 2017.

institutionalism and new modernism. For instance, constitutionalist socialists adopt the idea of a change process in the sense that traditional values need a constant updating to accommodate modernisation. This explains why constitutionalist socialists do not want simply to give up the socialist system.[12]

In summary, the debate on constitutionalism, which started in the early 1990s, is still going on. Just as Li Buyun said, most of the Chinese academy supports constitutionalist socialism or socialist constitutionalism. Han Dayuan indicated:

> Constitutionalism is a process or a state of implementing the constitution. There are different theoretical schools within constitutionalism. There are reasonable elements in the traditional Western constitutionalism. It is not a realistic or practical attitude either to accept the whole or [to] reject the total of it without any identification. Only through objective and comprehensive understanding can its essences be gained and utilised for our own purposes.[13]

Han rightly pointed out:

> The common sense of the history of human development tells us that as the achievement of the world civilisation, constitutionalism is the product of both socialism and capitalism. It is by no means the proprietary product of capitalism. The original intention of constitutionalism is to establish a system with broader participation and more adequate representation, to prevent the will of the state from being disintegrated, and to seek common values acceptable by social circles. Socialist constitutionalism helps to gain strength for common sense and re-establish the ideal of rule of law and national confidence.[14]

In fact, the key issue for China is how to deal with the problematic relationship between the Party and constitutionalism. President Xi Jinping addressed it in 2012 at the conference celebrating the thirty-year anniversary of the PRC 1982 Constitution. He indicated:

> The critical issue for China to maintain on the line of political development with Chinese characteristics is to insist on an organic unity of Party's leadership with deeming people as masters of the country and governance by law. It is to ensure the essence that people are masters of the country, and the goals to strengthen the vitality of the Party and the State and to

---

[12] Ibid.
[13] Han Dayuan, 'Socialist constitutionalism in world modern constitutional system' (2015) 8 *Law Science* 7.
[14] Ibid.

mobilise people's enthusiasm, in order to broaden socialist democracy and to develop socialist political civilisation.[15]

More importantly, President Xi emphasised that 'the priority of governing by law is governing by the constitution; the critical step for administration by law is administration by the constitution'.[16] It was his address that fanned the recent heated debate on constitutionalism or democracy that began in the early 1990s. Although it is unclear if there is any connection, CHRNGOs also started to develop at the beginning of the 1990s. Such development was undoubtedly triggered by the Fourth Women's Conference in Beijing.

3 CHRNGOs: how they started and developed

3.1 Definition of non-governmental organisation

NGOs are a very important part of civil society and international community, with the latter being a precondition for international constitutionalism. HRNGOs are more visible than other actors in the constitutionalisation of international law. There is no universally accepted definition of the term 'NGO'. The definition in the *Max Planck Encyclopedia of Public International Law* refers:

> to those organizations founded by private individuals, which are independent of States, oriented toward the rule of law, pursue public rather than private goals as an objective, and possess a minimal organizational structure. Concerning their reach, one may further distinguish between national and international NGOs, depending on whether the goals and the organizational structure transcend national boundaries or not.[17]

B. K. Woodward described NGOs' characteristics as follows:

(1) not-for-profit,
(2) non-governmental,
(3) voluntary (usually membership) groups,

---

[15] Xi Jinping, Address at the Conference of the Capital Circles Celebrating the 30 Years' Anniversary of the Promulgation and Implementation of the Existing Constitution (4 December 2012), available at http://news.xinhuanet.com/politics/2012-12/04/c_113907206.htm, visited on 4 February 2017.

[16] Ibid.

[17] Stephan Hobe, 'Non-governmental organizations', *Max Planck Encyclopedia of Public International Law* (MPEPIL), article last updated in March 2010, available at http://opil.ouplaw.com/view/10.1093/law:epil/9780199231690/law-9780199231690-e968?rskey=jxPF3j%26result=4%26prd=EPIL.

(4) organised on a local, national or international level,
(5) intended to address issues in support of the good of the general public or the world at large, and
(6) through either the provision of specific services or advocacy.[18]

Ideally, there should be three essential elements of NGOs: (1) they should not be established by the government; (2) they must not be established for profit, which is why corporations or enterprises cannot be called NGOs and why this term is often used interchangeably with 'non-profit organisations (NPOs)'; and (3) their aim should be the public interest or common good.

3.2 The role of HRNGOs in implementing international human rights law

HRNGOs are like bridges connecting civil society and the government on one hand and linking the country of origin and the world community on the other. They are playing important roles in the making and implementation of international human rights law. Their functions have been studied and summarised by many writers. These functions may include, as Peters stated, 'to represent special or global interests, to enhance the knowledge base for global governance, to ensure transparency, to support international secretariats, to shape a global public opinion, and thereby to globalise values and preferences'.[19] Apart from those mentioned earlier, the tasks of HRNGOs in implementing international human rights law may specifically include the monitoring of the enforcement of international human rights conventions and customary rules by participating in all kinds of mechanisms practised by charter-based bodies and human rights treaty bodies (HRTBs). The most popular mechanisms are state reporting, individual complaints (or individual communications in the HRTBs), enquiry and fact finding. The mechanism of state-to-state communications is also commonly provided in all core international human rights conventions; unfortunately, the practice is effectively nil. Since only state reporting is compulsory (i.e. contracting parties have no

---

[18] Barbara K. Woodward, 'Global civil society and international law in global governance: some contemporary issues' (2006) 8 *International Community Law Review* 247–355, at 345.
[19] Anne Peters, 'Membership in the global community', in Klabbers, Peters and Ulfstein (eds.) (n. 1), pp. 219–220.

choice but to accept the monitoring by the HRTBs), and since the Chinese government could not evade the reporting procedure when ratifying those conventions, the focus of the following discussion on CHRNGOs will be on state reporting.[20] There are chances for HRNGOs to participate in the procedure of state reporting under both the United Nations Human Rights Council and the ten (in China's case, six) treaty bodies. They may intervene in the process when the HRTBs raise questions about the report submitted by state parties, when HRTBs dialogue with state parties and when state parties implement the concluding recommendations made by HRTBs.[21] In fact, HRNGOs play a crucial role in the drafting of the report itself through writing shadow or parallel reports, which are very useful sources of information for HRTBs to find out the truth about the human rights records of the reporting state parties.[22]

3.3   Emergence and development of CHRNGOs

'CHRNGO' is an umbrella concept that covers Chinese NGOs aimed at promoting human rights research and education; seeking social justice; advocating anti-discrimination against women, disabled persons and all other vulnerable groups; etc. The term 'NGO' became widely known by the Chinese people only during the Fourth World Women's Conference (the 1995 World Women's Conference), though the phenomenon did exist long before. The first group of international NGOs (INGOs) came to China in the 1980s. The first seminar on the cooperation between international civil organisations was held in 1990 in Jinan, Shandong province, sponsored by the International Exchanging Centre of Economy and Technology in China and the United Nations Development Programme (UNDP). In the same year, a national non-profit, united, voluntary and independent legal entity as social organisation was

---

[20] To date, China has ratified six of the nine core human rights conventions, except for the International Covenant on Civil and Political Rights (signed in 1998 but not yet ratified), International Convention against Enforced Disappearance and Convention on the Rights of All Migrant Workers and Members of Their Family.

[21] See 'The reporting cycle under the human rights treaties' made by the OHCHR, available at www.ohchr.org/SiteCollectionImages/Bodies/ReportingCycle.gif.

[22] Taking the CEDAW as an example, Elizabeth Evatt, former chair of the committee, recognised that 'NGO support was an essential element in making the work of the Committee effective'. See Elizabeth Evatt, 'Finding a voice for women's rights: the early days of CEDAW' (2002–2003) 34 *The George Washington International Law Review* 515–553, at 535.

established, as suggested by Chinese and foreign experts. It was approved by the Ministry of Foreign Economics and Trade in 1992. This was the China Association for Promotion of Corporation of International Civil Organisation.[23] Nonetheless, there was almost no awareness of the concept of NGO or NPO. It was the 1995 World Women's Conference, specifically the Huairou NGOs Forum, that compelled the Chinese government to attend to the roles and influences of NGOs in internal and external affairs.

In order to organise the forum, many so-called NGOs were set up in China in the three years prior to the 1995 World Women's Conference. Those 'NGOs' were all composed of female public servants working in different areas (e.g. the Association of Women Judges, the Association of Women Prosecutors, the Association of Women Journalists, the Capital City Social Club of Women Professors, the Association of Women Mayors, the Association of Women Entrepreneurs). In fact, they were all set up as sub-organisations or group members of the All China Women's Federation (ACWF). There were only two NGOs outside the ACWF.[24]

The Huairou NGO Forum in 1995, an unprecedented international event in Chinese history, shocked the Chinese people culturally and at the same time encouraged the Chinese groups and broadened 'their view of what an NGO was, what it took to be an NGO and how it differed from a governmental agency'.[25] Many NGOs were set up with different foci, including women's rights, environmental protection, rights of the child, migrant workers' rights and other interest groups (such as homosexual groups, national minorities and HIV/AIDS carriers and hepatitis B carriers). Immediately and mostly inspired by that historical event there were, of course, Chinese women's groups. Many new Chinese

---

[23] Xie Xiaoqing, 'Thirty years' overview of international non-governmental organizations in China: history, current status and some responses' (2011) 6 *Oriental Law* 119.

[24] These are namely the National Council of Young Women's Christian Associations (YWCAs) of China and the Women Personnel Section of the All-China Trade Union. Both are considered politically reliable institutions by the Chinese Communist Party. There had been many more NGOs in addition to the ACWF before the Anti-Rightest Movement in 1957, when most of them were dissolved. In fact, the National Council of YWCAs of China did a very good job in the Huairou NGO Forum. See Zuo Furong, 'Chinese YWCA's social services and their features after 1949' (2006) 3 *Journal of East-China University of Science and Technology* 22.

[25] Chen Jie, 'The NGO community in China: expanding linkages with transnational civil society and their democratic implications' (2006) 68 *China Perspectives* (online), para. 30, available at http://chinaperspectives.revues.org/3083, visited on 4 February 2017.

women's NGOs were established in China before or after the Huairou Forum (e.g. the Rural Women Know-All Magazine, the Migrant Women's Club, the Jinglun Family Centre, the Centre for Women's Legal Studies and Legal Services of Peking University, the Centre for Women's Studies of Fudan University, the Chinese Women Health Network, the East-West Exchanging Group, the Women's Media Watch Network, the Lesbian Pager Hotline). Other NGOs include the AIDS Prevention Commonweal Alliance of Medical Students, Beijing Aizhixing Institute (protection of and anti-discrimination against AIDS carriers), Beijing Yirenping Centre (protection of and anti-discrimination against hepatitis B carriers), Tongyu (a lesbian NGO), Beijing Centre for Social Work Facilitators (an NGO for migrant workers), Rett's Family Care Centre (for children, the aged and disabled persons) and Youren Magazine (an NGO for visually impaired persons).

CHRNGOs are basically of two kinds: government-organised NGOs (GONGOs) and non-GONGOs or new NGOs. Besides the ACWF, there are another seven GONGOs of the same kind and fourteen social organisations that need not register.[26] The former are not state organs, and the latter are not actually governmental organisations. They are commonly called 'social organisations' (*shehui zuzhi* in Chinese). There are a huge number of them because there are branches at different levels, including national, provincial and county. However, there are only two that are relevant for human rights besides the ACWF, including the China Federation of Disabled Persons. Since they are all organised and sponsored by the government with staff members who are all public servants, they are typical GONGOs working for the government under the Party's leadership. It is not surprising that they are criticised by some commentators for their behaviour at the international level.[27]

Non-GONGOs or new NGOs went through three stages or, as Amy Gadsden observed, three generations of development. 'One might consider China's government-affiliated research centres as the first generation of Chinese civil society, and university-based centres might be considered a second generation. Today's community-based NGOs

---

[26] According to a notice of the Ministry of Civil Affairs in 2000, the seven other GONGOs and the fourteen registration-immune social organisations can be found at www .chinalawedu.com/falvfagui/fg22598/19989.shtml, visited on 15 February 2017.
[27] I disagree: the ACWF is changing, and it is wrong to see it as static. See Zhang Naihua, 'NGO's discourse and its impact on Chinese women's development' (2000) 5 *Collection of Women's Studies* 28. The ACWF has gone through three major stages. In the last, it has identified itself as a feminist group organisation.

represent a third generation.'[28] Government-affiliated research centres or institutes are those that are established or sponsored by the government but are relatively independent from the government (e.g. the Chinese Association of Development Strategy Studies, China Population and Development Research Centre, China Culture Institute). There are many university-based centres or institutes (e.g. the Centre for Protection of Rights of Disadvantaged Citizens, the former Women's Legal Research and Service Centre of Peking University, the Research Centre for Human Rights and Humanitarian Law of Peking University and the Centre for Human Rights Research and Education of Hunan University).[29] Community-based NGOs are more grass roots and independent, since their leaders come from the communities that they serve and their offices are 'in converted residential spaces or out of the way commercial properties'.[30] They belong to private non-enterprise units. The official statistics showed in 2015 that there were about 662,000 registered social organisations, including 329,000 social groups, 329,000 civil non-enterprise units and 4,784 foundations.[31] This multitude is not surprising if one considers that the 329,000 civil non-enterprise units include technical service groups, educational and social service groups and many other kinds of groups (e.g. in the arts).[32] NGOs, whose work is related to human-rights, anti-discrimination or protection of disadvantaged persons (such as women's rights groups, free press journalist groups, migrant workers' advocacy associations), are far fewer in number in the official statistics. The exact number of CHRNGOs is hard to know, but it is likely much bigger than what is indicated in these statistics, since many CHRNGOs are not registered or are registered as private companies, such as cultural communication or information centres. The reasons for this are manifold and will be discussed later.

[28] Amy E. Gadsden, 'Chinese nongovernmental organizations: politics by other means?' (American Enterprise Institute, July 2010), available at www.aei.org/wp-content/uploads/2011/10/TocquevilleChineseNGOs0710.pdf, p. 3.
[29] Statistics show that there are about twenty-eight centres or institutes of this kind in China. See the website of the China Society on Human Rights Studies, available at www.humanrights.cn/html/jypx/rqyjjg/index.html, visited on 15 February 2017.
[30] Gadsden (n. 28), p. 3.
[31] See part III of the Statistical Communique of the Ministry of Civil Affairs of the People's Republic of China on 2015 Social Service, available at www.mca.gov.cn/article/sj/tjgb/201607/20160700001136.shtml, visited on 15 February 2017.
[32] There is a government website hosted by the National Administration of Social Organisations, where all registered social organisations can be found, including non-enterprises. See www.chinanpo.gov.cn/40/11/wzmain.html, visited on 15 February 2017.

3.4 Relation of CHRNGOs with the global community

The relation of CHRNGOs with the international community has two dimensions: outside-in and inside-out. The outside-in relation means that international institutions or INGOs came to China and established cooperative relations with Chinese counterparts like those mentioned earlier in the field of economics and trade. INGOs came to China after the open-door policy was implemented by the Chinese government. Incomplete statistics showed in 2015 that there were up to 6,000 to 7,000 overseas NGOs operating in China.[33] Their activities cover many aspects, including economy, trade, investment, health, education, minorities and vulnerable people.

Take just one NGO in human rights education as an example. The Raoul Wallenberg Institute for Human Rights and Humanitarian Law (RWI) began its activities in human rights education early in 1998, when the first round of donations of human rights law books was made. Thirteen universities, academic institutions and libraries were selected throughout China to receive a collection of some 400 titles. There followed four other donation rounds (in 2002, 2003, 2006 and 2007), and in each, there were about 80 brand-new books in English published by famous publishers on international law and human rights law. Peking University was included in the first round, and for each round thereafter, the list of universities and academic institutions would include more recipients, especially in western China.[34]

For the period 2001–2007, the RWI, together with two other Nordic institutions, the Norwegian Centre for Human Rights and the Danish Institute of Human Rights, held annual training courses. They trained altogether more than 200 Chinese university teachers in how to teach international human rights law, many of whom have become leading human rights teachers in China. Since the training lasted for a long period, some of the first trainees became trainers for later courses. According to a follow-up study on the previous course participants carried out in 2010, undergraduate- and graduate-level human rights courses have now been established at around 100 universities in

---

[33] Huang Qingchang, 'Representatives of overseas NGOs in China: open China welcomes NGOs', *People's Daily* (Overseas Edition), 27 July 2015, available at http://paper.people .com.cn/rmrbhwb/html/2015-07/27/node_868.htm, visited on 15 February 2017.
[34] The twelve institutions mentioned here are the Chinese Academy of Social Sciences, Fudan University, Jilin University, Nanjing University, Tsinghua University, Sun Yat-sen University, Wuhan University, Xiamen University, China University of Political Science and Law, Sichuan University, Yunnan University and National Prosecutors College.

China.[35] In order to strengthen exchanges among Chinese human rights teachers, annual conferences started to be organised and sponsored by the three Nordic human rights institutions from 2008.[36] Such a mechanism attracted more and more human rights teachers from about 80 universities and research institutes. During the conferences, participants exchanged their human rights teaching experiences, experts from abroad were invited to give lectures on teaching and research as well as to share their thoughts and their working experiences in international human rights institutions (such as the UN Human Rights Council and human rights treaty bodies) with the Chinese participants, and model lessons were presented by Chinese human rights teachers. As a result, a human rights textbook was compiled by some of the leading participants of the annual conferences.[37]

There are many similar overseas NGOs conducting projects or collaborating in China with Chinese partners in the field of human rights education, research and other activities. Some are permanent, such as the Nordic institutions. Some are temporary, such as joint conferences, seminars or training courses and field studies. These activities have brought progressive influences to bear on the political reform in China.

The inside-out relation means that CHRNGOs participate in human rights activities at the international level, particularly in the procedures of the UN Human Rights Council and the human rights treaty bodies. Since China refuses to accept any optional mechanisms of individual communications or enquiry, this chapter will focus on the reporting system. It was a lengthy and arduous process for CHRNGOs to reach out to the international community. As a matter of fact, opportunities to contact or to have regular connection with UN human rights institutions have been controlled by the Chinese government or GONGOs. The most important link with the UN is to the Economic and Social Council, which is the gateway for NGO involvement in UN international processes on various issues, including human rights. According to the council's resolution,

---

[35] Rhona Smith and Guimei Bai, 'Higher education in human rights within China: a ten-year review of the Peking University model' (2015) 2 *Asian Journal of Legal Education* 81–99.

[36] The annual conference of 2015 was stopped for political reasons related to the award of the Nobel Peace Prize by the Norwegian Committee. One of the conference sponsors was found to be the Norwegian Human Rights Centre, when Norway was being sanctioned by China.

[37] Bai Guimei, *Human Rights Law*, 2nd ed. (Beijing: Peking University Press, 2015). This project was sponsored by the RWI. As a by-product also sponsored by the RWI, an online human rights textbook is being compiled.

member states of the council have the prerogative to grant, suspend and withdraw NGO consultative status through the Economic and Social Council and its Committee on Non-Governmental Organisations, as well as the interpretation of norms and decisions relating to this matter.[38] Of the total 4,665 NGOs that currently have consultative status in the council, 34 are Chinese NGOs, only 5 relate to human rights and all are unfortunately GONGOs.[39] As Peters pointed out:

> In some cases, reliance by governments on NGOs, especially when they *de facto* become part of national bureaucracies, may mask the inactivity of governments, and actually weaken the output legitimacy of governance. More important even is the outright abuse of the NGO garb by governments, especially in the human rights field. Numerous NGOs, such as Chinese para-state mass organizations in the Human Rights Council, only serve their state of origin or registration by constantly praising and imitating it in general or in country-specific debates.[40]

Peters's observation is partly true. Some GONGOs, being part of national bureaucracies, try to use the opportunities provided by the UN to support the Chinese government.[41] However, GONGOs such as the ACWF have changed their attitude towards the Universal Periodic Review (UPR) of the UN Human Rights Council and the reporting to treaty bodies somewhat over the past decade. In the previous cycles, shadow reports from mainland China were impossible. Even worse was that some shadow reports and other related materials were covertly put into a black garbage bag and thrown away by some GONGO representatives on the spot, an act that was considered patriotic. That has not happened since 2006. In 2006, non-GONGOs or new women's NGOs observed the review of the report submitted to the Committee of Elimination Discrimination against Women (CEDAW) for the first time.[42] About five years later,

---

[38] UN Economic and Social Council Resolution 1996/31, Consultative Relationship between the United Nations and Non-Governmental Organizations (25 July 1996), available at www.un.org/documents/ecosoc/res/1996/eres1996-31.htm, para. 15.

[39] The statistics are actual to 1 September 2015 and available at http://esango.un.org/civilso ciety/displayConsultativeStatusSearch.do?method=search%26sessionCheck=false, last visited on 15 February 2017.

[40] Peters, 'Membership in the global community' (n. 19), pp. 236–237.

[41] When, for instance, the second round of periodic reports was reviewed by the UN Human Rights Council in 2013, the side events organised by the China Society of Human Rights Studies were quite supportive, though without obvious praise or imitating the government at every step.

[42] About six new Chinese women's NGOs with eleven representatives sponsored by foreign funding went to New York in 2006 to participate in the review of China's fifth and sixth combined report. They were very active in contacting the members of the CEDAW.

CHRNGOs began to write shadow reports, which was a milestone in the development of CHRNGOs at the international community level.

It was One Plus One, an NGO for visually disabled persons, that was 'the first one to eat crabs'.[43] It started to prepare its parallel report at the end of 2011 and finished it the following year. It did so with great unease and wondered whether anything would happen to its organisation. Although it knew it was of great significance to participate in the state reporting process, it felt that it was doing something like 'ratting on the government to the UN, and this sounded very dangerous'.[44] Entitled Implementation of the Convention on the Rights of Persons with Disabilities: A Report from One Plus One, the report was submitted quietly to the UN Office of the High Commissioner of Human Rights (OHCHR) and was made public on the OHCHR's website.[45] It turned out that its worries about pressure from the government were misplaced; to its surprise its activities were actually accepted by the authority. Other CHRNGOs were encouraged and followed in its steps in subsequent years. More shadow reports and similar texts were written on rights of the child and women's rights, some of which were submitted to the OHCHR and transmitted to the Commission of Rights of the Child (CRC) and CEDAW and published on related UN websites.[46] Since it was the first time that CHRNGOs composed shadow or parallel reports, some of them were trained by international NGOs.[47] This is something to celebrate for CHRNGOs as a great step towards joining in the international community and contributing to international constitutionalism. NGOs remain, however, very cautious in selecting the topics of their reports, and they may still prefer to join the GONGOs in writing

In 2014, seven grass-roots NGOs were represented in Geneva during the review of China's seventh and eighth combined report.

[43] This Chinese idiom refers to the person who took the first step to challenge something that no one had dared to challenge before.

[44] See 'Case three: Chinese disabled persons organization participating CRPD state report review process', in Manual of Homosexual Rights and Interests Guidelines on Civil Organization's Participation in International Institutions, unpublished draft, pp. 1–2.

[45] See One Plus One's announcement (4 November 2012), available at www.yijiayi.org /black/index.php?id=160, visited on 15 February 2017.

[46] There are about nine such shadow reports for the Committee Against Torture (CAT), six for the CRC and thirteen for the CEDAW. See the website of the OHCHR, 'Reporting status for China', available at http://tbinternet.ohchr.org/_layouts/TreatyBodyExternal/ Countries.aspx?CountryCode=CHN, visited on 15 February 2017.

[47] For example, One Plus One's representatives and five other NGOs were trained in Hong Kong in 2011 by the International Disability Alliance, a cooperation between eight global and six regional organisations of persons with disabilities.

a combined shadow report.[48] It will take time for CHRNGOs and the Chinese authority to adjust themselves to the global civil society and the consequences brought about by the constitutionalisation of international law. CHRNGOs are currently confronted with many problems and challenges.

4 Problems and challenges

It has been more than two decades since CHRNGOs began to flourish in different fields. In this time, they have made various contributions to building up Chinese civil society, which remains very weak. CHRNGOs participate actively in the processes of decision making and law-making on their issues. For instance, influenced by the Huairou NGO Forum, Chinese new women's NGOs have been active, playing very important roles in legislation, including making new laws, such as the Anti-Domestic Violence Law, and amending existing laws, such as the amendment of the Chinese Marriage Law. They have also played a crucial role in decision making. Taking the debate on 'Women Go Home' as an example, Chinese women's NGOs successfully resisted recommendations by decision makers urging women to quit their jobs and go home periodically to take care of their children and family.[49] However, they have experienced many setbacks and frustrations due to the changing attitudes of the Chinese government towards both domestic and international NGOs, particularly after the Colour Revolutions and Tunisia's Jasmine Revolution.[50] That turbulence made some waves in China, leading to

---

[48] I joined in the drafting of the combined shadow report organised by the ACWF for the CEDAW with about four other women's NGOs before the Chinese seventh and eighth periodic report was reviewed in 2013.

[49] Such recommendations have been made several times by different decision makers or legislators. See 'Discussion on the historical and cultural causes of the current doctrine of "Women Go Home"' (23 March 2011), available at www.china.com.cn/blog/zhuanti/female/2011-03/23/content_22201352.htm, last visited on 15 February 2017. The latest similar recommendation was made by a member of the National Political Consultative Conference in discussing the influence of the Second Child policy, available at www .rmzxb.com.cn/c/2016-03-12/732983.shtml, last visited on 15 February 2017.

[50] 'Colour Revolution' is a term used by media worldwide to refer to related pro-democracy movements that developed in several societies of the former Soviet Union and the Balkans during the early 2000s. The term is sometimes connected with other similar movements elsewhere, such as the 'Jasmine Revolution'. The latter term originated from all movements taking place during the Arab Spring in the Middle East in 2011, which enflamed some pro-democracy activists in China that year. Both are generally deemed by Chinese authorities as a manoeuvre by Western powers to undermine governments that they dislike.

sensitive responses or even overreactions from the Chinese government. As a result, the safety belt was fastened to prevent foreign intervention and to maintain the country's stability and unity. Measures taken by the Chinese government variously affected CHRNGOs and brought problems and challenges for them in continuing their human rights work.

4.1   Difficulty of getting registered as non-enterprise units

According to common Article 3 of the 1998 Interim Regulation on Registration Administration of Private Non-Enterprise Units and the Regulation on the Administration of the Registration of Social Organisations (revised in 2016), 'to become established, social organisations must be approved by the authorised department and follow the registration procedure set out in these regulations'. The common problem for grass-roots CHRNGOs is to get registered in China as a non-enterprise unit, since finding an 'authorised department' is very difficult. This double administration policy frustrates many small-scale NGOs in China, especially those that lack funds and those that live mostly off of foreign donations. The reason for that is at least four-fold. First, the threshold of registration is too high. Second, what they do is politically sensitive. Third, registration is hard to maintain due to a lack of funds. Fourth, their administrative ability is poor. These problems are inter-related. The failure to register at the Ministry of Civil Affairs leaves them with two options:[51] not to register at all, which means they are illegal organisations, or to register as commercial units in the Industrial and Commercial Bureau, which means they are legal but not officially NGOs. The difficulty in registering as a non-enterprise unit puts CHRNGOs in a very awkward situation. First, they are not entitled to government support but must pay taxes like profit-making companies, though they are non-profit and live from donations. Moreover, if they want to solve the problem by making some money, their nature as an NGO will wither away.

Something even worse may happen to them. Since human rights advocates lack commercial experience, it is easy for them to make

---

[51] According to Liu Kangmai, the former secretary-general of the Chinese Association of STD and AIDS Prevention and Control, there were about 500 HIV/AIDS NGOs in China up to 2006. Only 200 among them were registered, most in the Industrial and Commercial Bureau. See 'AIDS NGOs facing a predicament in China' (30 November 2010), *Caixin Media*, available at http://money.163.com/10/1130/19/6MOSPS4O00253B0H.html, last visited on 15 February 2017.

financial mistakes. Some of them think they do not have to pay taxes because they are non-profit organisations. A typical example is the famous CHRNGO Open Constitution Initiative (in Chinese *Gongmeng*). *Gongmeng* was registered as a 'Consultant Firm of Limited Liability' in the Industrial and Commercial Bureau. It was, however, dissolved for tax evasion and fined 1,420,000 yuan (RMB) in 2009. Its head, Xu Zhiyong, was arrested five years later and sentenced to four years in prison for promoting human rights.[52]

4.2   Lack of funds

Most grass-roots CHRNGOs are faced with fundraising problems. It is very difficult to raise funds from Chinese domestic enterprises since 'their aim to commit to public service is, on one hand, to redound upon society and more important for themselves to build good image on the other. Therefore, when choosing cooperative partners enterprises would rather appreciate GONGOs or NGOs that gained legal status.'[53] Since most CHRNGOs cannot register with the Ministry of Civil Affairs as non-enterprise units, the likelihood of attracting domestic donations is almost zero, because Chinese domestic enterprises do not like to choose them as cooperative partners for the enterprise cannot enjoy the favourable tax treatment. Therefore, fundraising is one of the main ways for CHRNGOs to survive. Challenges for them are the following. First, as is well known, most CHRNGOs are living off of foreign donations. This is becoming more and more difficult as well since the fact that China has the world's second largest economy suggests to many Western donors that they should reduce their donations to China and turn instead to Africa. Second, as mentioned, one of the adverse effects of CHRNGOs' failure to get registered as non-enterprise units is that it is difficult for them to raise domestic funds because domestic companies prefer to sponsor those that have legal status as non-enterprise units so as themselves to enjoy favourable tax treatment and the like. Finally, the political sensitivity of CHRNGOs scares off potential donors, for these do not want to risk being watched by the authority. Furthermore, most

---

[52] Because he was found responsible for the public display of banners urging authorities to disclose their assets as a check against graft and for a sit-down protest in front of the Ministry of Education against discrimination in higher education, Xu was found by the Beijing intermediate court guilty of 'gathering crowds to disrupt public order'.

[53] See Li Li, 'Difficult situation for the development of grass-root NGOs in our country and the raising up of their social capital' (2011) 8 *Economic Observation* 52.

CHRNGOs are operating on projects sponsored by foreign foundations or doing projects jointly with foreign institutions. To put it another way, foreign donors prefer to support CHRNGOs' projects on human rights issues in China instead of directly providing them with funds. Due to the economic crisis in 2008, the number of projects has been reduced. In addition, there has been something worse for those CHRNGOs whose funds are mostly from foreign donations. In 2009, the State Administration of Foreign Exchange promulgated a new regulation, which came into force on 1 March 2010. According to it, the donation agreement should be notarised and the use of funds indicated; at the same time, CHRNGOs must provide certification showing that the overseas non-profit institution is registered and formed abroad according to law. This regulation has made the work of CHRNGOs that largely rely of foreign foundations more complicated and difficult.[54]

4.3   Political sensitivity: the most problematic issue for CHRNGOs

The concept of human rights is quite politically sensitive for many Chinese people, especially government workers. They prefer to avoid using that term when they handle related issues. When the Colour Revolutions and the Arab Spring or Jasmine Revolution inspired pro-democracy protests in China in 2011, the government harboured anxieties about social 'instability' and even the country's dismemberment. It took several measures to maintain the social order and to prevent external intervention. In such circumstances, CHRNGOs must keep a low profile and try to avoid doing projects that are politically sensitive, such as on freedom of religion, expression or assembly. CHRNGOs are now at their lowest ebb. The ones that have a foreign background and the ones that are financially supported or that carry out activities sponsored by Western countries are having a difficult time. The survival of some is in doubt.

The fate of the Centre for Women's Legal Studies and Legal Services of Peking University (the Women's Centre) is an example of the awkward situation of CHRNGOs due to political sensitivity. The Women's Centre was established with the financial support of the Ford Foundation in 1995 and has been active in cases on battered women. In order to avoid being involved in politically sensitive issues, Peking University (its authorised

---

[54]   See Art. 5, Notice of the State Administration of Foreign Exchange on Issues Concerning the Administration of Foreign Exchange Donated to or by Domestic Institutions.

department) terminated the agreement with the Women's Centre and detached it from the university in 2010. It had to register in another name, the Zhongze Centre for Women's Legal Consultation Service. Less than six years later, on 1 February 2016, the centre was shut down, and there is no hope of its being reopened soon.[55] The centre is not the sole example.[56] That does not mean, however, that CHRNGOs are dying out. Most of them support the idea of conserving their strength and avoiding critical action against the government. It is more important to keep going inside China with a moderate style or following the middle way. At the moment, they are undergoing a transition period, since the new law on administration of overseas NGOs came into force at the beginning of 2017. As there are many formalities to go through before formal registration, all joint projects with overseas NGOs must be suspended, as explained in the next section.

4.4   Law on administration of activities of overseas nongovernmental organisations

The new law has a long title: Law of the People's Republic of China on Administration of Activities of Overseas Nongovernmental Organisations in the Mainland of China (ONGO Law). It came into force on 1 January 2017. The Jasmine Revolution in 2011 triggered its drafting, which lasted for a couple of years, and the first and second Drafts for Comments aroused strong reactions from both Chinese and overseas NGOs. Many revisions were recommended, some of which were accepted and manifested in the third reading of the law in 2015. The third reading notably cancelled some prohibition provisions against ONGOs. (For instance, previous readings of the law had allowed ONGOs to set up only one representative office in China. Having considered comments from civil society that some ONGOs are active in different areas all over China and that having only one office is inconvenient, the third reading of the law cancelled the numerical limit.)[57] Nonetheless, the law remains

---

[55] See the Notice of Closing Business by the Centre, available at www.woman-legalaid.org .cn/news_detail/newsId=423.html, last visited on 15 February 2017. There was no explanation for the closing and no mention of reopening.

[56] When heads of NGOs are suspected of being against the government, they risk a similar fate as the head of the Women's Centre. For instance, Gao Yaojie, a famous human rights advocate for HIV-infected patients, and Wan Yanhai, head of another HIV/AIDS NGO, have sought asylum in the United States.

[57] See 'Three highlights on the 3rd reading of the draft of Law on the Administration of Activities of Overseas Non-Governmental Organisations within the territory of China',

very restrictive, and it will take time for ONGOs to accustom themselves to it.

Article 9 provides:

> An overseas NGO engaging in activities in the mainland of China shall, in accordance with the law, register an established representative office. Where an overseas NGO that has not registered an established representative office needs to carry out temporary activities in the mainland of China, it shall submit documents for the record to this effect in accordance with the law.
>
> Where an overseas NGO has not registered an established representative office, nor submitted documents for the record stating that it intends to carry out temporary activities, it shall not carry out or covertly engage in any activities, nor shall it entrust or finance, or covertly entrust or finance, any organisation or individual to carry out activities in the mainland of China on its behalf.

According to this article, ONGOs cannot engage in any activities unless they register a representative office or submit documents for temporary activities in order to get approval from the Public Security. Otherwise their activities will be illegal.

Since the ONGO Law came into force, ONGOs have been busy preparing for registration and for submitting documents to get recorded if they do not want to cease their activities in China. This is, however, difficult, because the ONGO Law also follows the principle of double administration, like the Regulation on the Administration of the Registration of Social Organisations (revised in 2016). Article 11 of the law provides:

> Overseas NGOs that apply for the registration of formation of representative offices shall obtain approval from the competent business authorities.
>
> The directory of competent business authorities shall be announced by the public security department of the State Council and the public security organs of provincial people's governments in conjunction with the relevant departments.

This article means that an ONGO must also obtain the approval of a competent business authority before applying for the registration of an office or get recorded for its temporary activities. Although the directory of competent business authorities has been made public, it is not easy to find the competent business authority, since ONGOs engage

available at http://news.xinhuanet.com/politics/2016-04/25/c_128930036.htm, last visited on 1 March 2017.

in different activities across disciplines. One competent business authority may not cover activities in another discipline. (For example, the RWI's activities range from education to justice. In the directory, two competent business authorities have been found: the Ministry of Education and the Ministry of Justice. It is obvious that the Ministry of Education cannot cover activities on justice and vice versa.) There is no doubt that solutions will be explored and that before everything is settled CHRNGOs' activities with ONGOs will have to be put off, but hopefully not for too long.

5   Conclusion

What is happening in China may seem antithetical to the ideas of global constitutionalism and human rights. That is not entirely true for the following reasons. First, the Chinese government's attitude towards human rights has changed a lot compared to thirty years ago. China has ratified more than twenty-six international human rights treaties, including six out of the nine core UN human rights conventions. Second, the Chinese government attaches much importance to the treaty bodies' review of its periodic reports on implementing the human rights conventions. The government delegation sent is always high level. The participation of CHRNGOs is no longer blocked, and shadow reports are allowed, though the 'quality' and content are of some concern to authorities. Third, three National Human Rights Action Plans have been promulgated to date, and some of their goals have been reached. (For instance, eight human rights education bases have been set up in Chinese universities.) Another five will be established in keeping with the third Action Plan. Since 2008, there have been annual conferences on human rights institutions organised by the China Society of Human Rights Studies, while the Beijing Human Rights Forum is also hosted by that institution each year. (Many more achievements could be mentioned, but this is not the place to list them.) Lastly, in the past twenty years, China has made some laws to implement its ratified international human rights conventions (including laws on women's rights, rights of the child, rights of persons with disabilities and recently domestic violence).

Why, after all, is the Chinese government so restrictive towards CHRNGOs and ONGOs? What is the problem, and what is its cause? Several reasons may be summarised. Historically speaking, China has been the main target of international criticism for human rights violations since the Tiananmen Square protests of 1989. China has espoused

defensive attitudes in almost all international forums, in the human
rights treaty bodies and UN institutions (particularly the former UN
Human Rights Commission) as well as during the China–foreign
human rights dialogues. In addition, the Colour Revolutions and the
Jasmine Revolution in 2011 scared the Chinese government about most
group activities, particularly those that are organised by CHRNGOs
supported or sponsored by ONGOs and foreign donors. This is an
understandable response from a government that prioritises national
security and unity, though much too restrictively. Finally, China has
consistently refused to follow Western ideas and the so-called universal
values. It wants to have a leading voice in the international discourse on
building the global order, including human rights protection. At the
Summit of Asian and African Nations, President Xi gave a speech urging
Asian and African countries to carry forward the 'Bandung Spirit' and to
enhance cooperation for jointly building 'a community of common destiny for all mankind'.[58] The concept of a community of common destiny
or shared future for all mankind was proposed in the Report to the 18th
Congress of the Communist Party in 2012 and was elaborated by
President Xi in the past years in international fora.[59] It seems that
China is seeking to build a unique leading role through this new concept
in international discourse on international relations and international
law, including human rights.[60]

That said, some solutions are proposed here to conclude this chapter.
First, since civil society in China is too weak, CHRNGOs should try to
develop solidarity among themselves. It might be a good idea to participate in the UPR process, especially when China's report is under review,

---

[58] See 'Xi raises three-point proposal on carrying forward Bandung Spirit' (22 April 2015),
Xinhua, available at www.chinadaily.com.cn/world/2015xivisitpse/2015-04/22/con
tent_20511293.htm, last visited on 4 March 2017 (emphasis added).

[59] Xi Jinping, 'Toward a community of common destiny and a new future for Asia', keynote
speech at the Boao Forum for 2015 Asia Annual Conference (Boao, 18 March 2015),
available at http://english.boaoforum.org/hynew/19353.jhtml, updated on 8 April 2015;
see also Qu Xing, 'Value bases of a community of shared future for mankind' (2013) 4
Qiushi 53.

[60] For instance, Ma Zhaoxu, head of the Chinese mission to the UN in Geneva, delivered
a joint statement on behalf of a cross-regional group of 140 countries during a high-level
meeting of the thirty-fourth session of the Human Rights Council on 1 March 2017. He
stressed that 'countries should foster partnership characterised by mutual respect, promote and protect human rights through dialogue and cooperation' and that the politici-
sation of human rights should be avoided. See 'China underlines "shared human future"'
(2 March 2017), *Xinhua*, available at http://china.org.cn/world/2017-03/02/con
tent_40389642.htm, last visited on 5 March 2017.

because only this report is comprehensive, covering all aspects and issues of human rights. CHRNGOs may use this opportunity to build their solidarity. Second, if they fail to be registered as non-enterprises, they should be encouraged to register for the moment at the Industrial and Commercial Bureau. They must, however, be careful about the matter of taxation. Concern about changing into a company and the nature of NGOs withering away is not warranted because the NGOs will not be transformed as long as they are authentic NGOs devoted to human rights. On the contrary, once they are registered as companies and obtain legal status, they can make a profit and use this to engage in human rights activities.[61] In the present Chinese political environment, it might be wise to choose this middle path. Third, regarding the political sensitivity of CHRNGOs, they should maintain a low profile and try to avoid direct confrontation with the government. Instead, they may take advantage of what the government is promoting in terms of international human rights and use the new concept of 'building a community of common destiny of all mankind'. Finally, it should be recalled that 'hard times can be the mother of invention'. CHRNGOs will survive and contribute to international constitutionalism by engaging actively in the process of UPR and the treaty bodies' review of the national periodic reports of China.

[61] There are many CHRNGOs that exist in this way and operate without any difficulty. For instance, one institute doing research on freedom of religion was registered as a cultural and arts company about ten years ago and is continuing the work it did as an NGO.

16

Global Constitutionalism and Private Governance: The Discrete Contribution of Voluntary Sustainability Standards

AXEL MARX AND JAN WOUTERS[1]

1 Introduction

As is aptly illustrated throughout this volume, there are many different strands of and approaches towards global constitutionalism.[2] In general, global constitutionalism constitutes a framework that aims to analyse (analytical dimension) or 'promote' (normative dimension) a set of global constitutional principles and norms that limit the degree of freedom of national legal orders. These constitutional principles and norms include inter alia the principles of the rule of law and democracy and a string of fundamental rights which 'comprehensively regulate the social and political life of a polity'.[3] This top-down approach from the international to the national might conflict with state-based perceptions on what constitutes a legitimate political order and the principles and norms underlying this order. Hence, several authors seek to understand how this 'global constitutionalist movement', based on a Western conception of a constitution, interacts with other legal orders. This volume aims to contribute to this endeavour by analysing in-depth non-Western, and mainly Asian, perspectives on global constitutionalism.

---

[1] We thank Anne Peters and the participants of the Global Constitutionalism Workshop in Leuven (11–12 February 2015) for comments on previous versions of this chapter.

[2] The contribution by Kotzé in this volume (Chapter 13, 'Conceptualising Global Environmental Constitutionalism in a Regional Context: Perspectives from Asia and Europe') briefly outlines some of the major strands. See also Matthias Kumm, Anthony F. Lang, James Tully and Antje Wiener, 'Editorial: how large is the world of global constitutionalism' (2014) 3 *Global Constitutionalism* 1–8.

[3] Anne Peters, 'Compensatory constitutionalism: the function and potential of fundamental international norms and structures' (2006) 19 *Leiden Journal of International Law* 579–610, at 581.

Several authors assess how different countries might fit, or not, in this global constitutionalist narrative. While interesting, these approaches tend to overlook a crucial dynamic in contemporary global governance. In a globalised world and economy, the monopoly of rule making and whether or not international rules are transposed to national rules no longer solely lie with states and their willingness to do so. An increasing number of private[4] and hybrid[5] actors play a role here. Indeed, a significant body of literature has pointed to the role of private actors in transnational rule making and enforcement.

The importance of these private actors has also been recognised in the literature on global constitutionalism.[6] Teubner makes a strong plea to include the private sector in the analysis of the processes which support or hinder the development of a 'global constitution', understood as the principles, institutions and mechanisms which improve 'the legitimacy of an international legal order and institutions without asking for a world state'.[7] Teubner argues that we are witnessing a privatisation of global rule making and that the private sector is becoming an increasingly relevant 'unit of observation' to analyse processes of 'constitutionalisation'.[8] Moreover, in his view, these private forms of rule making constitute quasi-legal orders which are growing to become 'societal constitutions' which are functionally equivalent to state constitutions.[9]

We agree with Teubner that private actors are important players in constitutionalisation processes. However, we do not necessarily consider them as functionally equivalent or distinct from (inter)governmental rule making. In our view they do not constitute quasi-legal orders which are

---

[4] Axel Marx, Miet Maertens, Johan Swinnen and Jan Wouters (eds.), *Private Standards and Global Governance* (Cheltenham: Edward Elgar, 2012).

[5] Joost Pauwelyn, Ramses Wessel and Jan Wouters, 'When structures become shackles: stagnation and dynamics in international lawmaking' (2014) 25 *European Journal of International Law* 733–763; see also Kenneth W. Abbott and Duncan Snidal, 'Strengthening international regulation through transnational new governance: overcoming the orchestration deficit' (2009) 42 *Vanderbilt Journal of Transnational Law* 501–578.

[6] Anne Peters 'Global constitutionalism', in Michael T. Gibbons (ed.), *The Encyclopedia of Political Thought* (New York: John Wiley and Sons, 2014), pp. 1–4. Available at http://www.mpil.de/files/pdf4/Peters_Global_Constitutionalism2.pdf.

[7] Peters (n. 6), p. 1

[8] See Gunther Teubner, 'Societal constitutionalism: alternatives to state-centred constitutional theory?', in Christian Joerges, Inger-Johanne Sand and Gunther Teubner (eds.), *Transnational Governance and Constitutionalism* (London: Hart Publishing, 2004), pp. 3–28; Gunther Teubner, 'Self-constitutionalizing TNCs? On the linkage of "private" and "public" corporate codes of conduct' (2011) 18 *International Journal of Global Legal Studies* 617–638.

[9] Teubner, 'Self-constitutionalizing TNCs?' (n. 8), at 626.

functionally equivalent to or separate from state (or intergovernmental) constitutions. Rather, we opine that they establish transnational mechanisms which enforce international law and global constitutional norms. This component of enforcement of existing public international law makes them especially relevant in the context of this volume. The private actors concerned have the potential to 'hollow out' the monopoly of sovereign states to oppose, or not accept, international rules and norms by obliging 'subjects'[10] within a polity to comply with these international rules and norms. In other words, a focus on non-state actors enriches our understanding of how constitutionalisation processes might work 'beyond the state', since they enforce international norms, even when they are being contested or rejected by sovereign states. Enforcement in this context refers to a dual process. First, global public or intergovernmental norms and principles are 'translated' into specific 'contextualised' rules (standards). Second, an assessment occurs as to whether rule-takers are complying with the rules and standards developed on the basis of the aforementioned global norms.

In this chapter, we aim to substantiate this argument by focusing on a specific type of private actor captured under the umbrella term 'voluntary sustainability standards' (VSS). VSS have received substantial academic interest as a major transnational regulatory instrument for non-state markets.[11] Recent inventories show that more than 400 VSS exist and are operational.[12] The majority of these VSS are private governance systems, in the sense that they are governed by non-governmental actors such as civil society organisations, firms or multi-stakeholder types of organisations.[13]

---

[10] With 'subjects' we mean individual or corporate 'rule-takers', i.e. subjects of (transnational) regulation.

[11] Graeme Auld, *Constructing Private Governance: The Rise and Evolution of Forest, Coffee, and Fisheries Certification* (New Haven, CT: Yale University Press, 2014); Tim Bartley, Sebastian Koos, Hiram Samel, Gustavo Setrini and Nik Summers, *Looking behind the Label: Global Industries and the Conscientious Consumer* (Bloomington, IN: Indiana University Press, 2015); Benjamin Cashore, Graeme Auld and Deanna Newsom, *Governing through Markets. Forest Certification and the Emergence of Non-State Authority* (New Haven, CT: Yale University Press, 2004); Richard Locke, *The Promise and Limits of Private Power: Promoting Labor Standards in a Global Economy* (Cambridge: Cambridge University Press, 2013); Marx, Maertens, Swinnen and Wouters (eds.) (n. 4); Walter Mattli and Ngaire Woods, *The Politics of Global Regulation* (Princeton, NJ: Princeton University Press, 2009).

[12] Ecolabel Index database available at http://www.ecolabelindex.com/.

[13] For an extensive discussion, see Abbott and Snidal (n. 5), at 501–578; see also Gary Gereffi, Ronie Garcia-Johnson and Erika Sasser, 'The NGO–industrial complex' (2001) 125 *Foreign Policy* 56–65.

This chapter proceeds as follows. First, we briefly introduce VSS, sketch their reach and show that they are increasingly integrated in other forms of governance, establishing them as significant transnational governance instruments. Next, we further elaborate our core argument, namely that they are in essence enforcement/compliance instruments of public international law contributing to a global implementation of international rules and norms. This argument is substantiated by detailing three steps in which VSS enforce public international law. Special attention will be given to examples which show that they operate 'beyond the state'. With a number of concluding remarks, we wrap up the chapter.

2 A short introduction to VSS

The United Nations Forum on Sustainability Standards (UNFSS)[14] defines VSS as 'standards specifying requirements that producers, traders, manufacturers, retailers or service providers may be asked to meet, relating to a wide range of sustainability metrics, including respect for basic human rights, worker health and safety, the environmental impacts of production, community relations, land use planning and others'.[15] Although the idea of voluntary standards is quite old,[16] their proliferation is of a more recent nature. Figure 16.1 shows the growth of the number of VSS over the last seven decades. It is especially since the 1990s that their number has grown exponentially.

This collection of voluntary standards comprises many different initiatives. A few examples illustrate the diversity. Some of these initiatives are mainly industry- and company-driven. Self-regulatory efforts which ensure sustainable and social performance have emerged from within the private sector with increasing speed since the early 1990s. These

---

[14] In the Spring of 2013 the UNFSS, a joint initiative by five UN agencies (Food and Agriculture Organization (FAO), United Nations Industrial Development Organization (UNIDO), International Trade Centre (ITC), United Nations Environment Programme (UNEP) and United Nations Conference on Trade and Development (UNCTAD)), was launched. The UNFSS is a platform created to generate knowledge and information on VSS with a particular focus on their potential contribution to development. The initiative is a recognition of the increasing importance of VSS in international trade.

[15] UNFSS, *Voluntary Sustainability Standards: Today's Landscape of Issues and Initiatives to Achieve Public Policy Objectives* (Geneva: United Nations Forum on Sustainability Standards, 2013), p. 3

[16] See Axel Marx and Jan Wouters, 'Competition and cooperation in the market of voluntary standards sustainability standards', in Panagiotis Delimatsis (ed.), *International Standardization: Law, Economics and Politics* (Cambridge: Cambridge University Press, 2015), pp. 215–241.

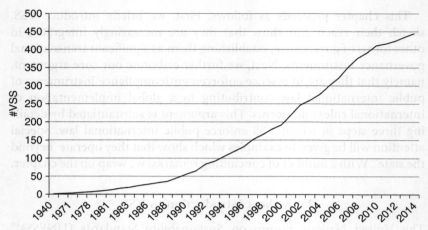

Figure 16.1   Number of Cumulative VSS: 1940–2014
Source: Own calculation on the basis of Ecolabel Index database

standards are commonly adopted as a corporate 'Code of Conduct' (CoC) or a set of 'business principles' by an individual firm or a group of firms organised in an industry association. Often the adoption of such codes is part of a risk-response strategy[17] with the aim of safeguarding a company or an industry's reputation. Adopting a code for social and environmental self-regulation can also help a company in 'recruiting and retaining certain types of employees', as well as 'attracting consumers or investors' who put value in sustainable corporate governance.[18] An interesting case of how corporate CoCs have evolved is offered by Unilever, one of the world's largest producers and sellers of consumer goods, ranging from beverages to personal hygiene products.[19] Introducing certain social, environmental and ethical standards, Unilever adopted a 'Code of Business Principles' for its own operations and a 'Suppliers Code', which has been revised several

[17] For example, after the 1984 Bhopal chemical plant disaster, the Chemistry Industry Association of Canada adopted a 'Codes of Practice' as part of the 'Responsible Care Program', which subsequently was adopted by chemical industry associations in other countries. The sportswear giant Nike introduced its 'Code of Conduct' in 1992 as labour conditions in the 'sweatshops' that were part of the company's supply chain received widespread media attention.

[18] James Brudney, 'Envisioning enforcement of freedom of association standards in corporate codes: a journey for Sinbad or Sisyphus?' (2012) 33 *Comparative Labor Law & Policy Journal* 555–604, at 555.

[19] The Unilever Sustainable Living Plan available at http://www.unilever.com/aboutus/introductiontounilever/unileverataglance/ and Unilever Supplier Centre available at http://www.unilever.com/aboutus/supplier/.

times and was recently replaced by a more elaborate 'Responsible Sourcing Policy'. Both codes include certain labour rights and partially reflect the International Labour Organization's (ILO) core labour standards, however with some important gaps.[20] As early as 2003, Unilever has been considered a forerunner in defining the social content and implementation of corporate standards.[21] Implementation of its corporate codes is overseen by a Global Code and Policy Committee, which reports regularly to the Executive Board's Corporate Responsibility and Reputation Committee. In order to ensure suppliers' compliance with the codes and principles, Unilever has sought to rely on 'external' verification mechanisms, in particular through multi-stakeholder initiatives such as the Sustainable Agricultural Network. In this way, a single company's policies on social and environmental standards influence other firms across the globe through a 'Suppliers Code'. Unilever has factories in 100 countries and directly employs 174,000 people.[22] Moreover, it purchases raw materials from 160,000 suppliers across 190 countries.

Other private regulatory initiatives emerge from civil society. In this case, there is no involvement of businesses in the setting of these social or environmental standards, which are usually drafted by a coalition of several civil society organisations, often including trade unions and environmental groups. One of the more successful and internationally recognised initiatives in this context has been the Clean Clothes Campaign (CCC). Launched in the Netherlands and the United Kingdom in 1989, the CCC was initially driven by a group of non-governmental organisations (NGOs) working on labour rights and women's rights, which reacted to a particular incident in a garment factory in the Philippines.[23] By 2014, the organisation had spread out and formed national branches in fifteen European countries, with an extended network of about 250 partner organisations worldwide.[24]

---

[20] Rachel Wilshaw, Liesbeth Unger, Do Quynh Chi and Pham Thu Thuy, 'Labour rights in Unilever's supply chain: from compliance to good practice; an Oxfam study of labour issues in Unilever's Viet Nam operations and supply chain' (2013) *Oxfam Research Report, Oxfam International* 44, 54–55.

[21] Wilshaw, Unger, Do and Pham (n. 20), p. 55; Ans Kolk, Rob van Tulder, and Bart Wesdijk, 'Poverty alleviation as business strategy? Evaluating commitments of frontrunner multinational corporations' (2006) 34 *World Development* 789–801.

[22] Unilever Sustainable Living Plan (n. 19) and Unilever Supplier Centre (n. 19).

[23] Clean Clothes Campaign, CCC Annual Report 2004, Amsterdam (2004), p. 3.

[24] Clean Clothes Campaign, CCC Annual Report 2013, Amsterdam (2013), http://www .cleanclothes.org/about/annual-reports/2013; a list of partner organisations is available on the CCC website at http://www.cleanclothes.org/about/annual-reports/2013/part ners-2013.

According to its own documentation, the CCC consists of a mix of women's organisations, consumer organisations, research institutes, organisations for fair trade, solidarity groups, youth groups, churches, NGOs and labour unions. The main standard which the CCC developed is the 'Code of Labour Practices for the Apparel Industry Including Sportswear', which includes core ILO labour standards as well as other basic labour conditions which are derived from the ILO conventions. The CCC's key goal is to campaign for the adoption and implementation of this code by companies, whereby it uses different tools including raising public awareness on labour conditions, lobbying and pressuring specific companies. The CCC's code stipulates obligations for companies which commit to implementing the code. While the CCC is not directly involved in monitoring corporate compliance with its code through certification or audits, it does have a complaint or 'urgent appeals' mechanism through which it highlights violations of its code.

Between these two types, several multi-stakeholder initiatives emerged bringing companies and civil society actors together. Several initiatives in this zone have gained significant scholarly attention. Some authors consider them 'one of the most innovative and startling institutional designs of the past 50 years'.[25] A leading example here is the Forest Stewardship Council (FSC).[26] The FSC was established in 1993 following the Rio Declaration of the United Nations Conference on Environment and Development in 1992 as a response to the slow process of formal discussions on the promotion of sustainable forest management. The FSC is a multi-stakeholder, membership-based organisation with a governance structure consisting of a general assembly in which the members are represented, a board of directors and an executive director. The general assembly of FSC members is the highest decision-making body in the FSC and is made up of the three membership chambers (a tripartite structure) – environmental, social and economic – which are further split into sub-chambers North and South. The purpose of the chamber structure is to maintain the balance of voting power between different interests without having to limit the number of members. Standards are developed on the basis of ten principles which are of equal importance. Specific standards, for the purpose of certification, are developed by national

[25] Cashore, Auld and Newsom, *Governing through Markets* (n. 11), p. 4.
[26] More information on the FSC can be found in Axel Marx, Emilie Bécault and Jan Wouters, 'Private standards in forestry: assessing the legitimacy and effectiveness of the Forest Stewardship Council', in Marx, Maertens, Swinnen and Wouters (eds.) (n. 4), pp. 60–97.

standard working groups and reviewed internationally via a two-tier consultation process. Forest management (FM) certification is the cornerstone of the FSC system and refers to the certification of forests. Chain-of-custody certification, a supply chain tracking system, refers to the fact that the product with the chain-of-custody certificate is made of products which originate from an FM-certified forest.

Other initiatives include, for example, the Fair Labour Association (FLA) and Social Accountability International (SAI). The FLA grew out of the Apparel Industry Partnership (AIP) initiative of the Clinton administration to protect workers worldwide and provide firms and consumers with the information they needed to make informed purchasing decisions. The partnership was composed of apparel and footwear firms, human rights groups, labour and religious organisations, and consumer advocates. The FLA now represents a multi-stakeholder coalition of business enterprises, colleges and universities, and NGOs (human rights, labour, religious and consumer groups). Its mission is to combine the efforts of these stakeholders to promote adherence to international labour standards and improve labour rights worldwide. SAI is a nongovernmental, international, multi-stakeholder and non-profit organisation whose mission is to promote the rights of workers worldwide and to improve working conditions by applying socially responsible standards. The SAI standards are based on internationally recognised guidelines, including various ILO conventions, the UN Convention on the Rights of the Child and the Universal Declaration of Human Rights.

An important feature of these VSS for the debate on global constitutionalism concerns their transnational nature. Little consolidated empirical data is available to make a full assessment of their global spread, but specific cases, such as the FSC, as well as an overview of which VSS are active across the world give us a glimpse of their global adoption. The FSC system is, for example, adopted in 117 countries.[27] Table 16.1 shows the adoption of VSS in different countries of the world. For this purpose, data was collected from the International Trade Centre (ITC) standards map.[28] Table 16.1 shows

---

[27] FSC Facts and Figures, March 2016 available at: https://ic.fsc.org/en/facts-and-figures

[28] This database contains fewer VSS than the Ecolabel database used for the analysis of institutional features but provides better information on the diffusion of standards. The ITC is an agency created jointly by the World Trade Organization and the United Nations. The ITC developed the standards map as a tool to enable producers and buyers to identify, compare and select the appropriate sustainability standard – out of more than 160 currently available. We use the ITC standards map to identify the number of VSS active in each country.

Table 16.1 *VSS Uptake by Country*

		# VSS			# VSS			# VSS
1	China	79	42	Norway	48	83	Cambodia	33
2	United States	78	43	Czech Republic	47	84	Malawi	33
3	Brazil	77	44	Greece	47	85	Mozambique	32
4	India	72	45	Ireland	47	86	Cameroon	31
5	Mexico	71	46	Philippines	47	87	Papua New Guinea	31
6	Canada	70	47	Ghana	45	88	Bosnia & Her.	30
7	United Kingdom	70	48	Uganda	45	89	Burkina Faso	30
8	Netherlands	69	49	Dominican Rep.	44	90	Senegal	30
9	Germany	67	50	New Zealand	44	91	Panama	29
10	Belgium	65	51	Romania	44	92	Rwanda	29
11	Thailand	65	52	Slovenia	44	93	Congo	28
12	Colombia	64	53	Bolivia	43	94	Namibia	28
13	Indonesia	64	54	Bulgaria	43	95	Venezuela	28
14	Peru	64	55	Ethiopia	43	96	Belize	27
15	Spain	64	56	Latvia	43	97	Laos	27
16	Denmark	63	57	Morocco	43	98	Lebanon	27
17	France	62	58	Tunisia	43	99	Saudi Arabia	26
18	Italy	62	59	Madagascar	42	100	Kazakhstan	26
19	South Africa	62	60	Nicaragua	42	101	Mali	26
20	Vietnam	60	61	Lithuania	41	102	TFRY Macedonia	26
21	Costa Rica	59	62	Pakistan	41	103	Albania	25
22	Switzerland	59	63	Singapore	41	104	Iceland	24
23	Australia	58	64	Slovakia	40	105	Oman	24
24	Austria	57	65	Zambia	40	106	Suriname	24
25	Sweden	57	66	Korea	40	107	Togo	24
26	Argentina	56	67	Estonia	39	108	Algeria	23
27	Ecuador	56	68	Russian Federation	39	109	Swaziland	23
28	Turkey	56	69	Paraguay	38	110	Bahrein	22
29	Chile	55	70	Zimbabwe	38	111	Georgia	22
30	Japan	54	71	Croatia	37	112	Myanmar	22
31	Poland	54	72	El Salvador	37	113	Niger	22
32	Portugal	53	73	Israel	37	114	Trinidad and Tobago	22
33	Malaysia	52	74	Uruguay	37	115	Azerbaijan	21
34	Guatemala	51	75	Bangladesh	36	116	Benin	21
35	Honduras	51	76	Cyprus	36	117	Botswana	21
36	Finland	50	77	Mauritius	36	118	Burundi	21
37	Kenya	50	78	Luxembourg	35	119	Guinea	21
38	Sri Lanka	50	79	Serbia	35	120	Iran	21
39	Egypt	49	80	Ukraine	35	121	Syrian Arab Rep.	21
40	Tanzania	49	81	Cote d'Ivoire	34	122	Afghanistan	20
41	Hungary	48	82	United Arab Emirates	34	123	Armenia	20

Table 16.1 (cont.)

		# VSS			# VSS			# VSS
124	Cuba	20	147	Central African Rep.	16	170	Palau	13
125	Gambia	20	148	Dominica	16	171	Bhutan	12
126	Guyana	20	149	Grenada	16	172	Eritrea	12
127	Uzbekistan	20	150	Guinea-Bissau	16	173	Sao Tome & Prin.	12
128	Angola	19	151	Kyrgyzstan	16			
129	Korea DPR	19	152	Mauritania	16			
130	Solomon Islands	19	153	Tajikistan	16			
131	Sudan	19	154	Vanuatu	16			
132	Turkmenistan	19	155	Yemen	16			
133	Fiji	19	156	Sierra Leone	15			
134	Gabon	19	157	Djibouti	14			
135	Seychelles	18	158	Iraq	14			
136	Barbados	17	159	Kiribati	14			
137	Kuwait	17	160	Maldives	14			
138	Lesotho	17	161	Somalia	14			
139	Liberia	17	162	Andorra	13			
140	Micronesia, Fed.	17	163	St. Vincent and Gren.	13			
141	Qatar	17	164	Cape Verde	13			
142	Samoa	17	165	Chad	13			
143	Timor-Leste	17	166	Comoros	13			
144	Antigua & Barbuda	16	167	Equatorial Guinea	13			
145	Bahamas	16	168	Libyan Arab	13			
146	Brunei Darussalam	16	169	New Caledonia	13			

Source: International Trade Centre – standards map – own calculation

that VSS are active in 173 countries; in many countries several dozen of these transnational governance instruments are in operation. It also shows the significant variation in the number of VSS which are active in a country. There are clearly some VSS hotspots or leaders, which are not limited to only Global North countries. Also, in several Asian and Latin American countries many VSS are active, which is probably explained by the countries' strong economic development over the last decades and the fact that companies often require VSS certification in order to export. In fact, following this analysis, VSS have spread out all over the world, thereby showing their potential to diffuse constitutional principles over a large number of countries.

These VSS do not operate in isolation: they interact increasingly, in different ways, with governmental policy.[29] Government actions are often instrumental in stimulating and promoting the adoption of VSS.[30] Moreover, VSS are increasingly becoming part of regulatory actions of governments. This happens in several ways. One way in which VSS are integrated in legislation and policies is through sustainable public procurement policies. Sustainable public procurement is an increasingly widespread practice that has been consolidated in policy frameworks at several institutional levels, particularly in Europe.[31] Policy initiatives also integrate VSS in the design of regulatory processes and public policies. In some cases the integration of VSS in legislation is direct, in the sense that VSS perform a specific function in the regulatory framework such as is the case with the 2009 EU Renewable Energy Directive (RED).[32] The RED requires 20 per cent of energy use in the EU to come from renewable sources by 2020. Under the RED, the European Commission set up an accreditation system for voluntary

[29] Jem Bendell, Anthony Miller and Katharina Wortmann, 'Public policies for scaling corporate responsibility standards expanding collaborative governance for sustainable development' (2011) 2 *Sustainability Accounting, Management and Policy Journal* 263–293; Eric F. Lambin, Patrick Meyfroidt, Ximena Rueda, Allen Blackman, Jan Börner, Paolo Omar Cerutti, Thomas Dietsch, Laura Jungmann, Pénélope Lamarque, Jane Lister, Nathalie F. Walker and Sven Wunder, 'Effectiveness and synergies of policy instruments for land use governance in tropical regions' (2014) 28 *Global Environmental Change* 129–140; W. J. Vermeulen, Y. J. Uitenboogaart, L. D. L. Pesqueira, J. Metselaar and M. T. J. Kok, *Roles of Governments in Multi-Actor Sustainable Supply Chain Governance Systems and Effectiveness of Their Interventions: An Exploratory Study* (Bilthoven: Netherlands Environmental Assessment Agency (PBL), 2011); Stephan Wood, 'Environmental management systems and public authority in Canada: rethinking environmental governance' (2003) 10 *Buffalo Environmental Law Journal* 129–210; Stephan Wood, 'Three questions about corporate codes: problematizations, authorizations and the public/private divide', in Wesley Cragg (ed.), *Ethics Codes: The Regulatory Norms of a Global Society?* (Aldershot: Edward Elgar Press, 2005), pp. 245–287.
[30] Cashore, Auld and Newsom, *Governing through Markets* (n. 11); Benjamin Cashore, G. Cornelis van Kooten, Ilan Vertinsky, Graeme Auld and Julia Affolderbach, 'Private or self-regulation? A comparative study of forest certification choices in Canada, the United States and Germany' (2005) 7 *Forest Policy and Economics* 53–69.
[31] D. d'Hollander and A. Marx, 'Strengthening private certification systems through public regulation: the case of sustainable public procurement' (2014) 5 *Sustainability Accounting, Management and Policy Journal* 2–22.
[32] Directive 2009/28/EC of the European Parliament and of the Council of 23 April 2009 on the promotion of the use of energy from renewable sources and amending and subsequently repealing Directives 2001/77/EC and 2003/30/EC, O.J. 2009, L 140/16.

standards in order to prove compliance of biofuel providers with the directive. The list currently comprises nineteen VSS, including inter alia International Sustainability and Carbon Certification, BonSucro, Roundtable on Responsible Soy, Roundtable of Sustainable Biofuels, Red Tractor and Roundtable on Sustainable Palm Oil.[33] As Ponte and Daugbjerg as well as Schleifer[34] point out, this type of hybrid governance is based on deep and mutual dependence and interconnection between public and private actors.

3 VSS as enforcement mechanism of international rules

How do VSS enforce international rules and contribute to global constitutionalist processes? They do this in three distinct steps. First, they embed the sustainability standards they develop in international law by including international legal commitments in their foundational principles. Second, they translate these principles in measurable indicators and action. Third, they develop a comprehensive institutional framework to monitor compliance with these standards. We will now further elaborate each step. In doing this, we 'aggregate' away from specific examples but discuss more in general how private systems enforce public international rules.

First of all, VSS integrate existing international rules and agreements, often developed in a multilateral context, in their set of rules and standards. In this way, they integrate public rules and standards in a private set of procedures. Let us take the example of the Forest Steward Council which was introduced earlier. It bases its transnational regulatory rules and standards on ten principles of which two explicitly refer to public international law (principle 1 and principle 4). Principle 1 prescribes that the standards which are developed in the context of the FSC should adhere to provisions included in inter alia the Convention on Nature Protection and Wild Life Preservation in the Western Hemisphere, the Convention Concerning the Protection of World Cultural and Natural Heritage, the Convention on International Trade in Endangered Species of Wild Fauna and Flora (CITES), the Convention on Biological

---

[33] The list of accredited biofuel providers (VSS) is available at https://ec.europa.eu/energy/en/topics/renewable-energy/biofuels/voluntary-schemes.

[34] S. Ponte and C. Daugbjerg, 'Biofuel sustainability and the formation of transnational hybrid governance' (2015) 24 *Environmental Politics* 96–114; P. Schleifer, 'Orchestrating sustainability: the case of European Union biofuel governance' (2013) 7 *Regulation and Governance* 533–546.

508 AXEL MARX AND JAN WOUTERS

Diversity (CBD), the UN Framework Convention on Climate Change (UNFCCC) and the International Tropical Timber Agreement. Another example is Social Accountability International. Its standards are based on internationally recognised guidelines, including various ILO conventions, the UN Convention on the Rights of the Child and the Universal Declaration of Human Rights. Almost all VSS state in their mission a commitment to international conventions and agreements and list them in their foundational documents and principles.

The aforementioned makes clear that private regulatory actors take as their starting point public international law. This grounding of private rules in international law is important to understand the potential of the private actors concerned to contribute to constitutionalisation in a context or country which has a 'different perspective' on global rule making or which does not align with the global constitutionalist agenda. Let us take the example of the right to freedom of association as a core global norm or principle. Freedom of association is a norm included in many international treaties and declarations. These include inter alia the Universal Declaration of Human Rights (Article 20), European Convention on Human Rights (Article 11) and the ILO Declaration on Fundamental Principles and Rights at Work adopted in 1998.[35] As stipulated by the ILO, the 'Declaration makes it clear that these rights are universal, and that they apply to all people in all States – regardless of the level of economic development'.[36] Reference to the ILO Fundamental Principles is, in turn, integrated in several international policies of nation states and regional organisations. For example, the United States and the European Union have integrated the fundamental principles in their multilateral, bilateral[37] and unilateral[38] trade policies.

---

[35] Freedom of association is one of the eight core conventions included in the declaration. See http://www.ilo.org/declaration/thedeclaration/textdeclaration/lang-en/index.htm (accessed 25 March 2016).

[36] See the ILO Declaration on Fundamental Principles and Rights at Work available at http://www.ilo.org/declaration/thedeclaration/lang-en/index.htm (accessed 25 March 2016).

[37] In a recent publication (2013), the ILO provided a full overview and discussion of social clauses in trade and economic partnership agreements.

[38] Besides bilateral economic instruments, labour standards are also referred to in unilateral trade measures such as the Generalised System of Preferences (GSP). The GSP grants preferential tariff cuts to developing countries in exchange for the implementation of human rights standards including the ILO core labour standards. See European Commission (2016), The EU Special Incentive Arrangement for Sustainable Development and Good Governance (GSP+) covering the period 2014–2015 accompanying the Report from the Commission to the European Parliament and the Council Report on the Generalised Scheme of Preferences during the period 2014–2015, Brussels.

However, as Pasture[39] notes, the right of freedom of association is also one of the most contested global values. Many Asian countries, including China, Vietnam, Laos and Malaysia, have not ratified the ILO convention on freedom of association. China, for example, tries to control as much as possible freedom of association. In a remarkable study, King, Pan and Roberts[40] analysed censorship by the Chinese government. They devised a system to locate, download and analyse the content of millions of social media posts originating from nearly 1,400 different social media services all over China before the Chinese government was able to find, evaluate and censor (i.e. remove from the Internet) the messages they wanted to block. Surprisingly, the researchers found that the Chinese government does not vigorously censor messages which are critical of the state, its leaders and its policies. The censorship strategy of the Chinese government is mainly focused on messages that initiate or spur social mobilisation, regardless of whether it is collective action in favour of or against the government. Censorship is oriented towards attempting to forestall collective activities that are occurring now or may occur in the future, and hence censorship is geared towards preventing any form of association or collective action.

Also, in the area of VSS, the Chinese government tries to exclude provisions on freedom of association through supporting Chinese-led VSS. An interesting case in this respect is the CSC9000 Code of Conduct (China Social Compliance for Textile and Apparel Industry), which is a voluntary initiative of the China National Textile and Apparel Council (an industry association) launched in 2005. The code is mainly based on Chinese labour law and some international conventions.[41] However, it does not make any reference to the ILO Fundamental Principles. The code has been criticised, for example, by the International Textile,

Available online at http://trade.ec.europa.eu/doclib/docs/2016/january/tradoc_154178 .pdf (accessed 25 March 2016).

[39] Patrick Pasture, 'The ILO and the freedom of association as the ideal of the Christian trade unions', in Jasmien Van Daele, Magaly Rodríguez García, Geert Van Goethem and Marcel van der Linden (eds.), *ILO Histories: Essays on the International Labour Organisation and Its Impact on the World during the Twentieth Century, in International and Comparative Social History*, Vol. 12 (Bern: Peter Lang, 2010), pp. 114–143.

[40] Gary King, Jennifer Pan and Margaret Roberts, 'How censorship in China allows government criticism but silences collective expression' (2013) 107 *American Political Science Review* 1–18.

[41] The code is available at http://www.csc9000.org.cn/PDF/SystemDocuments/ CSC9000T_ENG_2005.pdf.

Garment and Leather Workers Federation (ITGLWF) for not being rigorous enough and lacking key conventions such as the convention on freedom of association. The code does make reference to the role of unions but refers only to unions recognised by law. It is considered an initiative led by the Chinese government and national industry association to compete with more established international systems such as SA8000 (Social Accountability International).[42]

However, in many other private VSS schemes one can find references to freedom of association. ILO Convention 87 on 'freedom of association and protection of the right to organise' is explicitly integrated in many VSS. The ITC standards map offers some evidence of this. The standards map provides a wide range of information on approximately 150 VSS. This information includes the international legal commitments they aim to implement. Almost 90 VSS refer to freedom of association as one of their foundational principles. This includes the most prominent ones such as 4 C Association, Alliance for Responsible Mining, BonSucro, Ethical Trading Initiative, Fair Trade, Fair Wear Foundation, Fair Labour Association, GlobalGAP, Forest Stewardship Council, UTZ Certified and many others. As Table 16.1 shows, in some countries which have not ratified ILO Convention 87, such as China and Vietnam, many of these VSS are active.

For example, a leading VSS in the field of labour rights in the textile and apparel industry, Social Accountability International, has certified 654 firms in China which employ more than 350,000 workers. In Vietnam it has certified 91 companies (from a total of 3,490 certified firms worldwide). The Forest Stewardship Council has certified sixty-nine forests (and the workers working in these forests) for a total surface area of 859,555 hectares in China. In addition, almost 4,300 chain-of-custody operators (firms working in the wood-processing industry) have been FSC-certified in China (481 in Vietnam).[43] Overall, these figures remain modest when compared to the total number of firms active in the wood-processing or textile industries in China and Vietnam. However, the numbers are significant enough not to be disregarded entirely and generate some change in terms of implementing international rules. In addition, the number of certified entities in these countries is growing quite quickly. Compared to 2014, the number of FSC-certified chain-of-custody entities in China has

[42] Fibre2Fashion, Briefing on the Chinese Garment Industry, available at http://www.fibre2fashion.com/industry-article/1594/briefing-on-the-chinese-garment-industry?page=6.
[43] Data for March 2016 Facts and Figures for the FSC are available at https://ic.fsc.org/en/facts-figures.

grown with almost 1,000 additionally certified firms (representing an increase of almost 25 per cent in two years).

Moreover, and interestingly, some governments which did not ratify an international convention sometimes promote private regulatory initiatives which do so. Vietnam is an interesting case in point. As Putzel et al.[44] show, since 1992 the Vietnamese government has implemented far-reaching policies and programmes to increase the country's tree cover by promoting plantation forestry. In addition to providing environmental services, these efforts were intended to alleviate rural poverty through sustainable forestry. Towards this goal, more than four million hectares were assigned to households and rural cooperatives through forest-land reallocation or management contracts. In addition, in the last decade, Vietnam's economic policies have promoted the timber-processing industry. By 2008, the processing sector had expanded into a $3 billion industry, one of Vietnam's top live export sectors and a major source of demand for logs and sawn wood by the household managed forests. In this context several small forest owners were seeking certification through the Forest Sector Development project which was set up by the government of Vietnam in cooperation with the governments of Finland and the Netherlands and the World Bank. Focused on family forest owners it promotes forest certification by financing consulting services to carry out certification pre-assessment and assessment, as well as audits, training for local staff for the purpose of auditing for certification and market promotion of the certified products for export.[45]

Second, VSS operationalise international norms and principles in specific standards and benchmarks, which makes compliance assessment possible. Often VSS initiatives start with defining general principles as noted earlier and delegate the formulation of specific standards to working groups or committees which can take local conditions into account. In order to achieve its mission the FLA, for example, developed a Code of Conduct[46] which formulates basic principles related to different labour

---

[44] L. Putzel, A. Dermawan, M. Mocliono and L. Q. Trung, 'Improving opportunities for smallholder timber planters in Vietnam to benefit from domestic wood processing' (2012) 14 *International Forestry Review* 227–237; see also Hai Thi Nguyen Hoang, Satoshi Hoshino and Shizuka Hashimoto, 'Forest stewardship council certificate for a group of planters in Vietnam: SWOT analysis and implications' (2015) 20 *Journal of Forest Research* 35–42.

[45] Forest Stewardship Council US, Government Activities to Promote Forest Certification, available at https://ic.fsc.org/en/news/events/event-details/fsc-involvement-in-rio20/overview-02/government-activities-to-promote-forest-certification.

[46] See http://www.fairlabor.org/labor-standards.

BOX 16.1 Example – Compliance Benchmarks, FLA Freedom of Association and Collective Bargaining

1 General Compliance Freedom of Association
2 Right to Freely Associate
3 Legal Restriction/Alternative Means
4 Anti-Union Violence/Harassment or Abuse
5 Anti-Union Discrimination/Dismissal, Other Loss of Rights and Blacklisting
6 Restoration of Workers Rights/Reinstatement
7 Protection of Union Representatives
8 Production Shift/Workplace Closure
9 Severance Pay
10 Employer Interference
11 Employer Interference/Constitution, Elections, Administration, Activities and Programs
12 Employer Interference/Registration
13 Employer Interference/Favouritism
14 Employer Interference/Police and Military Forces
15 Facilities for Worker Representatives
16 Right to Collective Bargaining/Good Faith
17 Right to Collective Bargaining/Exclusive Bargaining and Other Recognised Unions
18 Right to Collective Bargaining/Unorganised Workers
19 Right to Collective Bargaining/Compliance with Collective Bargaining Agreement
20 Right to Collective Bargaining/Validity of Collective Bargaining Agreement
21 Rights of Minority Unions and Their Members
22 Right to Strike/Sanction for Organising or Participating in Legal Strikes Employers
23 Right to Strike/Replacement Workers
24 Deduction of Union Dues and Other Fees

Source: FLA Compliance Benchmarks[47]

issues (all relating to ILO conventions such as on the employment relationship, non-discrimination, harassment and abuse, forced labour, child labour, freedom of association and collective bargaining, health, safety and environment, hours of work and compensation). These general principles are next translated into specific 'compliance benchmarks'. These benchmarks contain more specific criteria which are related to

[47] See http://www.fairlabor.org/sites/default/files/fla_complete_code_and_benchmarks.pdf.

each of the broad principles. Each of these benchmarks is in turn further defined and operationalised into measurable indicators. Box 16.1, for example, illustrates the different components which are captured under the principle of freedom of association and collective bargaining in the FLA Code of Conduct. Each of these benchmarks, in turn, is further defined and operationalised into measurable indicators, resulting in a more than twenty-page document detailing very specific requirements which need to be met by standard adopters.

The way in which some of these VSS transform principles into specific 'private' rules and standards is remarkably democratic. Let us take the example of the Forest Stewardship Council. Many scholars have suggested that the FSC's standard-setting structures and procedures encompass several institutional features which could be considered democratic (i.e. inclusiveness, participation, transparency, deliberation).[48] These features include the organisation's membership structure and the decision-making procedures. One of the primary goals of the FSC is to provide voice to a whole range of forest stakeholders, such as forest owners and managers, stewards of the forest, resident forest-dependent people, local communities, indigenous people and forest workers.[49] As noted by several authors, this concern for broad representation and inclusiveness is particularly apparent in the organisation's open and chamber-based membership structure (see earlier discussion).[50] Membership in the FSC is open to any individual or organisation that shares the scheme's goals and vision, providing that they secure the support of two existing members and pay a membership fee. As Meidinger notes: 'Most rules and standards are developed through

[48] See inter alia Errol Meidinger, 'Forest certification and democracy' (2011) 130 *European Journal of Forest Research* 407–419; Graeme Auld, Lars Gulbrandsen and Constance L. McDermott, 'Certification schemes and the impacts on forests and forestry' (2008) 33 *Annual Review of Environment and Resources* 187–211; Klaus Dingwerth, *The New Transnationalism: Transnational Governance and Democratic Legitimacy* (Basingstoke: Palgrave Macmillan, 2007); Lars H. Gulbrandsen, 'Accountability arrangements in non-state standards organisations: instrumental design and imitation' (2008) 15 *Organization* 563–583; Jonathan Koppell, *World Rule: Accountability, Legitimacy and the Design of Global Governance* (Chicago, IL: Chicago University Press, 2010).
[49] Forest Stewardship Council (2003), FSC Social Strategy: Building and Implementing a Social Agenda, Version 2.1.
[50] Fred Gale, 'An institutional analysis of FSC governance', in Chris Tollefson, Fred Gale and David Haley (eds.), *Setting the Standard: Certification, Governance, and the Forest Stewardship Council* (Vancouver: UBC Press, 2009), pp. 274–292; Heiko Garrelts and Michael Flitner, 'Governance issues in the ecosystem approach: what lessons from the Forest Stewardship Council?' (2011) 130 *European Journal of Forest Research* 395–405.

extensive deliberative proceedings involving stakeholder consultation, "formal public notice and comment processes" and public explanations of decisions.'[51]

More in general several VSS follow the Code of Good Practice for Setting Social and Environmental Standards. This code was developed by the International Social and Environmental Accreditation and Labelling (ISEAL) Alliance[52] and identifies at least five components which are important in the setting of standards: (1) the identification of stakeholders via stakeholder mapping; (2) the development of a strategy to proactively approach and involve the identified stakeholders; (3) the bringing together of several major stakeholders on a more or less equal representative basis in a process of decision making; (4) the opening up of the decision-making process to all interested parties not initially identified in the first round of the stakeholder mapping; and (5) the deployment of consensus-based decision making in order to ensure that all interests are included.

Third, after operationalising international norms into specific standards, VSS put systems in place to monitor compliance with standards by VSS adopters. Monitoring allows for the assessment of compliance with specific standards. Monitoring in VSS is a function of two interrelated aspects, namely the design of top-down monitoring, audit-based systems and the design of bottom-up complaint systems.[53]

'Top-down monitoring' refers to the assessment of conformity with standards by independent third parties through a set of standardised procedures primarily based on audit procedures. In other words, conformity assessment often takes the form of auditing sites (production facilities and/or natural resources). These audits allow for quantification of conformity via different indicators (developed in step 2 described earlier) and comparison between certified entities.[54] Auditing in the context of VSS occurs via auditing protocols. A walk through a factory or forest with auditors relying on common sense is not considered effective monitoring. Initially auditing relied on a checklist/questionnaire approach. Auditors visited different units and filled out a questionnaire.

---

[51] Meidinger (n. 48), at 419.
[52] See https://www.isealalliance.org/sites/default/files/ISEAL%20Standard%20Setting%20Code%20v6%20Dec%202014.pdf.
[53] Axel Marx and Jan Wouters, 'Redesigning enforcement in private labor regulation: will it work?' (2015) 155 International Labor Review 435–461.
[54] Nina Ascoly and Ineke Zeldenrust, Considering Complaint Mechanisms: An Important Tool for Code Monitoring and Verification (Amsterdam: SOMO, 2003).

On the basis of the results of the questionnaire, an assessment was made. An advantage of this approach was that it allowed for the quantification of compliance with standards on the basis of different indicators. It also standardised auditing. However, this approach was criticised for not providing sufficiently reliable data on compliance with standards.[55] One of the criticisms was that standardisation leads to routinisation, resulting in auditors doing a 'quick' job and missing crucial information.[56] Consequently, more qualitative and participatory approaches to auditing were introduced, which include participation of workers, local communities and local governments in monitoring.[57]

Currently, a well-developed top-down monitoring/conformity assessment protocol consists of two main components. First of all, it implies a checklist approach which generates quantitative comparable information – via questionnaires and the assessment of company documents – on compliance with standards. This component of conformity assessment is most of the time outsourced to 'accredited' certifiers. In order to ensure that parties which carry out conformity assessments and certification activities are fit for their task, accreditation systems are sometimes put in place. Accreditation aims to guarantee that a conformity assessment body is competent to carry out such tasks as auditing and inspection. Accredited organisations may be either international consultancy firms such as SGS and Bureau Veritas, NGOs or local organisations.[58] Second, auditing is complemented with assessment tools that gather qualitative data – via participatory techniques – from the involved local stakeholders.

Top-down monitoring systems, however, are incomplete for monitoring compliance with standards on a continuous basis.[59] In order to overcome the constraints of top-down approaches, bottom-up complaint or dispute settlement procedures are being put in place, which allow

---

[55] Locke (n. 11); Marx and Wouters (n. 53).

[56] Charles Sabel, Archon Fung and Dara O'Rourke, *Ratcheting Labor Standards: Regulation for Continuous Improvement in the Global Workplace* (Washington, DC: World Bank, 2000); Clean Clothes Campaign, *Looking for a Quick Fix: How Weak Social Auditing Is Keeping Workers in Sweatshops* (Amsterdam: Clean Clothes Campaign, 2005).

[57] Stephanie Barrientos, *Corporate Social Responsibility, Employment and Global Sourcing by Multinational Enterprises* (Geneva: ILO, 2003); Stephanie Barrientos and Sally Smith, 'Do workers benefit from ethical trade? Assessing codes of labour practice in global production systems' (2007) 28 *Third World Quarterly* 713–729.

[58] Margaret Blair, Cynthia Williams and Li-Wen Lin, 'The new role for assurance services in global commerce' (2008) 33 *Journal of Corporation Law* 325–360.

[59] Locke (n. 11); Marx and Wouters (n. 53).

different stakeholders to constantly monitor and report any violations of standards. This has been referred to as the establishment of procedures which allow for 'retrospective accountability'.[60] This notion helps to capture the degree to which 'power wielders' meet 'the expectation of relevant constituencies', accept 'answerability' and act upon 'criticisms'.[61] These complaint and dispute systems allow 'internal' participants (members of VSS, VSS certificate holders, etc.) to appeal decisions. These systems also empower 'external' stakeholders by allowing them to raise issues relevant for the functioning of VSS. Complaint mechanisms provide a necessary complement to conformity assessment and auditing in order to guarantee compliance. Recently, we have observed the emergence of complaint and dispute settlement systems in many VSS. They take a variety of forms, but several VSS allow external stakeholders (NGOs, citizens, etc.) to file a complaint if they believe that a violation of standards has occurred.[62] In order to enable stakeholders to raise a complaint, several VSS have also installed transparency measures through information disclosure procedures. Information disclosure procedures can inform different stakeholders on compliance with standards. Publicly available information in this context includes specific information about certification procedures, auditing reports, reports on violations and reports on corrective action plans. This allows stakeholders to assess whether the reported information mirrors real conditions.

4 Concluding remarks

VSS enforce compliance with existing international law through three interrelated steps. First, they identify key principles on which the standards should be based. These principles often make explicit reference to and are based on existing international conventions and agreements. Next, they operationalise international rules into specific standards for the purpose of assessing whether standard adopters comply with the standards and international norms. In order to assess whether standard adopters comply, VSS make use of monitoring instruments which

---

[60] Nicolas Hachez and Jan Wouters, 'A glimpse at the democratic legitimacy of private standards: assessing the public accountability of GLOBALG.A.P.' (2011) 14 *Journal of International Economic Law* 677–710; see also Gulbrandsen, 'Accountability arrangements (n. 48), at 563–583.

[61] Gulbrandsen, 'Accountability arrangements' (n. 48), at 567.

[62] Axel Marx, 'Legitimacy, institutional design and dispute settlement: the case of eco-certification systems' (2014) 11 *Globalizations* 401–416.

according to Ostrom are necessary to generate compliance with rules and standards.[63]

Hence, do VSS contribute to the development of global constitutionalism 'beyond the state'? On the basis of the analysis in this chapter, we submit that VSS do contribute to constitutionalisation in two ways. First, they operationalise and enforce global public rules, norms and principles. In this way, they are not fully distinct from (inter)governmental constitutionalisation processes but more an extension of those. They contribute to a further strengthening and enforcement of principles and norms captured by the global constitutional framework. Second, they diffuse these norms and principles on a truly global scale: they are active in most countries of the world. VSS are clearly not a purely European or American phenomenon.

These arguments support the claims by authors in the global constitutionalism school, such as Teubner, that private actors play an increasingly important role in constitutionalisation processes. VSS potentially play an important role in the enforcement of constitutional values and principles and contribute to processes of constitutionalisation, even in countries which do not necessarily align with the global constitutionalist agenda.

---

[63] Elinor Ostrom, *Understanding Institutional Diversity* (Princeton, NJ: Princeton University Press, 2005).

17

International Courts and Tribunals and the Rule of Law in Asia

GEIR ULFSTEIN[*]

1 Introduction

International courts and tribunals (ICs) are evermore important in the regional and global legal order.[1] They increase in number but also in their substantive scope of jurisdiction, including human rights, trade and investment. Many of the new ICs have a compulsory character. Furthermore, they form integrated parts of legal regimes that are attractive to states, such as the World Trade Organization (WTO). Finally, several of the ICs are open to non-state actors as litigants, whether they are individuals or companies. The rise of the international judiciary brings hope to a world progressively governed by law.

In Section 2 of this chapter, I will first present some general reflections on ICs and the rule of law. The initial task is to define what is meant by the rule of law. Then, as the rule of law is a principle known from domestic law, I discuss whether this principle is at all useful in the international context. Finally, I examine to what extent an international rule of law should be seen as part of global constitutionalism.

Section 3 of the chapter deals with the significance of ICs for the rule of law in the Asian context. I compare the strong status of the Court of Justice of the European Union (CJEU) and the European Court of

[*] Department of Public and International Law, University of Oslo. This chapter was written under the auspices of ERC Advanced Grant 269841 MultiRights – on the Legitimacy of Multi-Level Human Rights Judiciary – and partly supported by the Research Council of Norway through its Centres of Excellence Funding Scheme, project number 223274 PluriCourts – the Legitimacy of the International Judiciary.
[1] Geir Ulfstein, 'The international judiciary', in Jan Klabbers, Anne Peters and Geir Ulfstein (eds.), *The Constitutionalization of International Law* (Oxford; New York: Oxford University Press, 2009), pp. 126–127; Karen J. Alter, *The New Terrain of International Law: Courts, Politics, Rights* (Princeton, NJ: Princeton University Press, 2014); Karen J. Alter, Yuval Shany and Cesare P. R. Romano, *The Oxford Handbook of International Adjudication* (Oxford: Oxford University Press, 2014).

Human Rights (ECtHR) with the weak development of regional trade courts and human rights courts in Asia. I also ask whether the use of global dispute settlement mechanisms, such as the International Court of Justice (ICJ), the WTO system and the International Tribunal for the Law of the Sea (ITLOS), by Asian states may compensate for the lack of regional ICs.

On this basis, I reflect on why the regional Asian judiciary is so weak and ask whether we may expect more regional judicialisation in the future. I also discuss whether there are viable alternative Asian procedures for dispute resolution. This discussion will be used to assess the status of the rule of law in Asia, but I also examine whether the sceptical approach to international judicialisation among Asian states may weaken the global rule of law.

2   The international rule of law and global constitutionalism

The purpose of the rule of law (or comparable standards like *Rechtsstaat* or *État de droit*) is to protect individuals against arbitrary governmental power.[2] This principle means that government shall be exercised by law and not by other means. The law should also fulfil certain standards. It should not be secret, retrospective or impossible to understand.[3] In other words, individuals should be able to foresee the content of the law and order their lives accordingly. It is worth noting that the rule of law applies to all government functions. In our context, it means that courts, as subjects of law, must themselves apply law and not extra-legal considerations. They should fulfil certain minimum standards with respect to their composition, procedure and style of interpretation to be credible judicial institutions. Courts are also essential as providers of the rule of law, by contributing to respect for the law. Indeed, it has been seen as an implication of the rule of law that everyone should, as a last resort, have access to courts to determine their rights and claims.[4]

Some writers distinguish between a formal and a substantive notion of the rule of law. Formal understandings will typically refer to procedural criteria and equal treatment ('thin theories'). Substantive theories will include a broader set of ideals, such as human rights or protection of certain minimum social or economic conditions ('thick theories').

---

[2] Martin Krygier, 'Rule of law', in Michel Rosenfeld and András Sajó (eds.), *The Oxford Handbook of Comparative Constitutional Law* (Oxford: Oxford University Press, 2012), p. 241.

[3] Ibid., p. 235.

[4] Tom Bingham, *The Rule of Law* (London: Penguin Books, 2011), p. 85.

Joseph Raz is sceptical of such a substantive character of the rule of law. He argues that 'if the rule of law is the rule of good law then to explain its nature is to propound a complete social philosophy. But if so the term lacks any useful function. We have no need to be converted to the rule of law just in order to discover that to believe in it is to believe that good should triumph.'[5]

While including a requirement of 'good law' as part of the rule of law may be going too far, setting certain minimum standards for the content of the law is less worrisome. I will come back to whether a formal or substantive notion of the rule of law should be applied. But first, I will discuss whether the rule of law is relevant not only for national courts but also for international courts and tribunals.

Jeremy Waldron raises the question of whether sovereigns should be entitled to the rule of law. He claims that applying the rule of law in international law is complicated by the fact that (1) there is no world government from which we need protection and (2) international law, in the first instance, affects states as opposed to individuals, which have traditionally benefitted from the rule of law.[6]

Now, there is reason to mention that the UN General Assembly clearly is of the view that the rule of law is of relevance in the international society and to international courts. In its Declaration of the High-Level Meeting of the General Assembly on the Rule of Law at the National and International Levels (2012), the importance of the International Court of Justice and other international courts and tribunals for the rule of law is explicitly recognised.[7] But this does not necessarily mean that it is useful to apply the concept of the rule of law in the international context. Let us have a look at the two critical points raised by Waldron.

First, there is the absence of a supreme international authority. International law has often been described as contract law writ large, among states. This may be an argument for seeing international rule of law as unfitting – as a 'category mistake'. However, the rising powers of international institutions, including ICs, make it appropriate to examine the application of rule of law standards to such institutions – taking duly into account the special characteristics of

---

[5] Joseph Raz, 'The rule of law and its virtues', in Joseph Raz (ed.), *The Authority of Law: Essays on Law and Morality* (Oxford: Oxford University Press, 2009), p. 211.

[6] Jeremy Waldron, 'Are sovereigns entitled to the benefit of the international rule of law?' (2011) 22 *European Journal of International Law* 315–343, at 323.

[7] UN Doc. A/RES/67/1, paras. 31 and 32.

the international legal system and the relationship between international and national law.[8]

Second, states, not individuals, are the primary subjects of international law. I agree that states in the international system are not analogous to individuals in the national system. I furthermore agree that states do not have the same legitimate reasons to claim standards of human dignity. But states may nevertheless claim a legitimate right to treatment on the basis of rule of law standards, such as the predictability of international obligations. States will also more likely submit to international obligations and implement them if they have reasonable guarantees that international organs, including ICs, will respect their mandates, that the voices of the states are heard and that all states are treated equally.

This is an argument for applying the international rule of law for instrumental as opposed to normative reasons. But there are also normative grounds for supporting rule of law standards for democratic as opposed to authoritarian states, since decisions of the national legislative, executive and judicial organs should be seen as expressions of the will of the individuals of such states. Finally, individuals are in some areas directly subject to international law, such as in international criminal law.

Next, we should ask whether an international rule of law should be considered part of global constitutionalism. Michael Zürn, André Nollkaemper and Randall Peerenboom argue that constitutionalisation

> refers to a process in which different legal orders are integrated by the establishment of an ultimate legal authority in the form of a (written or unwritten) constitution that serves as higher law and is grounded in shared fundamental values. [...] Although this vision is intimately bound to the concept of rule of law, it goes further by identifying an overarching authority and prescribing legal means through which it can be achieved. This project therefore contains a strongly utopian flavour.[9]

There is, however, reason to distinguish between constitutionalism and constitutionalisation.[10] The former refers to the end result, i.e. some form of international constitution, while the latter indicates a process towards an international constitution, while being agnostic about the end

---

[8] See also Michael Zürn, André Nollkaemper and Randall Peerenboom, 'Conclusion: from rule of law promotion to rule of law dynamics', in Michael Zürn, André Nollkaemper and Randall Peerenboom (eds.), *Rule of Law Dynamics: In an Era of International and Transnational Governance* (Cambridge: Cambridge University Press, 2012), p. 308.

[9] Zürn, Nollkaemper and Peerenboom, 'Conclusion' (n. 8), p. 316.

[10] Jan Klabbers, 'Setting the scene', in Klabbers, Peters and Ulfstein (eds.), *The Constitutionalization of International Law* (n. 1), pp. 3–4.

result or indeed whether an international constitution is desirable. My focus is on the process of constitutionalisation rather than constitutionalism in the form of an international constitution.

Constitutionalisation may be seen as having two elements: the empowerment of international institutions and the control of such institutions by constitutional standards, such as the rule of law. In our context, the empowerment of ICs may in itself be seen as an aspect of the constitutionalisation of international law. But ICs also serve a constitutional function in controlling governmental power, i.e. they are providers of the rule of law, and they are themselves subject to rule of law standards. It is those latter aspects of the rule of law that are discussed as features of international constitutionalisation in the present context.

It may be asked whether the content of the rule of law as it has been developed in a domestic constitutional setting is useful in the international setting. Zürn, Nollkaemper and Peerenboom claim that it is debatable whether it makes sense to conceptualise international rule of law based on an analogy from the domestic standard. They say that 'it may be better to try a radically different approach that does not begin with domestic rule of law as the model for rule of law at the international level'.[11]

This discussion is comparable to other aspects of the constitutionalisation of international law: Is it worthwhile to use principles developed for national legal systems in an international setting? I have argued earlier that there are good reasons for applying the rule of law standard in the international context. It also makes sense to regard this standard as having basically the same content as in the domestic setting: requiring that international authority should be based on law in order to avoid arbitrariness. But, of course, the more precise content of the rule of law standard should be adapted to the relevant differences between the domestic and the international setting.

As regards rule of law standards applicable to ICs, the content of such standards could vary, taking into account the following factors: the different mandates of ICs; who are the parties to the IC – whether they are states, individuals or private companies; the specific substantive area ICs are meant to serve; whether they are 'civil' or criminal courts; the extent to which they hand down binding judgments or non-binding recommendations, including advisory opinions; and, finally, whether they are global or regional tribunals.

[11] Zürn, Nollkaemper and Peerenboom, 'Conclusion' (n. 8), p. 317.

It may also be discussed to what extent ICs have an international legal obligation to respect rule of law standards. The standards set out in human rights conventions apply formally to states and their national courts, not to international courts. But the International Criminal Tribunal for the former Yugoslavia (ICTY) Appeals Chamber held in the *Tadic* case that an international criminal court 'ought to be rooted in the rule of law and offer all guaranties embodied in the relevant international instruments'. The rule of law requires that the court must be established 'in accordance with the proper international standards: it must provide all the guarantees of fairness, justice and even-handedness in full conformity with internationally recognized human rights instruments'.[12] Likewise, rule of law standards should apply to ICs other than international criminal courts. Whether this is a current legal requirement will not be further discussed in our context.

These legal requirements refer to ICs as *subjects* of the rule of law. The rule of law standard may, however, be seen to extend beyond any legal requirements and include the following political standards: that ICs should be composed of competent and independent judges, which also include credible nomination and selection procedures, gender representation, etc.; that they apply due process and transparency, including access to justice and the representation of third parties; that ICs fulfil their legal mandate and respect relevant principles for treaty interpretation and sound reasoning; and, finally, that their practice is consistent.

ICs as *providers* of the rule of law raise first of all the issue of whether ICs promote the rule of law *among* states. It is therefore of interest to study to what extent ICs are able to resolve the particular dispute, promote predictability in the specific legal field and enhance the general rule of law in the international society. The fragmentary character of the international judiciary may lead to inconsistent or contradictory judgments at the expense of consistency, as required by the rule of law.

But ICs may also promote the rule of law *within* states. ICs may enhance access to justice, ensure fair proceedings and promote non-discrimination in the national legal systems. It has been argued that to the extent international law is applied at the national level it should satisfy no lesser standards than what is required in a domestic context.[13] However, the practice by an IC may conflict with the national

---

[12] ICTY, *Prosecutor v. Duško Tadic* (Decision on the Defence Motion for Interlocutory Appeal on Jurisdiction, Case No. IT-94-1-AR72, A. Ch., 2 October 1995), paras. 42 and 45.

[13] Zürn, Nollkaemper and Peerenboom, 'Conclusion' (n. 8), p. 318.

legal system and create confusion about the applicable legal norms. Hence, as with the fragmentation between different ICs, the plurality of legal systems with their own international courts and tribunals may undercut judicial consistency.

ICs as providers of the rule of law make the distinction between *formal* and *substantive* approaches to the rule of law relevant. Nienke Grossman argues that ICs should at least uphold certain core human rights.[14] Indeed, it seems that there should be certain limits to the substantive content of international judgments of ICs if they should be seen as respecting the rule of law.

3 International courts and tribunals in Asia

After the end of World War II, two courts were established in Europe with profound effects on the region. The CJEU has competence far beyond those of international trade courts. It has been important in implementing the internal market in the EU. But it has now, under the former 'third pillar', also been delegated powers in the field of criminal and police cooperation. It has furthermore competence in immigration law and protects human rights by enforcing the EU Charter of Rights. Its judgments have direct effect in national jurisdictions and are claimed to be superior to national law.[15] The ECtHR is, on the other hand, not only protecting basic human rights, such as the most dramatic intrusions in human dignity. The court also deals with a broad range of human rights as incorporated in the European Convention of Human Rights. As a result, the ECtHR has led to significant structural changes in the legal systems in member states.[16]

What is the situation when it comes to regional courts in Asia?

It is commonly acknowledged that Asian states are more concerned with protecting their sovereignty than are Western states and that they prefer to resolve their disputes through bilateral consultations and negotiations, rather than through binding settlement by ICs.[17] There are no

---

[14] Nienke Grossman, 'The normative legitimacy of international courts' (2012) 61 *Temple Law Review* 61–106, at 100.

[15] See Hans-Wolfgang Micklitz and Bruno de Witte, *The European Court of Justice and the Autonomy of the Member States* (Cambridge: Intersentia, 2012).

[16] Helen Keller and Alec Stone Sweet, 'Assessing the impact of the ECHR on national legal systems', in Helen Keller and Alec Stone Sweet (eds.), *A Europe of Rights* (Oxford: Oxford University Press, 2008), p. 710.

[17] Tommy Koh, 'International law and the peaceful resolution of disputes: Asian perspectives, contributions, and challenges' (2011) 1 *Asian Journal of International Law* 57–60, at

courts covering the Asian region. We see, however, developments towards increasing acceptance of binding third-party dispute resolution among Asian states at the bilateral, sub-regional, transregional and global levels.

Dispute settlement mechanisms have been developed within the framework of the Association of Southeast Asian Nations (ASEAN) in recent years. This organisation is sub-regional rather than regional and is currently composed of ten member states: Indonesia, Malaysia, the Philippines, Singapore and Thailand, later joined by Brunei Darussalam, Vietnam, Lao PDR, Myanmar and Cambodia.

The relevant ASEAN instruments include the 1976 Treaty of Amity and Cooperation in Southeast Asia, the 2007 ASEAN Charter and the 2010 Protocol to the ASEAN Charter on Dispute Settlement Mechanisms. While peaceful settlement is central to the cooperation, it is also guided by the principles of equality, respect for each other's internal affairs and non-interference. Dispute settlement has been based on consent and has traditionally been of a non-binding character. Such settlement has also involved political rather than legal organs. This has been seen as the 'ASEAN Way'.[18]

The ASEAN Charter contains the possibility of resolving disputes by arbitration, but no court has so far been established. While the ASEAN Enhanced Dispute Settlement Mechanism (EDSM) of 2004 is modelled on the WTO Dispute Settlement Understanding (DSU), it has not been used by any ASEAN member.[19] The ASEAN Intergovernmental Commission on Human Rights (AICHR) and the ASEAN Commission on the Promotion and Protection of the Rights of Women and Children (ACWC) were established in 2009 and 2010 respectively, while the ASEAN Human Rights Declaration was adopted in 2012. However, these organs lack the competence to receive individual complaints, and no regional human rights court has been established.[20]

57; Ma Xinmin, 'China's mechanism and practice of treaty dispute settlement' (2012) 11 *Chinese Journal of International Law* 387–392, at 392.

[18] Hao Duy Phan, 'Procedures for peace: building mechanisms for dispute settlement and conflict management within ASEAN' (2013–2014) 20 *University of California Davis Journal of International Law and Policy* 47–73, at 52.

[19] Michael Ewing-Chow, Alex W. S. Goh and Akshay Kolse Patil, 'Are Asian WTO members using the WTO DSU "effectively"?' (2013) 16 *Journal of International Economic Law* 669–705, at footnote 12.

[20] See Haisen-Li Tan, *The ASEAN Intergovernmental Commission on Human Rights: Institutionalising Human Rights in Southeast Asia* (Cambridge: Cambridge University Press, 2011); John S. Ciorciari, 'Institutionalizing human rights in Southeast Asia' (2012) 34 *Human Rights Quarterly* 695–725, at 715 and 721; Vitit Muntarbhorn, *Unity in Connectivity? Evolving Human Rights Mechanisms in the ASEAN Region* (Leiden: Nijhoff, 2013).

On the other hand, Asian states have been willing to enter into – and use – global dispute settlement mechanisms. But Simon Chesterman writes that they are far more reluctant to accept such mechanisms than are states in other parts of the world. They have

> by far the lowest rate of acceptance of the compulsory jurisdiction of the International Court of Justice (ICJ) and membership of the International Criminal Court (ICC) [...] or to have joined the World Trade Organization (WTO). The proportion of Asian states that are contracting parties to the International Centre for Settlement of Investment Disputes (ICSID) is also the lowest of any region – though on that they are tied with Latin America.[21]

Asian states are parties to the 1982 UN Convention on the Law of the Sea (UNCLOS) with its compulsory dispute settlement through the ITLOS, the ICJ or arbitration. China's refusal to participate in arbitration under Annex VII initiated by the Philippines in 2013 concerning the Chinese claims in the South China Sea raised the issue whether it rejected the UNCLOS dispute resolution mechanism as such. But China participated sort of halfway by having issued a 'position paper' that the tribunal seems to have acknowledged as setting out the Chinese position for these proceedings.[22]

The WTO dispute settlement mechanism is also used by Asian states. Chesterman has found that 'India, Japan, and China are the fifth, seventh, and ninth most frequent to appear in WTO cases as applicant states; China and India are the second and third most frequent respondents. Japan is the most frequent participant as a third party; China and India are third and fourth.'[23]

And Asian states are parties to bilateral investment treaties (BITs) involving binding investor–state dispute settlement.[24] According to Chesterman, 'China is now party to the second largest number of BITs overall, with Korea and India in the top fourteen'.[25] Finally, the United States and eleven Pacific states, including Japan, Malaysia, Vietnam, Brunei and Singapore, concluded the Transpacific Partnership trade

---

[21] Simon Chesterman, 'Asia's ambivalence about international law and institutions: past, present, and futures' (2015), at 3. Available at SSRN: http://ssrn.com/abstract=2694408 or http://dx.doi.org/10.2139/ssrn.2694408; See also Simon Chesterman, 'International criminal law with Asian characteristics?' (2014) 27 *Columbia Journal of Asian Law* 129–164.

[22] PCA, *The Republic of the Philippines v. The People's Republic of China*, paras. 133 et seq. See also Chesterman, 'Asia's ambivalence' (n. 21), at 40.

[23] Chesterman, 'Asia's ambivalence' (n. 21), at 23.

[24] See for China Xinmin (n. 17).

[25] Chesterman, 'Asia's ambivalence' (n. 21), at 23.

accord (TPP) on 5 October 2015. This agreement also includes a chapter on binding dispute settlement.[26] This may be seen as a transregional development – unless the Pacific states are seen as a separate region.

Why do we not find regional courts in Asia, and why is there reluctance to accept and use global ICs? Several explanations may be possible. Chesterman points to four factors that may explain the more general reluctance to restrict national sovereignty in favour of more international law and international institutions: Asian states' historical experience with international law; the cultural and political diversity between these states; power disparities within the region; and, finally, that the current regime may serve the interests of many Asian states.[27] There may be also more specific factors that are relevant for acceptance and use of binding third-party dispute settlement. Michael Ewing-Chow et al. refer, for example, to the lack of capacity of states to engage in WTO litigation.[28]

Asian states have traditionally preferred resolving disputes through political processes and mechanisms, rather than by formal dispute settlement in ICs. But, as in the rest of the world, we have seen a trend towards more third-party dispute settlement.[29] This is demonstrated in the ASEAN Enhanced Dispute Settlement Mechanisms and the potential of an ASEAN human rights judicial organ. But, foremost, we see it through bilateral investment treaties with dispute settlement clauses, the use of global ICs, especially the WTO dispute settlement system, and, most recently, the adoption of the Transpacific Partnership trade accord with its binding dispute settlement procedure.

This means that Asia may be a reluctant fellow traveller. Asian states may also have special preferences about the design and use of international dispute resolution mechanisms. But we see no sign of an *Eastphalia*, as opposed to the Westphalian international legal system. Asian states rather prefer traditional Westphalian values, especially strong state sovereignty.[30]

---

[26] The text of the dispute settlement procedure is available at https://medium.com/the-trans-pacific-partnership/dispute-settlement-a5b4569a9a55#.qsukz0bsz.

[27] Chesterman, 'Asia's ambivalence' (n. 21), at 28–30.

[28] Ewing-Chow, Goh and Patil (n. 19), at 677.

[29] See Julian G. Ku, 'China and the future of international adjudication', Hofstra University Legal Studies Research Paper No. 12–17 (2012) 27 *Maryland Journal of International Law* 154–173, available at SSRN: http://ssrn.com/abstract=2129217; Rodman R. Bundy, 'Asian perspectives on inter-state litigation', in Natalie Klein (ed.), *Litigating International Law Disputes: Weighing the Options* (Cambridge: Cambridge University Press, 2014), pp. 164–165.

[30] Chesterman, 'Asia's ambivalence' (n. 21), at 34.

4 Conclusions

The relative absence of formal mechanisms for dispute resolution in Asia means, of course, that it is less meaningful to examine regional ICs as subjects of the rule of law. The distinction between the formal and substantive aspects of the rule of law is also of less importance. But what are the consequences for ICs as providers of the rule of law?

One cannot exclude that political mechanisms and processes have the potential to protect the rule of law: there is no necessary connection between the existence of ICs and respect for law. But ICs are generally established to ensure a better protection of the rule of law than if dispute resolution is left to politics. While investment can be protected by the BIT mechanisms and trade by the global WTO, issue areas that are typically resolved through regional ICs, especially human rights protection, will suffer from the non-existence of such regional courts in Asia.

Furthermore, the political and cultural diversity between Asian states is not only of interest as an obstacle for establishing ICs. The resulting lack of such organs means that Asia will not experience the integration seen in the European context, through both the CJEU and the ECtHR. This may or may not be regarded as desirable by Asian states. Neither will Asia see the transnational effects of courts like the CJEU and the ECtHR, in the sense that international court practice is accepted as part of the domestic legal order – with the concomitant merging of international and national law.

Karen Alter, Laurence Helfer and Jacqueline R. McAllister have also shown that regional and sub-regional courts in other parts of the world have exercised a considerable flexibility in adapting their practices to local needs and potentials.[31] However, with the exception of the sub-regional ASEAN Enhanced Dispute Settlement Mechanism there is no court in the region that can initiate such a development.

What is the importance of the attitudes of Asian states for the future development of regional and global ICs?

First, we may expect increasing pluralism between the approaches of different states, between different issue areas and between different geographic levels.[32] The ASEAN represents a sub-regional development that may result in further judicialisation. China, on the other hand, may

[31] Karen J. Alter, Laurence R. Helfer and Jacqueline R. McAllister, 'A new international human rights court for West Africa: the ECOWAS Community Court of Justice' (2013) 107 American Journal of International Law 737–779, at 774.
[32] See Chesterman, 'Asia's ambivalence' (n. 21), at 46–47.

exhibit greater power attitudes towards formal dispute resolution. The stance of China in the case brought by the Philippines in the South China Sea arbitration reminds one of the non-appearance of Russia in the *Arctic Sunrise* case[33] and of the United States in the *Nicaragua* case.[34]

We have also seen that increased judicialisation is more acceptable to Asian states in trade and investment than in human rights. This is reflected in the support for BITs, the TPP and the WTO – and the lack of support for human rights courts but also for the International Criminal Court, with its non-Westphalian character of holding individuals to account. The increase in ICs in the areas of trade and investment may continue while the dearth of ICs in the fields of human rights and criminal law becomes even more striking.

Finally, while there is a general reluctance to enter into regional dispute resolution mechanisms, we see a mosaic of bilateral (BITs), sub-regional (ASEAN), transregional (TPP) and global (ICJ, ITLOS, WTO) ICs. Such geographical pluralism may grow even further in the future. On the other hand, as Asian states become accustomed to ICs at other geographical levels, they may become less sceptical to establishing regional ICs.

The attitudes of the Asian states towards ICs are important far beyond this particular region, especially due to the rising economic and political power of China. While the preference of these states to protect sovereignty may slow down international judicialisation, such a development is not to be expected in areas of economic importance such as trade and investment. Neither is there any sign that the general trend towards increased international judicialisation will be reversed – although the enthusiasm for establishing new ICs may be somewhat restricted.

The scepticism of Asian states may weaken the development of more international rule of law protection and constitutionalisation. But the rule of law provided by existing ICs will continue to expand, also for Asian states: through their constant dispute resolution, their interpretation of treaties and general international law, and their judicial law-making functions.

---

[33] ITLOS, *The 'Arctic Sunrise' (Kingdom of the Netherlands v. Russian Federation)*, Case No. 22, Order of 22 November 2013.

[34] ICJ, *Military and Paramilitary Activities in and against Nicaragua (Nicaragua v. United States)*, Merits, Judgment of 27 June 1986, ICJ Reports 1986, 14.

PART V

Conclusion: East Asia and Global Constitutionalism

18

Global Constitutionalism for East Asia: Its Potential to Promote Constitutional Principles

TAKAO SUAMI

1 Introduction

The debate on global constitutionalism assumes the existence of universally accepted constitutional principles, such as the rule of law, human rights protection and democracy, and their application to the whole international society. By virtue of its universal character, global constitutionalism has not been yet discussed from the perspective of any particular region. It is widely accepted that EU law has been constitutionalised. However, the discussion on the constitutionalisation of EU law is not of it as a regional form of global constitutionalism but as a starting point leading to it. The lack of consciously regional approaches to global constitutionalism represents a gap in international legal scholarship. At present, both the contents of and the familiarity with constitutionalisation still vary by region. Accordingly, the idea of a 'global constitutionalism', which covers domestic and international law, cannot but have an uneven impact upon individual regions. It must be carefully examined whether the diversity in the world undermines the significance and effectiveness of global constitutionalism. My argument is that sensitivity to regional diversity is meaningful for the development of global constitutionalism and that such sensitivity is compatible with the applicability of global constitutionalism to any region including East Asia.[1]

Based on this understanding, the present chapter evaluates both persisting patterns and ongoing changes in constitutionalism in East Asia. It specifies and fleshes out how and to what extent global constitutionalism is significant for East Asia. The chapter's structure reflects the combination of both descriptive and normative elements that is inherent in global constitutionalism in taking an empirical as well as a theoretical approach.

[1] There is no established definition of East Asia. In this chapter, 'East Asia' means the so-called ASEAN (ten member states) Plus Three (China, Korea and Japan) countries.

To be concrete, the Section 2 summarises the overall situation of East Asia in terms of both legalisation and constitutionalisation. The history of East Asia may give us some clues to understand the present situations in East Asian constitutionalism. Section 3 focuses on the wartime discussion in Japan on 'overcoming modernity'. In the light of insights from this section, the situation of the constitution of Japan is studied in Section 4 in terms of global constitutionalism. As a whole, this chapter asserts that the traditional dichotomy between the West and the East is theoretically meaningless and useless for analysis of ongoing problems in international society.

2   Background for constitutionalism debate in East Asia

2.1   East Asia and international law: different approach to international law

In order to discuss global constitutionalism in the East Asian context, we have to begin by considering the current state of affairs in this region from a legal perspective.

Modern international law originated in relations among European states in the seventeenth century, and it became truly international through the expansion of European empires in the nineteenth century. It is true that international law had been formed not only through interaction among European states but also through their long-term engagement with the world outside of Europe.[2] Nonetheless, the idea of international law had been almost unknown in East Asia until the mid-nineteenth century, and it was exported as a self-contained system to East Asia through European imperialism. The first contact with international law for most East Asian states came in the form of unfortunate events.[3] North-East Asian states such as China, Korea and Japan were dragged into international society, disciplined by international law through the so-called unequal treaties.[4] International law was the product of

[2] Yasuaki Onuma, *International Law in a Transcivilizational World* (Cambridge: Cambridge University Press, 2017), pp. 55–84.
[3] Stephen C. Neff, *Justice among Nations: A History of International Law* (Cambridge; London: Harvard University Press, 2014), pp. 310–319.
[4] For example, Japan was forced to conclude unequal treaties with Western countries in the 1850s and 1860s. With the United States, these were the Kanagawa Treaty of 1854, Shimoda Treaty of 1857 and US–Japan Treaty of Amity and Commerce of 1858. The revision of these treaties was the most important diplomatic target for Japan for a long time (ibid., at 315–317).

European civilisation and as such was perceived to be the law of European states and applicable only to them. East Asian states were not treated in the nineteenth century as equal subjects of international law with European states, because the former were regarded as barbarian or savage, not as civilised. However, East Asian states in those days had no choice but to accept the international law system that was quite unfamiliar to them.

No international legal scholarship is free from unconscious national bias, even among Western states, and consequently it must be nationalised or regionalised.[5] Given East Asian states' unhappy encounters with international law, the approaches to international law that they generally take differ from those of Western states. Most East Asian states have perceived international law with 'deep scepticism and criticism', though the degree depends upon the state.[6] Such East Asian attitudes towards international law cannot but affect the comprehension of international law in the region. For example, an East Asian characteristic is a preference for absolute sovereignty. Traditional Westphalian-type or more absolute sovereignty continues to be widely praised in East Asia. The claims of non-interference in domestic affairs and full respect for territorial integrity are clearly shown in the recent territorial disputes in the region.[7] East Asian states are fully aware of the defensive function of sovereignty, which is useful for protecting their autonomy from Western powers. A corollary is that East Asian states also prefer non-binding measures to binding. The Asia Pacific region including East Asia has traditionally been exemplified by 'low or soft legalization'.[8] Even in

---

[5] Anne Peters, 'International legal scholarship under challenge' (2016) *MPIL Research Paper Series No. 2016-11* 1–7; Emmanuelle Jouannet, 'French and American perspectives on international law: legal cultures and international law' (2006) 58 *Maine Law Review* 291–335, at 292–323; Martti Koskenniemi, 'The case for comparative international law' (2009) 20 *Finnish Yearbook of International Law* 1–8, at 4.

[6] Hanqui Xue, 'Meaningful dialogue through a common discourse: law and values in a multi-polar world' (2011) 1 *Asian Journal of International Law* 13–19, at 15.

[7] Zuxing Zhang, 'A deconstruction of the notion of acquisitive prescription and its implications for the Diaoyu Islands dispute' (2012) 2 *Asian Journal of International Law* 323–338, at 334–337; Andrew Coleman and Jackson Nyamuya Maogoto, '"Westphalian" meets "Eastphalian" sovereignty: China in a globalized world' (2013) 3 *Asian Journal of International Law* 237–269, at 241–245, 252–255 and 260–261; Zhihua Zheng, 'Legal effect of maps in maritime delimitation: a response to Eril Francks and Marco Benatar' (2014) 4 *Asian Journal of International Law* 261–279.

[8] Miles Kahler, 'Legalization as strategy: the Asia-Pacific case', in Judith L. Goldstein, Miles Kahler, Robert O. Keohane and Anne-Marie Slaughter (eds.), *Legalisation and World Politics* (Cambridge; London: The MIT Press, 2001), pp. 165–175.

liberalising trade, states in this region have tended to rely upon non–legally binding measures.[9]

Nonetheless, a clear move to greater use of international legal instruments has been apparent in East Asia from the beginning of this century. Several legal changes in the last decades suggest a process of 'constitutionalisation'.[10] However, these are rather exceptional phenomena: most developments remain at the stage of mere 'legalisation', i.e. the 'thickening' of legal elements in the international relations involving East Asian states.[11] While 'legalisation' is an important starting point for 'constitutionalisation', it cannot be equated with 'constitutionalisation' itself. To be recognised as supporting 'constitutionalisation', East Asia must share higher law embodying constitutional principles.[12] Unfortunately, the reality of East Asia, especially North-East Asia, has yet to reach the stage of 'constitutionalisation' due to a lack or an insufficient incorporation of constitutional principles into its international law. This analysis is confirmed by the region's lesser interest in normative elements of international law. Although the instrumental use of international law is widespread, constitutional principles are generally considered less important there, because they originated in the West and are not shared as such by East Asian states.[13] The fact that many Asian states approach international criminal adjudications differently from non-Asian states evidences such inclination.[14]

---

[9] Takao Suami, 'Informal international lawmaking in East Asia: an examination of APEC', in Ayelet Berman, Sanderijn Duquet, Joost Pauwelyn, Ramses A. Wessel and Jan Wouters (eds.), *Informal International Lawmaking: Case Studies* (The Hague: Torkel Opsahl Academic Publisher, 2012), pp. 55–96.

[10] For example, in accordance with Art. 14 of the ASEAN Charter adopted in 2007, the ASEAN Intergovernmental Commission was established in 2009. The ASEAN Human Rights Declaration was adopted in 2012 (Gerard Clarke, 'The evolving ASEAN human rights system: the ASEAN Human Rights Declaration of 2012' (2012) 11 *Northwestern Journal of International Human Rights* 1–27).

[11] Takao Suami, 'Regional integration in East Asia and its legalization: can law contribute to the progress of integration in East Asia?', in Tamio Nakamura (ed.), *East Asian Regionalism from a Legal Perspective: Current Features and a Vision for the Future* (London; New York: Routledge, 2009), pp. 172–177.

[12] Aoife O'Donoghue, *Constitutionalism in Global Constitutionalisation* (Cambridge: Cambridge University Press, 2014), pp. 25–26.

[13] Due to its traditional philosophy and modern pragmatism, China tends to regard international law as just an instrument to achieve its policy objectives (Junwu Pan, 'Chinese philosophy and international law' (2011) 1 *Asian Journal of International Law* 233–248, at 234 and 238–239); Xue (n. 6), at 13–14.

[14] Among the state parties of the Rome Statute for the International Criminal Court (the ICC), thirty-three are from Africa, while only twelve are from Asia (Hanqin Xue, 'A point

2.2   East Asia and constitutionalism: implantation of constitutionalism into East Asia

East Asia has also taken a similar path as to the reception of domestic constitutionalism. Almost at the same time as they met international law, East Asian states met a Western-style law, constitution and constitution-alism for the first time. The transplantation of European law to East Asia was initiated in the second half of the nineteenth century. Since then, above all since the end of World War II, modern Western-style constitutions have been gradually accepted by East Asian states, mainly through decolonisation, and have taken root in their societies.[15] However, constitutional practice in East Asia remains very diverse due to differences in colonial history, political ideology, culture, as well as legal and constitutional developments. Some East Asian states with Western-style constitutions have a practice of liberal constitutionalism, but the constitutional practice of others (e.g. socialist states) is generally considered non-liberal. In short, 'there is no singular or monolithic conception or practice' of constitutionalism among East Asian states.[16]

Even in the case of East Asian states with liberal constitutions, their situations are quite distinct from many European states'. The importance of a modern constitution is not limited to the organisation of the government. It extends to the establishment of the constitutional principles that are expected to guide the development of society and to modify traditional social and economic structures. Although this function is also applicable to European states, modern written constitutions in East

---

[15] to meet: justice and international criminal law' (2014) 4 *Asian Journal of International Law* 35–39, at 36 and 38). South Korea and Japan are members of the ICC, but most ASEAN states and China are not.

[15] 'Constitutionalism' had gained universal recognition for the organisation and legitimation of political power by the end of the twentieth century (Dieter Grimm, *Constitutionalism, Past, Present, and Future* (Oxford: Oxford University Press, 2016), p. 357). East Asian states are no exception. For instance, the first Japanese Constitution, the Meiji Constitution incorporating Western principles of government, was promulgated in 1889, but it was not liberal, since sovereignty was in the emperor's hands (the '*Tenno*'). While this constitution provided for a Lower House composed of elected representatives and an independent judiciary, the bill of rights was subject to 'reservation of the law' (Hideo Tanaka (ed.), Malcolm D. H. Smith (assistant), *The Japanese Legal System: Introductory Cases and Materials* (Tokyo: University of Tokyo Press, 1976), pp. 621–641). The Meiji Constitution was replaced with the current constitution in 1947. The current constitution is much more liberal and democratic, and it guarantees the protection of fundamental human rights for the people.

[16] Wen-Chen Chang, Li-Ann Thio, Kevin Y. L. Tan and Jiunn-Rong Yeh, *Constitutionalism in Asia: Cases and Materials* (Oxford; Portland, OR: Hart Publishing, 2014), pp. 5–6.

Asian states were implanted from the outside world in societies whose specific identities had long been established. This fact has consistently led to gaps between East Asian states' constitutions and their actual social and economic structures: in particular, the difference between constitutional principles supported by their written constitutions and social principles upheld by their local societies is significant.[17] Irrespective of diversity in the region, East Asian constitutionalism is characterised by a weak tradition of the rule of law and of rights-based thinking, both of which have resulted in inadequate human rights protection.[18] Furthermore, the rule of law is inclined to be confused with the rule-by-law paradigm.[19]

2.3 Regional specification and global constitutionalism: paradigm of the West versus East confrontation

2.3.1 Acceptance of international law

The brief survey of legal developments in this region at both national and international levels reveals gaps between the West and the East (particularly East Asia) in many aspects of international law, national law and constitutionalism. These gaps seem to justify the confrontational relationship between the West and the East regarding global constitutionalism, but this finding is just an aspect of a larger whole.

Unlike the situation in the nineteenth century and the first half of the twentieth century, international law is nowadays applied to every part of the world, and a certain degree of consensus on the understanding of international law has been already attained worldwide. Therefore, one must recognise that every state, region and people have been fully incorporated into the legal framework of contemporary international law and that none objects outright to international law itself. In the past, China was negative towards and cautious about international law due to its Western-dominated contents as well as the historical role that it

---

[17] In Japan, the written constitution is based on modern Western constitutional principles such as the rule of law, human rights and democracy, but Japan's social and economic structures are organised in accordance with traditional values and principles, which differ considerably from those of the West (Takao Suami, 'Rule of law and human rights in the context of the EU-Japan relationship: are both the EU and Japan really sharing the same values?', in Dimitri Vanoverbeke, Jeroen Maesschalck, David Nelken and Stephan Parmentier (eds.), *The Changing Role of Law in Japan: Empirical Studies in Culture, Society and Policy Making* (Cheltenham; Northampton: Edward Elgar, 2014), pp. 247–266).

[18] Chang et al. (n. 16), pp. 5–6.

[19] Ibid., pp. 28–29; O'Donoghue (n. 12), pp. 28–29.

had played for China, but China has shifted towards a positive stance to international law.[20] As Christian Tomuschat argues, Asia has become a main contributor today to the development of international law through both international law-making and adjudication.[21]

2.3.2   Regional or national diversity about international law

The fact that international law is applied throughout the world does not mean that international law is uniformly understood, interpreted and applied. In reality, international law is applied diversely among states and regions.[22] Furthermore, the level of legalisation, particularly the recourse to legal rules and judicial adjudications, is not the same worldwide, and an optimal level of legalisation in each region must be found individually.[23] This argument holds also for the substance of constitutionalism, especially the application of constitutional principles. It is difficult to deny that there are differences in the understanding of these principles between Europe and East Asia.[24]

In discussing diversity or non-uniformity, the claim of 'Asian values' cannot be avoided. This claim was first asserted by some East Asian political leaders in the early 1990s and was taken over by some academics in East Asia.[25] Pluralism based on respect for diversity may well be sympathetic to this claim. The substance of Asian values is still being discussed in terms of the normative aspects of international law, mainly fundamental human rights.[26] The reason why the Asian values claim has attracted so much academic attention is quite simple: it seems to challenge the universal nature of human rights. Universality is essential to the

---

[20] In addition to participating in international law-making, China has made frequent use of international courts and dispute settlement mechanisms and has promised to respect international law (Pan (n. 13), at 242 and 245–247).

[21] Christian Tomuschat, 'Asia and international law: common ground and regional diversity' (2011) 1 *Asian Journal of International Law* 217–231, at 225–227; China is not a full member of the International Criminal Court (ICC). But, 'China has maintained a dialogue with the ICC and has involved itself in the process leading to its continuous evolution' (Dan Zhu, 'China, the crime of aggression, and the International Criminal Court' (2015) 5 *Asian Journal of International Law* 94–122, at 95–96). This practice demonstrates that Asian states can contribute to the development of international law despite not being members of international organisations.

[22] Anthea Roberts, 'Comparative international law? The role of national courts in creating and enforcing international law' (2011) 60 *International and Comparative Law Quarterly* 57–92, at 79–80.

[23] Kahler, 'Legalization as strategy' (n. 8), at 187.

[24] Suami (n. 17), at 248–263.

[25] Andrew Wolman, 'National human rights commissions and Asian human rights norms' (2013) 3 *Asian Journal of International Law* 77–99, at 82–83.

[26] Ibid., at 78–80; Pan (n. 13), at 227–231.

idea of human rights, and as long as the protection of human rights derives from the assumption that every individual must be respected and dignified as such, the Asian values claim that Asian history, development and culture may justify differences in human rights implementation is liable to undermine human rights' very foundation.[27] International society has already made some efforts to find a compromise between the universality of human rights and their national and regional peculiarities. The Bangkok Declaration in April 1993, the Vienna Declaration in June 1993 and the World Summit Outcome in 2005 are noteworthy in this respect. They take due account of national and regional particularities, while maintaining the universal nature of human rights.[28] By adopting them, international society has already achieved a certain consensus on the necessity of the process whereby international human rights instruments are localised or vernacularised as legitimate in non-Western environments.[29]

To our regret, these achievements have not brought the end of the Asian values claim. Some East Asian scholars still do not believe in discourse on human rights as well as the rule of law and democracy, which is deeply rooted in their scepticism about Western-oriented international law.[30] If one compares East Asia with Europe, several differences in philosophy, history, culture, religion and national law between the two regions are readily apparent. Since the West–East dichotomy is popular in both Europe and East Asia, their binary opposition seems to be a useful framework for recognising all sorts of ongoing phenomena relating to constitutional principles. Many scholars in various fields have, however, raised doubts about the effectiveness of such dichotomous thinking.[31]

[27] Wolman (n. 25), at 79.

[28] Final Declaration of the Regional Meeting for Asia of the World Conference on Human Rights (Bangkok Declaration), UN Doc.A/CONF.157/PC/59 (7 April 1993); Vienna Declaration and Programme of Action, UN Doc.A/CONF.157/23 (25 June 1993); 2005 World Summit Outcome, GA Res. 60/1, UN Doc.A/RES/60/1 (24 October 2005), paras. 121–122.

[29] National Human Rights Commissions in East Asia have been playing an important role in developing localised human rights norms. These norms reflect local values and cultures, while maintaining a fundamental consistency with the universal human rights (Wolman (n. 25), at 77–78 and 81); Sally Engle Merry, 'Human rights and transnational culture: regulating gender violence through global law' (2006) 44 Osgoode Hall Law Journal 53–75, at 55–56.

[30] Xue, (n. 6), at 17.

[31] Naoki Sakai, 'Resistance to conclusion: the Kyoto School philosophy under the Pax Americana', in Christopher Goto-Jones (ed.), Re-Politicising the Kyoto School as Philosophy (London; New York: Routledge, 2008), pp. 183–198; Bardo Fassbender and

Hence we have to consider whether the West–East dichotomy is useful or effective when examining the progress of globalisation from a legal perspective. This is the next question to be answered.

3 Wartime discourse on overcoming modernity in Japan: is the dichotomy between the West and the East really meaningful?

3.1 From the opening of the Pacific War to the Overcoming Modernity symposium

When facing a difficult question such as this, we can often find valuable suggestions from our history. Therefore, I look at the Japanese attempt during World War II to intellectually challenge Western modernity based on Japanese tradition, culture and values. Due to their shared critique of Western universalism, it overlaps with the Asian values claim.

With its surprise attack in December 1941 on Pearl Harbour, Japan joined World War II on the side of the Axis powers. In July 1942, the Overcoming Modernity (*Kindai no chokoku* in Japanese) symposium took place in Tokyo over two days.[32] The symposium was an initiative of the famous literary journal *Bungakukai* (*Literary World*), and its participants were carefully selected from among contemporary Japanese intellectual leaders in thought, literature, science, film, philosophy, theology, history and music. The symposium's proceedings were published and attracted considerable attention in wartime Japan.

The main theme of the symposium was a conflict between Western modernity and Japanese tradition, culture and ideology. Such a conflict was not an important issue in the Meiji era (1868–1912). In it, Japan fervently aimed to modernise itself in order to defend itself against the threat of Western imperialism.[33] The government's policy of 'civilisation and enlightenment' (*bunmei kaika* in Japanese) in the Meiji era was the wholesale incorporation of Western rationalism, science and technology into Japan for the purpose of rapidly constructing the modern nation state.[34] In those days, modernity was automatically identified with

Anne Peters, 'Introduction: towards a global history of international law', in Bardo Fassbender and Anne Peters (eds.), *The Oxford Handbook of the History of International Law* (Oxford: Oxford University Press, 2012), pp. 4 and 10.

[32] Richard F. Calichman, 'Preface', in Richard F. Calichman (ed. and trans.), *Overcoming Modernity: Cultural Identity in Wartime Japan* (New York: Columbia University Press, 2008), p. ix.

[33] Ibid., p. viii.

[34] Ibid., p. viii.

Western modernity.[35] Doubts or suspicions about Western modernity had not been so obvious until the start of the Pacific War. Its start transformed the whole situation. Since the war with the Allied powers was regarded as resistance to Western modernity, its start gave those intellectuals a prime opportunity to reconsider the legitimacy of Western modernity.

After World War II ended, the symposium was heavily criticised as being a project to ideologically uphold and justify Japanese aggression in Asia.[36] The phrase 'overcoming modernity' became shorthand for war and fascist ideology in wartime Japan, since the symposium had tried to explain the Pacific War under the paradigm of overcoming modernity.[37] Without a doubt, the objective of the overcoming modernity argument was to contribute to a far-reaching plan according to which Japan would defeat the Allies and assume hegemony over the whole world.[38] A successful symposium would have been likely to be beneficial to the justification of Japan's starting the Pacific War.

3.2   Legitimation of the Pacific War and Japanese values

Briefly put, overcoming modernity was an ideological project in wartime Japan that tried to discover a new paradigm originating in East Asia, particularly in Japan, in order to cope with the defects and limits of Western modernity.

On the day after the Pacific War started, the imperial Japanese government officially announced that Japan's actions in South-East Asia were intended to exclude the tyranny of both the United States and the United Kingdom from the area, not to harm any local peoples at all.[39] The Japanese government repeatedly declared the liberation of Asian peoples and the establishment of the 'Great East Asia Co-Prosperity Sphere' with the leadership of Japan as the objectives of the

---

[35] Ibid., p. ix; one of the symposium participants also said that 'in general, what is called "modern" means European' (Keiji Nishitani, 'My views on "Overcoming Modernity"', in Calichman (ed.), Overcoming Modernity (n. 32), p. 51).

[36] Kenichi Matsumoto, 'Kaidai [bibliographical introduction]', in Tetsutaro Kawakami and Yoshimi Takeuchi (eds.), Kindai no Cyokoku (Overcoming Modernity) (Tokyo: Toyamabo, 1979), p. vi.

[37] Yoshimi Takeuchi, 'Kindai no Cyokoku' (Overcoming Modernity), in ibid., pp. 274–275.

[38] Wataru Hiromatsu, Kindai no Cyokoku-ron; Syowa-Shiso-shi no Ichi-Shikaku (An Essay about Overcoming Modernity: One Perspective on the History of Thought in the Showa Era) (Tokyo: Kodansha, 1989), pp. 5, 51–53 and 225–227.

[39] The Imperial Government of Japan, Announcement of 9 December 1941.

Pacific War.[40] The symposium participants also presupposed that overcoming Europe's world domination was 'the reason why the Greater
East Asia War was currently being fought'.[41]

The Western colonial rule of wide-ranging territories in East Asia was
a product of Western modernity in one sense, because its legitimacy was
based on the distinction between developed and developing countries
relative to Western modernity. Now that it had launched an attack
against Western colonial rule, Japan could no longer invoke the same
rationale for Japanese leadership over other Asian states.[42] In addition,
the Japanese government had proclaimed the construction of a new style
of international order based on the Japanese traditional spirit, 'Hakko
Ichiu' (the spirit of universal brotherhood), among East Asian states from
prior to the Pacific War.[43] Taking account of these conditions, the
Japanese wartime intellectuals who were to justify the prosecution of
the Pacific War concluded that they could no longer rely upon Western
thoughts or ideology as before in order to accomplish their task.
Accordingly, they were forced to look for a new basis that was uncon-
nected to Western modernity, and they could not help depending on
their own traditional ideology, thoughts, culture, spirits and history.[44] In
other words, the intellectuals were strongly motivated to uncover limitations and insufficiencies inherent in Western modernity and to overcome
them by replacing Western modernity with something else based on
Japanese tradition.

Consequently, under the rubric of overcoming modernity, the symposium's primary aims were to consider critically the modernisation and
the Westernisation of Japan since the beginning of the Meiji era and,

[40] For example, by issuing the Great East-Asia Joint Declaration in November 1943, the
Japanese government declared together with its puppet East Asian governments that they
undertook to cooperate militarily, economically and politically in 'liberating their nation
from the yoke of Britain-American domination', 'ensuring their self-existence and self-
defence' and 'constructing a Great East Asia' (Daitoa-kaigi kaisai oyobi kaigi no jyokyou
(Holding Assembly of Great East-Asiatic Nations and Its Details), from 2 October 1943 to
6 November 1943 (https://www.jacar.archives.go.jp/das/meta/B02032955900)); Kosuke
Kawanishi, Daitoa Kyoei-Ken: Teikoku Nihon no Nanpou Taiken (The Great East Asia Co-
Prosperity Sphere: Southern Experiences of the Imperial Japan) (Tokyo: Koudansha, 2016),
pp. 77–85 and 136–139.
[41] Roundtable Discussion, 'Day one', in Calichman (ed.), Overcoming Modernity (n. 32), pp.
151, 154; the Greater East Asia War is a Japanese name for the Pacific War at that time.
[42] Takeuchi (n. 37), pp. 307–308.
[43] The Great East-Asia Joint Declaration made clear the principles to be observed for that
purpose (n. 40); Kawanishi (n. 40), pp. 105–128.
[44] Matsumoto (n. 36), pp. v–vi.

further, to re-establish Japanese society on a non-Western foundation. The symposium was not intended simply to justify the Pacific War but also to raise serious doubt about importing Western modernity into non-Western environments.[45] The meaning of 'overcoming Western modernity' was not self-evident, but a participant summarised it as 'the overcoming of democracy in politics, the overcoming of capitalism in the economy, and the overcoming of liberalism in thought'.[46] As his explanation indicates, considering whether Japanese intellectuals were capable of constructing their own non-Western identity without input from Western modernity was a chief subject of this symposium. In view of these historical details, it is not difficult to find many commonalities between the overcoming modernity discourse in wartime Japan and the Asian values claim after the 1990s.

The symposium participants carefully explored universal elements in Japanese philosophy, thoughts, culture and religion in order to overturn Western predominance in various fields.[47] All participants severely criticised deficiencies of European civilisation and seriously sought to look at from various angles how Western modernity could be replaced by a modernity that originated in Japan. Nonetheless, the symposium was a total failure.[48] It is accepted that the symposium never reached any meaningful theoretical conclusions. On the one hand, the phrase 'overcoming modernity' had considerable impact as a political slogan upon Japanese popular sentiment at the time and contributed something at least to the ideological justification of the Pacific War. On the other hand, the discussions did not offer any clear-cut answer to the question of how to substitute European modernity with something else. In short, the symposium failed to find non-Western values and principles that could replace Western values and principles.

---

[45] Ibid., pp. 15–16.

[46] Shigetaka Suzuki, 'A note on "Overcoming Modernity"', in Calichman (ed.), *Overcoming Modernity* (n. 32), p. 146.

[47] For example, Keiji Nishitani, a religious philosopher, stressed the importance of Japan's traditional spirit and argued that 'there is something at the deepest roots of Japan's traditional spirit that can provide a course of resolution to these present world problems' (Nishitani (n. 35), p. 59). Nishitani desired that 'Japan and, more broadly Asia as a whole should be seen in its unique identity as a simple outside of the West' (Richard F. Calichman, 'Introduction: "Overcoming modernity", the dissolution of cultural identity', in Calichman (ed.), *Overcoming Modernity* (n. 32), pp. 1, 20). Fusao Hayashi presented a similar argument (Fusao Hayashi, 'The heart of imperial loyalty', in Calichman (ed.), *Overcoming Modernity* (n. 32), p. 108).

[48] Takeuchi (n. 37), p. 275; Hiromatsu (n. 38), p. 53.

3.3   Reason for the symposium's failure

All the participants yearned for Japan's total victory over the Allies and were pleased to devote their intellectual energies and resources to the symposium. Despite such great efforts, why did the Overcoming Modernity symposium not reach any definite conclusion? The papers prepared by the participants reveal that when considering the subject of overcoming modernity, many faced a hard and unavoidable question: Would Japan be able to escape from the framework of Western modernity? In their papers, some participants were forthright about their distress at how Japanese modernity, nurtured with Western modernity, could be ahead of Western modernity itself.

In grappling with that question, these participants could not but acknowledge the fact that Japan had been deeply integrated into the system in which Western modernity was ubiquitous. As stated, Japanese modernisation had taken place under strong Western influence.[49] Through modernisation from the start of the Meiji era, many things, material and immaterial, were imported from the West into Japan, and these affected various aspects of Japanese society. As a result of this historical process, many elements making up wartime Japan were transplanted from the West, and traditional Japan had actually merged with the West.[50] Recognising such foreign transplantation, one participant had to acknowledge that rejecting the West was facile discourse, and he confessed that '(Western) influence has become so deeply rooted as to affect the foundations of our daily life'.[51] He finally concluded that 'it is unlikely that our rejection of Western culture at this point will save us from the source of this illness'.[52] Not only this participant but some others also observed the implantation of Western modernity into Japan and insisted that European civilisation was no longer merely an alien civilisation but was now actually a part of

---

[49] Roundtable Discussion, 'Day one', in Calichman (ed.), *Overcoming Modernity* (n. 32), p. 152.

[50] Jyunichi Isomae, '"Kindai no Cyokoku" to Kyoto-Gakuha: Kindaisei, Teikoku, Fuhensei' ('Overcoming Modernity' and the Kyoto School: modernity, imperial and universality), in Naoki Sakai and Jyunichi Isomae (eds.), *'Kindai no Cyokoku' to Kyoto-Gakuha: Kindaisei, Teikoku, Fuhensei* ('Overcoming Modernity' and the Kyoto School: Modernity, Imperial and University) (Tokyo: Ibunsha, 2010), pp. 31, 53–54.

[51] Mitsuo Nakamura thought that the Japanese were no longer able to be conscious of such influence and that this lack of consciousness revealed 'how deeply this influence has permeated our lives' (Mitsuo Nakamura, 'Doubts regarding "Modernity"', in Calichman (ed.), *Overcoming Modernity* (n. 32), pp. 136, 137–138).

[52] Ibid., p. 144.

Japan.[53] Japanese thoughts were usually believed to be unique and specific to Japan, but Naoki Sakai explains that the Japanese philosophy, particularly the Kyoto School, which attracted much attention in Japanese society before and during the war, was not based on Chinese classics and Buddhist texts but was instituted as Western philosophy.[54] This thought was actually nothing less than a kind of Western thought. In short, wartime Japan was no longer the traditional Japan that it had been before the middle of the nineteenth century in terms of thought, culture and ideology, though it was not the same as Europe.

If pure Japanese elements had been clearly distinguishable from later imported Western elements, specifying the location of the overcoming modernity question in the binary opposition would have been possible. The reality was that Western modernity had been fully integrated with and was almost inseparable from Japanese modernity at that time. Given such high-level integration, it was practically impossible to specify targets to be substituted for the sake of overcoming modernity. The participants had no choice but to acknowledge the absence of pure Japanese-ness in Japan.[55] Yet mere rejection of European modernity was self-denial of wartime Japan itself.[56] This stalemate was well proved by the debate at the symposium. Assuming that Western modernity is the target to be overcome, it must be an object of disapproval. Notwithstanding that, some participants ironically expressed their appreciation of Western modernity and could not help accepting the universality of European modernity.[57] Many

[53] Shigetaka Suzuki, a historian, took a similar view to Nakamura's. He stated that European civilisation had already become 'deeply internalised' in Japan (Suzuki (n. 46), p. 146). Torataro Shimomura, a philosopher, stated that 'for us at present, however, Europe is no longer a mere other' (Torataro Shimomura, 'Course of Overcoming Modernity', in Calichman (ed.), Overcoming Modernity (n. 32), p. 111).

[54] Sakai (n. 31), pp. 187–189. He argues that a dichotomous view of the West and Japan is futile in understanding modern Japanese thought (ibid., p. 191).

[55] Calichman, 'Introduction' (n. 47), pp. 1, 18.

[56] According to Shimomura, 'we must also criticise ourselves rather than simply criticise them. Modernity is us, and the overcoming of modernity is the overcoming of ourselves' (Shimomura (n. 53), p. 111); he said that 'it would be easy if the overcoming of modernity were simply a question of criticising others' (ibid.).

[57] Shimomura stated that 'regardless of modernity's origins in Europe, the fact that we ourselves could and indeed have become modern derives from the global nature of modernity. Regardless of the motives and manner of this reception, it must be said that European modernity could become our modernity because of that globality, even though we possess an entirely different historical ground' (Shimomura (n. 53), p. 111). Hideo Tsumura, a film critic, also discerned the universal power of European culture that 'enabled this culture to spread throughout the word' (Hideo Tsumura, 'What is to be destroyed?', in Calichman (ed.), Overcoming Modernity (n. 32), p. 115) and expressed his

participants paid respect to positive aspects of European modernity through referring to great intellectuals such as Plato, Kant, Kierkegaard and Bergson. In order to exceed Western modernity, they discussed the West within Japan and searched for parts that had firmly rejected foreign influence.[58] Approving the universal nature of European modernity was actually the sole choice to escape from such an impasse, but it contradicted by definition the aim of the symposium. All in all, contrary to their original intentions, the participants were forced to recognise how difficult it would be for Japan to escape the influence of Western modernity. In tackling these intractable problems, the symposium participants had exhausted most of their intellectual energies and resources and thus never reached their final destination.

The inseparability of the West and Japan further became manifest in the prosecution of the Pacific War. Japan fought the Pacific War in the name of liberating the Western colonies from Western imperial rule and establishing the new international order headed by Japan. In contradiction to this pretext, however, what Japan actually did against other Asian states was nothing more than impose its own imperialistic colonial rule.[59] The contradiction exists in the fact that 'the non-West (Asia) must essentially become Western in order to resist the West, or [. . .] become modern in order to resist modernity'.[60] According to Yoshimi Takeuchi, a famous critic and Chinese studies scholar in the post-war era, this contradiction has been 'the aporia of modern Japanese history' during the war and thereafter.[61] The topic of overcoming modernity pursued in the symposium was definitively refuted by the Japanese wrongdoings throughout East Asia during the war.

These details about the symposium cast deep doubt on the West–East dichotomy. The symposium's theme of overcoming modernity presupposed a confrontation between Europe and Japan. It assumed most fundamentally that Japan could be separate from the West. The first

belief that this modern (actually European) spirit still had much in itself that Japanese should respect and adopt (ibid., p. 126).

[58] Roundtable Discussion, 'Day two', in Calichman (ed.), *Overcoming Modernity* (n. 32), pp. 178–209.

[59] The reality was the mere replacement of Western imperialism with Japan's own colonial aggression throughout Asia (Calichman, 'Preface' (n. 32), p. xiii; Kawanishi (n. 40), at 130–159).

[60] Calichman, 'Preface' (n. 32), pp. xiii–xiv; Takeuchi (n. 37), pp. 307–308.

[61] Takeuchi (n. 37), pp. 338–339; according to Takeuchi, the idea of overcoming modernity presents an important thesis that Japan must tackle today (Calichman, 'Introduction' (n. 47), pp. 1, 30).

question then that had to be answered was whether it was possible for
Japan to remain outside the West in terms of modernity. Analysis of the
symposium demonstrates that we cannot conclude that wartime Japan
was inherently separate from the West. Metaphorically speaking, Japan
was no longer located outside the West in the 1940s. Consequently, Japan
could not avoid contradicting itself or falling into self-denial when
Japanese modernity, which had mostly developed based on European
modernity, sought to challenge European modernity.

In conclusion, the appropriateness and meaningfulness of a theoretical
framework in which Europe and Japan existed in opposition were questionable. It was inadequate to overcome Western modernity. In general,
the West–East dichotomy assumes Western universality and Eastern
particularity and may thereby strengthen Western hegemony over the
East.[62] Therefore, the validity of such overarching binaries is currently
criticised by more than a few intellectuals. The reason for the symposium's failure can be found in a structural defect connected with such a
binary framework. At the moment when the dichotomy between the
West and the East was adopted, the symposium was doomed to fail.

3.4 The Overcoming Modernity symposium and Asian values claim

3.4.1 Insignificance of Asian values claim

The outcome of the Overcoming Modernity symposium is instructive
when considering the Asian values claim in the context of global constitutionalism as well as of international law. The Asian values claim
assumes the West–East dichotomy and therefore shares problems with
the overcoming modernity debate of the 1940s. Their essence is the
question whether the Asian values claim can effectively challenge the
present system of international law.

Regional or national particularity in East Asia often induces East
Asians to adopt the West–East dichotomous approach to explain many
differences between Europe and East Asia. In other words, East Asians
are tempted to understand such particularity in terms of national or
regional exceptionalism.[63] The lack of equivalents in East Asia reinforces

---

[62] Sakai (n. 31), p. 184; Sakai shed light on the complicity of universalism and particularism
and criticised the structural complicity between the West and Japan (ibid., p. 186). He
further argued that 'the dichotomy of the West and the Rest or Asia is utterly irrelevant to
the comprehension, apprehension or critical evaluation of Japanese philosophy in general' (ibid., p. 189); Fassbender and Peters, 'Introduction' (n. 31), p. 4.
[63] Sakai (n. 31), pp. 194–195.

such exceptionalism in terms of law.[64] The dichotomy seems to East Asians to clarify the present problems in international society and plays persuasively on people's sentiments. The Overcoming Modernity symposium shows, however, that the binary opposition formula is not merely too simple to get a hold of complicated issues. More essentially, it is almost impossible for someone who is and remains within a given system to call the whole system into question by relying upon such a formula.

The application of the dichotomy is also problematic for international law issues including the Asian values claim. Nowadays, international law applies around the world. East Asia is a latecomer to international law, but all states in this region have, willingly or not, accepted the international law system. As stated, East Asian states have not only joined nearly all major international organisations but have also contributed in many ways to international law's development, though their impact might not be on par with that of Western states.[65] Contemporary international law is not simply a Western product but is partly a non-Western product. All in all, East Asia does not at present remain outside the sphere of international law and is fully integrated into the system of international law.[66] Therefore, proponents of Asian values must face difficulties similar to those that the symposium participants faced more than seventy years ago, and they will also have to succumb to self-contradiction or self-denial. Insofar as local factors have become inseparably combined with more universal factors through participation in that system, purely local factors have been transformed and no longer exist anywhere as they originally stood. For example, Japan's encounter with European modernity was not its first experience of being integrated into a wider system. Ancient Japan participated in the China-headed tribute system. Under this system, Chinese religion, culture, technology, legal and government system,

[64] This does not mean that East Asia did not have its own regional system. In East Asia, there was the Sino-centric 'Tributary' system in the pre-modern era (Onuma (n. 2), pp. 64–67).
[65] Fassbender and Peters, 'Introduction' (n. 31), pp. 5–6. According to Garwood-Gowers, China, an emerging great power, increasingly sees itself as a norm-shaper and norm-maker within the international system and has contributed to the evolving normative architecture on sovereignty and intervention in the context of non-consensual military intervention for civilian protection (Andrew Garwood-Gowers, 'China's "Responsible Protection" concept: reinterpreting the Responsibility to Protect (R2P) and military intervention for humanitarian purposes' (2016) 6 *Asian Journal of International Law* 89–118).
[66] As a basis of his argument for transcivilised international law, Onuma presupposes that international law has been accepted by non-Europeans and points out that all nations and peoples recognise it as the law of the international society (Onuma (n. 2), pp. 16 and 56); Tomuschat (n. 21), at 217–218 and 226.

and political thoughts inter alia were imported into Japan from the early seventh century, and they formed the foundation of traditional Japan.[67] Consequently, it is almost impossible to extract imported Chinese factors from today's Japan. No one in Japan at present seeks to challenge Chinese influence by invoking purely Japanese factors. There is, however, an exception to this argument. When a worldwide or regional system is modelled upon a given local system, one can at the same time maintain local elements as they stand and take part in the former system, because the former system does not directly contradict the latter. In this case, the development of the singular system is instead likely to guide that of the broader system.[68]

This logic holds true for international law. Yasuaki Onuma, a Japanese scholar of international law famous for his idea of a 'transcivilisational perspective' on international law, explains this perspective as developing a cognitive and evaluative framework based on the recognition of the plurality of civilisations and cultures that have long existed in human history.[69] He is critical of the West-centric nature of international law,[70] but he does not seek to negate 'the great asset of Western ideas and thoughts'.[71] His arguments are based on the past achievements, progresses and developments of international law, and they do not reject its values.[72] We have to recall that as the outcome of the Overcoming Modernity symposium suggests, such negation is unlikely to be conducive to the further development of international law.

[67] Kimio Kumagai, *Daio kara Tenno he, Nihon no Rekishi No. 3 (From a King to an Emperor: The History of Japan, Vol. 3)* (Tokyo: Kodansha, Japan, 2008).
[68] The development of international law exemplifies this exception. International law has been developed based on European international law. Irrespective of its local nature, the progress of European international law can therefore contribute to the further development of the whole international law without falling into self-contradiction.
[69] Yasuaki Onuma, *A Transcivilizational Perspective on International Law* (Leiden; Boston: Martinus Nijhoff, 2010), p. 81.
[70] Ibid., pp. 29–108.
[71] Onuma (n. 2), p. 14.
[72] For example, he criticises a narrow, liberty-centric notion of human rights and stresses the importance of economic and social rights. He admits the critical importance of human rights, mainly liberty for protecting the value of individuals from the power of sovereign states (Onuma (n. 69), p. 462). He does not espouse 'Asian values' or 'Asian human rights' claims, because such claims must assume the universal nature of the West-centric construct of human rights by juxtaposing the 'universality' of West-centric human rights theories and the 'particularity' of Asian human rights (ibid., p. 36; Onuma (n. 2), p. 385). An Indian professor also sees the rejection of all Western thought as deeply problematic (B. S. Chimni, 'Asian civilizations and international law: some reflections' (2011) 1 *Asian Journal of International Law* 39–42, at 40).

3.4.2 Inseparability of constitutional principles from contemporary international law

The doubt about the West–East dichotomy is related to another criticism of the Asian values claim. The symposium also indicates how difficult it is to justify cherry-picking only what one likes within one comprehensive system. Modernity impacts all of human society. Likewise, international law is an overall system that consists of many different elements (including legal notions, principles, values and instruments), and those elements are closely interrelated and reinforce each other. If each party may make partial use of the international law system according to his or her liking, international law's integrity will be undermined. Only when one part of the whole system is separable from the rest can partial rejection or non-acceptance be legitimate and justified. Accordingly, it must be examined whether constitutional principles that global constitutionalism embraces are detachable from the rest of international law.

To begin with, advocates of Asian values criticise Western-oriented normative structures and contents of international law, which reflect the basic values of Western liberalism.[73] Their targets are usually the trinity of 'the rule of law, human rights and democracy'. Although their claim is not entirely clear as a legal claim, they tend to insist on replacing these constitutional principles with other principles derived from Asian history, culture and thoughts or on exempting Asian states from the application of these principles. The incorporation of these constitutional principles into traditional international law has caused various problems and difficulties mainly for non-Western states.[74] Above all, disputes have arisen over human rights.[75] Since the Universal Declaration of Human Rights in 1948, however, many human rights treaties, regional and worldwide, have been successfully adopted and constitute a substantial part of today's international legislation.[76] Specific human rights have already crystallised into rules of customary international law. In East Asia, there are several states that have yet to ratify some major human

---

[73] Xue (n. 6), at 15 and 17.

[74] Ibid.; Niels Petersen, 'International law, cultural diversity, and democratic rule: beyond the divide between universalism and relativism' (2011) 1 *Asia Journal of International Law* 149–163, at 151.

[75] Tomuschat (n. 21), at 227–231; Onuma (n. 69), pp. 370–462.

[76] The UN itself is an international organisation for the protection of human rights. The Charter professes the UN's faith in human rights in its preamble and provides for the promotion and encouragement of respect for human rights as a purpose of the UN (Art. 1 (3)). In addition, bilateral or multilateral economic cooperation agreements often refer to human rights in relation to conditionality (Onuma (n. 2), pp. 411–412).

rights treaties, but there is no state that officially rejects the idea of human rights protection.[77] On the whole, every state has accepted the protection of human rights as a prerequisite for membership in international society. Therefore, constitutional principles represented by the trinity already constitute a fundamental part of contemporary international law.

Nevertheless, it remains an open question whether these constitutional principles can be separated from the rest of international law. The scope of the subjects of international law gives us a clue in answering it. Incorporation of these principles into international law has been closely associated with the expansion of international law subjects. In the nineteenth century, the main subjects of international law were nation states. In the twentieth century and thereafter, individuals have been gradually accepted as not only the objects but also the subjects of international law, and the practice of many states has conformed. Particularly after World War II, due to learning from the tragic genocide experiences in wartime, international law started embracing individuals as well as states among its subjects.[78] Further along this line lie the developments of international human rights law, humanitarian law and criminal law.[79] Due to this progress, individuals in any country are able now to benefit enormously from the incorporation of the trinity into international law. As long as it is considered useful in protecting their well-being, individuals, irrespective of the state to which they belong, will compel international law to maintain its present structure. Recognising individuals as subjects of international law presents an opportunity for them to confront their own government, since human rights were created to protect individuals from government oppression. It is true that individuals cannot be generally equated with states as well as other international law subjects in terms of capacity to act in international law. Their role in international law is still limited. But the inclusion of individuals as subjects of international law has given dynamism to the development of international law.

[77] China and some ASEAN states have not ratified the International Covenant on Civil and Political Rights (ICCPR) yet. However, the ASEAN has made much progress on human rights recently (Clarke (n. 10), at 1–27; Jean-Claude Piris and Walter Woon, *Towards a Rules-Based Community: An ASEAN Legal Service* (Cambridge: Cambridge University Press, 2015), pp. 55 and 111–112; Simon Chesterman, *From Community to Compliance? The Evolution of Monitoring Obligations in ASEAN* (Cambridge: Cambridge University Press, 2015), pp. 45–47).
[78] Petersen (n. 74), at 151; Tomuschat (n. 21), at 227.
[79] Neff (n. 3), pp. 370, 375–377, 396–404.

In sum, including individuals as subjects of international law combines constitutional principles closely with the rest of international law. Given these principles' deep embedment in contemporary international law, however, accepting the Asian values claim could serve to restructure the whole of international law. The only choice that a state has is to accept or not international law as a whole, though each state is free to join or leave any individual treaty. States have no other choice than this.

3.4.3   Positive signification of Asian values claim

Given the preceding, the Asian values claim, like the debates at the Overcoming Modernity symposium, cannot avoid confronting a difficult question: How can East Asia offer substitutes for the European-originated values and principles inherent in international law while being an insider of the international law system? The structure of this confrontation is very similar to that of the Overcoming Modernity symposium. In the case of international as well as national law, however, overcoming Western elements is more problematic than overcoming Western modernity. As regards modernity in general, East Asia could manage to rely on its own philosophy, culture and thoughts somehow, which still existed to a considerable extent in the 1940s. As regards law, the situation is otherwise. During the modernisation of East Asia from the middle of the nineteenth century, indigenous law in East Asian states, whether national or international, has been totally or almost totally replaced by modern Western law, and there is no or little vestige of indigenous law at present.[80] This point of difference is decisive for the success or failure of the Asian values claim. Constitutional principles in international law are presented as legal ideas, but it is not feasible to invoke principles of indigenous East Asian law to contest them. One might be able to discover some useful principles from non-legal elements such as tradition, customs and history, but these would likely be inconsistent with the principles of East Asian domestic law modelled upon Western law (the degree of inconsistency depending upon its affinity to Western law). After all, there is a higher probability that the Asian values claim would fail as a legal claim, because the claim cannot present any counter-paradigm based on purely Asian elements. Like the overcoming modernity debates,

---

[80] For example, a textbook on Japanese law gives short shrift to Japanese law before the mid-nineteenth century (Curtis J. Milhaupt, J. Mark Ramseyer and Michael K. Young (eds.), *Japanese Law in Context: Readings in Society, the Economy, and Politics* (Cambridge; London: Harvard University Asia Center, 2001), pp. 2–7 and 10–27). This makes clear the discontinuity of indigenous law and current law in Japan.

the Asian values claim is inevitably deficient. Finally, as a matter of fact, international human rights treaties will become almost meaningless, provided that regional values take precedence over their protection of individuals. As long as the Asian values claim insists on the partial non-application of international law to Asia, such a claim cannot be accepted.

This conclusion does not mean that each distinction between the West and the East in terms of constitutional principles is insignificant and useless. On the contrary, the fact that international society shares Western values and principles as frameworks does not undermine the importance of contributions from other regions to the development of international norms and standards. Assuming that international human rights instruments are interpreted only by the West and that such Western interpretation is universally applied, it is difficult to recognise the legitimacy of that interpretation.[81] Therefore, the input from all regions is necessary in establishing universal interpretation. The Asian values claim may well be valid, meaningful and fruitful for international law developments at this stage. The significance of reflection on national and regional particularities has been repeatedly endorsed by several regional and worldwide declarations,[82] but it is unclear how such particularities should be taken into consideration. First, too uniform application of the same principle is not adequate to the current diverse world. A margin of appreciation should be permitted and is desirable for each state and region.[83] Second, if each is free to interpret and implement provisions of human rights treaties to its own likening, these provisions will become almost meaningless. There are many questions to be answered in order to implement human rights treaties suitably. They include the definition of the scope of an individual right, the identification of the core content of such a right, justifiable restrictions taking account of the doctrine of the margin of appreciation, the hierarchy between or among different human rights and the justification of restrictions protecting other values and interests.[84] The Asian perspective on human rights will be able to contribute

---

[81] Petersen (n. 74), at 151.

[82] Bangkok Declaration, Vienna Declaration and 2005 World Summit Outcome (n. 28).

[83] Mary Arden, *Human Rights and European Law: Building New Legal Orders* (Oxford: Oxford University Press, 2015), pp. 58–59, 237–238 and 289–290; Titia Loenen and Lucy Vickers, 'More is less? Multiple protection of human rights in Europe and the risks of erosion of human rights standards', in Sonia Morano-Foadi and Lucy Vickers (eds.), *Fundamental Rights in the EU: A Matter for Two Courts* (Oxford: Hart Publishing, 2015), pp. 159, 162–166.

[84] Petersen (n. 74), at 151–156.

much towards finding answers and reaching worldwide consensus. Since the implementation of any human right must be made in the context of regional or national conditions, avoiding conflicts with regional or national perspectives is not easy. In this respect, Onuma stresses that even in Europe, 'it was through continued serious controversies as well as reinterpretation of the dominant culture and the teachings of Christianity that human rights took root in Europe'.[85] In contrast to Europe, international society has just started experiencing such controversies and reinterpretation of regional and national cultures.[86] It should be kept in mind, however, that there is a prerequisite for the worldwide discussion: any claim based on Asian values must namely sublimate Asian specificity to universal standards and norms. In other words, stressing Asian particularity only does not meet this requirement.[87] After all, East Asian states must present a universally acceptable explanation that legitimates their own interpretation to international society.

3.4.4   Overcoming binary opposition

Here, it must be stressed again that we will have to renounce the binary opposition between the West and the non-West. East Asian peoples tend to regard Europe as monolithic, since it shares many things in common including Christianity, Roman law, the Renaissance, the Enlightenment and the Industrial Revolution. Thus, the EU is considered to have the same values, as the EU Treaty clearly provides (TEU Article 2). This is, however, not always true. The fact that conflicts about the trinity of the rule of law, human rights and democracy among EU member states are taking place reveals that even Europe is diverse as regards normative values, though the degree of diversity may not be as great as in East

---

[85] Onuma (n. 69), p. 457.

[86] The establishment of regional academic associations of international law (such as the European Society of International Law and the Asian Society of International Law) indicates the progress for dialogues (Hélène Ruiz Fabri, 'Reflections on the necessity of regional approaches to international law through the prism of the European example: neither yes nor no, neither black nor white' (2011) 1 *Asian Journal of International Law* 83–98, at 84–85; Hisashi Owada, 'Asia and international law: the inaugural address of the First President of the Asian Society of International Law, Singapore, 7 April 2007' (2011) 1 *Asian Journal of International Law* 3–11.

[87] The Japanese government's argument in the UN stresses national particularity only. Its explanation about the application of the death penalty is a good example and does not satisfy this requirement (consideration of reports submitted by states parties under Art. 40 of the Covenant, sixth periodic report of states parties, Japan, UN Doc. CCPR/C/JPN/ 6, 9 October 2012, pp. 20–22).

Asia.[88] It should also go without saying that there is difference within the Western world outside Europe (e.g. between the United States and Europe).[89] All of these findings are evidence of the ineffectiveness and uselessness of the West–East dichotomy. The view that there is a single universal international law is a myth of a kind. International law has no choice but to be understood and interpreted in national and regional contexts, since international actors are not free from their own national or regional specificity.[90] All things considered, the ultimate aim must be to enter a world without hegemony, rather than to replace the European hegemony with another hegemony. Through serious controversies among all international actors, each of the West, the East and international law will be forced to transform further so that constitutional principles of international law can become more truly universal (though without more harmonisation and unification automatically).[91] In the next section, I examine how such controversies will have impact on East Asia. This examination clarifies the specific meaning of global constitutionalism to East Asia.

4   Global constitutionalism in East Asia: a case study of Japan

4.1   Global constitutionalism and national constitutionalism

As regards international organisations, it is not so difficult for East Asian states to see merits in global constitutionalism, because legal conflicts like those underlying the *Kadi* case may also occur in East Asia in the future. A reform of the United Nations (UN) system guided by the idea of global constitutionalism is desirable for East Asian states as well. It is more

---

[88] Onuma (n. 2), pp. 419–420; recent examples are the situations of both Hungary and Poland (Bojan Bugarič, 'Protecting democracy and the rule of law in the European Union: the Hungarian challenge' (2014) *LEQS Paper No. 79/2014* 1–38; 'Editorial comments: Union membership in times of crisis' (2014) 51 *Common Market Law Review* 1–12; Armin Von Bogdandy and Michael Ioannidis, 'Systemic deficiency in the rule of law: what it is, what had been done, what can be done' (2014) 51 *Common Market Law Review* 59–96; 'Editorial comments: the rule of law in the European Union, the rule of Union law and the rule of law by the Union: three interrelated problems' (2016) 53 *Common Market Law Review* 597–606).

[89] Jouannet (n. 5), at 297–323.

[90] Ibid., at 292–293; Koskenniemi (n. 5), at 4.

[91] According to Delmas-Marty, globalisation calls for hybridisation, which can be distinguished from harmonisation, because hybridisation 'does not impose absolutely identical rules on every state' (Mireille Delmas-Marty, 'Comparative law and international law: methods for ordering pluralism' (2006) 43 *University of Tokyo Journal of Law and Politics* 43–59, at 49 and 54).

difficult to identify benefits of global constitutionalism for their domestic issues. Here, specific sensitivities in the region must be taken account of. It is true that in many East Asian states, certain tension persists between the government and the people regarding constitutional principles, their interpretation and their application. On the one hand, national governments are wary of the domestic application of international law. On the other hand, ethnic minorities, political dissidents and non-governmental organisations (NGOs) tend to rely on international law to challenge oppression by their governments. This constellation inevitably provokes these governments' negative attitude towards global constitutionalism. Are there some strategies to overcome this high barrier to the development of global constitutionalism in East Asia?

National constitutionalism is important for the global constitutionalism discourse in each domestic setting. An argument of global constitutionalism is partly motivated by the transfer of powers from a national level to an international level, because constitutional principles are required wherever power is exercised. Initially, global constitutionalism had no option but to be largely proscribed by national constitutionalism.[92] Once constitutionalism beyond states begins, interaction between the two begins. As global constitutionalism is also able to affect national constitutionalism in various ways, these two types of constitutionalism cannot independently coexist, without any mutual influence. They are interacting with and reinforcing each other by resting on similar values and principles.[93] This reciprocity is compatible with the trend for boundaries between international and domestic law to be no longer maintainable and to blur.[94] In these circumstances, global constitutionalism is tasked with supplementing imperfections or shortcomings of domestic constitutionalism.[95] The following section undertakes a case study of

---

[92] O'Donoghue concludes that 'domestic constitutionalism is considered as indispensable to understanding the nature of the core principles relating to global constitutionalism' (O'Donoghue (n. 12), pp. 44–46 and 49).

[93] Ibid., pp. 31 and 49; Tom Bingham, *The Rule of Law* (London: Penguin Books, 2010), p. 110.

[94] Ibid., p. 6; Christian Walter, 'International law in a process of constitutionalization', in Janne Nijman and André Nollkaemper (eds.), *New Perspectives on the Divide between National and International Law* (Oxford: Oxford University Press, 2007), pp. 191, 204–205.

[95] Anne Peters, 'Compensatory constitutionalism: the function and potential of fundamental international norms and structures' (2006) 19 *Leiden Journal of International Law* 579–610; Joel P. Trachtman, *The Future of International Law: Global Government* (Cambridge: Cambridge University Press, 2013), pp. 259–260.

Japan from this point of view. The study focuses on current discussions about amendments to the constitution of Japan, particularly the recent proposal submitted by the ruling party.

4.2　Japan's constitution as a long-lasting political issue

The current constitution was adopted in 1946 and came into force in 1947 during the military occupation of the Allied powers (mainly the United States). Since the constitution was subject to strong American influence,[96] its provisions are fully consistent with Western constitutional principles such as the rule of law, human rights and democracy.

The constitution has yet to be amended,[97] but its revision has been a continuous political issue since Japan regained independence in 1952. It has been an issue because the then Japanese government prepared its draft together with the General Headquarters of the Allied powers (GHQ).[98] The GHQ's engagement in constitution making put into question the constitution's legitimacy. Constitutional revisionists in Japan always bring up this foreign involvement as justification for constitutional revision. From the constitution's early days, the biggest debate has been about how to interpret Article 9, a clause on 'renunciation of war'. It not only renounces war solemnly but also prohibits the maintenance of any military forces.[99] This clause has been a symbol of Japanese pacifism in the post-war period. Due to it the constitutionality of Japan's Self Defense Forces and Japan's participation in the collective security

---

[96] Tanaka (ed.) (n. 15), pp. 652–685. For example, the Japanese courts, like their US counterparts, are conferred the power of constitutional review, i.e. to determine whether a national law is consistent with the constitution (Art. 81 of the Constitution of Japan).

[97] Constitutional revision requires the approval of two-thirds of the members in both houses of the Diet as well as the majority of the votes cast in a mandatory national referendum (Art. 96 of the Constitution of Japan).

[98] Carl F. Goodman, *The Rule of Law in Japan: A Comparative Analysis* (The Hague: Kluwer Law International, 2003), pp. 29–30; Shoichi Koseki, *Nihonkoku-kenpo no Tanjyo, Zoho-kaitei-ban* (*The Birth of the Japanese Constitution, Enlarged and Revised Edition*) (Tokyo: Kodansha, 2017), pp. 175–222; Law Library of Congress, Japan, Art. 9 of the Constitution 4–8 (February 2006) (https://www.loc.gov/law/help/japan-constitution/interpretations-article9.php).

[99] Art. 9(1) provides that 'aspiring sincerely to an international peace based on justice and order, the Japanese people forever renounce war as a sovereign right of the nation and the threat or use of forces as a means of settling international disputes'. Para. 2 provides that 'in order to accomplish the aim of the preceding paragraph, land, sea and air forces, as well as other war potential, will never be maintained. The right of belligerency of the state will not be recognised.'

mechanism are focal points of constant political and legal disputes in Japan.

Initially, the main issue about Article 9 was whether Japan could maintain its own military forces under the current constitution.[100] Recently, the right of collective self-defence has been hotly disputed. The Supreme Court of Japan held in the so-called *SUNAGAWA* case of 1959 that Article 9 would not deny the right of self-defence.[101] Bearing in mind that pacifism was the fundamental principle of the constitution, however, subsequent governments interpreted the right of self-defence narrowly to mean the right of 'individual' self-defence only.[102] On their view, the constitution prohibited Japan from participating in a collective self-defence scheme (like NATO) under Article 51 of the UN Charter. The current government adopted a new interpretation in July 2014 so that Japan could exercise the right of 'collective' self-defence as well. It explained that the recent change in the security environment in East Asia forced Japan to change its interpretation.[103] This change provoked large-scale public protest. Most law professors and lawyers also criticised it as unconstitutional,[104] arguing that by modifying the previous interpretation drastically, the government exceeded the limits of interpretation that are permissible without recourse to constitutional revision.[105] The recent

---

[100] Hajime Yamamoto, 'Interpretation of the pacifist Article of the Constitution by the Bureau of Cabinet Legislation: a new source of constitutional law?' (2017) 26 *Washington International Law Journal* 99–125, at 106–111.

[101] Judgment of 16 December 1959, Sup. Ct. Grand Bench, 13 Keishu 3225; 'Judgment upon the so-called *SUNAGAWA* case' (1960) 4 *Japanese Annual of International Law* 103.

[102] The government's written answer submitted to the Audit Committee of the House of Councilors, Relationship between the Right of Collective Self-Defense and the Constitution, 14 October 1972; Keigo Komamura, 'Constitution and narrative in the age of crisis in Japanese politics' (2017) 26 *Washington International Law Journal* 75–98, at 75–76.

[103] Cabinet Decision on Development of Seamless Security Legislation to Ensure Japan's Survival and Protect Its People, 1 July 2014 (http://www.mofa.go.jp/fp/nsp/page23e_000273.html); Press Conference by Prime Minister Abe, 1 July 2014 (http://japan.kantei.go.jp/96_abe/statement/201407/0701kaiken.html); Yamamoto (n. 100), at 100–101 and 111–115.

[104] According to recent opinion polls, a majority of the public opposes the changed interpretation. Most constitutional law professors have also expressed their opposition (Komamura (n. 102), at 75–76).

[105] Under the previous interpretation, only an armed attack against Japan justifies its use of force as the exercise of the right of self-defence. The new interpretation allows recourse to the use of force when an armed attack occurs against a foreign state that is in a close relationship with Japan and, as a result, the attack threatens Japan's survival (Cabinet Decision, n. 103). Almost all professors of constitutional law oppose this change of interpretation (Komamura (n. 102), at 76; Yamamoto (n. 100), at 118).

dispute over Article 9 might actually be a prelude to even greater changes. Japan's constitution is at risk of being modified more fundamentally in the near future through its official revision procedures.

4.3 The LDP and amendments to the constitution of Japan

4.3.1 The LDP's constitutional policy

The Liberal Democratic Party (LDP) is the current ruling party in Japan. Its political belief is a complex combination of conservative, reactionary, as well as neo- and non-liberal tendencies. The LDP has always attached considerable importance to preserving a friendly relationship, including a military alliance, with the United States.[106] It does not earnestly reflect on Japan's past wrongdoings and is not very active in human rights protection or the rule of law.

As regards the current constitution, the LDP has continuously insisted on its amendment since the party's founding in 1955. In April 2012, it presented its own draft for a new constitution (the LDP Draft).[107] From the Upper House election of 2016, the ruling coalition of the LDP and the Buddhist party (a junior partner of the LDP) has retained more than a two-thirds majority in both the Lower House and the Upper House. Since that majority enables constitutional amendment procedures to be formally started at any time (per Article 96 of the constitution), revisionists will likely present the LDP Draft as the basis for constitutional deliberation in both chambers in the near future.

4.3.2 The spirit of the LDP Draft

An amendment to Article 9 in the draft has attracted the most attention in Japanese society, because it clarifies that Japan can maintain military forces (new Article 9–2). It is important for the pacifism of Japan whether the present Article 9 will be amended in such a way, but the issue of how Japan will forge its military and security policy remains within a range of reasonable policy choices. In contrast, the draft would totally refurbish the structure of the current Japanese society.[108] Modern constitutionalism assumes that a national constitution is not only to organise and

---

[106] Prime Minister Shinzo Abe, 'Toward an alliance of hope' (Address to a Joint Meeting of the US Congress) (April 29, 2015).

[107] Jiyu Minshu To (Liberal Democratic Party), 'Nihonkou Kenpo-Kaisei Soan' (Draft Constitution for the revision of the Constitution of Japan), 27 April 2012 (https://jimin.ncss.nifty.com/pdf/news/policy/130250_1.pdf).

[108] Komamura (n. 102), at 77–78.

legitimate state power but to constrain the exercise of state power within constitutional limitations.[109] The current constitution is in line with such an understanding of constitutionalism, whereas the LDP Draft is not.

The LDP Draft is characterised by a reactionary propensity. The current constitution expresses sympathy towards universal principles of humankind as well as international cooperation.[110] As its preamble reveals, the draft is based on old-fashioned, nationalistic and state-centred sentiments, and it stresses the importance of Japanese history, culture and tradition.[111] It is very evident that the draft's basic philosophy is quite different from the current constitution's. Although the current constitution and the draft have many provisions in common, the draft removes key passages and provisions from the current constitution in order to emasculate the essence of modern constitutionalism. If the draft is adopted as it stands, constitutional principles endorsed by the current constitution will be seriously damaged, and thus constitutionalism might be imperilled in Japan. How the draft modifies the protection of human rights is examined hereinafter.

4.3.3   Transforming the essence of human rights

The function of constitutionalism is firmly linked to the idea of human rights, whereas the LDP Draft will have significant impact on human rights protection in Japan. Since it retains many human rights provisions of the current constitution (with some slight modifications), it appears as if the draft will not weaken the current human rights protection much. However, the LDP Draft is premised on a different understanding of

---

[109] Dieter Grimm, *Constitutionalism, Past, Present, and Future* (Oxford: Oxford University Press, 2016), pp. 15 and 22. Most Japanese scholars of constitutional law share such an understanding of constitutionalism (Shojiro Sakaguchi, 'Jiminto Kaisei-soan to Kenpo-Soncyo-Yogo-Gimu' (The LDP's draft for revision of the Constitution and the duty to respect and defend the Constitution), in Horitsujiho Hensyubu (ed.), *'Kenpo-Kaisei-Ron' wo Ronzuru (Discussing Arguments for Constitutional Revision)* (Tokyo: Nihonhyoron-sha, 2013), pp. 105, 108–109.

[110] The current constitution's preamble expresses that 'we [the Japanese people] shall secure for ourselves and our prosperity the fruits of peaceful cooperation with all nations', and it refers to 'a universal principle of mankind upon which this Constitution is founded'. These sentences and passages are completely deleted in the LDP Draft.

[111] Unlike the current constitution, the preamble of the draft starts with reference to Japan's long history, unique culture and 'Tenno [Emperor]'. Komamura points out that though legal principles in the current constitution (e.g. popular sovereignty, fundamental human rights and pacifism) remain in the draft, the deletion of a few important passages (e.g. 'a universal principle of mankind' and 'we reject and revoke all constitutions, laws, ordinances, and rescripts in conflict herewith') from the current preamble will reduce the constitution's normative status (Komamura (n. 102), at 88).

human rights from the current constitution. Japanese constitutional scholars usually explain that fundamental human rights in the constitution derive from the Western theory of natural rights,[112] whereas the draft is very hostile to the natural rights theory. The hostility is not explicit in the draft; it is the LDP's explanatory brochure on the draft that makes clear its firm rejection of the natural rights theory and insists that natural rights be replaced with the Japanese style of human rights reflecting the country's history, culture and tradition.[113] In sum, even if human rights provisions in the draft do not appear so different from the current ones, it can be inferred from the explanatory brochure that human rights in the draft are something different from the present ones. For that reason, the draft had to remove Article 97 of the current constitution, which emphasises the inviolable and universal nature of human rights.[114] All things considered, the LDP Draft has the potential to transform the current liberal constitution into a more illiberal one. This anxiety has already provoked serious opposition to the draft in Japan.[115]

It is not entirely clear how the rejection of the natural rights theory will affect actual conditions of human rights in Japan, because the explanatory brochure does not offer any details. Bearing in mind the fact that the supreme nature of human rights is rejected with the deletion of Article 97, the draft seems to allow the restriction of human rights by ordinary legislation. Under the draft, the borderline between human rights guaranteed by the constitution and legal rights protected by ordinary legislation may, in other words, be considerably blurred. This change is nothing less than a return to the situation under the Constitution of the Great Empire of Japan (the Meiji Constitution) before the end of World War

---

[112] Noriho Urabe, *Zentei Kenpo-Gaku Kyoshitsu* (*Fully Revised Constitutional Law Study Classroom*) (Tokyo: Nihonhyoron-Sha, 2000), pp. 12–13; Miyoko Tsujimura, *Kenpo* (*Constitutional Law*) (Tokyo: Nihonhyoron-sha, 2000), pp. 143–145.

[113] Specifically, it explains that 'human rights provisions must presuppose the history, culture and tradition of Japan' and that 'while there are some provisions of the current Constitution which seemed to be drafted on the basis of the Western theory of natural human rights, these provisions have to be amended' (Jiyu Minsyu To (Liberal Democratic Party), *Nihonkoku-Kenpo Kaisei Soan Q&A, Zoho-Ban* (*Draft for Amendments to the Japanese Constitution Q&A: An Enlarged Edition*) (2012), p. 13 (https://jimin.ncss.nifty.com/pdf/pamphlet/kenpou_qa.pdf)).

[114] Art. 97 provides that 'the fundamental human rights by the Constitution guaranteed to the people of Japan are fruits of the age-old struggle of man to be free; they have survived the many exacting tests for durability and are conferred upon this and future generations in trust, to be held for all time inviolate'. The LDP Draft deletes this provision too.

[115] Komamura (n. 102), at 84–92.

II.[116] It makes sense that human rights NGOs as well as many scholars are strongly opposed to the draft: with good reason they are afraid that the current level of human rights protection will be lowered by changes proposed in it.[117]

4.3.4 The LDP Draft and international society

The LDP Draft can be understood as one instance of the Asian values claim. Overlap between the LDP Draft and other Asian values claims is easy to see. The draft's way of thinking about human rights is problematic for international society as well. This is because the draft does not deliberately provide for exchange with other international actors outside Japan in order to construct international standards and norms, which will be more mature and universal through input from all actors in international society. Whereas the current constitution takes a positive stance on international cooperation and dialogue, the draft is rather close-minded and passive. The draft seems to suppose that Japan is still isolated and cut off from the wider world.[118] Within the current international society, however, Japan cannot reject interaction with other states and international organisations. Indeed, Japan cannot avoid a nationalistic constitution being examined from the global perspective. This reality is further discussed in the next section.

4.4 The LDP Draft and international society: EU–Japan relationship

4.4.1 Freedom of sovereign state and the global society

The LDP Draft assumes that Japan is free to determine the contents of its constitution as it wishes, because Japan is a sovereign state, and that constitution making is still subject to its full discretion. Contrary to the drafters' expectation, it is no longer possible for any state to adopt a non-liberal or undemocratic constitution without any restrictions, because

[116] The Meiji Constitution guaranteed the rights of the Japanese people only within conditions laid down by parliamentary legislation (Arts. 18–32). These rights were not regarded as human rights, because they were not something that pre-existed the constitution. They were often infringed on by legislation (Tanaka (ed.) (n. 15), p. 637).
[117] Human Rights Now, Submission of Human Rights Now to the Committee of Civil and Political Rights in Advance of the Consideration of Japan's Report (2014); Komamura argues that the replacement of some key wording as well as the inclusion of some new provisions will also reduce human rights protection (Komamura (n. 102), at 91).
[118] The preamble of the LDP Draft does not refer to anything international or universal at all beyond 'strengthening friendship relation with other states' and 'contributing to international peace and prosperity'.

the adoption of such a constitution will necessarily bring about serious conflicts with international law as well as international society. This truth is demonstrated by the circumstances around recent constitutional amendments in Hungary. The current Hungarian government made a series of revisions to the Hungarian Constitution after taking office in 2010. As a consequence, the liberal constitution of Hungary has been transformed into the present illiberal and authoritarian constitution, which lacks real checks and balances to restrain public power, restricts independence of the judiciary, weakens human rights guarantees and limits jurisdiction of the Constitutional Court.[119] It is significant from the viewpoint of global constitutionalism that the new constitution causes many conflicts with the international and European legal obligations of Hungary and that various actors in international society do not leave Hungary to choose its own course freely.[120] In response to these revisions of Hungary's constitution, several international organisations, principally the Council of Europe (CE) and the EU, have continually pressured the Hungarian government in various ways to change course and maintain the conformity of the domestic human rights protection with international treaties.[121]

---

[119] Bugarič (n. 88), at 7–14; Committee on Civil Liberties, Justice and Home Affairs of European Parliament (Rapporteur: Rui Tavares), Report on the Situation of Fundamental Rights: Standards and Practices in Hungary, 1–39 (24 June 2013).

[120] International actors (such as the EU and its member states, the Organisation for Security and Cooperation in Europe (OSCE), the Council of Europe, the UN, NGOs, and international and national journalists' organisations) have criticised the situation in Hungary and made recommendations (Committee on Civil Liberties (n. 119), at 16–18 and 32).

[121] First, while any EU member state is free to review its constitution, it must not breach the European common values mentioned in Art. 2 of the EU Treaty (Committee on Civil Liberties (n. 119), at 7–10). The EU can put conditions on constitutional amendments of the member state. This means that the member state has already renounced some constitutional autonomy. The new constitutional order of Hungary basically undermines the rule of law, human rights and democracy in the country. As a result, the Hungarian situation may constitute the existence of 'a clear risk of a serious breach' of the values and may trigger an enforcement mechanism (Art. 7(1) of the EU Treaty) (Bugarič (n. 88), at 14–15; ' Editorial comments: Hungary's new constitutional order and "European unity"' (2012) 49 *Common Market Law Review* 871–883, at 877–878 and 882; Committee on Civil Liberties (n. 119), at 28). Therefore, the European Parliament adopted resolutions on Hungary. Second, the CE's Statute also obliges Hungary to uphold democracy, the protection of human rights and the rule of law. The Hungarian Parliament's sovereignty is thereby again limited in international law. As the compatibility of the new constitution with the European Convention on Human Rights is not guaranteed, the European Commission for Democracy through Law (Venice Commission) has published several critical comments on the new constitution of

Despite their pressure, the Hungarian government has only partly accepted the organisations' recommendations and to some extent improved deficiencies in its constitutional regime.[122] The constructive dialogue between the CE and the EU on one side and the Hungarian government on the other does continue to function. It is not easy, however, to assess how effective the dialogue is in ensuring conformity between the Hungarian Constitution and international law. Nonetheless, the ongoing situation of Hungary can be considered a good example of interaction between 'national constitutionalism' and 'constitutionalism beyond the states'.

By and large, the LDP Draft resembles the new Hungarian Constitution. They share several features such as admiring national history and undermining the inalienable nature of human rights.[123] If Japan were a member state of the EU and the CE, these regional organisations would likely have the same or similar reactions to the anticipated constitutional revision based on the LDP Draft. Japan is unfortunately not in Europe. Still, we can expect interaction about the Japanese Constitution and international law.

4.4.2 Conflicts with international treaties

Japan has already signed and ratified many major international human rights treaties. Accordingly, human rights conditions in Japan are periodically examined by the international human rights bodies established under these treaties. Yuji Iwasawa already appreciated two decades ago that thereby the overall human rights situation in Japan had much improved.[124] However, the human rights situation in Japan is not fully consistent with international law even today. For example, the Committee of Civil and Political Rights expressed in 2014 its deep concern about many aspects of the Japanese human

---

Hungary by adopting its opinions just after the Hungarian government started preparing constitutional revisions (Opinion no. 614/2011 (CDL-AD(2011)001), Opinion no. 618/2011 (CDL-AD(2011)016), Opinion no. 663/2012 (CDL-AD(2012)001), Opinion no. 665/2012 (CDL-AD(2012)009), Opinion no. 672/2012 (CDL-AD(2012)023), Opinion no. 683/2012 (CDL-AD(2012)020), Opinion no. 720/2013 (CDL-AD(2013)012) and Opinion no. 798/2015 (CDL-AD (2015)015)).

[122] Opinion no. 663/2012 (n. 121), para. 122; Opinion no. 672/2012 (n. 121), paras. 30–36; Opinion no. 683/2012 (n. 121), paras. 6 and 85; Opinion no. 7 20/2013 (n. 121), para. 75; Opinion no. 798/2015 (n. 121), para. 110.

[123] Bugarič (n. 88), at 7–14.

[124] Yuji Iwasawa, *International Law Human Rights and Japanese Law: The Impact of International Law on Japanese Law* (Oxford: Oxford University Press, 1998), p. 3.

rights situation.[125] If the draft is adopted as it stands, the situation will get worse and will cause more conflicts with international law. These human rights treaties will have a positive impact upon the Japanese situation in the long run, but the impact will not be so effective as to meet current concern over the LDP Draft. Fortunately, there is an alternative for Japan.

4.4.3   Trade agreement and political cooperation agreement

An alternative to the UN human rights scheme is a combination of bilateral agreements, namely a trade agreement and a political cooperation agreement (PCA). The EU and Japan are now negotiating a free trade agreement (FTA) and a strategic partnership agreement (SPA), which is a kind of PCA. Both the European Commission and the Japanese government anticipate that the EU–Japan FTA and SPA will be concluded at the same time in the near future. The combination of the two different agreements derives mostly from the EU's external policy. The EU has recently taken to integrating the promotion of constitutional principles (including human rights) into its trade agreements.[126] Linking an FTA with a PCA is no more than the realisation of this external policy. Pursuant to it, the EU concluded an FTA and a PCA together with South Korea in 2010 and Canada in 2016, respectively.[127] These political agreements are important precedents for the future EU–Japan SPA. Japan has

---

[125] The committee expressed its concern and recommendations about several aspects of the human rights situation in Japan. These included applicability of the Covenant rights by national courts, gender equality, hate speech and racial discrimination, death penalty, sexual slavery practices against 'comfort women', involuntary hospitalisation, substitute detention system (*Daiyo Kangoku*) and forced confessions, expulsion and detention of asylum seekers, surveillance of Muslims, restriction of fundamental freedoms on grounds of 'public welfare', Fukushima nuclear disaster and rights of indigenous peoples (Human Rights Committee, concluding observations on the sixth periodic report of Japan, 20 August 2014, UN Doc. CCPR/C/JPN/CO/6).

[126] Council, EU Strategic Framework and Action Plan on Human Rights and Democracy, 25 June 2012. The EU's external policy on human rights has a long history, dating back to the Lomé Conventions in the 1970s (Piet Eeckhout, *External Relations of the European Union: Legal and Constitutional Foundations* (Oxford: Oxford University Press, 2004), pp. 465–484). The external policy is currently grounded on provisions of the EU Treaty (Art. 3(5) and Art. 21(1)); Aravind Ganesh, 'The European Union's human rights obligations towards distant strangers' (2016) 37 *Michigan Journal of International Law* 475–538, at 476–478 and 530–538; Karen E. Smith, *European Union Foreign Policy in a Changing World*, 3rd ed. (Cambridge: Polity Press, 2014), pp. 100–103 and 110–111.

[127] The political agreement with South Korea is named the 'EU–Korea Framework Agreement' and that with Canada is named the 'EU–Canada Strategic Partnership Agreement'.

a long history of political cooperation with the EU from the early 1990s,[128] but the EU–Japan SPA will provide a more comprehensive framework for their political cooperation and will encourage new bilateral cooperation on many political issues.

The arrangements between the EU on the one side and South Korea and Canada on the other side are very suggestive for the ongoing negotiations between the EU and Japan from the viewpoint of global constitutionalism. First, the EU's PCAs are based on the sharing of common values with third states. All parties to the EU–South Korea and the EU–Canada agreements clearly express their strong commitment to these values. For example, the EU–South Korea Framework Agreement (EU–South Korea FA) lists democratic principles, human rights, fundamental freedoms and the rule of law as shared values (Article 1(1))[129] and provides that respect for these values constitutes an essential element of the agreement (ibid.). It is worth stressing that the EU and South Korea promise to respect these values both externally and internally.[130]

Second, the mutual relationship between the FTA and the PCA is quite important for global constitutionalism. This is because the close linkage between the two agreements constitutes a legal mechanism to ensure the observance of their commitments to shared values. In the case of the EU and South Korea, the EU–South Korea FA sets up a framework for their overall relationship, and the EU–South Korea FTA makes up an integral part of it.[131]

---

[128] The Hague Declaration in July 1991 was a turning point in the political cooperation between the EU and Japan. Since then, the EU–Japan cooperation on non-economic issues has gradually developed. Joint Press Statement of the 23rd Japan–EU Summit (29 May 2015) listed several subjects for political cooperation.

[129] The EU–Canada SPA refers to similar values. Like the EU–Korea FA, the EU–Canada SPA lists democratic principles, human rights and fundamental freedoms (as laid down in the Universal Declaration of Human Rights and existing international human rights treaties) (Art. 1(3)) and the rule of law (Art. 2(4)).

[130] Art. 1(1) of the EU–Korea FA stipulates that respect for these values 'underpins the internal and international policies of both Parties'; Art. 2(1) of the EU–Canada SPA also stipulates that 'respect for democratic principles, human rights and fundamental freedoms [. . .] underpins the Parties' respective national and international policies'.

[131] Art. 9(2) (Trade and Investment) of the EU–Korea FA stipulates that 'the Parties shall give effect to their cooperation in the trade and investment area through the agreement establishing a free trade area. The aforementioned agreement shall constitute a specific agreement giving effect to the trade provisions of this Agreement, within the terms of Article 43'. Art. 43(3) (Other Agreements) of the FA also provides that 'the Parties may complement this Agreement by concluding specific agreements in any area of cooperation. [. . .] Such specific agreements shall be an integral part of the overall bilateral relations as governed by this Agreement and shall form part of a common institutional framework.'

In other words, both the FA and the FTA are legally integrated into a single unit, though they are agreed in separate documents. This integration means that non-observance of their commitment in the FA will breach the whole unit including the FTA. Like other international agreements, the FTA provides for sanctions in response to any failure to meet obligations,[132] and such measures are interpreted to include the FTA's suspension or termination. It follows from the application of these sanctions as well as the integration of the two agreements that if one of the parties violates its own commitment to common values in the FA, it may be deprived benefits accruing from the FTA. Although their details are not exactly the same as those of the EU–Korea FA and FTA, the EU–Canada SPA and FTA also link the two agreements, clearly referring to the termination of the FTA.[133] The observance of the party's commitments to shared values can be protected by such trade sanctions, albeit not to the full extent.

4.4.4 The LDP Draft and the EU–Japan FTA and SPA

Both the EU–South Korea and the EU–Canada relationships include many suggestions about how international society should respond to the expected constitutional amendments in Japan. Although draft provisions of the EU–Japan FTA and SPA have yet to be published, they will probably be similar to the preceding agreements between the EU and South Korea and the EU and Canada. The Japanese government is confident that Japan has good records of human rights, democracy and the rule of law (though some human rights issues remain controversial domestically and internationally). Therefore, the EU–Japan Summit meeting loudly proclaims 'common values and shared principles' every year.[134] Even now, however, it is doubtful that Japan really shares the

---

[132] Art. 45(3) (Modalities for Implementation) of the EU–Korea FA prescribes that 'if either Party considers that the other Party has failed to fulfil its obligations under this Agreement, it may take appropriate measures in accordance with international law'.

[133] In the case of the EU and Canada, the integration of the SPA with the FTA is not so obvious. However, Art. 28 (Fulfillment of Obligations) clearly stipulates about the sanction for non-observance of values that 'a particular serious and substantial violation of human rights or non-proliferation, as defined in para. 3, could also serve as grounds for the termination of the EU-Canada Comprehensive Economic and Trade Agreement (CETA)'.

[134] Prime Minister Shinzo Abe, Joint Press Statement, The EU and Japan Acting Together for Global Peace and Prosperity, 22nd EU–Japan Summit (7 May 2014); the Joint Press Statement of the 23rd Japan–EU Summit (29 May 2015) states that '1. As close partners, Japan and the European Union are working together to address issues of vital importance to our citizens and the world based on common values and shared principles, and that 5. [. . .] enhancing cooperation and collaboration in this field at both global and

same constitutional principles with Europe as regards the rule of law and human rights.[135] First, as regards the rule of law, effective control of state power seems to be the main concern for the majority of Europeans. In Europe, the rule of law emphasises judicial control over public authorities. In Japan, constitutional law scholars take a similar view that the rule of law must govern the relationship between public administration and people, but this control does not function so well.[136] Second, as regards human rights, there is the aforementioned conflict between the UN bodies and Japan about the interpretation of human rights treaties. Likewise, there are differences between Europe and Japan over a range of human rights, duties to protect human rights and human rights as a common concern of international society.[137] The LDP Draft will expand these gaps, and then it will become very difficult under the new constitution for the EU and Japan to continue sharing 'common values and shared principles' in the same manner as today. Assuming that the EU–Japan FTA and SPA are successfully concluded, the EU will be able to take action against Japan in response to its revision of the constitution. If, having recourse to the exercise of rights under international treaties, the EU succeeds in persuading the Japanese government to follow internationally recognised values and principles, the EU's action will be highly appreciated as a great contribution to global constitutionalism.

5 Concluding remarks: pre-modernity, modernity and postmodernity

During World War II, Japanese intellectuals seriously explored how they could successfully deal with mistakes of the Western-originated modernity. In order to justify the Japanese invasions in the Asia Pacific area, many of those intellectuals looked for another source of justification within Japanese history, culture, arts and ideas. They discussed transcending Western democracy, capitalism and liberalism[138] and finally sought to transcend European modernity. They looked back on Japan's past, and they expected to identify there valuable ideas for the world in the future. Unfortunately, their efforts did not achieve the result desired. Their arguments seemed fairly persuasive, as long as they criticised

regional level, based on the common values of democracy, the rule of law, human rights and shared principles such as open markets and rule-based international system'.
[135] Suami (n. 17), p. 248.
[136] Ibid., pp. 249–254; Goodman (n. 98), pp. 32–33 and 326–335.
[137] Suami (n. 17), pp. 254–263.
[138] Hiromatsu (n. 38), p. 18.

deficiencies of Western modernity. They failed, however, to present an alternative paradigm. Wataru Hiromatsu explained that one reason for the failure was an anachronism inherent in their arguments, namely the search for a way of overcoming modernity by looking back to remnants of the pre-modern system that symbolised the imperial system of Japan.[139] Those wartime intellectuals believed that as long as Japan had accepted Western modernity and remained inside it, Japan could not go beyond modernity. In their view, Japan had to first escape Western modernity in order to challenge Western modernity. Since Japan was forced to identify its peculiarity and uniqueness based on Western modernity, however, it was almost impossible to correctly specify the objects that were supposed to be 'overcome' without relying upon Western modernity. When the intellectuals tried to replace the paradigm of Western modernity with a non-Western one, they had to fall into 'the complicity between Western universalism and Japanese particularism'.[140] The dichotomy between the West and Japan was useless and meaningless for Japan in extricating itself from Western modernity. Japan had to recognise that the only thing that it could do was to further develop the contents of modernity through infusing non-Western local elements. These lessons from wartime Japan are still useful, not only to Japan but to the whole region.

The LDP Draft reminds us of this wartime history. The LDP Draft tries to root Japan's constitution in Japan's history, tradition and culture. Its attention to these elements should not be disallowed, because they might be useful to the further development of constitutionalism within or beyond the state. However, one must carefully examine these elements from the viewpoint of constitutionalism and extract universally applicable principles from them. Not all local elements are worth keeping. Only through a continuous process of self-reflection can we make local principles grow into truly universal principles. Unfortunately, the intent to merely replace the natural rights theory with Japanese elements indicates that the LDP Draft is based on blind deference to these elements. Just as with the Overcoming Modernity symposium, it is likely that the LDP's attempt will, intentionally or unintentionally, bring about the weakening of constitutional principles and that it will inevitably fail.

---

[139] Ibid., p. 100.

[140] Sakai (n. 31), pp. 186 and 194–196; Naoki Sakai, 'Modernity and its critique: the problem of universalism and particularism' (1988) 87 The South Atlantic Quarterly 475–504, at 480.

There are many different types of constitutionalism in Asia at present. Although we can perceive some common features,[141] there is currently, even in Europe, diversity in national constitutionalism. Therefore, the axis of confrontation cannot lie in the West–East dichotomy at all. The real axis lies in the confrontation between 'liberal constitutionalism', which accepts the achievement of international law and contributes to its further development, and 'illiberal constitutionalism', which dismisses international law's achievement and has little interest in international law's future. The problem to be addressed is how to control and train illiberal constitutionalism. As regards human rights, Onuma insists that they must be reconceptualised in response to the diverse desires, views, perspectives and propensities of peoples with different cultures, religions and civilisations.[142] However, such reconceptualisation seems to be a bit misleading or should not be accorded priority, even if necessary. Before human rights are reconceptualised, such regional or national culture, religion and civilisation have to be critically examined from the viewpoint of constitutional principles. More important than reconceptualisation is improving human rights situations in the world through making all peoples, regions and states take equal part in building up global common standards and norms. Given that the Asian values claim is based on the binary framework of Western universality versus Eastern particularity, it will not succeed. Our course of action must be not to replace universal values that are actually dominated by the Western values with those dominated by the Eastern values.[143] Instead, we should encourage international law to attain more maturity, legitimacy and universality without hegemony by instilling non-Western, including East Asian, elements in it.[144] Although East Asian states have problems accepting parts of constitutional principles in international law, these problems must be solved by the development of these principles through the additional injection of East Asian local elements, not through their replacement with East Asian elements. This is exactly the same as overcoming modernity must exist in the process of thoroughly pursuing modernity, as the failure of the Overcoming Modernity symposium demonstrates.[145]

---

[141] Chang et al. (n. 16), pp. 9–64.

[142] Onuma (n. 69), pp. 374, 376 and 383–388.

[143] Isomae, '"Kindai no Cyokoku" to Kyoto-Gakuha' (n. 50), pp. 52–55.

[144] Hisashi Owada (n. 86), at 9–10; Yoshimi Takeuchi, *Nihon to Asia* (Japan and Asia) (Tokyo: Chikuma Shobo, 1993), pp. 442, 469.

[145] On 17 July 2018, the EU and Japan signed both the FTA and the SPA. But unlike the cases of the EU-South Korea and the EU-Canada, legal linkage between two agreements does not clearly exist. .

INDEX